Interdisciplinary Studies in Human Rights

Volume 16

Human rights are one of the normative cornerstones of contemporary international law and global governance. Due to the complexities of actual or potential violations of human rights and in light of current crises, new and interdisciplinary research is urgently needed. The series Interdisciplinary Studies in Human Rights recognizes the growing importance and necessity of interdisciplinary research in human rights. The series consists of monographs and collected volumes addressing human rights research from different disciplinary and interdisciplinary perspectives, including but not limited to philosophy, law, political science, education, and medical ethics. Its goal is to explore new and contested questions such as the extraterritorial application of human rights and their relevance for non-state actors, as well as the philosophical and theoretical foundations of human rights. The series also addresses policy questions of current interest including the human rights of migrants and refugees, LGBTI rights, and bioethics, as well as business and human rights.

The series editors are Members of the Centre for Human Rights Erlangen- Nürnberg (CHREN), an interdisciplinary research center at Friedrich-Alexander- University Erlangen-Nürnberg. The Advisory Board brings together human rights scholars from a wide range of academic disciplines and regional backgrounds. The series welcomes suggestions for publications of academic research falling into the series subject matter.

Raluca Grosescu • John G. Dale
Editors

Corporate Accountability for Human Rights Violations

Civil Society and Transnational Activism across the World

Springer

Editors
Raluca Grosescu
SNSPA
Bucuresti, Romania

John G. Dale
George Mason University
Fairfax, VA, USA

ISSN 2509-2960 ISSN 2509-2979 (electronic)
Interdisciplinary Studies in Human Rights
ISBN 978-3-032-05568-2 ISBN 978-3-032-05569-9 (eBook)
https://doi.org/10.1007/978-3-032-05569-9

This work was supported by National University of Political Studies and Public Administration.

This Springer imprint is published by the registered company Springer Nature Switzerland AG
The registered company address is: Gewerbestrasse 11, 6330 Cham, Switzerland

To all who fight corporate impunity across the globe.

Acknowledgments

This volume is the result of an international conference organised by Henry Rammelt, Andru Chiorean, and the editors in 2023, in Bucharest. As Colombian participant, Daniel Marín López, Romania was a rather unforeseen place for such an event, given the neoliberal thinking that has taken over Eastern Europe since the 1990s. Yet, the ERC-Consolidator Project *Transnational Advocacy Networks and Corporate Accountability for Major International Crimes* – implemented by the National University of Political Science and Public Administration (Bucharest) – brought us together in Romania, a country where corporate accountability and business and human rights are indeed incipient topics of activism. Despite this context, or maybe even because of it, we aimed to move forward the global debates on anti-impunity campaigns regarding transnational corporations and their involvement in human rights violations, with a conference on corporate accountability to take place in Eastern Europe. As Daniel put it, "manifestos" for corporate accountability can emerge in unexpected places, even in neoliberal dominated semi-peripheries.

We thank all speakers and discussants for their participation and their valuable contributions, comments and critiques. We are particularly grateful to Măriuca Petre, Mircea Vâlceanu, Roxana Robu and Cornelia Mareş (all from SNSPA) for the energy and effort they expended in organising the conference and the gracious hospitality they extended to all of us.

At different stages, Radu Mareş (Lund University), Sabine Michalowski (University of Essex), Ruxandra Ivan (Bucharest University), Daniel Marín López (University of Los Andes), Andrei Miroiu (SNSPA, Bucharest) and Arpad Todor (SNSPA, Bucharest) provided valuable feedback on different contributions and the volume as a whole. Their criticism has motivated, challenged, and inspired us. All mistakes and divergent opinions are of course ours.

We also kindly appreciate Markus Krajewski, Brigitte Reschke, and Peter Pushpanathan at Springer for their support.

This volume is part of the ERC-Consolidator project *Transnational Advocacy Networks and Corporate Accountability for Major International Crimes*. The project has received funding from the European Research Council (ERC) under the

European Union's Horizon 2020 research and innovation programme (grant agreement No. 101002993 — CORPACCOUNT), implemented by the National University of Political Science and Public Administration (Bucharest) between 2021 and 2026. In addition, our collaboration with the Movement Engaged Research Hub (George Mason University, US) has contributed to the improvement of many contributions to this volume through presentations at various conferences and seminars.

Contents

Introduction: Re-Envisioning Corporate Accountability for Human Rights Abuses. Civil Society and Transnational Action

Raluca Grosescu and John G. Dale

Abstract This introductory chapter highlights the value of socio-historical approaches for understanding the multiplicity of ideas and strategies for holding economic actors responsible for human rights violations and the massive degradation of the environment. It underlines the crucial role of transnational and intersectoral civil society alliances, but also the fragmentation of the global corporate accountability movement stemming from different ideological visions about human rights and economic development and globalisation. We argue that actor-focused analyses of corporate accountability are essential to moving beyond both depoliticised and technocratic accounts of justice in the name of supposed universalised human rights and structuralist interpretations that posit the impossibility of inclusive accountability processes due to the foundational arrangements inherent to the capitalist economic system and their legal legitimation.

1 Rethinking Corporate Accountability from an Actor-Focused Perspective

The early twentieth century witnessed a proliferation of legislative initiatives, civil and criminal litigation, and concerted demands by civil society groups across the world to hold economic actors responsible for human rights violations and environmental degradation. Scholarship from different academic disciplines has

This research was supported by the ERC-Consolidator project *Transnational Advocacy Networks and Corporate Accountability for Major International Crimes* under the European Union's Horizon 2020 research and innovation program (grant agreement No. 101002993—CORPACCOUNT).

R. Grosescu (✉)
SNSPA, Bucharest, Romania

J. G. Dale
George Mason University, Fairfax, VA, USA
e-mail: jdale@gmu.edu

R. Grosescu, J. G. Dale (eds.), *Corporate Accountability for Human Rights Violations*, Interdisciplinary Studies in Human Rights 16,
https://doi.org/10.1007/978-3-032-05569-9_1

begun to examine these accountability processes and their potential to overcome the limits of an international order that currently exempts business groups from liability for mass crimes, the destruction of nature, and the dispossession of large sectors of the global community. Nevertheless, these works have often been restrictive in their approach, confining their analysis within national borders,[1] specific spheres of activism,[2] or certain venues of norm construction, in particular the UN.[3] Moreover, this emergent literature has thus far privileged analyses of legal norms and public policies with limited insights into *why, how and by whom* they were created and enacted.[4] The dearth of socio-historical approaches to corporate accountability has resulted in either depoliticised accounts of norm formation and public policy creation[5] or in structuralist analyses that posit the impossibility of inclusive accountability processes due to the foundational arrangements inherent to the capitalist economic system and their legal legitimation.[6] The few works that have taken an actor-focused approach[7] have generally depicted the activism for corporate accountability as rather monolithic, overlooking the diversity of the actors involved and their different (and often competing) political agendas, visions of justice, and ways of rethinking the current economic order.

This volume moves forward the current academic debates by critically exploring the role, limitations, and internal fragmentation of social activism for corporate accountability across Africa, the Americas, Asia, and Europe. It analyses a variety of NGOs, trade unions, and grassroots movements and their transnational mobilisations in their attempts to hold accountable economic actors involved in massive infringement of human rights—from war crimes and crimes against humanity, to forced labour, extreme environmental degradation, and the violent targeting of human rights activists. It emphasises the diverse visions and strategies extolled by these civic actors, including civil and criminal litigation, efforts to prohibit and punish business misconduct through national and international legislation, political protests and memorialisation projects. We thus define corporate accountability as a wide series of mechanisms—both legal and non-legal—designed to denounce corporate abuses and enforce binding duties, sanctions, and remedies, as opposed to voluntary corporate self-regulation and corporate social responsibility projects, which have been heavily criticised by scholars and practitioners for their inefficacy.[8]

By adopting an actor-focused approach and examining their national and transnational forms of activism, the collection provides an innovative perspective across

---

[1] Verbitsky and Bohoslavsky (2016); García Martín (2020); for comparative works that include several national case studies, see Černič (2019); Van de Sandt and Moor (2017).

[2] Such works have focused in particular on the legal field: Michalowski (2013); Khoury and Whyte (2017); Baars (2019).

[3] See for example Rodríguez-Garavito (2017); Deva and Bilchitz (2017).

[4] See Olsen (2023); George (2021); Černič and Carrillo-Santarelli (2018); Krieger et al. (2020).

[5] Michalowski (2013); Olsen (2023); George (2021).

[6] Khoury and Whyte (2017); Tombs and Whyte (2018); Baars (2019).

[7] Dale (2011); Payne et al. (2020); The very few exceptions that have underlined fragmentation within the corporate accountability field are Grosescu (2019); Prem (2020).

[8] See Lim and Tsutsui (2011); Blowfield and Frynas (2005).

three main themes: the role of transnational and intersectoral alliances within civil society as key drivers of corporate accountability efforts; the fragmentation of the global corporate accountability movement across ontological, ideological, regional and professional lines; and the Janus-faced paradigm of transnational activism for corporate accountability. The book thereby argues that corporate accountability today does not, if ever it did, result from corporate self-governance, nor from states' determination to secure legal regulations. Rather, mobilisations initiated by civil society and social movements are the main driver advancing the criminalisation of corporate involvement in human rights violations. This is especially true when pro-accountability actors form coalitions across borders and professional sectors. Such transnational and intersectoral engagements create counter-hegemonic discourses against corporate impunity, push for more inclusive justice projects, and multiply spaces and notions of accountability.

However, their social action faces two significant obstacles. First, contemporary political, economic and legal structures more often constrain than enable binding sanctions against economic actors and durable accountability mechanisms. Such restrictive configurations include, among others, the veto power of business groups and technocrats in rapidly changing contexts of neoliberal and digital development; the weak international legislative environment that governs the relations between business, trade, and human rights; and the competing cultural structures of property rights, technology standards, and legal personhood. Second, civil society and social movements themselves are fragmenting over the meaning and scope of corporate accountability. This fragmentation is due to the different local, national and regional contexts, the variety of ideological views on human rights and economic development, and the different professional understandings of accountability processes. New human rights ontologies advocating for a posthuman order and the rights of nature also contribute to this diversity of discourses and create new challenges and opportunities for activists seeking to reckon with corporate violence.

The book thus provides a sociological alternative to previous studies that have explained the advancements and the push-backs of corporate accountability processes exclusively through institutional and structural factors. Norms and public policies do not enact themselves. They require actors to construct and endorse them. Placing these social actors at the centre of the analysis enables us to better understand *why* and *how* corporate accountability demands and their subsequent outcomes have gained global momentum, but continue to constitute a fragmented field of knowledge and activism.

2 Corporate Accountability and Transnational and Intersectoral Civil Society Coalitions

Since the publication of Keck and Sikkink's seminal work in 1998, socio-historical approaches to norm formation have flourished, underlining the role of civil society and social movements in progressively transforming human rights and environmental law, as well international justice and policy making.[9] Yet, the scholarship on corporate accountability continues to be dominated either by legal analysis with a limited focus on the social construction of norms, or by structuralist approaches that suggest practices of corporate accountability ultimately serve to create, reproduce, and legitimate the "good corporation," and thus inadvertently strengthen rather than restrain capitalist inequalities.[10] Based on case studies spanning the globe, the current volume demonstrates the crucial role of social activism in fighting corporate impunity and opening new avenues of justice. Civil society and social movement mobilisation, especially when it becomes transnational and intersectoral, constitutes the key driver of corporate accountability today, although structural constraints continue to limit these efforts. Even if confined to particular cross-border and cross-regional contexts, these transnational mobilisations, when multiplied, create discourses that counter the current status quo, generate emancipatory social projects, and propose novel understandings of rights that challenge the narrow definitions enshrined in international law.[11] While concrete results in terms of corporate accountability remain limited and ambivalent, there is an acceleration of cross-border and intersectoral mobilisations aiming to disrupt the corporate power enforced by neoliberal logics and, to a lesser extent, the dominant Eurocentric, liberal-focused discourse on rights.

Two chapters of the volume underscore the opportunities and limitations of global advocacy networks that attempt to enforce corporate accountability. Andru Chiorean analyses two major global coalitions fighting corporate impunity. He argues that class-based struggles and radical repertoires of action are impacting the landscape of corporate accountability, as the activities of the Global Campaign to Reclaim Peoples Sovereignty, Dismantle Corporate Power and Stop Impunity (Global Campaign) demonstrate. The programme of this network continues the anti-capitalist and anti-neocolonial claims of socialist and so-called Third World states during the Cold War—most clearly manifested in the project for a New International Economic Order. The Global Campaign advocates for a non-capitalist, people-centred economy that would reclaim peoples' sovereignty, ensure the equal distribution of wealth across the world, and curtail economic dispossession and the plunder of the Earth. While engaging in political negotiations within the UN, various members of the Global Campaign also employ contentious repertoires of action, such as protests, picketing, blockades, and Peoples' Tribunals against transnational corporations, free trade agreements, and international foreign debt. Nevertheless, the activity of the Global Campaign has often been eclipsed at an international level by the more institutionalised and socio-liberal International Network for Economic, Social and Cultural Rights (ESCR-Net). Encompassing more powerful and more resourceful NGOs—such as Amnesty International and the International Federation

[9] Keck and Sikkink (1998); Pellow (2007); Merry (2009); Hadden (2015); De Búrca (2021); Reiners (2022); Grosescu (2024).

[10] Khoury and Whyte (2017); Tombs and Whyte (2018); Baars (2019).

[11] For critics of the limited definitions of rights in international law see Goodale (2022); de Sousa Santos (2007); de Sousa Santos and Rodriguez-Garavito (2005); Rajagopal (2009).

of Human Rights—this coalition endorses discourses of social justice and solidarity without however promoting class struggle and radical anti-neocolonial critics.

Based on a quantitative analysis of 260 organisations, Henry Rammelt demonstrates how these organisations promote a left-leaning discourse of social inclusion, solidarity, struggle for socio-economic rights, and demands for reforming the neoliberal economic system. These ideological frames create a new ethos of political and economic change across the globe, but do not necessarily constitute a radical transformative project. In their search for funding and legitimacy, most organisations employ socially accepted repertoires of action, resort to strategies embedded in liberal forms of activism (such as litigation, political negotiations, and consumer boycotts). They also moderate their discourses and are thus unlikely to substantively change the configuration and systemic causes of current global inequalities. However, the struggle to hold economic actors accountable remains at the forefront in the fight for a better life and the empowerment of marginalised communities.

Moving from global coalitions to national and transnational corporate accountability campaigns, several chapters highlight how civil society and social movements from different world regions imagined and enforced successful justice and memorialisation projects. In his contribution on the transnationalisation of trial support groups in East Asia's war redress movement, Timothy Webster emphasises how transnational and intersectoral coalitions of activists from China, South Korea, and Japan succeeded in creating a powerful justice and memory agenda concerning forced labour perpetrated by Japan during the Second World War. Through this cross-border activism, victims of forced labour won trials or reached settlements in South Korean and Japanese courts. These linkages also contributed to a reconciliation process in a region still rife with misunderstanding, distrust, and suspicion. Furthermore, due to cross-border cooperation, forced labourers overcame many restrictions common to illiberal regimes, and were able to negotiate previously institutionalised limits to travel, to associate, and to assemble, thereby facilitating the formation of independent civil society organisations.

Victoria Basualdo examines how Argentinian trade unions formed coalitions across borders and professional fields to hold the economic accomplices of the last dictatorship (1976–1983) accountable. Such efforts resulted in guilty verdicts at the national level, as well as pro-accountability decisions by the Inter-American Court of Human Rights. They also generated memorialisation campaigns and historical reports that acknowledged the complicity of multinational corporations (including Ford, Mercedes Benz, and Techint) in mass atrocities. Moreover, they underlined the direct connections between the neoliberal economic project and the systematic infringement of labour rights and socio-economic rights during the dictatorship. Corporate accountability efforts resuscitated discourses of class struggle, enhanced long-term cooperation between Argentinian and European activists, and were widely discussed across Latin America, even if no Western company acknowledged its complicity with the dictatorship and its repressive policies.

In Brazil, as highlighted by Juan Pablo Bohoslavsky and Juan Cruz Goñi's chapter, corporate accountability efforts regarding the complicity of multinational companies with the previous dictatorship (1964–1985) also emerged in response to the mobilisation of trade unionists and the alliances they forged with other national and international justice and memory activists and NGOs. The contribution focuses on the recent agreement between the São Paulo Prosecutor's Office and the Volkswagen subsidiary in Brazil (VW do Brazil), signed in 2020. It demonstrates how—in a country marked by total impunity for dictatorial crimes—trade unions (especially in São Paulo state) played a crucial role in sparking debates about the role of Western corporations as accomplices in gross human rights violations and the interconnection between neoliberal economic doctrines and the systematic attack on labour and socio-economic rights in Latin America. Such mobilisations succeeded in enforcing this narrative through the work of the São Paulo Truth Commission, civil lawsuits against VW do Brazil, and the publicization of their cause in Western venues by cooperating with European human rights lawyers. Yet, unionists—and other Brazilian human rights groups—finally split over the terms of the agreement with VW do Brazil, a settlement that revealed the limits of civil litigation as a means of addressing corporate violence and the structural inequalities in the neoliberal economic system.

Transnational corporate accountability coalitions have also started to coalesce in Africa, as discussed in Rasul Minja's chapter on mobilisations in the East African Community (EAC). Organisations such as the East African Law Society and the East African Human Rights Institute have increasingly played a critical role in supporting lawyers and litigants across the region, as well as filing complaints on their own behalf at the East African Court of Justice.

Moving to Western Europe, Caroline Lichuma examines the mobilisations of German, French and Luxemburgish civil society for the adoption of due diligence laws (DDLs). She argues that both the French (2017) and German (2021) laws were the result of wide mobilisations from below that assembled a variety of organisations and professional groups, including NGOs, trade unions, epistemic communities, and church-based initiatives. While Luxemburg has not yet (2025) enacted such a law, civil society organisations succeeded in putting an initial legislative proposal on the agenda in 2023. Moreover, national coalitions for DDLs cooperated across borders, borrowing and adapting activist tactics and discourse frameworks employed by their counterparts. The importance of cooperation across professional sectors is also emphasised by Thomas Beckers' contribution on Dutch civil society organisations attempting to open civil law trials for corporate human rights violations committed abroad. Becker argues that in order to succeed, activists must fulfil several roles, including kickstarters, pacemakers, watchdogs, and informal assistant-prosecutors. Such functions require the involvement and cooperation of various professional groups, such as lawyers, political activists, journalists and epistemic communities.

Focusing on criminal and civil litigations in Argentina, Gabriel Pereira and Leigh Payne highlight the role of national institutional innovators and civil society groups as critical drivers of corporate accountability efforts. They revisit Keck and Sikkink's classic "boomerang model" of transnational pressure exercised by transnational advocacy networks to challenge the power of states that often protect or complicitly enable corporate malfeasance. They argue that the model does not capture significant local dynamics of power that are critical to the success of corporate accountability campaigns. In their view, while transnational mobilisations are important, intra-country and inter-sectoral collaborations are often more productive for achieving justice. Fernando Mendiola and Juan Carlos García Funes emphasise the ability of Spanish grassroot movements and trade unions to embed forced labour perpetrated under Franco's regime in twenty-first century Spanish memory politics. While the 1977 Amnesty Law remains in place and impedes prosecutions for human rights violations committed under the dictatorship, local victim groups and memory associations from Andalusia, Aragon, the Basque Country, and Valencia succeed in implementing memorialisation projects concerning forced labour perpetrated by both state and private companies and even include the right to recognition and reparation for such crimes in regional legislation. The Spanish case reflects the importance of national intersectoral activism versus transnational mobilisations, since local actors cooperated little across borders.

A similar case of grassroot activism is examined by Stephanie Triefus and Irina Velicu in their chapter on the Roşia Montana movement in Romania. Grassroots, anti-extractivist communities from a small village in Transylvania, supported by national and transnational advocacy networks, succeeded in stopping a Canadian mining project, engaged in cyanide extraction, and then inscribe their village—Roşia Montana—on the UNESCO world heritage list. However, the international investment arbitration procedure introduced by the Canadian company against the Romanian state perpetuated environmental injustice and illustrated what may be called "green crime," facilitated by a prevailing bias in arbitration procedures in favour of multinational corporate interests, even if Romania finally won.

The volume thus highlights that struggles around the inadequacies of the current international order and subsequent corporate impunity are starting to coalesce across the world. Transnational and intersectoral activism create spaces for new discourses and lines of action, even though securing a genuine counter-hegemonic victory against the neoliberal order and corporate power at a global level remains limited. The veto power of business actors in global affairs and the reluctance of governments to engage in radical reforms for social and environmental justice severely constrain the transformation of the current international order. Free trade agreements and subsequent international arbitration procedures are only one example—as illustrated by Triefus and Velicu—of how social and environmental injustices continue to affect local communities even after successful efforts to stop destructive extractivist projects. The fact that funding for social activism for corporate accountability remains dominated by state and international institutions and liberal-leaning foundations—as demonstrated by Rammelt—contributes to a deradicalisation of both discourses and actions. Judicial mechanisms, such as criminal trials and civil litigation, are severely limited by the current definitions of core international crimes and by the possibility of legal settlements that, while bringing some financial redress for victims, generally exonerate economic actors of any legal and moral responsibility (as emphasised by Bohoslavsky and Goñi, and by Raluca Grosescu's chapter on transnational cooperation for corporate accountability in Guatemala). Finally, national political constellations often impede accountability projects, such as the amnesty laws still in force in Brazil and Spain. Moreover, as demonstrated by Minja, human rights and environmental activists in the EAC face not only a legislative vacuum in terms of business and human rights, but also systematic repression exerted by their authoritarian governments.

While many case studies in this collection highlight the limitations of particular campaigns, they also reveal that civil societies working transnationally have gleaned lessons from their struggles for corporate accountability that can serve to sustain the broader movement. John G. Dale examines a transnational, indigenous-led rights of nature movement in Ecuador that successfully pre-empted the rights and extractive practices of transnational and state-owned mining corporations while creating new rights to protect indigenous communities, the Amazonian forests they inhabit, and novel legal forms of data ownership. He then compares this case to a U.S.-focused corporate accountability movement that differently constructed rights of nature to challenge corporate rights of extractivist development to demonstrate how the rights of nature project in Ecuador has subsequently influenced the political strategies of corporate accountability in the U.S. Indeed, U.S-based militants have shifted their strategy from using a "human right *to* nature" to a "rights *of* nature" discourse, realising that the former approach only served to reinforce environmental law as property law in U.S. courts, and that community arguments for protecting the environment (as "natural resources") continued to lose out to corporate property rights in corporate-friendly state courts. Although the "rights of nature" discourse has not yet resulted in U.S. court victories, an analysis of these campaigns should not be narrowly assessed in terms of immediate victory or defeat in the courts or legislatures. These campaigns are also deliberately engaged in symbolic politics to educate and mobilise support for and from other communities and movements. These rights projects—and the alternative discourses they generate within and disseminate beyond legal arenas—provide critical resources for sustaining the kind of public collective memory and activism that future movements can draw upon in the struggle for corporate accountability and the reform of rights' approaches that have often served the interests of corporations over the protection of communities and ecosystems.

3 Corporate Accountability as a Fragmented Global Cause

This volume thus shares the optimism of many scholars who underline the crucial role of civil society in positively transforming national and international norms, including in the field of corporate accountability. Nevertheless, the book also calls for a careful analysis of the ideologies and political narratives that underpin accountability claims. The scholarship that has taken an actor-focused approach to corporate accountability[12] has thus far paid little attention to the heterogeneity of groups

[12] Dale (2011); Payne et al. (2020). The very few exceptions that have underlined fragmentation within the corporate accountability field are Grosescu (2019); Prem (2020).

and networks involved in corporate accountability processes, and the way they build different—sometimes divergent—strategies for dealing with corporate violence, according to their different regional and professional backgrounds and diverse visions about world politics, economic doctrines, development, and human rights. Furthermore, current approaches have often confined themselves to (and have taken for granted) substantialist understandings of rights as promoted by the UN and most international organisations, providing no conceptual room for the way civil society and social movements imagine alternative, more inclusive visions of rights. Collective activism for creating rights from below (including to living non-humans) and their implications for corporate accountability remain understudied.

We argue that civil societies and social movements engaged in corporate accountability remain fragmented and often divided over the meaning of, and solutions for reckoning with corporate violence. This is another constraint that limits the formation of a unified and coherent global cause. Our collection thus challenges previous works which have depicted global pro-accountability movements as monolithic campaigns, driven by idealistic activists, bound together by shared values and common interests.[13] We contend that the locus of activism, within different political, economic and cultural contexts, generates diverse approaches to corporate accountability. Ideological divisions over the meaning of human rights, economic globalisation and development also create divergent visions of how to contend with corporate human rights violations.[14] Finally, different professional agendas of activism, as well as competition for funding and symbolic capital, frame different tactics and repertoires of action across corporate accountability campaigns.

The chapters by Andru Chiorean and Henry Rammelt reveal the diverse ideological inclinations of NGOs and social movements that participate in global coalitions for corporate accountability: from postcolonial and class-based approaches to liberal and socio-liberal frameworks. Such variations produce tensions between networks and have different impacts on national governments and international organisations, with the liberal version as the preferred approach of Western governments and donors. The cases of Global Campaign and ESCR-Net examined by Chiorean are two convincing examples, which are then sustained by Rammelt's wider quantitative analysis. In her contribution on transnational cooperation for corporate accountability in Guatemala, Raluca Grosescu highlights the tension between liberal discourses and Indigenous narratives. While positing the importance of transnational activism for the very survival of anti-extractivist movements in Guatemala, Grosescu also underlines that Western support for accountability campaigns has often been framed within a liberal lexicon of rights that has dominated global affairs since the mid-1970s and limited the capacity of Guatemalan Indigenous communities to assert a politics of alternative, non-liberal and non-Western autonomy. For his part, Rasul Minja demonstrates how in the EAC, activists are also

[13] Keck and Sikkink (1998). For similar approaches, see Dale (2011), Payne et al. (2020), Saage-Maaß et al. (2021).

[14] Our collection thus links the literature on corporate accountability to broader analysis on neoliberal globalization, human rights and development: Goodale (2022); Manfred Novak (2016); Rajagopal (2009); Kaltenborn et al. (2020).

divided over the best solution for dealing with corporate violence. On the one hand, some organisations accept the corporate social responsibility (CSR) frameworks and the self-regulatory agreements proposed by companies and their main representative, the East African Business Council. On the other hand, more contentious NGOs and networks, including the East African Law Society struggle for the adoption of binding norms and support legal actions in court.

Fragmentation over corporate accountability strategies also emerge within movements with similar ideological orientations. Bohoslavsky and Goñi highlight that despite the fact that leftist national and international NGOs achieved an initial consensus in launching civil litigation against VW do Brazil, activists ultimately split over the terms of the agreement reached between the company and the São Paulo Prosecutor's Office. While some hailed the settlement as the only (although limited) access to justice in a country marked by total impunity for dictatorial crimes, others criticised it as a form of "corporate wash" and even as a dangerous precedent for the perpetration of systematic corporate and state violence against human rights and environmental activists that has characterised contemporary Brazil. While underlining the role of trade unions in corporate accountability campaigns in Argentina, Basualdo's chapter underscores that the trade union movement was politically heterogeneous and varied in terms of their relationship with the dictatorship. This heterogeneity led to a fragmentation of their engagement in justice processes, and of their historical narratives about the past.

In a less contentions form, fragmentation results from the lack of dialogue between various movements working in different regions. While actors from South America, East Africa, and Southeast Asia frequently collaborate with Western European and North American militants, and across borders withing their own regions, South-South cooperation remains weak and knowledge about other regional contexts and social mobilisations poor. Minja's chapter also emphasises that while cross-border cooperation between NGOs from the EAC exists, it remains limited due to the existential threat that such organisations face from their own national governments. Moreover, Minja underlines the dominance and subsequent shortcoming of "upward accountability" in civil society activities at the expense of "downward" (bottom-up) accountability.

Yet, while this volume identifies how internal fragmentation operates to limit corporate accountability efforts, it also notes that this fragmentation can *enable* social action. The diversity of experiences, local understandings of (in)justice, cultural repertoires of collective action, modes of being, visions of the future, and historical relations to the corporations (and states) they target need not be understood only as constraining: it is also under conditions of internal diversity that new critical and progressive resistance narratives emerge. Movements that can manage these tensions and contradictions without dissolving *can* over time work to identify and address their own sources of contention and find ways to experimentally deploy a wider range of discourses as they confront a diverse array of challenges.[15] As Big

[15] See Sturgeon (1997); Latour (2018).

Tech-driven development of artificial intelligence and data mining becomes increasingly entangled with traditional practices of extractivist mining for oil, gas, coal, and precious metals and minerals,[16] the corporate accountability movement has stared to take into consideration nonhuman rights to adequately defend and mobilise support for the humans, communities, and ecosystems being impacted. Drawing on relational approaches to rights projects,[17] Dale observes in his chapter on the "rights of nature" movements in Ecuador and the United States, that this activism articulates a rights discourse that some scholars and practitioners argue will further fragment existing human rights projects (including those that advocate for the UN-recognised human right to a clean, healthy, and sustainable environment) and fail to hold corporations accountable in the Western legal systems of the Global North. However, a relational approach to understanding the rights of nature, humans, and corporations opens up strategic discursive possibilities for bridging and strengthening transnational corporate accountability activism without eclipsing the potentially emancipatory quest of human rights advocates to render us more fully human.

4 The Values and Limitations of Transnational Activism

The fragmentation of corporate accountability strategies also impacts the outcome of cross-border mobilisations. Consequently, this volume conceptualises transnational activism as a Janus-faced paradigm and provides a nuanced perspective on both the value of transnational cooperation and its shortcomings in terms of unequal power relations, discursive domination, and dependencies between organisations from the Global North and the Global South.

On the one hand, most contributions to this book argue that the formation of transnational coalitions for corporate accountability is essential. By connecting organisations, communities, and individuals across countries and regions, transnational activism brings attention to the global character of the structural inequalities and corporate violence that exemplify the contemporary world.[18] It also creates spaces of interaction that reconfigure relations of community, class, race, and gender beyond conflicting national interests and geopolitical anxieties. Coalitions across borders thus forge new solidarities and common causes against the oppressive state and market arrangements that underpin corporate impunity. Moreover, they help secure funding and offer support to local human rights and environmental activists repressed by their own governments (often in collaboration with transnational or national economic elites). It renders such groups more visible both internationally and in the home countries of the offending multinational corporations and,

[16] Crawford (2021).

[17] Jung 2024; Rodríguez-Garavito 2024.

[18] Khagram et al. (2022); Tarrow (1994); de Sousa Santos and Rodriguez-Garavito (2005).

thus, impacts the behaviour of international organisations, transnational networks of governance and the corporations themselves.[19] Finally, cooperation across borders opens up dynamic dialogues between different cultures and thus erodes powerful nationalist agendas and civilisational (mis)conceptions. It enables citizens living in different nation-states, regions, and cultural contexts to understand, and imagine alternative visions about the social world and comprehend how their (in)action affects or is affected by that of individuals living elsewhere. Transnational activism thus helps circulate alternative, more inclusive, ideas about rights, development and democracy that are rooted in non-Western, non-liberal forms of thinking—such as Indigenous cosmovisions or postcolonial and decolonial approaches to world politics. This volume thus posits the importance of moving beyond methodological nationalism to understand mobilisations for corporate accountability, and, in so doing, makes the case for inter-connected domestic, regional, and transnational contestations against injustice, inequality and impunity.[20]

On the other hand, critical studies of transnational activism have highlighted that global struggles for rights and justice remain a terrain dominated by organisations and institutions that are based in the richest countries of the Global North—which often function as donors for organisations in the Global South. Consequently, global issues are typically communicated and played out by professional groups and elites from Western Europe and North America—thereby perpetuating neo-colonial exclusion and injustice.[21] Moreover, NGOs from the Global North do not necessarily challenge hegemonic systems that generate structural inequality and dispossession. On the contrary, they frequently channel private or government funding, which arrives with particular conditions that impose Western values or serves certain Northern economic or political interests,[22] including the effective naturalisation of markets as the key driver of progress and development.[23] In most cases, discourses from the Global North remain confined to Western realities and liberal understandings of the social world, which are then deliberately or unintentionally exported to the Global South. Even when adopting more radical approaches, Western-based NGOs have to translate demands from the Global South into a vocabulary familiar to Western societies in order to gain support for their campaigns.[24] These translations often distort social realities and generate exotic and simplistic accounts of non-Western societies, particularly as far as Indigenous populations are concerned. The dependence of Global Southern civil society actors on Western institutional donors further limits their actions. Global Southern activists, and especially grassroot groups with few financial resources must market themselves and adapt to the political ideas and organisational behaviour of donors. They often have to frame

[19] Keck and Sikkink (1998); Dale (2011); Dale and Samara (2008).

[20] Dale and Kislenko (2022).

[21] Sénit and Biermann (2021); Struett (2008).

[22] Munck (2006).

[23] Mitchell (2002); Unger (2007); Block (2018).

[24] de Sousa Santos (2015); Gill (2009); Bueckert (2019); Freeman (2024).

their cause in legal categories and definitions that do not necessarily fit their own society's visions of the social world.[25] Dependence on Western funding risks a reformulation of goals, a de-radicalisation of discourses, and the use of a toolbox and a vocabulary provided by the Western (liberal) script.[26]

Several contributions in this volume highlight this two-sided feature of transnational activism for corporate accountability. Grosescu demonstrates the crucial role of Westren-based NGOs in supporting Guatemalan Indigenous human rights and environmental defenders. In a country marked by endemic corruption, pervasive racism against Indigenous populations, and violence against anti-extractivist campaigners, international support and transnational cooperation were crucial for securing the very survival of those who opposed extractivist development and the dominant economic elite. Nevertheless, the corporate accountability campaigns developed in the Global North must translate Global South, Indigenous discourses into a vocabulary embedded in liberal Western thinking about rights and economics. Such translation alters Global South narratives and emphasises the limits of transnational class and culture-based solidarities.

In his chapter on global coalitions for corporate accountability, Chiorean points to the connections between human rights approaches and economic questions. He shows how more radical organisations—most of them originating in the Global South—mobilise the language of human rights to explicitly denounce capitalism, demand the economic self-determination of people from the Global South, and advocate for a more equal redistribution of resources at a global level. In contrast, many organisations from the Global North vacate the economic arena and confine themselves to criticising violations of civil and political rights. In so doing, they allow for a shift in responsibility for global poverty and inequality away from international economic arrangements toward states in the Global South. They also cultivate an antipathy towards any politicisation of the economy, effectively serving to naturalise the market. The language of human rights is thus used to undermine an amalgamation of political solidarity capable of challenging the unequal tenets of the current international economy.

Examining the national coalitions for the adoption of DDLs, Lichuma highlights that while members of these coalitions collaborate with Global South counterparts, they have little power to incorporate Global South claims in Western European national legislations. Parliamentary debates on DDLs remain dominated by national political actors, without consultation with actors from the Global South. The emergence of norms on business and human rights in Europe reflects the asymmetrical power dynamic between the Global North and South with problematic ramifications for states, communities and individuals of the Global South that continue to be disenfranchised from the negotiation legal processes relevant to them. The contributions by Becker and Grosescu emphasise how corporate accountability activists in the Netherlands and Canada respectively act in the name of Global Southern victims

[25] Bob (2012).

[26] Saunders and Roth (2019); Samson (2020).

of corporate violence, but design their pro-accountability strategies within their own judicial and political contexts. Interested in opening avenues of justice, their reference point remains the Dutch or the Canadian systems with their own opportunities and constraints.

In terms of funding, Rammelt underscores how organisations from the Global South, due to their dependency on donors from the Global North, borrow established vocabularies of rights and subsequent repertoires of action that do not necessarily correspond to their economic and cultural contexts. In Guatemala, as highlighted by Grosescu, international funding for anti-extractivist activism is generally filtered through Western NGOs working in the country, which are able—by dint of their Western vocabulary and fundraising skills—to attract doners and become the legitimate redistributors of funding to local communities and NGOs. While Indigenous groups and other poorly resourced movements benefit from this financial support, they are forced to connect their demands to Western liberal activist agendas rather than to projects that can ensure their economic and political autonomy. Moreover, Western Europe and North America remain the main nodes of global entanglement in terms of corporate accountability, often at the expense of South-South cooperation. While several chapters in the book also underline the existence of regional cooperation within Latin America, EAC or South-East Asia, trans-regional networks that do not involve Western countries are rare. More research is needed to unpack the reasons behind this limited cooperation, but the lack of funding likely stands as one key explanation.

There are, however, more optimistic accounts in which the Janus-faced paradigm is less visible. Timothy Webster demonstrates the role of cross-border collaboration—between Japanese and Korean citizens on the one hand, and between Japanese and Chinese citizens on the other—in generating trust and reconciliation. Bohoslavsky and Goñi and Basualdo also provide convincing examples of the critical importance of transnational activism in the cooperation between Western and Latin American militants and in the corporate accountability coalitions formed within the Southern Cone itself.

To be sure, "going transnational" is not always a winning strategy for organisations or communities seeking justice.[27] Transnational activism encompasses both promises and perils for the corporate accountability movement. How corporate accountability activists organise the social relations upon which they forge their transnational solidarities clearly matters. This collection not only identifies how various ways of transnationally structuring these relations has enabled and constrained collective action for corporate accountability, but also provides readers with methodological (ethnographic, historical, statistical and comparative) insights into the sources, processes, and patterns of their reproduction. In so doing, it lays critical new groundwork for addressing the conditions under which thinking and acting transnationally is likely (or unlikely) to advance corporate accountability.

[27] See Bob (2005); Hersford and Kozol (2002); Dale (2013).

References

Baars G (2019) The corporation, law and capitalism. A radical perspective on the role of law. Brill, Leiden
Block F (2018) Capitalism: the future of an illusion. University of California Press, Los Angeles
Blowfield M, Frynas JG (2005) Critical perspective on corporate social responsibility. Spec Iss Int Aff 81(3):499
Bob C (2005) The marketing of rebellion: insurgents, media and international activism. Cambridge University Press, Cambridge
Bob C (2012) What issues rouse global civil society? In: Moksnes H, Melin M (eds) Global civil society: Shifting powers in a shifting world. Uppsala Centre for Sustainable Development, pp 83–89
Bueckert M (2019) Boycotts and revolution: debating the legitimacy of the African National Congress in the Canadian anti-apartheid movement, 1969–94. Radic Hist Rev 134:96–115
Černič JL (2019) Corporate accountability under socio-economic rights. Routledge, London
Černič JL, Carrillo-Santarelli N (2018) The future of business and human rights. Theoretical and practical consideration for a UN treaty. Cambridge University Press, Cambridge
Crawford K (2021) Atlas of AI: power, politics, and the planetary costs of artificial intelligence. Yale University Press
Dale JG (2011) Free Burma: transnational legal action and corporate accountability. University of Minnesota Press, Minneapolis
Dale JG (2013) Review of internal affairs: how the structure of NGOs transforms human rights by Wendy H. Wong. Am J Sociol 119(3):875–877
Dale JG, Kislenko I (2022) Invitation to transnational sociology. In: Muschert G, Budd K, Dillaway H, Lane D, Nair M, Smith J (eds) Global agenda for social justice, vol 2. Policy Press, Bristol, pp 109–119
Dale JG, Samara TR (2008) Legal pluralism within a transnational network of governance: the extraordinary case of rendition. Law Soc Just Glob Dev 12(2):1–19
De Búrca G (2021) Reframing human rights in a turbulent era. Oxford University Press, Oxford
de Sousa Santos B (2007) Another knowledge is possible: beyond northern epistemologies. Verso, London
de Sousa Santos BS (2015) Epistemologies of the south: justice against epistemicide. Routledge, London
de Sousa Santos B, Rodriguez-Garavito CA (2005) Law and globalization from below. Towards a cosmopolitan legality. Cambridge University Press, Cambridge
Deva S, Bilchitz D (2017) Building a treaty on business and human rights. Cambridge University Press, Cambridge
Freeman D (2024) Sovereignty, human rights and the regulation of transnational corporations: a critical spatial analysis of civil society proposals for a binding treaty. Globalizations 21(1):1–19
García Martín L (2020) Transitional justice, corporate accountability and socio-economic rights. Lessons from Argentina. Routledge, London
George E (2021) Incorporating rights. Strategies to advance corporate accountability. Oxford University Press, Oxford
Gill L (2009) The limits of solidarity: labor and transnational organizing against Coca-Cola. Am Ethnol 36(4):667–680
Goodale M (2022) Reinventing human rights. Stanford University Press, Palo Alto
Grosescu R (2019) Transnational advocacy networks and corporate accountability for gross human rights violations in Argentina and Colombia. Glob Soc 33(3):400–418
Grosescu R (2024) Justice and memory after dictatorship. Latin America, Central Eastern Europe, and the fragmentation of international criminal law. Oxford University Press, Oxford
Hadden J (2015) Networks in contention: the divisive politics of climate change. Cambridge University Press, Cambridge

Hersford WS, Kozol W (2002) Just advocacy? Women's human rights, transnational feminisms, and the politics of representation. Rutgers University Press, New Brunswick
Jung M (2024) Rights projects: a relational sociology of rights in globalization. Sociol Theory 42(3):256–281
Kaltenborn M, Krajewski M, Kuhn H (2020) Sustainable development goals and human rights. Springer, London
Keck ME, Sikkink K (1998) Activists beyond borders. Advocacy networks in international politics. Cornell University Press, Ithaca
Khagram S, Sikkink K, Riker JV (2022) Restructuring world politics: transnational social movements, networks, and norms. University of Minnesota Press, Minneapolis
Khoury S, Whyte D (2017) Corporate human rights violations. Global prospects for legal action. Routledge, London
Krieger H, Peters A, Kreuze L (2020) Due diligence in the international legal order. Oxford University Press, Oxford
Latour B (2018) An inquiry into modes of existence: an anthropology of the moderns. Harvard University Press, Cambridge
Lim A, Tsutsui K (2011) Globalization and commitment in corporate social responsibility: cross-national analyses of institutional and political-economy effects. Am Sociol Rev 77(1):69–98
Manfred Novak M (2016) Human rights or global capitalism: the limits of privatization. Pennsylvania University Press, Philadelphia
Merry SE (2009) Human rights and gender violence: translating international law into local justice. University of Chicago Press, Chicago
Michalowski S (2013) Corporate accountability in the context of transitional justice. Routledge, New York
Mitchell T (2002) Rule of experts: Egypt, techno-politics, modernity. University of California Press, Los Angeles
Munck R (2006) Global civil society: royal road or slippery path. Volunt Int J Volunt Nonprofit Org 17:325–332
Olsen T (2023) Seeking justice: access to remedy for corporate human rights abuse. Cambridge University Press, Cambridge
Payne LA, Pereira G, Bernal-Bermúdez L (2020) Transitional justice and corporate accountability from below: deploying Archimedes' lever. Cambridge University Press, Cambridge
Pellow DN (2007) Resisting global toxics: transnational movements for environmental justice. MIT Press, Boston
Prem B (2020) Private military and security firms as legitimate governors. From barricades to boardrooms. Routledge, London
Rajagopal B (2009) International law from below. Development, social movements and third world resistance. Cambridge University Press, Cambridge
Reiners (2022) Transnational lawmaking coalitions for human rights. Cambridge University Press
Rodríguez-Garavito C (2017) Business and human rights: beyond the end of the beginning. Cambridge University Press, Cambridge
Rodríguez-Garavito C (2024) More than human rights: an ecology of law, thought and narrative for earthly flourishing. NYU Law, New York
Saage-Maaß M et al (2021) Transnational legal activism in global value chains. The Ali Enterprises factory fire and the struggle for justice. Springer, London
Samson C (2020) The colonialism of human rights: ongoing hypocrisies of western liberalism. Polity Press, Cambridge
Saunders C, Roth S (2019) NGOs and social movement theory. In: Davies T (ed) Routledge handbook of NGOs and international relations. Routledge, London
Sénit C-A, Biermann F (2021) In whose name are you speaking? The marginalization of the poor in global civil society. Global Pol 12(5):581–591
Struett MJ (2008) The politics of constructing the international criminal court. NGOs, discourse, and agency. Springer, London

Sturgeon N (1997) Ecofeminist natures: Race, gender, feminist theory and political action. Routledge, London
Tarrow S (1994) Power in movement: social movements, collective action, and politics. Cambridge University Press, Cambridge
Tombs S, Whyte D (2018) Corporate criminal: why corporations must be abolished. Routledge, London
Unger RM (2007) Free trade reimagined: the world division of labor and the method of economics. Princeton University Press, Princeton
Van de Sandt J, Moor M (2017) La Paz, responsabilidad de todos. La responsabilidad corporativa en la justicia transicional: lecciones para Colombia. PAX, Utrecht
Verbitsky H, Bohoslavsky JP (2016) The economic accomplices to the Argentine dictatorship: outstanding debts. Cambridge University Press, Cambridge

Raluca Grosescu is a Lecturer in Politics at the National University of Political Science and Public Administration, Bucharest, where she leads the ERC-Consolidator Project "Transnational Advocacy Networks and Corporate Accountability for Major International Crimes." Her work focuses on the history of international criminal law, memory politics and corporate accountability. Her latest publications include the monograph *Justice and Memory after Dictatorship: Latin America, Central Eastern Europe and the Fragmentation of International Criminal Law* (Oxford University Press in 2024) and the co-edited volume *Socialism and International Law. The Cold War and its Legacies* (Oxford University Press in 2024).

John G. Dale is Associate Professor of Sociology and Director of Movement Engaged at George Mason University. He was a Science and Technology Innovation Program Fellow at the Woodrow Wilson Center for International Scholars (2019–20) where he researched the digital transformation of human rights, and a Japan Society for the Promotion of Science Visiting Research Fellow (2021–22) exploring efforts to integrate human rights into national policies on AI and robotics. He serves as Scientific Advisor on the ERC-Consolidator Project "*Transnational Advocacy Networks and Corporate Accountability for Major International Crimes.*" Dr. Dale was elected Council Member of the American Sociological Association's Section on Human Rights (2019–2022) and to the Steering Committee of the Science & Human Rights Coalition of the American Association for the Advancement of Science (2018–24). He is author of *Free Burma: Transnational Legal Action and Corporate Accountability* (University of Minnesota Press, 2011) and co-author of *Political Sociology: Power and Participation in the Modern World* (Oxford University Press, 2009).

Corporate Accountability: A Fragmented Global Cause?

“A World Where There Are Many Worlds.” Fragmentation of Civil Society Advocacy for a UN Business and Human Rights Treaty

Andru Chiorean

Abstract This chapter explores the activities of two key transnational advocacy networks concerned with holding economic actors accountable for human rights violations and massive environmental degradation. Over the past decade, the Global Campaign to Dismantle Corporate Power and Stop Impunity and the International Network for Economic, Social and Cultural Rights have become important actors in the ongoing drafting of a UN Binding Treaty on Business and Human Rights, as well as in engaging in political and legal activism and transnational cooperation to improve corporate accountability. The chapter argues that these two networks maintain important differences in terms of historical and political culture, membership, and funding, which affect their strategies for corporate accountability. It underlines their points of convergence, but also their divergent constitutive visions of resistance to the capitalist mode of production and, consequently, their different solutions for the alleviation of the consequences of corporate wrongdoing. It also highlights how the fragmentation of the global corporate accountability cause offers a fresh angle to explore the limitations of civil society advocacy at the international level.

1 Introduction

On the evening of 26 June 2014, activists from social movements and civil society organisations (CSOs) from all over the world gathered at the office of Franciscan International in Geneva to celebrate the passing of the long-awaited UN Resolution 26/9. Co-sponsored by Ecuador and South Africa, the resolution established a

This research was supported by the ERC-Consolidator project *Transnational Advocacy Networks and Corporate Accountability for Major International Crimes* under the European Union’s Horizon 2020 research and innovation program (grant agreement No. 101002993—CORPACCOUNT).

A. Chiorean (✉)
SNSPA, Bucharest, Romania

R. Grosescu, J. G. Dale (eds.), *Corporate Accountability for Human Rights Violations*, Interdisciplinary Studies in Human Rights 16,
https://doi.org/10.1007/978-3-032-05569-9_2

"working group mandated to develop an internationally legally binding instrument to regulate, in international human rights law, the activities of transnational corporations (TNCs) and other business enterprises". The atmosphere, predictably, was one of celebration. However, amidst the hearty congratulations and champagne-popping, questions about the limits of any future collaboration were already looming in the background. Recalling the scene, one activist contrasted the mildly optimistic tone of his speech to the general mood of the gathering: "let's see what happens from now on because the [political] differences between us regarding what we envision the Treaty should entail will not be worked out easily and most likely will pose further challenges".[1] The shared interest of civil society in passing the resolution for the Treaty had spawned unprecedented unity, but the activist was eager to add, this unity derived more from circumstantial agreement on the need for a Treaty than from deep political affinities: "in terms of the content of the Treaty, there will be disagreements between us [...]. Our mutual commitment to sustaining the Treaty process probably remains the sole factor that can continue binding us together".[2]

The mobilisation of civil society as a major force pushing for the adoption of the UN Treaty on Business and Human Rights (UN Treaty) has been widely acknowledged as a catalyst for systemic normative change in the UN's business and human rights strategy.[3] Remarkably, the Treaty process saw one of the highest participation from civil society in negotiating a UN international instrument.[4] Sympathetic observers, self-styled narratives, as well as more neutral analyses often depict the global civil society struggle for corporate accountability in idealistic terms. Such accounts consistently represent transnational advocacy networks (TANs) in a dialectical relationship with the state system and business interests, and herald them as "principled" actors in an amoral political and economic international system. They also emphasise common values and moral authority which ostensibly construct a counter-hegemonic project aimed at altering state or corporate power.[5] Even the evolving literature on TANs and their campaigns, despite extensively addressing questions of network formation and the material condition of their emergence, rarely considers the critical task of exploring the ideological and normative differences among various networks and actors.[6]

However, as I will show in this chapter, the transnational campaign for a UN Treaty to regulate business and human rights has been characterised by broad, dynamic and heterogenous coalitions. This global campaign intersects not only with the North/South divide, various polycentric fields of action, and contrasting formulations of sovereignty, but also competing visions of economic development, legal structures, and human rights. The chapter thus enriches previous scholarship by examining the corporate accountability movement at the level of the UN as a site of

[1] Personal interview with Gonzalo Berrón, 19.02.2024 (online).

[2] Ibid.

[3] Ibid.

[4] Personal interview with Alberto Villarreal, 02.04.20024 (online).

[5] Florini (2000); Edwards and Gaventa (2001).

[6] Keck and Sikkink (1998); Hertel (2006); Joachim and Loacher (2008); Bob (2009).

uneven political contention. In does so by examining two of the largest, transnationally active and influential networks involved in corporate accountability: the Global Campaign to Reclaim Peoples' Sovereignty, Dismantle Corporate Power and Stop Impunity (Global Campaign); and the International Network for Economic, Social and Cultural Rights (ESCR-Net). Encompassing more than 500 member organisations, these movements bring together a diverse range of local, national, and global actors consisting of transnational social movements, peasants and indigenous groups, trade unions, and local and international human rights NGOs. These TANs have mobilised political and legal strategies for corporate accountability at local, regional, and international scales, and notably, they are the only networks to have submitted their own proposals to the UN for a treaty on business and human rights.

Both networks are ardent advocates of the adoption of such an international legally binding instrument, and some of their constituent members are part of both organisations. However, ESCR-Net and Global Campaign reveal important differences in terms of historical and political culture, membership, and funding, which also impact their visions of corporate accountability. Since human rights law does not yet directly legally bind TNCs, a key normative objective of the proposed treaty is to establish obligations for businesses within international human rights law. However, the nature and extent of the obligations often give rise to divergent visions regarding the degree of regulation and the nature of enforcement mechanisms. As explored later in the chapter, these divisions are not solely of a technical nature. Rather, they reveal underlying ideological and political rifts, as well as differing historical and organisational time frames.

The chapter argues that political differences and expectations, whether overt or subtle, alongside diverse cultural and historical formations, and competing ideological and legal perspectives on the scope and nature of human rights, are just as important as the joint efforts of Global Campaign and ESCR-Net to advance the adoption of the UN Treaty. It further contends that these networks, given their positioning in the socio-legal debate on the politics of rights and engagement with global legal and economic structures, perpetuate the cleavage between the liberal type of civil society (ESCR-Net) and the counter-hegemonic type (Global Campaign). Unlike the former, the latter regards legality as attuned to the dynamic political struggle for social justice and upholds a more collectivist vision of (human) rights as an expression of popular sovereignty and peoples' right to self-determination.[7]

The formulation of sovereignty is key to devising international law to regulate TNCs. As other authors have argued, Global Campaign's aim is to create a "global sovereignty", in which "sovereignty is vertically displaced upwards to a global level and downwards to the people" and thus establish an emancipatory universal politico-economic order that would enable both the regulation of TNCs and the effective protection of the human rights of people and peoples.[8] The more liberal-oriented activist stream, represented by ESCR-Net, does not overtly politicise either the dominant economic model of neoliberal globalisation nor its political embodiment,

[7] Santos and Rodríguez-Garavito (2005), pp. 15–16; Brennan and Berrón (2020).

[8] Freeman (2024), p. 2.

liberal democracy. Although it includes some organisations with anti-neoliberal credentials, ESCR-Net remains largely anchored in the human rights framework that primarily addresses the negative consequences and human rights abuses stemming from the workings of global economy. In contrast to Global Campaign, ESCR-Net stands for extending horizontally the sovereignty of Northen states into the territories of the Southern states in order to protect human rights in the latter. It is what Freedman has called "imperial sovereignty", a conceptual framework grounded in the imperial spatiality of the Western-inspired human rights regime which, despite its support for TNCs regulation, does not challenge the Global North's "imperial spatial order".[9]

Comparing such contexts, ideas, and different visions of activism is key to understanding these TANs and their approaches to corporate accountability. Yet, in doing so, we must avoid conflating affinities with identities, and differences with animosities. To capture the political vocabulary and legal language in relation to the UN Treaty, this chapter compares the two networks in terms of what each identifies as their three major points of contention. First, there is the "depth" question of the UN Treaty (or *ratione personae*), which pertains to the types of business enterprises that should be subject to the Treaty. Second, the "breadth" question (*ratione materiae*), concerns the kinds of human rights that should be encompassed by the Treaty and the ways that corporate responsibility with to respect human rights can be operationalised. The third contentious issue pertains to mechanisms designed to offer justice and remedy to affected people and communities in the event that the Treaty is adopted.

My analysis combines discourse analysis of various written sources—including official submissions to the UN, reports, press releases, newsletters, advocacy and policy papers, and the proposal drafted by the networks themselves for a UN Treaty—and direct observation conducted at the 2022 session of the UN Business and Human Rights Forum, the 2023 session of the open-ended inter-governmental working group on TNCs and other business enterprises with respect to human rights, and during field research in South Africa in September 2023. I have also conducted over ten interviews with representatives of various organisational members of the two networks, which allowed to better make sense of internal dynamics and personal assessments of various discourses surrounding the Treaty process.

2 The Challenges of an Entrenched Neoliberal Orthodoxy of Human Rights

International organisations, governments, CSOs, and business associations, all agree on the necessity of managing the adverse impacts of corporate activities on human rights and state governance. However, there is discord regarding the approach required to achieve this goal. The main point of contention revolves around whether

[9] Ibid.

the governance of corporate behaviour leading to human rights violations should be addressed through a binding UN treaty in the area of business and human rights or through soft-law (voluntary) instruments. The latter approach has been favoured by the states of the Global North, while the consensus among the states of the Global South is towards the former. The disagreement over the legal nature of obligations is thus grounded in broader political divisions along the North-South axis, including competing visions of the global environment of capitalism, economic development, issues of national sovereignty, corporate responsibility, and beliefs about the role of the state in socioeconomic development.[10]

This political polarisation has also significantly influenced regulatory initiatives related to business and human rights at the UN level during the last half century. The most recent initiative—the ongoing negotiations for a UN Treaty on Business and Human Rights—was sparked by a resolution tabled by Ecuador and South Africa, co-sponsored by Bolivia, Cuba, and Venezuela, and adopted by the UN Human Rights Council on 26 June 2014 (Resolution 26/9). Robust backing for the Resolution also came from a large-scale global campaign led by civil society advocating for corporate accountability. For instance, the Treaty Alliance, a global network bringing together more than 600 CSOs, some of whom were involved in previous attempts at the UN to regulate TNCs, was formed in 2012 to support the adoption of Resolution 26/9.[11] By highlighting the struggles of victims in holding TNCs accountable for human rights violations, the Alliance played a pivotal role in both exposing the limitations of previously voluntary UN initiatives in terms of business and human rights, and rallying state support for a binding international instrument. In response to the adoption of the Resolution, in 2014, the UN Human Rights Council established an open-ended intergovernmental working group (OEIWG) to develop proposals to move forward inter-state negotiations for the achievement of a legally binding instrument to regulate the activities of TNCs.[12]

The political environment was favourable for the adoption of the Resolution and the creation of the OEIWG. The rise of the so-called "pink tide" of left-wing governments in the 2000s resurrected debates about the meaning of democracy and economic justice in Latin America. In terms of economic and diplomatic policies, "pink tide" governments were, to a large extent, a reaction to the state corporatisation accelerated by the "Washington Consensus" policies of unchained free

[10] Throughout the chapter the distinction between Global North and Global South is understood as dynamic rather than static. I use Global South in a broader sense, not strictly confined to its geographical connotations, but rather to encompass various forms of economic subordination associated with neoliberal globalisation. See de Sousa Santos (2005).

[11] See https://www.treatymovement.com (accessed 28.07.2024).

[12] Resolution 26/9 established an open-ended inter-governmental working group (OEIWG) to "elaborate an internationally legally binding instrument to regulate, in international human rights law, the activity of transnational corporations and other business enterprises." See UN Human Rights Council (UNHRC) Resolution 26/9 Elaboration of an International Legally Binding Instrument on Transnational Corporations and Other Business Enterprises with Respect to Human Rights (26 June 2014) UN Doc A/HRC/RES/26/9.

markets, the elimination of trade barriers, privatisation and economic deregularisation.[13] Such policies changed the structure of the state, trapped Latin American countries in asymmetrical free trade agreements with the United States and spearheaded the extractivist model.[14] As a general trend, these governments aspired to reconfigure national economies through reforms aimed at correcting the effects of the markets, redistributing national wealth and assuming control over key economic sectors.[15] The 2008 global financial crisis further spotlighted how national economic policies were subordinated to clusters of financial institutions and TNCs.[16] Against this political and economic backdrop, and influenced by Ecuador's long-standing case against Texaco-Chevron regarding the environmental damage sustained during the company's oil exploitation in the Amazon,[17] the left-leaning government of Rafael Correa sponsored the UN Resolution with the goal to create a binding instrument to regulate TNCs under international human rights law. The resolution came up against UN's "new regulatory dynamic", a "smart mix" of (mainly) voluntary and mandatory measures in the field business and human rights that aimed to foster a better alignment between public and private governance systems.[18]

In the aftermath of the Cold War, the UN had shifted toward a model of "polycentric governance" based on the premise that states alone could no longer adequately address their diverse societal needs. Thus, constructing a framework for business and human rights relied on "informal cooperation", "public-private partnerships", and "multistakeholder processes".[19] This approach led to the emergence of soft-law initiatives such as the Global Compact (2000) and the UN Guiding Principles on Business and Human Rights (2011), which were focused on flexible approaches to gaining the commitment of businesses to human rights obligations without, however, imposing binding norms.

The adoption of UN Resolution 26/9 brought new hope for a shift in this voluntary regime. Yet, despite the extensive support from CSOs and the mobilisation of countries from the Global South, the Treaty proposal was divisive from the outset.[20]

---

[13] Gold and Zagato (2020), pp. 7–8.

[14] Gills (2023); Chagnon et al. (2022); Gudynas (2018); Martín (2017).

[15] Buono and Lara (2007).

[16] Tooze (2008), p. 346.

[17] Pellegrini et al. (2020).

[18] Ruggie (2014), pp. 6–8.

[19] Ruggie (2015).

[20] Of the 47 member states of the Human Rights Council, the resolution was supported by 20 (Algeria, Benin, Burkina Faso, China, Congo, Cote d'Ivoire, Cuba, Ethiopia, India, Indonesia, Kazakhstan, Kenya, Morocco, Namibia, Pakistan, Philippines, Russia, South Africa, Venezuela, and Vietnam) and opposed by 14 (Austria, Czech Republic, Estonia, France, Germany, Ireland, Italy, Japan, Montenegro, South Korea, Romania, Macedonia, the United Kingdom, and the United States of America). 13 member states abstained (Argentina, Botswana, Brazil, Chile, Costa Rica, Gabon, Kuwait, Maldives, Mexico, Peru, Saudi Arabia, Sierra Leone, and the United Arab Emirates).

States from the Global North, aligned with influential corporate entities, opposed the idea of a binding treaty, thereby reaffirming their commitment to a governance framework reliant on existing voluntary initiatives.[21] Global North states and business actors also worried that the Treaty proposal might revive the 2003 proposal submitted by the UN Working Group on the Working Methods and Activities of the TNCs (known as UN Draft Norms), which imposed positive obligations on companies regarding the realisation of human rights, meaning that companies not only had to respect human rights, but were also obligated to promote such rights and refrain from any direct or indirect contribution to, or benefit from, human rights violations.[22]

For some, the Treaty proposal signalled a potential attempt to revisit the protracted debates of the 1970s and 1980s, during which the regulation of TNCs featured prominently in the New International Economic Order (NIEO) programme for reorganising the postcolonial economic order.[23] Adopted by the United Nations General Assembly in 1974, the NIEO declaration envisaged an international economic order that would correct global inequalities and redress the injustices of the postcolonial economic order through effective control over natural resources, debt forgiveness, fair commodity prices, technology transfers, and the regulation of TNCs.[24] As some scholars have noted, the strident defence of the sovereignty of newly independent states placed the project in direct opposition to the new human rights movement of the time.[25] While the latter was focused on individual rights, the NIEO inspired a vision of freedom and rights of individual citizens that derived from national independence and "equal state sovereignty".[26] It privileged collective rights, the rights of states and peoples, and the right to permanent sovereignty over natural resources as a complement to the political right to self-determination.[27]

[21] These initiatives comprise the OECD Guidelines for Multinational Enterprises (1976), the ILO tripartite Declaration of Principles Concerning Multinational Enterprises and Social Policies (1977), the United Nations Global Compact (2000), and the United Nations Guiding Principles (2011).

[22] See Surya Deva (2021), pp. 149–151.

[23] Between 1977 and 1990, negotiations for a draft Code containing standards for corporate conduct occurred that covered a broad array of government-TNCs relations: respect for national sovereignty, non-interference in internal political affairs, respect for human rights and fundamental freedoms. However, as the ideological climate became more radicalised in developed countries (unchaining free-marketisation) and the Soviet-led camp disintegrated, negotiations cooled. The pivot by developing countries towards attracting foreign investment and the proliferation of bilateral investment agreements also moved the focus from investor responsibility to investor protection. Negotiations for the Draft Code were thus abandoned in 1992. See Sauvant (2015) and Hamdani and Ruffing (2017).

[24] United Nations General Assembly (1974).

[25] Whyte (2018), p. 174.

[26] Freeman (2024), p. 7.

[27] Ishay (2008), Ch. 4; and *contra*, Moyn (2010).

Indeed, there was no mention of human rights, but an emphasis on the reform of the international trading and investment law regimes.[28]

Both the aforementioned initiatives ultimately failed due to staunch opposition from Global North states and corporations, or were rendered obsolete by unfavourable political and economic timing and legal uncertainties surrounding subjecting companies to norms usually demanded of the state.[29] Contemporary human rights law is focused, largely, on the same legal regimes—in trade, investment, and finance—that the NIEO contested.[30] Yet, unlike the NIEO, dominant human rights activism does not seek to radically alter these regimes, but only to mitigate certain damaging aspects of their functioning. As will be seen later in this chapter, the challenge of how to adapt human rights law to provide a mechanism for global redistribution, also challenges any collaboration between the largest civil society networks supporting the UN Treaty.

Thus far, scholarly research on the Treaty process has primarily centred either on normative issues—the normative potential, contribution, and impact of the Treaty on the international regulatory framework[31]—or on descriptive questions pertaining to the development of the drafts during the annual and inter-sessional negotiations of the OEIWG.[32] An examination of how various CSOs imagined different normative aspects of the Treaty according to their own political and ideological perspectives is still largely missing. The lack of such analysis can partially be explained by the formation of the Treaty Alliance, a large heterogenous alliance of CSOs that in many regards is the driving force behind the Treaty process. The Alliance was formed by Global Campaign, a network grounded in social movements, alongside other human rights NGOs, mainly from the Global North, most prominent among them being ESCR-Net, and For the Right of Food and Nutrition International (FIAN).[33] In addition, transnational coalitions such as the Global Interparliamentary Network, Feminists for a Binding Treaty, and the International Federation for Human Rights later joined the Treaty Alliance. The coalition publicly asserted itself as a "space for convergence of organisations and movements", a tactical alliance to advance international law in terms of business and human rights.[34] Its objective was not to eliminate the differences between various groups, whether material or normative, but to adopt an approach that fostered flexibility and created opportunities for individual members to pursue their agendas. Consequently, the Alliance endeavoured to mediate the diverse ideological nuances and political differences of its members.[35]

---

[28] Anghie (2019), pp. 435–438.

[29] de Schutter (2015). See also Bilchitz (2017), pp. 191–92.

[30] Anghie (2019), p. 438.

[31] Bilchitz (2016)

[32] Bantekas (2021).

[33] Personal interview with Gonzalo Berrón, 19.02.2024 (online).

[34] Suárez Franco and Fyfe (2018), p. 157; Civicus (2017).

[35] Suárez Franco and Fyfe (2018), p. 148.

Although the Alliance is united in advancing the Treaty process, its member organisations are far from embodying a unified front about its form and the content. According to one activist I interviewed in 2024, "we [Global Campaign], the International Commission of Jurists, FIAN, and ESCR-Net, attempted to establish a common political and ideological position but it was so problematic that at one point I just said: Why don't we give up on the Treaty Alliance? All these tensions just divide us!"[36] Another activist from Global Campaign confirmed to me that the political cleavages between Global Campaign and human rights-oriented organisations led to the recalibration of the Treaty Alliance as a forum for information exchange and analysis only. In his words, the Treaty Alliance is "only process oriented, but not content oriented ... there is no consensus on content issues, indeed the only issue we came together on was that we need to protect the Treaty process".[37] Consequently, the consensus among the members of the Alliance is that common statements on content issues related to the Treaty are impossible. Some activists from Global Campaign believe that the Alliance invariably tried to pressure them to water down their more radical demands,[38] but also concede that "occasionally our fellow members in the Alliance were subjected to the heat of the political discourse of our most radical members, but this is because the human rights NGOs are hesitant to challenge the entrenched orthodoxy of human rights".[39]

3 Global Campaign and ESCR-Net: Institutional Background and Historical Linkages

3.1 Global Campaign and the Radical Reformulation of an Emancipatory Legal Framework

Established in 2012 as a coalition of social movements, CSOs, trade unions, environmental NGOs, human rights advocates, citizens groups, women's groups, and other militant groups based mainly in Latin America, Global Campaign emerged from a frustration with the profound inequality, human rights violations, economic dispossession and environmental destruction brought about by the acceleration of neoliberal globalisation since the 1990s.[40] However, its political and organisational roots run deeper. The trade integration policies established in the Americas during the 1990s and 2000s, such as the Free Trade Area of the Americas (FTAA) and North American Free Trade Agreement (NAFTA), represented some of the most

[36] Personal interview with Gonzalo Berrón, 19.02.2024 (online).

[37] Personal interview with Alberto Villarreal, 02.04.20024 (online).

[38] Ibid.

[39] Personal interview with Gonzalo Berrón, 19.02.2024 (online).

[40] Goodman (2002); Scholte (2002); O'Brien et al. (2000).

ambitious trade integration efforts ever undertaken.[41] Nevertheless, the social and environmental costs of these neoliberal models of regional trade were severe. The new forms of governance that emerged exacerbated regional socioeconomic disparities, weakened public mechanisms to address social and economic exclusion, and, overall, diminished citizen participation in public policy.[42] Trade-related issues became arenas of contestation between formal representative democracy and more grassroots forms of citizen participation. It was against this backdrop that social movements across Latin America joined forces to establish the broad, cross-sectorial, Hemispheric Social Alliance (HSA) in 1997.[43]

The movement represented a transnational collaboration of social movements, trade unions, NGOs, indigenous groups, and advocacy groups from across the continent to oppose the advancement of the neoliberal agenda of the FTAA.[44] Through transnational organising and, the HSA connected resistance efforts with the development of alternatives to neoliberal economic globalisation from below.[45] Subsequently, the network expanded its scope with the formation of the Europe-Latin America and the Caribbean bi-regional network Enlazando Alternativas (EA), which brought together activists from Latin America and Europe through a partnership with the Amsterdam-based Transnational Institute.

The EA's strategies centred on empirically documenting the abuses of Western TNCs and the resistance experiences of the victims of these abuses. The alliance not only sought to develop a critique of neo-liberal economic globalization from a Latin American standpoint, but also attempted to imagine an alternative vision of the world. By challenging the prevailing political and ideological frameworks embedded in the economic and human rights discourse (the "market-friendly" vision of human rights),[46] EA aimed to articulate a transnational space that provided venues for a re-politicised perspective of the law more attuned to social justice.[47]

In the absence of legal mechanisms compelling TNCs to uphold the rights of the people, EA also accommodated new avenues for debate and public engagement by reimagining legal institutions from below such as the Permanent People's Tribunals (PPT), Peoples Summits and Social Forums. They understood that despite its limited individualistic focus, human rights law could advance social welfare at the national level and that governments had the duty to protect and promote it. Yet, similar to Marxist critics of human rights who argue that abstract equality and

---

[41] Salazar-Xirinachs and Maryse (2001).

[42] Gallagher (2005); Anderson and Arruda (2002).

[43] Saguier (2007), pp. 251–65.

[44] Ibid.

[45] The HSA's policy document centres on the premise that the people should have a voice in deciding the future of regional integration. In addition, labour and environmental rights were seen as key to any economic agreement, whilst the protection of key sectors such as food production had to be guaranteed by the state in order to ensure the rights and well-being of the people. See HSA, *Alternative for the Americas* (2002).

[46] Whyte (2018), p. 239.

[47] Icaza et al. (2009), pp. 9–11.

freedom only obscure substantive domination and inequality, EA activists rejected the political sovereignty imposed by such unequal relations of economic domination. A broader focus on people's economic and environmental rights would thus also revise and transform the language of human rights. By holding the PPT, the EA (and later Global Campaign) promoted a tradition of peoples' tribunals, building on a version of human rights anchored in decolonisation and concern for its of neocolonial and imperialist reverberations. It aimed to bridge the gap between international law and human rights violations by emphasising collective rights, in the form of economic and environmental rights, and the right to self-determination.[48]

The goal of the PPT was to expose violations of internationally recognised rights, as well as the failure of TNCs to comply even with established voluntary UN mechanisms. During its hearing sessions in Vienna (2006,) Lima (2008), Madrid (2010), South Africa (2016–18), the PPT identified, analysed and condemned the activities of TNCs in various sectors, including finance, agrobusiness, extractive industries, and infrastructure.[49] For instance, the Madrid session, which built on cases presented in Vienna and Lima, affirmed the "persistence of systematic violations of fundamental rights by European TNCs in Latin America", which demonstrated that "a regime of widespread permissiveness, unlawfulness and impunity exists and is manifested, in the behaviour of European TNCs in Latin America".[50] In the final judgement of the Madrid session, the Tribunal resolved to morally sanction and denounce in the international arena the political, economic, financial, productive and judicial conduct and practices of the neoliberal model, promoted and developed by the most industrialised States and international institutions such as the International Monetary Fund, the World Bank and the World Trade Organisation which, under the aegis of promoting growth and economic development to combat poverty and achieve sustainable development, are the cause of the increase in inequalities between a powerful minority and an extraordinary majority who suffer the adverse consequences of globalisation.[51] At the same time, it acknowledged the right of communities, Indigenous people, and all victims of the "development model imposed by TNCs" to resist and organise in defence of their territory, culture, and self-determination.[52] The PPT also formulated recommendations for regulating the political influence of corporations and their pursuit of profit.

Additionally, drawing on the NIEO's legacy, it proposed the establishment of new international mechanisms, including an International Economic Tribunal to

---

[48] The Permanent Peoples' Tribunal was established in 1979 in Bologna and was based on a conceptual militant-utopian vision of international law as a tool of liberation and an enabler of a dignified life. Yet, its origins go back to the two Russell Tribunals, the first of which (1966–67) investigated the crimes of aggression and war crimes perpetrated by the United Sates during the invasion of Vietnam, whilst the second considered the Latin American dictatorships. See Tognoni (2018), p. 42.

[49] See https://permanentpeoplestribunal.org/?lang=en

[50] Permanent Peoples Tribunal (2010), p. 11.

[51] Ibid., p. 23.

[52] Ibid., p. 24.

address economic and environmental crimes committed by TNCs, the creation of a Centre on Transnational Corporations within the UN,[53] and measures to protect against extraterritorial human rights abuses by TNCs.[54] By highlighting the centrality of the people as active subjects capable of advocating for truth and justice, popular tribunals served as a platform to explore avenues for shaping a legislative process that was responsive to and driven by the people.[55] Their aim was to cultivate people-centred transnational legal, social, and political strategies of resistance to neoliberalism, while also enhancing and adapting the exiting framework of international law for a "post-neoliberal system".[56]

The establishment of Global Campaign in Rio de Janeiro in 2012 incorporated this tradition of resistance into a more global project, serving as evidence for the evolving organisation of the counter-hegemonic movement worldwide.[57] With a foothold in Latin America, Europe, Africa, Asia, North America, Global Campaign currently represents a network of over 250 movements, social organisations, and trade unions that aim to "resist land grabs, extractive mining, exploitative wages and environmental destruction caused by TNCs globally".[58] Prominent members include international networks such as La Via Campesina, the Transnational Institute, Friends of the Earth, Amigos de la Tierra América Latina y el Caribe (ATALC), Jubilee South, Movimento dos Atingidos por Barragens (Movement of People Affected by Dams), FIAN International, and national networks such as Centre Europe Tiers Monde (CETIM), AIDC South Africa, and the Instituto de Direitos Humanos e Empresas (Homa) Brazil.[59]

In contrast to existing neo-liberal globalisation projects, the counter-hegemonic globalisation agenda articulated by Global Campaign is characterised by a redistributive ethos that encompasses material, cultural, political, and social dimensions. It embodies a struggle against social exclusion, infused with a radical utopianism.[60] It is a political project rooted in the belief that hegemonic economic and legal realities can be challenged and transformed through alternative conceptions of law and politics. An illustration of this approach is seen in the International Peoples Treaty on the Control of TNCs (hereafter Peoples Treaty), the Global Campaign's proposal for a legally binding instrument to address human rights violations committed by TNCs, submitted to UN in 2014.[61]

---

[53] The UN Centre on Transnational Corporations was established in 1975 and abolished in 1992. See Hamdani and Ruffing (2015).

[54] Transnational Institute and Enzalando Alternativas (2010).

[55] Fraudatario and Tognoni (2018), pp. 134–35.

[56] Enlazando Alternativas (2009).

[57] Ibid.

[58] See https://www.stopcorporateimpunity.org/call-to-international-action/ (last accessed 07 May 2023).

[59] Global Campaign (2012).

[60] de Sousa Santos (2005), pp. 30–31.

[61] Global Campaign (2016).

The Peoples Treaty exemplifies how law, typically a hegemonic tool, can be retooled and mobilised to serve counter-hegemonic relations in the furtherance of social justice. The proposal is open-ended in the sense that was updated several times between 2014 and its submission as a treaty text proposal in October 2017 on the occasion of the third session of the OEIWG.[62] It was thus conceived not only as an organic document that provides a glimpse into civil society's evolving opposition to neoliberal economic policies, but also a statement on the alternative political imaginary this movement represents. According to Global Campaign, the Peoples Treaty diverges from traditional juridical norms of international law, in so far as it was conceived as a collective effort where the priorities of social movements and communities supersede legalistic arguments. Its very title highlights the interconnectedness between an "international treaty", typically understood as a legal agreement among states, and a "peoples treaty", suggesting that communities and individuals, beyond the confines of the state, can actively participate in shaping legal norms, thereby reinforcing that grassroots engagement in law-making processes can serve to both defend and expand the scope of international law from below.[63]

Drawing from the diverse experiences of various social movement struggles for collective rights to the commons, justice, and public accountability, the Peoples Treaty emerged as a dynamic political document where in legal mobilisation is seen as an integral component of political mobilisation. As such, it emphasises that legal actions support broader political goals, rather than the other way around by building upon two central pillars: Firstly, it tackles the legal challenges associated with holding corporations accountable under international law. Secondly, it dedicates a substantial section to advocating for structural economic transformations away from the prevailing corporate economic model, while also promoting alternative economies and modes of development.[64] The latter provide alternatives to the current system of trade and investment, intellectual property rights, and environmental protection, but also explores issues central to Global Campaign's alternative vision of the world, such as gender, communications, sustainability, and indigenous living. The purpose of this structure is to show that the current economic structures have protracted, harmful consequences for broader society, and that an alternative model of economic integration must take into account a more far-reaching range of social and political issues.

[62] See Global Campaign (2017).

[63] Rajagopal (2003).

[64] Global Campaign (2015).

3.2 ESCR-Net and the Liberal Language of Human Rights

In contrast to Global Campaign, ESCR-Net is embedded in the tradition of Western-based, human rights-focused NGOs. In the aftermath of the Cold War, the international political environment became increasingly more receptive to promoting economic and social rights, which allowed for a de-linking of the human rights issue from the geopolitical conflict between East and West. This incremental openness created more favourable conditions for the adoption by NGOs (including mainstream Western NGOs) and various human rights networks of the cause of economic, social and cultural rights. As the anti-globalisation movement erupted in the late-1990s, the legitimacy of human rights organisations became even more closely linked to advocacy for economic and social rights.[65] While larger international human rights NGOs expanded their mandates to include socioeconomic and cultural rights, new human rights networks such as ESCR-Net were created specifically to address and promote these rights more broadly. Generous support from the Ford Foundation facilitated the sation of the first two planning meetings in New York (2000) and Cape Town (2001), followed by the 2003 conference in Bangkok, which ultimately led to the formation of ESCR-Net.

Highlighting its role to the international human rights community, the ESCR-Net inaugural conference drew considerable participation from activists, representatives of prominent NGOs, and influential figures in the human rights sector. Notably, Mary Robinson, the UN High Commissioner for Human Rights at the time, delivered the keynote address. Among the network's most prominent members are organisations such as the Centre for Constitutional Rights in New York, Amnesty International, Corporate Accountability, the Initiative for Social and Economic Rights (ISER), and the International Federation for Human Rights (FIDH), Association for Human Rights in Development (AWID), and Centro de Estudios Legales y Sociales (CELS, Argentina). As a collaborative network of over 250 members active in over 75 countries, ESCR-Net positions itself as a solidarity network dedicated to supporting the realisation of rights for the victims of dispossession, economic disparities and restructuring, environmental degradation, and widespread human rights violations. According to the network, its objective is to "secure economic and social justice through human rights". Members engage in shared analysis, strategy definition, and collective action primarily through issue-based working groups. ESCR-Net's overarching goal is to advance economic, social, and cultural rights (ESCR) in public discourse, decision-making processes, and political practices. To achieve this aim, it operates through six working groups: Corporate Accountability, Woman and ESCR, Strategic Litigation, Economic Policy, Social Movements, and Monitoring of ESCR.[66] These groups assess their

[65] Chong (2009), pp. 120–121.

[66] For ESCR-Net's organisation see https://www.escr-net.org/sites/default/files/ESCR-Net%20Brochure%20English.pdf (last accessed 30 January 2024).

progress annually, revise objectives, and prioritize collective action as part of shared work plans.[67]

In political terms, ESCR-Net can be understood as a liberal civil society network. While it shares certain commonalities in action with the counter-hegemonic approach of the Global Campaign, its political framing is more cautious. Similar to Global Campaign, ESCR-Net recognises "corporate capture" as a threat to the realisation of human and environmental rights. However, while Global Campaign advocates for the creation of alternative economic structures and the formation of non-capitalist subjectivities from grassroots movements, ESCR-Net's approach remains within the bounds of traditional (liberal) political frameworks. In placing the duty to guarantee ESCR rights exclusively on the state, ESCR-Net also regards these rights as uniting "women and men, migrants and indigenous people, youth and elders, of all races, religions, political orientations, and economic and social backgrounds, in a common realisation of universal human freedom and dignity".[68]

The realisation of social justice is consequently seen as inherently connected to defending and enjoying human rights. But conflating economic social justice with the fulfilment of human rights can also mean a de-politization of political action and resistance. In the words of ESCR-Net director, Chris Grove, "social justice is becoming a reality for growing numbers of people due to human rights realisation".[69] The network thus tends to anchor its economic critiques within "a human rights framework rather than an ideological one". For instance, when addressing the detrimental effects of privatization across different regions, ESCR-Net does not necessarily align itself with resistance efforts against privatization itself. Instead, it focuses on the adverse consequences of commercialization's profit-oriented approach, emphasising how such practices can negatively impact human rights.[70]

This distinction is reflected in ESCR-Net's emphasis on legal and juridical mobilisation as preferred methods of action. For instance, a 2014 report suggested that to combat corporate capture across various social domains, the network should focus on lobbying for achievable policy and legislative reforms, advocating for transparency legislation, garnering community support to expose corporate power, and utilizing court cases as tools for change. The network's weapon of choice is strategic litigation carried out through its Strategic Litigation Working Group at the domestic, regional, and international.[71] However, as some scholars have pointed out, relying on legal advocacy to achieve social justice may sidestep addressing deeper structural issues that are not easily remedied through legal means. Similarly, an overemphasis on the legal approach can lead to the portrayal of legal abuses as mere anomalies and may result in the neglect of other social and economic conflicts.[72]

---

[67] See https://www.escr-net.org/members

[68] See https://www.escr-net.org/rights

[69] Grove (2014), p. 356.

[70] ESCR-Net (2016a).

[71] See https://www.escr-net.org/strategiclitigation

[72] Baars (2019), p. 48.

ESCR-Net's pragmatic approach to the progressive potential of legal action is integral to its Ten Key Proposals for the Treaty submitted to OEIWG in 2016 (hereafter Key Proposals). These proposals emerged from the Treaty Initiative Project, a 2-year endeavour (2015–2017) conducted by ESCR-Net's Corporate Accountability Working Group in collaboration with the International Federation for Human Rights. The Treaty Initiative Project organised in-person consultations in the Asia-Pacific, Africa, the Middle East, and Latin America regions and collected written input and suggestions from human rights organisations and grassroots movements.[73] The Key Proposals serve as a legal resource designed to support advocacy efforts by members of the network, government officials, and other parties interested in engaging with the UN Treaty. It reaffirms the paramount importance of human rights law, particularly concerning states' obligations within legal frameworks governing trade and investment and investor-state dispute settlements. Furthermore, the Key Proposals acknowledge the necessity for special protections for various vulnerable groups, including women, children, indigenous peoples, individuals with disabilities, and migrants. They assert that all corporations must uphold human rights and respect the entire spectrum of interconnected and indivisible human rights. Additionally, the Key Proposals emphasise the importance of ensuring access to relevant, sufficient, and high-quality information regarding corporate activities. Given their focus on state sovereignty and home-state regulation, they follow an approach that both seeks to strengthen the UNGPs by requiring states to both adopt legislation that forces businesses to implement human rights due diligence, and carry out extraterritorial obligations to shield human rights.[74]

Nonetheless, different targets also invite different time frames; and varying objectives may require different time frames for action. Global Campaign, with its distinct history, sometimes perceives grassroots legal mobilisation as conflicting with the time frame of state judicial processes. While social movements within Global Campaign view the ongoing negotiations of the UN Treaty as integral to a broader and long-term resistance movement, human rights professionals from the Global North often approach these negotiations more in terms of "campaigns" defined by "achievable" results.

One can also look at the Peoples Treaty's human rights related proposals as drawing from two separate, albeit linked, traditions in the organisation of territorial political power and authority, internationalism and cosmopolitism. On the one hand, Global Campaign's proposal set aside the inviolability of state territoriality in favour of universal human rights, insofar as the indivisibility and inalienability of human rights are understood to be anchored in a cosmopolitan imaginary that sidesteps the nation-state. On the other hand, the political structure backing this cosmopolitan view, in line with the NIEO, is part of an internationalist tradition that aspires to promote cosmopolitan aims through multilateral organisations.[75] The later have the

[73] ESCR-Net (2016c).

[74] Ibid.

[75] Lynch (1999).

capability to constrain states and oblige them to abide by the obligations inscribed in international instruments. As Marc Doucet put it, this is the classic dilemma of internationalism: "Enacting universal human rights from the standpoint of internationalism both requires and simultaneously undermines the territorially bounded nation-state model".[76] To conclude, the different ideological and political positions of the two networks resulted, although not always overtly, in different advocacy and accountability strategies, that, as we will see, continue to structure their visions of how a future UN Treaty on Business and Human Rights should look.

4 The UN Business and Human Rights Treaty, Legal and Alternative Dimensions

Disagreements on the scope and content of a prospective Treaty, as well as on how to address human rights violations within human rights law, emerged from the inaugural meeting of OEIWG in October 2015. These differences can be assigned to three main categories: the "depth" question (or *ratione personae*), which pertains to the types of business enterprises that should be subject to the Treaty; the "breadth" question (*ratione materiae*), which concerns the kinds of human rights that should be encompassed by the Treaty; and the enforcement issue, namely, the most suitable mechanism for achieving the prevention and the sanction of human rights violations.

4.1 The "Depth" Question

From the beginning of the debates on the content of Resolution 26/9, ESCR-Net urged member states on the Human Rights Council not to confine any future UN Treaty solely to the activities of TNCs, since such a restrictive definition would overlook an opportunity to establish a level playing field for all corporations globally.[77] This position was reiterated in the network's 2016 Key Proposals. ESCR-Net asserted that, based on consultations conducted during the Treaty Initiative, CSOs and affected individuals demanded a treaty with broad applicability that should encompass all types of business enterprises, including those within supply chains, and should address all civil, political, social, economic, and cultural rights recognized under international human rights law.[78]

The concerns raised by ESCR-Net regarding the scope of any future UN Treaty were echoed by Human Rights Watch, which shared similar concerns.[79] Additionally,

[76] Doucet (2005), pp. 288–289.

[77] ESCR-Net (2016b).

[78] Ibid.

[79] Ganesan (2014).

the European Union, although not supportive of the Treaty, also advocated for broadening the scope of the instrument to include all companies, in order not to discriminate against businesses from Global North, where the great majority of TNCs are located.[80] In contrast, the Ecuadorian resolution specified in a footnote that the reference "to other business enterprises" in the title of the Treaty pertains only to businesses with a "transnational character in their activities" and excludes "local businesses registered in terms of relevant domestic law" from the scope of the Treaty.[81] Leading voices within ESCR-Net have also contended that including all business types in the Treaty could serve as a gesture of goodwill toward the Global North countries that are hesitant to engage in negotiations. As an alternative, they proposed a "hybrid option", whereby the Treaty would apply "to all business enterprises but would include special provisions tailored specifically for TNCs".[82] Furthermore, there was a readiness within ESCR-Net to collaborate and negotiate with transnational businesses and convince them to support the Treaty process.[83]

Moreover, in official submissions, brochures, and advocacy papers, ESCR-Net deliberately avoided using the term "TNC"—favoured by Global Campaign and a significant number of Global South countries—opting instead for the more inclusive term "corporations". This choice reflected ESCR-Net's commitment to inclusivity and its willingness to engage with a broader spectrum of businesses in the pursuit of human rights. However, as I elaborate below, this approach was criticized by other CSOs as inapplicable and intended to divert the discussion from the importance of regulating the behaviour of the most powerful contemporary economic actors. In contrast, Global Campaign, along with various Global South countries that voted in favour of Resolution 26/9, including South Africa, China, Cuba, Venezuela, Pakistan, and India, firmly maintained the position that the footnote in the Resolution should be interpreted literally, taking TNCs as the sole subject of any UN Treaty. Global Campaign, aligned with that of many Global South countries, asserted that—due to the immense power they wield, the impunity they enjoyed through investment and free trade agreements, and their ability to evade liability within national jurisdictions—TNCs should be the sole focus of international regulations. They argue that a significant legal gap exists in international human rights law that must be addressed to put an end to the impunity for human rights violations committed by TNCs.[84] Moreover, Global Campaign contends that treating TNCs and national economic actors, which are already subject to a certain degree of state control, equally would undermine the effectiveness of any future Treaty. They also highlight that if the UN Treaty establishes uniform provisions for enterprises with varying structures and activities, its enforcement mechanism would become

[80] European Union (2015)

[81] See footnote 2 in United Nations Human Rights Council (2014).

[82] Deva (2017), pp. 170–175.

[83] Personal interview with David Bilchitz, Johannesburg, 18 September 2023.

[84] Global Campaign (2015).

inefficient.[85] These points align with the economic concerns voiced by states from the Global South, who expressed apprehension that, if the Treaty were to apply to all types of business enterprises, their local and small-scale companies could face significant burdens resulting from international human rights norms.[86]

The political shifts in Ecuador (the key driver of the Treaty process since 2013)—marked by the ascension of Lenin Moreno to power in 2017, followed by conservative billionaire banker Guillermo Lasso in 2021—significantly altered the power dynamics of the negotiations. While outgoing President Rafael Correa steered Ecuador away from political and economic alignment with the United States between 2007 and 2017, his successors reinstated many neoliberal policies in an attempt to re-connect the country with the US regional interests. This change in Ecuador's foreign policy orientation was reflected in the draft treaties presented during the negotiations. The new Ecuadorian ambassadors at the UN, who also served as chairperson rapporteurs to the OEIWG, diluted the language of previous drafts to accommodate many of the demands of Global North countries, such as expanding the scope of the Treaty. Although, beginning with the first revised draft in 2018, the scope of the Treaty was expanded to include all business enterprises, civil society remained divided on this issue.

4.2 The "Breadth" Question

Until 2023, the Treaty's possible "breadth" also remained a highly contentious question. Two models have emerged: the "indirect" model, which focuses on the state's role in protecting individuals from human rights violations through the international legal obligation to ensure that corporations do not violate human rights, and the "direct" model, which would impose obligations on corporations through international law.[87] The indirect approach would thus absolve corporations of any direct obligations related to international human rights law. Relying solely on states to uphold these obligations may not be sufficient, since many states lack the political will and institutional capacities to effectively regulate corporate behaviour. Additionally, some states may face economic dependencies that limit their ability to enforce human rights standards within their jurisdictions.[88]

Global Campaign has been at the forefront of advocating for the inclusion of direct obligations for businesses as legal persons under the UN Treaty, a position supported by several states from the Global South, including the African Group, Cuba, Bolivia, Colombia, Pakistan, and Indonesia. According to them, the inclusion of direct obligations for TNCs under international law is crucial for addressing the

85 Global Campaign (2023).

86 Deva (2017), pp. 167–68.

87 Bilchitz (2017), p. 186.

88 Ibid.

legal gap and subsequent impunity generated by the multi-jurisdictional nature of their activity. Their proposed approach entails a dual model: a "vertical" direct application for states that imposes an obligation to take measures to protect human rights, and a "horizontal" application for TNCs, obligating them to refrain from violating human rights during their business operations.[89] This framework thus aims to establish clear responsibilities for both states and corporations, ensuring accountability for human rights violations within their respective spheres of influence.

Although the direct model proposed for a business and human rights treaty diverges from the current international law paradigm, it offers several advantages. Firstly, it acknowledges that states alone are not solely responsible for upholding fundamental rights. Given the limitations of states in effectively regulating corporations, direct obligations for corporations ensure that their failure to fulfil these obligations can be addressed even without state intervention. This could result in consequences such as reputational harm, extraterritorial litigation, and international accountability if appropriate forums are established. However, implementing direct obligations for corporations would require the treaty to establish structures to define the nature and extent of these obligations. Moreover, this approach is likely to face opposition from businesses and powerful states aiming to safeguard corporate interests. Additionally, some states may attempt to evade their own responsibilities by shifting the focus onto corporations. Furthermore, establishing direct obligations for corporations would necessitate the creation of an international mechanism to provide access to remedies. The effectiveness of such a mechanism would, in turn, rely on the cooperation and efficiency of national mechanisms.[90]

In contrast, ESCR-Net tends to advocate for an "indirect approach", wherein only states are bound by human rights obligations. Under this model, businesses have no direct obligations under international human rights treaties, but states are responsible for implementing measures that impose obligations on businesses. In this framework, states would be tasked with ensuring the effectiveness of any international direct obligations resulting from a UN Treaty. However, this approach also has its drawbacks. States may lack the capacity or willingness to effectively regulate powerful corporate interests. Major corporations may wield resources that surpass those of states, or they may exert influence over government officials. Additionally, this model allows corporations to argue that they bear no direct obligations regarding human rights, potentially undermining the universality of obligations placed on corporations. Different states may enact varying frameworks and obligations, leading to inconsistencies in corporate accountability for human rights violations.

Indeed, these different lines of argumentation are deeply rooted in specific political and ideological trajectories. The Latin American experience of social struggle during the twentieth century, coupled with political legacy of the NIEO, have influenced the Global Campaign's perspective, shaping its view of both the state as a

[89] Europe-Third World Centre (2019).

[90] Bilchitz (2016). Also undermining efforts to establish such national mechanisms is the transnational organisation of international commercial arbitration. See Dezalay and Bryant (1996).

social relation, and of the relationship between democracy and territoriality. Despite its contradictions, the state is regarded as a significant battleground. In many (neo) liberal states, public law and public power are closely intertwined with private interests; there is therefore a pressing need to shift the focus from serving corporate interests to transforming the "public" realm into the "common" sphere. Global Campaign advocates for reclaiming the state from corporate capture, viewing this as essential for democracy. By realigning the state's priorities away from serving corporate interests and toward promoting the common good, the aim is to establish a more democratic and equitable society. This perspective underscores the importance of challenging corporate influence over state institutions and policies to ensure that the state serves the interests of the people rather than those of powerful corporate entities.[91]

As such, in a dedicated section entitled "Obligations of Official International Economic and Financial Institutions Regarding Trade and Investment Agreements", Global Campaign expands upon the regulatory framework proposed for any future Treaty. According to the network's perspective, when participating in intergovernmental organisations, including economic and financial institutions, as well as free trade and investment agreements, states should adhere to the obligations established by the Treaty. This entails ensuring that such agreements do not contribute to the violation of human rights by TNCs.[92] Furthermore, financial institutions and international financial institutions are expected not to finance TNCs and their supply chains if they are aware or should be aware that doing so would nullify or violate human rights. This comprehensive approach aims to hold both states and international institutions accountable for their roles in promoting or mitigating human rights violations resulting from trade and investment agreements.[93]

While ESCR-Net agreed with the overarching principle of prioritizing human rights, it also recognized the significant impact of trade and investment treaties negotiated both within and outside the framework of the World Trade Organisation on human rights.[94] Their legal approach, however, emphasises the operationalization of corporate responsibility to respect human rights through a future Treaty, as outlined in the United Nations Guiding Principles on Business and Human Rights. Under this framework, states are required to enact legislation that legally obliges corporations to undertake human rights due diligence. This entails the identification, prevention, and mitigation of—and accountability for—adverse human rights impacts in line with existing international standards. By integrating these requirements into national legislation, states can ensure that corporations are held accountable for their human rights impacts and take appropriate measures to address them.[95]

[91] Global Campaign (2015).

[92] Ibid.

[93] Ibid.

[94] ESCR-Net (2016b).

[95] Ibid; United Nations Human Rights Office of the High Commissioner (2011).

4.3 The Enforcement Issue

Even more contentious is the question of which entities, whether national or international, should ensure the implementation of the UN Treaty and enforce the stipulated obligations. In 2016, Luis Callegos, former Ecuadorian ambassador to the UN and Chair of the OEIWG, proposed the concept of a "World Court on Business and Human Rights". Callegos sought to include the creation of a court as a "further measure against corporate impunity" in the draft of the UN Treaty.[96] The ambassador's proposal aligned closely with the Global Campaign's suggestion for an "International Tribunal on TNCs and Human Rights", which also found support among several states from the Global South. Global Campaign's proposal envisioned an international tribunal operating under the principle of complementarity, akin to the structure of the International Criminal Court. This tribunal would be affiliated with the UN system and, ideally, be headquartered in a country from the Global South.[97] This tribunal would have jurisdiction over TNCs as legal entities, regardless of the legal framework in the home or host country, or in the state where the violation occurred. In terms of the tribunal's material jurisdiction, Global Campaign envisions its extension to the obligations of TNCs outlined in the future treaty. Regarding its geographic jurisdiction, the tribunal would be empowered to adjudicate violations occurring in a state party to the statute, even if the TNC involved is located in a non-party state, provided that a clear relationship between the TNC and the entity responsible for the violation can be established.[98]

Additional provisions place the burden of proof on the accused violators of human rights and establishes cost-free access to justice and legal counsel. While this provision may conflict with the principle of presumption of innocence, it has been advocated by numerous NGOs.[99] The aim is to ensure a more equitable access to justice for victims of human rights violations who may lack sufficient resources.[100] Moreover, Global Campaign proposed the establishment of an International Monitoring Centre on TNCs, operating under the auspices of the UN, envisioned as an inclusive social platform providing legal and psychological assistance to affected individuals and communities, as well as support for social movements and states in their quest for corporate accountability.[101]

Perhaps the most radical proposal put forth by Global Campaign, the establishment of an international tribunal is not supported by other members of the Treaty Alliance, including ESCR-Net. Instead, ESCR-Net emphasises the importance of

---

[96] Gallegos and Uribe (2016).

[97] Global Campaign (2022).

[98] Ibid.

[99] In France, for instance, Sherpa advocated for the inclusion of such a provision in the 2017 Due Diligence Law. The proposal was however rejected by Parliament as it was against the constitutional principle of the presumption of innocence.

[100] See Sherpa (2022).

[101] Global Campaign (2022).

ensuring that states guarantee access to adequate, effective, and appropriate remedies for individuals affected by violations. From this perspective, the UN Treaty presents an opportunity to compel states to enact legislative, judicial, and other measures to ensure access to mechanisms for providing remedies. Indeed, beginning in 2017, the chairs of the Treaty process distanced themselves from the proposal for an international tribunal for TNCs and removed it from future drafts. In addition to the cost associated with establishing and maintaining an international tribunal, critics also highlight that such tribunals do not replace the role of the state. Even the International Criminal Court intervenes in a case only when a state is unwilling or unable to address it, and without state cooperation, no supranational court can effectively carry out its work or enforce its decisions.[102]

5 Conclusion

The involvement of transnational advocacy networks in the process of drafting a UN Treaty on Business and Human Rights reveals the substantive disagreements between the networks on how to deal with corporate infringements on human rights. The chapter has argued that the political affinities and visions, historical experiences and modes of resistance to neoliberal globalisation, and national backgrounds of their membership, of each network have led to the differences in repertoire that are also reflected in their differing substantive orientations. Focusing on this contentious political territory provides a critical site for assessing current efforts to reconstruct global rules and institutions and, not least, de-territorialise the democratic experience. Although many view advocacy by civil society as a site of progressive democratic ideas, little attention has been paid to how each network views the relationship between democracy, human rights, and territoriality.

Thus far, Global Campaign and ESCR-Net have succeeded in reconciling these political differences, largely due to the prevailing sense of inclusivity and respect for divergent opinions in pro-Treaty advocacy at the UN level. An important factor contributing to this convergence is the Treaty Alliance's flexible and politically minimalist approach to collaboration on the UN Treaty. While cleavages have emerged over time, primarily in the form of tensions between North and South-centred approaches, they have not led to outright exclusions.

Another factor that enhanced cooperation was the professionalisation among the activists, instilled by years of UN activism. Participation in UN proceedings necessitates the prioritization of legal knowledge, adherence to a proper dress code and a rigorous protocol for both formal and informal interactions. An activist from Global Campaign recalls, for instance, that before the vote on Resolution 26/9, "we had an advocacy bias – our tactics were outside tactics, not inside tactics. We did not want to change them. We did not know exactly what to do beyond denouncing corporate

[102] Ibid.

power. Our people did not want to go to Geneva, but afterwards we tried to understand what a binding treaty meant".[103] Activists from ESCR-Net also acknowledge the influence of Global Campaign on their operations. Members who are part of the both networks have played a role in smoothing out certain political cleavages. For example, Movement of People Affected by Dams is active both in Global Campaign and ESCR-Net, and has been credited for its role in exposing the North-based network to more critical political economic perspectives.[104]

Ultimately, the campaign for the UN Treaty highlights two central features of corporate accountability within the context of neoliberal globalization. Firstly, it underscores the necessity for the continued combination of political and legal strategies, encompassing both protest and the mobilisation of dynamic legal instruments at local, regional, and global scales. Secondly, it illuminates how social movements can utilize the law to establish countervailing possibilities to liberal visions of regulations and human rights. Taken together, these findings suggest a reason to be hopeful about the possibilities of overcoming fragmentation within the corporate accountability movement.

References

Anderson S, Arruda M (2002) Another integration is possible: sovereignty yes, FTAA no. Institute for Policy Studies and the Institute of Policy Alternatives for the Southern Cone of Latin America, Washington DC

Anghie A (2019) Inequality, human rights, and the New International Order. Hum Int J Hum Rights Humanit Dev 3(10):429–442

Baars G (2019) The corporation, law and capitalism. A radical perspective on the role of law. Brill, Leiden

Bantekas I (2021) Towards a treaty on business and human rights. In: Bantekas I, Stein M (eds) The Cambridge companion to business and human rights. Cambridge University Press, Cambridge, pp 583–610

Bilchitz B (2016) The necessity for a business and human rights treaty. Bus Hum Rights J 1(2):203–227

Bilchitz D (2017) Corporate obligations and a treaty on business: A constitutional law model? In: Deva S, Bilchitz D (eds) Building a treaty on business and human rights: context and contours. Cambridge University Press, Cambridge, pp 185–215

Bob C (2009) The international struggle for new human rights. University of Pennsylvania Press, Philadelphia

Brennan B, Berrón G (2020) Touching a nerve. How a peoples' campaign at the United Nations is challenging corporate rule. https://longreads.tni.org/stateofpower/touching-a-nerve

Buono R, Lara J (2007) Imperialism, neoliberalism and social struggles in Latin America. Brill, Leiden

Chagnon C, Durante F, Gills B, Hagolani-Albov S, Hokkanen S, Kangasluoma S et al (2022) From extractivism to global extractivism: the evolution of an organizing concept. J Peasant Stud 49(4):760–792

[103] Personal interview with Gonzalo Berrón, 19.02.2024 (online).

[104] Personal interview with Alberto Villarreal, 02.04.20024 (online).

Chong D (2009) Economic rights and extreme poverty: moving toward subsistence. In: Bob C (ed) The international struggle for new human rights. University of Pennsylvania Press, Philadelphia
Civicus (2017) Interview with Mónica Vargas Collazos. https://www.civicus.org/images/TNI-Mo%CC%81nicaVargas-11-29-17_FINAL.pdf_English.pdf
de Sousa Santos B (2005) Beyond neoliberal governance: the World Social Forum as subaltern cosmopolitan politics and legality. In: de Sousa Santos B, Rodriguez-Garavito C (eds) Law and globalisation from below. Cambridge University Press, Cambridge, pp 29–64
De Schutter O (2015) Towards a new treaty on business and human rights. Bus Hum Rights J 1(1):41–67
Deva S (2017) Scope of the proposed business and human rights treaty. Navigating through normativity, law and politics. In: Deva S, Bilchitz D (eds) Building a treaty on business and human rights: context and contours. Cambridge University Press, Cambridge, pp 154–182
Deva S (2021) The UN guiding principles on business and human rights and its predecessors. Progress at a snail's pace? In: Bantekas I, Stein M (eds) The Cambridge companion to business and human rights. Cambridge University Press, Cambridge, pp 145–172
Dezalay Y, Bryant G (1996) Dealing in virtue: international commercial arbitration and the construction of a transnational legal order. University of Chicago Press, Chicago
Doucet M (2005) Territoriality and democratic paradox. Contemp Polit Theory 4(2005):275–295
Edwards M, Gaventa J (2001) Global citizen action. Lynne Rienner, Boulder
Enlazando Alternativas (2009) Profit before people and human rights. European transnational corporations in Latin America and Caribbean. Submission to the United Nations Consultation on Business and Human Rights, 5–6 October 2009, Geneva. www.ohchr.org/sites/default/files/Documents/Issues/Business/Consultation2010/BiRegional.pdf
European Union (2015) Submission of the European Union to the First Meeting of the Open-Ended Intergovernmental Working Group on Transnational Corporations and Other Business Enterprises with Respect to Human Rights (12–15 July 2015). www.ohchr.org/en/hr-bodies/hrc/wg-trans-corp/session1/session1
Europe-Third World Centre (2019) Comments and proposals on the draft of the legally binding instrument presented to the Inter-Governmental Working Group on Transnational Corporations and Other Business Enterprises with respect to human rights. www.ohchr.org/sites/default/files/Documents/HRBodies/HRCouncil/WGTransCorp/Session4/SubmissionLater/CETIM.pdf
ESCR-Net (2016) *Corporate capture and the people's struggle for economic, social and cultural rights*. International Network for Economic, Social andCultural Rights, New York
Florini A (2000) The third force: the rise of transnational civil society. Brooking Institution Press, Washington, DC
Fraudatario S, Tognoni G (2018) The participation of the people and the development of international law. In: Brynes A, Simm G (eds) Peoples' tribunals and international law. Cambridge University Press, Cambridge, pp 133–154
Freeman D (2024) Sovereignty, human rights and the regulation of transnational corporations: a critical spatial analysis of civil society proposals for a binding treaty. In: Globalizations, pp 1–19
Gallagher K (2005) Putting development first: The importance of policy space in *the WTO and international financial institutions*. Zed Books, London
Gallegos L, Uribe D (2016) The next step against corporate impunity: A world court on business and human rights? Harv Int Law J 57:7–10. (Spring). Online Symposium. https://journals.law.harvard.edu/ilj/wp-content/uploads/sites/84/Gallegos-Uribe_0615.pdf
Ganesan A (2014) Dispatches: a treaty to end corporate abuses? www.hrw.org/news/2014/07/01/dispatches-treaty-end-corporate-abuses
Gills BK (2023) Extractivism and global social change. In: The Palgrave handbook of global social change. Palgrave Macmillan, Cham, pp 1–23
Global Campaign to Reclaim Peoples Sovereignty, Dismantle Corporate Power and Stop Impunity (2012) Call to International Action. For the economic, political, cultural, and environmental sovereignty of our Peoples: Let us put an end to the impunity of transnational corporations and corporate capture, let us defend democracy and our rights! www.stopcorporateimpunity.org/call-to-international-action/

Global Campaign to Reclaim Peoples Sovereignty, Dismantle Corporate Power and Stop Impunity (2015) Written contribution of the Global Campaign to Dismantle Corporate Power and Stop Impunity to the first session of the intergovernmental working mandated with the elaboration of an international legally binding instrument on transnational corporations (TNCs) and other business enterprises with respect to human rights, June 2015. www.ohchr.org/sites/default/files/Documents/HRBodies/HRCouncil/WGTransCorp/Session1/Global_Campaign_to_Dismantle_Corporate_Power_andStop_Impunity_June-2015_en.pdf
Global Campaign to Reclaim Peoples Sovereignty, Dismantle Corporate Power and Stop Impunity (2016) The International Peoples Treaty on the control of TNCs. www.stopcorporateimpunity.org/wp-content/uploads/2016/11/PeoplesTreaty-EN-mar2015-1.pdf
Global Campaign to Reclaim Peoples Sovereignty, Dismantle Corporate Power and Stop Impunity (2017) Treaty on transnational corporations and their supply chains with regard to human rights. Treaty text proposal. www.ohchr.org/sites/default/files/Documents/HRBodies/HRCouncil/WGTransCorp/Session3/CETIM-TNI_EN.pdf
Global Campaign to Reclaim Peoples Sovereignty, Dismantle Corporate Power and Stop Impunity (2022) Elements for the Statute of an International Tribunal on Transnational Corporations and Human Rights as a mechanism of enforcement and guarantee of the obligations of the legally binding instrument on transnational corporations and human rights. www.stopcorporateimpunity.org/wp-content/uploads/2022/10/Elements-Tribunal_Oct2022-1.pdf
Global Campaign to Reclaim Peoples Sovereignty, Dismantle Corporate Power and Stop Impunity (2023) Frontiers of an effective binding treaty. www.cetim.ch/wp-content/uploads/Frontiers-of-an-Effective-Binding-Treaty-2023.pdf
Gold M, Zagato A (2020) After the pink tide. Corporate state formation new egalitarianism in Latin America. Berghahn, New York
Goodman J (2002) Contesting corporate globalism: sources of power, channels for democratisation. In: Anderson A (ed) Transnational democracy: political spaces and border crossings. Routledge, London, pp 215–235
Grove C (2014) To build a global movement to make human rights and social justice a reality for all. SUR Rev Int Direitos Human 11(20):353–362
Gudynas E (2018) Extractivisms. Tendencies and consequences. In: Munck R, Delgado Wise R (eds) Reframing Latin American development. Routledge, London, pp 61–76
Hamdani K, Ruffing L (2015) *United Nations Centre on Transnational Corporations: Corporate conduct and the public interest*. Routledge, London
Hamdani K, Ruffing L (2017) Lessons from the UN Centre on Transnational Corporations for the current treaty initiative. In: Deva S, Bilchitz D (eds) Building a treaty on business and human rights: Context and contours. Cambridge University Press, Cambridge, pp 27–47
Hemispheric Social Alliance (2002) Alternatives for the Americas. Position Paper. www.iatp.org/documents/alternatives-americas
Hertel S (2006) Unexpected power. Conflict and change among transnational activists. Cornell University Press, Ithaca
Icaza R, Newell P, Saguier M (2009) Democratising trade politics in the Americas: Insights from the women's, environmental and labour movements, IDS Working Paper 328. Institute of Development Studies, University of Sussex, Brighton, pp 1–57
International Network for Economic, Social, and Cultural Rights (2016a) Webinar on privatisation and public-private partnerships. www.escr-net.org/news/2016/webinar-privatization-public-private-partnerships
International Network for Economic, Social, and Cultural Rights (2016b) Ten key proposals for the Treaty. A legal resource for advocates and diplomats engaging with the UN Intergovernmental Working Group on Transnational Corporations and Other Business Enterprises. https://www.escrnet.org/sites/default/files/attachments/tenkeyproposals_final.pdf
International Network for Economic, Social, and Cultural Rights (2016c) Statement of the ESCR-Net Corporate Accountability Working Group (CAWG). https://media.business-humanrights.org/media/documents/files/media/documents/cawg_statement_re_un_hrc_resolution_text.pdf

Joachim J, Loacher B (2008) Transnational activism in the UN and the EU. Routledge, London
Keck ME, Sikkink K (1998) Activists beyond borders. Advocacy networks in international politics. Cornell University Press, Ithaca
Lynch C (1999) The promise and problems of internationalism. Glob Gov 5(1):83–101
Martín F (2017) Reimagining extractivism. Insights from spatial theory. In: Engels B, Dietz K (eds) Contested extractivism, society, and state. Palgrave, London, pp 21–44
Moyn S (2010) *The last utopia: Human rights in history*. Belknap Press of Harvard University Press, Cambridge
O'Brien R, Goetz A, Scholte J, Williams M (2000) Contesting global governance: multilateral economic institutions and global social movements. Cambridge University Press, Cambridge
Pellegrini L, Arsel M, Orta Martínez M, Mena C (2020) International investment agreements, human rights, and environmental justice: the Texaco/Chevron case from the Ecuadorian Amazon. J Int Econ Law 2(2020):455–468
Rajagopal B (2003) International law from below: development, social movements and third world resistance. Cambridge University Press, Cambridge
Ruggie J (2014) Global governance and "new governance theory": lesson from business and human rights. Glob Gov 20(2014):5–17
Ruggie J (2015) Regulating multinationals: the UN Guiding Principles, civil society, and international legalization, Regulatory Policy Program Working Paper RPP-2015-04. Mossavar-Rahmani Center for Business and Government, Harvard University, Cambridge
Saguier M (2007) The hemispheric social alliance and the free trade area of the Americas process: the challenges and opportunities of transnational coalitions against neo-liberalism. Globalisations 4(2):251–265
Salazar-Xirinachs J, Maryse R (2001) Toward free trade in the Americas. Brookings Institution Press, Washington, DC
Santos de S, Rodríguez-Garavito C (2005) *Law and globalization from below: Towards a cosmopolitan legality*. Cambridge University Press, Cambridge
Sauvant K (2015) The negotiations of the United Nations code of conduct on transnational corporations: experience and lessons learned. J World Invest Trade 16(1):11–87
Scholte J (2002) Civil society and democracy in global governance. Glob Gov 8:281–304
Sherpa (2022) Sustainability due diligence: The proposal finally unveiled by the commission must be improved. www.asso-sherpa.org/directive-on-corporate-sustainability-due-diligence-the-proposal-finally-unveiled-by-the-commission-must-be-improved
Suárez Franco A, Fyfe D (2018) Voluntary vs binding: civil society claim for a binding instrument. In: Letnar Cernic J, Carrillo-Santarelli N (eds) The future of business and human rights. Theoretical and practical considerations for a UN Treaty. Intersentia, Cambridge, pp 139–160
Tognoni G (2018) The history of the permanent peoples' tribunal. In: Brynes A, Simm G (eds) Peoples' tribunals and international law. Cambridge University Press, Cambridge, pp 42–58
Tooze A (2008) Crashed. How a decade of financial crisis changed the world. Viking, New York
Transnational Institute, Enzalando Alternativas (2010) Permanent Peoples' Tribunal. The European Union and transnational corporations in Latin America: policies, instruments, and actors complicit in violations of the peoples' rights. Deliberating Session, Madrid, May 14–17, 2010. https://enlazandoalternativas.org/IMG/pdf/TPP-verdict.pdf
United Nations General Assembly (1974) Declaration on the establishment of a new international economic order. https://digitallibrary.un.org/record/218450?ln=en&v=pdf
United Nations Human Rights Council (2014) Resolution 26/9. Elaboration of an international legally binding instrument on transnational corporations and other business enterprises with respect to human rights
United Nations Human Rights Office of the High Commissioner (2011) Guiding principles on business and human rights. Implementing the United Nations "protect, respect and remedy" framework. www.ohchr.org/sites/default/files/documents/publications/guidingprinciplesbusinesshr_en.pdf
Whyte J (2018) *The morals of the market: Human rights and the rise of neoliberalism*. Verso, London

Andru Chiorean is a Researcher at the National School of Political Studies and Administration, Bucharest, in the ERC Project, "Transnational Advocacy Networks and Corporate Accountability for Major International Crimes." His research interests focus on transnational/global history, political sociology, and corporate accountability. After defending his PhD in history at University of Nottingham in 2019, he held postdoctoral positions at the New Europe College Institute of Advanced Studies in Bucharest, the Research Institute of the University of Bucharest, the Wilson Center in Washington, DC, and the Davis Center for Russian and Eurasian Studies at Harvard University. His work has been published in journals such as the *European Review of History* and in edited collections. He is currently investigating the role of transnational NGO coalitions and business associations in the production of corporate accountability international norms and regulations.

Transnational Advocacy Networks and Corporate Accountability: Visions, Divisions, and Convergences of a Global Cause

Henry P. Rammelt

Abstract Based on organisational and relational data comprising 260 organisations active in the field of corporate accountability, this chapter examines the diversity of actors that seek to redress business complicity in gross human rights violations at a global level. It maps the organisational field and disentangles the relationship between the structure of different organisations, their discursive underpinnings and network positions, and the way they attempt to hold corporations accountable. The chapter identifies divisions within the field leading to fragmentation in terms of ideology and repertoires of action and pinpoints existing and prospective points of convergence. It identifies a range of leftist anti-corporate rhetorical framing but also finds that the variance in frames is eclipsed by a variety of strategies. The leftist, and sometimes radical, discourse is often inconsistent with the corresponding action strategies. Overall, organisations active in the field make far less often use of movement-related repertoires, such as protest or blockades, than of classic, liberal advocacy repertoires, such as lobbying, other conventional forms of political participation, or strategic litigations. Finally, funding dependency and organisational embeddedness seem to moderate both the repertoires and claims of organisations. The findings of the chapter are relevant to the study of corporate accountability initiatives as they contribute to identifying the limits of pressure and relief civil society can bring about in this field.

This research was supported by the ERC-Consolidator project *Transnational Advocacy Networks and Corporate Accountability for Major International Crimes*. The project has received funding from the European Research Council (ERC) under the European Union's Horizon 2020 research and innovation program (grant agreement No. 101002993—CORPACCOUNT).

H. P. Rammelt (✉)
National University of Political Studies and Public Administration, Bucharest, Romania
e-mail: henry.rammelt@politice.ro

R. Grosescu, J. G. Dale (eds.), *Corporate Accountability for Human Rights Violations*, Interdisciplinary Studies in Human Rights 16,
https://doi.org/10.1007/978-3-032-05569-9_3

1 Introduction

At least since Keck and Sikkink's (1998) seminal work on transnational advocacy networks (TANs)[1] and the short-lived, alter-globalisation movement in the early 2000's, legions of students of international relations, political sociology, social movement studies, and comparative politics have mapped counter-hegemonic transnational campaigns emerging against neoliberal globalisation and the cross-border power of its main proponents and agents.[2] Some of these authors see transnational social movements as sources of opposition "from below" to these capital-centred processes that challenge the authority and practices of states, transnational governmental networks, and international institutions and thus play a role in shaping global governance. Some even claim to be mapping an emerging global civil society.[3] It might be too soon to say whether something resembling a coherent global civil society is forming that will be able to serve as an effective normative terrain from which to influence transnational politics. However, we can certainly see that there are important transnational processes and mechanisms that have had a profound effect on local politics. Likewise, social movements are creating and effectively using different means to influence social, cultural, political, and economic change. While many arguments can be made for why corporations continue to operate with global impunity, the role civil society plays in holding them accountable, the (potential) lack of effectiveness in their endeavours, and the consequences of power relations between donors and organisations are attracting increasing criticism.[4] This chapter presents the preliminary results of an exploratory quantitative study on the global universe of organisations, networks, and groups that are active in the field of corporate accountability (CA) and addresses a number of questions that either have not yet been asked or that remain unclear.

What are the main drivers mobilising anti-corporate campaigns? What frames are organisations constructing to convince their targeted audiences to join their cause? How do organisations struggle for corporate accountability, and what repertoires do they mobilise? Ultimately, whom do they hold responsible for wrongdoing, and what solutions do they advance?

This chapter examines a wide range of civil society organisations that are seeking to hold corporations accountable. I do this by mapping each organisation's structure, funding, and accountability strategies. I also provide evidence of each organisation's ideological leanings, goals, and mobilisation frames. I pinpoint existing divisions that suggest fragmentation in terms of repertoires of actions and ideology, as well as existing and prospective points of convergence.

---

[1] Keck and Sikkink (1998).

[2] della Porta (2007); della Porta and Tarrow (2004); Smith and Johnston (2002); Evans (2000); Klein (1999).

[3] Keane (2003).

[4] Banks et al. (2015); Dauvergne and LeBaron (2014); Edwards and Hulme (1996).

This research is significant for a number of reasons. A systematic conceptualisation of different visions of such organisations, national peculiarities, and the underlying discourses that inform their activities has yet to be achieved.[5] Against this empirical backdrop, the chapter attempts to contribute to broader theoretical debates, in particular to scholarship in the field of (non-electoral) political participation. I address the abovementioned questions through a theory-driven analysis of global networks of civil society organisations active in the field of corporate accountability. I employ the conceptual toolkits provided by the research literature on contentious politics[6] and the (critical) analysis of (transnational) civil society.[7] For data collection, I used an adapted version of Action Organization Analysis[8] that resulted in a population of 876 organisations of which a random sample of 260 organisations was coded. Descriptive statistics were carried out on this sample in order to answer the research questions.

In the second section, I elaborate my theory-driven analytical framework, drawing on scholarship dedicated to global civil society and corporate accountability, discussions of the diversity of civil society, and social movement theory. I use this framework to formulate a battery of hypotheses that structure the analysis. In Sect. 3, I present the method of data collection and analysis and consider its potential limits. The subsequent sections are dedicated to the results of the analysis (Sect. 4) and their interpretation (Sect. 5). The concluding section summarises the paper, highlights its main contributions to academic debate, discusses the limitations of the results, and identifies future avenues for research.

2 Conceptual Framework: Corporate Accountability, Civil Society, Social Movement Theory

2.1 Corporate Accountability and Global Civil Society

I consider a wide range of actors of diverse forms and configurations, including, for example, NGOs, loose protest networks, trade unions, epistemic communities, and mutual aid associations, to be a part of civil society. What all of these actors have in common is that they engage in activities that pursue shared goals and mobilise the public for these goals, and by so doing, they provide an interface between the individual and the political and economic arena. While some scholars argue that NGOs influenced international politics as early as 200 years ago,[9] civil society rose to

[5] Grosescu (2019).

[6] McAdam et al. (2001); McAdam and Snow (1996); Tarrow (1994).

[7] Banks et al. (2015); Kean (2003); Batliwala and Brown (2006).

[8] Kousis et al. (2018).

[9] Davies (2014).

prominence in international relations in the twenty-first century.[10] Notably in arenas where governmental action is reluctant, such as the field of climate and sustainability governance, some social movement scholars see actions by non-state actors, not least NGOs, as crucial.[11] The same seems likely to hold true for corporate accountability. The civil society I consider in this chapter is, to a greater or lesser extent, involved in providing relief from or responding to the social problems related to the activities of transnational corporations. In more detail, the universe of organisations active in the field of corporate accountability considered here refers to the civil society that is involved in holding corporations accountable for their wrongdoing or in exposing human rights abuse or environmental harm caused by corporations. Students of civil society have identified many different functions, often including its role in providing an interface between citizen and state and that of playing the role of a watchdog towards governments and authorities. In this vein, global civil society can (potentially) play a role in holding other influential actors, such as corporations, accountable. Scholarship shows that global civil society can exert pressure on corporations.[12] Scholars have also identified a variety of potential means for holding corporations accountable,[13] ranging from public pressure via information (including research and counter-accounting, or exposing corporate abuses) and advocacy (including the struggle for labour and environmental protection) campaigns, to supporting victims of human rights abuses through humanitarian or legal assistance, and legal action, particularly in the form of strategic litigation. Civil society can also hold states accountable for their inaction against illegal or immoral corporate conduct. Other attempts to provoke behavioural change in firms have included shareholder activism, a politics of influence or persuasion, as well as collaborative engagement between civil society organisations and corporations.[14] The latter respond to the pressure exerted by the former and other stakeholders by altering their discourses. They attempt to legitimise and consolidate their power by strategically shifting the focus of contestation to discourses that require minimal change in, or better reinforce, their ongoing behaviour—such as "corporate social responsibility (CSR)," "sustainability," "economic growth and prosperity," or "the promotion of voluntary principles."[15] Notably in the field of labour and environmental protection, companies pushed the narrative of an efficient self-regulating mechanism and voluntary principles and such initiatives are widely seen to have failed to deliver on their promises.[16] Moreover, increasingly, conservative transnational networks have emerged to challenge human rights initiatives in order to maintain the

[10] Davies and Peña (2021); Davies (2019); Kaldor (2003); Keane (2003); Smith et al. (1997).

[11] Hale (2020); Chan et al. (2019).

[12] Reinecke and Donaghey (2023); Reinecke and Donaghey (2015); Dale (2011).

[13] Birchall (2020).

[14] Dahan et al. (2010).

[15] Balsiger (2018); Banerjee and Bonnefous (2011); Banerjee (2008).

[16] Yan and Zhang (2020); Locke (2013); Zumbansen (2006).

human rights status quo.[17] For all these reasons, some contend that civil society is most efficient when mobilising different institutions, ranging from elite allies to governments[18] and when government-driven regulatory mechanisms and legal frameworks are implemented due to these mobilisations.[19] Against this backdrop, Payne et al. (2020) and Pereira et al. (2022) introduce the idea of corporate accountability "from below".[20] "From below," for them, does not exclusively refer to bottom-up civil society initiatives, but rather to weakly resourced groups in Latin America—such as victims associations—working together with institutional innovators benefitting from preferential institutional access. However, other scholars have found that activism is generally becoming more corporatised, that funding can facilitate co-optation, and that the lack of funding can create radicalisation; or, that advocacy elites assess issues on grounds other than the needs of their constituency.[21] Others argue that global civil society, and its most visible organisations—TANs—reinforce existing power dynamics, notably because most of the donors—both authorities and charities—are located in the Global North, or because they partner with governments and state institutions located in this hemisphere. Global civil society, then, risks, as Munck argued more nearly two decades ago, becoming "the social wing of the neoliberal offensive against the subaltern peoples and regions of the world".[22]

The means employed by civil society organisations (CSOs) have been widely discussed, ranging from advocacy and lobbying to service provision, or from mobilisation of the public and consumers to legal actions.[23] The same holds true for their goals, ranging from promoting democracy to speaking truth to power, or from being a watchdog to providing an interface between individuals and the economic and political sphere. However, scholarly discussions on the role of civil society have frequently taken an approach as normative as the perspective taken by many CSOs themselves. A classic way of distinguishing models of civil society follows the analytical differentiation between liberalism and communitarianism. While the former focuses on rights and freedoms and consequently on civil society as an additional layer of checks and balances to power, the latter focuses on responsibility and community and consequently on civil society as a means to empower communities and promote social cohesion.[24] In this vein, proponents of critical theory[25] look at underlying power structures, inequalities, and domination, and hence focus on the trans-

[17] Payne (2023).

[18] Seidman (2007).

[19] Scherer and Palazzo (2011).

[20] Payne et al. (2020); Pereira et al. (2022).

[21] Banks et al. (2015); Carpenter (2014); Dauvergne and LeBaron (2014); Yaziji and Doh (2013); Edwards and Hulme (1996).

[22] Munck (2006), p. 331.

[23] Edwards (2009); Anheimer (2004).

[24] Warren (2001).

[25] Fraser (1989); Habermas (1962).

formative power of civil society in creating a society ex negativo to the conditions in the existing society. Postcolonial approaches[26] refute these Western views altogether, understood as vehicles of imperialism and Western capital, and hence underline the role of Global Southern civil society in challenging the Western modes of organisation and striving for emancipation.

While the academic debate on the role of civil society is widely influenced by the epistemological position of its proponents, diverging visions within civil society regarding their role is not free of ideological leanings either. But, whereas the former impacts on the scholarly and public discourse regarding civil society and consequently the strategic orientation of the field, the latter shapes the actual tactics and repertoires. Understanding the relationship between visions and actions becomes essential for understanding the role civil society plays in provoking or hampering change.

2.2 Social Movement Theory and the Diversity of Modes of Engagement and Frames

I follow della Porta's (2020) instructive advice on using social movement studies as a toolkit to analyse the voluntary sector and civil society. Social movement theory seems suitable to study such organisations (both formal and informal) for a number of reasons.[27] Social movements frequently target businesses and play a key role in the struggle to hold corporations accountable.[28] Existing scholarship has pointed out the usefulness of social movement theory for the study of different types of organisation over the past 20–30 years.[29] Further, apart from the fact that many organisations and networks active in the field understand themselves as being part of a larger global movement—the corporate accountability movement—they also resemble in many regards social movements or social movement organisations. They mobilise around grievances and connect to social movement-driven causes such as climate change, labour rights, and fair distribution of wealth. They also engage in mobilisation strategies and repertoires known from social movements; different forms of conventional and unconventional political participation, advocacy, and reputation campaigns.[30] In particular, they often make use of protest.[31] They frequently form networks, alliances, and coalitions, often involving classic "elite allies"[32] such as

[26] Gabay (2013); de Sousa Santos (2002).

[27] della Porta (2020).

[28] Giugni and Grasso (2018); Soule (2018); McDonnell et al. (2015); King (2011).

[29] Campbell (2005); Davis and Zald (2005).

[30] George et al. (2023); Bereni and Dubuisson-Quellier (2020); Georgallis (2017); King (2014).

[31] Dubuisson-Quellier (2021); Banerjee and Case (2020).

[32] McAdam et al. (1996).

churches, politicians, or celebrities that serve as ambassadors for the cause.[33] Further, they use similar tactics to communicate their mobilisation frames.

Therefore, using social movement theory to analyse the universe of organisations active in the field of corporate accountability offers a sound theory-driven lens to study their mobilisation strategies, repertoires, and, in particular, their visions for their work and for society. For this purpose, we build on the "framing" perspective and repertoires of contention. As our analysis is dedicated to aspects that are either internal to, or directly mediated by the organisations, these two theoretical lenses enable us to conceptualize internal configurations of organisations, and, in particular, to analyse how the mobilisation frames impact the way these organisations struggle for holding corporations accountable.

Claims and issues brought forth or fought against by SMOs and their leaders, as well as the existing opportunity structures, need to be framed in a way that mobilises people to join the cause.[34] Framing in social movement studies thus describes the way in which social movements and movement organisations mobilise participants through the construction of mobilisation frames. Framing allows social movements to transform individual political orientations, values, and beliefs into collective action.[35] Movements need to pay close attention to whether their constructed frames are in accordance with the audiences they target to ensure that individual preferences correspond to the movement's goals, activities, and ideology.[36] Movements also need to ensure that the activities they engage in are sanctioned by their activists and participants. This 'frame resonance', in Snow and Benford's words, constitutes a deliberate compatibility between the preferences of the movement and those of activists, participants, and the targeted populations.[37]

Consequently, the framing approach allows us to conceptually disentangle and analyse the aim, ideology, and type of organisation. Repertoires of contention[38] are the way social movements and other organisation make claims and, hence, how their frames are transformed into action. From a classical perspective, disruptive repertoires are distinguished from conventional means. However, advances in information and communication technology, as well as constant innovation by societal actors made a broader understanding of repertoires necessary. Apart from frame resonance, also the tactics and repertoires employed by social movements, or all other relevant organisations, have to be compatible. Therefore, radical frames often come with radical repertoires, but radical repertoires almost always come with radical frames. On the other hand, given the corporatisation of activism, softened frames often lead to soft forms of activism.

---

[33] Reinecke and Donaghey (2015); Dale (2011); Keck and Sikkink (1998).

[34] Benford and Snow (2000); Gamson and Meyer (1996).

[35] Beck (2013).

[36] Snow et al. (1986).

[37] Snow and Benford (1988a); Snow and Benford (1988b).

[38] Tilly (2008); Tilly and Tarrow (2006); Tilly (1986).

Based on the scholarship presented above, I formulate a battery of three hypotheses. Informed by scholarship on global civil society, I expect to find a preponderance of organisations mobilising civil society repertoires over social movement specific repertoires (Hypothesis 1). Based on scholarship dedicated to the role civil society plays in the field of corporate accountability, I expect to find a preponderance of activities related to advocacy and information over contentious repertoires (Hypothesis 2). Drawing on social movement theory, I assume that the struggle to hold corporations accountable is, by its very nature, dominated by leftist or progressive frames (Hypothesis 3).

3 A Quantitative Approach to the Pluriverse of Corporate Accountability

The data collection followed the approach of Action Organization Analysis (AOE),[39] which has been successfully employed for data collection in multiple European projects (TransSOL, LIVEWHAT, EURYKA). AOE is an adaption of Protest Event Analysis that responds to the growing importance of the online sphere for civil society, that allows to map, sample, and code organisational data available on websites of organisations.[40] AOE relies on hub websites identified by national teams. Here, I used a slightly adapted version of AOE, notably regarding the sampling. Inspired by data collection methods suitable for network analysis,[41] I identified hub websites through the Global Civil Society Database.[42]

The database is compiled by the Union of International Associations (UIA), a Brussels-based non-profit research and documentation centre, mainly known for its reference work on international non-profit organisations, the Yearbook of International Organizations. Using the search routine "corporate accountability" and "corporate justice", I found four hub websites[43] (and hub-organisations). I followed Grant and Keohane's broad definition of accountability as the right of some actors "to hold other actors to a set of standards, to judge whether they have fulfilled their responsibilities in light of these standards, and to impose sanctions if they determine that these responsibilities have not been met".[44] Hence, these two search terms were chosen to identify organisations and networks that strive to hold corporations accountable for wrongdoings (hence, mainly post facto) or that promote fair

[39] Kousis et al. (2018).

[40] Ibid., p. 745.

[41] Jones (2020); Hughes et al. (2018).

[42] Union of International Associations (2022).

[43] The four initial organisations are the following: African Coalition for Corporate Accountability; Corporate Accountability; European Coalition for Corporate Justice; International Corporate Accountability Roundtable.

[44] Grant and Keohane's (2005), p. 29.

Table 1 Distribution by region

Region	North America	Europe	Africa	South America	Asia	Australia
Count	81	78	65	17	13	1
Percentage	31.8	30.6	25.5	6.7	5.1	0.4

treatment of people by corporations, rather than focusing on voluntary efforts by corporations (such as corporate social responsibility). Subsequently, 195 links to partner organisations have been extracted from these hub websites.

In a third step, the "about" sections of these partner websites have been scanned for references to corporate accountability and corporate justice. In a fourth step, links to partner websites from the websites that contained references to these terms were extracted, resulting in an additional 677 identified partners (see Table 1). By so doing, a global universe of formal and informal organisations active in the field of corporate accountability was identified.

The unit of analysis is, then, organisations (both formal and informal) active in the field of corporate accountability by striving to hold corporations accountable for wrongdoings or by enforcing and sanctioning fair treatment of individuals and groups affected by corporate actions. The link extraction resulted in a sample of 876 websites, as per three tiers (Graph 1), that allowed me to map and systematically analyse comparable cross-national data of a variety of types of organisations. Through this principle of data collection, biases created in methods based on the analysis of existing media content (such as Protest Event Analysis or Political Claims Analysis) could be limited by targeting the source rather than the representation. Consequently, the dataset is composed of an unmediated population of organisations that are both influential in the public discourse and informal, marginal or grassroots groups. Multiple pre-tests were performed which resulted in changes in the codebook, and an adapted sampling method.

In a final step, a cleaned and randomised sample of organisational websites was coded. In total, 260 websites of organisations,[45] groups, and networks were coded.

Africa has become the epicentre of human rights problems resulting from corporate activities,[46] while most TNCs are headquartered in Europe and North America. The dataset, although globally not representative due to the sampling based on the hub websites, provides a comprehensive exploratory sample of organisations located in these three world regions (Table 1). The data was collected between October 2022 and March 2023 and, as such, provides a snapshot of the publicly available data at this moment. Both the database and the present analysis are the first sources providing quantitative data on the pluriverse of organisations active in the field of corporate accountability and examining the organisational field.

Based on the theoretical framework presented in section one, I explore why and how organisations (both formal and informal) try to hold corporations accountable.

[45] This is a sub-sample of the dataset created by the author, that, in its complete version includes 290 organisations (Rammelt 2024).

[46] Olawuyi (2015).

Given the aforementioned fragmentation of civil society active in the field of corporate accountability,[47] my main focus is on internal factors, namely the repertoires and visions of organisations. To do so, I employ descriptive statistics to test the hypotheses based on the theoretical framework. The framing perspective informs our analysis of the type of organisation (variable 'type of organisation primary') and the three classic frames (variables 'values' for the motivational frame, 'blame attribution' for the diagnostic frame, and 'proposed route' for the prognostic frame). Additionally, descriptive statistics will reveal the trends in terms of funding sources (variable 'funders'), collaborations (variable 'partner organisations'), and on the interaction between different fields of activity (variable 'type of organisation primary' and 'type of organisation secondary'). The diversity of repertoires will be assessed through activities listed on the organisations' websites (variable 'field of activity').

The merits of the method are important (data collection on a global network of organisations through desk research, easy and accessible codebook, and dataset, etc.); however, three points deserve attention. First, while the data grasp a single universe of organisations, other universes of organisations are active. The universe under analysis is the extended network of the four TANs that were identified through the Global Civil Society Database (Fig. 1). The network and the extended network also only include partners that were mentioned or linked. It is worth noting that organisations collaborate with other groups, networks, and organisations that are not publicly acknowledged or discoverable online. This is probably not the case for donors, as most donors' funding regulations require public acknowledgement. When trying to generalise the results of this study for the universe of organisations included in the dataset, one has to take into account that the sampling mechanism recreated a single universe of organisations. Other universes might have slightly different characteristics and a slightly different composition (also in region terms) of organisations.

Secondly, quantifying data derived from qualitative analysis always implies a certain level of simplification. Subtle differences between organisations' visions, interests, and goals can remain hidden.

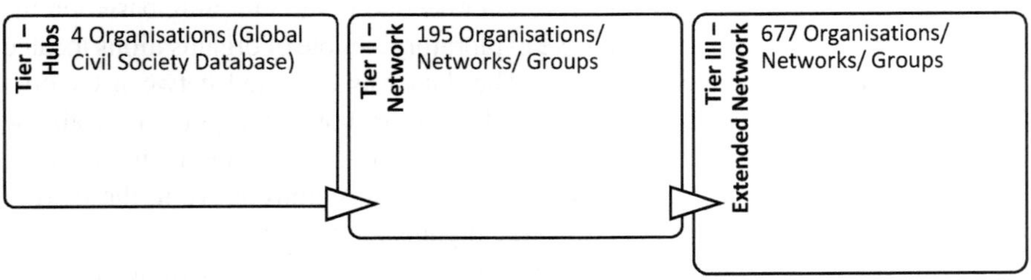

Fig. 1 Hubs and network

[47] Grosescu (2019).

Thirdly, organisations might describe their mission, vision, and their activities on their websites (e.g., to comply with funding requirements) in a certain way, while acting differently based on different motivations in reality. However, most of these limitations are to be encountered with other methods that are less comprehensive and that are affected by additional biases.

4 The Organisational Field in Numbers

In this section, I present the descriptive findings. The visions of organisations, what we consider the motivational frame, active in the field are assessed through their postulated values (see Table 2). "Ecology, environment, sustainability" is one of the main drivers of their activity, with 72.7% of websites referring to it. "Social justice", a value associated with progressive and left-wing ideologies, is placed second (56.3%), followed by the more generic values of "human rights" (55.9%) and "democratic principles" (49.6%). Another rather progressive value, "solidarity", is also a prominent reference (50.8%). A clear pattern emerges when looking at values that are more commonly associated with market-liberalism—"fairness" (14.1%),

Table 2 Motivational Frame

Values	Count	Percentage
Diversity and Sustainability—Ecology, environment, sustainability	186	72.7
Rights Based—Social Justice	144	56.3
Rights Based—Human Rights	143	55.9
Humanitarian—Solidarity	130	50.8
Democratic Principles	127	49.6
Humanitarian—Truthfulness, honesty, and sincerity	114	44.5
Rights Based—Political Equality	108	42.2
Humanitarian—Dignity	97	37.9
Diversity and Sustainability—Respect for difference	87	34
Community and Order—Preserving existing (local) communities	46	18
Rights Based—Fairness	36	14.1
Economic Virtues—Prosperity	32	12.5
Economic Virtues—Professionalism	32	12.5
Religion—Christian Values	12	4.7
Economic Virtues—Competitiveness	8	3.1
Community and Order—Tradition	5	2
Religion—Interfaith	4	1.6

“prosperity” (12.5%), and “competitiveness” (3.1%) are far less frequently referred to than their progressive counterparts.[48]

In agreement with the mobilisation frame (Table 2), the diagnostic frame (Table 3) displays a focus on blaming governments (78%) and companies (71%). The data shows a concurrence with regard to the institutions or actors responsible for social injustice and the construction of contemporary society, as Global North (27.6%), capitalist system (26.6%), and wealthy countries (21.5%) are in the second layer of blame attribution. The Poor (0%), General Population (1.3%) and Consumers (3.3%), broadly speaking, are at the bottom of the list of malefactors, showing the perception of civil society of individuals as subjects to corporate agendas and governments’ policy making.

While the diagnostic frame constructed by organisations identifies the problem or delivers a definition of the evil in society, they also need to advance solutions or encourage the public by developing scenarios for success. Table 4 summarises the prognostic frames. In first and fourth place, we find a preference for new domestic Legislation (59.2%) and New International Legislation (40.8%), and in second and third place, respectively, we find Collaborative efforts of Global Civil Society (53.7%) and Direct Intervention (45.1%). These latter two refer mostly to humanitarian aid and capacity building. Some (33%) see opportunities within the current legal framework or through the reinterpretation of existing laws (15.7%). The idea of voluntary principles (11.8%), strongly preferred and promoted by corporations themselves, is of limited influence in the universe of organisations included in the sample. A strong 33.3% of organisations believe the economic system should be reformed.

Table 3 Diagnostic Frame

Blame Attribution	Count	Percentage
Governments	168	78.5
Companies	152	71
Local Authorities	77	36
Politicians	63	29.4
The Rich	60	28
Global North	59	27.6
Capitalist System	57	26.6
International Regimes	54	25.2
Wealthy Countries	46	21.5
Greedy Company Personnel	39	18.2
Consumers	7	3.3
Global South	6	2.8
General Population	4	1.9
The Poor	0	0

[48] For a qualitative analysis of two major global coalitions for corporate accountability, including their political visions and repertoires of actions, see Andru Chiorean’s contribution in this volume.

Table 4 Prognostic Frame

Proposed Route	Count	Percentage
New domestic Legislation	151	59.2
Collaborative efforts of Global civil society	137	53.7
Direct Intervention	115	45.1
New International Legislation	104	40.8
Application of Existing Legislation	58	33.3
Reform the economic system	85	33.3
New International Regimes	55	21.6
Reinterpretation of existing law	40	15.7
Collaborative efforts of epistemic communities	31	12.2
Voluntary Principles	30	11.8

The findings concerning the field of activity and the tactics employed by organisations (Table 5), are in agreement with their mobilisation frames. The ranking of their activities, however, is a little different. Organisations' main activity is directed towards educating, informing, and empowering the general public, with the aim of mobilising public support. As such, we will find that raising awareness and providing information ranked first among their activities with 81.1%, and capacity building ranked third, with 58.3%. The second most common activity/strategy employed is directed towards authorities, lobbying and meetings with officials, scoring 62.9%. This Political/Advocacy activity shows their interest in garnering elite allies and influencing institutional actors through benign actions, making them more susceptible to incorporate the causes they advance. The collaborative component, networking (including federating national groups), with 47.5%, falls under the same logic. The watchdog role organisations have refers to documenting and making Human Rights Abuses public (51.4%) and counter-accounting other ways of gathering and spreading financial information on corporations (33.6%). The legal battle is another important arena for organisations in the field: 30.5% of organisations file complaints to relevant authorities, 32.4% provide legal assistance, 18.5% engage in litigation, and 9.3% (above our expectations) are active in prisoner support. Environmental activities constitute another pole of repertoires: Protection of the Environment (45.9%), fighting against extractive industries (24.7%), and alternative consumption or de-growth (20.8%) play an important role in the struggle against corporations. Although not as frequent, many organisations make use of social movement-related repertoires: Organising, or at least participating, in protests is an important element in terms of organisations activities (29.7%), organising or joining boycotts ranks second (20.8), followed by the more disruptive tactics of confrontational actions (12.4%) and occupations and blockades (10.8%). Externalising claims by addressing to international organisations and institutions (an avenue that requires a certain network position and access) is practised by 42.9%. As such, one can observe a

Table 5 Field of Activity and Repertoire

Field of Activity	Count	Percentage
Education—Awareness raising and Providing Information	210	81.1
Political/ Advocacy—Lobbying and Meetings with Officials	163	62.9
Education—Capacity Building	151	58.3
Documentation—Documenting Human Rights Abuses	133	51.4
Networking (including federating national groups)	123	47.5
Environmental—Protection of the Environment	119	45.9
Political/ Advocacy—Addressing to International Organisations and Institutions	111	42.9
Political/Advocacy—Conventional	106	40.9
Documentation—Financial Reports on Corporations	87	33.6
Legal—Legal Support	84	32.4
Legal—Complaints to Relevant Authorities	79	30.5
Political/Advocacy—Demonstrative	77	29.7
Community Support—Mutual Aid and Aid to Victims	72	27.8
Environmental—Extractive Industries	64	24.7
International Cooperation	56	21.6
Environmental—Alternative Consumption or De-Growth	54	20.8
Political/ Advocacy—Boycott	54	20.8
Legal—Litigation	48	18.5
Economic—Financial Support and Fundraising	46	17.8
Basic/ Urgent Needs—Health care/ mental health	36	13.9
Political/ Advocacy—Confrontational	32	12.4
Political/ Advocacy—Occupations and Blockades	28	10.8
Support to Indigenous People	27	10.4
Basic/Urgent Needs—Clothes, Food, Shelter	24	9.3
Legal—Prisoner Support	24	9.3
Political/Advocacy—Electoral (e.g., mobilising people to vote)	22	8.5
Cultural/Artistic initiative	13	5
Economic—Shareholder Activism	10	3.9
Economic—Pro-Business	7	2.7

tendency to use non-disruptive repertoires in their fight to convince governments or corporations to incorporate their agenda or to mobilise the public.

I was further interested in network embeddedness and availability of monetary resources: almost one-third of organisations (Table 6) do not have funding or do not provide information on funding (which is a strong indicator for the lack of funding, given that most grants require public acknowledgement of funding). The same holds true for network embeddedness. However, the latter comes with a reservation that does not necessarily apply to funding: while organisations frequently and positively identify themselves with their network, if it involves highly visible NGOs for reputational benefits, it is possible that some of the organisations that do not list or mention partners actually do work with other organisations and benefit from expertise and exposure provided by others. Table 7 summarises funding sources of

Table 6 Embeddedness and Resources

	Funding	Partners
yes,	68%	73%
no, or not public	32%	27%

Table 7 Funding Sources

Funding	Charities/ Philanthropies	Donations	Authorities	Membership Fees	Fundraising	Services
Count	145	143	83	45	41	36
Percentage	72.9	71.9	41.7	22.6	20.6	18.1

organisations included in the sample for which information on funding was available. They strongly rely on external funding, with less than a quarter of them being self-funded through fundraising (20.6%), membership fees (22.6%), or services (18.1%). Notably, membership fees and services (such as renting out spaces or selling beverages in self-managed locales) provide, at least partially, financial autonomy to organisations. Most organisations in the sample depend on funding through charities (72.9), donations (71.9%), and official funding by authorities (41.7%).

The field of corporate accountability is predominantly populated by human rights (~30%) and environmental organisations (~10%). Table 8 summarises the main types of organisations. Trade unions (3.5% and 0.5%) and organisations struggling for labour rights (1.2% and 4.1%) are much less frequent, which is surprising given that working conditions and slave labour are one of the more prominent anti-corporate frames visible to the public (e.g., anti-sweatshop campaigns). Also, very few law firms (1.6% and 0.5%) are involved in the CA network under study. A higher percentage for lawyer associations (2.3% and 2.6%) indicate that when legal expertise is provided to the network it is either coming from specialised organisations or from lawyers that try to hold corporations accountable in their spare time. Humanitarian organisations, mainly providing disaster (including human-made, such as oil spills) and poor relief account for around 6% of the network. Many organisations act in a secondary capacity also as donors; more than 8% function on the secondary plan as charities or foundations, often granting micro-funding to smaller and often local initiatives. Epistemic communities account for a very small share of the sample (1.6% and 1%), leaving intellectual input and research expertise mainly to think tanks (8.6% and 10.4%). Less organised groups and networks such as protest groups (1.9% and 4.7%) and informal citizen groups (2.7% and 1%) indicate that the field is dominated by more structured and professional organisations to the detriment of networks that could be considered the primary suppliers of opportunities for unconventional political participation.

Table 8 Type of Organisation

	Type of Organisation PRIMARY		Type of Organisation SECONDARY	
	Count	Percentage	Count	Percentage
Political—Civil/ human rights group	93	36.2	58	30.1
Political—Environmental group	28	10.9	22	11.4
Political—Protest Group	5	1.9	9	4.7
Political—Labour Rights	3	1.2	8	4.1
Professional Organisations—Unions/Labour organisations	9	3.5	1	0.5
Professional Organisations—Researchers, Academics, Intellectuals	4	1.6	2	1
Professional Organisations—Lawyer Associations	6	2.3	5	2.6
Law Firm	4	1.6	1	0.5
(International) Platform/ Federation	24	9.3	6	3.1
Humanitarian Organisation	15	5.8	11	5.7
Charity/ Foundation	12	4.7	16	8.3
Think Tank	22	8.6	20	10.4
Informal Citizen Group (like NIMBY)	7	2.7	2	1
Information Platform	10	3.9	20	10.4

5 Visions, Divisions, Convergences in the Organisational Field

5.1 Visions

There is far less variety than expected in the values that organisations in our sample claim. Concern for individual and group wellbeing prevails over corporate and governmental economic imperatives. This is consistent with the prognostic frames that organisations in the field construct. Given that 26.6% of the organisations analysed blame capitalism, 33.3% want to reform the economic system, and social justice is the second most prominent value (56.3), the data suggests a relatively strong left or progressive leaning. Our assumption that the field is mainly populated by leftist or progressive frames can be confirmed, with certain reservations (Hypothesis 3). The visions for the solution to the problems identified by organisations converge to creating new legal frameworks. While many organisations in the network do make use of movement-related repertoires, such as boycotts, confrontational or demonstrative repertoires, and blockades and occupations, conventional and more conformist repertoires are the preferred way of organisations in their respective struggles. However, anti-capitalist rhetoric and post-colonial approaches are quite prevalent in the sample (e.g., blame attribution to the Global North (27.6%), capitalist system (26.6%), and wealthy countries (21.5%).

5.2 Divisions

The most important division we observed within the field relates to the repertoires that organisations mobilise. Civil society deploys a diversity of means and tactics in their struggle, including significant proportions of advocacy and lobbying-related activities, capacity building and information, different forms of political participation (including more conflictual repertoires), and legal means; all are well represented within the population of organisations surveyed.

This division in repertoires also manifests in the type of organisations. Protest groups, citizen initiatives, and victims' associations (2.1% secondary type, not in the table) play a merely marginal role. Another major division can be observed between the haves and the have-nots and the connected and the not connected. If we consider that donor-civil society relations often de-radicalise and corporatize activism,[49] the data indicates that a considerable portion of organisations active in the field might be softened through their dependence on funding. The numbers for embeddedness and resources (around one-third of organisations without funding or no information on funding and no partners) are also concurrent with what we observed in terms of repertoires (less than a third of organisations engage in movement-related repertoires). The strong dependency on funding through donations, charities, and official funding to the detriment of more self-reliant funding sources indicate, can potentially explain the weak representation of movement-related repertoires. If we further consider that radical groups are often smaller, attract fewer resources, and are less structured,[50] our study can explain the toothlessness of civil society vis-à-vis corporations. Ultimately, both can be considered an indicator of the weak capability of non-state actors to provoke change. This becomes even more concerning in times of growing corporatisation, constantly increasing prerogatives for private security and weakening of civil liberties, and shrinking spaces for civil society. Unsurprisingly, H2 (Preponderance of advocacy and information over contentious repertoires) is confirmed. The quasi-absence of law firms in the network indicates that only a few firms active in anti-corporate litigations are clearly specialised as such and assume a more political role in the struggle against corporations. The fact that more than 18% of organisations in the network mention strategic litigation as one of their primary fields of activity, but only five out of 260 organisations are law firms indicates that either organisations have their own legal capacities (as it is the case for a number of high-profile NGOs, such as Sherpa in France, the European Centre for Constitutional and Human Rights, or the Centre of Legal and Social Studies in Argentina) or that for most law firms organisations, work with anti-corporate litigation is just one of many other businesses. This means that only very specialised organisations or very affluent organisations can engage in legal struggle.

[49] Saunders and Roth (2019); Banks et al. (2015); Edwards and Hulme (1996).

[50] Yaziji and Doh (2013).

5.3 *Convergences*

While the organisations included in the sample are diverse in terms of repertoires, embeddedness, and funding, the problems they identify and the values the problem is in contradiction with are quite convergent. Visions of the malaise of society and of the reasons for which it has to be overcome (diagnostic and motivational frame) allow for a coagulation of different forces from different ideological backgrounds employing different strategies and tactics in their struggle. First, civil society active in the field of CA considers it the state's responsibility to regulate and create a functional framework to control corporate activity (Table 4). Second, they believe they have the capacity, the know-how, and the network to provoke change and to influence the state into taking measures. Blaming the rich (or the Bourgeoisie) and the economic system (or the mode of production) follows a Marxist logic, and their prominence (Table 3) can indicate a strong ideological leaning to the left. In that case, the strong 33.3% for identifying a reform of the economic system as a solution could equally indicate such a leaning. Our data further shows a strong relationship between the field of CA and human rights and environmental protection. Environmental struggles are one of the key platforms in the struggle for CA. Also, while more radical and movement-related repertoires are, unsurprisingly, less frequently used than conventional means of political participation and information or expertise-related activities, many organisations engage in a diversity of tactics, and activities dedicated to mobilising the public often include calls for boycotts or, at least, the participation in protests. Other contentious repertoires embedded in the structure of contemporary society, such as strategic litigation (carried out by highly specialised or affluent organisations), are accompanied by efforts to mobilise the public (such as information campaigns or counter-accounting). By and large, many repertoires go hand-in-hand and provide additional pressure on different stakeholders. Overall, a prevalence of liberal advocacy repertoires is observed. Hence, the hypothesis regarding a preponderance of organised civil society repertoires over social movement-specific repertoires (Hypothesis 3) can be confirmed. Lastly, the prognostic frame indicates a strong belief in the power of civil society and epistemic communities while rejecting the business-driven idea of voluntary principles.

6 Conclusion

This chapter has attempted to pinpoint existing divisions within a universe of civil society organisations that are active in the field of corporate accountability, which leads to fragmentation in terms of repertoires and ideology. It has also identified existing and prospective points of convergence. I have done so by mapping the organisations' structure, funding, and accountability strategies, and by providing exploratory evidence of ideological leanings, goals, and mobilisation frames. The theory-driven analysis of a rich and innovative dataset enables us to answer the majority of the research questions. The main driver of mobilisation is a leftist, anti-corporate discourse, mainly advanced by human rights and environmental organisations. The frames they construct clearly follow this logic and—except for the prognostic frame, where also around 30% of organisations want to reform the economic system—identify elements of society as problems and as culprits that are deeply enshrined in the way contemporary capitalism functions. Overall, the variance in frames (and, thus, in ideological leanings) is eclipsed by the variety of repertoires, where the leftist and often rather radical discourse is not followed by the corresponding repertoire. Organisations show a tendency to cooperate with different institutions/governments while drawing upon a critical narrative of capitalism. Although they mostly reject voluntary initiatives to CA, they still trust governments, which they also identify as one of the main culprits, to remedy the situation. Similar to the classic dictum in social movement studied, that states are both the target and the fulcrum of social movements,[51] the organisations included in the sample identify the state as their target but also as the means to bring relief. Hence, we observe a situation where discourse and mobilisation strategy are radical, but actions are conforming to socially accepted forms. We can only speculate about the reasons for this value-practice contradiction, but fashion and trends in activism and funding (e.g., a current preference for topics such as social justice, climate justice, or discrimination). Notably the detrimental effect of state funding on civil society organizations active in the field has been demonstrated by a recent study using the complete dataset.[52] One of the main findings, then, and one of the main contributions to the field of this paper, is that civil society is further contained and, ultimately, contributes to maintaining the status quo, as cautioned by Munck almost 20 years ago.[53] This is even more relevant in the field of CA: in times when life is almost entirely colonised by corporations, and almost every aspect of it is commodified, provoking the weakening of labour protection standards and consumer rights and environmental destruction, CA could serve as some sort of a master frame similar to globalisation in the late 1990s and early 2000s. The struggle against corporations, or, at least, the struggle to hold them accountable, could (potentially) be at the forefront in the fight for a better life. From an empirical perspective, the contribution of this chapter is, then, that it is unlikely that civil society will challenge power configurations and the systemic causes of the malaise they identified. The chapter also demonstrated the usefulness of social movement theory in analysing civil society. From a conceptual perspective, the main contribution is related to global civil society, in general, and its functioning mechanisms. If civil society and non-state actors fail in the field of CA, civil society's role is reduced to supplement or assume functions formerly falling under the responsibility of the state (that it light-heartedly hands over because of the 'requirements' of constant crises) and becoming a toothless tool in the legitimation strategies of the economic system, neoliberalism, and the status quo.

---

[51] Tarrow (2009), p. 63.

[52] Rammelt and Kołczyńska (2025).

[53] Munck (2006).

In addition to the caveats and limitations of the sampling and data collection method mentioned above, other limitations of the approach have to be pointed out, and avenues for future research are to be identified. Amongst the most important ones is the fact that organisations might collaborate in a less discoverable way. For example, presidents or personnel of different organisations could be part of the same social network (in the sense of social capital), and a *multipositionnalité* of actors[54] could take effect. Frequently, chairpersons of large or influential NGOs are also on the board of other organisations etc. A network analysis of leading personnel (e.g., through an analysis of LinkedIn profiles or professional biographies) could provide invaluable insights on less visible, less official mechanisms of cooperation and domination. The interaction between donors and grantees and a potential process of conformity, although widely studied, is, until now, limited to case studies. More holistic approaches on 'controlled civil society' are needed. The impact of different context variables, such as the position in the World economy, regime type, political opportunity structures, or cultural backgrounds, could greatly contribute to the study of political participation and of global civil society. Lastly, power dynamics within civil society in the Global North and in the Global South require more attention.

References

Anheimer H (2004) Civil society. Measurement, evaluation, policy. Routledge, London

Balsiger P (2018) Explaining dynamic strategies for defending company legitimacy: the changing outcomes of anti-sweatshop campaigns in France and Switzerland. Bus Soc 57(4):676–705. https://doi.org/10.1177/0007650315619471

Banerjee SB (2008) Corporate social responsibility: the good, the bad and the ugly. Crit Sociol 34(1):51–79. https://doi.org/10.1177/0896920507084623

Banerjee SB, Bonnefous A-M (2011) Stakeholder management and sustainability strategies in the French nuclear industry. Bus Strateg Environ 20(2):124–140. https://doi.org/10.1002/bse.681

Banerjee T, Case B (2020) The leverage of protest: market, media, and reputational disruption in social movement success. Sociol Forum 35(1):95–125. https://doi.org/10.1111/socf.12569

Banks N, Hulme D, Edwards M (2015) NGOs, states, and donors revisited: still too close for comfort? World Dev 66:707–718. https://doi.org/10.1016/j.worlddev.2014.09.028

Batliwala S, Brown DL (2006) Transnational civil society: an introduction. Kumarian Press Inc., Bloomfield

Beck CJ (2013) Ideology. In: The Wiley-Blackwell encyclopedia of social and political movements. Blackwell Publishing Ltd.

Benford R, Snow D (2000) Framing processes and social movements: an overview and assessment. Annu Rev Sociol 26:611–639. https://doi.org/10.1146/annurev.soc.26.1.611

Bereni L, Dubuisson-Quellier S (2020) Au-delà de la confrontation: saisir la diversité des interactions entre mondes militants et mondes économiques. Rev Fr Sociol 61(4):505–529. https://doi.org/10.3917/rfs.614.0505

[54] Mathieu (2007).

Birchall D (2020) The role of civil society and human rights defenders in corporate accountability. In: Deva S, Birchall D (eds) Research handbook on human rights and business. Edward Elgar Publishing, Cheltenham, pp 422–445
Campbell J (2005) Where do we stand? Common mechanisms in organizations and social movements research. In: Davis GF, McAdam D, Scott RW, Zald MN (eds) Social movements and organization theory. Cambridge University Press, Cambridge, pp 41–68
Carpenter C (2014) "Lost" causes: agenda vetting in global issue networks and the shaping of human security. Cornell University Press, Ithaca
Chan S, Boran I, van Asselt H et al (2019) Promises and risks of nonstate action in climate and sustainability governance. WIREs Clim Change 10:e572
della Porta D (2007) Global justice movement. Cross-national and transnational perspectives. Routledge, Abingdon
della Porta D (2020) Building bridges: social movements and civil society in times of crisis. Volunt Int J Volunt Nonprofit Org 31:938–948. https://doi.org/10.1007/s11266-020-00199-5
della Porta D, Tarrow S (2004) Transnational protest and global activism. Rowman & Littlefield, Lanham
Dahan NM, Doh JP, Oetzel J, Yaziji M (2010) Corporate-NGO collaboration: co-creating new business models for developing markets. Long Range Plan 43(2–3):326–342. https://doi.org/10.1016/j.lrp.2009.11.003
Dale JG (2011) Free Burma: transnational legal action and corporate accountability. University of Minnesota Press, Minneapolis
Dauvergne P, LeBaron G (2014) Protest Inc.: the corporatization of activism. Polity Press, Cambridge
Davies, T (2014) NGOs: A new history of transnational civil society. Oxford University Press, Oxford
Davies TR (2019) Introducing NGOs and international relations. In: Davies TR (ed) Routledge handbook of NGOs and international relations. Routledge, London
Davies TR, Peña AM (2021) Social movements and international relations: a relational framework. J Int Relat Dev 24:51–76. https://doi.org/10.1057/s41268-019-00180-w
Davis GF, Zald MN (2005) Social change, social theory, and the convergence of movements and organizations. In: Davis GF, McAdam D, Scott RW, Zald MN (eds) Social movements and organization theory. Cambridge University Press, Cambridge, pp 335–350
De Sousa Santos B (2002) Toward a new legal common sense: law, globalization, and emancipation. Cambridge University Press, Cambridge
Dubuisson-Quellier S (2021) Anti-corporate activism and market change: the role of contentious valuations. Soc Mov Stud 20(4):399–416. https://doi.org/10.1080/14742837.2020.1731448
Edwards M (2009) Civil society. Polity Press, Cambridge
Edwards M, Hulme D (1996) Too close for comfort? The impact of official aid on nongovernmental organizations. World Dev 24(6):961–973. https://doi.org/10.1016/0305-750X(96)00019-8
Evans P (2000) Fighting marginalization with transnational networks: counter-hegemonic globalization. Contemp Sociol 29(1):230–241. https://doi.org/10.2307/26549
Fraser N (1989) Unruly practices: power, discourse, and gender in contemporary society. University of Minnesota Press, Minneapolis
Gabay C (2013) Civil society and global poverty. Hegemony, inclusivity, legitimacy. Routledge, Abingdon
Gamson WA, Meyer DS (1996) Framing political opportunity. In: McAdam D, McCarthy JD, Zald MN (eds) Comparative perspectives on social movements: political opportunities, mobilizing structures, and cultural framings. Cambridge University Press, Cambridge, pp 275–290
Georgallis P (2017) The link between social movements and corporate social initiatives: toward a multi-level theory. J Bus Ethics 142:735–751. https://doi.org/10.1007/s10551-016-3111-0
George S, Brown J, Dillard J (2023) Social movement activists' conceptions of political action and counter-accounting through a critical dialogic accounting and accountability lens. Crit Perspect Account 91:102408

Giugni M, Grasso M (2018) Economic outcomes of social movements. In: Snow DA, Soule S, Kriesi H, McCammon H (eds) The Wiley Blackwell companion to social movements. Wiley-Blackwell, Oxford
Grant RW, Keohane RO (2005) Accountability and abuses of power in world politics. Am Polit Sci Rev 99(1):29–43. https://doi.org/10.1017/S0003055405051476
Grosescu R (2019) Transnational advocacy networks and corporate accountability for gross human rights violations in Argentina and Colombia. Glob Soc 33(3):400–418. https://doi.org/10.1080/13600826.2019.1598947
Habermas J (1962) Strukturwandel der Öffentlichkeit. Untersuchungen zu einer Kategorie der Bürgerlichen Gesellschaft. Suhrkamp, Frankfurt/Main
Hale T (2020) Transnational actors and transnational governance in global environmental politics. Annu Rev Polit Sci 23(1):203–220. https://doi.org/10.1146/annurev-polisci-050718-032644
Hughes MM, Paxton P, Quinsaat S, Reith N (2018) Does the global north still dominate women's international organizing? A network analysis from 1978 to 2008. Mobil Int Q 23(1):1–21. https://doi.org/10.17813/1086-671X-23-1-1
Jones S (2020) Memory relations. Cross-border collaboration between mnemonic actors in Germany, Central Eastern Europe, and the MENA Region. Revue d'études comparatives Est-Ouest 2(2–3):225–259. https://doi.org/10.3917/receo1.512.0225
Kaldor M (2003) Global civil society: an answer to war. Polity Press, Cambridge
Keane J (2003) Global civil society? Cambridge University Press, Cambridge
Keck ME, Sikkink K (1998) Activists beyond borders. Advocacy networks in international politics. Cornell University Press, Ithaca
King BG (2011) The tactical disruptiveness of social movements: sources of market and mediated disruption in corporate boycotts. Soc Probl 58(4):491–517. https://doi.org/10.1525/sp.2011.58.4.491
King BG (2014) Reputational dynamics of private regulation. Soc Econ Rev 12(1):200–206
Klein N (1999) No logo. Knopf Canada, Toronto
Kousis M, Giugni M, Lahusen C (2018) Action organization analysis: extending protest event analysis using hubs-retrieved websites. Am Behav Sci 62(6):739–757. https://doi.org/10.1177/0002764218768846
Locke R (2013) The promise and limits of private power: promoting labor standards in a global economy. Cambridge University Press, Cambridge
Mathieu L (2007) L'espace des Mouvements Sociaux. Politix 77(1):131–151. https://doi.org/10.3917/pox.077.0131
McAdam D, Snow D (1996) Social movements: readings on their emergence, mobilization and dynamics. Roxbury Press, Los Angeles
McAdam D, McCarty JD, Zald MN (1996) Introduction: opportunities, mobilizing structures, and framing processes – toward a synthetic, comparative perspective on social movements. In: McAdam D, McCarthy JD, Zald MN (eds) Comparative perspectives on social movements. Political opportunities, mobilizing structures, and cultural framings. Cambridge University Press, Cambridge, pp 1–20
McAdam D, Tarrow S, Tilly C (2001) Dynamics of contention. Cambridge University Press, Cambridge
McDonnell M-H, King BG, Soule SA (2015) A dynamic process model of private politics: activist targeting and corporate receptivity to social challenges. Am Sociol Rev 80(3):654–678. https://doi.org/10.1177/0003122415581335
Munck R (2006) Global civil society. Royal road or slippery path? Volunt Int J Volunt Nonprofit Org 17(4):325–332. https://doi.org/10.1007/s11266-006-9019-z
Olawuyi DS (2015) The increasing relevance of rights-based approaches to resource governance in Africa: shifting from regional aspiration to local realization. McGill Int J Sustain Dev Law Policy 11(2):294–337
Payne LA (2023) The right against rights in Latin America: an analytical framework. In: Payne LA, Zulver J, Escoffier S (eds) The right against rights in Latin America. Oxford University Press, Oxford, pp 29–58

Payne LA, Pereira G, Bernal-Bermúdez L (2020) Transitional justice and corporate accountability from below: deploying archimedes' lever. Cambridge University Press, Cambridge
Pereira G, Payne LA, Bernal-Bermúdez L (2022) Justice from below: corporate accountability in Argentina. Int J Hum Rights 26(8):1418–1454. https://doi.org/10.1080/13642987.2022.2027764
Rammelt H (2024) Civil society active in corporate accountability dataset. Mendeley Data., V1. https://doi.org/10.17632/pfp7zmxcyx.1
Rammelt HP, Kołczyńska M (2025) Donor dependency, embeddedness and organizational structure of civil society: an analysis of a global sample of actors active in the field of corporate accountability. Global Networks 25:e70024. https://doi.org/10.1111/glob.70024
Reinecke J, Donaghey J (2015) After Rana Plaza: building coalitional power for labour rights between unions and (consumption-based) social movement organisations. Organization 22(5):720–740
Reinecke J, Donaghey J (2023) Stitching governance for labor rights. towards transnational industrial democracy? Cambridge University Press, Cambridge
Saunders C, Roth S (2019) NGOs and social movement theory. In: Davies T (ed) Routledge handbook of NGOs and international relations. Routledge, Abingdon, pp 138–152
Scherer AG, Palazzo G (2011) The new political role of business in a globalized world: a review of a new perspective on CSR and its implications for the firm, governance, and democracy. J Manag Stud 48(4):899–931. https://doi.org/10.1111/j.1467-6486.2010.00950.x
Seidman GW (2007) Beyond the boycott: labor rights, human rights, and transnational activism. Russel Sage Foundation, New York
Smith J, Johnston H (2002) Globalization and resistance. Transnational dimensions of social movements. Rowman & Littlefield, Lanham
Smith J, Chatfield C, Pagnucco R (1997) Transnational social movements and global politics: solidarity beyond the state. Syracuse University Press, Syracuse
Snow DA, Benford RD (1988a) Ideology, frame resonance, and participant mobilization. In: Klandermans B, Kriesi H, Tarrow S (eds) From structure to action: social movement participation across cultures. JAI Press, Greenwich, pp 197–217
Snow DA, Benford RD (1988b) Ideology, frame resonance, and participant mobilization. Int Soc Mov Res 1:197–217
Snow DA, Rochford BE Jr, Worden KS, Benford RD (1986) Frame alignment processes, micromobilization and movement participation. Am Sociol Rev 51(4):464–481
Soule SA (2018) Social movements and their impact on business and management. In: Bergh DD (ed) Oxford research encyclopedia of business and management. Oxford University Press, Oxford
Tarrow S (1994) Power in movement. Social movements and contentious politics. Cambridge University Press, Cambridge
Tarrow, S (2009) Power in movement. Social movements and contentious politics. Cambridge University Press, Cambridge
Tilly C (1986) The contentious French. Harvard University Press, Cambridge
Tilly C (2008) Contentious performances. Cambridge University Press, Cambridge
Tilly C, Tarrow S (2006) Contentious politics. Oxford University Press, Oxford
Union of International Associations (2022) Global civil society database. Union of International Associations
Warren ME (2001) Democracy and association. Princeton University Press, Princeton
Yan M, Zhang D (2020) From corporate responsibility to corporate accountability. Hastings Bus Law J 16(1):43–64
Yaziji M, Doh JP (2013) The role of ideological radicalism and resource homogeneity in social movement organization campaigns against corporations. Organ Stud 34(5–6):755–780. https://doi.org/10.1177/0170840613479235
Zumbansen P (2006) The conundrum of corporate social responsibility: reflections on the changing nature of firms and states. CLPE Res Pap 2(1)

Henry Rammelt is Researcher and Associate Lecturer at the National School of Political Studies and Administration, Bucharest. His research interests include social movements, corporate accountability, contentious politics, and civil society. He is author of *Activistes Protestataires en Hongrie et en Roumanie* (L'Harmattan, 2018) and co-editor of *Power and Protest in Central and Eastern Europe* (Palgrave Macmillan, 2025). His work has been published in journals such as *East European Politics and Society*, *Erdkunde – Archive for Scientific Geography*, *Global Networks*, and *Political Studies Review*. He is currently a Senior Researcher in the ERC Project "Transnational Advocacy Networks and Corporate Accountability for Major International Crimes" and leads the Romanian team of the Horizon Project "Protest as a Democracy Test: Protest Culture under Transformation and as a Transformative Power."

Corporate Accountability and the Ecological Turn: Mining Lessons from the Rights of Nature Movement

John G. Dale

Abstract As Big Tech-driven development of artificial intelligence and data mining becomes increasingly entangled with traditional practices of extractivist mining for oil, gas, coal, and precious metals and minerals, the corporate accountability movement now must take into consideration (living and non-living) nonhuman rights to adequately defend and mobilise support for the humans, communities, ecosystems, and knowledge being impacted. Drawing on relational approaches to rights projects, this chapter examines a transnational, Indigenous-led rights of nature movement in Ecuador that successfully pre-empted the rights and extractive practices of transnational and state-owned mining corporations while creating new rights to protect Indigenous communities, the Amazonian forests they inhabit, and novel legal forms of data ownership. I then compare this case to a U.S.-focused corporate accountability movement that had separately and differently constructed rights of nature to challenge corporate rights of extractivist development. I demonstrate how the rights of nature project in Ecuador subsequently engaged and influenced this U.S.-based rights project, including its relational discourse on rights of nature and community, political aims and strategies of corporate accountability, and its movement identity.

Special thanks to Daniela Kraiem for her insightful comments on this chapter, editorial scrutiny, and encouragement throughout this project. Appreciation to Maxwell Rollins and Karthik Ramanujam for their research assistance. Finally, my gratitude to Raluca Grosesçu for her steadfast partnership in the production of this co-edited volume.

J. G. Dale (✉)
George Mason University, Fairfax, VA, USA
e-mail: jdale@gmu.edu

R. Grosescu, J. G. Dale (eds.), *Corporate Accountability for Human Rights Violations*, Interdisciplinary Studies in Human Rights 16,
https://doi.org/10.1007/978-3-032-05569-9_4

1 Introduction

The extractivist practices of corporations mining for oil, gas, coal, as well as precious metals and minerals have for many decades despoiled watersheds, biodiverse forests, and other non-human living ecosystems. Scientists recently have drawn attention to how Big Tech corporations, long hyped as a "clean" industry, creates its own environmental and social harms. Now representing the most advanced practices of capitalism, Big Tech corporations have become the dominant actors shaping the digital transformation of the knowledge economy, with ill effects for workers who face economic stagnation and increasing global inequality.[1] Big Tech corporations have introduced new systemic practices of extraction: the mining and colonization of data.[2] As Big Tech and states invest heavily in the development of artificial intelligence (AI), we find them also increasingly building massive energy-sucking data centres in communities around the world to sustain their systems of data extraction, storage, and control.[3]

Communities are now seeing all too clearly the entanglement of extractivist practices that link the mining of data to the mining of precious metals, such as nickel, lithium, and especially copper, which is critical to the transformation of electricity that powers the data centres, and which, in turn, contribute to AI's "compute"—that is, the computer hardware, memory, and other resources—that is required to create, train and run AI models efficiently. As Kate Crawford, co-founder of the AI Now Institute at New York University and author of *Atlas of AI: Power, Politics, and the Planetary Costs of Artificial Intelligence*, explains:

> The stack required to power artificial intelligence systems goes well beyond the multilayered technical stack of data modelling, hardware, servers, and networks. [...] If we visit the primary sites of mineral extraction for computational systems, we find the repressed stories of acid-bleached rivers and deracinated landscapes and the extinction of plant and animal species that were once vital to the local ecology. [...] The corporate imaginaries of AI fail to depict the lasting costs and long histories of the materials needed to build computational infrastructures or the energy required to power them. The rapid growth of cloud-based computation, portrayed as environmentally friendly, has paradoxically driven an expansion of the frontiers of resource extraction.[4]

In response communities, activists, and scholars have demanded corporate accountability for the massive harms—environmental and social—caused by old and new extractivist industries. The corporate accountability movement, which has long struggled to prevent extractivist industries from destroying our communities and the ecosystems in which they are embedded, must now also address these industries' relations with Big Tech. Will regulatory agencies, responsible for permitting these extractive projects, and who already cede their mandates to business interests, be

---

[1] Unger (2019).

[2] Couldry and Mejias (2019); Mejias and Couldry (2024).

[3] Wong (2024).

[4] Crawford (2021), pp. 31, 36, and 47.

less likely to do so when Big Tech adds more pressure? These issues will only become more pressing, especially as they become aligned with the business interests of Big Tech corporations and their massive investment in the data centres required to maintain AI Systems and advance the projects that depend on them.

According to the Environmental Justice Atlas, there are currently 2225 registered cases of conflicts over extractive activities worldwide.[5] If we include registered cases of conflict over data centers (70), biodiversity conservation (161), waste management (326), and water management (528), the total number rises to 3310. In Latin America, the Observatorio de Conflictos Mineros (Mining Conflicts Observatory) reports 289 conflicts over mining alone.[6] When we consider that many of these conflicts are occurring in the Amazonian forest ("the lungs of the Earth"), we are reminded of the global consequences of these "Latin American" mining conflicts. Even in jurisdictions most friendly to environmentalist claims rooted in human rights and the rights of nature, such as Ecuador, which I will discuss in far more detail below, "losing cases tend to be ones versus large extractive interests."[7]

In their various campaigns to address the threats and ongoing harms posed by the extractive practices of corporations, corporate accountability movements have for decades invoked human rights discourse. Whether within or outside formal political and legal institutional channels, mobilising strategies typically rely on justificatory discourses, such as those based on human rights norms or claims, to account for their action. The threats posed by climate change, and fuelled more so by the environmental demands of AI, are leading many human rights and corporate accountability activists, advocates, and scholars to re-think how such discourses adequately speak to the changing relations between humans, corporations, technology, and natural ecosystems.

In this chapter I explore how some corporate accountability movements, scholars, and activists are taking an ecological turn, shifting to a more relational approach to human rights, in combination with rights for non-human actors (including the rights of nature itself), to combat the extreme harms caused by extractivist industries more generally. I consider how these new discourses might play out in the context of corporate accountability movements looking to rein in Big Tech, in which non-human actors, such as corporations, already exercise rights—often to the detriment of human beings and the health of ecosystems, such as forests, watersheds, and oceans.

I begin by describing how movements might think more relationally about rights, introducing Rodríguez-Garavito's concept of "More-Than-Rights"[8] and Jung's concept of the "rights project."[9] I reflect on how such an approach might help us better

---

[5] Available at https://ejatlas.org/ (accessed 3.02.2025). The search was conducted in January 2025, using the following categories: mineral ores and building materials extraction, fossil fuels and climate justice; energy and biomass and land conflicts.

[6] Available at www.ocmal.org/ (accessed 3.02.2025).

[7] Gordon (2019), p. 85.

[8] Rodríguez-Garavito (2024).

[9] Jung (2024).

understand the challenges (cultural, political, legal, ecological, and technological) that corporate accountability projects now face operating under conditions of a digitally transforming Anthropocene.

I draw on this approach to examine a case of a transnational Indigenous-led rights project that has been successfully struggling for corporate accountability against existentially harmful extractivist corporate practices in Ecuador. They have done this in part by constructing, defending, and advancing the rights of the Amazonian forest in which they live—a right of nature itself, not dependent upon harm to humans. Then, with an eye on protecting the data that they and transnationally allied scientists are collecting to monitor the ongoing protection and regeneration of their forest (and themselves), they are also constructing novel forms of collective data ownership rights, which they envision sharing with their Living Forest (*Kawsak Sacha*).

In order to illustrate how relationally configured rights projects in different contexts may converge,[10] and to explore the mutual effects of their engagement, I also examine a different rights project that began in 1995 in Pennsylvania in a U.S.-based mainstream environmental organisation. It initially focused on preventing extractivist corporations from proceeding with projects that would have negative impacts on local communities, such as pollution and health problems. By the mid-2000s, it had changed tactics to became the leading organisation working to forge rights of nature laws in local communities across the U.S. I examine its shift in strategy (and the impact of) pitting the legal personhood of nature against the legal personhood of corporations. I then draw on existing socio-legal historical and political anthropological ethnographic research to show that this organisation's eventual engagement with the Indigenous-led transnational rights of nature project in Ecuador, especially it's understandings of relations between humans and nature, and political community, helped to transform this U.S.-based rights project.

The new extractivism of the digitally transforming conditions of the Anthropocene has generated new ontological threats and politics that today challenge the prospects, and even the notion, of a global human rights project. As William Connolly, puts it, "to name the Anthropocene […] is to challenge human exceptionalism. […] And it is to invite the humanities [and social sciences] to forge intellectual and political alliances with geologists, glaciologists, climatologists, and palaeontologists who link this era to several other bumpy periods that preceded it. The preciousness of classical humanism must be challenged by…*entangled humanism.*"[11] The two rights projects I discuss offer reason for hope that it is at least possible to entangle extractivist development projects.

I conclude that relational approaches to understanding the construction of rights and agency of humans (social systems) and nonhumans (natural ecosystems and technological systems) must take into consideration the pluriversal politics that

---

[10] Ibid., p. 266, on comparing "multiscalar" yet differently contextualized rights projects as relational objects; See also Guarnizo and Smith (1998), on comparing "transnational social formations."

[11] Connolly (2017), p. 33.

have emerged in the wake of the ecological and technological turns across many fields of knowledge production. This can open up strategic discursive possibilities for bridging and strengthening multiscalar corporate accountability movements and their rights projects.

2 Relational Approaches to Rights

2.1 Entangling Rights Projects

"If the human rights project is to remain relevant in the Anthropocene," argues César Rodríguez-Garavito, Professor of Clinical Law and Director of the More-Than-Human Rights (MOTH) Project at New York University's School of Law, "it needs to take into consideration the rights of nonhumans."[12] He has in mind predominantly the living ecosystems and living nonhuman species that constitute them. He does not see humans as separate from nature but, rather, symbiotically and deeply entangled,[13] much in the way his MOTH colleague biologist and author Merlin Sheldrake describes in his best-selling book, *Entangled Life*.[14] Rodríguez-Garavito sees the rights of humans beings as "intrinsically entangled" with the rights of nonhumans and embedded within the rights of nature[15]—"all subjects of rights (from people to animals to forests) are ecosystems."[16] Provocatively yet seriously he asks, "if biology has become ecology, if individuals are ecosystems, where does that leave human rights, which arose to protect *Homo sapiens*?"[17]

A conceptual foundation of human rights is the hierarchical order that places humans above nonhumans. Philosopher of Human Rights (and MOTH Project affiliate) Will Kymlicka explains, "the theory and politics of human rights has been grounded in ideas of human supremacism and has been complicit in many harms and injustices done to the more-than-human-world. … Insofar as the theory and practice of human rights rests on supremacist views, it is in clear tension with the project of MOTH rights, which rejects the idea that intrinsic value is an exclusively human quality."[18] Anthropocentric approaches to the environment, such as the right to a healthy environment or the application of conventional rights to environmental protection, only protect nonhumans to the extent that it is necessary to redress harms to individual human beings. "Ecocentric understandings of rights," Rodríguez-Garavito explains, "aim to protect and redress harms to nonhumans themselves,

[12] Rodríguez-Garavito (2024), p. 33.

[13] Ibid., p. 34.

[14] Sheldrake (2020).

[15] Rodríguez-Garavito (2024), p. 29.

[16] Ibid, p. 35.

[17] Ibid., p. 34.

[18] Kymlicka (2024), pp. 56, 58.

above and beyond the associated harms to humans."[19] Both approaches will continue to exist—even if in tension. How might we shrink the gap?

Rodríguez-Garavito describes his approach to thinking about rights as "relational."[20] In seeking to call attention to the rights of marginalised, living nonhumans, this approach entails "relaxing the legal frontier between human and MOTH subjectivities"[21] to ground a different moral relation between them. There would seem to be a tension within this approach, perhaps a dual strategy, in which he first ascribes (moral) "intrinsic value" to living nonhumans as the ontological grounding from which the rights of these nonhumans derive, yet he then also works relationally (beyond the strategic essentialism of his starting point) to generate such subjectivities in the social world of human consciousness, relations and institutions.

The scholarship advancing relational approaches to rights and their subjects is robust, but also diverse. Sociologist Minwoo Jung advocates for a relational approach that altogether eschews conceiving of rights as substances, that is, as a given set of entitlements, privileges, or protections that can be granted, lost or possessed, say, as a derivative of intrinsic value such as rights as a universal norm, or as an Indigenous culture, or as a colonial and neo-imperial imposition.[22] Jung's relational approach emphasises rights (as well as agency and power) as social constructs that derive their meaning and significance within a relational setting.[23] Jung proposes the concept of the "rights project" as an analytical construct for focusing on how rights become a project, for whom, and what it does in a relational context. It is a "context-specific endeavour of marginalised communities to envision, claim, and achieve rights on their own terms and in their own ways."[24] A rights project asks, "how is the notion of rights envisioned, articulated, and enacted not just in relation to but also in opposition to, or even beyond, the global human rights discourse."[25] It has the advantage of allowing us to "capture actors' collective efforts, in the name of rights, to speculate, plan, strategise, and optimise toward meaningful ends in a multiscalar relational context,"[26] and to "denaturalise the politically charged notion of rights while acknowledging its ongoing significance in a globalizing world."[27]

Jung's relational sociology of rights also enables a reconsideration of the state's role in constituting rights projects. "The concept of the rights project redirects our analysis from the state's control over predetermined rights to the efforts of marginalized communities to define and enact rights as a context-specific project that

[19] Rodríguez-Garavito (2024), p. 40.

[20] Ibid., p. 38.

[21] Ibid., p. 41.

[22] Minwoo Jung (2024), pp. 257, 261, 273–274.

[23] Ibid., p. 261, drawing on Emirbayer (1997) and Desmond (2014) and Somers (1994).

[24] Ibid, p. 256.

[25] Ibid., p. 257.

[26] Ibid., p. 263.

[27] Ibid., p. 257.

sometimes aligns with...but other times challenges or goes beyond...the state's legitimacy over rights."[28] Thus, we can view the state as one powerful relational axis among many others (e.g., corporations, regulatory agencies, international NGOs, or international human rights systems) with which marginalised communities negotiate.

Both Rodriguez-Garavito's and Jung's relational approaches clearly focus on how rights are being socially constructed (and possibly, but not necessarily, institutionalised in law). Yet, Jung's relational analysis does not take into consideration the socially constructed agency and rights of nonhumans in the way Rodríguez-Garavito, importantly, does. How might we expand this analytical construct of the rights project to make conceptual room for understanding the emerging recognition of relations between humans and nonhumans?

Mark Goodale also promotes a relational approach to rights animated by the virtue of both human and nonhuman solidarity. He shows us how we might produce ethnographically rich relational subjectivities in which human rights principles and practices are generated from within overlapping temporal, spatial, and even cosmological networks within one's own social and political communities, past and future generations, and the wider non-human world.[29]

Goodale clearly identifies the tension that arises when decentring orthodox accounts of human rights subjectivity expressed through the normative category of human rights described within the Universal Declaration of Human Rights (i.e., "all members of the human family"), particularly when we subsume the associated rights, obligations, and interests of human beings "within a broader, indeed universal ontological interdependence."[30]

> Among other things, a regime of (human) rights based in ecological interconnectedness...implies a kind of antipodean system in which most of the key elements are reversed or inverted: the parts are the sum of the whole; duties give rise to rights; the (human rights) subject is not a person but persons in relations; and juridical identity is embedded in actions rather than individuals.[31]

But toward what kind of political strategies might thinking in terms of such universal ontological interdependence lead us? And who, then, is "us"? This challenge to sociocentrism, as William Connolly argues in *Facing the Planetary*,[32] renders problematic the projection of *any* smooth horizon into the future. "To what pluralities, human and non-human, might we belong – even if we decide that the term *belonging* must be suspended in favour of a pursuit of plural sites of attachment?"[33] Neither Goodale nor Connolly has an answer to this question.

[28] Ibid., 275.

[29] Goodale (2020, 2022).

[30] Goodale (2020), p. 61.

[31] Ibid.

[32] Connolly (2017).

[33] Ibid., p. 33.

Connolly does, however, offer important political insight as we seek to create new networks or relational assemblages of belonging:

> No single class, nation, faith, gender, state, order, party, racialized constituency, or age group can form an authoritative centre of the militant 'we' needed today. …Old notions of pluralism as a coalition of diverse interests [implied, for example, by the concept of "stake-holders"] are…insufficient [to the task]. We see an evolving, complex, cross-regional "we" that propels diverse constituencies into larger assemblages, even as each constituency retains a host of differences. It will assemble, if it does, to respond to a planetary condition asymmetrically distributed in its effects and dangers, as participants also pay attention to other local, regional, class, racial, [gender], state, and religious questions.[34]

Thus, in both Connolly and Goodale's relational politics we find echoes of the kind of "accountability" grounded in an "ethics of becoming." This means that the focus shifts from unitary to what Ray Braidotti calls "nomadic" subjectivity."[35] Rejecting self-centred individualism (and any notion of any ethical bond grounded in the self-interests of the individual)—but also rejecting relativism and nihilistic defeatism—her view promotes what she calls a "posthuman ethics for a non-unitary subject," which engenders "an enlarged sense of inter-connection between self and others, including the nonhuman or 'earth' others."[36]

2.2 *The Social Agency of Non-Living Nonhumans*

To push the question even further, what would emerge—for better or worse—from a relational approach to rights that takes into consideration the social construction of agency and rights of *non-living* nonhumans, like corporations or technological entities like AI? We already grant non-living, non-human corporations the social status of agency in our social systems. What about non-living non-human AI systems? Anicker et al. persuasively argue from a relational perspective that AI systems can exercise agency within social systems. "Agency," as they conceptualise it, "is neither a universal property of "the social" nor an ontic quality of humans but, rather, a culturally performed yet situationally flexible social status. It results from interpretations and pragmatic attributions that subjectify their objects by providing them with a [social] license to issue actions."[37]

They reject a social constructivism that sees the agency of things as a mere effect of the projections of humans.[38] "Not only do we attribute agency to AI systems—in certain domains, AI systems already attribute a status to us. Even algorithms and AI systems that do not 'know' they are ascribing intentionality and that are not treated as agents can issue decisions that have the social significance of recognizing or

[34] Ibid., p. 34; see also Danowski and Viveiros de Castro (2017), pp. 113–119.

[35] Braidotti (2013), p. 49.

[36] Idid., pp. 49–50.

[37] Anicker et al. (2024), p. 323.

[38] Ibid., pp. 318–319.

denying agency,"[39] for example, assigning credit scores or ranking job candidates in the hiring process or, in combination with facial recognition, monitoring borders to distinguish "suspicious" crossers.[40] They contend that even agents with the capability to institute agency in other entities exercise this ability because of social attribution.[41]

Because social processes continuously demarcate actors from nonactors, a theory of nonhuman agency, they assert, needs theoretical tools to observe this process, "not ontological theories of why only humans can act or why everything is already an agent by somehow influencing the course of events."[42] This relational conception of agency opens the path to understanding why some (but not other) nonhuman systems may gradually be granted the social power to act instead of merely behave, that is, granted behavioural latitude, intentions, a normative status, or legal standing in social practice. Furthermore, because agency attribution has the effect of normatively restricting actors, we can trace how actors differently become tied to certain standards of accountability and rationality.[43]

While they do not make a case for AI rights, Anicker et al.'s relational approach to understanding how AI systems can exercise agency within social systems lays conceptual groundwork for such a project. They note that the EU Parliament considered a motion for a resolution in 2017 entertaining the idea that AI systems may be granted legal status as "electronic persons,"[44] "which would have substantially changed authoritative norms for agency ascription in legal contexts."[45] And Crawford, quoted above, makes a convincing case for how a relational approach to AI soon forces us to confront how AI systems are inextricably linked to the ecological systems of which humans and their social systems are a part. If the corporate accountability movement is to remain relevant in the digitally transforming relations of the Anthropocene, it also needs to take into consideration the relationally constructed rights of Big Tech, as well as the alternative rights of data ownership and stewardship[46] now being constructed by and for marginalized communities, both human and nonhuman.

As climate change and the development of AI have become more entangled, the corporate accountability movement has had to contend with not only the longstanding challenge of the ontological politics of corporate personhood but also new political and legal challenges concerning humanity's changing relations to ecology and technology. In an effort to challenge the naturalising tendencies of ontological

[39] Ibid., p. 318.

[40] See, for example, https://thebulletin.org/2022/10/chinas-high-tech-surveillance-drives-oppression-of-uyghurs/ (accessed 3.02.2025).

[41] Ibid., p. 319.

[42] Anicker et al. (2024), p. 323.

[43] Ibid., p. 315.

[44] Committee on Legal Affairs (2017).

[45] Anicker et al. (2024), p. 319; See also Gellers (2020); Wojtczak (2022).

[46] I discuss alternative rights of data ownership in Sect. 3 of this chapter.

claims defending corporate personhood (and the ecosystems and their elements that corporations call "natural resources" and claim to rightfully control as property), corporate accountability activists, advocates and scholars have developed new relations, strategies, and notions of rights informed by more "pluriversal"[47] (and "transversal")[48] politics.

2.3 *Pluriversal Politics*

Pluriversal politics recognise that the world is more than one socio-natural formation. Movements worldwide supporting the pluriverse, or "world of many worlds"[49] challenge the Western-centric global coloniality of "universalism" and one-way diffusionism that positions Western modernity at the pinnacle of progress. Pluriversal politics challenge Western ontological claims of a "one-world world," which relegate all "other" realities to "beliefs" within a singular (Western) reality (knowable through Western forms of science). Pluriversal politics also challenge neoliberal economic development policy visions, reflected in slogans like "There is No Alternative," and which assert there are no possible other future paths of development. Pluriversal politics call for decolonial projects that might fracture Western-centric global coloniality in pursuit of attaining a pluriverse, that is, a more just co-existence of worlds that exceeds what is imagined to be possible.[50] Toward this end, pluriversal politics defend subaltern worlds as potential producers of theory and knowledge,[51] and sources of "radical alterity" (i.e., new conceptions of what is possible) beyond the confines of "Western modernity," which works to delegitimate such politics and the movements that sustain them.[52] In short, pluriversal politics inform serious reflection on the legal and social implications of embracing a wider and more dispersed understanding of "agency" then is traditionally recognised by Western legal and social theorists.

Growing numbers of scholars working loosely in this tradition are grappling with the political and legal interventions of "earth beings" in a range of situated contexts. As Erin Fitz-Henry observes, they focus disproportionately on Indigenous communities, "as if 'radical alterity' were to be found primarily among such communities."[53] While they have made timely provocations to engage with more pluriversal politics that do not share the epistemological assumptions and ontological categories of Western liberalism, particularly when it comes to demarcating the lines between

[47] de la Cadena (2010); Connolly (2017); Escobar (2020).

[48] Monsees et al. 2023); Tinnel (2012).

[49] Blaser and de la Cadena (2018).

[50] Rojas (2016), pp. 369–389.

[51] Dunford (2017), pp. 383, 387–389.

[52] Escobar (2020).

[53] Fitz-Henry (2018), p. 98.

humans and nature, they have remained largely inattentive to the other forms of alterity, such as "other" (marginalised) ways of constructing boundaries between person and property, that are *also* being mobilised in the United States,[54] which I discuss below in Sect. 4.

Pluriversal politics deploy radically relational and ecological concepts that contribute to the fragmentation of the concept of the human as isolated from nonhumans. They do not represent a challenge to regulate the powerful and conflicting forces of the world into some idealised, harmonious balance. Rather, they are a first (and necessary) step toward a relational understanding of ecologically embedded humanity, and to engendering "new institutional and ontological conditions that encourage people to encounter the world as a series of open and ongoing syntheses between partial, [relational] objects (as opposed to) regarding phenomena as objects-in-themselves, complete and isolatable."[55] How might corporate "persons" and their "property" in fictitious commodities[56] such as land, rivers, forests, and data be productively destabilised, or at least differently contextualised, by attention to the imaginings of other non-human "persons?"[57]

3 Uprooting Human Supremacy: An Indigenous-Led Transnational Rights of Nature Project in Ecuador

To explore how this might work in practice, I examine a case of an Indigenous-led transnational corporate accountability campaign in Ecuador that has been invoking not only human rights (specifically, collective Indigenous peoples' rights), but also constructing the rights of the forest in which they live, to successfully pre-empt the rights of a transnational oil corporation and hold it accountable for its extractive practices that have been harming the community and forest. It has also been constructing novel legal forms of data ownership whereby the data being collected to monitor the ongoing protection and regeneration of the forest would be collectively owned by the Indigenous people and the living forest they inhabit. This movement articulates a broader rights of nature paradigm included in the Ecuadorian Constitution and now incorporated into laws and court rulings around the world. As Rodríguez-Garavito points out, this paradigm is "a Western legal translation of a more fundamental notion that everything is alive, that all beings speak in their own ways – and that law, science, and spirituality are not mutually exclusive but rather

[54] Ibid.

[55] Tinnel (2012), p. 362.

[56] See Burawoy (2018), discussing knowledge as a fictitious commodity.

[57] Fitz-Henry (2018, p. 87). I elaborate Fitz-Henry's question to include property in fictitious commodities in order to address the intersection of data mining, which she does not address, and the mining of natural resources, as well as to bring alternative legal framings of property into play with those of personhood.

participants in a growing conversation about what human rights mean in the Anthropocene."[58]

On November 10, 2021, the Constitutional Court of Ecuador recognised Los Cedros Forest ("The Cloud Forest") as a bearer of rights.[59] Additionally, it invoked the precautionary principle that advises restraint in the face of unpredictable effects of mining on the forest's web of life to revoke the permits for mining in Los Cedros that had been granted[60] to Ecuador's state mining company, Empresa Nacional Minera (ENAMI), and its Canadian partner, Cornerstone Capital Resources (Cornerstone). It banned all future extractive practices within the forest.

The *Los Cedros* decision is one of the most promising legal cases among the over 500 initiatives on rights of nature that have been pursued in dozens of countries around the world and international venues like the United Nations.[61] Approximately two-thirds of these initiatives, which include court decisions, constitutional provisions, national or local laws, policy instruments and non-binding declarations, have been approved. According to the Eco Jurisprudence Monitor, an interactive online platform that compiles ecological jurisprudence initiatives around the world,[62] this global trend in the social attribution of rights of nature has been growing exponentially since the early 2000s.

Appreciation for the Court's decision begins with understanding the uniqueness, biodiversity, and critical ecological role of the Los Cedros Forest, located within the Chocó bioregion and tropical northwest Ecuadorian Andes. This 4800-hectare old-growth reserve of misty cloud forest ranges from 3000 to 9000 feet and is home to over 300 species of birds, 600 kinds of moths, 200 varieties of orchids, and a wide host of critically endangered wildlife, including the black-and-chestnut eagle, spectacled bear, and brown-headed spider monkey, among other species that live nowhere else on Earth. It also serves as a crucial water source for the four rivers that run through it, as well as the numerous streams in the surrounding area. The communities surrounding Los Cedros depend on sources of drinking water that

[58] Rodríguez-Garavito (2024), pp. 25–26.

[59] Constitutional Court of Ecuador, Case No. 1149-19-JP/21 (10 November, 2021), hereafter *Los Cedros* decision, available at http://celdf.org/wp-content/uploads/2015/08/Los-Cedros-Decision-ENGLISH-Final.pdf (accessed 3.02.2025).

[60] New York University (NYU) More Than Human Life (MOTH) Project and the Earth Rights Research and Action (TERRA) Program at NYU School of Law, (2024), p. 10. In March 2017, Ecuador's Ministry of the Environment, Water and Ecological Transition (MAATE, for its name in Spanish) issued two concessions (Rio Magdalena 01 and 02) approving copper and gold mining in two-thirds of Los Cedros. By December of that year, they granted an environmental registration permit for the initial exploration phase of mining.

[61] See Kauffman, Craig, et al. Eco Jurisprudence Monitor, available at https://ecojurisprudence.org/dashboard/?map-style=political (accessed 3.02.2025).

[62] See https://ecojurisprudence.org/about/ (accessed 3.02.2025).

originate in the forest or flow through it.[63] It was for this reason Ecuador's cloud forest was designated a protected area in 1994.[64]

The Amazonian rainforest is also home to many Indigenous peoples of Ecuador, including the Sarayaku, also known as the Midday People, who identify as Kichwa Indigenous people, and whose own struggle to protect the area of the Amazonian forest they inhabit helped lay the cultural, political, and moral groundwork for the *Los Cedros* decision. Working first, regionally, with the Coordinator of Indigenous Organisations of the Amazon Basin (COICA), and then, nationally, with partners in the Confederation of Indigenous Nationalities of Ecuador (CONAIE), the Sarayaku played a critical role in contributing to the incorporation of rights of nature in the 2008 Ecuadorian Constitution. It is the first in the world to enshrine constitutional protection for the rights of nature—or *Pachamama*, Mother Earth—providing another layer of defence to Los Cedros.

The Sarayaku and broader Indigenous movement's call for Ecuador as a plurinational polity, a form of multiculturalism that incorporates politicized versions of Indigenous beliefs about the environment along with demanding respect for Indigenous territories and ways of life, was especially important to putting forward an alternative ethical understanding of relations between society and nature.[65] The concept of *sumak kawsay*, a Kichwa phrase used in the constitution to refer to a development regime based on well-being as opposed to neoliberal economic growth, came to shape an understanding of plurinationality in this context that was associated with a broad critique of the country's economic development, especially the role of extractive industries.[66]

The Sarayaku's 1500 inhabitants (representing 320 families) comprise seven ancestral communities: Chuntayaku, ShiwaKucha, Kali-kali, Puma, Sarayakillu, Kushillu Urku, and Mauka Llakta.[67] In 1992, the Republic of Ecuador (Ecuadorian State) issued a collective title for 254,000 hectares of tropical forests to the Kichwa peoples of the middle and lower basin of the Bobonaza River. Of these, 135,000 hectares located in the middle course of the river basin in the province of Pastaza—southeast of the city of Puyo—belong to the Sarayaku.[68] Nearly all (95 percent) of the Sarayaku territory is primary forest and highly biodiverse.[69]

[63] Constitutional Court of Ecuador, Case No. 1149-19-JP/21 (10 November, 2021), at paragraphs 185–235, available at http://celdf.org/wp-content/uploads/2015/08/Los-Cedros-Decision-ENGLISH-Final.pdf (accessed 3.02.2025).

[64] See also R2HE Toolkit by NYU Law, Case No. 1149-19-JP/21 (Ecuador) – Los Cedros Decision, available at https://www.r2heinfo.com/casebook/los-cedros-forest/ (accessed 3.02.2015) (accessed 3.02.2025).

[65] Akchurin (2015), p. 951.

[66] Ibid., pp. 951, 954. See also Jameson (2011).

[67] [38] New York University (NYU) More Than Human Life (MOTH) Project and the Earth Rights Research and Action (TERRA) Program at NYU School of Law (2024), p. 9.

Indigenous Peoples Movement for Self-Determination & Liberation (2023), at paragraph 4.

[68] Pueblo Originario Kichwa de Sarayaku and Fundación ALDEA (2021), p. 5.

[69] See "Sarayaku, El Pueblo Del Medio Dia," available at https://sarayaku.org (accessed 3.02.2025).

The titling of territory to the Sarayaku occurred in the wake of a 1989 march (*Kawsaimanda allpamanda jatarishun)* mobilised by the Organisation of the Indigenous Peoples of Pastaza,[70] which triggered the Indigenous uprising of the 1990s.[71] In 1992, the government legally recognised the territory but granted titles that did not coincide with ancestral inter-community and inter-ethnic boundaries.[72] The grant included the provision that the subterranean resources, and the right to exploit them, pursuant to environmental protection laws, remain property of the State.[73] Nevertheless, the titles served as instruments for defending the territory against the expansion of agricultural and cattle ranching frontiers.

However, only four years later, the Ecuadorean State authorised a partnership between PETROECUADOR (the State oil company)[74] and a consortium consisting of the Argentinian company Compañía General de Combustible (CGC) and Petrolera Argentina San Jorge S.A,[75] and granted an oil block concession comprising an area (Block No. 23) that overlapped 65 percent with the Sarayaku territory.[76] The permit to CGC was granted without complying with its duty to carry out a free, prior, and informed consent [FPIC] consultation.[77] In April of 1999, Indigenous peoples of the area destroyed oil workers' camps and interfered with their work, leading the state to temporarily suspend oil activities in Block No. 23.[78]

Over the next several years, in an effort to gain access to Sarayaku territory, the CGC resorted to a number of divide-and-conquer tactics, including bribery schemes (offering money, jobs, and medical care programs to surrounding communities in an effort to sow division between them and the Sarayaku);[79] hiring Daymi Services, sociologists, and anthropologists, to develop and implement strategies to internally divide the Sarayaku, manipulate their leaders, and discredit them within the community;[80] and even created a group called the "Community of Independents of Sarayaku" to secure an agreement to allow it to enter the Sarayaku territory.[81]

---

[70] Pueblo Originario Kichwa de Sarayaku and Fundación ALDEA (2021), p. 5. The Organisation of the Indigenous Peoples of Pastaza are now known as the Pastaza Kikin Kichwa Runakuna (PAKKIRU).

[71] Witten and Witten (2011); Paige (2020).

[72] Pueblo Originario Kichwa de Sarayaku and Fundación ALDEA (2021), p. 5.

[73] Kelly (2017, p. 1469*); Kichwa v. Ecuador*, Petition to the Court, Inter-American Commission of Human Rights, Case No. 12.465, (April 26, 2010), paragraph 60.

[74] Kelly (2017), p. 1470.

[75] *Kichwa Indigenous People of Sarayaku v. Ecuador*, Merits and reparations, Judgment, Inter-Am Ct. H.R., (Series C) No. 245 (June 27, 2012), at paragraph 64.

[76] *The Kichwa Peoples of the Sarayaku community and its members v. Ecuador (2004), at paragraph 22.*

[77] Gualinga Montalvo et al. (2024).

[78] Kelly (2017), p. 1470.

[79] *Kichwa Indigenous People of Sarayaku v. Ecuador*, Merits and reparations, Judgment, Inter-Am Ct. H.R., (Series C) No. 245 (June 27, 2012), at paragraph 73.

[80] *Ibid.*, at paragraph 74.

[81] Ibid, at paragraph 75.

When these tactics failed to secure CGC the access they sought, they resorted to coercive violence. Between October 2002 and February 2003, CGC oil company workers, accompanied by the Ecuadorian armed forces, entered—without permission—the Sarayaku people's territory to carry out drilling, plant explosives and launch seismic prospecting activities.[82] During this period they also destroyed woodlands, sources of food, medicines, and cultural heritage, and committed a series of assaults, illegal detentions, and abuses against members of the Sarayaku people,[83] including the detainment of young Sarayaku girls whom CGC workers threated to rape, until an army unit intervened.[84]

The Sarayaku subsequently launched a legal and political campaign to defend their rights and those of the territory. They pursued a national and international strategy to oppose the entry of corporations and the exploitation of oil in their territory, and made clear that their right to consultation was not an end but a means of their resistance. Their aim was to defend their territory which they have long understood (and in 2018 formally declared in the General Assembly of the Kichwa Indigenous people of Sarayaku[85]) to be a "Living Forest" (*Kawsak Sacha*), that is, a living, conscious being and a subject of rights that are independent of, yet inseparable from, the rights of human beings. The Sarayaku asserted that the oil exploitation not only contravened FPIC, but also the rights of the land itself to remain whole and to continue to regenerate human and non-human life.[86]

At the national level, the Sarayaku worked with the non-governmental organisation Pachamama Foundation[87] and lawyers such as Mario Melo to go before the Ecuadorian courts, but the CGC continued to proceed with oil exploitation, burying 1.5 tons of explosives in the process with the intention of detonating them as part their prospecting work. So, at the international level, they sought legal assistance from the Centre for Justice and International Law (CEJIL), a non-profit, non-governmental organisation with consultative status before the Organisation of American States (OAS) and the United Nations. The CEJIL works to ensure that public policies and practices are in line with international human rights law, to create a hemisphere where national government protections are reinforced by a system of complementary regional protection that is prompt and effective in protecting the fundamental rights of individuals and peoples.[88] The Sarayaku filed a claim against the Ecuadorian State in the Inter-American Human Rights System, first to the Commission (IAHRC) in 2003, and then, after a background report in which the

[82] Kelly (2017), p. 1472.

[83] *The Kichwa Peoples of the Sarayaku community and its members v. Ecuador (2004), at paragraphs 21, 24, 26.*

[84] *Kichwa v. Ecuador, Petition to the Court, Inter-Am. Comm'n H.R., Case No. 12.465 (April 26, 2010), at paragraph 93.*

[85] Pueblo Originario Kichwa de Sarayaku and Fundación ALDEA (2021), p. 6.

[86] Gualinga Montalvo et al. (2024).

[87] See https://www.pachamama.org.ec/sobre-nosotros (accessed 3.02.2025).

[88] See https://cejil.org/en/who-we-are/ (accessed 3.02.2025).

IACHR concluded that Ecuador violated the rights to (among others) life, integrity, property and judicial guarantees,[89] to the Court (IACtHR) in 2004.

After working its way through the IACtHR, in 2010, a series of recommendations were issued to the Ecuadorian state, including reparations and non-repetition measures,[90] some of which have still not been implemented.[91] The decision issued by the Court is of great importance because it strengthens jurisprudence on Indigenous peoples' rights in the Inter-American system.[92] In 2012, IACtHR recognized that, by authorising oil exploration in Sarayaku territory, Ecuador has disregarded the right of the people to be heard in prior consultation and in a free and informed manner. The Court ruled in favour of the Sarayaku people and ordered the Ecuadorian state to do the following: (1) issue norms guaranteeing the right to free and informed consultation (FPIC); (2) to remove the explosives; (3) to apologize; and (4) to pay compensation to the Sarayaku people.[93]

It is also worth noting that prior to the IACtHR's globally unprecedented ruling on behalf of the protection of Indigenous rights, the Court engaged in additional and related unprecedented action: (1) it organised a public hearing at the Court's headquarters in Costa Rica; (2) it visited an Indigenous territory (Sarayaku's living forest); and (3) it held a hearing in San José, where a shaman and Sarayaku spiritual leader (Sabino Gualinga) explained how the oil company and Ecuadorian military violated the rights and led to the displacement of members of the Sarayaku people and hundreds of other living forest beings. Finally (4), the judges asked questions and listened to the Sarayaku people's statements.

Successive governments in Ecuador did present a public apology and paid compensation, but they did not remove the explosives, nor did they issue norms guaranteeing (regulating and protecting) the right of Indigenous peoples to FPIC. Not accepting the state's half-compliance in this landmark ruling—the Sarayaku continued their mobilisation and campaign. On December 20, 2023, The Constitutional Court of Ecuador ruled on the action brought by the Sarayaku people to demand that the state comply with the orders issued over a decade earlier by the IACtHR.

This case illustrates how the Sarayaku displaced human supremacy in seeking both protection for their Living Forest and accountability from CGC, the corporation responsible for the destruction of their forest. Rodríguez-Garavito's claims, "The ecological turn would require concepts different from those that have dominated human rights."[94] The Sarayaku's concept of the Living Forest (an interconnected living entity) put the forest on an equal footing with the Indigenous People of Sarayaku themselves, and was the root of their claim that the forest is inextrica-

---

[89] *Kichwa Indigenous People of Sarayaku v. Ecuador, Merits, and Reparations, Judgment, Inter-Am. Ct. H.R. (Series C) No. 245 (June 27, 2012).*

[90] Ibid.

[91] Gualinga Montalvo et al. (2024).

[92] Ibid.

[93] *Kichwa Indigenous People of Sarayaku v. Ecuador, Merits, and Reparations, Judgment, Inter-Am. Ct. H.R. (Series C) No. 245 (June 27, 2012).*

[94] Rodríguez-Garavito (2024), p. 34.

bly linked to their human rights as a people. Recall that this relational approach advises we relax the frontiers between human and MOTH subjectivities. The Inter-American Court, unlike the Ecuadorian Court, was open to taking a pluriversal approach toward the Sarayaku's claims (or at least suspending disbelief until first visiting the Sarayaku People and their Living Forest).

This case also illustrates how, following Jung's relational approach, the analytical construct of the rights project enables us to trace the state's role in constituting this Indigenous-led transnational rights project, directs our analysis away from the state's control over predetermined rights (e.g., the Ecuadorian Constitution's recognition of the rights of nature, or the Ecuadorian Federal State's recognition of the its ownership of the minerals beneath the Sarayaku's territorial land, and recognition of the corporate rights of the transnational mining company to "whom" it had issued mining concessions). It instead directs our analysis to the efforts of marginalized communities, such as the Sarayaku and (if we subject Jung's concept to an ecological turn) the Living Forest, to define and enact rights as a context-specific project that sometimes aligns with, but other times challenges or goes beyond the state's legitimacy over rights.

In this case, we find the Sarayaku negotiating with an Ecuadorian state operating at multiple scales of action (Provincial and Federal, and across multiple ministries acting in contradictory ways (simultaneously and over time) in response to the claims of the Sarayaku. We also find the Sarayaku negotiating beyond the Ecuadorian State to seek recognition for its rights claims in the Inter-American Human Rights System, where it ultimately secured a favourable ruling and, consistent with the "boomerang model" of transnational pressure,[95] the IACtHR pressured the Ecuadorian Constitutional Court to finally recognize the Sarayaku's claims and the IACtHR's ruling, and ultimately ordered the Ecuadorian State to enforce the mining corporation's (CGC) compliance. We also find the Sarayaku negotiating the meaning of their rights along non-state axes of power, with the Pachamama Foundation and the CGC. Thus, we are able to see the ways in which the state (and other actors) did (and did not) play a role in constituting the rights of the Sarayaku and their Living Forest as they struggled within shifting situational contexts over time and at multiple scales to define, enact, and ultimately institutionalize them—for now.

The Sarayaku have also been working transnationally with civil society organisations in the U.S. to build their rights project. In the next section, we will see how their transnational engagement transformed a separate rights of nature project in the U.S., while also benefitting their own work shaping Ecuador's 2008 Constitution. But first, we will see how the Sarayaku have been working with the NYU MOTH Project to ensure remaining aspects of the Ecuadorian Federal ruling are fully implemented, and to devise strategies for mobilising data in support of its implementation. We will also see how their transnational initiatives are re-imagining data ownership (i.e., property in data).

[95] Keck and Sikkink (1998); See also Dale (2008).

The MOTH Project has been working over the past several years to support the campaign of the Sarayaku to defend their territories from extractive industries such as oil drilling and mining. Following the Ecuadorian Constitutional Court's landmark rulings in 2021 (the *Los Cedros* decision) and 2023 (recognizing the right the Sarayaku Nation and the Living Forest), the Sarayaku launched the Kawsak Sacha—or, Living Forest—Initiative. To support this initiative, the MOTH Project began working with the Sarayaku and a team of researchers from the Society for the Protection of Underground Networks (SPUN)[96] and the Fungi Foundation[97] to launch the *Science Across Cultures* Initiative. It aims to use data from comprehensive mycorrhizal fungal surveys to allow ongoing monitoring of fungal communities, and mobilise this data in support of the implementation of a recent court ruling as well as the broader Kawsak Sacha Initiative.

According to a description of the initiative in a brief report on the MOTH Project's website:

> The fungal data will likely elucidate critical biodiversity present in the territory, triggering domestic and international obligations and norms around the protection of biodiversity; this, in turn, would strengthen the Sarayaku's opposition to extractive activities within their territory. The data and analysis will also clarify how above-ground ecosystems depend on and are connected to below-ground ecosystems, including mycorrhizal fungi; this will help elaborate the interconnectedness underpinning the Sarayaku's claim for recognition of their territory as a subject of rights.[98]

The plan, they emphasise, is not to use the assessment of fungal diversity to try and "prove" in scientific terms the Sarayaku concept of the living forest, but rather to provide additional evidence that the Sarayaku can use in support of their Living Forest Initiative and legal mobilisations. They argue that, "to make effective arguments against the destruction of underground ecosystems through, for example, mining, it is important to draw attention to the countless organisms that live underground and the vital roles they play in mitigating climate change and supporting above-ground biodiversity."[99] In the long view, they imagine this collaborative work developing tools for more general application that would advance the case for inclusion of fungi in environmental frameworks and legal actions.

The MOTH Project claims that one of the core concerns is how Western scientists and Indigenous knowledge holders and scientists might enter into generative, two-way collaboration, both to bring forth insight and understanding and to apply that understanding technologically. One way they plan to achieve this is through dialogue around the fungal sampling process: discussing the limits and possibilities of their sampling techniques and devising hypotheses together with the Sarayaku based on particular questions the Sarayaku have about fungal communities in their territories. They also plan to participate in ceremonies hosted by the Sarayaku and

---

[96] See https://www.spun.earth/ (accessed 3.02.2025).

[97] See https://www.ffungi.org/ (accessed 3.02.2025).

[98] See https://mothrights.org/project/science-across-cultures/ (accessed 3.02.2025).

[99] Ibid.

in sustained dialogue about how the modern sciences and Indigenous knowledge systems might inform each other and work together to advance protections for the living world.

Might this initiative be a good example of what William Connolly describes as "entangled humanism" (as mentioned above)? It is a reassembling of knowledge production, application of new and evolving technologies, and mobilisation of data to address planetary crises that also works to create new, democratic, relational identities that recognize our interconnected natures and bridge existing institutional dividing lines between humans and nonhumans. A next question, one that the MOTH Project also recently has raised, is "how do we protect our data – data that in this case is central to the strategies of sustaining their rights projects and corporate accountability?"

Jacqueline Hicks tells us, "one issue with contemporary discussions of data ownership is their narrow definitions of property rights […] as they are currently conceived in the West. […] In other legal systems around the world, some of the main functions of property rights are to protect rights use, or to support particular social obligations."[100] The MOTH project has been pursuing their own rights project. Understanding how extractive corporations and the Federal State have interests in the forest management data that they are collecting and planning to use hold both accountable for fully implementing the orders of the Ecuadorian Constitutional Court, the activists, scientists, and lawyers supporting this project have been working to construct new legal forms of collective data ownership. As they put it, "to help instantiate the content of MOTH rights, the MOTH Project has been exploring ways to create a licensing framework in which the fungal datasets collected in an Indigenous territory in Ecuador would be owned by the forest itself, as a holder of rights, together with the Indigenous community."[101] This would be the first instance in which an Indigenous nation co-owns data rights with its territory, a development which the MOTH Project believes would help advance both human and more than human rights. They intend for this work to serve as a prototype illuminating the practical implications of MOTH rights and developing data ownership and licensing models that respects the needs and interests of the more-than-human world.[102]

This case has illustrated how a relational approach to rights allowed for pluriversal politics. It also has demonstrated how pluriversal politics created an opening for decentring human supremacy and lead to recognising the rights of the Living Forest. This social attribution of agency in the form of legal personhood then gave the forest the tools needed to defend itself in the Anthropocene. As a result it strengthened the rights of the Sarayaku People as well, whose lives and well-being are inextricably connected to the Living Forest. Together, they successfully pre-empted the corporate rights of the mining company that had threatened their joint existence.

---

[100] Hicks (2023), pp. 551–552.

[101] https://mothrights.org/project/rethinking-data-technology-and-the-more-than-human-world/ (accessed 3.02.2025).

[102] Ibid.

4 Grass Rooting Corporate Personhood: Ecuador's Influence on the Politics of Corporate Accountability in the United States

While in Ecuador environmental and Indigenous groups have successfully worked to construct and include rights for nature in their *national* Constitution, in the U.S., people of cities, townships, counties, and even First Nation tribes[103] have been turning to *local* constitutions and law to render the hazardous practices of extractivist companies violations of the rights of nature.[104] One reason that communities and lawyers in the U.S. have pursued local legal strategies is that they have been unable to find points of leverage in struggles with federal and state governments and regulatory agencies that defer to claims of corporate rights to exploit natural resources held as property.[105]

Legal scholar Elizabeth Macpherson explains that there is an opening at the local level because in the U.S. states have their own constitutions and can enact environmental and human rights protections in their state legislative codes. Within each state, local government authorities with varying regulatory powers also have the authority to pass ordinances that may include human rights and environmental protections.[106]

Even so, claims rooted in human rights meet with stiff resistance, "even as they are co-opted, adapted, and 'stretched' to pursue improved environmental outcomes and constitutional protections are secured to 'trump' business as usual."[107] A new corporate accountability strategy was necessary in the United States, and some organisations began to turn the rights of nature. One of the most creative organisations advancing claims to a right of nature in the U.S. is the Community Environmental Legal Defence Fund (CELDF), a small, not-for-profit, public interest legal organisation, established in 1995.

The CELDF was among the first organisations in the U.S. to work with local community groups to agitate for rights of nature, with the aim of simultaneously subordinating constitutional protections for corporations. CELDF has also promoted legal doctrine that defines state law as a "floor" to which local communities can add civil, human and ecological rights protections. The CELDF works with local communities and government across the U.S. to draft and advance laws to establish rights for ecosystems as well as human rights to water and a liveable climate, and to ban practices such as fracking, factory farming, sewage sludging of farmland and water privatisation.

[103] Eco Jurisprudence Monitor (October 15, 2024).

[104] Fitz-Henry (2018), p. 85.

[105] Ibid.

[106] Macpherson (2021), p. 339.

[107] Ibid., p. 338.

CELDF also has been working with First Nation communities to establish Rights of Nature in tribal law that recognise the rights of ecosystems and natural communities to exist and thrive, and empowering people and their governments to defend and enforce these rights. Their tagline is that they are "helping build a decolonial movement for community rights and the rights of nature to advance democratic, economic, social, and environmental rights – building upward from the grassroots to the state, federal, and international levels."[108] CELDF is not simply targeting the state for legal inclusion of rights of nature, but also targeting civil society's cultural ways of thinking and being with regard to the relations between humans and nonhuman life.

However, CELDF's initial corporate accountability strategy in their first decade of work was typical of mainstream environmental organisations in the U.S.—appealing state-issued environmental permits. This strategy proved largely fruitless in terms of scoring legal victories. Companies were able to remedy any procedural errors CELDF identified and eventually gain the approval of the state—rendering CELDF's lawyers helpful, if unintentional, facilitators of the permitting process.[109]

By the mid-2000s, they increasingly began pitting the legal personhood and rights of nonhuman ecosystems against the legal personhood and rights of nonhuman corporations (which already were recognized in U.S. law). In other words, the CELDF and the activists with whom they work began prioritizing strategies for legally transforming natural communities and ecosystems from forms of *property* to types of *persons* with the aim of extending legal standing to intervene in environmental contestations.

How did this change in CELDF's thinking and strategy by the mid-2000s come about? As the debates over Ecuador's 2008 Constitution were unfolding, Fundación Pachamama, one of the organisations that had been promoting the idea of nature as a subject of rights, invited lawyers from CELDF to have a conversation and share their experiences in writing rights of nature into city ordinances in the United States.[110] While the CELDF was at first reticent to attend, seeing Ecuador's efforts as distant from their own work, they agreed to travel to Ecuador to participate in the discussions,[111] which included many diverse environmental groups from the Global South rights of nature movement as well as Indigenous groups who spoke of the need to recognise plurinational collective rights (*plurinacionalidad*)[112] and the long-standing worldviews (*cosmovisiones*) in which the Earth (*Pachamama*) is a living being. This transnational engagement was not just another example of importing ideas from the Global North, nor of how notions of rights are exported from the Global North to the Global South through hegemonic flows of transnational

[108] See https://celdf.org/about-celdf/ (accessed 3.02.2025).

[109] Fitz-Henry (2018), p. 88.

[110] Akchurin (2015), p. 952; Pietari (2016), pp. 41–42; Huneeus (2022), p. 146.

[111] Huneeus (2022), p. 146.

[112] Akchurin (2015), p. 954.

relations. Rather, as Professor of Law Alexandra Huneeus argues, "it was clearly a fruitful moment of exchange that would reshape the U.S. movement."[113]

Political and legal anthropologist Erin Fitz-Henry notes that CELDF's new strategic approach is substantially different from those used by other environmental groups who have been working to extend to ecological systems legal standing to challenge that of corporations. She cites research documenting a wide range of strategies pushing for the following: more robust forms of federal compliance with FPIC commitments; an international tribunal to prosecute crimes of ecocide; more serious consideration of the environmental justice concerns of affected communities before granting environmental permits; and extension of human rights to include the right to a healthy environment, and the right to a safe climate. However, "[the strategy of deploying] the 'rights of nature' in the United States are unique," argues Fitz-Henry, "in that they are framed explicitly by way of juxtaposition with the rights of corporations in order to perform a kind of moral-political double labour – simultaneously extending ecological rights and undermining corporate constitutional rights."[114]

Appreciation for the CEDLF's ecological turn and unique strategy cannot be well measured in terms of its legal impact. As Huneeus observes, "While much has been written about the emerging rights of nature movement's recent legal gains around the world, scholars are just beginning to study the U.S. experience, which unfolds at the humble level of small-town and city ordinances and so often ends in swift legal or political defeat. …It is not that these groups are creating a new path to legal success. Rather they are re-defining success, using law in a symbolic way so as to ignite new conversations."[115] In a recent press release for his new book *Wouldn't You Say? A Collection of Essays about Environment and Community*, CELDF's Education Director Ben Price, describes how CELDF explained the new strategy to the communities with whom they were working: "we shared our hope that gradually, eventually, the idea of legal rights for living ecosystems would be normalised and accepted. We were, we explained, not so much engaged in legal strategy as we were testing a theory of experiential education and cultural change."[116]

Rather than challenging corporate personhood by starting with a blueprint for dropping an untested constitutional amendment into the U.S. Constitution, as organisations such as Move To Amend[117] are pursuing, CELDF is thinking pluriversally and transversally, spurring broader conversations across different relational contexts and building a body of law that begins to confront a greater multiplicity of "persons" and ways that local communities are embedded in and connected through ecosystems. Such a strategy might, as Fitz-Henry suggests, serve to recontextualise

---

[113] Ibid.

[114] Fitz-Henry (2018), p. 90.

[115] Huneeus (2022), pp. 136–137.

[116] See CELDF, "Press release: New book reflects on 30 years of activism for community and nature's rights," (December 23, 2024), available at https://celdf.org/2024/12/new-book-reflects-on-30-years-of-activism-for-community-and-natures-rights/ (accessed 9.26.2025).

[117] Fitz-Henry (2018), p. 96.

local understandings of corporate personhood and nature as property by attending to the knowledge and imaginings of other nonhumans.[118]

At a minimum, this strategy's multiple, local legal experiments—such as passing municipal ordinances affirming rights of nature to educate the public while knowing they eventually will be pre-empted by states—operate as a democratic stress test for the viability of destabilizing corporate personhood. By drawing state and corporate legal responses, they more publicly expose the legal relations of power that support corporate persons at the expense of those human communities and living nonhuman ecosystems. As for this strategy's impact on public understanding and cultural change, it is too soon to say. CELDF points to the rising rate of growth in such community ordinances across the United States as evidence of positive cultural change.[119] However, there also recently have been a spree of anti-rights of nature legislation passed by the states of Florida,[120] Ohio,[121] and Utah,[122] which pre-emptively reject localities within their states from passing rights of nature legislation or ordinances.

This transnational exchange between CELDF and the activists and lawyers fuelling the movement in Ecuador served as a catalyst for CELDF's rethinking its own discourse on the relations between local communities and the ecosystems in which they are embedded, and its commitment to experiential education through rights of nature legislation as critical groundwork for cultural change. It also helps to account for the shift in their political aim and strategies of corporate accountability, of denaturalising the rights of corporate persons and the state pre-emption laws that ensure corporate personhood goes unchallenged at the local level. Furthermore, their efforts to newly engage with First Nation communities only began after their experience with Indigenous groups in Ecuador.

Ultimately, this transnational exchange transformed how CELDF identified the rights project in which it is embedded. It now identifies as part of an Indigenous-led transnational rights of nature movement, working from the grassroots up to state, federal and international levels, to help build a decolonial movement for community rights and the rights of nature to advance democratic, economic, social, and environmental rights.[123]

Most critically, opening up space for pluriversal politics in the United States created room to conceptualize a right of nature on an equal footing with the rights in

[118] Fitz-Henry (2018), p. 87.

[119] Ibid. For work by political anthropologists and sociologists exploring the material and ideological effects of the legal doctrine of corporate personhood and of the corporate form more generally, see Fligstein (1990); DiMaggio (2001); Dale (2011); Welker et al. (2011); Bashkow (2014); Kirsch (2014); Welker (2014).

See https://celdf.org/about-celdf/ (accessed 3.02.2025).

[120] See https://www.centerforenvironmentalrights.org/news/oi8znm3xqubni1otrk3lv4t17mj2tk (accessed 3.02.2025).

[121] See https://celdf.org/2019/07/rights-of-nature-ban/ (accessed 3.02.2025).

[122] See https://www.earthlawcenter.org/blog-entries/2024/2/utah-advances-anti-rights-of-nature-bill-with-implications-for-ai (accessed 3.02.2025).

[123] See https://celdf.org/about-celdf/ (accessed 3.02.2025).

property held by corporate persons. Anicker et al.'s relational conception of agency, as we saw in Sect. 2, opens the path to understanding why some (but not other) nonhuman systems may be socially granted agency. They persuasively argue that AI, operating in specific domains, already exercises such agency. It also lays the conceptual groundwork for socially attributing *rights* to all manner of non-living nonhumans, including (corporately owned) AI. If we are moving in the direction of socially attributing rights to AI, then nature must have the tools to defend itself as well.

This case shows how an Indigenous-led rights of nature movement in Ecuador transformed corporate accountability practices in the U.S., illustrating how conceptions of rights do not flow only from North to South, or "from the West to the Rest." The rights of nature movement in the U.S. that began over two decades ago in local municipalities and townships was an effort to pit two legal fictions against each other—the nonhuman legal personhood of nature against the nonhuman legal person of Corporations. The strategy was meant to destabilize the predominant discourses on the legal personhood of corporations. Yet this approach was largely contained by state courts in the U.S.

The legal success of the right of nature movement in the Global South (at the national, regional, and international levels) have provided a critical source of moral, if not legal, legitimacy to U.S.-focused corporate accountability struggles, which have continued to pursue rights of nature claims in U.S. courts as a strategy of symbolic politics and public awareness raising. This case suggests how this Indigenous-led transnational rights of nature movement, with which the CELDF now identifies, may be serving to strengthen both the corporate accountability movement and the human rights movement at a time in which climate change and digital data colonization—and the corporations contributing to these mutually reinforcing processes—pose existential threats to human and nonhuman living beings.

5 Conclusion

The new extractivism of the digitally transforming conditions of the Anthropocene has generated new ontological threats and politics that today challenge the prospects, and even the notion, of a global human rights project. Rodríguez-Garavito argues, "if the human rights project is to remain relevant in the Anthropocene, it needs to take into consideration the rights of nonhumans." I agree that human rights must take an ecological turn. So must the corporate accountability movement. In this chapter, I have argued that both of these movements are confronting a technological turn as well, and that if the corporate accountability movement is to remain relevant in the digitally transforming relations of the Anthropocene, it also needs to take into consideration the relationally constructed rights of Big Tech, as well as the alternative rights of data ownership and stewardship now being constructed by and for marginalized communities, both human and nonhuman.

The digital transformation of our social and ecological relations will require us to construct new rights that have not yet been imagined, much less institutionalized. In this chapter I have argued for relational approaches to understanding rights, and for self-reflexively constructing them together.

Relational approaches open opportunities for pluriversal and transversal politics and thinking. Pluriversal and transversal politics are radically relational and ecological concepts that contribute to the fragmentation of the concept of the human as isolated from nonhumans. They do not represent a challenge to regulate the powerful and conflicting forces of the world into some idealised, harmonious balance. Rather, they are a first (and necessary) step toward a relational understanding of ecologically and technologically embedded humanity, and to engendering new institutional and ontological conditions that encourage people to encounter the world as a series of open and ongoing syntheses between partial, relational objects.

The two rights projects I have discussed offer reason for hope that it is at least possible, in some contexts, to rein in extractivist development projects. In both of the rights projects I examined, we saw successful efforts to uproot the conceptual human supremacy that has remained a cornerstone of global human rights as a legal project. We saw in both cases as well how destabilizing the concept of human supremacy leads to attributing *agency* to nonhumans. The question is whether that, then, leads to *rights*.

In the case of the Sarayaku, it has opened a path to novel forms of data rights. Nature too needs data to protect itself from human supremacy so that it can "speak" in terms that are cognizable (rational) to humans, but also in terms that do not take away from other ways of listening and knowing. In the case of CELDF, we saw how their symbolic politics aim for recognition that nature is not *property* (owned by nonhuman corporate persons).

Comparing these cases also reveals another significant distinction. In the U.S., generally, corporations own the minerals beneath the land that they own. In Ecuador, by contrast, the state owns the minerals under the land. This is true in *Los Cedros* ("The Cloud Forest") as well as *Kawsak Sacha* ("The Living Forest"). This is in part why the Sarayaku, the MOTH Project, Society for the Protection of Underground Networks and the Fungi Foundation jointly launched Science Across Cultures. The fungal data they collect and analyse will also clarify how above-ground ecosystems depend on and are connected to below-ground ecosystems, including mycorrhizal fungi; this will help elaborate the interconnectedness underpinning the Sarayaku's claim for recognition of their territory *as a subject of rights*. Thus, movements might need to take different strategies and tactics depending on who owns the underlying resources.

I conclude that relational approaches to understanding the construction of rights and agency of humans (social systems) and nonhumans (natural ecosystems and technological systems) that take into consideration the pluriversal and transversal politics that have emerged in the wake of the ecological and technological turns across many fields of knowledge production can open up strategic discursive possibilities for bridging and strengthening multiscalar corporate accountability movements and their rights projects.

References

Akchurin M (2015) Constructing the rights of nature: constitutional reform, mobilization, and environmental protection in Ecuador. Law Soc Inq 40(4):937–968

Anicker F, Flaßhoff G, Marcinkowski F (2024) The matrix of AI agency: on the demarcation problem in social theory. Sociol Theory 42(4):307–328

Bashkow I (2014) What kind of a person is the corporation? PoLAR: Polit Leg Anthropol Rev 37(2):296–307

Bennett J (2010) A vitalist stopover on the way to a new materialism. In: Cole D, Samantha F (eds) New materialisms: ontology, agency, and politics. Duke University Press, pp 49–69

Blaser M, de la Cadena M (2018) Pluriverse: proposals for a world of many worlds. In: de la Cadena M, Blaser M (eds) A world of many worlds. Duke University Press

Braidotti R (2013) The Posthuman. Polity Press, Cambridge and Medford

Burawoy M (2018) Marxism after Polanyi. In: Williams M, Sagtar V (eds) Marxisms in the 21st century: crisis, critique & struggle. Cambridge University Press, Cambridge, pp 34–52

Committee on Legal Affairs (2017) Report with Recommendations to the Commission on Civil Law Rules on Robotics: Procedure: 2015/2103(INL), available at: https://www.europarl.europa.eu/doceo/document/A-0-2018-0005_EN.html?redirect#_section1

Connolly WE (2017) Facing the planetary: entangled humanism and the politics of swarming. Duke University Press

Couldry N, Mejias UA (2019) The costs of connection: how data is colonizing human life and appropriating it for capitalism. Stanford University Press

Crawford K (2021) Atlas of AI: power, politics, and the planetary costs of artificial intelligence. Yale University Press

Dale JG (2008) Burma's Boomerang: human rights, social movements and transnational legal mechanisms 'from below'. Int J Contemp Sociol 45(1):151–184. https://www.semanticscholar.org/paper/BURMA%27S-BOOMERANG-%3A-HUMAN-RIGHTS%2C-SOCIAL-MOVEMENTS-Dale/d5e3872040840094bb557532a8200055a84e5977

Dale JG (2011) Free Burma: corporate accountability and transnational legal action. University of Minnesota Press

Danowski D, Viveiros de Castro E (2017) The ends of the world. Polity Press, Cambridge and Medford

de la Cadena M (2010) Indigenous cosmopolitics in the Andes. Cult Anthropol 25(2):334–370

Desmond M (2014) Relational ethnography. Theory Soc 43(5):547–579

DiMaggio P (2001) The twenty-first century firm: changing economic organization in international perspective. Princeton University Press

Dunford R (2017) Towards a decolonial global ethics. J Global Ethics 13:380–397

Emirbayer M (1997) Manifesto for a relational sociology. Am J Sociol, 103 (2): 281-317

Escobar A (2020) Pluriversal politics: the real and the possible. Duke University Press

Fitz-Henry E (2018) Challenging corporate 'personhood': energy companies and the 'rights' of non-humans. Polit Leg Anthropol Rev 41(S1):85–102. https://doi.org/10.1111/plar.12255

Fligstein N (1990) The transformation of corporate control. Harvard University Press

Gellers JC (2020) Rights for robots: artificial intelligence, animal and environmental law. Routledge, available at: https://www.taylorfrancis.com/search?key=Rights%20for%20Robots

Goodale M (2020) The Misbegotten Monad: anthropology, human rights, belonging. In: Celermajer D, Lefebvre A (eds) The subject of human rights. Stanford University Press, pp 48–63

Goodale M (2022) Reinventing human rights. Stanford University Press

Gordon GJ (2019) Environmental personhood. Columbia J Environ Law 43(1):49–91

Gualinga Montalvo J, Baquero-Diaz JA, Rodríguez-Garavito C (2024) Sarayaku victory against oil exploitation is an inspiration for the entire Amazon. Sumaúma (5 February), available at: https://sumauma.com/en/a-vitoria-do-povo-sarayaku-contra-as-petroleiras-e-os-abusos-do-estado-inspira-a-amazonia/

Guarnizo LE, Smith MP (1998) The locations of transnationalism. In: Smith MP, Guarnizo LE (eds) Transnationalism from below. Transaction Publishers, pp 3–34
Hicks J (2023) The future of data ownership: an uncommon research agenda. Sociol Rev 7(3):544–560. https://doi.org/10.1177/00380261221088120
Huneeus A (2022) The legal struggle for rights of nature in the United States. Wis Law Rev 1:133–161, available at: https://wlr.law.wisc.edu/volume-2022-no-1/
Indigenous Peoples Movement for Self-Determination & Liberation (2023) Kawsak Sacha, Living Forest, available at: https://www.ipmsdl.org/news/kawsak-sacha-living-forest/
Jameson KP (2011) The indigenous movement in Ecuador: the struggle for a plurinational state. Latin Am Perspect 38:63–73. https://doi.org/10.1177/0094582X10384210
Jung M (2024) Rights projects: a relational sociology of rights in globalization. Sociol Theory 42(3):256–281. https://doi.org/10.1177/07352751241265366
Keck ME, Sikkink K (1998) Activists beyond borders: advocacy networks in international politics. Cornell University Press
Kelly J (2017) Kichwa Indigenous People of Sarayaku v. Ecuador. Loyola Los Angeles Int Comp Law Rev 40(3):1469–1491, available at: https://iachr.lls.edu/sites/default/files/iachr/Cases/kelly_kichwa_indigenous_people_of_sarayaku_v._ecuador.pdf
Kirsch S (2014) Mining capitalism: corporations and their critics. University of California Press
Kymlicka W (2024) Rethinking human rights for a more-than-human world. In: Rodríguez-Garavito C (ed) More than human rights: an ecology of law, thought and narrative for earthly flourishing. New York University Law School, pp 55–81
MacPherson E (2021) The (human) rights of nature: a comparative study of emerging legal rights for rivers and lakes in the United States and Mexico. Duke Environ Law Policy Forum 31:327–377, available at: https://scholarship.law.duke.edu/delpf/vol31/iss2/3
Mejias UA, Couldry N (2024) Data Grab: the new colonialism of big tech and how to fight back. University of Chicago
Monsees L et al (2023) Transversal politics of big tech. Int Polit Sociol 17:1–23. https://doi.org/10.1093/ips/olac020
New York University (NYU) More Than Human Life (MOTH) Project and the Earth Rights Research and Action (TERRA) Program at NYU School of Law, (2024) The Impact of the Rights of Nature: Assessing the Implementation of the *Los Cedros* Ruling in Ecuador. (June), available at: https://mothrights.org/project/report-assessing-the-implementation-of-the-los-cedros-ruling-in-ecuador/
Paige JM (2020) Indigenous revolution in Ecuador and Bolivia, 1990–2005. University of Arizona Press. https://doi.org/10.2307/j.ctv1131hhn
Pietari K (2016) Ecuador's constitutional rights of nature: implementation, impacts, and lessons learned. Willamette Environ Law J 5:37–93, available at: https://my.willamette.edu/site/law-journals/pdf/2016/2016-f-welj-cover.pdf
Pueblo Originario de Sarayaku ALDEA (2021) Sarayaku: The Living Forest of the Midday People in the Ecuadorian Amazon. (19 March), available at: https://report.territoriesoflife.org/territories/sarayaku-ecuador/
Rodríguez-Garavito C (ed) (2024) More than human rights: an ecology of law, thought and narrative for earthly flourishing. New York University Law School, available at: https://mothrights.org/more-than-human-rights-an-ecology-of-law-thought-and-narrative-for-earthly-flourishing/
Rojas C (2016) Contesting the colonial logics of the international: towards a relational politics for the pluriverse. Int Polit Sociol 10:369–382. https://doi.org/10.1093/ips/olw020
Sheldrake M (2020) Entangled lives: how fungi make our worlds, change our minds & shape our futures. Random House
Somers M (1994) The narrative constitution of identity: a relational and network approach. Theory Soc 23(5):605–649. https://doi.org/10.1007/BF00992905
Tinnel JC (2012) Transversalizing the ecological turn: four components of Félix Guattari's Ecosophical perspective. Deleuze Stud 6(3):357–388, available at: https://www.jstor.org/stable/45331514

Unger RM (2019) The knowledge economy. Verso
Welker M (2014) Enacting the corporation: an American mining firm in post-authoritarian Indonesia. University of California Press
Welker M, Partridge D, Hardin R (2011) Corporate lives: new perspectives on the corporate form. Curr Anthropol 52(S3):3–16
Witten NE, Witten DS (2011) Histories of the present: people and power in Ecuador. University of Illinois Press
Wojtczak S (2022) Endowing artificial intelligence with legal subjectivity. AI Soc 37:205–213
Wong Y-K (2024) How many data centres are there and where are they being built? ABI Research (16 July), available at: https://www.abiresearch.com/blogs/2024/07/16/data-centers-by-region-size-company/

John G. Dale is Associate Professor of Sociology and Director of Movement Engaged at George Mason University. He was a Science and Technology Innovation Program Fellow at the Woodrow Wilson Center for International Scholars (2019–20) where he researched the digital transformation of human rights, and a Japan Society for the Promotion of Science Visiting Research Fellow (2021–22) exploring efforts to integrate human rights into national policies on AI and robotics. He serves as Scientific Advisor on the ERC-Consolidator Project "*Transnational Advocacy Networks and Corporate Accountability for Major International Crimes.*" Dr. Dale was elected Council Member of the American Sociological Association's Section on Human Rights (2019–2022) and to the Steering Committee of the Science & Human Rights Coalition of the American Association for the Advancement of Science (2018–24). He is author of *Free Burma: Transnational Legal Action and Corporate Accountability* (University of Minnesota Press, 2011) and co-author of *Political Sociology: Power and Participation in the Modern World* (Oxford University Press, 2009).

The Values and Limitations of Transnational Activism for Corporate Accountability in Post-Civil War Guatemala

Raluca Grosescu

Abstract This chapter examines the role of transnational activism for corporate accountability in post-1996 Guatemala. It argues that, in a country marked by extensive neoliberal economic experiments, endemic corruption, pervasive racism against Indigenous populations, and violence against anti-extractivist campaigners, transnational cooperation between Guatemalan and Western activists, NGOs, and donors was crucial for strengthening local struggles against the development of mining operations and other extractivist projects. Nevertheless, Western support for accountability campaigns has often been framed within a liberal lexicon of rights that has dominated global affairs since the mid-1970s that has limited the capacity of Guatemalan Indigenous communities to assert a politics of alternative, non-liberal and non-Western autonomy. Furthermore, in their pursuit of Western public support for Indigenous demands, NGOs from the Global North often constructed communication strategies that oversimplified and depoliticised not only the economic conflicts unfolding in Guatemala, but also Indigenous thought, by employing simplistic narratives borrowed from Western blockbusters and bestsellers.

1 Introduction

The early twenty-first century has witnessed the acceleration of social activism for corporate accountability, and, to a lesser extent, the struggle against neoliberal economic development and its inequalities. A variety of activists and networks have begun to collaborate across national borders and world regions to challenge national and international norms that exempt business for their direct involvement or

This research was supported by the ERC-Consolidator project *Transnational Advocacy Networks and Corporate Accountability for Major International Crimes* under the European Union's Horizon 2020 research and innovation program (grant agreement No. 101002993—CORPACCOUNT).

R. Grosescu (✉)
SNSPA, Bucharest, Romania

R. Grosescu, J. G. Dale (eds.), *Corporate Accountability for Human Rights Violations*, Interdisciplinary Studies in Human Rights 16,
https://doi.org/10.1007/978-3-032-05569-9_5

complicity in human rights violations and massive environmental degradation. While socio-historical accounts of these transnational mobilisations remain rare, three approaches have thus far dominated the existing academic literature on this topic.

An initial series of works has drawn inspiration from constructivist theories of international relations and norm formation.[1] They depicted transnational activism for corporate accountability as rather monolithic campaigns driven by idealistic activists bound together by a shared human rights culture, a common moral commitment to justice, and similar repertoires of action.[2] Such accounts emphasised cross-border collaborations as a crucial counterpoint "from below" to the absence of a national and international will to regulate and sanction corporate violations of human rights and environmental norms. They underlined the capacity of transnational action to enforce new legislation, pressure corporations to withdraw from conflict zones and countries ruled by dictatorial regimes, pay compensation to victims of corporate wrongdoing, and raise public awareness about the involvement of multinational corporations in human rights violations and environmental destruction. Yet such analyses often overlooked not only the competing professional agendas of the activists involved, but also the conflicting visions of various transnational advocacy networks (TANs) regarding the most effective means of achieving justice and re-envisioning the current economic order. Furthermore, these works did not address the way cooperation between the Global North and the Global South often reinforced longstanding relations of domination, inequality and epistemic colonisation.[3]

A second body of literature challenged this idealistic view of TANs through the sociological lens of Pierre Bourdieu. These works examined the gradual reformulation of transnational norms in terms of "turf battles"[4] between competing networks and professionals that each aim to transform international regulations, but seek at the same time to control the financial and symbolic resources of these regulatory processes. Such analyses have identified a diverse array of networks fighting for corporate accountability and underlined how their actions were informed by a multitude of professional cultures, ideological agendas, and financial dependencies.[5] However, this literature has frequently exhibited a Eurocentric perspective by primarily concentrating on the most influential global and Western-based NGOs and on the most vocal and well-funded Global South civil society organisations (CSOs). This approach overlooked the collaboration and potential conflicts between these organisations and less visible or marginalised groups affected by corporate violence, such as trade unions, farmers and Indigenous communities.

[1] Haas (1992); Keck and Sikkink (1998); *Finnemore* and *Sikkink (*1998*).*

[2] Pellow (2007); Dale (2011); Bieri (2013); Basualdo et al. (2015); Saage-Maaß et al. (2021).

[3] For Global South human rights epistemologies and the risks of Global North epistemic colonisation, see de Sousa Santos (2015); Mutua (2002).

[4] Dezalay and Garth (2012).

[5] Grosescu (2019); Henry Rammelt's chapter in this volume.

To challenge such Eurocentric perspectives, a third category of studies has centred its analysis on how Global South actors construct corporate accountability and evaluate and re-think transnational cooperation in this arena. On the one hand, some scholars have argued that transitional cooperation plays a limited role in advancing corporate accountability. Mobilisations of local and weakly resourced groups, including victims' associations and local judicial officials from the Global South, have often been more successful in advancing justice than have transnational campaigns.[6] As such, scholars, activists and funding organisations should prioritise such local mobilisations and de-centre the value of transnational activism. These studies remained however embedded in a liberal narrative of corporate accountability and its "best" levels of actions, without engaging with global inequalities and ideological conflicts within national and transnational activism. On the other hand, while neo-Marxist or decolonial scholars argued for the importance of transnational activism, they also emphasised how cross-regional cooperation reinforces existing power dynamics and dominant liberal and neoliberal narratives on corporate accountability. They pointed to the disjuncture between the goals of Southern and Northern activists, the challenges of coordinating the varied objectives of transnational social movements, and the limitations of transitional solidarity, particularly when classed-based struggles and visions about sovereignty from the Global South must be advocated for in Global North venues.[7] In addition, due to the fact that they are situated in the Global North and receive funding from Global North donors, the most powerful NGOs tend to support projects that enhance "the neoliberal offensive against the subaltern peoples and regions of the world",[8] as prompted by international financial institutions, such as the World Bank and the International Monetary Fund. Furthermore, in their quest to market Global South causes to Western publics, Western NGOs often employ language and activist tactics that are familiar and acceptable in the West, but do not necessarily reflect the world visions and demands of the Global South groups with whom there have partnered.[9] Such marketisation can lead to the weakening or even abandonment of principles fundamental to the activism in question.[10]

This chapter aims to contribute to the critical literature on transnational activism for corporate accountability by emphasising the values and limitations of cross-border cooperation between Guatemalan activists and Western NGOs and donors after the end of the Guatemalan civil war in 1996. I argue that numerous organisations from the Global North supported local mobilisations against the extractive industry and other projects of Western economic modernisation, including large hydroelectric dams and monoculture plantations, through legal and scientific

[6] Payne et al. (2020); Pereira et al. (2022). See also the chapter by Leigh Payne and Gabriel Pereira in this volume.

[7] De Sousa (2005); Gill (2009); Baars (2019); Bueckert (2019); Freeman (2024).

[8] Munck (2006), p. 331. See also Brett (2015).

[9] Gill (2009); Seay (2015).

[10] de Waal et al. (2015).

assistance, funding and the "protective accompaniment" (*acompañamiento*).[11] of different communities and local NGOs. This Western backing was crucial for both the economic survival of Guatemalan CSOs and the protection of human rights and environmental activists in country plagued by systematic repression against individuals and communities that oppose neoliberal, extractivist projects.

Nevertheless, Western support came with several limitations. First, support was generally contingent upon a non-violent culture of protest rooted in contemporary Western liberal tactics aimed at de-radicalising political action. When anti-extractivist protests gained violent character, Western NGOs largely withdrew their support. Second, funding was predominantly directed towards the defence of the civil, political and cultural rights of Indigenous groups or towards the promotion of the soft-law international instruments in the domain of business and human rights. Only rarely did Western donors support projects of economic emancipation and autonomy that reflected Indigenous visions and interests. Third, transnational litigation brought against Global North companies in their home countries primarily focused on cases of corporate complicity in physical violence against human rights and environmental activists rather than on land grabbing or the imposition of an economic model that impoverished Indigenous communities and radically altered their culture and way of life. Such strategies were not only designed to comply with restrictive Global North legislation: they also reflected the structural constraints inherent to moving beyond the liberal lexicon of rights that has dominated global affairs since the mid-1970s. Finally, in their pursuit of Western public support for Indigenous anti-extractivist struggles, Global North NGOs often constructed communication strategies that oversimplified and depoliticised the economic conflicts unfolding in Guatemala and even reduced Indigenous perspectives on the world to crude narratives inspired by Western blockbusters and bestsellers.

By examining a series of transnational campaigns for corporate accountability in Guatemala, and drawing upon twenty interviews conducted with both Guatemalan and Western activists, the chapter underlines how cross-border mobilisations bolstered and legitimised local struggles against extractivist development. However, such transnational activism also re-enforced liberal and Western vocabularies of rights that restricted the capacity of Indigenous activists to assert their own world visions and subsequent approaches to economic development.

[11] "Protective accompaniment" or "acompañamiento" is a strategy pioneered by the International Peace Brigades in the 1990s to support and protect human rights and environmental activists at risk.

2 Neoliberalism, Extractivism and Indigenous World Visions in Post-1996 Guatemala

After the end of civil war in 1996, Guatemala embarked upon a broad programme of neoliberal development, which included the privatisation of various economic sectors and foreign investment in extractivist industries, large hydroelectric plants, and monocrop agro-industrial projects.[12] This economic reconfiguration was designed to increase economic growth and participation in global markets and was supported by the national elite and international institutions such as the World Bank, the Inter-American Development Bank, and the International Monetary Fund.[13] Extractivist projects, including in the mining sector,[14] were frequently implemented in the traditional territories of Indigenous groups, which continue to represent around forty-five per cent of the country's population.[15] While the 1995 Agreement on the Identity and Rights of Indigenous Peoples (signed as part of the peace process following the civil war) established political and cultural rights for Indigenous people and redefined Guatemala as a multiethnic, multicultural, and multilingual nation, it did not touch upon economic rights, including the restitution of ancestral Indigenous lands that had been progressively colonized since the sixteenth century.[16] Although Guatemala ratified the 1989 ILO Convention No. 169—which mandates that Indigenous people be consulted prior to any economic or infrastructure development on their traditional territories—in 1996, the government did not organise such consultations or ignored them when they resulted in opposition to the dominant economic trend. What is more, such neoliberal advances often involved new land grabs, the forced displacement of Indigenous and other rural populations, forced economic migration, environmental degradation (including massive pollution, the deviation of rivers, and deforestation) and the use of the military to repress protests.[17] They also exacerbated struggles over the ownership of lands and resources, insofar as natural resources in Guatemala are for the most part located on

[12] While such projects were implemented from the 1970s onwards, neoliberal development accelerated after the 1996 Peace Agreements, as a reflection of the global Washington Consensus and its economic doctrine and practice.

[13] On neoliberalism and extractivism in post-1996 Guatemala, see for example Nolin and Stephens (2010); Yagenova (2012); Spalding (2023), pp. 107–116; Batz (2023).

[14] In 2021, there were nearly 300 active mining exploitation licenses to extract a range of minerals and metals, with the largest operations controlled by Canadian and US corporations, See Batz (2023).

[15] Guatemala is predominantly Indigenous: There are twenty-one Mayan linguistic communities, in addition to two other Indigenous groups, the Xinca and the Garífuna. The remainder of the population is mestizo or ladino (non-Indian), mixed race descendants of Indigenous groups, Spanish settlers and other immigrants who colonized Guatemala beginning in the sixteenth century. In many municipalities in the highland departments, over 95% of the population is Mayan.

[16] Sieder (1997); Brett (2015); Spalding (2023), p. 293.

[17] Batz (2023); Willems (2010).

Indigenous territories, but the communities that reside there continue to be the most affected by poverty and pervasive racism.[18]

Indigenous reactions to these projects have been mixed and complex. Many saw mining exploitation and the construction of mega-hydroelectric projects as a source of jobs, income and development. In contrast, others considered them an overt attack on their culture, ways of being, and the very survival of their communities. To understand this opposition and the subsequent organised resistance, one must reflect on Indigenous worldviews and economic activities. From an economic perspective, most of Guatemala's Indigenous population lives in rural areas, sustained by subsistence farming and fishing. As mining operations often entail water and soil contamination, a loss of biodiversity, and deforestation, they have a direct negative impact on such economic activities. They also result in severe health problems for the local population, especially near operations that involve tailing and the use of cyanide. The construction of mega-hydroelectric dams has also impacted the Indigenous farming and fishing economy through deforestation and the deviation of rivers, cutting access to water and reconfiguring the fish population. This environmental degradation accelerated the pauperisation of Indigenous and other rural communities, resulting in forced economic migration to urban areas or across borders, in addition to the forced displacement of communities in order to implement various mega-development projects.[19]

From a cultural perspective, Western development and modernisation projects stand in stark conflict with Indigenous cosmovisions that understand the (Western) categories of nature, culture, and human as being, in fact, inseparable.[20] In contrast to the Western cartesian divide between nature and humans, which has been translated into international law as the separation of human rights law and environmental law into two distinct subfields, Indigenous philosophies postulate the essential connection between humans, animals and plants as part of "life". They thus represent a radical rethinking of a Western ontology and epistemology that replaces "a binary view of the world with a relational one," and "stress[es] the reproduction of life as against the reproduction of capital accumulation."[21] For instance, in an interview from 2019, a Guatemalan Indigenous activist pointed out that:

> for Indigenous Peoples, everything has life, and therefore it should have rights just like people have; for many Indigenous communities, this is very clear, but this is not true for the capitalist West, which sees every living thing as something to be exploited. […] I do not want to talk about human rights. I want to talk about the right of life. For us, everything has life, and therefore it should have rights just like people do.[22]

[18] IWGIA (2024). For racism in Guatemala, see Adams (2005); Casáus Arzú (2008).

[19] Shipton (2017); Batz (2023).

[20] MacNeill (2020), Chapter 6.

[21] Munck (2021), p. 171. See also Altman (2020).

[22] Personal Interview with with anonymous activist, Guatemala City, Guatemala, 19 August 2019. See also Iñigo (2023).

Consequently, Indigenous groups have an alternative discourse on development and rights than the dominant Western one: a discourse that "promotes an ethics of development that subordinates economic objectives to ecological criteria including food sovereignty, control of natural resources and water as a human right."[23] They aspire to—and to a certain extent have, in some communities, achieved—"an economic organisation through practices of reciprocity and solidarity, community-level action and self-management" that stands as an alternative to capitalist relations of production and distribution.[24] From this perspective, Western modernisation and economic projects not only impact the livelihood conditions of Indigenous groups, but also affect their cultural and spiritual essence, defined as the interconnected trilogy between the human being, the spirit, and the natural world.[25] Moreover, the arrival of extractivist industries has been labelled by Indigenous groups as the "fourth invasion," after Spanish colonization, the creation of the plantation economy beginning in the late nineteenth century, and the state-sponsored genocide during the civil war (1960–1996).[26]

3 The Guatemalan Anti-Extractivist Resistance and Its Selective Transnational Support

The expansion of extractivist politics after 1996 and especially in the mid-2000s generated strong opposition across the country. Guatemalan Indigenous communities and other militants fighting against mining and other mega-development projects began to build multisectoral coalitions that included local communities, Catholic Church officials, human rights and environmental NGOs, and associations of lawyers. Their main tactics comprised protests, roadblocks, scientific activism, demands for free and informed consultations at the local level, and judicial interventions.[27]

Such mobilisations took place across the country and against a variety of mining operations. The stronger and more mediatised anti-mining movements included the resistance against gold exploitation by Gold Corporation in the western highlands of Guatemala (Mina Marlin) and by Radius Gold in La Puya (Mina El Tambor), near Guatemala City; silver extraction by Tahoe Resources in San Rafael Las Flores, near Guatemala City (Mina El Escobal); and nickel exploitation by Sky Resources and HudBay in El Estor, on the shores of Izabal lake in eastern Guatemala (Mina

[23] Munck (2021), p. 171.

[24] Acosta (2018), p. 108.

[25] For ethnographic work on the Indigenous cosmovision in Guatemala see MacNeill (2020).

[26] Batz (2022).

[27] On the Guatemalan anti-mining movements and their strategies, see Spalding (2023), Chapter 4.

Fenix)—all corporations headquartered in Canada.[28] Nevertheless, despite their common goals, these resistance movements did not evolve into a unified national network.[29] In particular, this continued regional focus was due to the inadequacy of Guatemalan transportation infrastructure which renders travel extremely challenging, and to the limited access to digital technologies that hindered online communication. Moreover, the absence of any prominent Indigenous or leftist political party impeded alliances between activists and political elites, resulting in a nearly non-existent level of anti-extractivist political advocacy.[30]

Consequently, the Guatemalan government had significant leeway in countering anti-mining movements through the forced eviction of Indigenous and other rural communities, the unlawful arrest of protestors based on fabricated evidence, and the imposition of a state of emergency in various regions of the country, followed by arbitrary police and military violence. In addition to official state repression, activists were subject to violent attacks and assassination attempts, the majority of which remained without judicial response.[31] Into 2025, Guatemala continued to be one of the most dangerous countries in the world for defenders of land, territory and the environment.[32]

Since the signing of the Peace Agreements in 1996 that ended the civil war, the most important Guatemalan organisations involved in anti-extractivist campaigns included the ecological association Madre Selva (founded in 1996), the Centro de Acción Legal-Ambiental y Social (established in 2000), the Nim Ajpu Association of Maya Lawyers and Notaries (founded in 2004), the Xinka Parliament (founded in 2004), and the Peoples Council of the Western Highlands (created in 2008 and later renamed the Consejo del Pueblo Maya-CPO). Each of these organisations engaged in political and legal activism, with much of their work funded by Western governments, NGOs, and religious foundations. International NGOs offered a wide range of assistance, from the publication of reports and media articles and the release of documentary films exposing governmental violence against protestors, to public campaigns in support of activists illegally arrested, to *acompañamiento* provided to Indigenous and rural communities during protests or negotiations with state authorities. Additionally, Western actors initiated transnational litigation against Western companies accused of complicity in human rights violations. Organisations such as the International Peace Brigades Guatemala (PBI Guatemala), the International Accompaniment Project (ACOGUATE), the Network in Solidarity

[28] For the history of these mining projects and the subsequent resistance against them, see Yagenova et al. (2020); Sveinsdóttir et al. (2021).

[29] Spalding (2023), p. 316.

[30] Ibid.

[31] On the violence against anti-mining and anti-megaproject development protests in Guatemala, see for example Paredes Marín (2016); Sieder (2017); Yagenova et al. (2020); Sveinsdóttir et al. (2021).

[32] The Unit for the Protection of Human Rights Defenders – Guatemala (UDEFEGUA) reported 3.574 (in 2022) and 5.965 (in 2023) attacks against human rights defenders, including threats, killings, harassment and arbitrary detentions.

with the People of Guatemala (NISGUA) or Collectif Guatemala played a leading role in defending activists and promoting their cause abroad. They often collaborated with other international NGOs such as Amnesty International, the Front Line Defenders or the International Federation of Human Rights to organise global solidarity campaigns.[33]

In a country marked by endemic corruption, pervasive racism against Indigenous populations, and violence against anti-extractivist campaigners, international support and transnational cooperation were crucial for securing the very survival of those who opposed the dominant economic elite. The global campaign against the imprisonment of Bernardo Caal Xol, the leader of *Mayan Q'eqchi* resistance against mega-hydroelectric dams in Cahabón, Alta Verapaz, in northern Guatemala, serves as a compelling illustration of the importance of transnational activism in standing with activists at risk. In January 2018, Bernardo Caal was imprisoned for defending the rights of the Mayan Q'eqchi' communities affected by the construction of a hydroelectric project on the Cahabón river. In November 2018, he was sentenced to seven years in prison for property destruction and incitement to public violence. PBI Guatemala promptly launched a campaign protesting against his arrest, arguing that the sentence was unjust and based on fabricated evidence. PBI continued to monitor the case and systematically documented its progress. According to Bernardo Caal, "knowing that PBI is looking out for me in prison dissuades those who want to cause me harm."[34] PBI also called for the support of international institutions, including the UN. In Decembre 2018, various UN special rapporteurs on the rights of Indigenous populations and the situation of human rights defenders, as well as members of the UN Working Group on Business and Human Rights denounced Bernardo Caal's arrest as an "attempt to silence and discredit the legitimate exercise of the rights of the Indigenous community" and urged the Guatemalan government to "ensure the effective protection of Indigenous human rights defenders."[35] In July 2020, Amnesty International designated Bernardo Caal a "prisoner of conscience" and launched a two-pronged global campaign. On the one hand, it demanded his immediate release, engaging with both Guatemalan and international institutions, including the UN Committee on Human Rights. On the other hand, it gathered over 30.000 letters of solidarity from citizens worldwide. Other global NGOs, such as the International Organisation against Torture, the International Federation of

---

[33] For detailed information about the activities of these organisations in Guatemala, see their websites https://pbi-guatemala.org/; https://nisgua.org/ and https://collectifguatemala.org/ (accessed 21.04.2024). Other international NGOs involved in supporting anti-extractivist campaigns in Guatemala were MiningWatch Canada, the Washington DC-based Center for International Environmental Law (CIEL), the Justice and Corporate Accountability Project at York University in Toronto, and the Canadian Centre for International Justice, among others. Spalding (2023), p. 132.

[34] Statement by Bernardo Caal Xol, available at https://peacebrigades.org/en/our-work/what-we-do/protective-accompaniment (accessed 7.11.2024).

[35] OHCHR Press Release, Guatemala: UN experts concerned indigenous leader convicted in retaliation for opposition to Oxec hydro project, available at www.ohchr.org/en/press-releases/2018/12/guatemala-un-experts-concerned-indigenous-leader-convicted-retaliation?LangID=E&NewsID=24031 (accessed 24.11.2024).

Human Rights, and the International Service for Human Rights filed amicus curiae and organised media campaigns in Bernardo Caal's support. Following this extensive international mobilisation, Bernardo Caal was released from prison in March 2022, three years early. The campaign's success was however limited, as Bernardo Caal was not acquitted of the charges against him and served four years for what most international NGOs considered as baseless accusations.

However, not all movements and communities received assistance. International NGOs made their aid conditional on the use of pacifist and non-violent resistance (*resistencia pacifica y no-violenta*), to the point that it became a mantra for the involvement of Western organisations in specific cases. In her comparative analysis of anti-mining resistance in La Puya and San Rafael Las Flores, Ana Eugenia Paredes Marín demonstrates how the later movement lost international backing because it engaged in disruptive and violent forms of protests.[36] The San Rafael Las Flores anti-mining campaign began in 2010 with peaceful protests, such as laying flowers at the entrances of the land acquired by Tahoe Resources, the Canadian embassy, and the company's headquarters in Guatemala City. Various communities also organised local consultations and declared their opposition to the mining project, but both the state and Tahoe Resources simply ignored them. Starting in January 2012, in the absence of any response to these peaceful actions, protestors began to use disruptive and violent tactics, including the construction of roadblocks, the expulsion of the company's employees from the communities in which they resided, house arrests, the destruction of company trucks, grocery stores, and employee housing, and even the detonation of a grenade on mine property.[37] Despite the denials by community leaders of their involvement and accusations of external provocation, the government labelled the protestors "terrorists" and members of "organised crime". In May 2013, the government declared a state of emergency and initiated a substantial crackdown on anti-mining leaders and their communities. After the events of 2012, as protests escalated to violence, Western NGOs continued to document governmental abuses, but refrained from providing direct support. In the words of one activist from San Rafael Las Flores:

> I was in touch with organisations, for instance the Peace Brigades. They did not grant any support to me or to our resistance, because "it wasn't peaceful". I had guns and this disqualified me as a human rights defender, and, in the end, (the support from these) organisa-

---

[36] Paredes Marín (2016).

[37] Based on the "frustration-aggression hypothesis" (Dollard et al. 1939), aggressive behaviour, including collective behaviour, can been explained by the immediate frustration or bocking of desired goals. Over time, studies increasingly complicated this direct causal relation. Researchers of contentious politics began to analyse various conditions, notably poverty, oppression, and discrimination (Gurr 1970), as the root causes of violence. Today, social movement studies, as well as conflict and terrorism studies, explain the turn by previously non-violent protest movements towards greater disruption, violence, and potentially terrorism through the procedural lens of "radicalisation" (Bosi and Malthaner 2015). Radicalisation is frequently considered to be the result of "reciprocal adjustments" during encounters between social movements and authorities (della Porta 2018). Notably, clashes with law enforcement are considered to provide a justification for the use of more violent forms of action (Ibid.).

> tions was not significant. Madre Selva at the beginning, then CALAS and ACOGUATE, Collectif Guatemala y NISGUA, but one more occasionally than the other. It was a matter of personal engagement with these organisations, more than the organisations' engagement with the resistance.[38]

In El Estor, one of the most contentious sites of anti-mining resistance, protestors also employed disruptive and violent tactics, such as the construction of roadblocks, the severing of electrical wires, raising barricades in front of the mine, and violent assaults against the mining company's employees and security personnel. With the exception of Rights Action, none of the major international NGOs working in Guatemala supported the movement. According to Julio Gonzalez from Madre Selva, "when protests are violent and when communities are highly divided over the implementation of a mining project, it becomes more difficult to back those who protest. NGOs are very cautious in such cases."[39]

The lack of Western support for movements that employ disruptive and violent tactics has two explanations. On the one hand, from an instrumental and pragmatic perspective, violent protests are regarded as unproductive. They are presumed to elicit retribution and further violence from the state, pose risks to participants, and divide and alienate different sectors of society.[40] Indeed, Guatemalan state violence against anti-mining protestors has often targeted not only the militants themselves, but also independent observers and representatives of NGOs providing *acompañamiento* (who were then criminalised based on fabricated evidence).[41] For instance, in 2021, representatives of the transnational organisation ACOGUATE participated as observers in the "March for Dignity" in Guatemala City—a demonstration commemorating the international day of Indigenous Resistance. During the demonstration, participants attempted to remove the statutes of Cristopher Columbus and José María Reina Barrios, president of independent Guatemala (1892–1898), who led a national campaign to "civilise" Indigenous communities according to Western values. While ACOGUATE issued a statement denouncing all violent or illegal acts, the NGO was criminally investigated for vandalism, "attacks against the national security" and destruction of cultural heritage. ACOGUATE's representatives were subsequently the victims of anonymous death threats and defamation campaigns on social media,[42] leading the NGO to withdraw from Guatemala in 2022, due to security concerns. Such actions against Western organisations engaged in human rights work in Guatemala are a major reason for refraining from involvement in and support for social movements that resort to disruptive and violent tactics.

On the other hand, ideological issues are also at stake. Violent protests are typically seen as antithetical to liberal democracy, as they challenge the purportedly peaceful democratic institutions and their system of dispute resolution. Such actions

[38] Quoted by Paredes Marín (2016), p. 60.

[39] Personal Interview with Julio Gonzalez, Guatemala City, 5.09.2024.

[40] Chenoweth and Stephan (2008).

[41] Sibrián and van der Borgh (2014); Yagenova (2016).

[42] UDEFEGUA (2021), pp. 154, 157.

are also considered detrimental due to their destructive potential for property and persons. Liberal democracies, through the narrative of pluralism, are willing to co-opt opposition—even radical opposition—as long as it does not attack the very foundations of this system of thought: the inviolability of property. Conversely, non-state violence become an evil to be eliminated or at least mitigated.[43] The rise of neoliberalism in the 1970s and its accelerated pace in the 1990s has only reinforced this narrative, contributing to the gradual delegitimisation of radical social protests. The neoliberal moment also demarcated an important shift towards a new international individualist discourse on terrorism, which ultimately worked to discredit radical collectivist goals and national liberation struggles,[44] and establish a new moral order in which the right answer to state oppression is not collective struggles but individual dissidence. Following the events of 9/11 and similar attacks that occurred in Europe during the early twenty-first century, concerns regarding money laundering and terrorism financed through NGOs led to the implementation of robust financial controls and reports of risk management reporting by CSOs across the world. Violence and the defence of human rights became irreconcilable concepts in the vocabulary dominating within governments and NGOs. However, according to Anne Bordatto, a French engineer and environmental activist working with Guatemalan Indigenous communities since 2002:

> It is very difficult to keep making your claims in a pacifist tone when both the companies and your own government inflict so much violence against you. It is impossible. Nothing would have changed in Guatemala if they [Indigenous communities] would have resisted peacefully according to so-called international standards.[45]

While making funding and public support conditional on nonviolent resistance corresponds to current Western and international canons, it may inadvertently overlook the pressing local political context that renders nonviolent protests ineffective and pacificist rhetoric a weapon to suffocate social change.[46]

Another problematic issue in the Western selection of anti-extractivist movements is gender equality and representation. Not only did Western NGOs refrain from collaboration with Indigenous organisations that they considered to be misogynistic,[47] but they often prioritised movements that included women in their leadership positions. According to Anne Bordatto:

> The communities elect their own representatives, but NGOs come with other visions: they want more women, they want people who can talk outside [Guatemala]... and sometimes they think that there are individuals who are more representative to be heard at the international level than the community leaders themselves. [...] In most cases that I have participated in, most of the leaders were men because women decided to take care of the families

[43] Greenwood-Reeves (2023), p. 3.

[44] Slaughter (2018), p. 737.

[45] Personal Interview with Anne Bordatto, 12 September 2024, online.

[46] See the influential work of American anarchist Peter Gelderloos (2007) and, more recently, Malm (2021).

[47] Paredes Marín (2016), p. 59.

and the house. I think that sometimes we want to force things: sometimes women do not want to take part in these visible spaces or speak in public.[48]

Indeed, as part of a broader global movement to promote gender equality and women's empowerment, governments and NGOs have increasingly tied their aid agendas to feminist causes. While various funding requirements imposed by Global North donors on Global South beneficiaries, notably institutional capacity, financial accountability, and reporting standards, have been widely debated as potentially hindering the financing of projects that address local needs, requirements related to gender equality and gender quotas also frequently present significant challenges. Such demands by funders can present serious obstacles to organisations operating in cultural contexts where women have societal restrictions on their participation in civil society organisations, or in sectors where structural inequalities, such as access to education and the labour market, or cultural norms have led to the underrepresentation of women.

Finally, the selectivity of Western support is visible in the discrepancy between funding allocated to projects based on liberal frameworks of human rights and projects aimed at enhancing alternative economic development and the autonomy of Indigenous communities. One the one hand, Western donors contributed critical resources to Guatemalan NGOs for a variety of activities related to anti-extractivism: from research and reports on human rights violations and state violence, to the assessment of the environmental risks of different mining projects, to increasing awareness about the rights of Indigenous communities to local consultations, to supporting strategic litigation that challenged the legality of different megaprojects.

For instance, the Centro de Acción Legal-Ambiental y Social (CALAS), the most prominent Guatemalan legal organisation leading strategic litigation from 2000 to 2020, was funded by European religious foundations such as Trocaire (Irland), Pan Para el Mundo (Brot für die Welt, Germany), and Diakonia (Sweden), and by Scandinavian governments and Oxfam. With the support of these international donors, CALAS played a crucial role in developing legal strategies that determined the Guatemalan Constitutional Court to temporarily suspend various operations across the country until the government organised the required consultations with neighbouring Indigenous communities.[49] The Nim Ajpu Association of Maya Lawyers and Notaries, established in 2004 by a group of Mayan lawyers and legal rights experts, also offered free legal services to Maya communities, drawing on donations from European funders, including the European Commission. As with CALAS, their activities resulted in the temporary suspension of several mining licences, but also in the publication and dissemination of works on legal pluralism and the importance of Indigenous law and political organisation.[50] These examples

[48] Personal Interview with Anne Bordatto, 12 September 2024, online.

[49] For CALAS's legal strategies, see van de Sandt (2009); Spalding (2023a).

[50] For the activity of the Nim Ajpu Association, see https://nimajpu.org/ (accessed 22.12.2024).

are indicative of the importance of Western funding in supporting anti-extractivist discourses and strategic litigation.

While these cases were decisive for suspending some extractivist projects, they were however not based on customary Indigenous law, but on the above-mentioned 1989 ILO Convention No. 169. According to Ana Eugenia Paredes Marín, lecturer in politics at the Rafael Landívar University and former Madre Selva activist, using international law was probably the most pragmatic solution, but it did not intrinsically contribute to the autonomy of Indigenous communities. As the Guatemalan Constitution continues to place the exploitation of natural resources under the authority of the state, the government has the final say over the implementation of various economic projects, as well as the power to control local consultations. In Paredes Marín's view, legal and political activism should have been directed more substantially towards the acknowledgement of customary Indigenous law, because from the Indigenous perspective, the authority and jurisdiction to act does not arise from Guatemalan legislation. The authority arises from the inherent rights that come with being an Indigenous people.[51] Despite this critique, anti-mining legal cases have continued to underline Guatemala's obligation to respect ILO Convention No. 169 and enforce the right of Indigenous communities to free and informed consultations.[52]

In contrast, some projects funded by Western NGOs were at odds with the Indigenous cosmovision and contestation of capitalist development. One such example is the promotion of the 2011 UN Guiding Principles on Business and Human Rights (UNGPs) to Indigenous communities. For instance, in 2019, Oxfam tasked Ajkemab'—a Guatemalan NGO established in 2010 to provide legal, political and technical assistance to Mayan Ixil communities in Santa Cruz del Quiché—with the dissemination of the UNGPs and their importance in contexts related to violence against environmental activists. The programme included the production of flyers, audio-video materials and trainings in various communities.[53] The International Platform against Impunity sponsored similar activities in various regions of Guatemala in 2022 and 2023.[54] Drafted by John Ruggie and endorsed by the UN Human Rights Council in 2011, the UNGPs have attracted numerous critiques in terms of both their lack of efficiency and their Western ideological foundations.[55] The Principles are widely considered an instrument without teeth, as they place the burden of the duty to protect human rights on states and not on corporations. While Guatemalan activists often agree with this criticism, they have nonetheless embarked on projects aimed at promoting the UNGPs. For Rafael Herrarte from the International Platform against Impunity: Whether we like it or not, big business is present everywhere. It is important for local communities to know that the UNGPs exist and that

[51] Personal Interview with Ana Eugenia Paredes Marín, Guatemala City, 9.09.2023.

[52] For the different outcomes of various local consultations regarding mining projects and the role of the Guatemalan state in these processes, see Spalding (2023a).

[53] Ajkemab' (2020).

[54] Personal Interview with Rafael Herrarte, 15.02.2024 (online).

[55] See for instance Baars (2011); Khoury and Whyte (2017); Karp (2023).

the Guatemalan state has the duty to enforce legislation to protect human rights from corporate abuses. We live a world dominated by big corporations and in a country run by powerful economic elites. Sometimes is better to take a pragmatic approach and use any available instrument to at least limit the harm.[56]

This pragmatic approach is often paralleled by the need to conform to the political agendas of Western donors. According to Ajkemab' activists, the Oxfam funded project on the dissemination of the UNGPs was important for their NGO, because it offered the opportunity to continue their work on the rights of Indigenous communities and to also promote other international instruments, including ILO Convention No. 169 and the Escazú Agreement.[57] Nevertheless, the UNGPs are rooted, at best, in a Western tradition of "embedded liberalism" and, at worst, in a neoliberal framework that imposes certain ethical standards on business activities, but insulates them from sustained public intervention in the name of maximising shareholder value.[58] The ideological underpinnings of the UNGPs are thus Western-centric, accept capitalism as the "only game in town," and do not reflect Indigenous visions about rights and development in any way. While Guatemalan activists perceive the UNGPs as a useful (although insufficient) tool that can be used to (at least) raise awareness about corporate violence, from a decolonial perspective, their uncritical dissemination represents a new form of epistemic colonisation and neoliberal domination.

Relatedly, Western donors contributed far less to projects aimed at enhancing the economic autonomy of Indigenous communities based on their alternative models of life.[59] For instance, one major issue confronting Indigenous communities in Guatemala is the lack of access to electricity. This problem continues to be systemic, despite the recent construction of major hydroelectric dams by private firms on Indigenous lands across the country. These mega-hydroelectric projects produce significant amounts of electricity, most of which is however exported without providing local communities with the minimum consumption levels they need. Facing numerous political and legal barriers to accessing the electricity produced on their lands,[60] various Indigenous communities have mobilised to build small community hydroelectric facilities (*hidroeléctricas comunitarias*) and gain energy sovereignty. Such projects have been successful in Zona Reina (in the Quiché department, central-north Guatemala) with the establishment of four micro-dams from 2000 to

[56] Personal Interview with Rafael Herrarte, 15.02.2024, online.

[57] Personal Interview with Mario López, Guatemala City, 21.09.2023. The Escazú Agreement or the Regional Agreement on Access to Information, Public Participation and Justice in Environmental Matters in Latin America and the Caribbean was adopted in 2018 and entered into force in 2021. However, numerous Latin American states, included Guatemala, have yet to ratify it.

[58] As noted by David Jason Karp, "the sharp separation of the 'state duty to protect' from the 'corporate responsibility to respect' replicates the same divisions between the political and the economic, between the public and the private, between states and markets, which have characterized the neoliberal world order since the 1980s" (2023), p. 142.

[59] According to Brett (2015), p. 69: international support for projects aimed at achieving Indigenous economic autonomy and emancipation was almost inexistent in Guatemala.

[60] See Torres Hernández (2017).

2017, benefiting nine communities and around 9.000 people.[61] These projects were financially backed by the Canarian government through the NGO Siembra and by the Norwegian Church Aid and the Dan Church Aid. Other European governments, the European Commission and the UN did not support the initiative, despite various applications submitted to different calls for funding. According to José Cruz, who accompanied these projects on behalf of Madre Selva, it is unclear why funding was not granted: "the project was very ambitious, because it offered energy sovereignty and maybe this is why the European Union did not back it."[62] Mario Minera, from Madre Selva, also acknowledged that after 2021, when the communities in Zona Reina decided to build three further micro hidroeléctricas, funding from international organisations was again difficult to obtain. However, in 2022, Madre Selva found a partner in the Catalan Network for Energy Sovereignty, who helped draft an application for a low interest loan (3% per year) from the Spanish branch of the Ethic Bank, which they obtained in 2024. The application coincided with the election of the first progressive Guatemalan president since 1996, Bernardo Arévalo, who guaranteed part of the funds necessary to obtain the loan. According to Minera, these types of projects are most relevant for the autonomy of Indigenous communities: first, they do not require the deviation of rivers or wide deforestation, as do the larger hydroelectric dams; second, they ensure easier, lower cost, access to electricity than the private sector, which sets prices according to the global market.[63]

Despite these clear benefits, such projects receive less funding than those based on liberal frameworks of rights and capitalist economic principles. As underlined by Roddy Brett, international political and financial support for Indigenous movements and the Guatemalan state in the aftermath of the Peace Agreements was limited to a liberal narrative that combined the free market, civil and political rights, and identity rights. In contrast, "support for broader rights frameworks, such as a collective right to land or political and territorial autonomy, was excluded from international assistance, ultimately illustrating how aid would undercut true emancipation".[64] As we will see below, transnational litigation against multinational corporations accused of complicity in human rights violations and environmental destruction follow a similar pattern. The next section examines the lawsuits surrounding the operations of HudBay Minerals in the El Estor region and their limitations in ending extractivist structural violence and promoting a legal and social discourse based on Indigenous worldviews.

[61] Personal interview with Mario Minera, Guatemala City, 25.09.2024. For the history of the hidroeléctricas comunitarias in Zona Reina, see Colectivo MadreSelva (2014).

[62] Apud. Colectivo MadreSelva (2014), pp. 77–78.

[63] Personal interview with Mario Minera, Guatemala City, 25.09.2024.

[64] Brett (2015), p. 69.

4 The Limits of Transnational Litigation and the Westernised Translation of the Mayan World: The Case of the HudBay Lawsuits in Canada

Over the past seven decades, the history of El Estor—a small municipality on the shores of Lake Izabal in eastern Guatemala—has been marked by extreme violence connected to the mining operations located there, from forced evictions, protests against them to the subsequent governmental repression of the Indigenous communities. In the 1960s, the Canadian company INCO began to develop an open pit nickel mine in El Estor. To facilitate the extractivist project, Mayan Q'eqchi' communities residing in the area were forcibly displaced from their villages by state authorities. Despite opposition from these communities, both the Guatemalan and Canadian governments supported the project. Throughout the 1970s, Mayan protests against the mine were met with violent repression by the Guatemalan military, resulting in an estimated 3000 to 6000 fatalities.[65] In 1982, INCO shut down their operations due to a global decline in the market value of nickel. Subsequently, the evicted Indigenous groups began to return to their lands.

The project was, however, revived in 2004 when another Canadian company, Skye Resources, acquired the mine, now known as Fenix and operated by Skye's Guatemalan subsidiary, Compañia Guatemalteca de Níquel (CGN). Notably, Mayan Q'eqchi' communities were not consulted prior to the reopening of operations, as mandated by the ILO Convention No. 169.[66] Mayan Q'eqchi' communities protested once again, occupying various areas around the mine and organising road blockades. In response, armed police officers and members of the military once again conducted forced evictions in January 2007, during which numerous homes were destroyed. Eleven Mayan women from the small settlement of Lote Ocho were allegedly gang-raped by police, military and Fenix security personnel.[67] Both Skye Resources and CGN denied any involvement, stating that the rapes had not happened and declaring that a peaceful atmosphere was maintained during the evictions.[68]

Fenix underwent another ownership change in 2008 when HudBay Minerals purchased Skye Resources. In 2009, nickel prices experienced a surge, prompting the company to consider investing one billion Canadian dollars in the resumption of operations. This decision sparked local protests, leading to violent clashes between

---

[65] For the repression of anti-mining activists in the El Estor area, see for example Comisión para el Esclarecimiento Histórico (1999), pp. 674–679. See also Nolin and Stephens (2010).

[66] Despite its ratification, Guatemala has a long history of non-compliance with the Convention's provisions. For instance, in 2007, the ILO issued a report denouncing the absence of free and informed consultations with Mayan communities from El Estor regarding the opening of the Fenix mine. International Labour Organization (2007), paragraphs 48–51.

[67] *Margarita Caal Caal v. HudBay Minerals Inc.* (2011), available at https://chocversushudbay.com/legal-documents/ (accessed 24.03.2024).

[68] Imai et al. (2014), p. 288.

Indigenous groups, police and CGN security personnel on September 27, 2009. Tragically, community leader Adolfo Ich Chamón lost his life, while another protestor, German Chub Choc was left paralysed. Five security guards were also injured in the incident. Indigenous representatives accused CGN security personnel of participating in the violence; HudBay Minerals denied any involvement of its subsidiary and asserted that the crimes were the result of self-inflicted clashes between protestors.[69] It maintained this line even after the arrest of CGN's head of security for the murder of Ich in 2012.

In 2010 and 2011, the Toronto (Canada) law firm Klippensteins initiated three interrelated lawsuits in Canada on behalf of Mayan community members from El Estor.[70] Canada was selected as the jurisdiction for two reasons: First, the Guatemalan justice system is widely recognised as one of the most corrupt in the world.[71] Numerous complaints filed by Indigenous groups regarding their rights to land and to prior consultation concerning the utilisation of resources within their territories have often resulted in unfavourable verdicts or been subject to protracted delays. Consequently, the plaintiffs and their legal representatives argued that a lawsuit against CGN in Guatemalan courts was likely to encounter a similar outcome. Second, a trial in Guatemala would have focused specifically on CGN's possible liability without examining the responsibility of the parent company. A lawsuit in Canada was thus more appropriate to address the broader liability of transnational corporations for their operations aboard.[72] In their filings, the plaintiffs alleged negligence on the part of HudBay Minerals in failing to prevent the 2009 murder of Adolfo Ich and the severe injury of German Chub. Additionally, they accused mining security employees, the police and military personnel of committing gang rapes during the 2007 evictions. Amnesty International backed the cases and intervened as amicus curie on behalf of the victims.[73] Rights Action, a Canadian NGO, actively promoted the lawsuits to international audiences through public events and media campaigns. Since its establishment in 1995, Rights Action has engaged in extensive collaboration with Indigenous groups in Guatemala, and provided support to community struggles against mining projects in the El Estor area since 2004.[74]

---

[69] HudBay Minerals, HudBay Minerals Provides Update on CGN, 29 September 2009; available at https://hudbayminerals.com/investors/press-releases/press-release-details/2009/Hudbay-Minerals-Provides-Update-on-CGN/default.aspx (accessed 28.12.2024).

[70] *Angelica Choc v. HudBay Minerals Inc.* (2010)—Lawsuit regarding the murder of Adolfo Ich; *German Chub Choc v. HudBay Minerals Inc.* (2011)—Lawsuit regarding the shooting of German Chub; *Margarita Caal Caal v. HudBay Minerals Inc.* (2011)—Lawsuit regarding rapes in the community of Lote Ocho. For further details and legal documents, see https://chocversushudbay.com/legal-documents/ (accessed 24.03.2024).

[71] See for instance the World Justice Project's 2023 Rule of Law Index, available at https://worldjusticeproject.org/rule-of-law-index/global (accessed 11.12.2024).

[72] Imai et al. (2014), pp. 291–293.

[73] For details about Amnesty International's involvement, see www.amnesty.ca/legal-brief/angelica-choc-v-hudbay-minerals/ (accessed 24.12.2024).

[74] For the history of Rights Action, see https://rightsaction.org/who (accessed 24.12.2024).

The HudBay lawsuits reflect the importance of transnational cooperation in supporting corporate accountability initiatives. However, they also highlight the challenges and limitations of transnational civil litigation in dealing with corporate violence, as well as the difficulties involved in translating Indigenous anti-extractivist demands and their vocabulary of rights, the environment and development into legal terms and political Western discourses. From the outset, Klippensteins strategically selected the accusations to fit Canadian law. Consequently, the case did not focus on halting extractivist exploitation or protecting Indigenous populations' rights to land and cultural preservation. Instead, the law firm highlighted HudBay's "duty to care" and duty to prevent specific human rights violations, such as murder or rape, from being committed by its subsidiaries abroad. Klippensteins drew upon Canadian jurisprudence on the "duty to care": as all previous cases had referred to operations in Canada, the lawyers aimed to create a legal precedent and ensure the application of a "duty to care" outside Canadian territory. However, in public statements, Klippensteins underlined that the crimes in question were part of the longstanding history of violence against Indigenous resistance to mining projects in Guatemala and to Western models of development.[75] The firm also condemned the infringement of Indigenous communities' rights to free and informed consultation regarding the operation of the Fenix mine on their lands, although this aspect was not part of the legal complaint per se.[76]

In its defence, HudBay asserted that Canadian law did not impose a corporate "duty to care" on operations aboard. Consequently, the parent company could not be held liable for the actions of its subsidiaries in foreign countries. HudBay also contended that the lack of geographical proximity hindered the parent corporation from anticipating and preventing acts of violence against anti-mining protestors committed by Guatemalan state authorities or the subsidiary's personnel. Moreover, Guatemalan courts were deemed more appropriate to adjudicate the case, as Guatemala was the location of the alleged crimes and the residence of most witnesses.[77]

In 2013, the Ontario Superior Court of Justice dismissed the defence's argument and allowed the case to proceed to trial. The Court stated that Canadian legal precedent upheld a "duty to care" and imposed duties on companies to conduct risk assessments and establish clear parameters for the prevention of human rights violations.[78] Although previous cases had only addressed human rights violations

[75] The position espoused by Klippensteins's lawyers is described in Rachel Schmidt's documentary "Defensora" (2013), available at https://rightsaction.org/videos (accessed 25.12.2024).

[76] On 8 February, 2011, the Guatemalan Constitutional Court ruled that Mayan Q'egchi' communities had a valid claim to the contested land and ordered the Government of Guatemala to formally recognize the community's collective property rights. HudBav Minerals and the Guatemalan government disregarded this ruling.

[77] Imai et al. (2014), p. 298.

[78] Lexpert Business of Law, Ontario Superior Court Decision in Choc v. Hudbay Minerals paves way for defining responsibility of Canadian companies with foreign operations, 1 November 2013, available at https://www.lexpert.ca/archive/ontario-superior-court-decision-in-choc-v-hudbay-

committed in Canada, the same reasoning could apply to operations abroad. A subsequent trial had to evaluate the case on its merits and determine HudBay's involvement in the events and the extent to which extra-territorial "duty to care" applied.

Between 2011 and 2013, various Canadian NGOs, in particular Rights Action and Mining Injustice Solidarity Network (MISN), organised a series of events to garner public support for the lawsuits. In 2012, Mayan plaintiffs travelled to Canada to testify in court. In their view, the lawsuits empowered them to bring their anti-mining stances to Western attention. Wining was a secondary concern: being heard in Canadian courts was already important, since "other communities had not had the chance to get this far."[79] Rights Action and MISN also facilitated meetings between Guatemalan activists and Canadian Indigenous communities fighting against extractivist projects in their own territories. The two groups produced collective public statements and solidarity actions that condemned the role of the Canadian mining industry in displacing and harming Indigenous people in Guatemala, Canada and beyond. Canadian media covered the events.[80]

Such campaigns are crucial for ensuring that transnational litigations remain the subject of public discourse. However, since the majority of these law cases occur in Global North countries, NGOs often employ vocabularies that are familiar to Western audiences, but do not necessarily reflect the cultural and economic circumstances of the affected groups, particularly those of the Global South.[81] Rights Action adhered to a similar strategic communications pattern. For instance, its director, Grahame Russell, utilised James Cameron's blockbuster *Avatar* to discuss both Mayan culture and society and its resistance to extractivism:

> Like many resource extraction conflicts around the world, both historically and on-going today, this story of Canadian nickel companies trying to operate a mine in the Qeqchi territories of eastern Guatemala (starting with INCO in the 1960s and 70s, continuing with Skye Resources and HudBay after 2004) is like the documentary version of the Avatar movie. In Avatar, a powerful mining company brings a battalion of heavily armed men to a remote, far off place, uses extreme violence to forcibly remove the local indigenous people from their ancestral and sacred homelands, so as to get at a mineral that – once mined and processed – will sell for gargantuan profits, somewhere far away. In general terms, this is the story of nickel companies in Guatemala. Indeed, it is the story of many resource extraction struggles around the world, today and going back centuries.[82]

While such a discourse may be effective in triggering Western empathy, it is a crude rendering of Mayan society and cosmovision. Avatar is a Western fantasy, narrated in the language of American blockbusters. As Elise Marubbio observed, the movie

---

minerals-paves-way-for-defining-responsibility-of-canadian-companies-with-foreign-operations/348931 (accessed 25.12.2024)

[79] German Chub, quoted in "Defensora". Available at https://rightsaction.org/videos (accessed 25.11.2024).

[80] See for example Glynn (2013).

[81] Gill (2009), pp. 667–680.

[82] Russel (2012).

> weaves together antimilitary imperialism, environmentalism, pro-Nativism and Indigenous sovereignty into a deceptively familiar critique of western manifest destiny and settler nations' relationships with Indigenous people. [...] The film remains trapped within its own formula, relying heavily on the standard Western generic tropes rather than a truly pro-Native or Native film focus on the results of imperialism on the earth and her peoples.[83]

In the end, Avatar promotes an "imperialist nostalgia for ecologically pure Natives whose subsistence lifestyle and spiritual connection to nature marks them as noble, primitive and exotic."[84] These critiques have also resonated with Guatemalan activists who have seen the film. For instance, during an interview in 2023, a Mayan lawyer responded with amusement when asked about the parallels between the film and their own culture:

> Well, in the end it's a reproduction of Western stereotypes about us, Indigenous people in general. They probably think we still live in the trees and other similar stereotypes. There are some common aspects, such as the respect that we have for nature. But it is simplistic, because we don't live like that. Like in *Avengers*, where there is this African population – also a sort of Indigenous group – but it's not based on real African realities. To be honest, I don't think that there is any movie – except for documentaries, but people do not watch documentaries – that really shows how we live: there is a lot folklorisation and fiction.[85]

In addition to the potential exoticisation of the Indigenous world, it is important to note that in *Avatar*, a Western soldier sacrifices himself for the survival of the Indigenous world. This narrative falls into the category of white saviourism,[86] wherein Indigenous groups are depicted as requiring Western assistance and martyrdom to overcome capitalist extractivism. Similarly, in his depiction of Klippensteins, Russell drew inspiration from John Grisham's best-selling legal thrillers[87] that portray idealistic white lawyers and journalists working pro bono to defend poor, marginalised (often black) individuals and communities against repressive state authorities or corporations.[88] While using American blockbusters and bestsellers to promote the Mayan cause might resonate with Western audiences, it also oversimplifies complex realities and reinforces a narrative of Indigenous dependency on Western support. As Makau Mutua has argued in his critique of Global North struggles for human rights, Western NGOs often provide a Eurocentric construct for the reconstitution of non-Western societies and peoples with a set of culturally biased norms and practices. Such narratives revitalise an international hierarchy of race and colour and can privilege white people as models and saviours of racialised subjects as victims/savages.[89] Despite the problems underlying its campaign, Rights Action remained one of the very few NGOs to collaborate with anti-mining activists

83 Marrubio (2015), p. 171.

84 Ibid.

85 Personal Interview with Adriana Sunin, Guatemala City, 21.09.2023.

86 On "white saviorism" in the Global South, see for instance Mathers (2022).

87 Russel (2012).

88 One such famous novel was *A Time to Kill* (1989), whose 1996 screen adaptation stared Samuel L. Jackson and Matthew McConaughey.

89 Mutua (2002).

in El Estor. As discussed in the previous section, other Western NGOs did not support the cause due to the fact the community's protests had escalated into attacks on police officials and the mine's security personnel.

Ultimately, the impact of the Canadian lawsuits and the ensuing public campaigns was ambiguous. The Ontario Superior Court of Justice opened Canadian jurisdictions to transnational litigations regarding Canadian companies' omission of the "duty to care" and the obligation to prevent their subsidiaries' involvement in gross human rights violations abroad. This decision established a legal precedent that could potentially transform Canadian customary law.[90] However, the Ontario court did not address the structural problems generated by extractivism, leaving unresolved fundamental political issues such as the precarious socio-economic and environmental conditions for Indigenous people in Guatemala, the decades-long dispute over land rights, and the inequalities that the mining industry often creates between the Global North and the Global South. As critical scholarship on criminal and civil litigation concerning corporate accountability has underlined, such trials generally have a limited effect in terms of rethinking and adjusting the structural inequalities of capitalism, extractivism, and of neoliberalism in particular. While they represent a genuine response to oppression, they continue to legitimise capitalist interests and narrate corporate violence as an exceptional act by a limited number of villainous companies.[91]

In connection to the previous point, in 2011 (as the law suits were winding their way through the Canadian court system), HudBay sold Fenix to Solway Investment Group—a company underwritten by Russian capital, headquartered in Switzerland. Violence surrounding mining operations continued in El Estor up to the writing of this chapter in 2024. The reasons for the sale remain unclear. According to Klippensteins, "the sale was prompted in part by the severe human rights issues at HudBay's Fenix Project that dogged the company at every turn."[92] While the strong resistance of El Estor Mayan Q'eqchi' communities, including the systematic reoccupation of land and the blockade of roads and access points to the mine may also have played a role, further research is needed to substantiate this claim.

As the lawsuits against HudBay proceeded despite the sale of the company, other Canadian corporations continued their operations in Guatemala, with similar effects to those in the El Estor region.[93] In 2014, the Ontario Superior Court of Justice's previous decision provided the impetus for another complaint: Seven Guatemalan citizens filed a lawsuit against Tahoe Resources, seeking damages for injuries

[90] For the assessment of strategic litigation see Jeßberger and Steinl (2022); Mégret (2023).

[91] Baars (2019); Mehta (2024). See also Juan Pablo Bohoslavsky's and Juan Cruz Goñi's chapter in this book.

[92] Declaration of Klippensteins Barristers & Solicitors, 10.11.2011, available at https://www.globenewswire.com/news-release/2011/08/10/1345584/0/en/Ontario-Lawsuits-Against-HudBay-Regarding-Alleged-Human-Rights-Abuse-Continue-Despite-Sale-of-Fenix-Project.html (accessed 7.11.2024).

[93] See for instance the conflicts generated by Tahoe's operations in San Rafael Las Flores, or by Radius Gold in La Puya—both near Guatemala City—from 2011 onwards.

sustained during a shooting outside the company's Escobal silver mine in Sal Rafael Las Flores, near Guatemala City, in April 2013. In January 2017, the British Columbia Court of Appeal ruled that Canada courts had sufficient jurisdiction to proceed with the case, as a trial in Guatemala was considered futile. Although Tahoe Resources appealed the decision, the Supreme Court of Canada declined to hear the case, clearing the way for a trial in Canada. In February 2019, Pan American Silver acquired Tahoe Resources and, in July 2019, reached a settlement with the Guatemalan plaintiffs. The company publicly apologised to the victims and the community, but did not accept any legal responsibility. Tahoe Resources also stated that "the resolution of the lawsuit does not impede in any way the ability of the victims to exercise their rights of protest related to the mine in the future."[94] Yet, operations continued. According to Guatemalan activists who supported the anti-mining resistance in San Rafael Las Flores, the case had little impact in Guatemala. Moreover, it did not put a stop to the company's efforts to evade free and informed consultations regarding its operations on Indigenous lands.[95]

In October 2024, HudBay also opted to settle and pay compensation. As is customary in settled civil cases, the company refrained from acknowledging any legal responsibility. The specific terms of the agreement including the compensation amount also remain undisclosed.[96] Hudbay's decision to settle reveals that legal and public pressure can constraint companies to at least pay reparations in order to mitigate further legal and reputational risk. Notably, both Klippensteins and Rights Action successfully mobilised activists, researchers and journalists to support and publicise the Mayan anti-mining protests.

However, for strategic communication purposes, the NGO translated the plight of Mayan communities for Western audiences through the oversimplified *Avatar* narrative, a blockbuster that epitomises the very capitalism that Indigenous communities are struggling to resist. Such an account might lead to misunderstandings among Western audiences about the Indigenous cosmovision and even to an auto-colonisation of the Indigenous vocabulary in order to conform to Western (mis) perceptions. Furthermore, once the legal settlement was finalised, both Klippensteins and Rights Action severely adjusted their tone. During the early years of the litigation (2011–2013), they framed their campaign in terms of confronting corporate impunity and immunity, as well as fighting global inequality imposed by multinational corporations.[97] In contrast, in 2024, both the law firm and the NGO announced that the "parties have agreed to a quiet period following settlement, to allow for everyone, and in particular the plaintiffs, to focus on getting on with their lives."[98]

[94] See Business & Human Rights Resource Centre, "Tahoe Resources Law Suit (Guatemala), available at https://www.business-humanrights.org/en/latest-news/tahoe-resources-lawsuit-re-guatemala/ (accessed 11.04.2024).

[95] Personal Interview with Julio Gonzalez, Guatemala City, 29.09.2023; personal Interview with Ana Eugenia Paredes, Guatemala City, 9.09.2023.

[96] Mach (2024).

[97] Russel (2012).

[98] See https://rightsaction.org/ (accessed 30.10.2024).

While plaintiffs are indeed entitled to decide whether to accept or reject a settlement (especially considering that financial compensation often serves as an important aid in addressing acute economic challenges faced by impoverished societies), the shift in the Western discourse from assertive narratives of corporate accountability to "a quiet period" and the acceptance of a secret settlement only serves to support corporate interests, as noted by HudBay's vice president of investor relations: "We are thankful that this settlement finally brings these matters to a close, and we note the settlement was reached without any admission of liability."[99] Such legal settlements also enforce the idea of "good" and "responsible" corporations, despite their systematic record of human rights violations.

5 Conclusion

This chapter examined the values and limitations of transnational advocacy for corporate accountability in post-civil war Guatemala. While demonstrating the crucial role of transnational Western support for the very survival of anti-extractivist, human rights and environmental activism in Guatemala, the chapter also noted a series of limitations to this assistance. These limitations stem from Western militantism's embeddness in a dominant liberal vocabulary that posits the importance of civil and political rights, while marginalising the relevance of economic rights and of alternative economic projects that challenge not only extractivist development, but the liberal capitalist system itself. This ideological stance has led to the development of criteria that severely limits the provision of transnational support for Guatemalan social movements: conditioning Western aid on pacifist and non-violent resistance and gender representativity; promoting Western, liberal views on human rights and economics at the expense of sustaining Indigenous world visions; providing funding only to projects embedded in liberal economic thinking rather than in practices of reciprocity and solidarity, community-level action and self-management as an alternative to capitalist relations of production and distribution. Moreover, in their pursuit of Western public support for Indigenous demands, NGOs from the Global North often constructed communication strategies that oversimplified and depoliticised economic conflicts unfolding in Guatemala. They filtered Indigenous claims through both a Western lens and Western legislation, and even through the narratives of Western blockbusters that epitomise the very capitalism against Indigenous communities in Guatemala have fought since 1996.

These shortcomings demand a more responsible Global North activism that challenges not only the current international economic order and the status-quo of corporate impunity, but also Western cultural hegemony. Even if Indigenous worldviews and alternative economic development continue to be either ignored or seen at best as utopian visions (since they are nearly impossible to operationalise and hard to

[99] Quoted by Mach (2024).

envisage as a programme for government in the context of underdevelopment), they are considered by a number of researchers and activists as a valuable contribution to global development theories, as it "breaks the northern grip on development theory and the dominant approach to ecology in the shape of a vague sustainable development strategy."[100] A more attentive analysis of the potential of Indigenous alternative development projects, as well a more careful focus on Indigenous vocabularies could provide a more inclusive platform for political contestations and alternative economic development, such as envisioned in the Global South.

References

Acosta E (2018) Living well from an Ecuadorian perspective: philosophies without philosophers actions without theories. In: Munck R, Wise RD (eds) Reframing Latin American development. Routledge, London

Adams RN (2005) The evolution of racism in Guatemala: hegemony, science, and antihegemony. Hist Anthropol Annu 1:132–180. https://doi.org/10.1353/haa.0.0011

Ajkemab' (2020) Diseño de campaña para la promoción de los principios rectores de Naciones Unidas sobre empresas y derechos humanos en contextos de pueblos indígenas. Ajkemab, Santa Cruz del Quiché

Altman P (2020) The Commons as colonisation: the well-intentioned appropriation of Buen Vivir. Bull Latin Am Res 39(1):83–89

Baars G (2011) "Reform or revolution"? Polanyian versus Marxian perspectives on the regulation of the economic. North Ireland Leg Q 62(4):415–431

Baars G (2019) The corporation, law and capitalism. A radical perspective on the role of law. Brill, Leiden

Basualdo V, Quintana TO, Varsky C (2015) The cases of Ford and Mercedes Benz. In: Verbitsky H, Bohoslavsky JP (eds) The economic accomplices of the Argentine dictatorship: outstanding debts. Cambridge University Press, Cambridge, pp 159–173

Batz G (2022) La Cuarta Invasión. Historias y resistencia del Pueblo Ixil, y su lucha contra la Hidroeléctrica Palo Viejo en Cotzal, Quiché, Guatemala. Guatemala. Instituto Avancso

Batz G (2023) Extractive industries in Guatemala. Historic Maya resistance, ovements. Harvard Review of Latin America (online) https://revista.drclas.harvard.edu/extractive-industries-in-guatemala-historic-maya-resistance-movements/

Bieri F (2013) From blood diamonds to the Kimberley process: how NGOs cleaned up the global diamond industry. Routledge, New York

Bosi L, Malthaner S (2015) Political violence. In: della Porta D, Diani M (eds) Oxford handbook of social movements. Oxford University Press, Oxford, pp 439–451

Brett R (2015) The Janus face of international activism and Guatemala's Indigenous people. In: de Wall A et al (eds) Advocacy in conflict. Critical perspectives on transnational activism. Zed Books, London, pp 68–94

Bueckert M (2019) Boycotts and revolution: debating the legitimacy of the African National Congress in the Canadian anti-apartheid movement, 1969–94. Radic Hist Rev 134:96–115

Casáus Arzú M (2008) Genocidio: ¿la máxima expresión del racismo en Guatemala? F&G Editores, Guatemala

Chenoweth E, Stephan MJ (2008) Why civil resistance works: the strategic logic of nonviolent conflict. Int Secur 33(1):7–44

[100] Munck (2021), p. 184.

Colectivo MadreSelva (2014) El camino de la luz. Historias del proyecto comunitario de energía eléctrica "Luz de los Heroes y Martires de la Resistencia" Uspantan, Zona Reina, Quiche, Guatemala. Colectivo MadreSelva, Guatemala

Comisión para el Esclarecimiento Histórico (1999) Guatemala: Memory of Silence, available at http://www.aaas.org/sites/default/files/migrate/uploads/mos_en.pdf

Dale JG (2011) Free Burma: transnational legal action and corporate accountability. University of Minnesota Press, Minneapolis

de Sousa BS (2005) Beyond neoliberal governance: the World Social Forum as subaltern cosmopolitan politics and legality. In: Boaventura de Sousa S, Rodriguez-Garavito C (eds) Law and globalisation from below. Cambridge University Press, Cambridge, pp 29–64

de Sousa Santos BS (2015) Epistemologies of the South: justice against epistemicide. Routledge, London

de Waal et al (2015) Advocacy in conflict. Critical perspectives on transnational activism. Zed Books, London

della Porta D (2018) Radicalization: a relational perspective. Annu Rev Polit Sci 21(1):461–474

Dezalay Y, Garth B (2012) Lawyers and the construction of transnational justice. Routledge, New York

Dollard J, Miller NE, Doob LW, Mowrer OH, Sears RR (1939) Frustration and aggression. Yale University Press

Finnemore M, Sikkink K (1998) International norm dynamics and political change. Int Organ 52(4):887–917

Freeman D (2024) Sovereignty, human rights and the regulation of transnational corporations: a critical spatial analysis of civil society proposals for a binding treaty. Globalizations 21(1):1–19

Gelderloos P (2007) How nonviolence protects the state. South End Press, Cambridge

Gill L (2009) The limits of solidarity: labor and transnational organizing against Coca-Cola. Am Ethnol 36(4):667–680

Glynn T (2013) Angelica Choc's fight is our fight too: Mayan widow suing mining company in Canada stands with Wabanaki shale gas resisters. NB Media Co-op, 5th November, available at https://nbmediacoop.org/2013/11/05/angelica-chocs-fight-is-our-fight-too-mayan-widow-suing-mining-company-in-canada-stands-with-wabanaki-shale-gas-resisters/ (accessed 25.03.2024)

Greenwood-Reeves J (2023) Justifying violent protest. Law and morality in democratic states. Routledge, London

Grosescu R (2019) Transnational advocacy networks and corporate accountability for gross human rights violations in Argentina and Colombia. Global Soc 33(3):400–418

Gurr TR (1970) Why men rebel. Princeton University Press, Princeton

Haas PM (1992) Introduction: epistemic communities and international policy coordination. Int Organ 46(1):1–35

Imai S, Mehranvar L, Sander J (2014) Access to justice and corporate accountability: a legal case study of HudBay in Guatemala. Can J Dev Stud 35(2):285–303

Iñigo M (2023) Conversation with Aura Cumes on Maya epistemology, postcolonial theory and the struggle for identity. Re-visiones 7 (2017), available at http://www.re-visiones.net/index.php/RE-VISIONES/article/view/239/431

International Labour Organization (2007) Report of the committee set up to examine the representation alleging non-observance by Guatemala of the Indigenous and Tribal Peoples Convention, 1989 (No. 169), available at http://www.ilo.org/dyn/normlex/en/f?p=1000:50012:0::NO:50012:P50012_COMPLAINT_PROCEDURE_ID,P50012_LANG_CODE:2507321,en:NO

IWGIA (2024) The Indigenous World 2024: Guatemala. Available at https://iwgia.org/en/guatemala/5384-iw-2024-guatemala.html

Jeßberger F, Steinl L (2022) Strategic litigation in international criminal justice. J Int Crim Justice 20:379–401

Karp DJ (2023) Business and human rights in a changing world order: beyond the ethics of disembedded liberalism. Bus Hum Rights J 8(2):135–150

Keck ME, Sikkink K (1998) Activists beyond borders. Advocacy networks in international politics. Cornell University Press, Ithaca
Khoury S, Whyte D (2017) Corporate human rights violations. Global prospects for legal action. Routledge, London
Mach J (2024) Hudbay minerals settles lawsuit alleging human rights abuses in Guatemala. Canadian Lawyer, 7 October, available at www.canadianlawyermag.com/practice-areas/litigation/hudbay-minerals-settles-lawsuits-alleging-human-rights-abuses-in-guatemala/388983
MacNeill T (2020) Indigenous cultures and sustainable development in Latin America. Palgrave Macmillan, London
Malm A (2021) How to blow up a pipeline. Verso Books, London
Marrubio EM (2015) Decolonizing the Western: a revisionist analysis of Avatar with a twist. In: Paryz M, Leo JR (eds) The post-2000 film western: contexts, transnationality, hybridity. Palgrave Macmillan, London, pp 167–190
Mathers K (2022) White saviorism and popular culture: imagined Africa as a space for American salvation. Routledge, New York
Mégret F (2023) Immunities of foreign officials for international crimes: the dilemmas of strategic litigation. J Hum Rights Pract 15(1):66–83
Mehta K (2024) Strategic litigation and corporate complicity in crimes under international law: a TWAIL analysis. Routledge, New York
Munck R (2006) Global civil society. Royal road or slippery path? Voluntas: Int J Volunt Nonprofit Organ 17(4):325–332
Munck R (2021) Rethinking development. Marxist perspectives. Palgrave Macmillan, London
Mutua MW (2002) Human rights: a political and cultural critique. University of Pennsylvania Press, Philadelphia
Nolin C, Stephens Q (2010) "We have to protect the investors": "Development" & Canadian mining companies in Guatemala. J Rural Commun Dev 5(3):37–70
Paredes Marín AE (2016) Industria minera y represión en Guatemala. Los casos del Comité en Defensa de la Vida y la Paz de San Rafael Las Flores y La Resistencia Pacífica La Puya, MA Thesis Instituto Mora. Mexico City
Payne LA, Pereira G, Bernal-Bermúdez L (2020) Transitional justice and corporate accountability from below: deploying Archimedes' lever. Cambridge University Press, Cambridge
Pellow DN (2007) Resisting global toxics: transnational movements for environmental justice. MIT Press, Boston
Pereira G, Payne LA, Bernal-Bermúdez L (2022) Justice from below: corporate accountability in Argentina. Int J Hum Rights 26(8):1418–1454
Russel G (2012) Guatemala-Canada: clashing world views at a crossroads. Upside down world 19 December, available at https://upsidedownworld.org/archives/guatemala/guatemala-canada-clashing-world-views-at-a-crossroads/ (accessed 24.03.2024)
Saage-Maaß M et al (2021) Transnational legal activism in global value chains: the Ali enterprise fire and the struggle for justice. Springer, London
Seay L (2015) Conflict minerals in Congo: the consequences of oversimplification. In: de Wall A et al (eds) Advocacy in conflict. Critical perspectives on transnational activism. Zed Books, London, pp 115–141
Shipton L (2017) Canada's mining industry in Guatemala and the right to health of Indigenous peoples. Health Hum Rights J:1–20
Sibrián A, van der Borgh C (2014) La Criminalidad de los Derechos: La Resistencia a la Mina Marlin. Oñati Socio-Legal Series 4(1):63–84
Sieder R (1997) Reframing citizenship: Indigenous rights, local power and the peace process in Guatemala. Accord: Int Rev Peace Initiat 2:344–393
Sieder R (2017) Indigenous sovereignties in Guatemala: between criminalization and revitalization. NACLA Rep Am 49(3):370–372. https://doi.org/10.1080/10714839.2017.1373971
Slaughter JR (2018) Hijacking human rights: neoliberalism, the new historiography, and the end of the Third World. Hum Rights Q 40(4):735–775

Spalding RJ (2023) Breaking grounds. From extraction booms to mining bans in Latin America. Oxford University Press, Oxford
Spalding RJ (2023a) The politics of implementation: social movements and mining policy implementation in Guatemala. Extract Ind Soc 13:1–11
Sveinsdóttir AG, Aguilar-Støen M, Bull B (2021) Resistance, repression and elite dynamics: unpacking violence in the Guatemalan mining sector. Geoforum 118:117–129
Torres Hernández SA (2017) Luchas por la defensa del territorio y los bienes naturales. Represión, Criminalización y judicialización en el Norte de Huehuetenango (2006-2016)
UDEFEGUA (2021) Situación de personas, organizaciones y comunidades defensoras de derechos humanos. UDEFEGUA, Guatemala City
Van de Sandt J (2009) Mining conflicts and Indigenous peoples in Guatemala. Cordaid, The Hague
Willems L (2010) Mining and Indigenous peoples in Guatemala: the local relevance of human rights, MA thesis, University of Ghent
Yagenova SV (2012) La Industria Extractiva En Guatemala: Políticas Públicas, Derechos Humanos, y Procesos De Resistencia Popular En El Período 2003-2011. FLACSO, Guatemala City
Yagenova SV (2016) Guatemala: El Estado y procesos de resistencia popular frente a la industria extractiva 2003–2013. In: Cisneros P (ed) Política minera y sociedad civil en América Latina. Instituto de Altos Estudios Nacionales, Quito, pp 95–146
Yagenova SV et al (2020) Casos de gestión de seguridad ambiental y humana, relacionadas con la industria minera de metales en las cuencas de los Ríos Cuilco, Motagua, Los Esclavos, y Ostúa-Guija, en la República de Guatemala. Madre Selva, Guatemala City

Raluca Grosescu is a Lecturer in Politics at the National University of Political Science and Public Administration, Bucharest, where she leads the ERC-Consolidator Project "Transnational Advocacy Networks and Corporate Accountability for Major International Crimes." Her work focuses on the history of international criminal law, memory politics and corporate accountability. Her latest publications include the monograph *Justice and Memory after Dictatorship: Latin America, Central Eastern Europe and the Fragmentation of International Criminal Law* (Oxford University Press in 2024) and the co-edited volume *Socialism and International Law. The Cold War and its Legacies* (Oxford University Press in 2024).

Transnational Campaigns Against Corporate Impunity

The Transnationalisation of Civil Society in East Asia's War Redress Movement

Timothy Webster

Abstract Transnational human rights litigation is commonly associated with developments in Europe and the Americas during the 1990s. But Asian actors have used legal mobilisation to hold corporate actors to account since at least the 1970s. This chapter charts the first usages of transnational litigation in East Asia's Word War II redress movement, akin to the Holocaust Restitution movement of the West. Korean and Chinese forced labourers liaised with Japanese attorneys, activists and academics to press compensation claims against Japanese corporations for wartime human rights abuses in Tokyo. Legal mobilisation did not succeed in the traditional sense. Yet, the formation of epistemic communities (activists, attorneys, academics) across East Asia reflected new modalities of transnational cooperation that produced settlement agreements in the 1990s and 2000s that resolved some of the plaintiffs' demands.

1 Introduction

For decades, victims of World War II have demanded accountability from the actors who tortured, raped, maimed and imprisoned them. In the West, victims worked with civil society groups, state actors, international institutions, and human rights lawyers to press claims against Swiss banks, German corporations, and Austrian art

I appreciate the perceptive feedback of John Dale, Raluca Grosescu, and other participants of the *Conference on Corporate Accountability for Gross Human Rights Abuses*, National University of Political Science and Public Administration, Bucharest, Romania, May 25, 2023.

T. Webster (✉)
Faculty Research and Development, Western New England University, Springfield, MA, USA
e-mail: timothy.webster@law.wne.edu

R. Grosescu, J. G. Dale (eds.), *Corporate Accountability for Human Rights Violations*, Interdisciplinary Studies in Human Rights 16,
https://doi.org/10.1007/978-3-032-05569-9_6

museums.[1] Ultimately, these efforts yielded state-sponsored remedial mechanisms, from Germany's Remembrance Fund to the Zurich Claims Resolution Tribunal.

In East Asia, the accountability movement differs. After a small wave of redress activism in the 1970s, a broader effort reemerged in the early 1990s. Chinese scholars, Korean activists, and Japanese lawyers knit together a dense web of connections to demand compensation from the Japanese actors, state and corporate. These efforts continue in various forms to the present (2024).[2]

Transnational legal mobilisation has played a critical role in Asia's redress movement, with some 200 civil lawsuits filed in half a dozen jurisdictions.[3] As the only liberal democracy in the region during the relevant period (1972-present), Japan served as the epicentre of this social-legal campaign until 2010s. But Japanese courts rarely ordered damages, and firm opposition from the Japanese government, especially under Prime Minister Abe Shinzo, pushed the movement elsewhere. A Korean wave of lawsuits following favourable verdicts from its Supreme Court (2012, 2018) suggests continued court involvement in East Asia's war redress movement.[4]

While these lawsuits have attracted sustained media attention and intermittent legal analysis, their sociology remains obscure. Like other socially complex activities, transnational litigation does not just "happen." Attorneys, academics, and activists assist plaintiffs, often out of their own pocket. Transnational litigation hinges upon domestic mobilisation within each pair of states (Japan and China, Japan and Korea). The ensuing interactions will determine whether the Japanese will form the necessary "ligatures of trust" with Asian forced labourers.[5]

This chapter contributes to a growing body of literature that explains how non-Western actors mobilise across borders, with a special focus on corporate

---

[1] Bradfield (1998) describes the origins, functions, and personnel of this group, tasked with investigating "dormant accounts of victims of Nazi persecution in Swiss banks." Ibid. at 231.

[2] In March 2023, the South Korean government, under conservative President Yoon Suk-yeol, announced the creation of a foundation to pay Korean forced labourers, ostensibly to cover the damages award ordered by the South Korean Supreme Court against Mitsubishi and Nippon Steel-Sumitomo. The Japanese companies, with the backing of the conservative Japanese government, refused to pay the judgments that were handed down in late 2018. Because the Korean foundation will source funds from Korean (not Japanese) companies, most Koreans oppose the scheme, including two of the plaintiffs. In this way, the current scheme repeats a feature often criticised in prior schemes: that the money is not coming from the parties most liable for the harm but from well-meaning bystanders. Qiu (2013) criticises the 1995 Asian Women's Fund, which funnelled money from private Japanese citizens to a fund established by the Japanese government to pay compensation to former "comfort women" as an empty gesture.

[3] I approximate 102 (Japan), 56 (South Korea), 48 cases (United States), 6 (China), 2 (Netherlands), and 1 (Philippines).

[4] Since 2012, South Korean courts have delivered a series of verdicts against Japan and Japanese corporations that reconfigure the issue of wartime responsibility. Webster (2022b).

[5] "Asian plaintiffs" refer to litigants from four Asian countries: China, Taiwan, Philippines and South Korea. Asia is a vast landmass comprising most of humanity's 8 billion people, and Japan, of course, is part of Asia. But I differentiate Japanese actors from Asian actors due to the fact that Japan conducted inhumanities across Asia. Finally, I use Korean to mean *South* Korean.

accountability processes.[6] Most work on transnational social movements focuses on developments in the West. Theories of transnational movements cannot, however, exclude Asia. This is not to discount the models of transnational activism—spirals, boomerangs, two-level games, and so on. But if models begin from the premise of a preordained troupe of transnational actors or "global civil society," they do not explain the coalescence of such groups *ab initio*.[7] Tilly and Tarrow note the importance of international institutions in forming transnational coalitions; transnational activists flourish in the "coral reefs" of the European Union, United Nations, and World Trade Organisation.[8]

But what about regions far from the cosmopolitan hubs of Brussels, Geneva, or New York? What if language barriers, cultural differences, geographical distance, geopolitical inequalities, procedural barriers or restrictions on civil society limit recourse to such institutions? Put plainly, how do actors mobilise transnationally in *unintegrated* areas? They rely on a combination of expertise, ideology, and resources to overcome historical injustices and structural failures. To unpack these processes, the chapter focuses on two case studies of transnational litigation, *Geng Zhun vs. Kajima* and *Park Chang-hwan v Mitsubishi*, which are examined in the broader context of the Asian transnational redress movement.

2 Bridges and Abutments: East Asian Mobilisation

This paper begins from the ground up, providing a framework by which to understand transnational mobilisation in the contested issue of war redress. Three distinct phases apply to cases from East Asia: domestic mobilisation within Japan and the other Asian state, investigation by Japanese attorneys in the Asian state, and filing of litigation in Japan.

2.1 Mobilisation

First, grassroots groups mobilise domestically. While political opportunity structures vary from one state to the next, the uniting of citizens towards a common cause generates all social movements. That does not mean that mobilisation is uniform across jurisdictions. It is more difficult to mobilise in authoritarian regimes, which do not protect the rights of assembly, association or free speech to the same extent

[6] *See, e.g.*, Kim (2024) (arguing that early success in a movement's trajectory may hamper its ability to win redress in transnational contexts); Arrington (2016) (describing how transnational litigation in Japan and Korea, in concert with other tactics, serves as a "powerful tool for mobilizing third-party supporters and using them to gain leverage over decision makers").

[7] Tilley and Tarrow (2015).

[8] Ibid.

as liberal democracies. Repertoires of contention—demonstrations, strikes, occupations, and so on—might attract the regime's attention, surveillance, threats, violence or other discouragement. In politically restrictive environments, protest activities might be limited to "safe spaces" like college campuses, professional associations, or private residences. A couple of examples reveal the political delicacy of war redress in repressive regimes: Taiwan in the 1970s and China in the 1980s. Both the Kuomintang (KMT) in Taiwan and the Chinese Communist Party (CCP) in China looked askance at war redress mobilisation within their respective territories. Their ambivalence contrasts with the relative ease with which Japanese actors mobilised and confronted their government with redress claims.

With Taiwan's 1971 ouster from the United Nations and severance of diplomatic ties with longstanding allies, the KMT encouraged nationalistic protests against external actors, especially Japan.[9] College campuses, such as National Taiwan University, hosted protests. Yet, when students and professors demanded social and political reform from the KMT, party elites quickly shut down opportunities to protest.[10] Sensing an opportunity in the shifting terrain, Taiwanese veterans began to mobilise. Specifically, veterans who served Japan—*against* the KMT and CCP during World War II—gathered in central Taiwan. They sought the same benefits that Japanese law provided to veterans with Japanese nationality. Needless to say, many Taiwanese veterans experienced decades of marginalisation and abuse in a state run by the "victorious" KMT—their wartime enemy. While their claims targeted Japan and thus provided a potential escape valve to domestic political actors, KMT authorities still rejected their application to form a grassroots group. This did not deter the veterans from meeting, clarifying their demands, and pressuring the Taiwanese and Japanese governments. But it impeded the group's realisation of those demands.

In the liberalising China of the 1980s, as explored more fully below, a Chinese soldier sought war redress. Geng Zhun served as a captain in the KMT Army but was captured by Japanese forces and trafficked to northern Japan where he performed forced labour in a Japanese mine. Decades later, with the help of Japanese attorneys and activists, Geng began a movement to demand compensation from Kajima, the Japanese mining company. He founded China's first war redress group, the Hanaoka Victims Association, during a brief "warming" in China's political liberalisation. But when he tried to register his group, Chinese authorities rejected his application, suspicious that *any* group mobilising at the time of the Tiananmen Massacre (June 4, 1989) constituted cause for concern. In 1995, Geng became the first of hundreds of Chinese citizens to file war redress lawsuits in Japan, overcoming the barriers that the P.R.C. government erected against him, his fellow victims, and other Chinese.

In Japan, war redress mobilisation took several forms: vanguard groups, rearguard groups, and lawyers' groups. These groups typify the small-scale "trial

[9] Wright (2001).

[10] Ibid.

support groups" (*shienkai*) and related entities that Patricia Steinhoff and others write about.[11] According to Steinhoff, in the cause litigation context, attorneys provide the acumen needed to operate in the Japanese legal system, while trial support groups provide the "energy and constant dedication that keeps the [plaintiffs] in the legal case from giving up the fight . . . ."[12] These grassroots groups serve an important purpose in Japanese society: challenging state and corporate policies in a jurisdiction where civil society is putatively weak or underdeveloped.[13]

Academics, journalists, and other professionals created *vanguard* entities to lobby politicians, conduct historical and legal research, and strategise on advancing the cause, domestically and internationally. These self-appointed "committees" included outfits such as the Committee to Consider Taiwanese Veterans[14] (active 1977–1992), Committee to Consider Chinese Forced Labor[15] (active 1988-present), Committee to Clarify the Postwar Responsibility of Japan[16] (active 1990–2008), and Committee to Support Demands of Chinese War Victims[17] (active 1994-present). These groups concentrated their energies on uncovering facts, negotiating compensation arrangements, seeking out Asian (Chinese, Korean, Taiwanese) plaintiffs and convincing them to sue in Japan.

Rearguard groups, on the other hand, congeal in the wake of litigation. They provide financial support, arrange travel, attend hearings, plan protests, liaise with traditional media, and propagate online. Representatives of rearguard groups include the dozens of trial support groups that emerged after Chinese and Korean plaintiffs sued in Yamaguchi (1992), Hiroshima (1995), Sapporo (1999), and elsewhere. To be sure, vanguard and rearguard groups engage in similar conduct; their activities may well overlap. But the scholarly, proactive, and strategic roles of vanguard entities contrast with the reactive, supportive, and supplemental functions of rearguard groups.

---

[11] Steinhoff (2015).

[12] Steinhoff (2015), p. 10.

[13] Pekkanen (2006), p. 185.

[14] The group's name is more cumbersome in Japanese: the Group to Consider the Compensation Problem of Taiwanese Who Served as Japanese Soldiers (台湾人元日本兵士の補償問題を考える会).

[15] The name is streamlined by comparison: the Group to Consider the Forced Mobilisation of Chinese People (中国人強制連行を考える会). "Forced mobilisation" (強制連行) refers to the process by which Chinese and Korean men and women were abducted from villages in mainland Asia, transported by train to ports like Busan and Qingdao, and thence shipped to Japan to perform "forced labour" (強制労働). The term "forced mobilisation" challenges the dominant Japanese interpretation of history, which portrays the mobilisation of Korean labour as conscription (徴用), the legal consequence of Japan's 1938 National Mobilisation Law.

[16] The name itself (日本の戦後責任をハッキリさせる会) differs from all other groups in using the causative verb form (*saseru*), meaning to *cause* clarity, to *make* something clear. Most groups use active verbs—to consider, to support, to help—to describe what they aim to do. This group wanted to make Japanese society 'clear' about where its war responsibilities lay, a bolder claim than most other groups.

[17] The group, 中国人戦争被害者の要求を支える会, formed in 1994.

Attorneys, on the other hand, form lawyers' groups (*bengodan*). Often affiliated with the Japan Federal Bar Association and Japan Civil Liberties Union, these attorneys generally adhere to progressive ideas about Japan's colonial and wartime past and conclude that Japan has not adequately atoned for the harm visited upon former imperial subjects (Koreans, Taiwanese), enemy civilians (Chinese, Filipinas), and enemy combatants (Chinese, American, Dutch and other Allied POWs). Lawyers' groups devoted enormous amounts of time, money and effort to represent plaintiffs from Asia. Scouring Chinese villages, interviewing Taiwanese plaintiffs, and attending rallies in Busan, Japanese attorneys worked locally, nationally and transnationally to earn plaintiffs' trust, collaborate with local lawyers and scholars, and devise litigation strategies.[18]

2.2 Investigation

With vanguard, lawyers, and rearguard groups formed in Japan and plaintiffs' home country (Taiwan, China, Korea, etc.), Japanese actors investigated claims in East Asia. They visited war sites, interviewed victims, spoke to experts, and consulted local lawyers. They gathered evidence: photographs, diaries, ordnance, and personal testimonials. By interviewing survivors, Japanese lawyers learned about the human rights abuses performed by Mitsubishi, Mitsui, Japan Steel, and other major corporations. These overseas trips uncovered the facts necessary to ground legal claims and built relationships of trust with victims, families, local lawyers, and activists in Asia.

For many Asian plaintiffs, the idea of suing a Japanese corporation—in Japan, with the assistance of Japanese counsel—was hardly intuitive. Transnational human rights litigation, or transnational public law litigation, was alien to most people in the 1970s and 1980s.[19] These forms of litigation have engrained themselves into the dockets, scholarly repertoires, and discourse of liberal democracies since the 1980s. Submitting human rights violations or historical injustices to the local judiciary would have confounded the average Korean or Chinese citizen for the relevant period (1970s to 1990s). While legal consciousness has risen in China, Korea, and Taiwan, the use of courts to seek redress from corporations for historical injustices remains, in many places, novel.

---

[18] Tanaka (2005). Tanaka is a key architect in the war redress movement and the founder of the Association Chinese Forced Labor Committee.

[19] Beth Stephens defines international human rights litigation as lawsuits that seek remedies "for the most egregious human rights abuses, as to which there is widespread consensus around the world, such as torture, genocide, summary execution, war crimes and forced labor." Stephens (2002), p. 488. Harold Koh delimits transnational public law litigation to tort lawsuits where plaintiffs seek "compensation, norm-enunciation, and deterrence through judicial declarations of international law violations, and more ambitious 'institutional reform' suits," where they seek to reform U.S. foreign policy. Koh (1991), p. 2368.

Why, after all, would a Chinese forced labourer trust the legal system of his former enemy? Why would a Korean comfort woman, after decades of poverty, stigma and alienation, trust a Japanese attorney to defend her rights in Japan? Japanese activists had to build trust with their Asian clients, a multifaceted process involving repeated visits to Asian countries, support from plaintiffs' compatriots (e.g., Chinese lawyers in China, Korean academics in Korea), and busy travel itineraries before and after their hearings in Japan. While months and sometimes years were needed, Korean, Chinese, Taiwanese, and Filipina plaintiffs came to repose sufficient confidence in Japanese attorneys and activists so as to entrust their cases within the Japanese legal system.

2.3 Litigation

Third, after ascertaining facts, collecting documentary evidence, and recording conversations, Asian victims sued in Japan. No longer passive victims of wartime human rights abuses or recipients of second-class treatment, foreign plaintiffs—assisted by Japanese lawyers, activists, and interpreters—initiated the proactive enterprise of formal rights assertion. For many, this was a new identity and novel activity. Many plaintiffs came from the most precarious strata of their home societies. Taiwanese veterans of the Imperial Japanese Army were long oppressed by the Nationalist Party (Kuomintang), which fought Japan during the war (1937–1945) and ruled Taiwan as an authoritarian dynasty from 1949 to 1987. Korean *hibakusha* knew little about their illnesses or how radiation exposure would affect them. They eked out marginal lives on the outskirts of Korean society. Chinese forced labourers were branded as traitors and "running dogs" of imperial Japan during various political campaigns, most harshly during the Cultural Revolution.

Transnational litigation is, in several senses, a bridge: an emotional, logistical, procedural, and ritual set of linkages reinforced by civil society abutments in Japan on one side and Korea, China, and Taiwan on the other. The bridge places victims of humanity's most destructive war on a path towards rights assertion, legal accountability, monetary compensation, and dignity reclamation. Litigation cannot, of course, guarantee that plaintiffs *arrive* at these destinations. Plaintiffs often express deep regret with the results of their lawsuits, especially in Japan. A few plaintiffs, however, enjoyed a measure of reconciliation, which derived from relations forged with Japanese academics, activists, and attorneys during the plaintiffs' visits to Japan for hearings, celebrations, and memorials. They observed genuine demonstrations of Japanese remorse, communicated with Japanese activists dedicated to the cause of war redress, and actually extracted compensation and apologies in a few instances.[20]

[20] Webster (2019).

The transnational litigation at issue in Asia's war redress cases is both similar to and different from the attempts to hold former dictators to account in the West. The "Pinochet effect," a prime example of the "Atlantic" model, refers to transnational efforts to hold authoritarian leaders criminally liable for human rights violations, in their individual capacity, outside of their home jurisdiction.[21] By contrast, the "Pacific" model examined herein focuses on civil litigation, filed by foreign plaintiffs, against corporate and state defendants in their home jurisdiction. The legal claims, parties' nationalities, and nature of the proceeding (criminal vs civil) thus vary widely between the Atlantic and Pacific models. Structurally speaking, Pacific plaintiffs challenged society's strongest players—multinational corporations and the state—at home, a very significant set of obstacles to surmount. Atlantic activists, by comparison, prosecuted South American and African leaders in European courts. Both models thus used the judiciary of richer, more powerful states to preside over cases against parties from economically weaker states, but the equities of the two models differ significantly.

Where East meets West, to mangle Kipling, is in the bottom-up mobilisation by grassroots legal actors. As Roht-Arriaza writes, "it was ordinary people, acting mostly on their own time and their own dime" who demanded justice for Pinochet and others in criminal courts.[22] In the Pacific, a similar constellation of ordinary folks—lawyers, activists, and victims—collaborated to seek accountability from corporate and state actors. The bonds formed through domestic mobilisation in China, Korea, Taiwan, etc. ultimately enabled Japanese attorneys to represent Chinese and Korean forced labourers and hundreds of other war victims from the Asia-Pacific.

3 Background on War Redress

The transnational war redress movement first surfaced in East Asia during the 1970s. The first claimants came from Japan's former colonies (Taiwan, Korea), not its former enemies (China, Philippines, US, UK). Having once been Japanese subjects, the first wave of redress seekers pressed equality-based claims against the Japanese state, demanding Japan provide them with the same benefits Japan provided to its own citizens. Under a 1952 law, for instance, Japan gave pensions, medical treatment and social benefits to veterans of Japanese nationality. Seeing their former colleagues so rewarded, Taiwanese veterans, who lost their Japanese nationality in 1952, banded together in Taiwan to demand similar treatment from Japan. With the assistance of Japanese activists and lawyers, Taiwanese veterans filed a seminal lawsuit in 1977.[23]

---

[21] Roht-Arriaza (2006).

[22] Roht-Arriaza (2006), p. 224.

[23] Deng Sheng et al. v. Japan, filed 13 August 1977.

Similarly, under a 1958 law, survivors of the atomic bomb (*hibakusha*) qualified for pensions and medical treatment from Japan's health ministry. In 1972, a Korean *hibakusha* illegally entered Japan to seek medical treatment for illnesses linked to radiation exposure. At the time, medical treatment for atomic—bomb survivors was far more developed in Japan than in South Korea. When the Fukuoka health minister refused to issue the necessary certificate, Plaintiff Son Jin-doo sued—the first war redress plaintiff in East Asia. Son enjoyed a string of court victories at trial, appellate, and supreme courts.[24] Supporting Son during his time in Japan were various Japanese and Korean groups.[25]

The lawsuits of the 1970s and those of the present moment (1990-present) share common support among civil society actors. In the early 1970s, Taiwanese civil society was still constrained by the authoritarian leadership of Generalissimo Chiang Kai-shek. Nonetheless, a group of wounded Taiwanese veterans formed an unregistered, grassroots group to demand compensation from Japan. At the same time, groups in Japan mobilised around the issue of providing benefits to Taiwanese veterans. Two professors at Meiji University formed the Consideration Committee, which comprised over a dozen intellectuals from Tokyo, which ultimately supported the 17-year lawsuit filed by Taiwanese veterans in the Tokyo District Court. They raised money to fund the court costs, protested and ran signature campaigns, and meticulously recorded their activities, hearings, and legal developments in dozens of newsletters.

Second, Japanese activists liaised with individuals and grassroots groups in other Asian jurisdictions. Attorneys visited Taipei, Seoul, Beijing and other cities to meet their clients, ascertain historical facts, and collect evidence of Japanese war crimes. They also had to earn the trust of local people, persuading their Asian interlocutors that litigation in Japan constituted a proper course of action. In this sense, attorneys also acted as brokers, uniting previously unconnected groups of Japanese activists and Asian victims and supporters. Throughout the war redress movement, the brokerage role has fallen primarily to Japanese attorneys, though activists without legal training (e.g. Hiroshi Tanaka, Ichiba Junko, Yano Hideki) have played an active role in developments from the 1990s onward.

The first wave of war redress litigation, from the 1970s, mainly targeted the Japanese government.[26] But even when state and corporate interests align, these actors conduct themselves according to a different set of rules. Corporations exercise flexibility that states cannot. The Japanese government, under the conservative Liberal Democratic Party (LDP), has consistently opposed war redress on almost all accounts. Indeed, one can trace the hardening of the LDP's position to the profusion of war redress cases from the 1990s.[27] Hard-right Prime Ministers such as Abe

[24] Webster (2022a).

[25] Duro (2018).

[26] Two suits were filed against private actors: a Japanese bank and a Japanese insurance company. Webster (2025).

[27] The leading conservative civil society groups include Nippon Kaigi (日本会議) and the Japanese Society for History Textbook Reform (新しい歴史教科書をつくる会). Both groups oppose

Shinzo (2006–2007, 2012–2020), Taro Aso (2008–2009), and Suga Yoshihide (2020–2021) consistently downplayed carnage, denigrated victims, denied evidence, and dissembled about state involvement.

Japanese companies, on occasion, adopted a more emollient approach. As the second wave of war redress litigation crested in the 1990s, Korean and Chinese plaintiffs filed some two dozen lawsuits against Mitsubishi, Mitsui, Sumitomo and other powerful *zaibatsu* that armed, financed and sustained Japan's war machine.[28] Plaintiffs demanded compensation and apologies for the forced labour they performed on behalf of these companies during the war. A small fraction of these lawsuits settled in response to pressure from shareholders, unfavourable media coverage, changes in public opinion, and the threat of transnational litigation in the United States.[29] Japanese companies expressed remorse, showed creativity in designing remedies, and paid modest amounts of compensation. They conducted memorial ceremonies for deceased Korean forced labourers, apologised poetically to Chinese forced labourers, and erected monuments and museums around Japan. In less fraught times, corporations agreed to modest solutions.

Because corporations enjoy greater flexibility than state actors—they need not win popular elections, for example—a more cooperative outcome is possible. Corporate positions can evolve in response to pressures, whether political (ties between large Japanese corporations and the ruling Liberal Democratic Party extend back decades), public (consumer boycotts, protests), judicial (damages awards, suggested settlements), international (International Labour Organisation, UN reports), and peer (other companies). Given changes in power, public opinion, and political pressure, corporate defendants have, at times, assumed a less oppositional stance vis-à-vis plaintiffs. When confronted with Chinese demands for compensation in the 1980s, Kajima Construction Company staked out a flexible position, only to drag its feet once negotiations focused on how much compensation they would have to pay.

I will further present two case studies of transnational activism against Japanese corporations: one from China and one from Korea. Chinese forced labourers filed sixteen lawsuits against Japanese corporations, while Korean forced labourers filed eleven. These cases illuminate differences in transnational activism between authoritarian states (China, Korea in the 1970s) and liberal democracies (Japan, Korea now). Transnational activism never takes place in a vacuum. It is always subject to prevailing socio-cultural practices, political pressures, rights limitations, and organisational constraints. Informational constraints also influenced the selection. Trial support groups record their events in mesmerising detail but do not store that information in accessible places. Certain groups canonise themselves by publishing extensive compendia of their newsletters, verdicts, legal documents, and petitions.

---

what they call a "masochistic view of history," which acknowledges Japan as a perpetrator, not just a victim, of the Second World War.

[28] Webster (2020).

[29] Webster (2019).

Other groups leave no trace at all. While the internet can be a valuable source of information, most groups fail to maintain their websites; broken links abound. By reading secondary materials in Japanese, Chinese, and Korean, as well as newsletters from TSGs, media reports, and other materials, I trace the transnational activism of the first Korean (Park Chang-hwan) and first Chinese (Geng Zhun) forced labourers to seek corporate accountability from Japanese corporations.

4 Asia's First Transnational Mobilisation for Corporate Accountability: Pak Chang-hwan v. Mitsubishi Heavy Industries

4.1 Mobilisation in Korea

The origins of Pak's lawsuit date to the late 1960s. In 1965, Japan and South Korea signed the Basic Treaty, reinstating diplomatic ties for the first time since World War II. While the instrument smoothed over relations between the estranged states, it enraged many Koreans and animated popular resistance to its ratification. Two hundred intellectuals, opposition politicians, and religious leaders constellated the "Committee against Humiliating Diplomacy with Japan."[30] Students rallied against the Treaty, with protests ricocheting across Seoul university campuses on June 3, 1965, and later throughout the country.[31] Pupils at the country's most elite institution, Seoul National University, entered a hunger strike. Despite popular objections, Tokyo and Seoul signed and ratified the Basic Treaty.

In 1967, the Korean Atomic Bomb Victims Association (KABVA) was formed. This group did not challenge the Korean government, like the aforementioned Humiliation Committee. Instead, it advocated for "forgotten Koreans," whose exposure to radiation during the bombings of Hiroshima and Nagasaki produced a lifetime of anxiety, disease, and disfigurement. KABVA resembles the citizens groups (*simin*) that proliferated in the niches of Korean society at this time.[32] The Association created linkages among the thousands of atomic survivors living in South Korea, advocated for better medical treatment, and later organised trips to Japan for medical treatment. In 1968, former forced labourers at Mitsubishi formed an offshoot of the Association.

---

[30] The Committee against Humiliating Diplomacy with Japan (대일굴욕외교 반대투쟁위원회) consisted of Yun Posun (former president), Chang tae-sang (former prime minister), and other opposition leaders.

[31] Lee (2014). Known as the June 3 Movement (6.3 항쟁), it asked Japan to apologise and compensate Koreans for 35 years of colonial oppression. Movement members also opposed Korean President Park Chung-hee's waiver of the right to claim compensation against Japan in the 1965 Treaty.

[32] Shin (2020).

In April 1974, Korean activist Jeong Chang-hee compiled a list of fellow conscripts who had worked for Mitsubishi. Jeong observed his former colleagues in the following way: "Conscripts were poor, and lived in mountainside huts on the outskirts of Seoul. After work, I would drag my tired feet up the mountains, and stop at each hut for a visit. This was how the Association formed." Jeong recorded the names, addresses, dates of conscription, and worksites of each conscript. He later founded a grassroots entity, the Mitsubishi Conscript Association (MCA), to press claims against Mitsubishi.[33]

In Japan, Fukagawa Munetoshi—a poet and former worker at Mitsubishi—used Jeong's list to launch negotiations with Mitsubishi. During the war, Fukagawa oversaw Korean conscripts as a foreman in Mitsubishi's shipbuilding operations in Hiroshima. Himself a *hibakusha*, Fukagawa represented the MCA members in talks with Mitsubishi, forwarding their request for compensation and support.[34] Mitsubishi replied

> We feel really bad about this. But as a corporation, we bear no duty to assist bereft families. In 1948, we deposited the unpaid wages of workers with the Hiroshima Ministry of Justice, and a list of Korean conscripts after the war. If you'd like to discuss compensation or other matters, please consult corporate headquarters.[35]

Thus began a campaign of deflection, disinformation, and denial that Mitsubishi would practice for decades.

In August 1974, MCA members accepted Mitsubishi's offer to negotiate at the corporate headquarters. Leading figures in Korea's atomic bomb compensation movement—including Shin Yeong-su[36] and Kwak Kwi-hoon[37]—visited Tokyo and Hiroshima at this time. But their meeting with Mitsubishi was perfunctory. The company proffered four defences against their request for compensation: (1) the present site in Eba-chô, Hiroshima was not the site of the atomic bombing, (2) since

[33] Yonhap (2007). The group is referred to as both Mitsubishi Conscript Association (미쓰비시 징용자 동지회) and Korean Atomic Bomb Victims Mitsubishi Conscript Association (한국 원폭피해자 미쓰비시 징용자 동지회). It was likely affiliated with the Atomic Bomb Victims Association. The association's foundation became a key legal issue. Both Pusan District and High Courts used the 1974 date as the starting point for the ten-year statute of limitations on Pak's legal claims. The judgments use the second (longer) name.

[34] Mitsubishi Hiroshima Trial Support Group (2010).

[35] Ibid, p. 51.

[36] Kobayashi (2019). Shin Yeong-su (辛泳洙) founded KABVA in 1967 and ran it for forty years. As a former forced labourer and hibakusha, Shin spoke with broad authority on both issues. During his 1971 return to Japan, Shin lectured about the dire predicament of Korean hibakusha and sought the support of Japanese civil society. In August 1972, during Vice-Prime Minister Miki Takeo's visit to Seoul, Shin raised the compensation issue with Japanese officials directly. Shin also inquired about Japan's Atomic-Bomb Survivor Protection Law and the possible creation of medical facilities in South Korea. Miki did little in response.

[37] In the 1990s and 2000s, Kwak was the lead plaintiff in two of the most successful cases of the redress movement. One case is credited with forcing the Japanese Health Ministry to withdraw a discriminatory regulation after 30 years and countless denials to foreign atomic bomb survivors. Webster (2022a). Chairman Cho Hanseok and Secretary-General Pak Hae-gun were also present.

all wages were paid at the time, there are no "unpaid" wages, (3) other companies also used conscript labour, so Mitsubishi alone cannot bear responsibility, and (4) Mitsubishi had no duty to ensure safe passage back to Korea.[38] Mitsubishi would refine, reconfigure, and reinforce these defences in the lawsuits of the 1990s and 2000s. But in the mid-1970s, transnational litigation against corporate actors for human rights violations would have been a rarity anywhere, especially in East Asia. Without a credible threat of litigation, MCA members had few options to press their claims.

The MCA members pursued other forms of redress. Taking advantage of a 1974 verdict that found in favour of a Korean *hibakusha*, they successfully applied for certificates issued by Japan's Health Ministry to enable medical treatment.[39] They obtained theirs without litigation. On August 6, 1974, they participated in a ceremony to mark the 29th anniversary of the bomb. For the next several decades, the MCA remained active, liaising with Japanese groups and activists throughout the 1970s and 1980s. In the 1990s and 2000s, many MCA filed lawsuits in Japan and later in Korea.

4.2 Mobilisation in Japan

Grassroots groups sympathetic to Asian war victims have proliferated in Japan since the 1970s. Hiroshima, the site of humanity's most enormous war crime, attracts a disproportionately large number of peace activists. Indeed, many of Japan's most active adherents in the transnational war redress movement reside in Hiroshima. But even outside of that war-torn city, Japanese intellectuals—including Tokyo-based Attorney Takagi Ken'ichi and Professor Onuma Yasuaki—sought to understand the damage that Japan had inflicted upon its Asian neighbours and compensate those injured by Japanese war crimes.[40]

The Trial Support Group (TSG) for the Mitsubishi Hiroshima Conscripted Atomic Bomb Survivors was formed on December 10, 1995.[41] At the launch party, Korean conscripts and Japanese activists pledged to continue the fight against impunity of Mitsubishi and Japan.[42] Plaintiff Hwang Jong-ho implored the audience, "Please answer me. Have I led a normal life? First, I was abducted, then tormented by Mitsubishi, and finally irradiated? When I returned home, I had no land to farm. How hard has my life been? What do Japanese people think?"[43] Plaintiff Yang

[38] Mitsubishi Hiroshima Trial Support Group (2010), p. 52.

[39] In 1974, the Fukuoka District Court found in favour of Son Jin-doo, the first Korean hibakusha to demand a health certificate (*kenkô techô*) from the Japanese government. Building on Son's success, Shin successfully applied for a health certificate in Tokyo.

[40] Webster (2022b).

[41] Mitsubishi Hiroshima Trial Support Group (2010), p. 59.

[42] Ibid., p. 60.

[43] Ibid., p. 60.

Gi-seong noted his advanced age and the large number of fellow hibakusha who had already died. He queried, prophetically, whether he would live to see the verdict of his own trial.[44] Kim Sun-gil, a Korean hibakusha with litigation pendent against Mitsubishi in Nagasaki, also appeared.[45]

The TSG performed many acts in the repertoire of contention common in Japanese cause litigation. They organised protests and activities outside the Tokyo District Court after the case was filed in December 1995 and after subsequent hearings. On April 18, 1996, TSG members protested outside a Mitsubishi factory and a branch office of the Tokyo Mitsubishi Bank in Hiroshima. They waved signs that read "Mitsubishi: Pay the Unpaid Wages" and "Take Responsibility for Abducting Pak Chang-hwan."[46] The next day, before the first hearing, plaintiffs and activists called on Mitsubishi for one last attempt at settlement, but were turned away at the door.[47] Later, when Judge Katô Makoto dismissed the case on March 25, 1999, TSG members stood outside the Hiroshima District Court and unfurled the customary "unfair verdict" banner.[48]

The TSG also engaged in more conventional modes of activism, inflected with a litigious twist. The group gathered some 87,000 signatures from Japanese citizens, who demanded a "just verdict" in the lawsuit. On June 25, 1996, activists delivered a five-foot stack—comprising some 87,000 pages—to the Hiroshima District Court.[49] The reams of paper signified the broad support of Japanese citizens, quite apart from the Korean litigants and their supporters.

The Hiroshima TSG also collaborated with other groups to amplify pressure on Mitsubishi. On June 13, 2002, members of TSGs in Nagasaki, Nagoya, and Hiroshima gathered outside Mitsubishi's headquarters in Tokyo. Supporters held portraits of plaintiffs who had died during the litigation, conducted memorial services on their behalf, and set up family altars (*saidan*) on the sidewalk. Seven female plaintiffs, each wearing a sash that identified them as plaintiffs in the Nagoya trial, joined the Japanese activists in front of Mitsubishi headquarters. They carried a banner that read "It lives: my grudge," using a Korean term (*han*) to conjure the deep-seated and unremitting animosity borne by many Koreans against Japan.[50] Next to

---

[44] Ibid., p. 61. Yang died in 2001, after the disappointing trial court decision but before the victorious appeal.

[45] Kim filed the second corporate case in Japan. In 1992, he sued Mitsubishi Heavy Industry in Nagasaki District Court. Venue matters in Japan, as it does everywhere. Tokyo courts view war reparations claims dimly, dismissing the overwhelming majority. Lower courts in smaller cities (Fukuoka, Kyoto, Niigata, Yamaguchi), as well as those in Hiroshima and Nagasaki, have issued partial or full rulings for plaintiffs. In 1991, Kim Kyeong-seok—no relation to Kim Sun-gil—filed the first lawsuit against a Japanese corporation for war redress in Tokyo District Court. His case was dismissed four years later.

[46] Mitsubishi Hiroshima Trial Support Group (2010), p. 66.

[47] Ibid., p. 67.

[48] Ibid., p. 70.

[49] Ibid., p. 68.

[50] The word is 恨 or resentment, grudge, hatred.

the seven plaintiffs was a table with portraits of deceased plaintiffs from the three lawsuits, festooned with flowers, fruit and other offerings. After the events, supporters split up: some conducted negotiations with Mitsubishi, while others headed to Kasumigaseki to meet members of the Koizumi Cabinet.

When the Hiroshima High Court partially found for plaintiffs on January 19, 2005, the TSG took full advantage of the positive result. At a press conference at the Hiroshima Bar Association, Attorney Zaima Hidekazu discussed key features of the decision: (1) recognition of facts, (2) waiver of sovereign immunity, and (3) nullification of an "illegal" regulation to exclude foreign hibakusha.[51] Japanese and Korean media, echoing Zaima's formulation, repeated his characterisation of the case as a "landmark decision" that both acknowledged the state's liability for "abandoning" foreign hibakusha and ordered the state to pay ¥1.2 million (US$12,000) to each plaintiff.[52] The verdict did not, however, reverse the trial court's decision to dismiss the case against Mitsubishi due to statutes of limitation.[53]

In a rare "victory lap" for trial support groups, a small delegation flew to South Korea that weekend. At the Seoul headquarters of the KABVA, attorneys and activists explained the ruling to Chairman Kwak Kwi-hoon, Jeong Sang-hwa, Kim Dae-book, and other officials. After much exuberance ("We did it", "Great job!") and hugging, supporters, lawyers and plaintiffs went out to dinner. At the *noraebang* (karaoke bar) after dinner, Korean supporters sang a rendition of the Korean song "Let's win, Korea."[54] The next day, TSG members visited Pyongtaek, the city where most plaintiffs lived. Plaintiff Hwang Jong-ho raised his fist to protest Mitsubishi's exculpation. He posed more questions: "After sixty years of neglect, what can the statute of limitations possible mean? Mitsubishi cannot be forgiven."[55]

The transnational mobilisation against Mitsubishi did not produce the result that Korean plaintiffs sought, at least as a matter of law. Mitsubishi certainly felt pressure from the lawsuit and related incidents of activism at its headquarters and office buildings in Japan. However, Japanese courts have viewed Korean forced labour as *legal*, in the narrow sense that the statutory basis for recruiting wartime Korean labour was Japan's 1937 National Mobilisation Law. Japanese courts have taken a dimmer view of Japan's use of Chinese forced labour, which lacked a legal basis and was often much more violent and coercive. As the next section suggests,

[51] Japanese Community Party (2005). Since many conservative politicians and corporate officers reject the factual nature of Japan's war crimes, factual recognition by Japanese courts provides a meaningful bulwark against denialism and revision. *See* Webster (2018).

[52] The decision did not order Mitsubishi or the state to pay unpaid wages. See Daily Yomiuri (2005) (predicting the decision would have "substantial impact on other cases" as the "first time that a high court recognised the responsibility of the central government in compensation lawsuits"); Dong-A Ilbo (2005) (describing the ruling as the "first time that a Japanese court ordered compensation for atomic bomb victims overseas").

[53] Dong-A Ilbo (2005).

[54] The song was written in the late Park Chung-hee era (1976), and performed at the Olympics, Asian Games, Korea-Japan World Cup (2002), and other sporting events. The song has a martial feel and nationalist message.

[55] Mitsubishi Hiroshima Trial Support Group (2010), p. 85.

lawsuits from Chinese forced labourers rarely yield the results that plaintiffs demanded.

5 Mobilisation and Its Discontents: Geng Zhun v. Kajima Construction Company

5.1 Mobilisation in China

Geng Zhun was a leading figure in China's war redress movement, the rare victim-turned-activist.[56] His leadership manifested early. As a captain in the KMT Army, Geng was captured by the Japanese military, forcibly transported to northeastern Japan, and compelled to mine copper for the Kajima Corporation in Odate. On June 30, 1945, Geng led hundreds of his compatriots, who had also been effectively enslaved by the Japanese, to mount an insurrection known as the Hanaoka Incident in Japanese and the Hanaoka Uprising in Chinese. For his role in instigating the unrest, Geng was sentenced to death by the Akita District Court, but the verdict was commuted after Japan's defeat in the war. Decades later, having survived the vicissitudes as a Nationalist soldier in Communist China, Geng launched a movement to demand compensation from Kajima.

In 1985, Geng read an article about a Japanese commemoration of the "Hanaoka Uprising." Unbeknownst to Geng, Japanese activists and politicians annually gathered at the mine to commemorate the 486 Chinese victims of the Uprising. Four-plus decades after bloodily suppressing the incident, Japanese government officials, including the mayor of Odate, canonised the event in front of hundreds of Japanese citizens. Geng tracked down Liu Zhiqun, a participant in the ceremony and former forced labourer who lived in Japan. Through correspondence with Liu and close collaboration with state actors and private citizens in Japan, Geng attended the ceremony in June 1987. His first visit to Japan since the war made headlines across Japan; a photograph of his arrival at Narita International Airport appeared on the front page of many prominent dailies.

At the ceremony, Geng met Japanese politicians, Chinese envoys, and activists of various ethnicities: Tanaka Hiroshi, a Japanese professor then at Akita Prefectural University; Lin Boyao, the Taiwanese leader of the Overseas Chinese Association; and Niimi Tadashi, a Japanese attorney with a decade of criminal and civil experience.[57] Geng sensed the sincerity of Japanese activists, lawyers, politicians and audience members. From his reception at Narita to cultural events he attended in

[56] While many Korean forced labourers turned to activism in the 1970s and 1980s, only a few Chinese forced labourers became activists in their own right. This may reflect the depth of Korean resentment towards Japan, the difficulty of mobilising in an authoritarian state, or some other set of social factors.

[57] Niimi had worked with the Japanese left on cases like movement to end fingerprinting resident Koreans.

Tokyo (including a dramatic reenactment, "Roar Hanaoka," by journalist Ishitobi Jin), to his participation in the June 30 ceremony in Odate, Geng observed hundreds of sympathetic Japanese citizens recognise their collective guilt, even if they were not individually guilty for any wartime crime.

Chinese media also reported on Geng's return to Japan, leading many other Chinese forced labourers to reach out to him. In 1989, Geng founded China's first war redress group,[58] the Hanaoka Victims Association, with forty other forced labourers.[59] Unable to register in China, the group nonetheless advocated for redress for the 986 Chinese citizens forced to work at Hanaoka Mine. Members also demanded redress from Kajima.

One of the Hanaoka Victims Association's first acts was to draft an open letter to the Kajima Company. The letter asked Kajima to "wake up, respect historical facts, walk the road of peace, educate the next generation, using Hanaoka as an example."[60] The letter sought an apology, the building of memorial halls in China and Japan, and ¥5 million (US $35,000) in compensation to each forced labourer for physical injuries and emotional suffering.[61] With Attorney Niimi as their representative, the Chinese forced labourers agreed to a Joint Statement with Kajima in 1990. The company admitted its "corporate liability," an important concession that Chinese labourers wanted. It also expressed "deep apology."[62] Because this was still relatively early in the war redress movement, clear modes of apology, acknowledgement, and atonement were still possible, even if unlikely. Unfortunately, the parties could not agree on the amount of compensation Kajima should pay. After five more years of intermittent negotiations, Geng filed China's first war redress lawsuit.[63]

5.2 *Mobilisation in Japan*

The primary Japanese group dedicated to China's first wave of war redress efforts was the "Committee to Consider Chinese Forced Mobilisation" (Consideration Committee).[64] Formed in 1988 by Tanaka Hiroshi and Niimi Tadashi, the

---

[58] China here refers to the People's Republic of China. In Hong Kong, Ng Yat-hing founded the Reparation Association of Hong Kong in 1968. In Taiwan (Republic of China), a group of veterans coalesced in 1973.

[59] Nozoe (2014), p. 152. The Chinese name changed over time but is currently known as花岡受難者聯誼會.

[60] Nozoe (2014), p. 153–154.

[61] Nozoe (2014), p. 154.

[62] For a translation and analysis of Kajima's statement and the developments that led to it, *see* Webster (2019).

[63] Geng Zhun v. Kajima Construction Corp, filed 28 June 1995.

[64] In Japanese, 中国人強制連行を考える. A second wave of Chinese suits emerged in the mid-1990s, headed by Onodera Toshitaka and Oyama Hiroshi. These suits focused on the sexual violence and the "comfort women" lawsuits, as well as.

Consideration Committee conducted research, liaised with Chinese actors, and disseminated research and activist activities through newsletters.[65] Given its early genesis, foundational role in highlighting Chinese forced labour, and academic orientation, the Committee constitutes a vanguard group. Its initial aim was not litigation. Instead, a separate TSG, headed by a Consideration Committee member, emerged to support Geng's suit. TSG members devoted themselves to court-related activities: attending and reporting hearings, objecting to procedural irregularities, and staging protests after unfavourable rulings or verdicts.[66] The Consideration Committee, which predated the TSG by many years, had a broader remit. By unearthing chapters of Japan's wartime past, cultivating the ligatures of trust necessary for transnational litigation (and other cross-border initiatives), and assembling like-minded people across the Asia-Pacific, the Committee unearthed Japan's wartime labour practices for the first time.

The Consideration Committee focused primarily on forced labour, not sexual violence, indiscriminate bombing, or medical experimentation. In the short term, it assisted Chinese forced labourers to negotiate with Kajima. In the long term, the committee investigated the wartime history of Chinese forced labour, collaborated with Chinese academics, students and activists on recovering this history, and advocated for redress. In November 1990, Chinese forced labourers, bereft families, students, and members of the public gathered in Beijing to conduct China's first memorial service for the Hanaoka Uprising. Committee members from all over Japan flew in to attend. They met Chinese activists and intellectuals, interviewed former forced labourers, and visited sites of wartime abduction.[67] When a Chinese academic wanted to learn about his father's wartime death in Japan, the Committee arranged for his visit to Miike and a consultation with a local historian.[68] Later, when he sought the repatriation of his father's remains, the Committee represented him in negotiations with the Japanese corporation that once enslaved his father, Mitsui Mining.

The Committee also unearthed documentary evidence. During a visit to the United States Library of Congress in 1991, Tanaka Hiroshi exhumed a cache of documents compiled during the American occupation of Japan (1945-1952). A July 1945 report from the U.S. Army described the grim conditions of Chinese forced labour at the Kajima mine, as well as the whereabouts of the leader of the uprising,

[65] The Committee published approximately 100 issues of its Newsletter, 中国人強制連行を考える会ニュース, between 1990 and 2010.

[66] The Hanaoka Trial Support Liaison Conference (花岡裁判支援連絡会議) was formed after Geng filed his lawsuit.

[67] Asahi News (1990). When a judge cut off a plaintiff from testifying on March 3, 1997, TSG members filed a motion with the Diet to censure the judge. See Asahi News (1997b). When the Tokyo District Court dismissed the case in December 1997, TSG members protested in Akita City, objecting particularly to the summary (5-second) verdict read by the judge. See Asahi News (1997a).

[68] Asahi News (1991).

Geng Zhun.[69] Later, these documents ballasted a 1993 exhibit on the Hanaoka Incident at Beijing's Museum of the War of Japanese Resistance. The Consideration Committee also arranged for a Japanese soldier, who had once forcibly recruited Chinese men in Shandong province, to visit the museum and to apologise for his wartime misdeeds.[70]

The mobilisation against Kajima delivered mixed results. Geng's 1995 lawsuit was, from one perspective, delayed for decades; but from the perspective of corporate accountability, the lawsuit was filed early enough in East Asia's redress movement to gain a "first-mover" advantage. Under pressure from the Tokyo High Court judge and the possibility of litigation in the more plaintiff-friendly United States, Kajima settled Geng's case through a *wakai,* or conciliation agreement. Chinese media reported that 500 forced labourers accepted the terms of the settlement, which included a compensation payment and a subsidy to be used to educate the descendants of the forced labourers.[71] But Geng rejected the payout, claiming that Kajima showed insufficient remorse and did not make a meaningful apology.[72] Despite Geng's strong objections, the fact that hundreds of Chinese forced labourers accepted the terms of the settlement suggests that reconciliation is possible, even if unlikely.

6 Conclusions

Transnational public law litigation, whatever its rulings, reflects a tight linkage of social activism in contemporary East Asia. Park Chang-hwan's case "failed" in Japan but later succeeded in South Korea. Geng Zhun's case focused attention on Chinese forced labour and ultimately produced a settlement agreement that many other plaintiffs—Korean and Chinese alike—might envy, even if Geng himself refused to accept its terms. What lessons can we draw from these exercises in transnational corporate accountability?

First, activists must expect resistance, denial, and evasion from corporations. Like governments, corporations often bury their shameful past. Since they enjoy various advantages— wealth, influence, marketing budgets, political connections, etc.—corporations are unlikely to come clean without sustained pressure. Japanese corporations might have possessed, secreted, or destroyed relevant materials about Chinese and Korean forced labour from the war: work logs, payment records, bank accounts, and so on. But they rarely shared this information with plaintiffs. Nevertheless, with perseverance, research skills, and a bit of good luck, academics,

[69] The U.S. report described inadequate food and clothing, lack of payments, and the fact that "they treated the Chinese the same way that they treat cattle."

[70] Asahi News (1993).

[71] Legal Weekend (2011).

[72] Webster (2019), pp. 355–356.

activists and attorneys unearthed documentary evidence in archives, libraries and government agencies in Japan and the United States. This information lent credence to claims that corporations illegally used forced labour during World War II. Yet, corporations rarely offered redress, conceded legal liability, or made amends. The peculiar matrix of domestic, transnational, judicial and social pressures that corporations felt did, in some instances, produce settlement agreements (conciliations). But even then, we must remember that Geng Zhun rejected the settlement after fifteen years of bilateral negotiations, largely because Kajima had backtracked from its 1990 promises.

Second, activists should vary their stance and tactics. It is notable that Korean forced labourers first approached Mitsubishi in 1974, and Chinese forced labourers made their first plea to Kajima in 1989. Since those initial pleas, forced labourers and their Japanese representatives implored, cajoled, and browbeat Japanese corporations. Together with activists, they shouted slogans and brandished signs outside company headquarters. They met corporate executives to discuss appropriate terms of settlement. They sued, using court hearings as rituals to enact their resistance, attract media coverage, and win potential adherents to the redress cause. But they did not act alone. In Japan, in particular, trial support groups were formed to provide financial, logistical, and moral support to Chinese and Korean plaintiffs. Japanese activists provided the human touch necessary to ensure the human component did not subside in the technical, dry and lengthy processes of transnational litigation. Activists must develop a diverse toolkit to engage meaningfully with corporate actors to repair human rights abuses.

Third, when all else fails, sue. The lag between the demand for compensation and the filing of litigation can be measured in months, years, and sometimes decades. Civil litigation was *not* the first choice of any East Asian plaintiff. China, Taiwan and South Korea had not engendered legal systems with strong traditions of "cause litigation" before the advent of war redress litigation. Nor was it the first resort of Japanese activists. However, civil litigation has proven to be a central forum for airing the grievance, attracting media coverage, converting adherents, and demanding compensation. Understanding litigation as part of the activist toolkit may satisfy sociolegal scholars, but it also risks inflating plaintiffs' expectations. Many thought they would win, only to face grave disappointment when judges dismissed the case. Attorneys and activists must manage expectations by speaking clearly, and perhaps in a foreign language, to people without a sophisticated sense of what litigation can and cannot accomplish. Few victims, activists or even lawyers would claim that transnational litigation yielded the full panoply of redress initially sought. Yet, cross-border mobilisation brought East Asian victims into contact with Japanese attorneys, activists and academics who showed sincerity, assiduity and endurance in their attempts to address, if not redress, a spate of historical wrongs.

References

Arrington CL (2016) Accidental activists: victim movements and government accountability in Japan and South Korea. Cornell University Press, Ithaca

Asahi News (1990) Chugoku Pekin de Hanaoka Jiken no 'Tsuichokai' ['Memorial Service' for Hanaoka Incident in Beijing, China]. 10 Nov 1990

Asahi News (1991) Chichi no Saiki Shiritai Musukora Miike Kozan Tazureru: Chugokujin Kyosei Renko [Wanting to Know about Father's Last Days, Sons Visit Miike Mine: Chinese Forced Mobilisation]. 1 Aug 1991

Asahi News (1993) Pekin de 'Hanaoka Jikenten' Chugokujin Kyosei Renko no Shiryo 200-ten ['Hanaoka Incident Exhibition' in Peking: 200 Documents about Chinese Forced Mobilisation]. 30 June 1993

Asahi News (1997a) Genkoku, Saibankan Sotsui Seikyu e Tokyo Chisai ga 'Hanaoka Jiken' Shinri Uchikiri [Plaintiffs Request Prosecution of Judge after Tokyo District Court Ends Hearing in "Hanaoka Incident" Trial]. 5 Mar 1997

Asahi News (1997b) 'Senso Sekinin Kakusu' to Hanpatsu: Shijishara Fuman 'Hanaoka Jiken' Uttae Kikyaku [Supporters Dissatisfied with Dismissal of 'Hanaoka Incident:' Object to 'Concealing War Responsibility']. 11 Dec 1997

Bradfield M (1998) The role of the independent committee of eminent persons. Ame Univ Int Law Rev 14(1):235–255

Daily Yomiuri (2005) Govt Ordered to Pay ROK Slave Workers. 20 Jan 2005

Dong-A Ilbo (2005) Japan Court Rules 1.2 million Yen Compensation for Each South Korean Atomic Victim. 19 Jan 2005

Duro A (2018) Medical Assistance for Korean Atomic Bomb Survivors in Japan. Asia-Pacific J | Japan Focus 16(2), https://apjjf.org/2018/08/duro. Accessed 6 June 2024

Japanese Community Party (2005) Kyosei Renkode Hibaku, Kunini Sekinin Mitsubishi Juko Choyo Kankokujin Genkokuga Gyakuten Shoso [Korean Plaintiffs/Mitsubishi Conscripts Win on Appeal: State Liable for Forcibly Abducting Hibakusha] 20 Jan 2005, https://www.jcp.or.jp/akahata/aik4/2005-01-20/01_01.html. Accessed 6 June 2024

Kim CJ (2024) Colonial redress and the unintended consequences of global opportunities. Int Stud Q 68(2):125–178. https://doi.org/10.1093/isq/sqae036

Kobayashi S (2019) Zaikan Hibakusha Kyugo o Meguru Nikkan Kosho: 1960s-1970s [Japan-Korea Negotiations to Assist Korean Atomic Bomb Survivors: 1960s-1970s], 2 Proc Historical Soc Japan Inst Int Aff 2(4), https://www.jiia.or.jp/JIC/pdf/2-4.pdf. Accessed 6 June 2024

Koh HH (1991) Transnational public law litigation. Yale Law J 100(6):2347–2401

Lee H (2014) Remembering June 3, JoongAng Daily, 2 June 2014, https://koreajoongangdaily.joins.com/news/article/article.aspx?aid=2990036. Accessed 6 June 2024

Legal Weekly [Fazhi Zhoumo] (2011) Huagang Shijian Wuyi Riyuan Lipeijin Qu Xiang Chengmi [Whereabouts of 500 Million in Compensation for Hanaoka Incident Goes Missing] 19 October 2011, http://news.sina.com.cn/c/sd/2011-10-19/102823327556.shtml. Accessed 6 June 2024

Mitsubishi Hiroshima Moto Choyo Hibakusha Saiban o Shien Suru Kai [Mitsubishi Hiroshima Trial Support Group] (2010) 'Han:' Mitsubishi, Hiroshima, Nihon—46-nin no Kankokujin Choyoko Hibakusha ['Grudge:' Mitsubishi, Hiroshima, Japan, and 46 Korean Conscripted Hibakusha]. Soshisha, Tokyo

Nozoe K (2014) Hanaoka o Wasareru Na: Ko Jun no Seigan [Don't Forget Hanaoka: The Life of Geng Zhun.). Shakai Hyoronsha, Tokyo

Pekkanen, R (2006) Japan's dual civil society: members without advocates. Stanford University Press, Palo Alto

Qiu P (2013) Chinese comfort women. Oxford University Press, Oxford

Roht-Arriaza, N (2006) The Pinochet effect: transnational justice in the age of human rights. University of Pennsylvania Press, Philadelphia

Shin J (2020) Changing patterns of South Korean social movements, 1960s-2020s. In: Chiavacci D, Grano S, Obinger J (eds) Civil society and the state in democratic East Asia: Between entanglement and contention in post high-growth societies. Routledge, London, pp 239–260

Stephens B (2002) Taking pride in international human rights litigation. Chicago J Int Law 2(2):485–512

Tanaka H (2005) Sajô no Shôheki: Chûgokujin Sengo Hoshô Saiban Jûnen no Kiseki [Obstalces of Sand: A Decade of Chinese Postwar Compensation Trials]. Nihon Hyoronsha, Tokyo

Tilley C, Tarrow S (2015) Contentious politics, 2nd edn. Oxford University Press, Oxford

Webster T (2018) Discursive Justice: World War II litigation in Japan. Virginia J Int Law 58(2):281–343

Webster T (2019) The price of settlement: World War II reparations in China, Japan and Korea. New York Univ J Int Law Pol 51(2):301–384

Webster T (2020) Disaggregating corporate liability: japanese multinationals and World War II. Stanford J Int Law 56(1):175–243

Webster T (2022a) Japan's transnational war reparations litigation: an empirical analysis. Harv Int Law J 63(3):673–752

Webster T (2022b) South Korea shatters the paradigm: corporate liability. historical accountability and the second world war. UCLA J Int Law For Aff 26(2):123–148

Webster T (2025) The Taiwanese Roots of East Asia's war redress movement. Am J Comp Law 72(2) (forthcoming)

Wright T (2001) The perils of protest. University of Hawaii Press, Honolulu

Yonhap News, Weonpok Pihae Sosong 'Somyeol Shi-hyo' Keollyeo Paeso [Atomic Bomb Damage Lawsuit Dismissed on Statute of Limitations] 2 Feb 2007

Timothy Webster is Professor of International and Comparative law at Western New England University. He has published dozens of articles about the intersections of international law and the domestic legal systems of East Asia in fields such as human rights, international trade, foreign investment, and transnational litigation. His latest work examines East Asia's current Second World War reparations movement from a legal, political, and sociological perspective, and has appeared in the *Harvard International Law Journal, the Stanford Journal of International Law*, and the *Virginia Journal of International Law.* He is a member of the US-Japan Network for the Future (Mansfield Foundation), and the Public Intellectuals Program (National Committee on US-China Relations)—the only lawyer selected for both groups. Previously, he practiced international dispute resolution in Tokyo and New York, and clerked for a federal judge in Boston.

Trade Unions and Corporate Accountability in Argentina: Transnational and Intersectoral Alliances

Victoria Basualdo

Abstract This chapter examines the mobilisation of Argentinean trade unions to hold economic actors responsible for massive human rights violations committed during the last Argentinean dictatorship (1976–1983). It places the efforts of workers and trade unions in the wider context of actions undertaken by other state and non-state actors and highlights how different sectors of worker organisations had different attitudes towards the dictatorial past and ways of reckoning with its political and economic legacy. The chapter takes a transnational and historical perspective, starting with campaigns denouncing violations of human rights during the dictatorship in the 1970s, to judicial achievements during the early transition to democracy in the mid-1980s, to the post-2003 period, which marked a turning point that accelerated the debates on corporate responsibility for human rights violations and subsequent results in the judicial realm. It shows that the relationship between trade unions and human rights struggles, while certainly not linear and homogeneous, made an impact with implications, both at the national and the transnational level, for the evolution of the corporate responsibility agenda.

1 Introduction

This chapter examines the role of trade union organisations in reckoning with corporate complicity in crimes against humanity perpetrated by the last Argentinean dictatorship between 1976 and 1983. During this period business actors and technocrats actively collaborated not only in the implementation of economic and labour

This research was supported by the ERC-Consolidator project *Transnational Advocacy Networks and Corporate Accountability for Major International Crimes*. The project has received funding from the European Research Council (ERC) under the European Union's Horizon 2020 research and innovation program (grant agreement No. 101002993 — CORPACCOUNT).

V. Basualdo (✉)
CONICET-FLACSO Buenos Aires and SNSPA Bucharest, Buenos Aires, Argentina

R. Grosescu, J. G. Dale (eds.), *Corporate Accountability for Human Rights Violations*, Interdisciplinary Studies in Human Rights 16,
https://doi.org/10.1007/978-3-032-05569-9_7

policies, but also in the brutal political repression of opposition forces. Within the emergent field of corporate responsibility for human rights violations, this analysis contributes to a better understanding of the importance of movements "from below" and their national and transnational mobilisations for accountability.[1] Argentina, relevant both in terms of the depth of repression and of the active process of "memory, truth and justice"[2] after the fall of the dictatorship, has been a privileged terrain of research.[3] However, there are no specific contributions that focus on workers and trade union organisations and their role in this process.[4] In response, this chapter locates the efforts of workers and trade unions in the wider context of actions undertaken by other state and non-state actors. It highlights how these organizations had different attitudes towards the dictatorial past and the ways in which to reckon with its political violence at both the national and the international level—through methods such as criminal trials, civil litigation, and public campaigns. These findings are crucial not only for a more nuanced understanding of the Argentinean case, but also for underlining the importance of specific actors and movements that are frequently overlooked in the literature on corporate accountability.

The first section examines the impact of the last Argentinean dictatorship on the trade union movement, which, in the 1970s, was among the strongest in Latin America—with a tradition encompassing national confederations, national industrial-type trade unions with regional leaderships, and a firm presence in workplaces with shop stewards and "comisiones internas".[5] The core of this movement was the industrial working class, consolidated after decades of import-substituting industrialization, which developed from the 1930s to the mid-1970s. During the two previous dictatorships in 1955–1958 and 1966–1973, the economic elite and the military shared the concern that workers, particularly those in the most dynamic industrial sectors, such as the steel, automobile, and chemical industries, were at the centre of a process of increased confrontation, wherein they demanded political representation and the redistribution of wealth. Despite deep internal contradictions and conflicts in the worker's movement, military forces and the business elite

[1] Payne et al. (2020).

[2] The memory, truth and justice process (Proceso de Memoria, Verdad y Justicia) refers to a series of policies, promoted by both civil society and the state, designed to reckon with the crimes of the Argentinean dictatorship, from 1983 onwards. See Crenzel (2011) and Feierstein (2015), among others.

[3] Verbitsky and Bohoslavsky (2016), Grosescu et al. (2019), Grosescu (2019), García Martín (2019), Payne et al. (2020), Basualdo et al. (2021).

[4] One significant exception is García Martín (2019). However, García Martín's account is mainly written from a legal perspective that aims, in particular, to theorise the relationship between transitional justice and reparations for violations of socio-economic rights.

[5] Shop stewards and "comisiones internas" (CI) engage in direct worker representation on the shop floor. Workers at any company with ten or more employees are entitled to elect a representative. The number of shop stewards for each firm is directly related to the number of wage workers employed in the company and is regulated by legislation. The shop steward committee is a collective institution that comprises all shop stewards in a particular factory. The "comisión interna," also known as "comisión interna de reclamos," is a smaller body of shop stewards. See Basualdo (2011).

considered workers and trade union organizations to be a major player standing in opposition to their desire to impose a pattern of regressive income distribution. Consequently, one of the main goals of the 1976 coup was the reconfiguration of this labour power.

The second section analyses the lines of action of both the working class and the trade union movement during the dictatorship. It stresses that, while a segment of the trade union leadership initially supported repression of the more "combative" wings of the movement and attempted to secure benefits and positions of power for themselves (which a number of leaders managed to achieve), the dictatorial policies were aimed at transforming the power of the trade unions as a whole. The purpose was to fundamentally reconfigure the labour relations system within a framework that weakened labour rights and the income participation of wage earners. The combination of extremely repressive economic and labour policies was opposed by a large sector of the working class and the trade union movement throughout the country, who engaged in a wide range of traditional protests as well as clandestine activities, such as sabotage and other means of boycotting production. Workers and trade unionists also challenged the dictatorial policies by means of transnational campaigns that denounced human rights violations and advocated for economic, social and labour rights in different international forums, such as the International Labour Organization (ILO). These activities, which were backed by world labour confederations and numerous trade union organizations at the international level, emphasized that, during the dictatorship, many workplaces had become arenas of labour repression. Moreover, organizers underscored the strong links between the armed forces and segments of the business elite.

Finally, the third section analyses the post-dictatorial process of memory, truth and justice from 1983 onward as Argentina began to transition to democracy, paying particular attention to questions of corporate accountability. It examines different sub-periods: from the activities of the National Commission on the Disappearance of Persons and the Juntas Trial in the 1980s, to the period of impunity in the 1990s, to the reopening of the process of judicialization in the early 2000s. I show that the post-2003 period marked a turning point in the acceleration of debates on corporate responsibility and subsequent visible results both in the judicial and social and political spheres. Moreover, during the entire period from 1983 to 2023, various Argentinean trade unions became increasingly involved in reckoning with the dictatorial past, with a particular focus on the repression of the working class and the participation of the business sector in that repression. This section also explores experiences of transnational cooperation across Latin America and beyond and assesses the progress and limitations of corporate accountability in connection to the struggles for memory, truth and justice worldwide. In this context, I pay special attention to the "Ford trial", whose oral proceedings between 2017 and 2018 resulted in the conviction of one military officer and two Ford Motor Argentina executives for their participation in crimes against humanity, committed against twenty-four Ford workers in the 1970s. The concluding remarks summarise the main findings, contextualizing them within the most recent academic contributions to the field of corporate accountability.

2 The Last Argentine Dictatorship and Its Impact on the Trade Union Movement and the Working Class

The military coup carried out on 24 March 1976 attempted to put an end to the increasing confrontation between military forces, various political and social organizations, guerrilla movements, and paramilitary organizations fighting to establish rival national economic projects. The overthrow of Juan Domingo Perón in 1955, who along with the Peronist Party was banned until 1973, was followed by several military coups and increasing political violence. In the late 1960s, during the dictatorship led by Juan Carlos Ongania (1966–1973), a series of social upheavals led by workers and students sparked, in line with the global "'68 movements", a social mobilization for economic, labour and political rights. Among many others, the "Cordobazo", which took place in the industrial city of Córdoba in 1969, eventually forced the retreat of the dictatorship, a call for elections in 1973 and Juan Domingo Perón's return to power. During the democratically elected government (1973–1976), led first by Perón until his death in 1974 and then by his widow and former Vice-President María Estela Martínez de Perón, tensions within the labour movement—including the profound differences between the "combative" wing (which considered trade union action as part of a process of radical transformation) and the "conciliatory" sector (which focused on bargaining for improvements with no intention of challenging the economic and political order)—led to violent clashes. The death of Perón in 1974 deepened confrontations between the right and left wing of Peronism, a political movement established in the 1940s with a nationalist, industrialist and social justice agenda that encompassed a wide range of positions. In June and July 1975, massive labour mobilisations took place to oppose the austerity policies imposed by the government, which had lost credibility and support within a wider context of increasing repression by the armed forces and paramilitary groups such as the Argentinean Anti-Communist Alliance (AAA – La Triple A).

The economic elite and the armed forces both hoped to limit the strength of the labour movement and to stop political radicalization; they found the sitting government to be merely a partial and unsatisfactory solution to the problem of the working class, which not only underpinned the social and political order, but also opposed right-wing economic projects. The 1976 coup engendered the establishment of a terrorist state in Argentina well-known throughout the world for its record of violence and human rights violations. The figures support the notoriety: an estimated 30,000 disappeared people; thousands of political prisoners, tortured, murdered, or forced into exile. The personal property of the disappeared was seized, and 400 to 500 of their children abducted and put up for illegal adoption.[6] These crimes were denounced by human rights organizations and were recognized by the Argentine judiciary, which – as early as 1985 – convicted some of the most prominent military

[6] 137 of them have been located and have had their identity restored; the search continues. See: https://www.abuelas.org.ar/.

leaders in the so-called "Juicio a las Juntas", the first of many trials concerned with mass atrocities during the dictatorship.[7]

Workers, labour militants, and trade union leaders were prominent targets for the dictatorship.[8] Trade union activity was severely affected by the suspension of civil liberties and the military's direct control and management of the national labour confederation—the *Confederación General del Trabajo* (CGT)—as well as other major trade unions.[9] In the first three years of the dictatorship, dozens of organizations, such as the metal, construction, press, oil, textile, telephone, meatpacking, port, automobile and mechanic, and shipyard workers' union, were placed under military supervision, while others were deprived of their legal status.[10] The appointment of military officials to one third of the leadership of national labour organizations severely undermined the national union's centralized power structure. Labour rights, beginning with the right to strike, were suspended, along with any form of collective organization or bargaining.[11] At the same time, the military dictatorship introduced normative changes that legalised repressive activities and military presence at labour institutions, and established new regulations that undermined the institutional and financial foundations of union power.[12] For instance, the Law of Professional Associations passed in 1979 suppressed the existence of any labour confederation, thereby abolishing the CGT.[13]

Moreover, economic policies that increased commercial openness and financial liberalisation simultaneously decreased the participation of the industrial sector in the economy, thereby promoting the establishment of a new economic model that fostered the role of the financial sector. These economic transformations were imposed in a context of terror and control and had severe implications for the industrial working class and its ability to organise. Labour, economic, and repressive policies were closely interrelated and influenced each other, dramatically transforming the situation of workers and unions.[14] In economic terms, the structural changes of the mid-1970s, which fostered a process of acute deindustrialization, greatly eroded labour power. Moreover, a 1977 financial reform established internal interest rates that were considerably higher than international ones, dramatically

[7] Galante (2019).

[8] Fernández (1985, 1990), Abós (1984), Delich (1982, 1983), Barrera and Fallabella (1990).

[9] Communiqué 58 of the Military Junta informed that the CGT was going to be placed under military supervision, and afterwards a military authority appointed. See Fernández (1985), p. 62.

[10] For a list of the main organisations placed under military supervision from 24 March 1976 onwards, see Fernández (1985), pp. 135–137.

[11] Some of the major legal norms affecting labour: Law 21,261 prohibiting the right to strike; Law 8,596 authorising dismissals in state agencies without justification; Law 21,297 in April 1976 that changed hiring procedures, among many others. For the situation of workers under the dictatorship and the labour policies affecting trade union activity, see Pozzi (1988a, 1988b), Abós (1984), Fernández (1985), Munck (1998).

[12] Gallitelli and Thompson (1990), pp. 28–30.

[13] Gallitelli and Thompson (1990).

[14] James (1988); Drake (1996), and Barrera and Fallabella (1990).

altering the structure of internal prices in the domestic economy by favouring financial speculation over industrial production. The rise of external debt during this period provided funds for the internal financial market, generating profits from high interest rates, which were then sent abroad via capital flight.[15]

The industrial sector's impact on the GDP thus diminished, sparking a negative evolution in absolute terms. This restructuring process benefited the largest companies, most of which secured oligopolist positions in their markets by absorbing smaller firms, thereby significantly strengthening their position over their workforce. Furthermore, the military dictatorship developed a programme of subsidies, supposedly aimed at "industrial promotion" that benefited these oligopolies, which received considerable tax exemptions in return for establishing their productive activities in new areas.[16] These policies also affected labour organization. Several large-scale factories located in areas with existing traditions of union organization closed down or were reduced in size, leaving workers unemployed and weakening the power of those still employed. At the same time, new factories were established in areas with no previous tradition of industrialisation and union organisation.

Repression against the working class was another prominent feature of the period. The armed forces targeted industrial workers in particular, especially shop stewards and members of the "comisiones internas" of the large industrial factories. Repressive policies against industrial workers and union leaders included kidnapping, forced disappearance, murder, imprisonment, and persecution that internally displaced or drove many of them to exile. Testimonies and documents demonstrate the extreme concern of the armed forces and the economic elite about the growth in militancy on the shop floor during the late-1960s, which reached a high point in the mid-1970s, as well as about the links between workers, their immediate representatives, and left-wing organizations. They also reveal the involvement on part of the management of some of the most prominent industrial enterprises in the repression against their own workers, who were sometimes kidnapped in company vehicles or taken to clandestine detention centres located within the boundaries of the industrial estates.[17] One of the most prominent figures at the confluence between the economic elite and the armed forces was José Alfredo Martínez de Hoz, President of Acindar, a steel mill in Villa Constitución, until 1976 and then Minister of the Economy from 1976 to 1981. Acindar became emblematic of both the labour mobilization led by a combative leadership and the severe repression they suffered from 1975 onwards.[18]

On the one hand, the repressive policies had a strong economic impact that resulted in a dramatic increase in productivity and a decrease in real wages—an aspect facilitated by the persecution of activists and the strict prohibition of bargaining activities.[19] On the other hand, economic policies strengthened the impact of

[15] Azpiazu et al. (1986), Basualdo (2006) and Schvarzer (1987).

[16] Basualdo (2006).

[17] Basualdo (2006), AEyT FLACSO et al. (2015) and Basualdo et al. (2021).

[18] Basualdo (2020a).

[19] Basualdo (2006).

political and labour repression, as the structural change they caused altered the place of workers in the economy and society. Under the import substitution industrialization model, profits depended on the purchasing power of workers, which contributed, along with labour struggles and the key role of the industrial sector, to limit regressive income distribution. Under the new economic model, with its strong emphasis on financial valorisation and industrial restructuring, profits became increasingly independent from these factors. As such, the economic and social structural changes reinforced the attack on industrial workers that repression and the prohibition of union activities had instigated.

3 Responses to the Dictatorship: National and Transnational Trade Union Action Between 1976 and 1983

The 1976 coup ushered in important transformations within the Argentine labour movement. The once wide range of positions narrowed, as the most radical sectors were persecuted, killed, imprisoned, or driven into exile, and those who could still act maintained less combative positions from moderate and conciliatory to conservative or pro-military.

Despite the damaging effects of the offensive against labour movements, various sectors of the working class continued to challenge dictatorial policies in various ways. Beyond the different perspectives informing trade union action, it is vital to consider: (1) the initiatives of both the leadership and the rank and file; (2) the actions that took place within Argentina and those developed abroad; and (3) the forms of protest, including less visible underground movements. Nonetheless, if a significant segment of the rank and file as well as leadership found ways to engage in resistance and express their discontent with the dictatorship, there were also trade union leaders that sought accommodation with the regime, attempting to take advantage of some of the benefits offered, and playing an important role in legitimizing the dictatorship, both internally and abroad.

In the factories, the previously analysed history of shop floor organising played a decisive role in the early years of the regime, when the repression of union activity reached its high point. From 1976 to 1979, despite a relatively significant number of "traditional" strikes and protests, workers involved were severely punished, many of them by imprisonment, disappearance, or death. These circumstances forced the development of underground strategies to express labour unrest. Shop stewards and members of the "comisiones internas" resorted to previous traditions of organization. Militancy on the shop floor critically facilitated workers' efforts to develop different strategies: sabotage; methods for lowering the rhythm of production (*trabajo a desĝano, trabajo a tristeza*); repeated individual claims; and written petitions.[20]

[20] See Pozzi (1988a, b).

In April 1979, a sector of the union leadership represented by the "Commission of the 25," called for a National Day of Protest that marked the transition to a period of more open mobilization and a slow return to the traditional forms of struggle, such as massive mobilizations, strikes and protests. However, repression, if not as severe, continued, and many of the labour leaders were imprisoned for periods that ranged from days to months. In 1981 and 1982, further massive protests followed; after the defeat to Great Britain in the Falklands War, the transition to democracy was consolidated, opening the way for a slow recovery of labour rights after 1983. Despite strategies developed by workers and unions to repeal the attack on these various fronts, the dictatorship and the structural changes it implemented had a profoundly negative impact on industrial workers and their ability to organise.[21]

At the same time, trade unionists and trade union organisations developed lines of action in the international arena. From 1976 onwards, the international campaign by workers and union leaders in exile against the dictatorship received the support of local workers and leaders, as well as many national and international labour organizations, including the three world confederations: the World Confederation of Labour (WCL), the World Federation of Trade Unions (WFTU) and the International Confederation of Free Trade Unions (ICFTU).[22] This international support yielded progress both in terms of disseminating information about human rights violations and increasing pressure on the dictatorship to improve the conditions of persecuted workers. In 1975, the Argentinean General Confederation of Labour (CGT) was invited to participate in the up-coming ICFTU Congress, and later that year joined the organisation as a member.[23] After the 1976 coup, the ICFTU, along with the WFTU, the WCL and the ILO, played a substantial role in denouncing and opposing the persecution of the Argentine working class and its organisations. The anti-dictatorial campaign launched by militants in Argentina and abroad was accompanied by labour protests.

In this critical context, the ICFTU backed the CGT in several ways. First, it provided some labour leaders with the resources to live abroad. Second, from 1976 onward, the ICFTU not only issued various declarations protesting the dictatorial policies against labour, but also sent various missions to the country to discuss the conditions of the movement. Third, it supported complaints at the ILO against the Argentine dictatorship. In fact, immediately after the military coup, the WFTU and the WCL, together with the National Confederation of Workers of Perú and other Peruvian workers organisations, submitted complaints to the ILO's Committee on

[21] Basualdo (2010b).

[22] Basualdo (2006a, c) and especially (2010a).

[23] The ICFTU Bulletin *International Trade Union News*, dated June 1975, noted that: "The Argentine CGT has requested affiliation to the ICFTU. The Secretary General, Otto Kersten, had a meeting on May 22, 1975, with four representatives of the Argentine CGT, who submitted the demand for affiliation of the CGT to the ICFTU. See World Confederation of Labour archives (KADOC, Leuven, Belgium), Document "El movimiento obrero argentino y sus relaciones internacionales", signed by the Ateneo Justicialista Latinoamericano, August 1975. The document partially reproduces the *Boletín de la CIOSL, Noticias Sindicales Internacionales*, No. 11, 1/6/75, p. 3.

Freedom of Association (CFA). ILO Case Number 842 (Argentina) became the main case against the dictatorship's anti-labour policies and referred to two main complaints: the imprisonment and disappearance of union leaders, militants, and workers; and the violations of union rights, including the replacement of CGT's leadership with members of the armed forces and the restrictions imposed on union activities and workers' rights.[24]

Although the WFTU supported demands for the restoration of labour rights in Argentina, it initially held a contradictory position toward the military dictatorship, influenced by strong commercial ties to the Soviet Union and the line of the Communist Party of Argentina, which believed that the military junta belonged to the "moderate" sector of the armed forces. Although they denounced the disappearance of workers, they attributed them to right-wing "terrorist bands" and demanded that the government to put a stop to them. Eventually, as the responsibility of the Argentine state for human rights violations became undeniable, the WFTU hardened its position towards the government.[25]

In December 1976, the Executive Committee of the ICFTU demanded that the Argentinean government release all imprisoned trade union leaders, allow the return to the country of those exiled, eliminate all legislation that deprived the trade union leaders and workers of their civil, political and labour rights, and restore the free exercise of all union rights, including the right to strike.[26] The Executive Committee also asked all ICFTU affiliates, as well as regional organisations and the International Trade Secretariats, to participate in this campaign. It demanded that trade unions exert pressure on their own governments and urge them to engage with the Argentine government regarding all these urgent matters by expressing the intention to organise a delegation to visit Argentina.

The ILO thus became a key arena of protest. First, Case 842 became a central point of confluence for the numerous organisations attempting to build solidarity with the Argentine labour movement. This case did not occur in a vacuum. As labour repression was on the rise in the late 1960s and early 1970s, the CFA of the ILO had received various complaints related to Argentina, including Case 809 submitted in 1974 by the Graphic Federation of Buenos Aires relating to the withdrawal of its trade union status and the imprisonment of some of its leaders, and Case 836, submitted by the WCL in January 1976, concerning the government's interference in the exercise of union rights.[27]

---

[24] Zorzoli (2018).

[25] See for example the WFTU press release "Stopper l'action des groupes terroristes en Argentine!" (1 October 1976) in Confédération Général du Travail-Federation Syndicale Mondiale Archives, France.

[26] World Confederation of Labour archives (KADOC, Leuven, Belgium), Circulaire No. 59 (1976), ICFTU, signed by the General Secretary Otto Kersten, 3 December 1976.

[27] Regarding Case 809, see for example 157th report of the Committee on Freedom of Association (CFA), GB. 199 (February-March 1976), pp. 14–16. Regarding case 836, see for example 160th report of the CFA, GB. 201 (November 1976), p. 51.

The evolution of Case 842 reflects both the potential and the limitations of the CFA at the time. On the one hand, the pressure on the Argentine government engendered by the case had important effects, such as the release of some trade unionists, the legalization of the situation of others who had been kidnapped, and certain concessions in terms of trade union activity.[28] On the other hand, the strategy followed by the Argentine government of full formal collaboration allowed the dictatorship to differentiate its case from those of Uruguay and Chile. These neighbouring countries, also governed by military dictatorships, attracted considerably more criticism that Argentina. The lobbying power of Ambassador Gabriel Martínez, head of the Permanent Mission of Argentina to the International Organisations in Geneva, his connections, apparent willingness to collaborate and a solid defence strategy, as well as the explanations and justifications provided by the Argentinean government were successful in dismantling attempts to move the case to a Commission of Enquiry, the highest-level investigative procedure at the ILO. Moreover, structural problems in the functioning of the CFA itself hampered its operations: from insufficient equipment, staff, and resources to the reality that, once states made certain concessions, the CFA was forced to moderate its pressure on them.[29] However, even when the procedures and resources of the CFA were amended to increase pressure, the Argentine case provides an excellent example of the intrinsic limits of organisations like the ILO in dealing with labour and human rights violations committed by sovereign states, especially ones that carefully and dutifully comply with requests for information and collaboration.

Nevertheless, the ILO was important in another way. As previous research has demonstrated, the military junta paid special attention to its image on the international stage. Concerned with the international campaign against its human and labour rights violations, the Argentinean government deemed it important to send a tripartite delegation to the ILO's yearly conferences to preserve the image of a

[28] An illustration of the widespread appreciation that workers and trade unionists expressed for the international campaign against the dictatorship is the statement by Ricardo Pérez, leader of the truck drivers' union who was in prison for a short period during the dictatorship and integrated the "Commission of the 25", that "I would argue that, in a way, our lives were saved thanks to the international solidarity. […] There was a strong pressure of the ICFTU, and of the ILO, in defence of our liberties. […] The dictatorship had certain fears of international criticism, especially when abroad there was a lot of information that in Argentina had been hidden". Testimony by Ricardo Pérez, in Calello and Parcero (1984) cited by Basualdo (2010a).

[29] An example of a discussion on the insufficiency of CFA action is a letter submitted by the WCL to the CFA in March 1976, which criticised the lack of equipment, staff, and resources, yearly meetings (three), the dilatory process, and the generous deadlines granted to governments. It also lamented the fact that governments always had the last word, since its reply was not forwarded to the complainant as soon as it was received and before the Governing Body committee had reached its own conclusion on the case. See GB. 199/8/29, 199th Session (2–5 March 1976). To improve the situation, the WCL proposed that the Committee act promptly when circumstances required. When human life was in danger or trade union representatives were imprisoned or suffered collective dismissal, the Director General should be empowered to do more than simply transmit complaints to governments. They proposed a more proactive attitude, the abandonment of the "diplomatic language", and the declaration of guilt when warranted. See Basualdo (2010a).

certain "normality" in labour relations—except in 1977 and 1980, when only the government's delegate attended. In the context of censorship and control over the press, international meetings such as the yearly ILO conferences had the potential to spark a discussion about the situation in Argentina, a controversy that had been silenced inside the country. For Argentinean trade union leaders, the ILO became a forum in which they could heard by representatives from all over the world. However, as we shall see, the ILO conferences also became the object of constant confrontations between the two main sectors of the labour movement: one openly critical of the dictatorship, the other one more inclined to endorse the government's official narrative.

In most cases, the trade union delegates to the conference belonged to groups linked to the armed forces and the employers.[30] Although, in certain years (such as 1978), a greater number of autonomous trade union leaders could make their voices heard, most other trade unionists that appeared superficially as critics of the dictatorship were in fact close to the military government. However, the ILO conference also offered a place for persecuted and exiled union leaders, such as Raimundo Ongaro, former Secretary General of CGT, who attended every year as an observer. Ongaro was an important figure in a more extensive network of labour solidarity that included organisations such as the TYSAE (Trabajadores y Sindicalistas Argentinos en el Exilio), with members in various countries. The ILO allowed Ongaro to develop an essential network of both international and national organisations that participated in the campaign of denunciating violations of labour rights.[31]

In sum, mobilizations within Argentina, movements of international solidarity, encompassing trade union confederations from various countries, world labour federations and activities within organisations such as the ILO were integral to the process of documenting, assessing and analysing the economic and labour dimensions of repression. While the focus during this period was on the dictatorship and not on corporate responsibility, the corpus of evidence generated about human rights violations through the transnational solidarity campaign was key to illuminating the connections between the economic, social and repressive policies of the dictatorship, and unveiling the links between the armed forces and different economic actors—all of which was fundamental to the eventual transition to democracy.

4 The Role of the Trade Union Movement in the Process of Memory, Truth and Justice in Argentina After 1983

The process of memory, truth and justice (MTJ) concerning severe human rights violations between 1976 and 1983 was at first based on the activities carried out during the dictatorship by human rights organisations, victims groups and trade

[30] For an extensive analysis of this history, see Basualdo (2010a).

[31] Basualdo (2006a, c).

unions, among others. Given the complexity of this process, which lasted decades and included several dimensions that have been examined at length elsewhere, this section will only emphasize important turning points and narratives relevant to the issue of repression of workers and trade unionists and subsequent corporate accountability actions.[32]

During the initial stages of the MTJ process, from 1983 to 1989, both the work of the National Commission on the Disappearance of Persons (CONADEP) and its 1984 *Nunca Más* (Never Again) report, and the Trial of the Juntas (held in 1985) provided evidence for the involvement of the corporate sector in the repression of workers and trade unionists. The report emphasized the high proportion of workers among the victims of enforced disappearance. In a special section dedicated to trade unionists, the report detailed the significant number of collective disappearances that occurred *within* the workplace: shipyards, automobile factories, steel mills, public offices and sugar mills, or in neighbourhoods nearby, where the workers lived. It was clear from the testimonies gathered that the coup marked a negative turning point in labour relations between directors and managers and their staff. However, this early analysis of repression in industrial factories and disappearances in the agrarian labour milieu required a periodization beyond the strict limits of the dictatorship to include the repressive tactics that took place during the presidency of María Estela Martínez de Perón. The report included incidents that occurred at the Acindar steel mill in Villa Constitución, the Ledesma sugar mill, the Ford automobile factory, the shipyards in the north of the country, particularly Astarsa, among others, as well as repression of rural workers and the agricultural leagues in the Northeast.[33]

During the Juntas Trial in 1985, the diversity of trade union voices became evident. On the one hand, many survivors explicitly referred to the persecution of workers and trade unions and alluded to the previous process of international denunciation and international solidarity. On the other hand, additional testimonies revealed the complicity of some trade union leaders. This was the case, for instance, for Jorge Triaca (leader of the plastic workers trade union) and Antonio Baldassini (leader of the postal workers) who testified that the authorities had treated them extremely well, and that they had not heard of any "disappeared" within the labour movement. Following the Juntas Trial, groups of workers initiated, sometimes successfully, civil lawsuits demanding reparations, as in the case of three Ford Motor Argentina workers who were compensated by the company for their dismissal while under illegal detention by the armed forces.[34]

During the transition to democracy, certain segments of the trade union movement that had managed to attain positions of power during the dictatorship managed to consolidate their leadership and even gain positions in international labour organisations, despite the fact that some of them had been implicated in the regime of

[32] See Basualdo (2020b, 2022) and Payne et al. (2020).

[33] CONADEP (1984).

[34] About these trials, see Martínez (2021).

repression. Among the most emblematic examples was José Rodríguez, leader of the automobile union, SMATA, who testified during the "Truth Trials" (see below) in the late 1990s about the disappearance of Mercedes-Benz workers, and who was dismissed from his position as vice-president of the International Federation of Metalworkers in response to the protests of victims, families and human rights organisations.[35] Similarly, Gerardo Martínez, leader of the construction union, UOCRA, whose name was found on a list of civilian personnel of the 601 Battalion, the most important intelligence centre of the armed forces. Victims, families and human rights organisations sued him for his involvement in the repression, but he was acquitted for lack of evidence, although his presence on the list was not challenged or denied. [36] Despite all this, he managed to build an extensive international career which included key positions such as Secretary of International Relations of the CGT and, since 2005, member of the *ILO* Governing Body. These individuals, including the previously mentioned Triaca and Baldassini, are representative of leaders that explicitly distanced themselves from any connection to human rights organisations and their demands. Others, such as the top leaders of the metallurgical union UOM, also distanced themselves from the human rights movement. Underlining that some of their leaders, Augusto Timoteo Vandor and José Ignacio Rucci, had been killed by guerrilla organisations in the 1970s, they avoided for decades any involvement in human rights approaches focused on State repression on left-wing political and trade-union militants.

In contrast, other sectors of the labour movement, building on the strong leadership of trade unionists such as Víctor De Gennaro, Victorio Paulón, Alberto Piccinini, and Hugo Yasky, who had been victims of persecution during the dictatorship, maintained deep connections with human rights organisations. An important coordinating network for these initial efforts was the Coordinadora de Centrales Sindicales del Cono Sur, created in 1986 by the ICFTU and its regional organisation for Latin America, the Organización Regional Interamericana de Trabajadores (ORIT). The Buenos Aires constitutive act of September 1986 defined as central objectives the defence of democracy and human rights by fighting authoritarian regimes that still existed in the region (Chile and Paraguay) and the articulation of a joint trade union action against the external debt and its effects.[37]

The end of the 1980s marked a turning point in the MTJ process in Argentina. In the context of military unrest and challenges, President Raul Alfonsín adopted two impunity laws (the Due Obedience Law in 1986 and the Full Stop Law in 1987) that severely limited prosecutions against military officials involved in mass crimes

[35] See "Murió José Rodríguez, ex Secretario General de SMATA", Página 12, November 7, 2009. Link: www.pagina12.com.ar/diario/elpais/1-134851-2009-11-07.html.

[36] See "El jefe de la UOCRA no negó ser espía de la dictadura", Diario La Capital, July 21, 2011. Last access: August 6, 2024. Link: museodelamemoria.gob.ar/page/noticias/id/165/title/El-jefe-de-la-Uocra-no-neg%C3%B3-ser-esp%C3%ADa-de-la-dictadura- and "Un gremialista sospechado por su pasado", Página 12, July 13, 2011. Last access: August 6, 2024. Link: www.pagina12.com.ar/diario/elpais/1-172148-2011-07-13.html.

[37] Gordillo (2017).

during the dictatorship. Moreover, between 1989 and 1990, President Carlos Menem pardoned all previously convicted officers, inaugurating an era of impunity that lasted until the beginning of the 2000s. Nevertheless, various initiatives managed to keep the repression of workers and evidence of corporate complicity in this process on the national and international agenda throughout the 1990s. One prominent step, rooted in longstanding discussions within the Coordinadora de Centrales Sindicales, was the 1998 petition, by the Central de los Trabajadores de la Argentina (CTA)—an organisation born as a Congress in 1992 and transformed in a trade union confederation in 1997, to Spanish Judge Baltasar Garzón, which included a collection of testimonies and complaints that made it possible to identify thousands of disappeared workers. This was one of the first documents that not only underlined that workers and trade unionists had been key targets of dictatorial repression, but also pointed to the participation of several companies, such as Acindar, Ford, Astarsa, Mercedes-Benz, Ledesma, among others, in these crimes. These documents were submitted to the Spanish judiciary as it investigated mass crimes committed in Argentina based on the principle of universal jurisdiction.[38]

Another crucial initiative promoted by human rights organisations to overcome impunity were the Truth Trials, which began in 1998 in La Plata, and later expanding to most Argentinean cities. These trials, which had no criminal implications, focused instead on guaranteeing the "right to know the truth," giving rise to intense debate and controversy within the human rights movement. While some human rights organisations considered these trials a defeat, since they did not allow for punishment, others underlined the importance of the "right to truth" about human rights violations, and considered it a step forward marking it as a turn away from the impunity of the 1990s.[39] Indeed, the Truth Trials enabled, particularly in regards to corporate responsibility for the repression of workers and trade unionists, several witnesses from different parts of the country to make their voices heard. Their testimonies added new evidence about the persecution of the labour sector and the different ways economic actors participated in repressive processes. For instance, the repression against Ford and Mercedes-Benz workers was extensively analysed in the Truth Trials (among others), and the evidence provided was later crucial for the criminal cases presented after the impunity laws of the 1980s were declared unconstitutional in 2005.[40]

During this period, a trial centred around victims with Argentinian-Italian citizenship also took place in Italy. Many of these victims, who were kidnapped and forcibly disappeared, had been workers of the Astarsa shipyard in the northern industrial belt of Buenos Aires. In 2000, this trial ended in a historic conviction (in absentia) of several Argentinean military officials. The case was supported by trade union organisations from both countries. While not prosecuting corporate actors,

---

[38] For transnational investigations and prosecutions based on universal jurisdiction in Spain, see Roht-Arriaza (2005).

[39] See https://www.hrw.org/reports/2001/argentina/argen1201-04.htm (accessed 16.06.2024).

[40] See Basualdo et al. (2015).

they emphasized however that they had been persecuted as workers and in connection with their trade union activities. Furthermore, in 1999, a lawsuit was filed in Germany on behalf of Héctor Ratto, a Mercedes-Benz worker kidnapped on the premises of Mercedes-Benz Argentina in 1977. It accused Mercedes-Benz production manager Juan Tasselkraut of aiding and abetting the murder of another worker, Diego Núñez, who was kidnapped and disappeared, after Ratto overheard Tasselkraut providing key personal information about Núñez to the armed forces over the phone. The public prosecutor in Nuremberg-Fürth initiated investigations, but suspended the proceedings in November 2003. Enforced disappearances were not codified in the German criminal code at that time and, in the absence of Ratto's remains—which are missing to this day—the prosecutor argued that he had no legal basis for prosecution.[41]

4.1 Renewal of Human Rights Struggles and the Rise of Corporate Accountability Claims

From 2003 to 2015, prosecutions of crimes against humanity were reactivated in Argentina, and the issue of complicity of civil actors in human rights violations became an increasingly important issue. This new turn was determined by a series of transformations. In 2001, a court in Buenos Aires declared "the invalidity, unconstitutionality and irreversible nullity" of the Due Obedience and Full Stop laws.[42] On 21 August 2003, the Senate also annulled these laws, a decision confirmed by the Supreme Court of Justice in 2005. Moreover, the executive came out in support of the MTJ process, with a number of policies that included signalling and recognizing memory sites, opening the archives, assuming state duties for the protection of victims, and promoting scientific and academic research connected with human rights violations. This context opened new possibilities for prosecuting human rights violations committed under dictatorship, including the complicity of economic actors in such crimes.

In November 2002, Pedro Troiani, a former Ford worker, and other shop stewards and union militants at Ford petitioned for investigations into the alleged complicity of Ford managers in the illegal arrest and torture of so-called "subversive workers" in the 1970s. In 2006, the prosecution identified several participants in the crimes: the president of the company at the time, Nicolás Enrique Courard (who had died and therefore could not be summoned), the Manager of Production and member of the Board of Directors Pedro Müller, Guillermo Galarraga (who died before oral arguments could begin) and the Chief of Security Héctor Francisco Sibilla. In

[41] See Basualdo et al. (2015), and Basualdo (2015).

[42] Case 8686/2000, "Simón, Julio, Del Cerro, Juan Antonio s/sustracción de menores de 10 años" (Simón, Julio, Del Cerro, Juan Antonio a/abduction of minors under 10 years old), Registry of Secretariat No. 7 of Federal Criminal and Correctional Court No. 4.

2002, another group of plaintiffs accused Mercedes-Benz of having formed a criminal alliance with then Minister of Labour Carlos Ruckauf, as well as with the leadership of the Union of Mechanics and Related Automobile Transport (SMATA), to persecute union representatives considered "undesirable".[43] In reponse to the delays and difficulties encountered during the Argentinian judicial process, a group of delegates and workers decided to initiate a civil lawsuit in the United States in 2004 against Daimler Chrysler AG, the parent company of Mercedes-Benz, which was, however, unable to move forward for jurisdictional reasons.[44]

Also in 2004, a US law firm working in collaboration with Argentinean lawyers agreed to sue Ford Motor Company under the Alien Tort Claims Act (ATCA), which enabled foreigners to seek remedy in US courts for gross human rights violations committed by individuals and companies abroad. The complaint was filed in a California court and raised expectations that were however dashed when the US lawyers decided to withdraw shortly before the company was notified of the lawsuit. From Buenos Aires, the workers insisted on moving forward with the lawsuit, but the decision of the American lawyers was final.[45]

In 2006, against the backdrop of the reopening of trials in Argentina, various human rights organisations, trade unions and academic actors took up the issue of "business-military complicity" as a rallying cry in their repudiation of the thirty years since the coup d'état, highlighting the accumulated evidence and the demands of the victims.[46] At this stage, the trials in different parts of the country had produced a large number of testimonies and documents, as well as court decisions that underlined the importance of investigations into the participation of companies and businessmen in the repression of workers and trade unionists, as well as the persecution of labour lawyers. However, the power of these companies and the influence of their top officials in political and judicial sectors, the complexity of these cases, which demanded legal conceptualizations and criteria that had not yet been consolidated hindered the prosecution of corporate responsibility.[47] The "Task Force 5" trial in 2015 however allowed for the identification of a large number of cases of corporate complicity in gross human rights violations in the southern industrial area.[48] The Operativo Independencia case in Tucumán opened an investigation into sugar mills such as La Fronterita, which will soon begin oral proceedings, while

---

[43] Case 17.735/02.

[44] See Basualdo et al. (2015), and Basualdo (2015).

[45] Ibid., p. 165.

[46] Basualdo (2006b).

[47] All of this became visible in the cases linked to the Ledesma sugar mill and the "El Aguilar" mining company (Jujuy), La Nueva Provincia (Bahía Blanca) and Loma Negra (Province of Buenos Aires), as well as in the large number of cases involving companies in the northern industrial area, such as the Astarsa, Mestrina and Forte shipyards, the Lozadur and Cattaneo ceramics companies, Dálmine Siderca, and Mercedes-Benz. See Basualdo (2020, 2022).

[48] It shed light on cases such as Propulsora Siderúrgica, Astilleros Río Santiago, Petroquímica Sudamericana, Swift, SIAP, Molinos Río de la Plata among many others.

various trials in the province of Córdoba, such as Fiat, have also shed light on cases of corporate responsibility.

Worthy of note are also attempts at judicialization in civil law and labour jurisdictions. In April 2007, the Supreme Court of the province of Buenos Aires ordered Siderca, part of the Techint group, to pay compensation to the widow of Oscar Orlando Bordisso—a union delegate who was kidnapped and disappeared in June 1977—based on the law on work accidents, as the kidnapping occurred on the road between the metallurgical plant and his home. Similarly, in 2008, María Gimena Ingegnieros sued Techint for reparations based on the same law for the forced disappearance of her father, Enrique Roberto Ingegnieros, in May 1977. Ingegnieros was abducted by "a task force dependent on the National Government" during work hours and on work premises. The company objected on the grounds that the statute of limitations had expired. After court rulings at various levels, the case was resolved by the Supreme Court of Justice on 9 May 2019, which decided that labour actions aimed at obtaining compensation for damages arising from crimes against humanity are subject to the statute of limitations.[49] While this was a major step back for corporate accountability efforts, a new Civil Code adopted in November 2020 enshrined that civil claims connected with crimes against humanity did not fall under a statute of limitations, thus opening new possibilities for future prosecutions.

In addition to these civil litigations, human rights activists and researchers also collaborated to hold economic actors to account. One major achievement in this sense was the publication in 2013 of *Outstanding Debts: The Economic Accomplices of the Dictatorship*, coordinated by Horacio Verbitsky and Juan Pablo Bohoslavsky. With contributions from over twenty-five experts, the book explored the multiple connections between key economic actors and the armed forces.[50] Another relevant step was the publication, in 2015, of a two-volume report on corporate responsibility for crimes against humanity and the repression of workers.[51] This was the result of the coordinated work of a team of nearly twenty experts from the Economics and Technology Area of the Facultad Latinoamericana de Ciencias Sociales (FLACSO), an academic institution, the Centro de Estudios Legales y Sociales (CELS), an Argentinean NGO, and the Truth and Justice Programme and the Secretariat for Human Rights of the Argentinean government, with contributions from several trade union leaders and organisations. The report documented the role of twenty-five national and transnational companies in the illegal detention, torture or enforced disappearance of 900 workers and trade unionists in the 1970s. Several contributors presented the results internationally, in Brazil, Germany and Spain, arguing for the need of further research in Latin America and justice for such human rights violations by companies and their representatives.

---

[49] Basualdo (2021).

[50] The volume was translated into English by Oxford University Press and is among the most quoted publications on corporate accountability in Latin America.

[51] AEyT FLACSO et al. (2015).

The analysis of these cases demonstrated that there was a pattern of corporate involvement in human rights violations during the dictatorship (1976–1983). Based on a vast range of sources, the research provided evidence of the contribution of companies and their top officials to the development of the repressive policies, including key resources and information, as well as of the existence of clandestine detention spaces in five of the analysed companies.[52] The report thus had not only historical and political implications, but also legal consequences. Moreover, the project underlined the connection between repression and the implementation of neoliberal policies that transformed the economic structure of the country. It showed that this extreme pattern of repression was associated with a process of "militarization" in large factories, as well as with numerous setbacks and losses in labour rights and forms of shop floor organisation. It also demonstrated that labour had to relinquish many of the advances it had made in terms of labour conditions, safety measures in production processes, and the right to protest; the expansion of subcontracting and regressive changes in labour relations also accompanied the repression.

Among the many dialogues with various counterparts across the Southern Cone, Argentinean academic experts travelled in 2014 to provide technical support to the Brazilian Workers' Working Group (WG), which encompassed ten trade union confederations and was working within the National Truth Commission of Brazil. The final report of this WG emphasised corporate participation in the repression and culminated in the opening of investigations into various companies and a civil lawsuit against Volkswagen do Brazil. The lawsuit led to an agreement signed in 2020 by Volkswagen Brazil and the Prosecutor's office that established reparations and funding for a research project on the corporate responsibility of ten large companies in Brazil during the dictatorship.[53] In Chile, the lawyers and researchers of the human rights organisation and the memory centre "Londres 38, espacio de memorias" working on human rights violations during the dictatorship also fostered discussions and connections with counterparts from Argentina, Brazil and beyond to help advance research and trials through the dissemination of Argentinean historical and legal methodologies.[54]

5 Corporate Accountability: A Highly Contested Field

2015 marked a further turning point in justice and memory processes concerning the dictatorial past in Argentina. Immediately before Mauricio Macri's right-wing administration (2015–2019) was inaugurated, the Argentinean Congress approved

[52] AEyT FLACSO et al. (2015), pp. 408–409.

[53] CAAF-UNIFESP coordinated this project, which published a public report in 2023 that was presented at a conference in Sao Paulo that same year. See: CAAF-UNIFESP (2023) and the chapter by Juan Pablo Bohoslavsky and Juan Cruz Goñi in this volume.

[54] See Araya Gómez and Garcés Fuentes (2021).

the creation of a Congressional commission on corporate collaboration with the military dictatorships, a proposal that had been included in the book "Cuentas Pendientes".[55] The project was promoted by CELS in coordination with several political parties and trade unions, the international support of the UN Human Rights Council, Amnesty International, and the International Commission of Jurists. However, to this day, the establishment of the commission has been delayed due to pressure from political and economic actors, many of them associated with the Macri administration.

A similar contradictory movement occurred in the courts. In 2016, Marcos Levín, the owner and president of the transportation company La Veloz del Norte, and his right-hand man, Víctor Hugo Bocos, were convicted for their participation in the illegal deprivation of liberty and torture suffered by Víctor Cobos, a driver and union representative—a milestone judicial decision. However, a year later, a higher court of appeals reversed the verdict, arguing that although the crimes had been proven, they could not be considered crimes against humanity. This decision was again reversed in November 2023, when the Cámara Federal de Casación Penal convicted Levín to twelve years of imprisonment, while another court convicted him to sixteen to eighteen years' imprisonment for his responsibility in the kidnapping and torture of seventeen workers at the Salta bus company.[56]

Another prominent case was that of the Ledesma sugar mill in Jujuy. Businessman Carlos Pedro Blaquier—a close friend of Martínez de Hoz, Minister of Economy from 1976 to 1981 and a central figure of the business-military groups that played a key role in the organisation of the 1976 coup—and his right-hand man Alberto Lemos were indicted in 2013 for their participation in human rights violations, in particular for providing trucks used in the kidnapping of workers. However, in 2015, a court decided that the case lacked merit, based on technicalities and procedural issues. In 2021, the Court of Casación however reversed the order, and called for the continuation of the trial.[57] By that time, however, Blaquier was facing health problems, and the trial was postponed. In 2023, he died without having been brought to court, a fact that victims and human rights organisations considered a major symbol of impunity. Moreover, in 2018, a trial concerning a disappeared rural worker connected with the Las Marías company, in Gobernador Virasoro, ended with the

[55] See Law 27217 creating the Comisión Bicameral de la Verdad, la Memoria, la Justicia, la Reparación y el fortalecimiento de las instituciones de la democracia, Date: November 25, 2015, Promulgation: December 2, 2015. Link: https://servicios.infoleg.gob.ar/infolegInternet/anexos/255000-259999/256130/norma.htm Last access: August 6, 2024.

[56] See "Salta: condenan al exdueño de La Veloz del Norte a 18 años de prisión por crímenes de lesa humanidad cometidos contra los trabajadores de la firma", Ministerio Público Fiscal, November 3, 2023. Last access, August 6, 2024. Link: www.fiscales.gob.ar/lesa-humanidad/salta-condenan-al-exdueno-de-la-veloz-del-norte-a-18-anos-de-prision-por-crimenes-de-lesa-humanidad-cometidos-contra-los-trabajadores-de-la-firma/.

[57] See "La Corte Suprema de Justicia revocó la falta de mérito a Carlos Blaquier por delitos de lesa humanidad", Ministry of Justice, Secretariat of Human Rights, July 8, 2021. Last access: August 6, 2024. Link: www.argentina.gob.ar/noticias/la-corte-suprema-de-justicia-revoco-la-falta-de-merito-carlos-blaquier-por-delitos-de-lesa.

acquittal of the accused businessman, First Lieutenant (RE) Héctor María Torres Queirel.[58]

However, in 2020, two top officials at Acindar steel mill were indicted for their involvement in human rights violations in Rosario province, while Juan Tasselkraut, the high-ranking officer at Mercedes-Benz is currently (June 2024) being investigated for having provided information and a blacklist of workers who were subsequently kidnapped. New criminal trials concerning workers at Propulsora Siderúrgica (Techint group), Petroquímica Sudamericana, Astilleros Río Santiago, SIAP, Swift, and Molinos Río de la Plata, among others, are also in the early stages. In Tucumán, business officials of Ingenio "La Fronterita" were indicted for possible corporate involvement in human rights violations, and oral proceedings should begin soon.[59]

6 The "Ford Case" and Its Impact

In 2017–2018, the "Ford Case" constituted a milestone in the process for corporate responsibility, while also revealing its limitations. This criminal trial aimed to determine the responsibilities of military officer Santiago Omar Riveros and two senior officials of the Ford Motor Argentina, Héctor Sibilla, head of security, and Pedro Müller, manufacturing manager, in the repression of twenty-four Ford workers and trade union delegates. Between 1976 and 1977, the workers had been kidnapped (many of them from their workplaces), several taken to a company barbecue area where they were tortured, and then to police stations and different penitentiary units where they were further abused, while their families were forced to endure endless hardships.

Oral proceedings began in 2017 and included the testimonies of the surviving victims, their spouses, children and other relatives, as well as expert witnesses. The defence lawyers also called witnesses, who provided important information on the dynamics of the plant and the roles of the accused business officials. In addition, the trial also included visual inspections of the two police headquarters where workers had been detained and at the Ford Motor Argentina plant: the space used as a detention and torture centre on the premises was inspected particularly carefully. Defence lawyers did not dispute the human rights violations, but argued that the armed forces

[58] In July 2018, proceedings began in the trial on the disappearance of rural worker Marcelo Peralta on 29 June 1977, in a production plant linked to the Las Marías yerba mate company in Gobernador Virasoro. Torres Queirel, who had been the municipal controller of Virasoro during the dictatorship and supplier of raw material to the factory, was accused of being a necessary participant in Peralta's forced disappearance. Against the backdrop of a heavy presence of security forces in the court room and the extreme animosity against the family and friends of the victim, the court acquitted Torres Queirel, disregarding the evidence introduced at trial, on 23 August 2018.

[59] For more details about the "La Fronterita" case, see Leigh Payne and Gabriel Pereira's chapter in this volume.

alone had been responsible, denying the involvement of the accused in any of these crimes. While Ford Motor Argentina declared it would collaborate with judicial authorities, it made no official statement regarding the events.[60]

The verdict was announced on 11 December 2018, at a venue packed with victims, their families, political leaders and trade unionists, as well as a massive crowd waiting in an adjacent room and in the street. The judges found the three defendants guilty, sentencing them to various prison terms.[61] They considered Sibilla and Müller "necessary participants" in the illegal detentions and torture, a fact that garnered media attention around the world, and silenced significant segments of the Argentine media.

The judges released their reasoning behind this landmark decision on 15 March 2019. First, they explained that the acts qualified as crimes against humanity. They invoked rulings by the Argentine Supreme Court and referred to the verdicts of several international tribunals to clearly affirm that civilians could, indeed, be perpetrators of such crimes. Further, they analysed the ways in which Ford Motor Argentina officials had been involved in the repression, though collaboration with military authorities and providing information about the workers to be kidnapped.[62] Concerning the motives behind these criminal actions, the judges underlined that the elimination of the "comisiones internas" and the trade union organisation as "symbols of the working-class strength and resistance to the demands of higher efficiency, was a common goal between business leaders and the military who seized the government," giving extraordinary importance to the dictatorship's broader engagement in structural economic transformation. They claimed that in order to understand the specific facts of their repressive intent, it was imperative to place them in the wider framework of economic and labour policies imposed by the dictatorship. In this sense, they considered that the dynamic of the labour market was yet another dimension of the social and economic transformation put into motion by both the military and segments of the corporate elite. They highlighted the common denominator among the twenty-four victims—"their labour relation with Ford." The judges added that there was "a strategic relationship between the military and a segment of the business leadership" as the two groups had common interests, namely, to ensure a "normalization" of labour relations and to profoundly transform the economic and social structure of Argentina for their own benefit.[63]

---

[60] www.business-humanrights.org/en/ford-statement-regarding-legal-claims-brought-by-former-employees-who-say-they-were-kidnapped-and-tortured-on-ford-argentina-premises-during-the-1976-83-military-dictatorship"\l"c36643".

[61] Santiago Omar Riveros, the military chief in charge of the region, was sentenced to fifteen years imprisonment (not house arrest), Sibilla twelve, and Müller ten.

[62] Criminal Federal Court N° 1 of San Martín, integrated by Dr. Osvaldo Alberto Facciano, Mario Jorge Gambacorta, and Eugenio J. Martínez Ferrero, and the Chamber Secretary Déborah E. Damonte, Basis for the verdict for trials N° 2855 and 2358, March 15th, 2019, p. 201.

[63] Ibid., p. 247.

The judges concluded that the two top business officials were "responsible for complicity by means of necessary participation." This implies that, while the responsibility for the crimes lay with public officials (in this case, military chief Santiago Omar Riveros), Müller and Sibilla made effective contributions to aid the perpetrators who had control over the criminal act. These crimes had thus only been possible due to the deployment of state resources in the hands of the military, and the use of the factory's resources and facilities—that is, the everyday workplace of the victims, who considered it a vital part of their development, their lives, and the lives of their family members. In short, Ford business officials "contributed to the repressive apparatus of the state, providing information, means and facilities for the execution of crimes against humanity."[64] This verdict was confirmed in September 2021 by the Cámara de Casación Penal, which also underlined the role of economic structural transformation and the interconnections between the criminal acts and contemporary economic and labour policies in the 1970s.

The Ford trial also influenced other strategies for corporate accountability that had been inactive for decades. Pedro Troiani, a former worker and shop steward at Ford Motor Argentina who was kidnapped, tortured and imprisoned from 1976 to 1977 and was one of the twenty-four victims included in the trial, had previously submitted a petition in September 1992 to the Inter-American Commission of Human Rights (IACHR). He had accused Argentina of denying his access to justice when his civil claim against Ford—for having been kidnapped on Ford premises and then dismissed for abandonment of his work post—was thrown out of court for falling outside the statute of limitations. In March 2021, the Commission deemed the Argentinean state responsible for these violations; in December 2021, Troiani's family and representatives of the government signed an agreement. Within this framework, the Argentinean state not only began the process for financial reparations, but also other forms of collective reparations, including institutional support and funding for research and publications on other cases of corporate responsibility, organised public events on corporate responsibility with victims in the presence of IACHR authorities, in what constituted a major step in the Inter-American system.[65]

Following the Ford trial, representatives of over thirty trade unions established the "Intersindical de Derechos Humanos" (inter-trade union network for human rights) in 2019, an organisation committed to supporting the advancement of the MTJ process. This was a result of a long process of increasing institutionalization on the issue of human rights within trade unions, many of which now have a human rights department. The creation of this network enabled the coordination of efforts to encourage workers to actively participate in public campaigns for human rights. One such campaign is a special joint initiative with the Abuelas de la Plaza de Mayo called "Identidad en lucha", which consists of talks, events and activities in union

[64] Ibid., p. 364.

[65] See https://www.boletinoficial.gob.ar/detalleAviso/primera/271183/20220908.

facilities to collaborate on the search for the remaining sons and daughters of the disappeared.[66]

Moreover, some trade unions have become plaintiffs in criminal trials concerning affiliated workers who were victimized during the dictatorship. UOM, the metallurgical union, became a plaintiff in a criminal trial investigating the repression in Acindar, Villa Constitución. Similarly, the Federación de Trabajadores del Complejo Industrial Oleaginoso, Desmotadores de Algodón y Afines de la República Argentina (edible oil workers) is now a plaintiff in a suit concerning the responsibility of Molinos Río de la Plata (Buenos Aires); the Federación de Trabajadores de Industrias de la Alimentación in the case of Las Marías (Corrientes); the Sindicato de Obreros y Empleados del Azúcar del Ingenio Ledesma in the case of the Ledesma sugar mill; the Asociación Gremial de Trabajadores del Subte y Premetro (subway workers of Buenos Aires) in the case of "Puente 12". Trade union organisations have also become involved in the signalling (*señalización*) of several companies and factories as memory sites of crimes against humanity and political repression, such as the Ford plant near Buenos Aires, Siderar (formerly Propulsora Siderúrgica, near La Plata), La Fronterita sugar mill in Tucumán, Acindar in Villa Constitución (Province of Santa Fe), and Astarsa shipyard in Tigre, Province of Buenos Aires. They have also begun to promote the recovery of archives, such as in the case of the Federación Obrera Tucumana de la Industria del Azúcar, which has indicated the discovery of crucial documents concerning repression in the sugar mills of Tucumán, such as La Fronterita.

7 Concluding Remarks

The Argentinean case underlines the importance of analysing the interconnections between the repressive economic, labour, social, and political policies instituted by the Cold War dictatorships in Latin America and long-term historical perspectives that are critical to understanding and reframing issues related to corporate accountability. It also demonstrates that workers and trade union organisations, widely overlooked in the existing literature, played a central role in this history. While some segments of the trade union leadership accommodated and even contributed to the repression, others became key anti-impunity actors. Highlighting this fragmentation contributes to a more subtle analysis of workers' mobilization against, as well as collaboration with, authoritarian right-wing forces.

Workers and trade union organisations were central targets of dictatorial repression. Although the trade union movement was heterogeneous and diverse in terms of political perspectives and lines of action, the dictatorship persecuted this movement as a whole, attempting to drastically restructure it via repressive economic,

[66] See "Identidad en lucha, una campaña para la búsqueda junto a los sindicatos", Asociación Abuelas de Plaza de Mayo, June 8, 2023. Last access: August 6, 2024. Link: https://www.abuelas.org.ar/acciones/121.

labour and (other) policy changes. Moreover, even if the relationship between trade unions and the human rights struggle was not linear and homogeneous, trade unions have begun to play an increasingly important role in the international denunciation of the crimes perpetrated against workers. International solidarity was key to advancing justice campaigns in the international arena, including at the ILO, although structural factors limited its effects in the Argentinean context. World labour confederations, the ICFTU, WFTU and WCL, as well as many national labour confederations around the world were also instrumental in highlighting the restrictions on workers' rights and its connections to broader political and economic factors, such as the expansion of neoliberalism in the late 1970s.

After the transition to democracy in 1983, both the CONADEP and the Juntas Trial recorded the repression of workers and trade unionists and marked some labour establishments as significant territories of repression. Furthermore, the formation of the Coordinadora de Centrales Sindicales del Cono Sur in 1986, in line with the previous activities of the ICFTU and ORIT, along with the WCL and the WFTU, enabled the articulation of efforts among trade union organisations and explicitly included the issue of human rights in regional discussions. When the process of local judicialization was halted in the 1990s, in response to impunity laws and presidential pardons, sectors of the trade union movement participated in the Truth Trials, which gave voice to people who had not been heard in the 1980s. Simultaneously, transnational articulations were key to fostering the CTA's 1988 petition in Spain, as well as the trials on the repression of workers in Italy, Germany and the United States.

All of this was central to reactivating the MTJ process in the 2000s. Between 2001 and 2005, when trials were resumed in Argentina, cases investigating the responsibility of companies and businessmen in the repression of workers and union leaders gained momentum. Progress was achieved, but not without obstacle, including resistance from important sectors of the judiciary, delays in the judicial process, and a lack of personnel and resources. In this context, trade unions and human rights organisations pursued other initiatives, such as the marking of sites where companies collaborated with dictatorial authorities, the opening and cataloguing of archives, public communication on corporate complicity in gross human rights violations, and the strengthening of transnational cooperations for corporate accountability.

In 2015, when the first criminal trial of the owner of a company began (Marcos Levín, owner of La Veloz del Norte), the involvement of trade union organisations was already on the rise. From that moment onwards, their support for criminal trials became more explicit and concrete, not only through the presence of workers and trade union members as plaintiffs and witnesses in court, but also though their role as key actors opening their archives and providing documentation. The establishment of the Intersindical de Derechos Humanos – an umbrella organisation that articulated the union officials and areas in charge of human rights constituted another important step in this direction. The Argentinean efforts influenced other countries and facilitated counter-attacks on regressive state policies similar to those implemented between 2015 and 2019 in Argentina. This process culminated in the

2021 Inter-American Commission on Human Rights' decision in the Troiani case and the subsequent agreement with the Argentinean government.

While political and legal challenges in the analysis, investigation and prosecution of corporate responsibility remained significant throughout this history, the intersectoral involvement and transnational cooperation of trade unions, human rights lawyers and academics, proved to be a crucial factor in progressing the struggle for corporate accountability. This chapter thus calls for further research on trade unions—as collaborative, but also fragmented, movements "from below"—in understanding processes of corporate accountability.

References

Abós A (1984) Las organizaciones sindicales y el poder militar. CEAL, Buenos Aires

Araya Gómez R, Garcés Fuentes M (2021) 'El modelo tiene rostro de sangre': Responsabilidad empresarial en procesos represivos durante la dictadura de Pinochet en Chile (1973-1990). Revista Latinoamericana de Trabajo y Trabajadores 2:151–181

Área de Economía y Tecnología de FLACSO, Centro de Estudios Legales y Sociales, Secretaría de Derechos Humanos and Programa de Verdad y Justicia (2015) Responsabilidad empresarial en delitos de lesa humanidad. Represión a trabajadores durante el terrorismo de Estado. Ministerio de Justicia y Derechos Humanos de la Nación, Buenos Aires

Azpiazu D, Basualdo E, Khavisse M (1986) El nuevo poder económico en la Argentina de los años 80. Legasa, Buenos Aires

Barrera M, Fallabella G (eds) (1990) Sindicatos bajo regímenes militares. Argentina, Brasil, Chile. CES-Naciones Unidas, Santiago de Chile

Basualdo E (2006) Estudios de historia económica argentina. Desde mediados del siglo XX a la actualidad, Siglo Veintiuno Editores, Buenos Aires

Basualdo V (2006a) La participación de trabajadores y sindicalistas en la campaña internacional contra la última dictadura militar argentina, Revista Sociedad No. 25, Facultad de Ciencias Sociales-UBA

Basualdo V (2006b) Complicidad patronal-militar en la última dictadura argentina. Los casos de Acindar, Astarsa, Dálmine Siderca, Ford, Ledesma y Mercedes-Benz, in Suplemento especial de Engranajes a 30 años del golpe militar, FETIA-CTA

Basualdo V (2006c) Dictadura militar, sindicalismo combativo y relaciones internacionales: apuntes para una historia reciente de los trabajadores industriales, Antología. A treinta años del golpe. Secretaría de Cultura de la Nación Argentina-Central de los Trabajadores Argentinos

Basualdo V (2010a) The ILO and the Argentine dictatorship. In: Van Daele J, Rodríguez García M, van Goethem G, van der Linden M (eds) ILO Histories. Essays on the international labour organization and its impact on the world during the twentieth century, Peter Lang, Berlin, pp 1976–1983

Basualdo V (2010b) La clase trabajadora durante la última dictadura militar argentina (1976-1983): apuntes para una discusión sobre la resistencia obrera, Dossier "Memoria en las aulas" 13. Comisión Provincial por la Memoria, La Plata

Basualdo V (2011) Shop-floor Labour Organization in Argentina from Early Peronism to the "Proceso" Military Dictatorship. Working USA: J Labour Soc 14:305–332. https://doi.org/10.1111/j.1743-4580.2011.00343.x

Basualdo V (2015) Contributions for the analysis of the participation of sectors of the trade-union leadership in labor repression in Argentina during the 1970s. In: Verbitsky H, Bohoslavsky JP (eds) The economic accomplices of the Argentine dictatorship: outstanding debts. Cambridge University Press, Cambridge, pp 201–216

Basualdo V (2020a) El caso de Acindar Villa Constitución y El Ciclo de Transformaciones Represivas, Productivas y Laborales entre Dictadura y Democracia. Revista Continentes 8(16):44–75
Basualdo V (2020b) Empresas, crímenes de lesa humanidad y justicia transicional. In: Dossier Especial "Empresas y Derechos Humanos. Avances, desafíos y propuestas para acelerar una agenda de trabajo colaborativa", Consejo de DDHH-Defensoría del Pueblo CABA, ACNUDH y CERALC
Basualdo V (2021) Business and the military in the argentine dictatorship (1976–1983): institutional, economic, and repressive relations. In: Basualdo V, Berghoff H, Bucheli M (eds) Big business and dictatorships in Latin America: a transnational history of profits and repression. Palgrave Macmillan, London
Basualdo V (2022) Dimensiones económicas de los procesos represivos: herramientas, políticas e iniciativas para el avance de la búsqueda de Memoria, Verdad y Justicia en el caso de Argentina. In: Dossier Especial "Memoria, Verdad y Justicia", Defensoría del Pueblo de la Ciudad Autónoma de Buenos Aires
Basualdo V, Quintana TO, Varsky C (2015) The cases of Ford and Mercedes Benz. In: Verbitsky H, Bohoslavsky JP (eds) The economic accomplices of the argentine dictatorship: outstanding debts. Cambridge University Press, Cambridge, pp 159–173
Basualdo V, Berghoff H, Bucheli M (2021) Big business and dictatorships in Latin America. A transnational history of profits and repression. Palgrave, London. https://doi.org/10.1007/978-3-030-43925-5
Calello O, Parcero D (1984) De Vandor a Ubaldini, vol I. CEAL, Buenos Aires
CONADEP (1984) Nunca Más. informe de la Comisión Nacional sobre la desaparición de personas. Eudeba, Buenos Aires
Crenzel E (2011) The memory of the Argentina disappearances. The political history of Nunca Mas. Routledge, London
Delich F (1982) Después del diluvio, la clase obrera. In: Rouquie A (ed) Siglo XXI, Mexico
Delich F (1983) Desmovilización social, reestructuración obrera y cambio sindical. In: Waldmann P, Garzón Valdés E (eds) El Poder militar en la Argentina, 1976-1981. Editorial Galerna, Buenos Aires, pp 101–116
Drake PW (1996) Labor movements and dictatorships. The Southern Cone in comparative perspective. Johns Hopkins University Press, Baltimore
Feierstein D (2015) Juicios: sobre la elaboración del genocidio II. Fondo de Cultura Económica, Buenos Aires
Fernández A (1985) Las prácticas sociales del sindicalismo, 1976-1982. CEAL, Buenos Aires
Fernández A (1990) Sindicalismo e Iglesia (1976-1987). CEAL, Buenos Aires
Galante D (2019) El Juicio a las Juntas: Discursos entre política y justicia en la transición argentina. Universidad Nacional de La Plata, La Plata
Gallitelli B, Thompson A (1990) La política laboral en la Argentina del "Proceso". In: Barrera M, Fallabella G (eds) Sindicatos bajo regímenes militares. CES-Naciones Unidas, Santiago de Chile, Argentina, Brasil, Chile
García Martín L (2019) Transitional justice, corporate accountability, and socio-economic rights. Lessons from Argentina. Routledge, New York. https://doi.org/10.4324/9780429277702
Gordillo M (2017) Activismo sindical transnacional en el Cono Sur: algunas experiencias, Clepsidra. Revista Interdisciplinaria de Estudios sobre Memoria 4(7):68–83
Grosescu R (2019) Transnational advocacy networks and corporate accountability for gross human rights violations in Argentina and Colombia. Glob Soc 33(3):400–418. https://doi.org/10.1080/13600826.2019.1598947
Grosescu R, Baby S, Neumayer L (2019) Justice, memory and transnational networks. European and South American Entanglements. Glob Soc 33(3):307–315. https://doi.org/10.1080/13600826.2019.1598949
James D (1988) Resistance and integration. Peronism and the Argentine working class, 1946-1976. Cambridge University Press, Cambridge

Martínez MJ (2021) El terrorismo de Estado en la fábrica Ford: mensajes y secuestros. In: Sarrabayrouse Oliveira MJ, Martínez MJ (eds) Crímenes y juicios. Los casos de lesa humanidad en Argentina. Teseo Press, Buenos Aires

Munck G (1998) Authoritarianism and democratization. Soldiers and Workers in Argentina, 1976-83. Pennsylvania State University

Payne L, Pereira G, Bernal-Bermúdez L (2020) Transitional justice and corporate accountability from below. Deploying Archimedes' Lever. Cambridge University Press, Cambridge. https://doi.org/10.1017/9781108564564

Pozzi P (1988a) Argentina 1976–1982: labour leadership and military government. J Latin Am Stud 20(1):111–138

Pozzi P (1988b) Oposición obrera a la dictadura (1976-1982). Contrapunto, Buenos Aires

Roht-Arriaza N (2005) The Pinochet effect: transitional justice in the age of human rights. University of Pennsylvania Press, Philadelphia

Schvarzer J (1987) La política económica de Martínez de Hoz. Hyspamérica, Buenos Aires

Verbitsky H, Bohoslavsky JP (eds) (2016) The economic accomplices of the Argentine dictatorship: outstanding debts. Cambridge University Press, Cambridge. https://doi.org/10.1017/CBO9781316287026

Zorzoli L (2018) Las intervenciones a organizaciones sindicales durante la última dictadura militar argentina: un estudio cuantitativo. Desarrollo Económico 57(223):487–510

Victoria Basualdo holds a PhD in History from Columbia University (New York). She is a Researcher at CONICET Argentina and coordinates the programme "Labor Studies, Trade Union Movement and Industrial Organization" in the area of Economics and Technology at the Facultad Latinoamericana de Ciencias Sociales (FLACSO), Argentina. He is also a member of the ERC Project "Transnational Advocacy Networks and Corporate Accountability for Major International Crimes," at the National University of Political Sciences and Public Administration, Bucharest. She is the author and co-editor of various publications on Latin American labour history and corporate accountability, including the *Responsabilidad empresarial en delitos de lesa humanidad. Represión a trabajadores durante el terrorismo de Estado* (Infojus, 2015), and *Big Business and Dictatorships in Latin America. A Transnational History of Profits and Repression* (Palgrave Macmillan, 2021).

Social Mobilisations and Corporate Accountability in Brazil: The Volkswagen Case and the Limits of Legal Settlements

Juan Pablo Bohoslavsky and Juan Cruz Goñi

Abstract This chapter examines the legal and political strategies designed and implemented by victims, prosecutors, civil society organizations, and trade unions in Brazil and Germany against Volkswagen do Brasil for its complicity in crimes against humanity perpetrated during the Brazilian dictatorial regime. These strategies gave rise to a controversial agreement, signed in 2020, between Volkswagen do Brasil and the Federal Prosecutor's Office. We provide a framework for critically evaluating the potential and pitfalls of these strategies and analyze the process and terms of the agreement, through an actor-focused perspective that might be useful for subsequent comparative analysis.

1 Introduction

In response to its involvement in the repression of its own workers during the Brazilian dictatorship (1964-1985), the Volkswagen subsidiary in Brazil (VW do Brasil) signed a settlement agreement with the public prosecutor's office in September 2020.[1] As a mechanism designed to advance justice in the field of corporate responsibility for complicity in human rights violations in the region, this settlement was an innovation.[2] The agreement terminated the civil actions filed by

This chapter builds upon Bohoslavsky and Goñi (2024), which focuses on the legal implications of the agreement studied in this chapter, including the limitations in achieving its goals in the fields of truth, memory, justice, compensation and deterrence.

[1] VW do Brasil and Public Prosecutor's Office (2020).

[2] Timothy Webster studied the experience of the lesser-known settlement agreements related to Asian victims of Japanese military aggression committed in the context of World War II. He pointed out that an important number of large Japanese companies decided to settle -in spite of

J. P. Bohoslavsky · J. C. Goñi (✉)
CONICET, Buenos Aires, Argentina

R. Grosescu, J. G. Dale (eds.), *Corporate Accountability for Human Rights Violations*, Interdisciplinary Studies in Human Rights 16,
https://doi.org/10.1007/978-3-032-05569-9_8

former workers of VW do Brasil who were victims of the dictatorship and who had alleged their employer was complicit in those crimes.[3] The format of the agreement was the outcome of a much activism and a unique set of strategies coordinated and deployed by victims, prosecutors, civil society organizations and trade unions in Brazil and Germany.

In this chapter, we discuss the case against VW do Brasil as an instance of domestic and transnational activism aimed at holding a multinational corporation accountable for its complicity in gross violations of human rights. These cross-border and intersectoral mobilization efforts took place in a variety of arenas, including truth commission, the courts, the media, civil society activism, victim advocacy, national politics, trade unions, corporate governance and academia. These efforts eventually crystalized into a negotiated and agreed upon alternative means to conclude the ongoing civil litigation over the corporate complicity of VW do Brasil. We construct a framework for critically evaluating the promises and pitfalls of these strategies, analyze the process and terms of the agreement, and provide an actor-focused perspective that might be useful for subsequent comparative analysis. In line with the larger thesis of this edited volume, this chapter also underlines that corporate accountability mainly results from the synergistic combination of mobilizations promoted and sustained by civil society and social movements.

2 VW do Brasil During the Dictatorship and Its Extraordinary Profits

In 1964, concerned about the economic slowdown and the interventionist measures of Brazilian President João Goulart, the Industrial Association of São Paulo looked favourably upon the overthrow of the government by the military. Friedrich Schultz-Wenk, the CEO of VW do Brasil at that time, was euphoric after the "first coup of the South" and even celebrated the arrest of left-wing sympathizers.[4] More recently, referring to the 1964 coup d'état in an interview with the German journalist Stefanie Dodt, Carl Hahn, the president of the VW Group between 1982 and 1993, simply said: "At that time, it did not bother me. I don't remember crying about the demise of democracy".[5] To understand VW's sympathy for the military coup, one can

their guaranteed judicial victory- in cases in which victims of forced labor from China and South Korea have filled against them. He remarks that the process as well as the terms of settlements contributed to the project of war reconciliation and highlights that the effectiveness of settlements agreements relies, in good measure, on the presence of what he calls "affective remedies" such as statements, expressions, and manifestations of apology and remorse, beyond the pecuniary. "Satisfaction, and not monetary compensations, primary drives these settlements". See Webster (2019), p. 316; see also Webster's chapter in this volume.

[3] VW do Brasil and Public Prosecutor's Office (2020), clause 8, paragraph 1, 2 and 3.

[4] Kopper (2020), pp. 327–328.

[5] Hahn (2017).

examine the company's 1964 financial disclosures, published in April 1965, wherein the company states that "the revolutionary movement unleashed on March 31 by the democratic forces of the country – and the consequent change of government – provided the conditions for an economic reformulation […] In 1965, the political and economic situation must be consolidated, creating conditions for a positive development in Brazil".[6]

The coup inaugurated a period of strong growth and the increased concentration of wealth in the country– of which VW do Brasil directly benefitted.[7] During the early years of the dictatorship, the company also benefitted from protectionist policies, including tax exemptions, state loans with negligible interest rates, and import protections. In its 1965 disclosures, VW do Brasil noted that "with the change in the legislation on foreign capital, a new provision for investments is verified. Negotiations for foreign financial assistance concluded successfully".[8] In addition, the state imposed harsh labour policies, in an attempt to discourage and repress the activities of the unions. Between 1964 and 1970, 536 unions were subject to interventions, and thousands of union leaders were impeached and expelled from their positions in their respective unions.[9] Despite the extraordinary increase in VW do Brasil's sales during the period, wages nonetheless shrank. By 1975, the company had expanded considerably, and the number of workers increased dramatically, as a result of state policies that favoured land transport and urbanization.[10] According to Christopher Kopper, until 1979, profits within Volkswagen's Brazilian subsidiary "remained at a considerably higher level than in the German parent company".[11]

3 The Search for Truth and Justice: Actors and Dynamics

After the return to democracy, VW's participation in gross violations of human rights during the dictatorship remained outside the spotlight. Everything began to change in 2014, when the Comissão Nacional da Verdade (CNV, National Truth Commission of Brazil) delivered a report to President Dilma Rousseff (2011–2016) which furnished preliminary evidence regarding the collaboration of the VW do Brasil management and the political police (Departamento Estadual de Orden Política e Social, DEOPS) in *Operação Bandeirantes* (OBAN).[12] Among their

[6] Volkswagen do Brasil (1965).

[7] Bresser-Pereira (2016).

[8] Volkswagen do Brasil (1965).

[9] Text II of Volume II, CNV (2014).

[10] Almeida de Carvalho Silva (2018).

[11] Kopper (2019).

[12] The Brazilian National Truth Commission (CNV) was established by Law n. 12,528/2011. It began its efforts in May 2012, bringing them to a close in December 2014. The second volume of the CNV offers conclusions on civil complicity with the dictatorship, with a special emphasis on corporate participation.

conclusions: In June 1969, the Brazilian Army, the Police of São Paulo State (Polícia Estadual) and the Federal Police had established a special plan to combat armed and unarmed left-wing activists with direct support from São Paulo-based companies.[13] One of the targets of this special operation was Dilma Rousseff, then a 23-year-old student.[14]

The inclusion of the issue of corporate accountability in the second volume of the CNV report was noteworthy given the fact that truth commissions rarely focus on corporate conduct as part of their institutional mandate.[15] In fact, corporate complicity received unprecedented attention in the CNV report. Two chapters in volume II were devoted to civil complicity with the dictatorship: text 2 refers to the violation of worker's human rights, and text 8 raised the issue of civilians who collaborated with the dictatorship. Moreover, among the truth commissions in Latin America, the Brazilian truth commission reported on the largest number of companies complicit in human rights violations, based on collected testimonies and documents.[16]

In addition to a focus on truth commissions, one of the peculiarities of transitional justice in Brazil is its high degree of decentralization. Alongside the CNV, twelve parallel local truth commissions were set up, in which universities, groups of workers and other autonomous entities participated.[17] These commissions, which encouraged significant social involvement, worked in coordination with the CNV to promote public hearings and the collection of testimonies.[18] The Rubens Paiva São Paulo State Truth Commission was the first to be created, and it completed its work on March 14, 2015.[19] This truth commission collected a large number of testimonies from militant workers who stimulated stronger civil mobilization, and was the only one to make specific recommendations in its final report regarding corporate complicity and the need to carry out further accountability processes.[20]

In 2015, the "Forum of Workers for Truth, Justice and Reparation" took it upon itself to continue the work of the CNV and realize its recommendations by further

---

[13] Prado Soares y Fecher (2016), p. 477.

[14] See testimony by Dilma Vana Rousseff (2001).

[15] See Payne et al. (2020), p. 73. It is worth noting that in 2006, the Office of the High Commissioner for Human Rights recommended the inclusion of economic issues as part of any truth commission's mandate. See: UN, Rule-of-Law tools for Post-Conflict States: Truth Commissions, (New York: United Nations), p. 9; Also see Federman (2021), who states "as of 2020, the Corporate Accountability and Transitional Justice database reports the half of the approximately forty truth and reconciliation commissions held in recent decades named complicit corporations. Since 2000, for example, commissions in Sierra Leone, East Timor, Peru, the Philippines, and South Africa considered the role of business and industry, positioning these actors as possible perpetrators ... In most of these instances, the reports simply note corporate complicity without describing next steps" (2021), p. 131.

[16] Payne et al. (2020), pp. 123–124.

[17] Moreira da Silva Filho (2023).

[18] *Ibid.*

[19] *Ibid.*

[20] Almeida de Carvalho Silva (2021).

investigating the role of complicit companies during the dictatorial period.[21] Barred from prosecuting their torturers in criminal trials, a group of thirteen trade unions filed a civil case—running more than 600 pages—against VW do Brasil before the Federal Public Prosecutor's Office (MPF).[22] This action included the major national unions, such as the Central Workers' Union (CUT), and regional unions, including the Union of Workers in the Mechanical Metallurgical and Electric Material Industries of Osasco, the Central of Brazilian Trade Unions, and Força Sindical, as well as the Association of the Amnestied Politicians, Retirees, Pensioners and Seniors of the State of São Paulo, among others. Given the context of absolute impunity, civil proceedings were, as one of the former workers said, "the only possible avenue" available at that moment.[23] The claimants called for technical expertise, public hearings, interviews with witnesses and the collection of documents to support the opening of a civil investigation into VW do Brasil's collaboration in the violation of human rights, including the practices that made these violations possible, the level of participation of the company's management in the perpetration of crimes, and any benefits obtained by the company as a result of this collaboration.[24]

Among the individuals who filed the case, we need to highlight Rosa Cardoso, lawyer and president of the Rio de Janeiro State Truth Commission, a member of the CNV, and one of the main authors of the aforementioned Volume II of the commission's final report. She was one of the main "innovative actors" who, in combination with other civil mobilization activities, made it possible to achieve some level of corporate accountability against VW do Brasil. As coordinator of the work group "Dictatorship and Repression of Workers and the Union Movement", Cardoso was a key actor in collecting and classifying worker testimonies, as well as in promoting the need for public hearings. After contributing to the work of truth telling from below, she played a pivotal role in demanding "institutional accountability" for illegal business behaviour during the coup through the filing of the civil lawsuit. Further signatories of the lawsuit included former deputy Adriano Diogo, president of the São Paulo State Truth Commission, Lúcio Bellentani, Tarcísio Tadeu Garcia, José Braz Sobrinho and Expedito Soares Batista, all former workers at VW do Brasil, and Intercâmbio, Informações, Estudos e Pesquisas (IIEP), an organization that went on to play a key role during the subsequent discovery process. Tarcísio Tadeu would later become the president of the Heinrich *Plagge Association*, an organization established to summon those workers who were involved in the legal process and provide them with legal assistance. The organization was also a forum for the former workers to discuss their strategy in the context of the legal inquiry against the company as well as in the resulting settlement. As Tarcísio Tadeu points

[21] Moreira da Silva Filho (2023), p. 128.

[22] *Ibid.*

[23] BBC (2020).

[24] Almeida de Carvalho Silva (2021).

out, their positions were widely discussed among the former workers in assemblies organized by the association.[25]

Once filed, the charges were redirected to the São Paulo Regional Procuracy of Citizens' Rights (Procuradoria Regional dos Direitos do Cidadão, PRDC), an agency attached to the MPF. In response to the pressure exerted by the claimants, prosecutors decided to carry out a thorough investigation.[26] Authorities commissioned political scientist Guaracy Mingardi and criminal lawyer Martin Carone dos Santos to collect evidence, documents, and testimonies to support any claims.[27] A civil inquiry was opened in 2016, supported by three departments internal to the Brazilian Prosecution Service (MP): the MPF, through the São Paulo Procuradoria Regional dos Direitos do Cidadão (PRDC), the Prosecution Service of the State of São Paulo, and the Public Labour Prosecution Office (MPT), through São Bernardo do Campo's procuracy.[28] In practice, this allowed the discovery process to become a kind of *sui generis* truth trial, ultimately facilitating the reconstruction of the complicity between the company and the dictatorship.[29]

In 2016, the Brazilian Ministry of Justice devoted an entire edition of its *Revista Anistia Política e Justiça de Transição* (Political Amnesty and Transitional Justice Journal) to "Cooperação Econômica com a Ditadura" (Economic Cooperation with the Dictatorship).[30] The research contained therein reveals the volume, depth, and persistence of the complicity of a significant number of companies and businesspeople with the Brazilian dictatorship.[31] It analyses how this concerted campaign by various companies and the state against workers and anyone who opposed the economic policies that concentrated wealth among the elite resulted in a deterioration of the living conditions of the majority of the population and increased inequality across the country.[32] Yet, the prospects for corporate accountability remain daunting. After so many years, impunity for state and non-state actors persists nearly absolute in Brazil. The Amnesty Law of 1979 (No. 6683) has deprived victims of the dictatorship of their right to take the perpetrators to court to be tried and punished for their crimes. In addition, victims have suffered the effects of an official denialism promoted by the highest levels of the state during the Bolsonaro administration (2019–2022).[33]

---

[25] Tadeu (2022).

[26] The actions were processed first by the Federal Public Prosecutor's Office (Public Civil Lawsuit No. 1.34.001006706/2015-26) and then the Public Prosecutor's Office of the State of São Paulo (Public Civil Lawsuit No. 14.725.0001417/2015-7) and the Ministry of Labor (Public Civil Lawsuit No. 000878.2016.02.001/3).

[27] See Ministério Público Fiscal, Ministério Público do Estado do São Pablo (2020). See Mingardi & Carone dos Santos (2017).

[28] Moreira da Silva Filho (2023), pp. 128–129.

[29] Payne et al. (2020).

[30] Bohoslavsky and Torelly (2016).

[31] *Ibid.*

[32] *Ibid.*

[33] Caroline Silveira Bauer (2019).

In April 2010, the Federal Supreme Court affirmed the constitutionality of the Amnesty Law.[34] Conversely, that same year, the Inter-American Court of Human Rights, in *Gomes Lund et al. v. Brasil*, concluded that the Amnesty Law did not comply with Brazil's international obligations and ruled that Brazil was required to take the necessary steps to repeal the law and ensure accountability.[35] Subsequently, on March 15, 2018, the Inter-American Court of Human Rights condemned the state of Brazil in *Herzog et al. v. Brazil* for violating the rights and judicial guarantees and protection of life of the journalist Vladimir Herzog, who was tortured and murdered in a detention centre (Destacamento de Operações de Informação - Centro de Operações de Defesa Interna) in the city of São Paulo in 1975. During the proceedings, the Court reiterated the incompatibility of the Brazilian Amnesty Law with the American Human Rights Convention in cases of serious human rights violations.[36]

4 The Complicity of VW do Brasil: Main Findings

In its joint report entitled, "Human Rights, Business and Transitional Justice: The role of the VW do Brasil in political repression during the military dictatorship", published in 2020 by the Federal Public Prosecutor's Office,[37] the Public Ministry of the State of São Paulo and the Public Ministry of Labor, concludes that the company's cooperation with the dictatorial regime went well beyond political sympathies or commercial interests: "In collusion with the management of the parent company in Germany, the Brazilian branch, by decision of its management, became directly involved in the political persecution of opponents of the dictatorial regime". The report describes the routine practice of betraying workers to the political police, exposing them to illegal abductions and torture, the use of company resources to illegally detain workers, physical and mental torture on company premises, and the participation of the company's Industrial Security Department as a *longa manus* of the political police in conducting interrogations and investigations even outside the company, among other criminal acts. The report notes that the company participated in the fabrication of false information about the whereabouts of workers while they were imprisoned and subjected to torture. The surviving records of the political

[34] Federal Supreme Court (2010).

[35] Inter-American Court of Human Rights (2010).

[36] Inter-American Court of Human Rights (2018).

[37] Volkswagen Assina Acordo com Ministério Público Sobre Repressão na Ditadura, Ministério Público do Estado de São Paulo, https://mpsp.mp.br/w/volkswagen-assina-acordocom-ministério-público-sobre-repressão-na-ditadura [https://perma.cc/3SYW-2JWW] (translated by authors); Direitos Humanos, Empresa e Justica de Transicao: O Papel da Volkswagen Do Brasil na Repressao Política Durante a Ditadura Militar, Relatorio Conjunction, Ministerio Publico Federal, https://www.mpsp.mp.br/documents/portlet_file_entry/20122/2679806.pdf/55488978-129e-6f5d-5abf-50e4fb8824f5 [https://perma.cc/NAU4-URLA].

police show how VW's industrial security department, which was presided by a military, provided the police with information about its workers, including full name, picture, affiliation, physical features, worker ID, employment period, political activities, and any known participation in strike actions or the creation and distribution of pamphlets.[38] For instance, Idalécio Custodio da Silva was reported to be involved in the distribution of political propaganda and, therefore, was "under observation".[39]

One major target of labour repression policies was the Communist Party of Brazil (PCB), which had cells in several companies. Once identified by internal VW controls, such cells were reported to the police, thus providing information about Communist engagement within the industrial sector.[40] The archives of the political police contain a document that identifies the specific PCB cell operative in VW, and provides evidence of the close cooperation between the company and the repressive forces.[41] After the creation of the document, in 1972, six VW workers were arrested: Amauri Danhone, Annemarie Buschel, Antonio Torini, Geraldo Castro del Pozzo, Heinrich Plagge and Lúcio Antonio Bellentani. According to Bellentani, VW not only provided the information, but also facilitated the facilities for the illegal arrests, interrogations and torture.[42] After the initial abduction, they were transferred to clandestine detention centres.

In the second volume of its report, the CNV identified a litany of documents that prove VW do Brasil's cooperation with police security organs.[43] One document from 1980 mentions a report written by a security guard who witnessed a speech to VW employees by Luiz Inácio Lula da Silva, who was a union leader at the time and would later become president of Brazil, in which he warned workers that the company was probably monitoring them. In particular, he called attention to Colonel Adhemar Rudge, the head of security who participated in the arrest of Lúcio Antonio Bellentani.[44]

[38] Federal Public Prosecutor's Office, Public Ministry of the State of São Paulo and Public Ministry of Labor (2020), p. 58.

[39] Arquivo Público do Estado de São Paulo (1974).

[40] *Ibid.*

[41] *Ibid.*

[42] CMV (2012), p. 49.

[43] CNV (2014).

[44] *Ibid*, Volume II, p. 67.

5 VW do Brasil's Strategy

Faced with these allegations, the head of VW's historical archive, German historian Manfred Grieger, decided to launch an investigation in 2014 to establish their authenticity.[45] In a public statement, Grieger stated that the company would investigate "all indications of possible participation by Volkswagen do Brasil employees in human rights violations during the military dictatorship, and identify those responsible for these acts".[46] He subsequently travelled to Brazil to collect and evaluate evidence of the company's involvement with the authoritarian regime.[47] In September 2015, he also took part in a meeting with Pedro Machado, a trade unionists, researchers and victims at the MPF in São Paulo.[48] According to the BBC, Grieger's intention was to "get in touch with victims of the Brazilian military dictatorship and seek more information about the relationship between Volkswagen do Brazil and Brazilian institutions at that time".[49] He proposed to "develop a memorial concept together with other Brazilian institutions, such as trade unions, and to put it into practice".[50] The increasing international pressure on VW in addition to the bad publicity generated by the investigation in the public domain seems to have strained the relationship between Grieger and his employer; the historian was subsequently dismissed in October 2016.[51]

Several reports connected Grieger's dismissal with his investigation of VW's Nazi past or to his criticism of a study that linked the involvement of Audi—a Volkswagen subsidiary—with the Nazi party. Grieger was critical of the report, which, in his opinion, underestimated the relationship between Audi and the Nazi party and minimized the use of slave labour in the concentration camps. Grieger's dismissal mobilized the German academic community: In an open letter signed by seventy-five scholars, they not only accused VW of constraining Grieger's academic freedom, but also expressed their doubts about the continuation of investigations into the company's past, "in particular into allegations of collaboration with Brazil's military leaders in the 1970s".[52]

In response to the public scandal surrounding Grieger's removal,[53] VW hired a professor of economic history at the University of Bielefeld in Germany, Christopher Kopper, to replace him.[54] VW assigned him the task of re-analyzing the case to assess company's complicity with the dictatorship and its participation in any viola-

[45] Silva et al. (2022), p. 171.

[46] Neher (2014).

[47] Silva (2018).

[48] Neher (2014).

[49] BBC (2020).

[50] Neher (2014).

[51] Silva et al. (2022).

[52] Smale and Ewing (2016)

[53] H-Soz-Kult (2016).

[54] Silva et al. (2022), p.171; Kopper (2017), p. 126.

tions of the human rights of its workers.[55] As such, the company continued to hire experts instead of subjecting the case to a court investigation. This is problematic in view of the conflict of interest inherent to experts evaluating the persons or companies that hired them.

In his report, "VW do Brasil in the Brazilian Military Dictatorship, 1964-1985. A Historical Study", Kopper concluded that, "the leadership of Brazil's VW exhibited unreserved loyalty to the military government and shared the objectives of its domestic and economic policy".[56] The investigation also revealed the close and ongoing links between VW's Department of Occupational Safety and the police, which resulted in the abductions and torture of several employees who were involved in union activities or were critical of the government or the company.[57] On the profits made by VW, the report reveals: "Government wage controls and restrictions on trade unions kept pay levels lower than they would have been in a pluralistic democracy with freedom of pay bargaining and the right to strike. VW do Brasil, and ultimately also parent VW, profited from the suppression of fundamental workers' rights".[58] According to Kopper, both VW do Brasil and VW executives in Germany looked favourably on the military dictatorship and deliberately ignored growing concerns about human rights violations, tactically approving the ongoing institutionalized cooperation between the Department of Occupational Safety and the repressive political police.[59]

This cooperation had severe consequences for the six staff members who were detained, arrested, and tortured in 1972. The political police could never have identified those engaged in subversive activities if VW do Brasil's Department of Occupational Safety had not to spied on company employees and delivered the relevant information to authorities regardless of the consequences. However, the seriousness of the criminal consequences that could arise from this fact pattern—whether it be at the level of authorship, necessary participation or complicity—went unnoticed by the author. In his report, Kopper instead highlighted the role of the head of VW do Brasil's Industrial Security Department, the Brazilian Army officer Adhemar Rudge, and attributed all responsibility for the crimes committed to him, as if these crimes had been the work of an isolated and single-handed agent, devoid of any economic rationale.[60]

In 2018, at the annual assembly of the Association of Critical Volkswagen Shareholders in Germany, Christian Russau, a member of the association and activist, demanded that VW take a stand on the findings in the report, and accused the executive board and board of management with negligence. In his statement, Russau set out the contents of both Kopper and Mingardi's reports and demanded that the

[55] Silva et al. (2022), p.171; Kopper (2017), p. 126.

[56] Kopper (2017), p. 126.

[57] *Ibid.*

[58] Kopper (2017), p. 112.

[59] Kopper (2020), p. 343.

[60] Kopper (2017), p. 50.

company apologize "in full and in a sincere and public manner to the victim workers [...] so that Volkswagen finally assumes its historic responsibility".[61]

On 14 December 2017, the company held a ceremony at its headquarters in São Bernardo do Campo featuring Christopher Kopper, Pablo Di Si (the Argentinian president of Volkswagen in Latin America), and the president of the ABC metal-workers' union, Wagner Santana, during which the publication of Kopper's report was announced and a plaque for the victims of the dictatorship was unveiled.[62] Volkswagen do Brasil, in a statement released during the ceremony and unveiling of the plaque, declared that "Volkswagen recognizes its moral responsibility for the injustices that occurred during the military dictatorship in Brasil. Volkswagen do Brasil negotiates constructively with victims of the dictatorship and with the Brazilian Public Prosecutor's Office".[63] Pablo Di Si said in his speech that "we deeply regret those episodes that may have occurred at that historic moment in open disagreement with the values of the company". The plaque reads: "In memory of all the victims of the military dictatorship in Brasil. For human rights, democracy, tolerance and humanity. Volkswagen".[64] Certain former workers, including Lúcio Bellantani, were invited to take part in the ceremony, but they opted to stay outside the factory next to a banner that read "We don't want a party. We want justice". The workers criticized the isolated way in which the report was produced, without any dialogue with workers or reference to the previous MPF-São Paulo investigation.[65]

On 14 March 2021, VW do Basil published a three-paragraph declaration in the two main newspapers in the state of São Paulo. The company failed to acknowledge any liability for its actions or those of its directors and employees, and instead argued that the amounts to be paid out were in fact voluntary "donations" for social and cultural projects related to the promotion of truth and memory regarding gross human rights violations during the civil-military dictatorship.[66] As such, the company signed the agreement without publicly acknowledging its participation in gross human rights violations.[67] The final paragraph stated: "In unconditional defence of the democratic state of law, Volkswagen deeply regrets the human rights violations which occurred at this historical moment which are in total disagreement with the company's values and regrets eventual episodes involving former employees and their families. Volkswagen recognizes that respect and promotion of human rights is a shared responsibility of all economic actors and society".[68]

Yet, the former workers' strongest critique focused on the company's position that collaboration with the regime stemmed solely from certain members of the

---

[61] Russau (2018).

[62] Maciel (2017); Struck (2017).

[63] Agencia EFE (2017).

[64] Struck (2017).

[65] Bedinelli (2017).

[66] See Silva et al. (2022).

[67] Almeida de Carvalho Silva (2018).

[68] Volkswagen do Brasil (2021).

industrial safety department, instead of acknowledging it an institutionalized/corporate practice. This argument was based on a sentence in the Kopper report that stated that the head of the company's industrial safety department "acted on his own initiative, but with the tacit knowledge of the management". The company was criticized for trying to individualize responsibility without acknowledging the collaboration of the organization. As Lúcio Bellantani argued, their participation in the ceremony proposed by Volkswagen would suggest that they agreed with the content of the report and could be "used by them [Volkswagen] as a sign of 'done, we've dealt with the past'".[69]

The company adopted an obstructive stance through the process. In addition to numerous attempts by its lawyers to delay the process, Volkswagen also refused to respond to a request from prosecutors for information on its revenues, profit remittances and assets, claiming that such information "would have no relevance on the ongoing investigation".[70] According to the coordinator of the IIEP, Sebastião Neto, Volkswagen also attempted to divide and coopt the solidarity of the workers' movement, including contacting some of the victims individually to offer them direct compensation and thus undermining the union movement.[71]

VW do Brasil's lawyers contested the final report produced by the MP by means of their own 40-page document. The company argued that despite the researcher Christopher Kopper having found VW responsible for human rights violations and complicit with agents of the dictatorship, this was not the position of the company, but only the conclusion of a research. In reference to different parts of the MP's final report, the company stated that the conclusions were based on assumptions and generalizations, supported only by circumstantial evidence.[72] Conversely, the company's own external experts had cross-checked Kopper's conclusions with VW's archives and found several inconsistencies. VW argued that Kopper's report did not present sufficient evidence, and that the researcher failed to specify which documents he was referring to, or if the documents mentioned were ever presented by the company.[73]

---

[69] Struck (2017).

[70] Colla de Amorim et al. (2024), p. 273.

[71] *Ibid.*

[72] Almeida de Carvalho Silva (2021).

[73] Moreira da Silva Filho (2023).

6 The Agreement and Its Interpretations

On September 23, 2020, VW do Brasil signed an adjustment of conduct agreement with the Federal Public Prosecutor's Office that closed any claims of complicity initiated by former workers who were victims of the Brazilian dictatorship.[74] It is noteworthy that despite the fact that the IIEP and other civil entities were initially involved in the campaign to open a civil inquiry in 2015, the *Compromise of Adjustment Conduct* (TAC) was negotiated exclusively by the MP after the civil case started. In other words, the agreement was entirely negotiated and settled between VW do Basil and the MP, but excluded the participation of those entities that had provided the initial impetus. The TAC stipulated a payment of R$ 4.5 million to the Fund for the Defence of Diffuse Rights, and the same amount again to the Special Fund for the Reparation of Injured Diffuse Interests, as well as R$10.5 million to the Memorial for the Struggle for Justice—an initiative developed by the São Paulo chapter of the Brazilian Bar Association (OAB/SP) and the Centre for the Preservation of Political Memory—and the Federal University of São Paulo (UNIFESP). After the conclusion of the agreement, the company decided to grant the additional amount of R$16,8 million to the Volkswagen Workers' Association (Heinrich Plagge Association) as "reparations". The amount paid to the victims was not part of the TAC, although it was included in the case file and subsequent communications made by the MP. In return, the three civil actions filed against VW were closed and any future lawsuits involving these crimes blocked.[75]

The agreement can be interpreted from different perspectives. On the one hand, this settlement, unprecedented in Brazil, has played a key role in disclosing the relationship between VW do Brasil and the dictatorial regime. Corporate responsibility for serious human rights violations during Brazil's civil-military dictatorship had never before been discussed in-depth in Brazilian society, nor had there been any attempt to judicialize it given the Brazilian state's hostility to accountability for gross human rights violations committed by the dictatorship. From this point of view, the organizations and actors linked to the victims interpreted the agreement with VW do Brasil as a great achievement, since a large multinational company was, for the first time, forced to acknowledge human rights violations committed against workers. In various public demonstrations, Rosa Cardoso, and representatives of the Heinrich Plagge Association and IIEP, among others, stressed the unprecedented nature of the agreement and emphasized that it should serve to launch further investigations into other companies accused of serious human rights violations.[76] This event had an extraordinary impact in the national and international

---

[74] The *Compromise of Adjustment Conduct* (TAC) was signed by representatives of the Federal Public Prosecutor's Office, the Public Ministry of the State of São Paulo, the Public Ministry of Labor and VW do Brasil (2020) (VW do Brasil and Public Prosecutor's Office 2020).

[75] Prado Soares and Ferreira Bastos Arantes (2022).

[76] Cardoso et al. (2020).

media, which resulted in strong pressure on the company to negotiate with the public prosecutor's office.

On the other hand, these same social actors were unequivocal in pointing out the limits of the agreement, including the failure to guarantee a memorial to the workers' struggles. In a document made public in August 2020, certain signatories of the initial agreement, such as Adriano Diogo, Christian Russau, Rosa Cardoso, and Sebastião Neto (IIEP coordinator), highlighted the importance of building a place of memory conceived and managed by the organizations involved in the case that could be "visited and known, and that also works to produce and disseminate knowledge on the subject [because] it means reaffirming that the memory of the workers, as well as that of all those who resisted the civil-military dictatorship, is not for sale".[77] The aim of a memorial was thus not promote the collective right to the truth and the memory and educate people about corporate complicity during the dictatorship.[78] Despite the fact that memory-work has long been considered a useful transitional justice tool throughout the world to re-build civil society after mass violence,[79] the construction of a space of memory –initially considered a non-negotiable outcome—was not included in the final version of the agreement. In all the public demonstrations held after the TAC was signed, civil society organizations and other actors involved in the process pointed out that the lack of a memorial site was one of the main flaws of the agreement. In this sense, the social actors sought to mobilize people against the agreement in public demonstrations and online events.[80] As the TAC was signed during the COVID-19 pandemic during a period of enforced social distancing, online events were often the only means to demonstrate.

Despite the absence of a memorial, the agreement was signed and ratified by the public prosecutor's office, thereby rejecting the requests for reconsideration by trade unions and other civil society organizations seeking to challenge the TAC. In addition to the absence of a memorial, the TAC made no mention of VW do Brasil's responsibility or the payment of direct reparations to affected workers. On the contrary, the agreement made clear that "VW do Brasil enters into this conduct adjustment without acknowledging any responsibility of its own or of its managers, employees or agents for the acts and facts investigated".[81] For this reason, the signatories of the initial agreement appealed the decision to the Federal Civil Rights Prosecution (PFDC). The trade union organizations that had initially assisted the MPF and contributed to the opening of the inquiry argued that the organizations that were to benefit from VW's financial contributions had no links to the working class. Their arguments were based on the fact that the Fund for the Defence of Diffuse Rights "has its main initiatives related to the areas of combating corruption and consumer law, while the OAB-SP's Memorial for the Struggle for Justice is known

[77] Diogo et al. (2020).

[78] See Inter-American Commission of Human Rights (2014).

[79] See Lessa (2013), Darn (2015), Federman (2021).

[80] *Ibid.*

[81] Public Prosecutor's Office (2021), p. 2.

to be focused on the work of lawyers who resisted the military dictatorship and which, although praiseworthy, is not related to the working class memory that is the subject of the Inquiry".[82]

The request also pointed out a contradiction between the civil inquiry and the TAC proposal wherein the inquiry highlighted the company's responsibility, while the TAC absolved the company of any responsibility of its own or that of its executives, employees or agents. In addition, the agreement did not fulfil the demands made in the initial claim for an investigation into corporate complicity and the economic benefits accrued by the company. In addition to these issues, the payments were made "merely as a donation (as if out of benevolence on the part of VW) […] which would mischaracterize the real nature of these sums as compensation for human rights violations".[83] Thus, the signatories criticized the lack of acknowledgement on the part of VW do Brasil, as well as the ostensibly charitable nature of the payments earmarked for future research, while recognizing the value of the agreement as a milestone for accountability and the fight for reparations. They stated that "VW do Brasil, by its own deliberation, will promote donations to entities that develop projects to promote memory and truth in relation to human rights violations that occurred in Brazil during the military dictatorship from 1964 to 1985".[84]

Despite these critiques, the Federal Prosecutor's Office for the Rights of the Citizen confirmed the agreement on 15 January 2021, and thereby rejected the complaints presented by trade unions and other civil society organizations. In denying the request for reconsideration, the Public Prosecutor's Office responded to the questions, alleging the lack of a prior project for the construction of the memorial, the Fund for the Defence of Diffuse Rights' commitment to history and memory, the long period of the investigation which, due to its duration, ran the risk of "never reaching any conclusion, resulting in irreversible damage to the memory and truth of the workers affected by VW do Brasil's conduct in the period under analysis". In addition, it emphasized that the term "donation" did not distort the real nature of the funds paid, as well as the educational value of the investigation, since "Brazilian society, through this civil investigation, will have access to consistent and in-depth information to recover the memory and the truth, with the unequivocal demonstration of VW do Brazil's participation in the violations perpetrated by the organs of repression during the military regime".[85]

Neglecting the opportunity to carry out a conventionality control under the Inter-American human rights system regarding the obligations negotiated by the company and the public prosecutor's office, the reviewing authority concluded that the arguments of the complainants were insufficient to declare the agreement invalid. Indeed, the Prosecutor considered that the agreement constitutes "a true administrative *leading case* that paves the way for future proceedings that will allow Brazilian

[82] Diogo et al. (2020).

[83] *Ibid.*

[84] VW do Brasil and Public Prosecutor's Office (2020).

[85] Public Prosecutor's Office (2021).

society to move forward in terms of respect of human rights, especially those of workers, by companies established in the national territory".[86]

Although it was contested, the TAC was signed, highlighting the payment of R$19.5 million. The remaining R$16.3 million, intended as compensation to affected workers, was not part of the TAC agreement, but was included in the inquiry through a Private Instrument of Donation. R$4.5 million were earmarked for research projects; these funds, managed by Universidade Federal de São Paulo, resulted in a public call for scholars to submit research projects on the subject of corporate complicity during the dictatorship. In work that is still underway, approximately 55 experts are investigating the activities of Petrobras, Fiat, Companhia Docas de Santos, Itaipu, Josapar, Paranapanema, Cobrasma, Companhia Siderúrgica Nacional (CSN), Aracruz and Folha de S. Paulo – a list has drawn up by the public prosecutor's office based on previously gathered evidence. According to the project's general coordinator, the objective is not limited to academic research, but research "aimed at gathering evidence for the public prosecutor's office to open legal actions, inquiries or administrative procedures against these companies".[87] Thus, despite its limitations, the VW do Brasil case has provided some value through the formation of a consensus among the organizations involved, the funding of new investigations, and the creation of new possibilities for the judicialization of complicit companies. This reflects the ambiguous nature of the TAC, which was both celebrated by the network of organizations that worked with the public prosecutor's office on the investigation and critiqued by them for falling short of its ambitions, revealing the distance between "the possible agreement" and "the ideal agreement".[88]

This ambiguity is illustrated by the first clause of the TAC, which required VW do Brasil to make a public statement about the facts contained in the investigation but did not require the public prosecutor's office to approve the wording of this statement. On the contrary, the secrecy of the statement was guaranteed by the TAC, meaning that other interested parties did not have access to its content until after it was published. As part of the TAC, the company was only obliged to make a public statement to be published in the Sunday newspapers with the highest circulation in the state of São Paulo, noting the facts uncovered as part of the investigations that were the subject of the TAC. When it was finally published, VW do Brasil's statement made it appear as if the company was acting voluntarily and transparently, motivated by its "long-term commitment to the country", by claiming to have been "the first company in the automotive sector to examine its history during the period of the military dictatorship in Brazil." In so doing, the company insinuated that it had initiated the investigation itself, neglecting to mention that the whole process had only been carried out after a mass mobilization by sectors of civil society together with the public prosecutor's office.[89] Instead, the company stated its com-

---

[86] Ibid.

[87] Domenici (2023).

[88] Valério et al. (2021).

[89] VW do Brasil and Public Prosecutor's Office (2020); Sindicato Popular (2021).

mitment to transparency and the sharing of available information, and highlighted its collaboration with the public prosecutor's investigation, all the while omitting how it withheld and delayed the delivery of documents and information.[90]

Furthermore, the payment agreed in the TAC is described in the published statement as a voluntary action by the company with the aim of promoting the defence of diffuse interests and reparations for the victims of diffuse rights violations. As such, VW do Brasil used a punishment provided for in the TAC, namely the obligation to communicate the content of the investigation, to instead promote its brand and the company's role as a corporate citizen. If communication to society is part of the instructive and educational process that guarantees that acts of this nature are not repeated, then VW do Brasil's statement reveals the ambiguity and deficiency of the TAC's terms, in so far as a public statement that should have been used by the company to publicly assume responsibility, was unable to obtain any kind of statement of guilt on the part of the company. Upon publication of VW do Brasil's public statement, the TAC moreover noted that "there will be no additional statement, response or reply from the MPF, MPSP and MPT, or from VW do Brasil itself". This declaration, however, did not include statements by any of the other organizations involved in the TAC or VW do Brasil's victims.

7 Conclusions

A number of factors make this process worthy of detailed study: the variety of actors that participated in the process and the intersectoral alliances they established; the different interests and agendas promoted by each of them; the transnational, national and federal dimensions of the case itself; the often controversial involvement of academia in the investigations; the innovative tools used by the parties involved to promote their views; the use of public shaming as a means of achieving some level of justice; the creative remedies implemented to achieve transitional justice goals in adverse contexts; and the ambiguous outcome of the agreement reached.

We have identified certain lessons that can be drawn from the case studied in this chapter. First, the degree of corporate accountability reached—even if insufficient as compared to the intended objectives—was mainly due to the concerted national and transnational activism of victims and their lawyers, human rights organizations, and trade unions. The role of "innovative actors" constitutes a key driver, even in tardy and adverse transitional justice processes. They were the main protagonists, filing the initial complaint and then sustaining it momentum over the following years.

Second, the specific investigative work engaged in by truth commissions and the fact that many companies involved in gross violations of human rights during the

[90] *Ibid.*

dictatorship were mentioned in their reports helped make the arguments more compelling within the public discourse. Indeed, the context in which the São Paulo State Truth Commission made specific recommendations about corporate accountability paved the way for victims and civil society to bring their case to court. Without the important work carried out by truth commissions, civil proceedings and even the subsequent negotiations would have been impossible.

Third, the pressure exerted on VW headquarters in Germany was crucial to forcing the company to launch an internal investigation on its involvement during the dictatorship. Yet, it is worth remembering that corporations do not take their commitments to full disclosure and the respect of scholarly independence beyond what is strictly needed to protect their reputations, while still making sure that (legally) sensitive information is not revealed.

Fourth, as this case shows, academia can play a significant role in the elucidation of the truth, but it cannot replace knowledge processes carried out by the legal system. The report prepared by Mingardi & Carone dos Santos was vital to clarifying the facts and identifying those responsible for the crimes committed, and is thus a prime example of an effective cooperation between the public prosecutor's office and academia in the investigation of corporate complicity in crimes against humanity. As for the Kopper report, despite the criticism of its limitations, it was also a crucial document in so far as it not only revealed important information, but also represented a—circumscribed – acknowledgement of responsibility on the part of VW.

Fifth, the commitment of and coordination between the three organs of the Brazilian Prosecution Service—the Federal Public Prosecutor's Office, the Public Ministry of the State of São Paulo, and the Public Ministry of Labour—were key to advancing the investigation and eventually opening the door to the final agreement.

Sixth, once the claim was "institutionalized" in courts, the original claimants (victims, trade unions and social organizations) were no longer decisive or veto players in the process, and their claims became sidelined. The process ultimately expropriated the conflict from the groups that had initially formulated the claim and thus ignored the voices of its main protagonists—many of whom had contributed a great deal to the implementation of these transitional justice measures in the first place.

Seventh, the case shows that careful consideration should be given to the corporate tactic of attempting to negotiate with victims separately as a way of undermining the collective nature of any claims for reparations. Given the asymmetries that often exist between the parties engaged in transitional justice measures such as the case of Brazil, state agencies should be called to address imbalances, including by carrying out a "control of conventionality", which means verifying that the terms of agreements are in line with Inter-American standards for the protection of human rights.[91]

[91] Bohoslavsky and Goñi (2024), p. 517.

Eighth, the agreement reached by the prosecutor's office and VW do Brasil was heavily critiqued by both victims and other claimants. When designing transitional justice measures, the continued participation of those affected by human rights violations should be an indispensable component of the process before, during and after the implementation of any transitional justice measures. The voices of the victims should never be dismissed.

Ninth, as the terms of the agreement were not seriously tested against existing human rights standards, the final outcome evinces remarkable lacunae in terms of its ability to achieve any type of lasting transitional justice or strengthen accountability standards in terms of corporate complicity—all of which weakened the social and political legitimacy of the accountability process and its outcome.

References

Agencia EFE (2017) Volkswagen negocia para indenizar vítimas da ditadura militar no Brasil. 1 December, at https://epocanegocios.globo.com/Empresa/noticia/2017/12/volkswagen-negocia-para-indenizar-vitimas-da-ditadura-militar-no-brasil.html

Almeida de Carvalho Silva M (2018) Estudos Organizacionais e Ditadura Brasileira: a normalização da violação dos direitos humanos por empresas durante o regime militar brasileiro, Ph.D. Thesis. PUC-Rio, Rio de Janeiro

Almeida de Carvalho Silva M (2021) Volkswagen and the dictatorship: The factory of violence of the German multinational during the Brasilian civil-military regime, Rio de Janeiro, Ed. Consequência

Arquivo Público do Estado de São Paulo (1974) APESP. DEOPS inventory, Condenação de seis ex-operários da Volkswagen pelo STM. 1974. Localização: 50-Z-341 11350001

BBC (2020) Volkswagen: la "histórica" disculpa y la indemnización del fabricante alemán de autos por entregar a sus trabajadores "subversivos" al gobierno militar de Brasil hace 50 años, *Estadão*, 28 September, at www.bbc.com/mundo/noticias-america-latina-54288272

Bedinelli T (2017) Volkswagen admite laços com a ditadura militar, mas falha ao não detalhar participação, diz pesquisador". *El País*, 18 December. https://brasil.elpais.com/brasil/2017/12/15/politica/1513361742_096853.html

Bohoslavsky JP, Goñi JC (2024) Limits to negotiated accountability of economic accomplices: the case of Volkswagen do Brasil. Human Rights Quart 46(4):492–522

Bohoslavsky JP, Torelly M (2016) Dossier "Cooperação Econômica com a Ditadura" Revista Anistia Política e Justiça de Transição. 10. Brasileira". 3 August, at https://portal.unicap.br/w/caso-volkswagen-em-defesa-da-mem%C3%B3ria-dos-trabalhadores-e-das-lutas-contra-a-ditadura-brasileira

Bresser-Pereira LC (2016) Manufacturing export model and growth in the 1964 regime. Revista Anistia Política e Justicia de Transicao 10:336–367

Cardoso R et al (2020) Lições do caso Volkswagen com os que enfrentaram a empresa, 29 September. www.youtube.com/watch?v=t5ususiILyo

Caroline Silveira Bauer C (2019) La dictadura cívico-militar brasileña en los discursos de Jair Bolsonaro: usos del pasado y negacionismo. Relaciones Internacionales 28(7):37–51

CMV (Comissão Municipal da Verdade de São Paulo Vladimir Herzog) (2012) Relatório final. Câmara Municipal de São Paulo, São Paulo

Colla de Amorim F, Sion V, Machado R (2024) Los actores económicos y los límites de la justicia transicional. In: Payne L, Bernal-Bermúdez L, Pereira G (eds) Los actores económicos y los

límites de la justicia transicional. Verdad y justicia por la complicidad empresarial en las violaciones a los derechos humanos. Editorial Dejusticia, Bogotá
Comissão Nacional de Verdade. Relatório, 3 vols., Brasilia 2014.
Darn A (2015) Amending the past: Europe's Holocaust commissions and the right to history. University of Wisconsin Press, Madison
Diogo A et al (2020) Caso Volkswagen: em defesa da memória dos trabalhadores e das lutas contra a ditadura at: https://portal.unicap.br/documents/475032/1847759/volks-manifestolugardememoria-03082020-final.pdf/df247136-acc1-e40b-fd09-16f8fcd77afb?t=1634149290086
Domenici T (2023) Empresas cúmplices da ditadura: 'É preciso fazer das informações um ato de justiça'. Publica, 30 May, at https://apublica.org/2023/05/empresas-cumplices-da-ditadura-e-preciso-fazer-das-informacoes-um-ato-de-justica/
Federal Public Prosecutor's Office, Public Ministry of the State of São Paulo and Public Ministry of Labor (2020) Human Rights, Business and Transitional Justice: the role of the VW do Brasil in political repression during the military dictatorship, at https://mpsp.mp.br/w/volkswagen-assina-acordo-com-minist%C3%A9rio-p%C3%BAblico-sobre-repress%C3%A3o-na-ditadura
Federal Supreme Court (2010) Allegation of Non-Compliance with Fundamental Precept (ADPF) no. 153
Federman S (2021) Last Train to Auschwitz: The French national railways and the journey to accountability. University of Wisconsin Press, Madison
Hahn C (2017) Como a Volkswagen colaborou com a ditadura, TV interview, at www.youtube.com/watch?v=feJsXRP_nYw
H-Soz-Kult (2016). Erklärung von Wissenschaftlerinnen und Wissenschaftlern zum Ausscheiden des VW-Chefhistorikers, Kommunikation und Fachinformation für die Geschichtswissenschaften, 3 November, at www.hsozkult.de/text/id/texte-3936
Inter-American Commission of Human Rights (2014) The Right to Truth in the Americas 21-22
Inter-American Court of Human Rights (2010) *Gomes Lund et al. ("Guerrilha do Araguaia") v. Brasil*, Judgment of November 24, Accessed February 20, 2024: www.corteidh.or.cr/docs/casos/articulos/seriec_219_ing.pdf
Inter-American Court of Human Rights (2018), *Herzog Et al. v. Brasil*, Judgment of March 15, www.corteidh.or.cr/docs/casos/articulos/seriec_353_ing.pdf
Kopper C (2017) VW do Brasil in the Brazilian military dictatorship 1964-1985: A historical study. Volkswagen AG Wolfsburg
Kopper C (2019) Volkswagen do Brasil during the military dictatorship: an economic and political assessment. In: Schneider N (ed) The Brazilian truth commission: local, national and global perspectives. Berghahn, New York, pp 182–199
Kopper C (2020) Business as usual under a military regime? Volkswagen do Brasil and the military dictatorship in Brazil (1964–1980). In: Basualdo V, Berghoff H, Bucheli M (eds) Big business and dictatorships in Latin America: a transnational history of profits and repression. Springer Nature, Munich
Lessa F (2013) Memory and transitional justice in Argentina and Uruguay: against impunity. Jonathen Allen & Maria Guadulupe Arenillas
Maciel C (2017) Volkswagen admite que dentro da empresa havia colaboradores da ditadura", Agencia Brasil, 14 December, at www.volkswagenag.com/en/news/2020/09/Volkswagen_do_Brasil_signs_agreement.h
Mingardi, G, Carone dos Santos, M (2017) A participação da indústria paulista na repressão política: O Caso Volkswagen - Relatório Final. www.mpf.mp.br/sp/sala-de-imprensa/docs/relatorio-guaracy-mingardi-tac-volkswagen
Ministério Público Fiscal, Ministério Público do Estado do São Pablo (2020) "Direitos humanos, empresas e justiça de transição: O papel da Volkswagen do Brasil na repressão política durante a ditadura militar. Relatório conjunto", October, at www.mpsp.mp.br/documents/portlet_file_entry/20122/2679806.pdf/55488978-129e-6f5d-5abf-50e4fb8824f5

Moreira da Silva Filho JC (2023) Corporate accountability for involvement in gross human rights violations during the Brazilian civil-military dictatorship – the role of the truth commissions and the case of Volkswagen Do Brasil. J White Collar Corp Crime 4(2):124–138
National Truth Commission (CNV) (2014) Relatório, Brasilia
Neher C (2014) CNV revela caso de tortura em fábrica da Volkswagen, *DW*, 12 December. www.dw.com/pt-br/relat%C3%B3rio-da-cnv-revela-caso-de-tortura-em-f%C3%A1brica-da-volkswagen/a-18126119
Payne L, Pereira G, Bernal-Bermúdez L (2020) Transitional justice and corporate accountability from below – deploying Archimedes' lever. Cambridge University Press, Cambridge
Prado Soares I, Ferreira Bastos Arantes L (2022) Caso Volkswagen: entre violações pretéritas aos direitos humanos e dilemas sobre uma reparação coletiva atual e efetiva. In: Ruy Cardia Atchabahian A, Pamplona, y Girardi Fachin D (eds) Mulheres, Direitos Humanos e Empresas, Almedina Brazil
Prado Soares IV, Fecher V (2016) Private companies and human rights violations: possibilities of accountability for complicity with the dictatorship in Brasil, Amnesty Magazine, 10
Public Prosecutor's Office (2021) Decision n° 14/2021-PFDC/CAV do MPF, at www.conjur.com.br/dl/vo/volkswagen-pagar-36-milhoes-colaborar.pdf
Rousseff DV (2001) Termo de Depoimento. Rio Grande do Sul Commission for Compensation to Victims of Torture. CNV Archive. Accessed February 20, 2024: http://cnv.memorias-reveladas.gov.br/images/documentos/Capitulo9/Nota%20212%20241%20243%20-%2000092_001027_2012_80.pdf
Russau C (2018) Colaboração da Volkswagen do Brasil com a ditadura militar brasileiral, 3 May. www.kooperation-brasilien.org/pt-br/temas-1/direitos-humanos-sociedade/colaboracao-da-volkswagen-do-brasil-com-a-ditadura-militar-brasileira
Silva M, Costa A, Santos C (2022) A responsabilidade política corporativa por atos de violência no passado: A colaboração da Volkswagen Do Brasil com a ditadura civil-militar Brasileira. REAd 28(1):154–179
Sindicato Popular (2021) Volkswagen cumpre acordo e reconhece que violou os direitos humanos durante a ditadura. Revista Forum. 16 March. https://revistaforum.com.br/opiniao/2021/3/16/volkswagen-cumpre-acordo-reconhece-que-violou-os-direitos-humanos-durante-ditadura-93491.html
Smale A, Ewing J (2016) Volkswagen parts ways with the historian who chronicled its Nazi past. New York Times, 2 November. www.nytimes.com/2016/11/03/world/europe/volkswagen-vw-emissions-scandal-nazi.html?ref=business
Struck JP (2017) Relatório da Volkswagen não satisfaz vítimas da ditadura no Brasil. Deutsche Welle., at www.dw.com/pt-br/relat%C3%B3rio-davolkswagen-n%C3%A3o-satisfaz-v%C3%ADtimas-da-ditadura-no-brasil/a-41803773
Tadeu T (2022) Document delivered to the Regional Attorney for Citizens' Rights of the State of São Paulo requesting investigation and opening of civil proceedings; at www.youtube.com/watch?v=rwtbDEKObEY
UN, Rule-of-Law tools for Post-Conflict States: Truth Commissions, (New York: United Nations)
Valério E et al (2021) SÁBADO RESISTENTE Vitória da classe trabalhadora a longa luta operária na VW do Brasil, 15 September, at www.youtube.com/watch?v=rwtbDEKObEY
Volkswagen do Brasil (1965) Volkswagen do Brasil. National Library Digital of Brazil. http://memoria.bn.br/DocReader/docreader.aspx?bib=030015_08&pasta=ano%20196&pesq=Volkswagen%20do%20&pagfis=67517
Volkswagen do Brasil (2021) Press release. https://static.poder360.com.br/2021/03/ComunicadoVolks14032021.pdf
VW do Brasil and Public Prosecutor's Office (2020) Compromise of Adjustment Conduct (TAC). At www.mpf.mp.br/sp/sala-de-imprensa/docs/TAC_Final_VW_Assinado_Sem_Anexo.pdf
Webster T (2019) The Price of settlement: World War II reparations in China, Japan, and Korea. New York Univ J Int Law and Polit 51:301–384

Juan Pablo Bohoslavsky is a Researcher at the National Scientific and Technological Research Council (CONICET) and UNRN-CIEDIS (Interdisciplinary Centre on Rights, Inclusion and Society Studies, Universidad Nacional de Río Negro, Patagonia) in Argentina. Between 2014 and 2020, he was a UN Independent Expert on Debt and Human Rights.

Juan Cruz Goñi Lecturer in Law at the National University of Comahue (Argentina), Doctoral fellow at the Argentine National Scientific and Technological Research Council (CONICET). Lawyer specialized in Criminal Law (UNComa), Master's in Criminology (UNL) and PhD in Human Rights (UNLa). Between 2011 and 2021, he was legal representative of victims and human rights organizations in Argentina. His work has been published in prestigious international journals, such as Human Rights Quarterly and in edited volumes.

Structural Constraints and Civil Society Mobilisations for Corporate Accountability and the East African Community

Rasul Ahmed Minja

Abstract Within the East African Community (EAC), corporate accountability (CA) is a relatively novel phenomenon, and human rights discourses underpinning a corporate accountability ethos are evolving but have yet to crystallize into legally binding norms. Besides the EAC partner states and corporate actors, a prominent set of civil society organisations (CSOs) has left a notable imprint on the business and human rights landscape in the region. The chapter explores three CSOs in the EAC partner states of Kenya, Uganda, and Tanzania, delving into their mobilizational strategies, impact on CA practices, and the structural constraints they encounter. I posit that the mobilisation of civil society has notably influenced businesses' practices, including the embrace of soft law, the organisation of human rights trainings by corporate entities, adjustments to business human rights policies, and measures of redress and remedy to victims of corporate malpractice. While these are significant steps, more robust forms of corporate accountability, such as binding regulations or the criminalization of corporate violence, are still pending. Moreover, such mobilisations have been dominated by "upward accountability" in CSO activities at the expense of "downward" (bottom-up) accountability.

1 Introduction

In the East African Community (EAC), corporate accountability is a relatively novel phenomenon compared to corporate governance and social responsibility. However, there has been a growing focus on corporate accountability in recent years. This is partly due to the increasing operations of multinational corporations in the EAC region and the growing attention to their business and human rights records. Moreover, human rights discourses underpinning a corporate accountability ethos in the EAC region are evolving but have not yet crystallized into legally binding

R. A. Minja (✉)
Department of Political Science and Public Administration, University of Dar es Salaam, Dar es Salaam, Tanzania

R. Grosescu, J. G. Dale (eds.), *Corporate Accountability for Human Rights Violations*, Interdisciplinary Studies in Human Rights 16,
https://doi.org/10.1007/978-3-032-05569-9_9

norms. As is the case at the international level, the EAC integration arrangement lacks an all-encompassing legal framework for holding corporate entities accountable for their actions or inactions. According to a mapping of the East African Business and Human Rights (BHR) sector conducted by Advocates for International Development (A4ID), the region has eight of the most common BHR concerns. The most prevalent BHR violations are unsafe working conditions in mines, forced evictions, low wages, displacement of Indigenous communities due to tourism, sexual violence against women, internet shutdowns by telecom companies that limit freedom of expression and access to information, pollution and health concerns related to the oil sector, exploitation, and human rights abuses of migrant workers. The most notorious sectors for BHR violations are the mining and extractive sectors (oil and gas).[1]

After several years of active involvement in corporate social responsibility and corporate governance, civil society organisations (CSOs) in the East African region have increasingly ventured into corporate accountability (CA) as one of their targeted sectors. Some of the prominent CSOs address CA practices and issues as part and parcel of their broader strategic objectives (including the promotion of the rule of law and good governance). In contrast, others were explicitly formed to enhance and monitor CA. Both types of CSOs have adopted several vital mobilisational strategies to address CA practices in the region. Such strategies include litigation (public interest/strategic lawsuits[2] and legal assistance/representative action), advocacy, watchdog activism, research, and capacity building.

I argue that in undertaking these roles and actions, CSOs have recorded mixed results, the positive ones being soft law adoption, human rights training by corporate actors, adjustments to business human rights policies, redress, and remedy to victims of corporate malpractice, and collaboration between corporate actors and CSOs. These results generally corresponded to business approaches and not with more radical revendications regarding the need for binding norms and the criminalization of corporate violence. In fulfilling such mobilisational roles, CSOs in the region face two critical forms of structural constraint: first, the external limitations in policy, regulatory, and institutional frameworks, and second, the internal challenges, such as the dominance of "upward accountability" in CSO activities at the expense of "downward" (bottom-up) accountability. According to Baur and Schmitz (2012),[3] upward accountability occurs when CSOs excessively prioritize their financiers over their beneficiaries, resulting in accountability being reduced to financial reporting without fully engaging those affected by their activities. This form of

[1] See Idemudia et al. (2022), pp. 1–8. See also IHRB (2016) and HRW (2023).

[2] Unlike conventional litigation, which typically resolves private conflicts, Public Interest Litigation (PIL) lawsuits aim to protect the rights of the broader public. PIL lawsuits often involve judicial activism to address societal concerns and defend marginalized groups, potentially leading to significant policy changes, government involvement, or the establishment of new legal precedents benefiting the larger society.

[3] Baur and Schmitz (2012).

accountability ultimately leads to co-optation.[4] Within the realm of downward accountability, a notable emphasis is placed on integrating input from beneficiaries into the decision-making process through the implementation of 'bottom-up' measures. This method guarantees that the recipients' viewpoints and input are thoroughly considered. This chapter will focus on a selective list of CSOs who are pioneering corporate accountability strategies in the East African Community partner states of Kenya, Tanzania, and Uganda,[5] highlighting not only their strategies but also their mobilising roles, impact on CA practices, and the structural constraints they face.

Sections 2 and 3 of this chapter review the extant literature, definitions of key terms, and an overview of the EAC's legal framework for corporate governance matters. Sections 4 and 5 present extensive narratives of the results and impacts of the strategies employed by three CSOs based in the countries mentioned above: the East African Law Society (EALS), the Uganda Consortium on Corporate Accountability (UCCA) and the Legal and Human Rights Centre (LHRC). Sections 6 and 7 analyze the challenges encountered and provide a conclusion.

2 Minding the Gap of Corporate Accountability

Most of the literature reviewed in this section dates back to 2003, following the initial two unsuccessful attempts by the global community to adopt norms regulating business and human rights issue areas. Both the latest draft of the United Nations Code of Conduct for Transnational Corporations, initially proposed in 1972, and the 2003 UN Draft Norms on the Responsibilities of Transnational Corporations and Other Business Enterprises concerning Human Rights (UN Draft Norms) failed to garner the much-needed international consensus on binding regulation of corporate accountability. This is important because, by the time of John Ruggie's mandate as the UN Secretary-General Special Representative (SGSR) in 2005, the EAC treaty had been in operation for barely 5 years.[6]

Several strands of the theoretical literature, henceforth, have either focused on or referred to the two failed attempts to reach an international consensus on a normative framework and the subsequent 2011 UN Guiding Principles on Business and Human Rights (UNGPs, also popularly known as the *Ruggie Principles*[7]). The

---

[4] Baur and Schmitz (2012) define co-optation as the strategic alignment of NGOs' interests with those of corporations, ultimately diminishing the former's autonomy.

[5] These are the three founding Partner States that signed the Treaty for the Establishment of the East African Community on November 30, 1999.

[6] The Treaty for the Establishment of the East African Community on November 30, 1999, which came into force on July 7, 2000. The formal launching of the Community took place on January 15, 2001.

[7] The principles are named after John Ruggie, a distinguished political scientist, human rights scholar, and international lawyer. Appointed as the Special Representative of the UN Secretary-

Ruggie Principles have become a prominent point of reference in analytical scholarly works envisioning a future that legally binds the business and human rights (BHR) treaty,[8] the process of human rights norms diffusion,[9] the potential to address the corporate accountability gap,[10] and the corporate implementation of the UNGPs.[11]

Other works have accentuated the power asymmetries between states and transnational or multinational corporations, on the one hand, and between communities and corporate actors, on the other.[12] Equally pertinent themes like corporate accountability reports,[13] corporate transparency,[14] human rights due diligence (HRDD) and mandatory due diligence (MDD) for corporations and global supply chains,[15] as well as the impacts of human rights litigation on corporate actors' human rights policies,[16] also shape the extant literature.

A substantial body of scholarship offers critical reviews of the form and substance of the Ruggie Principles (i.e., the protect, respect, and remedy framework). As summarized in Table 1, on the positive side, the Ruggie Principles are viewed as offering a much broader coverage of corporate actors and serve as an essential tool for advocacy for all relevant stakeholders working in the business and human rights issue areas.[17] They are also hailed for moving beyond state-centric conceptions of human rights and eventually received considerable support from states and corporations.[18] Furthermore, those interested in bridging the corporate accountability gap view the UNGPs as potentially influencing corporate human rights and environmental behaviors, especially in multilateral environmental agreements (MEAs).[19]

Nonetheless, a barrage of criticism has been directed at what the Ruggie Principles could not offer. Scholars have taken issue with the UNGPs' failure to bridge the governance gap,[20] attributing it to either a lack of any enforceability mechanism—owing to their voluntary and remedial nature[21]—or limited

General on Business and Human Rights in 2005, Ruggie formulated the UN Guiding Principles on Business and Human Rights, which was unanimously adopted by the UN Human Rights Council in 2011.

8 Bernaz (2022) and Thielbörger and Ackermann (2017).

9 Wolfsteller and Li (2022).

10 Rouas (2022), Schilling-Vacaflor and Lenschow (2021), Hughes-Jennett (2019) and Khoury (2018).

11 McVey (2022) and McVey et al. (2023).

12 Oshionebo (2018), Knöpfel (2017) and Connolly and Kaisershot (2015).

13 Christensen (2016), de Villiers and Dimes (2021) and de Felice (2015).

14 Ardigó and Zúñiga (2019).

15 Gustafsson et al. (2022).

16 Schrempf-Stirling and Wettstein (2017).

17 Bernaz (2022).

18 Thielbörger and Ackermann (2017).

19 Rouas (2022).

20 Hughes-Jennett (2019).

21 Bernaz (2022).

Table 1 Summary of the selected literature

Analytical frameworks/approaches			
Bernaz (2022) Seven-questions about the framework based on Gupta and van Asselt's framework: 1. Who is being held to account? 2. Accountable to whom? 3. What is the expected behavior? 4. What is the standard legal force? 5. What is the process by which to assess if standards are being met? 6. What remedial processes are in place? 7. What forms of reparation are available to victims?	Schilling-Vacaflor and Lenschow (2021) framework based on Mashaw's six questions: 1. Who is being held to account? 2. To whom is accountability owed? 3. For what are they accountable? 4. What standards does an agent use to demonstrate accountability? 5. What process demonstrates accountability? 6. What happens when the agent fails to meet these standards?	Gustafsson et al. (2022) Discourse analytical approaches: 1. The state-centric discourse. 2. The market-based discourse. 3. The polycentric-discourse.	de Villiers and Dimes (2021) Research framework on corporate governance reporting based on a review of the following theories: 1. Agency theory. 2. Stakeholder theory. 3. Stewardship theory. 4. Resource dependency theory. 5. Market theory.
Positive reviews			
• UNGPs cover all companies; important tool for advocacy.			Bernaz (2022)
• Move beyond the state-centric conception of human rights; gained support from states and corporations.			Thielbörger and Ackermann (2017)
• MEAs have the potential to influence corporate environmental behavior.			Rouas (2022)
Critiques			
• No enforceability mechanism; they are only remedial.			Bernaz (2022)
• The "Too Soft", "Too Pragmatic", and "Too Short" critiques.			Thielbörger and Ackermann (2017)
• UNGPs did not sufficiently plug the "governance gap".			Hughes-Jennett (2019)
• Voluntary and lack the necessary buy-in from corporations			Oshionebo (2018)

enforcement of the principles.[22] More elaborately, Thielbörger and Ackermann (2017) provide three sets of critiques of the Ruggie Principles. In the first set (or the "too soft" critique), they argue that the SGSR failed to recognize the limitations of the soft law approaches, which proved ineffective in human rights protection. In the second set (the "too pragmatic" critique), they cite those denouncing the SGSR's "principled pragmatism" approach, which sought to incorporate a large, diverse set of stakeholders, yet at the cost of "overemphasis[ing] an elusive consensus [and in the process] leaving ambition and the normative understanding of human rights

[22] Palmer (2015).

behind".[23] The third and final set (the "too short" critique), sums up the views of detractors who find Ruggie's work too cautious, lacking ambition, and bypassing many crucial questions. Drawing from these critiques, Thielbörger and Ackerman have highlighted three primary shortcomings of the UNGPs: (a) their non-binding nature undermines their effectiveness as they cannot enforce legal obligations on business and state actors; (b) their reliance on soft law and voluntary commitments is insufficient to address the systemic issues that contribute to human rights abuses in the business environment; and (c) there is a notable implementation gap, particularly in contexts where state institutions lack the capacity or the political will to uphold human rights standards. Consequently, the UNGPs' framework for preventing human rights violations is compromised by the absence of robust oversight mechanisms to monitor compliance and hold corporate actors accountable. These critical assessments of the UNGPs are essential for the EAC context due to concerns about effectiveness, lack of focus on structural issues, over-reliance on voluntary initiatives by businesses, and implementation gaps affecting CSOs involved in corporate accountability.

Seeking to contribute to the BHR treaty negotiation process, Bernaz (2022) adopts a "seven core-elements" analytical framework (see Table 1) to assess four models that, in his view, could inform a future BHR treaty: (1) the UNGPs model with corporate accountability-based on a do-no-harm requirement; (2) the Universal Declaration of Human Rights (UDHR) model with accountability situated in principles of international law but without any specific enforcement mechanism; (3) the progressive model with corporate accountability grounded in international law and relying on domestic enforcement mechanisms, including extra-territorial enforcement; and (4) the transformative model with corporate accountability also grounded in international law, but which, unlike the progressive model, relies on both international enforcement and domestic (including extra-territorial) mechanisms.[24] Bernaz favors a BHR treaty that will embrace a progressive model of corporate accountability. In contrast, Thielbörger and Ackerman are skeptical about the prospects for a new legally binding international treaty.[25] These models inform the ongoing BHR treaty process and have a bearing on current and future mechanisms for addressing CA. It is essential to revisit, albeit briefly, the literature on mechanisms addressing corporate accountability.

Khoury (2018) provides a fascinating account of regional human rights discourses while distinguishing three doctrines relating to mechanisms to address corporate accountability: the "positive obligations doctrine" whereby a state has to intervene to prevent violations or protect human rights guarantees; the "negative obligations doctrine" requiring a state to refrain from committing human rights breaches, and the "horizontal effect doctrine" in which a state assumes

[23] Thielbörger and Ackermann (2017), p. 51.

[24] Bernaz (2022), pp. 54–56.

[25] Thielbörger and Ackermann (2017).

responsibility for human rights violations by a third party.[26] Khoury concludes that both the European Court of Human Rights and the Inter-American Court of Human Rights allow the application of the positive obligations doctrine in their case law. Scholarly works on the state of corporate accountability focusing exclusively on the EAC integration scheme or her Partner States are few and far between. There is still a paucity of research dedicated to this issue. At present, there are hardly any regional or countrywide scholarly works within the EAC region addressing norms diffusion, actors' roles, and contextual factors, all within a single inquiry. While an exclusively EAC focus is lacking, a few country-based studies have explored themes like corporate governance,[27] corporate social responsibility processes,[28] environmental human rights litigations,[29] corporate human rights obligations in Kenya,[30] Tanzania's Extractive Industries Transparency Initiative (EITI) implementation process,[31] and resource nationalism in the Tanzanian extractive sector.[32] The works offer insights into CSR practices, power relations between multinationals and host countries, industrial pollution, and corporate governance for improving accountability. They conclude that local and global actors influence CSR practices in East African countries. Some call for a governance approach responsive to local challenges, while others highlight the power imbalances between multinational corporations and host countries.

Let us now turn to the key terms of this paper. While commonly accepted definitions of the three central concepts in this chapter—namely, corporate governance, corporate social responsibility, and corporate accountability—remain elusive, it is imperative to differentiate among them. I have adopted the EAC's definition of corporate governance. I chose to do so not only because the Community is the central focus of the chapter but also because it is currently the most comprehensive explanation of the term provided by an intergovernmental integration scheme in the entire Eastern African region.

The EAC defines corporate governance as "the process and structure used to direct and manage the business and affairs of a company towards enhancing business prosperity and corporate accountability with the ultimate objective of realizing long-term shareholder value whilst taking account of the interests of other shareholders."[33] The definition provided by the EAC includes three crucial elements. First, companies are the main target entities of the process and structure that

---

[26] Khoury (2018).

[27] Nakpodia et al. (2018), Katamba and Nkiko (2015), Wanyama et al. (2013) and Wanyama (2006).

[28] Muthuri and Gilbert (2011) and Kivuitu et al. (2005).

[29] Mwanza (2020).

[30] Osiemo (2016).

[31] Poncian and Kigodi (2018).

[32] Poncian (2021).

[33] See Article 1 of the Directive of the EAC on Corporate Governance for Listed Companies, Directive 2014/13/ of EAC Council of Ministers, Annexure VII. Article 1 of the EAC Draft Protocol on Good Governance as "the procedures and processes by which companies are directed and controlled."

enable corporate governance. Second, corporate governance focuses not only on the business aspects of the companies but also on their conduct. Third, and related to the second element, its dual goals are advancing the entities' interests (usually business prosperity) and corporate accountability. This suggests that corporate governance, as conceptualized by the Community, encompasses a broader scope than corporate accountability. Additionally, and more importantly, corporate governance endeavors to strike a delicate balance between the interests of companies and those of other stakeholders.[34] Thus, the EAC's corporate governance definition encompasses mechanisms (process and structure), scope (company's enterprise and affairs), and goals (business prosperity and corporate accountability), providing a comprehensive view of the term.

I adopt Morton Winston's (2009) conception of corporate social responsibility (CSR) or corporate social and environmental responsibility (CSER), which embraces both the *legal obligations* of business enterprises and their *moral responsibilities* to society, as well as what he refers to as *corporate philanthropy*[35] (Emphasis mine). Winston's conception presents CSR/CSER as a pyramid of corporate responsibilities "in which legal obligations (such as the fiduciary duties of corporate directors and regulatory requirements imposed by either an MNC's home or host country) are the base; additional moral responsibilities that fulfil emerging social expectations (for instance, concerning human rights and environmental protection) are the middle, and corporate philanthropy (such as gifts to causes that are unrelated to the core activities of the business enterprise) are at the top, these last being optional and non-obligatory, but praiseworthy."[36] Corporate social responsibilities are not inherently rooted in human rights or articulated in human rights terminology. Examples of CSR initiatives encompass the provision of scholarships, the establishment of healthcare facilities, the drilling of boreholes, the construction of educational institutions, and the facilitation of access to electricity.

Grant and Keohane's (2005) definition of accountability, which implies that "actors have the right to hold other actors to a set of standards, to judge whether they have fulfilled their responsibilities in light of these standards, and to impose sanctions if they determine that these standards have not been met",[37] has gained traction in the extant literature. The United Nations Research Institute for Social Development (UNRISD) conceptualizes corporate accountability with a more expansive menu of responsibilities placed on corporations. The UNRISD views corporate accountability as featuring "proposals to establish institutional mechanisms that hold corpora-

[34] The EAC defines a stakeholder as "a party that has an interest in a listed company and includes investors, employees, customers, community, government and trade associations." See Article 1 of the Directive 2014/13/ of EAC Council of Ministers.

[35] Maphosa and Maunganidze (2021) refer to corporate philanthropy as "corporate giving" or "corporate do-gooding" (p. 18).

[36] Winston (2009), p. 380. Winston belongs to the school of thought that makes a compelling argument that the conception of CSR as voluntary action separate from legal compliance is artificial (p. 381).

[37] Grant and Keohane (2005), p. 29.

tions to account rather than simply urging companies to improve standards or report voluntarily. Corporate accountability initiatives promote complaints procedures, independent monitoring, compliance with national and international law and other agreed standards, mandatory reporting, and redress for malpractice".[38] Compared with CSR, which emphasises instituting rights and duties for companies, corporate accountability focuses more on setting up institutional mechanisms to implement those rights and duties. The next section builds on this definition to provide a detailed account of corporate accountability within the EAC regional economic arrangement.

3 The EALS's Legal Framework on Corporate Governance

As is the case at the international level, the EAC integration arrangement lacks an all-encompassing legal framework for holding corporate entities accountable for their actions or inactions. This does not imply that the Community lacks regional instruments (policies, laws, and regulations) that speak to various aspects of corporate accountability. As some of these regional instruments will be referred to in the subsequent passages, they were adopted chiefly to cover different phases of the EAC deepening integration project without an exclusive focus on corporate accountability. Articles 6 and 7 of the Treaty for the Establishment of the EAC commit the regional integration body to conform to the principles of democracy, the rule of law, and the maintenance of universally accepted human rights standards. Article 6 of the EAC Treaty espouses the regional entity's commitment to promote and protect human and peoples' rights per the African Charter on Human and Peoples' Rights (ACHPR) of 1986.

A separate move was initiated at the beginning of the last decade to adopt a sound governance framework. The efforts culminated in the development of a draft "good governance protocol that incorporated the following pillars: human rights and promotion of equal opportunities; transparency, accountability through economic governance; access to justice, equality, and equal opportunities; democracy and democratization; and adherence to the rule of law, constitutionalism, and access to justice.[39] Some EAC partner states have since raised doubts about whether good governance is an area of cooperation that warrants the conclusion of a full-fledged Community protocol.[40] Interestingly, the EAC Draft Protocol on Good Governance does not refer to 'corporate accountability' in any of its provisions but defines 'corporate governance' as "the procedures and processes by which companies are directed and controlled".[41] As mentioned earlier, the EAC has adopted several

---

[38] UNRISD (2017).

[39] EALA (2014).

[40] Ibid.

[41] Article 2 (Definitions) of the EAC Draft Protocol on Good Governance (EAC, n.d.).

regional instruments addressing corporate accountability. These include the EAC Common Market Protocol (2010), which sets out provisions for the free movement of goods, services, and capital within the EAC. The Common Market Protocol includes competition policy, investment, and consumer protection provisions. Other relevant regional initiatives include the 2017 EAC Corporate Governance Code, which sets guidelines for corporate actors to promote transparency, accountability, and ethical conduct in their activities.

4 Civil Society's Mobilisational Strategies

Three main sets of actors are involved in the business and human rights regime in the EAC region, as is often the case in other areas. Besides the EAC Partner States and corporate actors, who often find themselves bound by positive and negative human rights obligations referred to in the previous section, a prominent set of actors has left a notable imprint on the business and human rights landscape in the EAC region. For brevity, a select active group operating in the three EAC founding states of Kenya, Tanzania, and Uganda will be highlighted. We will now turn to this set of actors who can act as a resolute bulwark against corporate abuse of power.

4.1 East African Law Society

The East African Law Society (EALS) is the apex regional bar association of East Africa, founded in 1995. Its membership is institutional and individual, comprising all Bar Associations within the EAC regional grouping. The Society's major mobilisational strategies include public interest litigation, advocacy, lobbying, research, and capacity building.

The EALS has used its observer status in the EAC to its advantage, specifically for advocacy and lobbying. As an observer member of the EAC, the EALS has often participated in the EAC's Secretary General's Forum and the Consultative Dialogue Framework and was thus able to make incisive presentations related to themes of common interest, including the promotion of regional integration. The most recent EALS intervention relevant to the chapter's theme is its legal reform submissions in extractives, human rights, good governance, the rule of law, and democracy. For instance, on February 19, 2020, the EALS submitted a policy brief to EAC analyzing the Community's Gender Policy[42] and proposed ways to execute it for the benefit of women, particularly those involved in extractive industry projects.[43]

[42] EAC Gender Policy, May (2018).

[43] See the EALS (2020) 25th Annual Report for the Financial Year 2019–2020; EAC Gender Policy and the Extractives Sector: Where are the Gender Dimensions? East Africa Law Society Secretariat Policy Brief, Arusha, David Sigano (2021), "Tanzania; and EALS Undertakes to Champion

Business and human rights training sessions are one of the intervention areas in which the EALS has registered its indelible mark. In 2020, for instance, EALS, in partnership with its Institute and the Advocates for International Development, A4ID, and ROLE UK, held capacity training sessions in four EAC Member States (Kenya, Rwanda, Tanzania mainland and Zanzibar, and Uganda).[44] These BHR training sessions targeted, in EALS terms, "responsible corporate practices" in the East African region. EALS capacity-building support has also been extended to the East African Court of Justice (EACJ) staff to strengthen its operational capacity. There have been attempts to bring legal services closer to communities affected by extractive industry activities through mobile clinics. For instance, the Tanganyika Law Society and the East Africa Support Inclusive Resource Development (TLS SIRD) mobile clinic training sessions were conducted in Geita, one of the regions in the Lake zone of Tanzania, on January 2 and 3, 2021. The focus of the legal assistance was women involved in mineral sites, human rights violations, and revenue collection arising from mining activities.[45] These mobile legal clinics were crucial in extending legal services to marginalized and vulnerable communities, promoting awareness of rights and dispute resolution mechanisms. Nonetheless, they frequently encounter challenges related to logistics and funding. Furthermore, in partnership with A4ID, the EALS conducted training sessions on human rights due diligence for over 500 lawyers and business leaders in East Africa.[46] The EALS-A4ID partnership to deliver professional development workshops on the UNGPs dates back to 2017.[47]

Research is another robust intervention by the EALS. Under the 4-year project supported by the Canadian Bar Association and the Government of Canada, known as Supporting Inclusive Resource Development in East Africa (SIRD), and jointly implemented by the Law Society of Kenya (LSK), Uganda Law Society (ULS), and Tanganyika Law Society (TLS), the EALS has played a leading role in conducting research and participating in deliberations on the EAC Mining Bill (2017) and the potential adoption of the EAC Mining/Mineral Value Addition Policy. It is worth noting that the EALS has also adopted a litigation approach to promote human rights in the EAC region, among other issues. Driven by its public-interest advocacy program, the EALS played a critical role in supporting lawyers and litigants in the cases (before the EACJ) "by filing amicus curiae and by having their lawyers appear in court together with the litigants' lawyers, or on behalf of the litigants' lawyers when they could not travel to Arusha".[48]

Implementation of the EAC Gender Policy", SIRD (2021) Bulletin, October - November, pp. 1–2. In February 2021, the EALS approached the EAC Gender Department to deliberate on the challenges hindering the execution of the EAC Gender Policy and explore the possibilities of establishing an implementation support framework.

[44] The 2020 training sessions were held in Kenya on June 11, Rwanda on October 29, Tanzania mainland and Zanzibar on September 22, and Uganda on July 29.

[45] See Nelson Frank (2021), p. 7.

[46] See A4ID (n.d.).

[47] A4ID (2017).

[48] Gathii (2016), p. 57.

4.2 *Uganda Consortium on Corporate Accountability*

The Uganda Consortium on Corporate Accountability (UCCA), a coalition of civil society actors, was founded in 2015. The UCCA has been at the forefront of popularizing the UNGPs in Uganda and actively engaged in developing the country's National Action Plan on business and human rights.[49] Its primary goal is to promote corporate accountability, focusing on the three key actors: states, non-state actors, and business corporations.

The UCCA brings together the following CSOs: the Initiative for Social and Economic Rights (ISER), the Public Interest Law Clinic (PILAC), the Legal Brains Trust (LBT), and the Center for Health, Human Rights and Development (CEHURD). In 2016, the Consortium published a report, "The State of Corporate Accountability in Uganda", assessing the findings of a baseline study on the impact of corporate activities on human rights. The study showed that corporations positively and negatively impact rural communities.[50] Local communities appreciate the expansion of business and employment opportunities, improved infrastructure, access to services, and corporate social responsibility initiatives by some corporations.[51] On the other hand, concerns raised by the communities encompass the exploitation of local miners and employees, failure to provide protective gear and medical care, land rights abuses, environmental pollution, corruption, lack of employment opportunities for residents, discrimination, social discord, and lack of consultation in decisions related to land acquisition and environmental impact assessments.[52]

Assessment of UCCA's official pronouncements and activities indicates that the Consortium supports a legally binding international instrument (a BHR Treaty) that addresses human rights and environmental abuses associated with businesses. The UCCA's stance is akin to Bernaz's progressive model, cited in Sect. 2, that embraces corporate accountability grounded in international law but relies on domestic enforcement. For UCCA, a binding legal instrument would be an appropriate approach to prevent corporate impunity if there is a firm intervention from states that are responsive to the demands and interests of individuals and communities they represent. However, there are two caveats to the legal obligations set by the binding Treaty: ensuring that human rights take precedence over trade and investment agreements and that a committed legal liability standard for acts or omissions by businesses is in place.[53]

---

[49] UCCA Statement on "Commemorating A Decade of the UN Guiding Principles on Business and Human Rights", July 2021. See also UCCA's Position paper on the European Union's Corporate Sustainability Due Diligence Directive and Forced Labour Regulation, *undated.*

[50] UCCA (2016), p. x.

[51] Ibid.

[52] Ibid.

[53] Byomuhangyi (2022).

In the absence of a globally mandated legal framework setting standards, and while the process of developing the BHR treaty continues, it seems that CSOs, including those highlighted in this chapter, have prioritized efforts to ensure the effective implementation of the UNGPs and NAPs, despite their voluntary nature. Their active participation in deliberations attests to this via in-country and international conferences and their increasing coordination of training sessions on the UNGPs and NAPs. Their current strategy seems to be let us settle with what (instruments) we have, but we need to advocate for a legally binding treaty. As the African Coalition for Corporate Accountability (ACCA) noted in its November 2020 submission, the UNGPs have recorded significant achievements in injecting renewed awareness.[54] The UNGPs have enjoyed global recognition in setting the "Protect, Respect, and Remedy" framework, and the adoption momentum has been perceptible at the continental and regional levels. Nonetheless, the voluntarism of the UNGPs partly explains the slow pace of implementation. There needs to be faster progress in incorporating the Ruggie Principles in domestic legal systems through NAPs and binding legislation.[55]

In what appeared to be a landmark intervention, UCCA commissioned a research study to examine the capacity of the state to regulate corporations in the Ugandan labor sector, to document deficiencies, and to highlight some best practices key to enhancing corporate accountability in that country.[56] UCCA has also ventured into BHR training sessions. It has conducted BHR training sessions in Fort Portal, Hoima, Buliisa, and the Karamoja region. In UCCA's view, these training sessions have offered "a platform to engage various corporate actors, company representatives, CSOs and officers in the Justice Law and Order Sector appreciate issues of corporate accountability".[57] Besides creating awareness of the Protect, Respect, and Remedy Framework of the UNGPs, these training sessions exposed participants to concrete cases of corporate abuses and available remedial and grievance mechanisms to hold corporations accountable for human rights violations.[58] Other topics featured in these trainings included corporate responsibility, human rights due diligence, sector-specific issues, and stakeholder engagement.

4.3 Legal and Human Rights Centre

In Tanzania, the Legal and Human Rights Centre (LHRC) is a human rights advocacy non-governmental organisation with an operational mandate in Tanzania Mainland and specific interventions in Zanzibar. The LHRC is a private,

---

[54] ACCA's submission to the call for inputs on "Business and human rights: towards a decade of global implementation - UNGP 10+", November 02, 2020.

[55] ACCA (2020), p. 7.

[56] See UCCA (2018), p. 2.

[57] UCCA (2017), p. 10.

[58] UCCA (2023).

autonomous, voluntary, non-governmental, non-partisan and non-profit sharing organisation envisioning a just and equitable society, established in 1995. Besides preparing and submitting shadow human rights reports, the LHRC was actively involved in preparing the Tanzania Universal Periodic Review (UPR) of October 2019. Like the EALS, the LHRC's successful employment of the strategic litigation approach at the EACJ has contributed to the organisation's growing reputation as a lively and persistent human rights defender. LHRC has a dedicated department on corporate accountability and environmental justice.[59] LHRC boasts of being the first-ever authoritative human rights organisation in Tanzania to pursue the BHR agenda.[60] It can further be argued that it is the only autonomous non-state actor in the East African region carrying out and publishing exclusive BHR surveys annually. Based on the LHRC's self-assessment, the BHR survey reports have positively impacted various aspects, including awareness, the BHR agenda, law reforms, and oversight institutions. Since the inaugural report was published in 2012, the following outcomes have been realized:

i) Increased awareness of human rights norms applicable in the business sector. For instance, several violations associated with the practices of business enterprises in almost all economic sub-sectors, e.g., relating to unlawful termination of employment contracts, are relatively decreasing compared with the trends in the early 2010s.

ii) Incorporation of the BHR agenda into the national human rights frameworks. For instance, the Tanzanian Commission for Human Rights and Good Governance (CHRAGG) has a specific portfolio (unit and thematic area) on BHR. The CHRAGG has also reflected BHR in its current Strategic Plan.

iii) Reforms of some laws and regulations, e.g., an enactment of the Non-Citizens (Employment Regulations) Act of 2015;[61] incorporation of requirements of corporate social responsibilities (CSR) and local contents in mining legal framework since 2018;[62] new legal position transparency of investment concessions, e.g., in the mining sector;[63] and enactment of several laws and rules to safeguard natural resources for the people of Tanzania.[64]

---

[59] LHRC (2019).

[60] LHRC (2022a), p. xix.

[61] Report 2013. At that time, there was a perceived trend of foreigners, particularly of Asian origin, dominating the business sector, including the petty market in Kariakoo International Market, Dar es Salaam. This caused concern among SMEs and other local traders who felt foreigners were using their financial power to push them out of the market and exploit them as cheap labor. LHRC proposed legal measures to protect local traders with limited capital and skills. The 2015 Act broadly addresses this recommendation.

[62] The Mining (Local Content) Regulations of 2018 and the 2017 Petroleum (Local Content) Regulation.

[63] In 2017, an amendment to the Mining Act of 2010 mandated the submission of all mineral and petroleum agreements for review by the National Assembly.

[64] Key legislation includes the Natural Wealth and Resources (Permanent Sovereignty) Act of 2017 and the Natural Wealth and Resources Contracts (Review and Re-negotiation on Unconscionable Terms) Act of 2017.

> iv) Increased performance of the State's regulatory authorities or agencies with oversight mandates, especially on environmental management and revenue collection. Incidents of environmental pollution caused by business practices are reportedly low....[65]

Similar to the EALS, LHRC does not proclaim a specific definition of corporate accountability in its publications (human rights reports, annual reports, survey reports, policy briefs, and newsletters). Instead, one can get a glimpse of the Centre's conception of corporate accountability from a range of thematic areas addressed by its BHR reports.[66] There is no doubt that LHRC has integrated the corporate accountability theme into its modus operandi. As alluded to earlier, it is a very recent "learning by doing" experience for LHRC. Unlike the UCCA, LHRC and EALS were not envisioned to address corporate accountability matters exclusively, but later, they found it imperative to incorporate them incrementally.

LHRC has also included legal aid clinics in its operational plans. The most recent finding is that most legal aid clinics have received complaints concerning land rights violations. In 2023 alone, their legal aid clinics in just the three cities of Dar es Salaam, Arusha, and Dodoma received 12,205 land rights violations.[67] The proportion of complaints involving or triggered by corporate actors is, however, not indicated in the BHR reports. LHRC has also supported local communities in accessing remedies for violations of human rights by corporate actors involved in the mining sector. The next section provides further details on the extent of its involvement. LHRC claims that the employment of strategic litigation has been fruitful in effecting legal reforms, especially when other advocacy initiatives have been unsuccessful. For instance, LHRC won three landmark cases, two in the regional courts (EACJ and AfCHBR) and one at the High Court of Tanzania, but none of which fall within the BHR thematic area.[68]

5 Results and Impact of EALS, UCCA and LHRC Strategies

In this section, I evaluate the strategies of the three organisations (EALS, UCCA, and LHRC) on a triple-level impact assessment scale with *massive*, *modest*, and *minimal* results. The analysis is based on a desk review of the reports (annual progress reports, human rights reports, and BHR reports) compiled by the three studied organisations. Results with *massive* impact refer to those that have a game-changing effect or influence in the BHR thematic area and have the potential to positively alter the situation of the majority of the affected communities. These achievements

[65] LHRC (2022b), pp. 1–2.

[66] Strangely, while the title of its reports is "Human Rights and Business Reports," the content refers to "Business and Human Rights", i.e., the widely referred BHR abbreviation.

[67] LHRC (2023), p. xxvii.

[68] The cases concerned reforming the Political Parties Act, the mandatory death penalty, and a constitutional case against Tanzania's Controller and Auditor General (CAG).

were recorded following the adoption of legal reforms, strategic litigation, and redress and remedy for affected communities and individuals. *Modest* results relate to accomplishments whose impact is contingent upon further action by the affected person or community, beneficiary, or subject of the specific intervention. For example, published reports will have an impact only if the findings therein are worked upon or when their recommendations are fully implemented. Likewise, the impact of training sessions and legal aid clinics will be felt only after further intervention by the target individuals and communities. *Minimal* results cover attainments linked to the organisations' naming and shaming of BHR breaches in their annual reports, published survey results, and collaboration with like-minded organisations. These are the minimal results a human rights activist organisation worth the name undertakes in its routine operations. Their impact range would vary depending on the organisation's operational context. Table 2 summarizes results from eight different types of strategies that the EALS, UCCA, and LHRC have employed. The strategies and their results are not mutually exclusive.

As explained in the previous section, EALS, as the name suggests, has gained prominence in the region for its strategic litigation endeavors rather than any other of its mobilisation strategies. The only downside to its strategic public interest litigations is that all reported cases filed before regional courts fall outside the BHR purview. More telling is the fact that more recent actions, whether pro-bono legal representation or filing of amicus curiae by its East African Bar partners (i.e., LSK, TLS, and ULS), have focused more on the extractive industry at the expense of other mainstream corporate businesses. Training sessions across the East African region for lawyers involved in policy and governance of natural resources have also benefited from the SIRD project, launched in 2019.

Table 2 An inventory of results and impact of EALS, UCCA and LHRC strategies

Impact level	Results	EALS	UCCA	LHRC
Massive	Adoption of legal reforms in the BHR thematic area (Public interest advocacy)	v	v	v
	Successful strategic lawsuits (Strategic litigation)	v		v
	Compensation to victims of corporate practices (Redress and remedy)		v	v
Modest	Publication of study results in the BHR thematic area (Evidence-based research)		v	v
	BHR training sessions (Capacity building)	v	v	v
	Provision of zonal and mobile clinics to grassroots communities (Pro-bono legal representation)	v	v	v
Minimal	Collaboration with government agencies and other CSOs working in the BHR thematic area (The logic of cooperation)	v	v	v
	Naming and shaming of perpetrators of corporate malpractices (Watchdog activism)	v	v	v

Source: Author's compilation, May 2024
Key: Strategies employed to achieve the results appear in parentheses

UCCA, which has an exclusive founding mission to tackle corporate accountability matters, has recorded relative results in four of its several interventions. These are legal advocacy, capacity building, research, and strategic litigation. It is the only CSO in the region with a straightforward distinction between 'corporate social responsibility' and 'corporate accountability'; whereas the former entertains voluntarism or "self-regulation," the latter embraces more concrete or enforceable strategies of influencing corporate behavior.[69]

The Consortium has also invested massively in propping up the legal capacity of local communities, human rights defenders, activists, and lawyers. BHR training sessions have, henceforth, featured prominently in UCCA's annual action plans. Unfortunately, the direct or indirect impact of its training sessions has not yet been established due to a lack of comprehensively compiled reports. As pointed out earlier, research on business and human rights observance remains the mainstay of CSOs in the East African region. UCCA is one such grouping that unravels not only the state of corporate accountability in Uganda but also the capacity of the state to regulate corporations, particularly in the labor sector.

LHRC's advocacy is also credited for successfully deterring the Tanzanian government from uranium mining. As part of the LHRC's collaboration with the Rosa Luxembourg Foundation, a report on the impact of Uranium Mining on Health and the Environment was launched on May 28, 2014, to increase public awareness about the dangers posed by uranium mining in Tanzania.[70] Ten years after the release of the LHRC flagship report on the potential hazards of uranium mining, actual exploration of this natural resource has yet to start. The Tanzanian government conceded that conducting a strategic environmental assessment (SEA) before any exploration is imperative, given that significant uranium reserves in the Mkuju River are located within the Nyerere National Park.[71] After the report, there was a stronger focus on ensuring that mining operations included proper health and safety measures to protect workers and nearby communities from the risks of uranium mining, such as radiation exposure.

Other notable results recorded in LHRC's interventions, particularly in the business and human rights thematic area, include the adoption of the 2022 Wage Order, compensation of villagers by an international mining company, and improved business compliance with acceptable working standards on such issues as work contracts, standard working hours, and an increase in knowledge on compensation regulations and procedures. Following LHRC's successful follow-up and intervention, Mr George Joseph Bwisige, who in January 2013 was shot multiple times by security officers of the Williamson Diamond mine, was awarded a settlement of 150 million Tanzanian shillings in 2021.[72] Bwisige, represented by the British law

[69] See UCCA, 2016, "The State of Corporate Accountability in Uganda Report," especially chapter two.

[70] LHRC (2014), p. 74. See also Uranium Mining Report, 2014.

[71] In 2022, it was estimated that Tanzania had about 55,000 tones of commercially viable uranium deposits. See Mirondo (2024).

[72] LHRC (2021), p. 26.

Table 3 Status of recommendations of LHRC's Tanzania Human Rights Reports

Human rights category	# Recommendations	I	PI	NI	U
Civil and political rights	71	26	30	15	0
Economic, social, and cultural rights	45	17	18	10	0
Rights of special groups	28	8	10	9	1
Other human rights	7	3	2	1	1
Total	151	54	60	35	2

Source: LHRC (2023), p. 296
I Implemented, *PI* partially implemented, *NI* not implemented, *U* unknown

firm Leigh Day, led 71 Tanzanian individuals who had been abused by the security personnel of Williams Diamonds Ltd., a subsidiary of Petra Diamonds. As a resolution, Petra Diamonds agreed to a compensation settlement of 4.3 million pounds and set up an independent grievance mechanism to address future complaints.[73] Furthermore, the LHRC backed the compensation for 98 Nyakunguru residents in Musoma Mara by the North Mara Gold Mine. The payout was successful following the LHRC's intervention.

Moreover, LHRC documents in its annual reports that the release of its human rights reports has often prompted action on the government and corporate side (See Table 3). During 2021–2022, civil and political rights were the most commonly recommended (47%) issues. In addition, recommendations concerning civil and political rights accounted for the majority of recommendations that were implemented (48%) and not implemented (43%). Besides, following the release of its 2013 human rights report, the National Environmental Management Council (NEMC) of Tanzania took steps to address the issues highlighted in the report.[74] The government adopted the Wage Order 2022, which replaces the Wage Order 2013, as suggested in the Human Rights and Business Report of the LHRC. The LHRC has been advocating for an increase in the minimum wage to ensure fair compensation for workers since 2017. The wage order established new minimum wage thresholds across sectors to uplift workers' living standards and enhance worker protection. Subsequently, the relentless push for strict compliance with the wage order has decreased incidences of unfair payment, but concerns about substantial minimum wage hikes in specific sectors persist.

LHRC, like several other CSOs, made submissions in all three of Tanzania's Universal Periodic Review (UPR) cycles in 2011, 2016, and 2021. Unfortunately, the activities of multinational corporations, their human rights implications, and human rights due diligence have not been featured prominently in the national reports and CSOs' submissions during the UPR cycles. However, the UPR process has managed to subject Tanzania to international scrutiny concerning its human rights practices in general. It has led to the incorporation of the BHR theme in its National Human Rights Action Plans (NHRAPs, 2013–2017, 2018–2022). Thus,

[73] The Guardian (2021).

[74] LHRC (2014), p. 72.

the effect of the UPR process has been about raising awareness and creating discussions rather than a substantial, systemic change in the BHR landscape.

The cases discussed in this chapter demonstrate that civil society organisations (CSOs) widely embrace the Ruggie Principles as part of their corporate accountability mechanisms. These principles serve as a valuable advocacy tool, encouraging state intervention to prevent abuses, uphold human rights guarantees, and ensure that government authorities abstain from committing human rights violations. This reflects both the positive and negative obligations doctrines espoused by Khoury.[75]

Despite the acknowledged shortcomings of the UNGPs, such as their non-binding nature, reliance on soft laws, and enforcement gap, as pointed out by Thielbörger and Ackerman[76] and other critics, CSOs like EALS, UCCA, and LHRC are advocating for the creation of an international BHR treaty based on domestic enforcement, following Bernaz's progressive model.[77] While the protracted BHR treaty negotiations show little sign of concluding, these CSOs collaborate with state agencies like NHIRs, corporate actors, international partners, and like-minded CSOs to address the domestic corporate accountability gap. They are doing this by enhancing capacity through research and conducting training sessions on BHR. My perspective is that it would be beneficial for all relevant parties to support a transformative model of CA based on international law and involving both international enforcement and domestic mechanisms, as opposed to a progressive model. In the EAC region and other parts of the continent, it has been evident that domestic mechanisms alone are not effective without the political will of state actors.

6 Challenges

As is often the case, undertakings by business enterprises involve high stakes. Any attempt at identifying, monitoring, voicing, and documenting corporate malfeasance is bound to face challenges. Even employing more reformist strategies, like drastic changes in laws and regulations and resorting to strategic litigation, comes with risks and trade-offs. In this section, I highlight two basic sets of challenges emanating from the observation of recent corporate accountability experience in the three East African states: state and corporate actors-related challenges and CSOs' self-inflicted hindrances.

The central state and corporate actors-related challenges noted in the case studies include corporate bureaucracy, inadequate capacity, and shrinking CSOs' operational space. In the first place, there is still a dearth of information on the state of corporate accountability in the East African region, despite some initiatives by some of the case studies (UCCA and LHRC) to fill the gap by instituting their

[75] Khoury (2018).

[76] Thielbörger and Ackermann (2017).

[77] Bernaz (2022).

independent surveys. There is still no regionally exhaustive comparative study on corporate accountability. Furthermore, the 2016 UCCA study will need to be updated, and LHRC's annual BHR surveys should be expanded in terms of geographical and sectoral scope, as they currently cover only a handful of Tanzania's regions and focus on small and medium enterprises. Therefore, the available surveys, notwithstanding their enlightening findings, provide a sketchy picture of the states' and corporate entities' compliance or lack thereof with the UNGPs. Related to this challenge is how best to confront two menacing and mutually reinforcing hindering forces: the state itself and corporations conspiring as violators. An extract of the UCCA state of corporate accountability report notes that abuses and violations by corporations "are happening with the knowledge of, and sometimes committed with the collusion of the government".[78] It goes on to claim that "The challenge for corporate accountability in Uganda is thus the challenge of finding ways of holding both the state and corporations accountable for their respective human rights obligations".[79]

Second, corporations and some regulatory authorities are reluctant to cooperate or share information during BHR surveys conducted by CSOs. As documented in the LHRC's 2022 BHR report, the reluctance to cooperate with survey teams is driven mainly by the fear of exposing internal deficiencies and "damaging information". Third, both studies by UCCA and LHRC found that the capacity of state regulatory authorities to monitor business corporate practices is insufficient. Another challenge is the shrinking operational space for CSOs. The LHRC cites this challenge in its 2018 report, released during the fifth phase of Tanzania's administration under President John Magufuli.

Besides the inability or struggle to manage community expectations, CSOs engaged in the BHR sector have created their own predicament, either consciously or inadvertently. The tenacity and vibrancy of CSOs' monitoring, watchdog, and even supportive roles are increasingly linked to donor-funded projects, which as presented in previous sections, have prioritized governance of natural resources, specifically the extractive industry. Other economic sectors, such as agriculture and manufacturing, have been generally overlooked despite critical human rights violations. This skewed attention on some business sectors, owing to where donor funds are channelled, amounts to the dominance of "upward accountability" at the expense of "downward accountability". This follow-the-money approach does not guarantee the sustainability of mobilisation strategies targeting grassroots communities, particularly vulnerable groups.

CSOs in the East African region, as is the case in many other areas on the continent, face structural constraints relating to the contraction of civic space. Three primary constraints experienced by the LHRC and partner CSOs in the operational context of Tanzanian civil society illustrate the worrying situation in East Africa. First, the Tanzanian government adopted controversial law amendments deemed to

[78] UCCA, 2016, p. 86.

[79] Ibid.

limit recourse to the justice system. On June 15, 2020, the Tanzanian President assented to the Written Laws (Miscellaneous Amendments) Act No. 3, which amended 13 laws, including Section 4 of the Basic Rights and Duties Enforcement Act. The amendments to Section 4 effectively abolished public interest litigation (PIL) unless a person submits their application and an affidavit stating how the contravention of constitutional provisions (12–29) has personally affected them.[80]

There has also been a notable concern regarding the amendment to the NGO Act (Cap 56), which conferred excessive powers to the NGO Registrar.[81] The amendments have granted the registrar the authority to suspend NGOs and seek assistance from law enforcement agencies in carrying out their duties. These changes were met with disapproval from the LHRC and its partner CSOs, leading to a collective legal action to contest them. The LHRC, in collaboration with the Tanzania Human Rights Defenders (THRDC), Pan African Lawyers Union (PALU), Tanganyika Lawyers Society (TLS), and Centre for Strategic Litigation (CSL), filed Reference No. 25 of 2020 against the Attorney General of the United Republic of Tanzania at the First Instance Division of the EACJ, aiming to challenge the amendments to Section 4 of the Basic Rights and Duties Enforcement Act.[82]

Arbitrary arrests, detentions, and frequent adjournment of cases have created difficulties for the smooth operations of CSOs. In December 2019, a staff member of the LHRC, Tito Elias Magoti, was arrested and charged with money laundering offenses, among others.[83] Mr. Magoti's arrest and detention were arbitrary for several reasons. Firstly, he was not properly informed about the reasons for his arrest. Secondly, he was interrogated without the presence of his lawyer, thus infringing upon his right to legal representation. Thirdly, he was not promptly brought before a judge or other judicial officer to face charges contrary to Tanzanian and international laws.[84] The LHRC staff faced formal charges despite the prosecutors claiming their investigation was incomplete. This delaying tactic involved prosecutors frequently appearing in court, asserting that the investigation was ongoing, and requesting adjournment of the case. In addition, on August 13, 2020, the police ordered the freezing of THRDC's bank accounts.[85] THRDC collaborated with LHRC on various human rights issues, including jointly filing public interest lawsuits in Tanzania and at the EACJ. Due to the frozen accounts, THRDC was forced to terminate all staff employment contracts, serving as a warning to other CSOs.

---

[80] See Section 4 of the Written Laws (Miscellaneous Amendment) Act No. 3 of 2020.

[81] The issue of excessive powers granted to the Registrar of NGOs was also raised in the report of the Human Rights Council on its 33rd session, 22 April 2020.

[82] See Reference No. 25 of 2020, THDRC, PALU, TLS, LHRC, and CSL versus the Attorney General of the United Republic of Tanzania.

[83] LHRC (2019), pp. 72–74.

[84] Article 14(3) of the United Republic of Tanzania Constitution, 1977; Article 7 (1) (C) of ACHPR and Article 14 (3) (d) of ICCPR.

[85] See THRDC (2021), pp. 37–38.

7 Conclusion

The adoption of the UNGPs by the international community was hyped as a "paradigm shift" for business,[86] and John Ruggie called them a "game changer" for business and human rights. Nevertheless, the "game-changer effect" has not yet been felt within the EAC arrangement. Human rights discourses underpinning a regional corporate accountability ethos are evolving but have not yet crystallized into legally binding norms. While a transformative wave from voluntary to mandatory corporate accountability is taking shape in Europe and other regions, EAC Partner States are yet to incorporate human rights due diligence, as provided under principle 17 of the UNGPs, into their respective domestic laws. As noted earlier, the EAC arrangement needs a more specific and comprehensive legal framework for business and human rights. Due to the slow uptake of the UNGPs, civil society groups have been calling upon state actors to view the parallel processes of developing and implementing NAPs and adopting a BHR treaty not as competing initiatives but rather as reinforcing one another.[87] Moreover, a formalized process to assess corporate accountability standards does not exist. This is not a situation peculiar to the EAC region. The corporate accountability assessment gap remains a global one.

CSO actors and national human rights monitoring institutions have played crucial roles in investigating, tracking reporting, and researching business and human rights breaches in different social and economic sectors. Reports from this set of actors in the international human rights system are awash with success stories, as well as the challenges of their experiences in auditing or overseeing compliance with mediation settlements between corporate entities and local communities. Nonetheless, their annual country-focused human rights reports hardly mention or reserve a section on the EAC business and human rights instruments. What does this entail? It may imply that the EAC human rights system (i.e., normative and institutional frameworks) is relatively undeveloped and unknown to draw the interest of the region's human rights advocates and defenders.

Unlike the UCCA, the LHRC and EALS were not envisioned to address corporate accountability matters exclusively. However, soon, they found it imperative to do so incrementally. Corporate accountability is still a relatively recent undertaking for these organisations. The current chapter does not present a systematic comparative evaluation of the three organisations. It has established eight main strategies CSOs employ to address corporate accountability matters. These are public interest advocacy, strategic litigation, seeking redress and remedy, evidence-based research, capacity building, provision of legal aid, creating collaborative networks, and embracing watchdog activism. Evidence-based research on business and human rights observance remains the mainstay of CSOs in the East African region. They have taken bold steps to unravel not only the state of corporate accountability but also the capacity of the state to regulate corporations, particularly in the labor sector.

[86] Hughes-Jennett (2019).

[87] ICAR, UCCA, and ISER (2017).

References

A4ID (2017) A4ID provides inaugural business and human rights training for the East African legal community, 17 June. https://www.a4id.org/a4id-provides-inaugural-business-and-human-rights-training-for-the-east-african-legal-community-in-partnership-with-the-east-africa-law-society/

A4ID (n.d.) Improving Business and Human Rights (BHR): mapping the East African BHR sector. www.roleuk.org.uk

African Coalition for Corporate Accountability (2020) ACCA's submission to the call for inputs on "Business and human rights: towards a decade of global implementation - UNGP 10+", November 02. https://www.ohchr.org/sites/default/files/Documents/Issues/Business/UNGPsBHRnext10/inputs/acca.pdf

Ardigó IA, Zúñiga N (2019) Corporate transparency: overview of issues and literature review. Transparency International

Baur D, Schmitz HP (2012) Corporations and NGOs: when accountability leads to co-optation. J Bus Ethics 106:9–21. https://www.jstor.org/stable/41413241

Bernaz N (2022) Conceptualizing corporate accountability in international law: models for a business and human rights treaty. Hum Rights Rev 22(1):45–64. https://doi.org/10.1007/s12142-020-00606-w

Byomuhangyi J (2022) Voluntary measures will not curb corporate impunity, a legally binding instrument is essential. https://ucca-uganda.org/743/voluntary-measures-will-not-curb-corporate-impunity-a-legally-binding-instrument-is-essential

Christensen DN (2016) Corporate accountability reporting and high-profile misconduct. Account Rev 91(2):377–399. https://doi.org/10.2308/accr-51200

Connolly N, Kaisershot M (2015) Corporate power and human rights. Int J Hum Rights 19(6):663–672. https://doi.org/10.1080/13642987.2015.1074458

de Felice D (2015) Business and human rights indicators to measure the corporate responsibility to respect: challenges and opportunities. Hum Rights Q 37(2):511–555. https://www.jstor.org/stable/24518328

de Villiers C, Dimes R (2021) Determinants, mechanisms and consequences of corporate governance reporting: a research framework. J Manag Gov 25(1):7–26. https://doi.org/10.1007/s10997-020-09530-0

East Africa Law Society (2020) Annual report for financial year 2019–2020. www.ealawsociety.org

East African Community (n.d.) Draft protocol on good governance

East African Legislative Assembly (2014) Report of the Committee on Legal, Rules and Privileges on the assessment of adherence to good governance in the EAC and the status of the EAC Political Federation 2nd – 6th September 2013, Kampala

Frank N (2021) TLS SIRD mobile clinics: bringing legal services closer to the community. SIRD Bulletin, October-November

Gathii JT (2016) Variation in the use of subregional integration courts between business and human rights actors: the case of the East African Court of Justice. Law Contemp Probl 79:37–62

Grant RW, Keohane RO (2005) Accountability and abuse of power in world politics. Am Polit Sci Rev 99(1):29–43. https://doi.org/10.1017/S0003055405051476

Gustafsson MT, Schilling-Vacaflor A, Lenschow A (2022) Foreign corporate accountability: the contested institutionalization of mandatory due diligence in France and Germany. Regul Gov 17(4):891–908. https://doi.org/10.1111/rego.12498

Hughes-Jennett J (2019) What role for human rights in business? Polit Q 90(3):457–461. https://doi.org/10.1111/1467-923X.12710

Human Rights Watch (2023) "Our Trust is Broken": loss of land and livelihoods for oil development in Uganda, July. www.hrw.org

ICAR, UCCA, and ISER (2017) Remarks by the International Corporate Accountability Roundtable (ICAR), Uganda Consortium on Corporate Accountability (UCCA), and the Initiative for Social and Economic Rights (ISER) Geneva, 27 October. https://ucca-uganda.org/wp-content/uploads/2020/03/ICARUCCAISERStatementOEIWG.pdf

Idemudia U, Tuokuu FXD, Essah M (2022) The extractive industry and human rights in Africa: lessons from the past and future directions. Resour Policy 78:102838. https://doi.org/10.1016/j.resourpol.2022.102838

Institute for Human Rights and Business (2016) Human rights in Tanzania's extractive sector: exploring the terrain, December. www.ihrb.org

Katamba D, Nkiko CM (2015) The landscape of corporate social responsibility in Uganda: its past, present and future. In: Idowu SO, Vertigans S, Schmidpeter R (eds) Corporate social responsibility in Sub-Saharan Africa. Springer, London

Khoury S (2018) Corporate (non-) accountability and human rights. Asian J Soc Sci 46:503–523

Kivuitu M, Yambayamba K, Fox T (2005) How can corporate social responsibility deliver in Africa? Insights from Kenya and Zambia, CRED perspectives, International Institute on Environment and Development (IIED) briefing paper no. 3. https://about.jstor.org/terms

Knöpfel LD (2017) Multinational corporations, affected communities and NGOs. In: Contesting the UN guiding principles on business and human rights from below. Swisspeace, pp 12–15. http://www.jstor.com/stable/resrep17665.5

Legal and Human Rights Centre (2014) Annual Progress Report 2014: engaging the public in the constitution review process - promotes citizens' right to participation

Legal and Human Rights Centre (2019) Human Rights and Business Report 2018/2019 Tanzania Mainland

Legal and Human Rights Centre (2021) Annual Report 2021

Legal and Human Rights Centre (2022a) Human Rights and Business Report 2021/22 Tanzania Mainland

Legal and Human Rights Centre (2022b) Annual Report 2022

Legal and Human Rights Centre (2023) Tanzania Human Rights Report, Part One: Tanzania Mainland

Maphosa F, Maunganidze L (2021) Business and society: an introduction. In: Maphosa F, Maunganidze L (eds) Corporate citizenship: business and society in Botswana. Palgrave Macmillan, Cham, pp 1–30. https://doi.org/10.1007/978-3-030-67766-4

McVey M (2022) Untangling the authority of external experts in the corporate implementation of the UN guiding principles on business and human rights. J Hum Rights 21(5):620–638. https://doi.org/10.1080/14754835.2022.2105646

McVey M, Ferguson J, Puyou FR (2023) "Traduttore, Traditore?" Translating human rights into the corporate context. J Bus Ethics 182(3):573–596. https://doi.org/10.1007/s10551-021-05028-3

Mirondo R (2024) Why uranium mining has yet to start in Tanzania. The Citizen, 3 September 2024. https://www.thecitizen.co.tz/tanzania/news/national/why-uranium-mining-has-yet-to-start-in-tanzania-4747764

Muthuri JN, Gilbert V (2011) An institutional analysis of corporate social responsibility in Kenya. J Bus Ethics 98:467–483. https://doi.org/10.1007/sl0551-010-0588-9

Mwanza R (2020) Toxic spaces, community voices, and the promise of environmental human rights: lessons on the Owino Uhuru pollution incident in Kenya. Nord J Hum Rights 38(4):279–304. https://doi.org/10.1080/18918131.2021.1904617

Nakpodia F, Adegbite E, Amaeshi K, Owolabi A (2018) Neither principles nor rules: making corporate governance work in sub-Saharan Africa. J Bus Ethics 151:391–408. https://doi.org/10.1007/s10551-016-3208-5

Oshionebo E (2018) Corporations and nations: power imbalance in the extractive sector. Am J Econ Sociol 77(2):419–446. https://doi.org/10.1111/ajes.12209

Osiemo L (2016) Securing corporate accountability for violation of human rights: towards a legal and policy framework for Kenya. PhD thesis, School of Law, University of Witwatersrand. http://hdl.handle.net/10539/22370

Palmer C (2015) What can post-democracy tell us about TNCs and extraterritorial violations of human rights? Polit Q 87(1):76–80. https://doi.org/10.1111/1467-923X.12211

Poncian J (2021) Resource nationalism and community engagement in extractive resource governance: insights from Tanzania. Rev Afr Polit Econ 48(170):529–551. https://doi.org/10.1080/03056244.2021.1953975

Poncian J, Kigodi HM (2018) Transparency initiatives and Tanzania's extractive industry governance. Dev Stud Res 5(1):106–121. https://doi.org/10.1080/21665095.2018.1486219

Rouas V (2022) Corporate accountability and access to justice in international and European legal frameworks. In: Achieving access to justice in a business and human rights context: an assessment of litigation and regulatory responses in European civil law countries. University of London Press, Institute of Advanced Legal Studies, pp 34–80. https://www.jstor.org/stable/j.ctv293p4bn.8

Schilling-Vacaflor A, Lenschow A (2021) Hardening foreign corporate accountability through mandatory due diligence in the European Union? New trends and persisting challenges. Regul Gov 17(3):677–693. https://doi.org/10.1111/rego.12402

Schrempf-Stirling J, Wettstein F (2017) Beyond guilty verdicts: human rights litigation and its impact on corporations' human rights policies. J Bus Ethics 145:545–562. https://www.jstor.org/stable/45022279

Tanzania Human Rights Defenders Coalition (2021) Situation report on human rights defenders and civic space in Tanzania. https://thrdc.or.tz/online-center/reports-viewssearch?_token=WaQmF4weXnV6jlRYKVpxuui4eWFtJD6G5PVFZx4Z&search=2021

The Guardian (2021) Petra Diamonds pays £4.3m to Tanzanians 'abused' by its contractors. May 18. https://www.theguardian.com/global-development/2021/may/18/petra-diamonds-pays-43m-to-tanzanians-abused-by-its-contractors

Thielbörger P, Ackermann T (2017) A treaty on enforcing human rights against business: closing the loophole or getting stuck in a loop? Indiana J Glob Leg Stud 24:43–79. https://www.jstor.org/stable/10.2979/indjglolegstu.24.1.0043

Uganda Consortium on Corporate Accountability (2016) The State of Corporate Accountability in Uganda A Baseline Study Report for the Uganda Consortium on Corporate Accountability.https://iser-uganda.org/wpcontent/uploads/2022/07/16_09_21_UCCA_The_State_of_Corporate_Accountability_in_Uganda.pdf

Uganda Consortium on Corporate Accountability (2017) Pursuing corporate accountability in Uganda, issue no. 1, December

Uganda Consortium on Corporate Accountability (2018) The capacity of the state to regulate corporations: analysis of Uganda's labour policies, legal and institutional framework within the context of business activities, October

Uganda Consortium on Corporate Accountability (2023) Training Manual for Media Practitioners on Business and Human Rights. https://ucca-uganda.org/wp-content/uploads/2023/05/New-UCCA-Training-Manual.pdf

United Nations Research Institute for Social Development (2017) Corporate social responsibility and business regulation. UNRISD research and policy brief 1. www.unrisd.org

Wanyama S (2006) Corporate governance and accountability in Uganda: an analysis of stakeholder perspectives. PhD thesis, University of Dundee

Wanyama S, Burton B, Helliar C (2013) Stakeholders, accountability and the theory-practice gap in developing nations' corporate governance systems: evidence from Uganda. Corp Gov 13(1):18–38. https://doi.org/10.1108/14720701311302396

Winston M (2009) Multinational corporations and global responsibilities. In: Hayden P (ed) The Ashgate research companion to ethics and international relations. Ashgate, Surrey, pp 375–391

Wolfsteller R, Li Y (2022) Business and human rights regulation after the UN guiding principles: accountability, governance, effectiveness. Hum Rights Rev 23(1):1–17. https://doi.org/10.1007/s12142-022-00656-2

Rasul Ahmed Minja is a Senior Lecturer at the Department of Political Science and Public Administration at the University of Dar es Salaam. He has a PhD in political science from the Institute for Political Science at the University of Duisburg-Essen, Germany. His main research interests include regional integration, regional security, governance and legitimacy issues related to natural resource extraction and management, extractive industry and human rights observance, and election management. He has extensively published on regional integration; community policing; election management; regional security; civil-military relations; the Tanzania Union; the East African Community (EAC) federation; local government elections, and participatory democracy.

Luxembourgish Civil Society Mobilising for Corporate Accountability: Prospects and Challenges for Law Making from Below?

Caroline Omari Lichuma

Abstract Civil society organisations (CSOs) and social movements have been instrumental in the progress made towards holding transnational corporations responsible for violations of human rights and environmental degradation, particularly in global value chains. Increasingly, CSOs have also been advocating for binding obligations within the regime of business and human rights nationally, regionally as well as internationally. This chapter examines the mobilisation of civil society in Germany and Luxembourg for the adoption of mandatory human rights due diligence (mHRDD) laws. Arguably, both the French *Loi de Vigilance* adopted in 2017 as well as the German *Lieferkettengesetz* (*LkSG*) adopted in 2021 were the result of widespread mobilisation from below that assembled a variety of organisations and professional groups, including NGOs, trade unions, epistemic communities, and church-based initiatives. While Luxembourg has not yet enacted an mHRDD law, CSOs succeeded in putting an initial legislative proposal on the government's agenda in 2023. The chapter critically analyses how such national coalitions for mHRDD laws cooperate across borders, borrowing and adapting activist tactics and discursive frameworks employed by their counterparts to agitate for more responsible business conduct.

C. O. Lichuma (✉)
University of Nairobi, Nairobi, Kenya

New York University, New York, NY, USA

Georg-August Universität Göttingen, Göttingen, Germany

Friedrich Alexander University (FAU) CHREN, Nuremberg, Germany
e-mail: caroline.lichuma@fau.de

R. Grosescu, J. G. Dale (eds.), *Corporate Accountability for Human Rights Violations*, Interdisciplinary Studies in Human Rights 16,
https://doi.org/10.1007/978-3-032-05569-9_10

1 Introduction: Civil Society Actors and Progress Towards Corporate Accountability in Luxembourg

Civil society has played a central role in holding transnational corporations (TNCs) accountable for human rights violations and environmental norms. The kind of bottom-up approach to human rights realisation implicit in civil society mobilisation has contributed to the empowerment of numerous stakeholders, including rights-holders affected by the activities of TNCs.[1] As John Ruggie observed, "[a]t the global level, corporate conduct is shaped by three distinct governance systems…the second is a civil governance system involving stakeholders affected by business enterprises and employing various social compliance mechanisms such as advocacy campaigns and other forms of pressure."[2] Within this context, civil society actors have emerged as a key source of governance in this new paradigm. This is because, as Birchall notes, "they can be more responsive, flexible, focused and better networked than state machineries."[3] "Civil society" is a broad term, and civil society organisations (CSOs) are neither part of the state, nor do they operate for profit. Indeed, they have been described as "voluntary entities formed by people in the social sphere that are separate from the state and the market."[4] Whatever shape or form civil society takes, it is clear that civil society actors play a crucial role in trying to make TNCs engage in reponsible business conduct.

Mandatory human rights due diligence (mHRDD) laws compel in-scope companies to meet a number of human rights and environmental due diligence obligations within the context of their operations. Despite textual variations in the various existing mHRDD laws, these obligations will generally require covered companies to: incorporate responsible business conduct into their operations, including by devising a human rights policy or a vigilance plan; execute a risk analysis to identify and assess actual and potential adverse impacts associated with business operations; take actions to stop, prevent, and mitigate any adverse impacts of their business activities, including by implementing a risk management system; publicly report on their performance in this regard; and remediate any adverse impacts.[5] Seen in this light, while due diligence obligations are not synonymous with human rights and environmental obligations, compliance with the former is capable of contributing to realisation of the latter.

Unlike neighbouring France and Germany, Luxembourg has yet to enact and implement an mHRDD law. However, this may soon change since, in 2023, CSOs succeeded in putting an initial legislative proposal on the Luxembourg government's agenda. Appreciation for this tentative achievement, and what is at stake in

---

[1] Jochnick (2017, p. 130).

[2] Ruggie (2014, p. 9).

[3] Birchall (2020, p. 422).

[4] Shift and Mazars LLP (2015).

[5] Lichuma (2024).

this struggle, begins with understanding what due diligence laws are, how they work, and how they are being enacted and implemented outside Luxembourg.

The French law (the *Loi de Vigilance*)[6] was enacted in 2017 and came into force shortly thereafter for companies employing more than 5000 employees in France or more than 10,000 employees both in France and abroad. Similarly, the German law (the *Lieferkettensorgfaltspflichtengesetz, LkSG*)[7] was enacted in June 2021 and came into force in January 2023 for enterprises based in Germany with more than 3000 employees or German-registered branches of foreign companies with over 3000 employees. Since the 1st of January 2024, the *LkSG* also applies to companies with 1000 employees and above. Notably, as a consequence of recent developments in both EU and in Germany there are plans to abolish the LkSG and replace this with a new law implementing the EU Corporate Sustainability Due Diligence Directive (CSDDD).

Crucially, the German and French[8] experiences are exemplars of the important role that civil society can play in the process of mobilising for mHRDD laws, as well as in their implementation. For instance, the German *Initiative Lieferkettengesetz* (Supply Chain Law Initiative) is a broad civil society alliance of over 130 human rights, development and environmental organisations, unions and church-based initiatives founded in September 2019, that played an important part in the processes leading to the enactment of the *LkSG.*[9] In France, since the *Loi de Vigilance* took effect, non-governmental organisations (NGOs) have been instrumental in bringing cases before the French courts to test the opportunities and the limits of the law.[10] The *Loi de Vigilance* provides for a two-step enforcement mechanism that requires parties to first issue the in-scope company in question with a formal notice to comply with its due diligence obligations, and only after this step can the claimants request the competent court to issue an injunction against the errant company coupled with a potential periodic penalty payment.[11] NGOs such as Sherpa, the European Center for Constitutional and Human Rights (ECCHR),[12] Friends of the

[6] *Loi no 2017-399 du 27 mars 2017 relative au devoir de vigilance des sociétés mères et des entreprises donneuses d'ordre 2017* (France), https://www.legifrance.gouv.fr/jorf/id/JORFTEXT000034290626/ (accessed 31 August 2023).

[7] Act on Corporate Due Diligence Obligations in Supply Chains, BGBl I 2021, 2959 (Germany) Official English translation available at https://www.bmas.de/SharedDocs/Downloads/DE/Internationales/act-corporate-due-diligence-obligations-supplychains.pdf, https://www.bmas.bund.de/XXX (accessed 31 August 2023).

[8] Evans (2019, pp. 662–664).

[9] *Initiative Lieferkettengesetz* Website, https://lieferkettengesetz.de/en/ (accessed 1 September 2023).

[10] Bueno and Bright (2020, p. 802).

[11] Savourey and Brabant (2021, p. 149).

[12] Business and Human Rights Resource Centre, 'EDF Group sent formal request urging company to comply with its duty of vigilance under French law' (2 October 2019), https://www.business-humanrights.org/en/latest-news/edf-group-sent-formal-request-urging-company-to-comply-with-its-duty-of-vigilance-under-french-law/ (accessed 20 March 2024).

Earth[13] and others have made use of these enforcement provisions, albeit unsuccessfully (so far).

As a consequence of a little neighbourly pressure, a number of CSOs in Luxembourg formed an initiative similar to the German one and geared towards pressuring the government of Luxembourg to commit to the enactment of a Luxembourgish due diligence law.[14] On 16th May 2023, members of this so-called "Duty of Care Initiative" held a press conference where they announced a bill on the duty of vigilance of companies and contacted all the political parties represented in the Luxembourg Chamber of Deputies to formally submit the due diligence proposal in Parliament. Only two parties, *Déi Lénk* and the *Piratepartei* responded positively.[15] This bill is still under consideration in the Luxembourgish parliament.[16] Nevertheless, given the recent adoption of the EU Corporate Sustainability Due Diligence Directive (CSDDD) in May 2024,[17] the government of Luxembourg (like other EU countries that have not yet enacted an mHRDD law) will soon be compelled to implement such a law.

Focusing on the experiences of the Luxembourg Duty of Care Initiative—an understudied mobilisation in the current literature—this contribution critically analyses the complexities and nuances of law-making "from below", where civil society actors pressure the state to legislate on corporate accountability issues. The intention here is two-fold. First, to trace and contextualise how civil society can have important symbolic effects on public discourse around corporate accountability even where the pertinent state has not yet enacted an mHRDD law. Second, using the comparative experiences of Luxembourg and Germany to critically analyse how CSOs learn from their cross-border counterparts in these processes.

This chapter is divided into four sections. Following this brief introduction, Sect. 2 critically analyses the role that German CSOs have played in the enactment and implementation of the *LkSG* so far. Section 3 delves into the Luxembourgish experience in order to highlight how CSOs contributed to the national dialogue around a potential due diligence law. Section 4 concludes, paying particular attention to the impact of the EU CSDDD legislative process.

[13] Friends of the Earth International, 'Oil Company Total Faces Historic Legal Action in France for Human Rights and Environmental Violations in Uganda' (23 October 2019), https://www.foei.org/oil-company-total-faces-historic-legal-action-in-france-for-human-rights-and-environmental-violations-in-uganda/ (accessed 20 March 2024).

[14] *Initiative Pour un Devoir de Vigilance Luxembourg* Website. https://www.initiative-devoirdevigilance.org/about (accessed 3 September 2023).

[15] *Initiative Pour un Devoir de Vigilance, 'Enfin une Proposition de loi au Luxembourg'*, https://www.initiative-devoirdevigilance.org/post/enfin-une-proposition-de-loi-au-luxembourg (accessed 3 September 2023).

[16] Chamber of Deputies Grand Duchy of Luxembourg, Proposal for a law on the duty of vigilance of companies in the field of sustainability, https://www.chd.lu/en/dossier/8217 (last accessed 25 March 2024).

[17] European Council, 'Corporate Sustainability Due Diligence Directive: Council Gives its Final Approval' (24 May 2024), https://www.consilium.europa.eu/en/press/press-releases/2024/05/24/corporate-sustainability-due-diligence-council-gives-its-final-approval/ (accessed 11 June 2024).

2 Civil Society Made in Germany: The German *Initiative Lieferkettengesetz* (Supply Chain Law Initiative) and Progress Towards Corporate Accountability

2.1 Putting Pressure on the German Government to Enact an mHRDD Law

One of the most enduring contributions made by CSOs to the corporate accountability landscape is the consistent and strategic use of social and public pressure to push governments such as Germany's to enact an mHRDD law. From as early as September 2006, German CSOs were already agitating for a supply chain law within the ambit of the Corporate Accountability Network (*CorA-Netzwerk*).[18] This network, made up of human rights organisations, trade unions, church and development policy organisations, consumer and environmental associations and other CSOs with social and socio-political objectives, sought to strengthen the social debate about the economic and political actions of TNCs and stand up for corporate accountability by calling for binding instruments. Notably, *CorA-Netzwerk* did not focus on binding law only in Germany but also emphasised the importance of hard corporate accountability obligations both within Europe as well as internationally.

In its founding declaration, the *CorA-Netzwerk* stressed the failures of voluntary corporate social responsibility (CSR) initiatives and instead proposed binding corporate rules that are effective across borders as an ethical imperative.[19] More specifically, the founding declaration (rather prophetically) urged "the Bundestag and the Federal Government of Germany, as well as the European Parliament, the European Council and the European Commission to take concrete steps to introduce a binding framework for corporate responsibility."[20] While it is difficult to quantify the exact impact of *CorA-Netzwerk's* efforts on the eventual adoption of the *LkSG*, this chapter argues that the network played an important role in planting the seeds of the mHRDD debate in Germany, seeds that were subsequently watered by the *Initiative Lieferkettengesetz*. In fact, most of the CSOs that are a part of the *CorA-Netzwerk* subsequently went on to join both the *Initiative Lieferkettengesetz* as well as the European Coalition for Corporate Justice (ECCJ).[21] This latter network, the ECCJ, has been particularly active in the legislative and socio-political processes surrounding the enactment of the EU CSDDD.

---

[18] Corporate Accountability: *Netzwerk für Unternehmensverantwortung,* https://www.cora-netz.de (last accessed 10 November 2023).

[19] *Gründungserklärung des Netzwerkes für Unternehmensverantwortung* Corporate Accountability (CorA) (July 2006), https://www.cora-netz.de/alt/wp-content/uploads/grundungserklarung-netzwerk-fur-unternehmensverantwortung.pdf(last accessed 25 February 2024).

[20] Ibid, p. 2.

[21] European Coalition for Corporate Justice, https://corporatejustice.org (last accessed10 January 2024).

The idea for a new network to champion mHRDD in Germany was suggested during a *CorA-Netzwerk* meeting. In autumn 2017, a first strategy workshop was held,[22] which culminated in the founding of the *Initiative Lieferkettengesetz* in September 2019. At the time, the network was composed of over 80 CSOs (18 founding organisations[23] and 69 supporting organisations), including, *inter alia*, human rights organisations, development and environment organisations, trade unions and church-based initiatives.[24]

The decision to form the Initiative was strategic as well as pragmatic and was driven by a number of factors, including the desire to pool relevant financial resources; coordination of a common set of demands and the development of a communication strategy that included the publication of position papers and background material; the central strategy of coalition building "as the initiators assumed that they 'would need considerable reinforcement that goes beyond the CorA network.'"[25] Ultimately, one of the great strengths of the Initiative lies in the fact that it "positioned itself as a broad alliance that simultaneously acted as a unified actor."[26] The size of the *Initiative Lieferkettengesetz* increased considerably since its formation and now has grown to include more than 140 organisations in 2024. As observed by Weihrauch et al., this growth of the Initiative partly resulted from the membership of church-based organisations, which brought with it a particular strategic importance given that the invocation of Christian values was seen as a crucial tool necessary to obtain the support of centre-right German political parties such as Christian Democratic Union (CDU) and Christian Social Union (CSU).[27]

This alliance of CSOs was particularly instrumental in the run up to the adoption of the German due diligence law, mobilising in a number of significant ways. For example, on 10th September 2019, during the 7th anniversary of the tragic Ali Enterprises Textile Factory Fire,[28] the Initiative tabled a petition urging the then German Chancellor, Angela Merkel to introduce a German supply chain law.[29] This

---

[22] Weihrauch et al. (2023, p. 916).

[23] The 18 founding organisations were*: Arbeitsgemeinschaft der Eine Welt-Landesnetzwerke in Deutschland e.V. (agl), Brot für die Welt, Bund für Umwelt und Naturschutz Deutschland e.V., Christliche Initiative Romero e.V. (CIR), CorA-Netzwerk für Unternehmensverantwortung, Deutscher Gewerkschaftsbund (DGB),* European Center for Constitutional and Human Rights (ECCHR*), Forum Fairer Handel e.V., Germanwatch e.V., Greenpeace e.V., INKOTA-netzwerk e.V., Bischöfliches Hilfswerk MISEREOR e. V.,* Oxfam *Deutschland e.V., SÜDWIND e.V., ver.di—Vereinte Dienstleistungsgewerkschaft, WEED—Weltwirtschaft, Ökologie & Entwicklung e.V., Weltladen-Dachverband e.V., Werkstatt Ökonomie e.V.*

[24] Background Paper: *Initiative Lieferkettengesetz* (January 2020), https://www.fairtradestadt-hamburg.de/wp-content/uploads/2020/02/Background-Paper-Initiative-Lieferkettengesetz_January-2020.pdf (last accessed 20 November 2023).

[25] Weihrauch et al. (2023, p. 916).

[26] Ibid.

[27] Ibid.

[28] Saage-Maaß (2021, p. 28).

[29] *Initiative Lieferkettengesetz*, Press Release (10 September 2019), https://lieferkettengesetz.de/pressemitteilung/broad-civil-society-alliance-calls-for-supply-chain-law/ (last accessed 30

was accompanied by a public protest on the 11th of September before the German *Bundestag*, with the various CSOs shining a spotlight on the numerous human rights and environmental violations involving German companies.[30] Carrying placards with powerful messages such as, "*Gegen gewinne ohne gewissen hilft nur noch ein gesetzlicher rahmen*," which loosely translates as "only a legal framework will help against profits without conscience," these CSOs helped to put corporate accountability squarely on the public and legislative agenda.[31] In addition, the Initiative is credited with commissioning a representative survey that indicated that, at the time, 75% of the German population was in favour of a supply chain law.[32] This was an additional tactic aimed at putting the government under pressure to enact a much-needed mHRDD law. One especially noteworthy tactic employed by the *Initiative Lieferkettengesetz*, and that arguably contributed to the success of its mission, was its masterful public relations campaign that managed to firmly cement the debate on the need for an mHRDD law in the collective public psyche. This was achieved, *inter alia*, through the use of a dedicated website where updates could be obtained; press releases issued; public campaigns outside government offices organised, educational online videos distributed, and more.

Nevertheless, while German CSOs played an important role in applying significant social and public pressure both on German corporations, as well as on the Federal Government, such CSOs' actions must be understood as operating in confluence with additional factors extending beyond Germany.

2.2 *The Catalytic Effect of Europe-Wide HRDD Norm Diffusion and Transnational Solidarity Among CSOs*

In addition to the internal factors within Germany, such as the monitoring of the implementation of the 2016 German National Action Plan on BHR (following the recommendations of the 2011 UN Guiding Principles on Business and Human Rights) that propelled the CSOs championing the LkSG, there were also external factors at play that influenced both the CSOs contributions and strategies, as well as eventual outcomes leading to a German mHRDD law. As empirical research undertaken by Weihrauch et al. confirms,

> ... many interviewees spoke about the recent proliferation of laws on FCA [Foreign Corporate Accountability] in the United Kingdom, the Netherlands, and France; or the

November 2023).

[30] INKOTA, Initiative Supply Chain Act: Stop Profits Without Conscience. https://www.inkota.de/themen/unternehmen-verantwortung/initiative-lieferkettengesetz (last accessed 30 November 2023).

[31] Ibid.

[32] Infratest dimap, *Lieferkettengesetz -KW 37/2020: Eine Umfrage von Infratest Dimap im Auftrag von Germanwatch e.V.,* (10 September 2020), https://lieferkettengesetz.de/wp-content/uploads/2020/09/infratest-dimap_Umfrage-Lieferkettengesetz.pdf (last accessed 10 March 2023).

> debates on a European directive that started in 2019. Most of them shared the conviction that these laws strengthened German MDD [Mandatory Due Diligence] supporters.[33]

Similarly, in the background document explaining the *Initiative Lieferkettengesetz*, the CSOs made reference to European countries such as the Netherlands, France and the UK which, by that time, had already adopted various laws to encourage the respect of human rights in overseas business operations.[34]

Arguably, transnational dialogue by European CSOs within the context of mHRDD processes in countries such as Germany and France, as well as the EU CSDDD process, may be said to have symbiotic effects on the development of binding HRDD norms, simultaneously strengthening both national as well as European efforts. As some scholars have shown, a global (or at least European) norm diffusion on mHRDD seems to be taking place, a trend Gustafsson describes as a "cascade of a new norm on foreign accountability."[35] Crucially, this kind of transnational solidarity continues to shape the strategies employed by CSOs in countries such as Luxembourg that are yet to enact mHRDD laws, with CSOs in these countries often presenting to their national legislatures the mHRDD success stories of neighbouring states. In a sense, these different national CSOs in the area of corporate accountability can be regarded as forming transnational "competence communities." Such communities allow actors in the corporate responsibility field to engage in continuous learning and to sustain and improve their knowledge and performance despite being geographically dispersed.[36]

2.3 The Significance of Narratives: Packaging the Call for an mHRDD Law as an Extraterritorial Human Rights Issue

As sociologist Francesca Polleta argues, the value of storytelling in creating a foundation for collective action cannot be understated.[37] In agitating for an mHRDD law, German CSOs carefully and strategically shaped the corporate accountability narrative as an extraterritorial human rights issue, a case of German companies behaving well at home but poorly when abroad. For example, in the "why was the Initiative

---

[33] Weihrauch et al. (2023, p. 912).

[34] Background Paper: *Initiative Lieferkettengesetz* (January 2020), https://www.fairtradestadt-hamburg.de/wp-content/uploads/2020/02/Background-Paper-Initiative-Lieferkettengesetz_January-2020.pdf (last accessed 20 November 2023), p. 2.

[35] Gustafsson et al. (2023a, p. 853).

[36] Backer et al. (2015, p. 270).

[37] Polletta (2006, p. 7), "… storytelling helps to make sense of the anomalous, …it elicits and channels emotions, and …it sustains individual and group identities. These processes are critical to collective action, and we can draw on them to develop the microfoundations of collective action that we still lack."

founded" section of the background paper to the *Initiative Lieferkettengesetz*, these CSOs emphasised the negative human rights and environmental impacts that German companies have around the world and particularly in the Global South.[38] Using this kind of narrative tool to personalise the extraterritorial harm caused by German companies abroad is a powerful and emotive way to make otherwise far away harms to distant strangers more relatable to the Germany populace. Formulations such as "[w]hen it comes to production of *our clothes*, for example, catastrophic textile fires and collapses are merely the tip of the iceberg," or "[*w*]*e* destroy the natural resources people rely on for their very existence to extract the raw materials we need to make *our* cars and electrical appliances" (emphasis added)[39] are an impactful way to raise the (German) society's concern and ensure support for mHRDD laws.

This kind of storytelling, coupled with petitions aggressively advertised by the *Initiative Lieferkettengesetz* inviting members of the public to sign on in support of an LkSG, undoubtedly helped to generate democratic debate and deliberation around the need for an mHRDD in Germany. In September 2020, for instance, members of the *Initiative Lieferkettengesetz* organised a demonstration in Berlin and presented a petition signed by over 222,222 people urging the Federal Cabinet to stop delaying the passing of the LkSG.[40] The use of this kind of "human rights storyline" and accompanying tactics deliberately relies upon a "moralising strategy that invokes the normative power of universally acknowledged human rights."[41] The strategy simultaneously vilifies opponents to a proposed mHRDD law by putting them under suspicion for being ready to "disregard human rights as a matter of principle."[42]

Relatedly, this moralising strategy of German CSOs involved invocations of the three major factory accidents in the Garment industry: the Ali Enterprises factory fire in Pakistan,[43] the Tazreen Factory Fire in Bangladesh,[44] and the collapse of the Rana Plaza factory also in Bangladesh—that occurred between September 2012 and

---

[38] Background Paper: *Initiative Lieferkettengesetz* (January 2020), https://www.fairtradestadt-hamburg.de/wp-content/uploads/2020/02/Background-Paper-Initiative-Lieferkettengesetz_January-2020.pdf (last accessed 20 November 2023), p. 1.

[39] Ibid.

[40] INKOTA, "Initiative Protests With More Than 222,222 Signatures at the Federal Chancellery—Cabinet Debate on Supply Chain Act Postponed Again" (9 September 2020), https://www.inkota.de/presse/pressemitteilungen/initiative-protestiert-mit-mehr-als-222222-unterschriften-am (last accessed 10 November 2023).

[41] Weihrauch et al. (2023, p. 913).

[42] Ibid.

[43] Worker Driven Social Responsibility Network, "Case Study: Ali Enterprises (Pakistan)", https://wsr-network.org/what-is-wsr/csr-and-msis/msi-case-study-ali-enterprises-pakistan/ (last accessed 21 June 2024).

[44] Clean Clothes Campaign, "Tazreen Fire: Fight for Compensation" https://cleanclothes.org/campaigns/past/tazreen (last accessed 21 June 2024).

April 2013, but whose tremors are still felt today in the BHR landscape especially given the intense international media attention that accompanied them.[45]

2.4 Countering Corporate Narratives and Redressing Power Imbalances Between TNCs and Rightsholders

Closely related to the human rights moralising strategy discussed above, CSOs also play an important role in countering the narratives of TNCs about how/whether they respect human rights and the environment in the context of their global operations. For instance, the Mercedes-Benz group widely publicises its compliance with human rights in their own operations as well as in their supply chains. In this regard, they have devised the so-called human rights respect system (HRRS), made up of four steps: risk assessment, program implementation, monitoring, and reporting. As the group states, "The HRRS is unique in our industry… [and] is designed to identify and avoid risks and possible negative effects of our business activities on human rights early on."[46]

In order to counter these and similar company narratives of adequate compliance with human rights and environmental standards, CSOs conduct and publicise research on identified companies' human rights and environmental records, particularly where the companies in question seek to paint a more attractive picture of their performance in reality. By reframing the narrative in this way, yet still within the bounds of the evidence presented, CSOs can more convincingly reiterate the case for binding laws, resonating with both lawmakers and the general public. For instance, in 2023, the European Centre for Constitutional and Human Rights filed a complaint with the German Federal Office of Economics and Export Control (BAFA), alleging that the Mercedes Benz Group (and others) are not adequately responding to the risk of forced labour within their supply chains in the Xinjiang Autonomous Uyghur Region (Uyghur Region).[47] This kind of action by CSOs, directly challenging abstract company narratives about the effectiveness of their risk management systems in concrete contexts, is a useful way to re-shape the conversation about what companies are or are not doing in reality.

Implicit in this strategy is the rebalancing of the asymmetrical power relations between TNCs and rightsholders, particularly with regard to power over

---

[45] Vanpeperstraete (2021, p. 157).

[46] Mercedes Benz Group, "The Mercedes-Benz Human Rights Respect System", https://group.mercedes-benz.com/responsibility/society/human-rights/human-rights-respect-system.html (last accessed 21 June 2024).

[47] ECCHR, "German economic engine roars thanks to forced labor: Complaint filed against VW, BMW and Mercedes Benz" (21 June 2023), https://www.ecchr.eu/en/press-release/deutscher-wirtschaftsmotor-brummt-dank-zwangsarbeit-beschwerde-gegen-vw-bmw-und-mercedes-benz-eingereicht/ (last accessed 10 June 2024).

knowledge.[48] Turning the spotlight on a case of alleged human rights and environmental violations offers the affected individuals and communities, often in the Global South, a platform to air their grievances with the backing of CSOs working through transnational advocacy networks. Crucially, shining the spotlight on alleged violations by companies can change the power dynamics between powerful TNCs and vulnerable rightsholders, as the former may be particularly careful about the potential damage to their reputations and accompanying public perceptions internationally or in key (European) countries. In following through on this strategy, the *Initiative Lieferkettengestez* has, for example, published detailed case studies of human rights and environmental violations by German companies all around the world.[49]

2.5 *Working Across Enemy Lines: Building Alliances with German Companies*

It is impossible to imagine the success of mHRDD laws without the active participation of covered or in-scope companies themselves. These are the companies which fall within the ambit of mHRDD laws and are required to comply with the identified due diligence obligations. On the one hand, business entities such as TNCs enjoy vast amounts of power and resources, and are oftentimes able to lobby law and policymakers in their favour—exerting their influence to ensure that mHRDD laws are not passed or that such laws are significantly weakened.[50] On the other hand, the eventual success of mHRDD laws in any given context will, to a large extent, depend on how effectively such in-scope companies actually discharge their due diligence obligations rather than engaging in tick-box or cosmetic compliance.[51] Seen in this light, companies may very well be said to occupy the position of a double-agent—being both enemy and (potential) ally in mHRDD debates.

Perhaps in acknowledgement of this reality, German CSOs took targeted steps to build alliances with German companies and economic actors likely to support the passing of an mHRDD law. These were "companies that either had expressed their position for such a law or were known for having advanced due diligence measures."[52] One example of such companies' involvement stands out. Under the coordination of the BHR Resource Centre, more than 40 companies, including, *inter alia*, Hapag-Lloyd, Nestlé Germany, Ritter Sport, Tchibo and Vaude, signed a joint statement

---

[48] Birchall (2021, pp. 61–63).

[49] *Initiative Lieferkettengesetz*, "Case Studies", https://lieferkettengesetz.de/fallbeispiele/ (accessed 20 March 2024).

[50] ECCJ, "Off the Hook? How Business Lobbies Against Liability for Human Rights and Environmental Abuses" (June 2021), https://corporatejustice.org/wp-content/uploads/2021/06/OffThe-Hook.pdf (last accessed 10 January 2024).

[51] Landau (2019, pp. 222–223).

[52] Weihrauch et al. (2023, p. 916).

supporting the enactment of a German mHRDD law.[53] However, a note of caution is necessary here. The utility of CSOs' strategies in building alliances with companies must be tempered by the fact that the support of companies is sometimes obtained at the expense of weaker mHRDD law designs. In this regard, corporate lobbying may seek to make mHRDD laws "toothless" by "restricting or even banning strong liability provisions and access to courts for victims."[54] In fact, even though many individual companies seem to support the imposition of due diligence obligations, company lobby groups have been quite active in seeking to dilute strong proposals both nationally as well as regionally in the context of EU legislative processes.[55]

2.6 *You Win Some, You Lose Some: How the Final mHRDD Law Failed to Live Up to CSO's Expectations*

The eventual enactment of the LkSG was a victorious moment for numerous stakeholders in Germany (and abroad), particularly for the CSOs who had worked so hard to make this happen. Yet, it was not a complete victory. The final law did not satisfy all the demands that the *Initiative Lieferkettengesetz* had made in the periods preceding the legislative drafting process. In fact, the Initiative presented a model mHRDD law in early 2020 with a number of proposed provisions, including, *inter alia*, a broad scope of application of the law to encompass companies with over 250 employees or even lower for businesses in high risk sectors; all companies with a genuine link to Germany should be liable; the due diligence obligations should account for both human rights as well as environmental degradation; an array of sanctions including civil liability; and a reversed burden of proof in favour of claimants.[56]

The final draft of the mHRDD adopted by the German government in June 2021 was clearly a political compromise.[57] As the *Initiative Lieferkettengesetz* observed,

---

[53] Business and Human Rights Resource Centre, "German Businesses Call for Legal Duty of Care for Human Rights and the Environment" (9 December 2019), https://www.business-humanrights.org/en/blog/german-businesses-call-for-legal-duty-of-care-for-human-rights-and-the-environment/ (last accessed 10 January 2024).

[54] Friends of the Earth and Others, "Off the Hook?: How Business Lobbies Against Liability for Human Rights and Environmental Abuses" (June 2021) https://friendsoftheearth.eu/wp-content/uploads/2021/06/Off-the-Hook-Lobby-report.pdf (last accessed 14 June 2024), p. 4.

[55] Friends of the Earth and Others, "Inside Job: How Business Lobbyists Used the Commission's Scrutiny Procedures to Weaken Human Rights and Environmental Legislation" (June 2022), <https://corporateeurope.org/sites/default/files/2022-06/INSIDE%20JOB%20How%20business%20lobbyists%20used%20the%20Commission%27s%20scrutiny%20procedures.pdf (last accessed 14 June 2024), p. 9.

[56] Hering (2020).

[57] Krajewski et al. (2021, p. 552).

with the adoption of the *LkSG*, Germany was "not there yet, but finally at the start."[58] On balance, in comparison to the French law and other mHRDD laws, the German law is the most detailed mHRDD law that currently exists.

However, according to the *Initiative Lieferkettengesetz* the law contains a number of weaknesses. First, the scope of the law is narrower than CSOs had hoped for, applying as it does to large companies with 3000 employees from 1st January 2023, and 1000 employees from 1st January 2024.

Second, the comprehensive due diligence obligations apply only to the company's business operations and any direct suppliers. As per section 9 of the Act, due diligence in the context of indirect suppliers need only be carried out where there is "substantiated knowledge" of violations, which is problematic given the heightened vulnerability experienced by rightsholders in the deeper, less visible tiers of GVCs.

Third, section 3(3) of the *LkSG* categorically states that the law does not create a new civil liability regime. This makes it difficult for aggrieved rightsholders to be able to bring claims of human rights and environmental violations before German civil courts.

Fourth, CSOs have argued that the law takes environmental aspects into consideration only marginally, with only three environmental conventions being annexed to the *LkSG*: the 2013 Minamata Convention on Mercury, the 2001 Stockholm Convention on Persistent Organic Pollutants and the 1992 Basel Convention on the Control of Transboundary Movements of Hazardous Wastes and their Disposal. Other important instruments, such as those that deal with biodiversity and habitat protection (*inter alia*, the Convention on Biological Diversity and the Cartagena Protocol on Biosafety) or pollution of the marine environment (*inter alia*, the International Convention for the Prevention of Pollution from Ships—MARPOL and the United Nations Convention on the Law of the Sea -UNCLOS), are not taken into consideration.

Fifth, the *LkSG* has also been criticised for its failure to mandate meaningful stakeholder engagement, instead granting, in its section 4(4), covered companies an arguably too-wide discretion to only give "due consideration" to the needs of stakeholders.[59] As the *Initiative Lieferkettengesetz* highlighted, unlike the UNGPs which foresees meaningful engagement of stakeholders, including by requiring companies to consult with potentially affected groups in order to carry out risk analysis and implement effective measures, the *LkSG* does not mandate the consultation of such affected parties.[60] Moreover, as Third World Approaches to International Law (TWAIL) critiques have emphasised, the exclusion of Global South stakeholders (including victims of corporate crimes, NGOs and trade unions) from the legislative

---

[58] *Initiative Lieferkettengesetz*, "What the new Supply Chain Delivers and What it Doesn't: An Analysis by *Initiative Lieferkettengesetz*" (11 June 2021), https://media.business-humanrights.org/media/documents/Initiative-Lieferkettengesetz_Analysis_What-the-new-supply-chain-act-delivers.pdf (last accessed 10 January 2024).

[59] Lichuma (2024, p. 12).

[60] *Initiative Lieferkettengesetz* (n 73), p. 5.

processes preceding the enactment of mHRDD laws such as the *LkSG* is another cause for concern.[61]

Certainly, it would be impractical (and perhaps even a little naïve) to expect that CSOs in any given context will be able to ensure that governments enacting mHRDD laws include all the provisions that such CSOs would like. There is only so much power that CSOs wield, even when they act through formidable networks such as the *Initiative Lieferkettengesetz*. Ultimately, this contribution posits that the biggest challenge to "law making from the bottom" is that elected governments will always retain the final say on which laws will be passed and what such laws will contain. Thus, while CSOs may be able to influence legislative processes leading to the adoption of mHRDD laws, they can only do so indirectly.

One final observation is necessary in this regard. The German NAP process may be said to have triggered the eventual adoption of the LkSG. After the German general elections in September 2017, the Social Democratic Party (SPD) and the CDU/CSU entered into a coalition agreement. One paragraph of this agreement played a key role in setting the stage for an mHRDD law. The English translation of the paragraph in question provided as follows:

> We are committed to the consistent implementation of the National Action Plan on Business and Human Rights (NAP), including public procurement. If the effective and comprehensive review of the NAP 2020 comes to the conclusion that the voluntary commitment of companies is not sufficient, we will take legal action at a national level and advocate for EU-wide regulation.[62]

Subsequently, "[t]he results of this monitoring were published on 14 July 2020 and indicated that only 13%–17% of German companies properly executed human rights due diligence."[63] This result, coupled with the promise made in the coalition agreement, reinvigorated the cause of the supporters of an mHRDD law.

2.7 The Ongoing Role of German CSOs in Implementing the LkSG

Section 11 of the *LkSG* grants German trade unions and NGOs a special capacity to sue on behalf of rightsholders whose rights are violated by in-scope companies. This is an important mechanism to rebalance the unequal power dynamic between large German corporations and the victims of human rights and environmental

---

[61] Lichuma (2021, pp. 522–524), Bose (2023, p. 19), Dehbi and Martin-Ortega (2023, p. 930).

[62] CDU, CSU and SPD (2018, p. 156), which provided in German: "Wir setzen uns für eine konsequente Umsetzung des Nationalen Aktionsplans Wirtschaft und Menschenrechte (NAP) ein, einschließlich des öffentlichen Beschaffungswesens. Falls die wirksame und umfassende Überprüfung des NAP 2020 zu dem Ergebnis kommt, dass die freiwillige Selbstverpflichtung der Unternehmen nicht aus- reicht, werden wir national gesetzlich tätig und uns für eine EU-weite Regelung einsetzen."

[63] Weihrauch et al. (2023, p. 918).

violations.[64] This provision has set the stage for German CSOs to continue taking an active part in the implementation of the *LkSG*. Given the fact that the *LkSG* only recently came into force, no complaints have thus far been made in German courts. However, a number of complaints have already been raised with the administrative body responsible for the monitoring and implementation of the Act, that is, the Federal Office for Economic Affairs and Export Control, or *Bundesamt für Wirtschaft und Ausfuhrkontrolle* (BAFA).[65]

Notably, CSOs such as FEMNET and the European Center for Constitutional and Human Rights (ECCHR) have filed complaints against IKEA and Amazon alleging that the failure of such brands to sign the Bangladesh Accord is a violation of the German due diligence law, given the fact that the Bangladesh Accord is meant to ensure workplace safety in supplier factories in Bangladesh.[66] Relatedly, CSOs have also lodged complaints against German automobile companies Volkswagen, Mercedes, and BMW alleging that these companies have been linked to potential human rights violations (particularly forced labour) in their supply chains in the Xinjiang Autonomous Uyghur Region.[67] The international NGO Oxfam has also filed complaints against two German supermarkets Rewe and Edeka, alleging that they have breached their obligations under the *LkSG* by contributing to human rights abuses on Latin American banana and pineapple plantations. The accusation asserts a disregard for evidence of low wages, deplorable working conditions, and suppression of trade unions.[68] While BAFA has not publicized adminsitrative actions taken against any of these companies,[69] one thing is for certain. The role of CSOs in corporate accountability processes does not end with the enactment of mHRDD laws. This chapter argues that, in fact, CSOs become even more important once such laws are passed and must utilise their resources and transnational

[64] Deva (2023, p. 411).

[65] BAFA, 'Information on the Supply Chain Act', https://www.bafa.de/DE/Lieferketten/Multilinguales_Angebot/multilinguales_angebot_node.html (last accessed 20 January 2024).

[66] Business and Human Rights Resource Centre, 'NGOs File Complaint Under new German Supply Chain Act Against IKEA and Amazon Over Alleged Failure to meet Their Due Diligence Obligations by not Signing Bangladesh Accord' (24 April 2023), https://www.business-humanrights.org/en/latest-news/ngos-file-first-complaint-under-new-german-supply-chain-act-against-ikea-and-amazon-over-alleged-failure-to-meet-their-due-diligence-obligations-by-not-signing-bangladesh-accord/ (last accessed 20 March 2024).

[67] ECCHR, 'German Economic Engine Roars Thanks to Forced Labour: Complaint Filed Against VW, BMW and Mercedes Benz' (June 2023), https://www.ecchr.eu/fileadmin/user_upload/Q_A_BAFA_FINAL_website.pdf (last accessed 15 January 2024).

[68] Business and Human Rights Resource Centre, 'Germany: NGOs File Complaint Under Supply Chain Act Against two Supermarket Chains Over Alleged Labour Rights Abuses on Plantations in Ecuador and Costa-Rica' (3 November 2023), https://www.business-humanrights.org/en/latest-news/germany-ngos-file-complaint-under-supply-chain-act-against-two-supermarket-chains-over-alleged-labour-rights-abuses-on-plantations-in-ecuador-and-costa-rica/ (last accessed 15 January 2024).

[69] Krajewski and Dey (2023).

networks to help victims of violation seek redress in the home states of in-scope companies.

3 Imitation Is the Sincerest Form of Flattery: A Luxembourgish *Lieferketten Initiative* and Its Mobilisation for a Due Diligence Law

3.1 Same Script Different Cast: The Initiative Pour un Devoir de Vigilance Enters the Stage

In March 2018, 17 CSOs in Luxembourg came together to form the Initiative for a Due Diligence law. This included, *inter alia*, Amnesty International Luxembourg, Caritas Luxembourg, Fairtrade Luxembourg, and Greenpeace Luxembourg, among others. The Initiative called for the government of the Grand Duchy to enact binding legislation establishing a duty of vigilance for companies based in Luxembourg.[70] While the number of CSOs involved is significantly smaller when compared to the CSOs making up the *Initiative Lieferkettengesetz*, the varying sizes in this context may very well be a factor of the different country sizes. Quite simply, Germany is much bigger than Luxembourg, and the number of CSOs in the former is much higher than in the latter, by extension. The timing of the coordination of this Initiative was strategic, as Luxembourgish political parties were in the process of developing their electoral programs for the parliamentary elections scheduled in October 2018.[71] Agreeing to commit to the adoption of an mHRDD law could, therefore, have been a selling point for any political party that chose to accept the Initiative's call. Additionally, the Initiative attempted to link their proposal with the then ongoing Luxembourg NAP in the BHR process by asking the Ministry of European and Foreign Affairs to include their proposals in the draft NAP.[72]

[70] *Initiative pour un devoir de Vigilance au Luxembourg*, "Proposal", https://www.initiative-devoirdevigilance.org/_files/ugd/af0254_047f82c62ba44621b3b109b9b92b5012.pdf (accessed 20 February 2024).

[71] *Initiative pour un devoir de Vigilance au Luxembourg,* https://www.initiative-devoirdevigilance.org/about (accessed 20 February 2024).

[72] *Initiative pour un devoir de Vigilance au Luxembourg*, "Launch of the Initiative for a duty of vigilance for transnational companies in Luxembourg" (17 April 2018), https://www.initiative-devoirdevigilance.org/post/lancement-de-l-initiative-pour-un-devoir-de-vigilance-des-entreprises-transnationales-au-luxembourg (accessed 20 February 2024). The Luxembourg NAP was adopted in XXX. Maybe 2–3 words about it's result?

3.2 Generating Publicity Around the Need for a Luxembourgish (and European) mHRDD Law

One notable goal that the Initiative has achieved since its inception is the generation of significant and consistent publicity within Luxembourg about the need for a due diligence law. The Initiative has accomplished this through, *inter alia*: the holding of numerous meetings with various parties across the political divide (e.g., the Luxembourg Socialist Workers' Party (LSAP), the Christian Social People's Party (CSV), etc.); organising and participating in conferences and roundtables on BHR; holding press briefings; issuing position papers, for instance, one explaining the potential scope of an mHRDD law in Luxembourg;[73] organising protests in front of the offices of companies alleged to have committed violations;[74] and other activities.[75] A particularly cheeky approach to generating publicity was the use of a so-called "postcards action" that invited interested citizens to send a postcard with a caricature to the then Minister of Foreign Affairs, Mr. Jean Asselborn, urging him to support an mHRDD law. The postcard included a reference to the already enacted German and French laws and encouraged citizens to voice their support for a Luxembourgish due diligence law.[76] Arguably, this kind of catchy tactic should be lauded for its potential to make an otherwise niche discussion on mHRDD laws more accessible to ordinary members of the public (Fig. 1).

Relatedly, the Initiative has publicised cases of human rights and environmental violations by Luxembourgish companies in order to "appeal to senses of guilt, compassion, and justice."[77]

Like its German counterpart, the Initiative has also used the results of public surveys to support its calls for a due diligence law. A survey carried out at the behest of the Initiative and through the national polling agency, the Luxembourg Institute for Social Science Research (*Institut Luxembourgeois de Recherches Sociales*—ILRES) indicated that 87% of the population of Luxembourg supported the enactment of an mHRDD law.[78] The interviews were conducted online via ILRES'

[73] *Iniatiative pour un devoir de Vigilance*, "Human Rights and Companies: What Law for Luxembourg" (3 February 2022), https://www.greenpeace.org/luxembourg/fr/communiques-de-presse/13529/droits-humains-et-entreprises-quelle-loi-pour-le-luxembourg/ (accessed 20 January 2024).

[74] Le Quotidien, "Duty of Vigilance: Activists at the Headquarters of Five Companies" (21 October 2021), https://lequotidien.lu/politique-societe/devoir-de-vigilance-place-a-laction/ (accessed 10 January 2024).

[75] *Initiative pour un devoir de Vigilance au Luxembourg*, "News", https://www.initiative-devoirdevigilance.org/news (accessed 25 March 2024)

[76] *Initiative pour un devoir de Vigilance au Luxembourg*, "Postcards Action" (10 May 2021), https://www.initiative-devoirdevigilance.org/post/action-cartes-postales (accessed 20 January 2024).

[77] Gustafsson et al. (2023b, p. 897).

[78] Le Quotidien, "Waiting for an Exemplary Luxembourg" (30 January 2024), https://lequotidien.lu/a-la-une/en-attendant-un-luxembourg-exemplaire/ (last accessed 30 March 2024).

Fig. 1 Postcard action for a Luxembourgish mHRDD law. Credit: *Initiative Pour un Devoir de Vigilance*

MyPanel platform and took place between the 13th and 19th December 2023. The use of public surveys is a tried and tested tactic used by CSOs to achieve the twin targets of raising public awareness on the importance of mHRDD laws while simultaneously placing pressure on the government to act accordingly.

The Initiative has been a quite vocal supporter of the EU CSDDD, repeatedly urging the government of Luxembourg to vote in favour of the Directive in Brussels[79] and sharply critiquing the government's failure to take a firm position on the EU Directive. In a bold move challenging the transparency (or lack thereof) of Luxembourg's position in Brussels, the Initiative went as far as referring the matter to the Commission on the Access to Documents, within the framework of the law of 14th September 2018 on a transparent and open administration,[80] in order to have access to all existing documents defining Luxembourg's position on the European EU CSDDD.

Crucially, one niche area of focus for the Initiative has been the call for due diligence laws that regulate all sectors, including the financial sector.[81] This is an important point of concern given the fact that Luxembourg is a powerhouse of financial activity and the fact that this issue of whether the financial sector should fall within the ambit of mHRDD laws has been a bone of contention in the EU CSDDD process.[82]

---

[79] *Initiative pour un devoir de Vigilance au Luxembourg*, "Action before the Chamber of Deputies: for a YES from Luxembourg to the CSDDD" (28 February 2024), https://www.initiative-devoirdevigilance.org/post/action-devant-la-chambre-des-députés-pour-un-oui-du-luxembourg-à-la-csddd (accessed 25 March 2024).

[80] Commission on Access to Documents, https://cad.gouvernement.lu/en.html (accessed 10 March 2024).

[81] Heindrichs (2022), ASTM (2022).

[82] EU Council, "Corporate sustainability due diligence: Council and Parliament strike deal to protect environment and human rights" (14 December 2023), https://www.consilium.europa.eu/en/press/press-releases/2023/12/14/corporate-sustainability-due-diligence-council-and-parliament-strike-deal-to-protect-environment-and-human-rights/ (accessed 12 February 2024); Costa (2024).

3.3 Cross-Border Collaborations with Other CSOs

The Initiative has, in numerous instances, adopted common strategies with other CSOs working both nationally as well as within the broader European context. Such collaborations are significant domestically, regionally, and transnationally in the area of corporate accountability for human rights and the environment and contribute to the convergence of norms on responsible business conduct.[83] By forging new links among various civil society actors, these collaborative networks make it possible for dialogue and exchange to take place and help clarify the shared goals as well as aligned strategies necessary to achieve them.

In this regard, one notable collaboration among various CSOs in Europe involves the "lady justice campaign". The lady justice statue is a 10-meter-tall inflatable 3D sculpture depicted on bent knees and a knife in the back. Commissioned by environmental campaigners, Friends of the Earth, the statue critiques the lack of corporate accountability for human rights and environmental violations by corporate actors.[84] CSOs across Europe, including in Paris, Vienna, Brussels, and Stockholm, organised public events calling attention to corporate impunity, with the lady justice statue as the centrepiece of these concerted actions. In November 2022, at the behest of the *Initiative pour un devoir de Vigilance*, the lady justice statue was presented in Luxembourg as part of the Initiative's public strategy geared at enhancing debate on the need for a Luxembourgish due diligence law.[85]

The lady justice campaign is a good example of how transnational advocacy networks frame issues of public concern, making them comprehensible to target audiences and attracting attention that will hopefully encourage action on the part of law and policymakers.[86]

3.4 Securing the Support of the Business Sector

The Initiative has also employed the tactic of cultivating relationships with those companies in the business sector that are likely to support the enactment of a Luxembourgish mHRDD law. In this regard, and very similarly to the German CSOs, the Luxembourg CSOs contributed to the signing of a statement by around 50 businesses and other economic actors supporting a national due diligence law.

[83] Keck and Sikkink (2018, p. 65).

[84] Glow inflatables, "Inflatable Statue for Friends of the Earth: European Tour" (26th September 2023), https://www.glowinflatables.com/inflatable-blog/inflatable-statue-friends-of-the-earth-europe (last accessed 15 June 2024).

[85] *Initiative pour un devoir de Vigilance au Luxembourg,* "With Lady Justice for Legislation Alongside Victims of Human Rights Violations" (2 November 2023), https://www.initiative-devoirdevigilance.org/post/avec-lady-justice-pour-une-législation-aux-côtés-des-victimes-de-violations-de-droits-humains) (last accessed 15 June 2024).

[86] Keck and Sikkink (2018, p. 66).

The companies in question comprised actors in key sectors of the Luxembourg economy, such as finance, construction, and mass distribution (including notable corporations, such as Aldi, Backbone Investment, Rinnen Construction company, among others).[87] The Luxembourg Association of the Social and Solidarity Economy (ULESS), which comprises over 200 economic actors with 20,000 employees, was also one of the signatories of this Business Statement.

This is a crucial aspect of CSOs' coalition building in the area of corporate accountability. Without the commitment of companies to comply with HRDD obligations, mHRDD is unlikely to change the quotidian realities of vulnerable rights-holders on the ground. Thus, where CSOs agitating for mHRDD laws are able to orchestrate alliances that garner the support of business entities, this is a necessary step in the journey towards truly transformative mHRDD laws. Importantly, companies that align with CSOs in this way provide credible testimony that due diligence is feasible, thus debunking arguments by detractors that mHRDD laws overburden business entities.

3.5 The Initiative Pour un Devoir de Vigilance Presents a Model mHRDD Law to the Grand Duchy Parliament

CSOs were instrumental in the adoption of both the German *LkSG* as well as the French *Loi de Vigilance*.[88] Notably however, despite the shared intention of these laws to regulate the impact of corporate actors on human rights and the environment, there are a number of salient differences between them, as depicted in Table 1.

Adopting a similar strategy to the *Initiative Lieferkettengesetz*, the Luxembourgish Initiative also drafted a model mHRDD law and presented it to political parties for discussion in the Chamber of Deputies.[89] In the explanatory memorandum to this bill, explicit reference is made to the Rana Plaza factory disaster and the global reactions it triggered. This is arguably part of the moralising strategy adopted by CSOs when trying to generate public support for an mHRDD law. As Weihrauch et al. observe, "[p]articularly the Rana Plaza incident is 'until today a reference point'... and thus occupies a central spot in the moralising strategy of civil society."[90]

[87] *Initiative pour un devoir de Vigilance au Luxembourg*, "Call for actors in key sectors of the economy to go beyond voluntary measures" (17 September 2021), https://www.initiative-devoirdevigilance.org/post/appel-d-acteurs-de-secteurs-clés-de-l-économie-pour-aller-au-delà-des-mesures-volontontaires (accessed 28 February 2024).

[88] Gustaffson et al. (2023, p. 892).

[89] *Initiative pour un devoir de Vigilance au Luxembourg* "Finally, a Proposal for a Law in Luxembourg!" (16 May 2023), https://www.initiative-devoirdevigilance.org/post/enfin-une-proposition-de-loi-au-luxembourg (accessed 28 March 2024).

[90] Weihrauch et al. (2023, p. 914).

Table 1 A comparison of the German *LkSG and* the French *Loi de Vigilance*

Issue	France	Germany
Personal scope of the law	French companies with 5000 employees in France or 10,000 in France plus abroad	From 2023, companies with 3000 employees or more with a registered office/ branch in Germany, and from 2024, companies with 1000 or more employees
Nature of due diligence obligations	Mandatory vigilance plan that includes: risk analysis to identify, analyse, and categorise risks; procedures for regular evaluation of the situation of subsidiaries and suppliers; appropriate measures to mitigate risks or to prevent serious violations; a whistle-blower mechanism for existing or emerging risks and, a system to evaluate the effectiveness of the implemented measures.	More detailed **than** the French law and obliging companies to: establish a risk management system (section 4(1)); designate a responsible person within the enterprise (section 4(3); perform a regular risk analysis (section 5); issue a policy statement (section 6(2)); lay down preventive measures in own operations (section 6(3)), and vis-à-vis direct suppliers (section 6(4)); take remedial action (section 7(1) to (3)); establish a complaints procedure (section 8)); implement due diligence in regards to indirect suppliers where there is "substantiated knowledge" of violations (section 9)); document (section 10(1)); report (section 10(2)).
Consequences of breach	Injunctive relief and potential civil liability	Fines, exclusion from public contracts, but no civil liability
Administrative enforcement	No public body responsible for administrative enforcement	Enforcement through BAFA

The key elements of the proposed bill included, *inter alia*:[91] a wide scope of application covering companies which meet 2 out of 3 criteria—250 employees, an annual turnover of EUR 50 million or a balance sheet total of EUR 43 million (Article 3); inclusion of the entire financial sector within the ambit of the mHRDD law; an obligation for covered companies to prepare and implement a vigilance plan similar to the one required under the French *Loi de Vigilance* (Article 5); the creation of a supervisory authority, the Regulator, similar to BAFA under the *LkSG* (Article 6); a provision granting Luxembourgish CSOs legal standing to bring representative cases before the courts (Article 19); civil liability (Article 20); a reversal of the burden of proof (Article 21). Notably, in both the French as well as the German contexts, suggestions to include a reversal of the burden of proof were unsuccessful. In the French case, for instance, intense lobbying by powerful business associations resulted in the provision on reversal of the burden of proof being dropped from the final law.[92]

One notable difference between the Initiative's draft and the French *Loi de Vigilance,* as well as the German *LkSG,* is the provision on stakeholder engagement.

[91] Chamber of Deputies, "Proposal for a Law on the Duty of Vigilance of Companies in the Field of Sustainability", https://www.chd.lu/fr/dossier/8217 (accessed 4 April 2024).

[92] Cossart et al. (2017, p. 317).

Whereas both the French and the German laws contain very vague meaningful engagement provisions, Article 5 (2) of the Luxembourg bill contained a very detailed provision on stakeholder consultation requiring covered companies to: publicly announce any calls for consultation; provide stakeholders with adequate information; and carry out consultation for a minimum of 4 weeks. Such consultation would require covered companies to involve stakeholders in carrying out their risk analysis and coming up with suitable measures to prevent, mitigate and remediate violations of human rights and the environment. One potential practical effect of mandating meaningful engagement in this way is the rebalancing of otherwise asymmetrical power relations between powerful companies and vulnerable rights-holders by allowing the latter to participate in due diligence processes.[93]

The Luxembourgish due diligence Bill was tabled in the Chamber of Deputies on 16th May 2023. Subsequently, in June 2023, the mHRDD bill was debated in the Committee on the Economy in the Luxembourg Chamber of Deputies.[94] Representatives of two political parties, *Déi Lénk* and the *Piratepartei,* had agreed in advance to present the bill in Parliament in association with the Initiative. The two speakers, Swen Clement and Nathalie Oberweis, explained that the bill had been drafted jointly with the *Initiative pour un devoir de Vigilance* and outlined the purpose of the law as enhancing more responsible business conduct in Luxembourg.[95] During the debate, one member of the Christian Social People's Party (CSV) party, MP Laurent Mosar, opposed the bill arguing that a European rather than a national response was the better approach and repeated the oft-expressed fear that such a law would unduly burden companies operating in Luxembourg and expose them to additional costs and competitive disadvantage.[96] In response, MP Charles Margue from the Green party argued that the defence of human rights takes precedence over the economic costs of such measures and thus welcomed mHRDD initiatives. The meeting ended with opinions divided on whether Luxembourg should enact an mHRDD law before an EU Directive on the same topic is adopted, a mood which seems to prevail to date.

As the above analysis clearly demonstrates, CSO coalitions such as the *Initiative pour un devoir de Vigilance* can only go so far in contributing to the legislative processes surrounding mHRDD laws. Other than drafting model laws, putting public pressure on governments to enact due diligence laws, and even forging alliances with the business sector, there is not much more that CSOs can do in this context. The Luxembourg experience highlights the reality of how political will and government support are indispensable elements in the quest to "harden" the human rights and environmental obligations of TNCs.[97]

---

[93] Lichuma (2023).

[94] Chamber of Deputies, "Minutes of the meeting held on 15 June 2023", https://wdocs-pub.chd.lu/docs/exped/0141/024/282244.pdf (accessed 10 January 2024), pp. 3–8.

[95] Ibid

[96] Ibid.

[97] Macchi and Bright (2020, pp. 218–219).

4 Final Reflections: A Luxembourgish mHRDD Law in the Shadow of the EU CSDDD and the Continuing Importance of Civil Society Mobilisation in Enhancing Responsible Business Conduct

4.1 Learning from Each Other: Comparing and Contrasting the Experiences of German and Luxembourgish CSOs

As previous sections of this chapter have illuminated, to a large extent, CSOs operating in the area of mHRDD laws seem to employ similar tactics in their struggles to convince national governments to adopt such laws. The similar experiences of the German *Initiative Lieferkettengesetz* and the Luxembourgish *Initiative pour un devoir de Vigilance* allow us to distil a number of common strategies in this regard.

First, in order to amplify their voices and widen their resource pools (human, as well as financial), such CSOs do not act individually. Instead, they combine in order to form a dedicated intersectoral network: the *Initiative Lieferkkettengesetz,* in the case of Germany and the *Initiative pour un devoir de Vigilance,* in Luxembourg. This allows the involved CSOs to come together and speak with a unified voice while simultaneously taking advantage of the economies of scale. In both cases, the use of a dedicated website devoted to updating readers on all the actions undertaken by the network helped cement the role of the respective Initiatives in the national due diligence debates.

Second, the most powerful tool that both Initiatives wielded was the continuous use of publicity to advance their respective causes and generate attention. Both the *Initiative Lieferkettengesetz* as well as the *Initiative pour un devoir de Vigilance* aggressively publicised their demands for a due diligence law. This was done on their websites, through press briefings, newspaper articles, etc. To some extent, publicity shapes public perception, and public perception is, in turn, capable of influencing political action. Thus, publicity by CSOs around the need for an mHRDD law not only increases public awareness about the problem of a lack of corporate accountability but also puts governments under sustained pressure to act. Granted, valid concerns may be raised about such media-centred political activism and accompanying publicity. For instance, Sarah Sobieraj highlights three possible concerns in this regard. Firstly, where activism is media-centred, the focus on public relations may result in participants being viewed as potential liabilities to be managed rather than as trusted peers able to make valuable contributions to the cause being advocated. Secondly, a media campaign requires actors to speak in a unified voice. This implicitly suppresses disagreement while privileging consensus. Thirdly, political and philosophical discussions may be marginalised in favour of more logistical organisation geared towards ensuring successful public campaigns.[98]As Sobieraj cautions, "the relentless concentration on impression management that

[98] Sobieraj (2011, p. 136).

accompanies the pursuit of media attention" could result in suppression of internal dialogue.[99] Nevertheless, despite these concerns, this contribution posits that media campaigns, such as those conducted by CSOs advocating due diligence laws, can be powerful tools when properly managed.

Third, in both cases, the CSO coalitions drafted a model mHRDD law to help augment their positions. The model laws in question were quite ambitious in many respects, including by: having a relatively large scope that would have brought more companies within the ambit of the law; creating a civil liability regime that would have allowed victims of violations to bring civil suits on the basis of the mHRDD law; a reversal of the burden of proof, which would have worked in favour of complainants and against covered companies. Ultimately, however, the German law deviated in some respects from CSOs' demands, leading the *Initiative Lieferkettengesetz* to decry the law for being "weak" and "having gaps." To be fair, given the highly political process of drafting an mHRDD law and the many conflicting interests at play, perhaps the best strategy for CSOs is to aim for the moon and maybe land on the stars. Which is to say, the model mHRDD laws they put forward should be as ambitious as possible so that even if some provisions are lost within the inevitable political compromises that follow, at least some CSOs' suggestions will remain in the end.

Fourth, in debates surrounding the enactment of an mHRDD law both in Germany as well as in Luxembourg, constant references were made to developments in other EU countries, such as France and the Netherlands, as well as to the EU progress towards a binding Directive. These were deliberate strategies geared towards appealing to legislators not to be left behind. The norm diffusion of binding HRDD obligations across Europe is a useful selling point for CSOs advocating a due diligence law. The power of the "see what our neighbours are doing card" cannot be overstated. Notably, this strategy of highlighting developments in comparable states in order to call for progress nationally is not a uniquely European strategy. For instance, within the East African context, Kenya was the first country to adopt a NAP on business and human rights.[100] This has been used as a rallying point to call for similar developments in Uganda (which now has a NAP in BHR) and Tanzania.[101] Similarly, the preferred Japanese regulatory strategy for BHR has, so far, been guidelines on responsible business conduct.[102] This has spurred calls for similar developments in Taiwan, for example.[103]

Fifth, it is clear that mHRDD laws cannot be effective tools to shape corporate behaviour and ensure redress for the victims of corporate human rights and

---

[99] Ibid

[100] Republic of Kenya, "National Action Plan on Business and Human Rights: For the Implementation of the UN Guiding Principles on Business and Human Rights (2020–2025)" (2019), https://statelaw.go.ke/wp-content/uploads/2020/11/NATIONAL-ACTION-PLAN-ON-BUSINESS-AND-HUMAN-RIGHTS-NOV-2020.pdf (last accessed 15 June 2024).

[101] Houerbi and Muchunguzi (2021, p. 1, 4). See also Rasul Minja's chapter in this volume.

[102] Ito (2024).

[103] Ling (2024).

environmental violations without the genuine acceptance of covered companies. To this end, one particularly noteworthy strategy employed by the *Initiative Lieferkettengesetz* and the *Initiative pour un devoir de Vigilance* has been to orchestrate the support of companies and other economic actors for mHRDD laws. This has culminated into "Business Statements of Support" in both cases, sending a strong message to both the government as well as to other companies that it is not only CSOs who are interested in due diligence laws. At the same time, however, care should be taken not to sacrifice more stringent mHRDD laws' design upon the altar of building coalitions with business entities. As clearly illustrated by the German context, the business support for the due diligence law came at the expense of a civil liability provision in the final *LkSG*.[104]

Sixth, both the Luxembourgish CSOs as well as their German counterparts have made use of existing NAP in BHR processes to agitate for binding mHRDD laws. Even though NAPs have been on the receiving end of criticism for being "cosmetic devices that states use to deflect attention from persisting abuses and needed regulation,"[105] they can be useful markers of progress towards corporate accountability. As the German example highlights, where an NAP contains monitoring provisions, this becomes a formidable tool to assess whether companies are voluntarily complying with HRDD obligations. Where the monitoring reveals a failure to act, as was the case in Germany, this may be an additional catalyst for binding obligations. As O'Brien has observed in this regard, NAPs may "trigger government commitments to implement business and human rights standards, so delivering better 'vertical' alignment of national laws, policies, and institutional practices with international commitments."[106] In fact, as the German experience confirms, NAPs may be said to be "pre-regulatory, in as much as they may lead to or create conditions encouraging the adoption of substantive policies, legislation or other measures."[107]

At the end of the day, however, no matter how effectively CSOs deploy the above tactics in their quest for mHRDD laws, one major challenge persists. In order for due diligence laws to be enacted and implemented, there must be political will and government support for the cause. As Part 2 has illuminated, the German experience is instructive in this regard. Without the support of the SPD and the CDU/CSU—and a coalition agreement that committed to coming up with more intrusive HRDD measures depending on the results of the NAP monitoring, it may very well be the case that the *LkSG* would not have been enacted. Or at least that its enactment would have taken a little more time. Luxembourg has only had two NAPs in BHR so far (2018–2019 and 2020–2022), and, to date, the government has not committed itself to implementing a due diligence law if the NAP monitoring process yields a dismal performance by companies. Thus, as the final section will outline, the tactic that might work best for Luxembourgish CSOs now is placing pressure on the

[104] Weihrauch et al. (2023, p. 919).

[105] O'Brien et al. (2021, p. 72).

[106] O'Brien et al. (2016, p. 121).

[107] O'Brien et al. (2021, p. 94).

government to tranpose the recently adopted EU CSDDD into the Luxembourgish context as ambitiously as possible.

4.2 A Note on Transnational Cooperation Between Global North and Global South CSOs in the Area of mHRDD Laws

Due diligence laws operate extraterritorially and are intended to influence the actions of suppliers in the Global South. Yet, Global South actors are not properly represented, both in the processes preceding the enactment of due diligence laws as well as in the implementation of such laws.[108] Valid questions may be raised about whether Global North CSOs are doing enough to include Global South CSOs in these mHRDD laws transnational advocacy networks and the conversations surrounding the development and implementation of binding due diligence obligations. Even though many Global North CSOs partner with Global South CSOs, the mere existence of such partnerships does not always mean that the interests of Global South rightsholders are properly considered and factored into the decisions taken.[109]

This contribution argues that more must be done to ensure that Global South CSOs and other grassroots organisations have a seat at the table and are able to actively and directly participate in processes surrounding mHRDD laws. It is not enough for Global North CSOs to speak on behalf of Global South CSOs, individuals, and communities. Recognition of the agency and autonomy of Global South stakeholders in matters that concern them necessarily requires a less Eurocentric transnational advocacy network.

4.3 Conclusion: The EU Corporate Sustainability due Diligence Directive and a Lingering Role for CSOs Advocating mHRDD Laws

For the EU CSDDD, the year 2024 got off to a tumultuous start.[110] For some months, the future of the Directive hang in the balance as a result of the 11th-hour backtracking of countries such as Germany, France and Italy, which threatened the compromise agreement that had been reached by the European Council and the European Presidency in December 2023.[111] This compromise agreement included now deleted

---

[108] Lichuma (2023, p. 764).

[109] Sénit and Bierrmann (2021, pp. 581–591).

[110] Blenkinsop (2024).

[111] EU Council (note 69).

provisions that covered a much larger number of companies and required due diligence in high-risk sectors.[112] Fortunately however, due to the tireless efforts of numerous actors, agreement was finally reached, albeit on a significantly watered down version of the Directive.[113] These actors included: the Belgian presidency of the Council of the EU (1st January to 30th June 2024);[114] Individual MEPs of the European Parliament such as Lara Wolters and Axel Voss; and CSOs mobilising primarily through the European Coalition of Corporate Justice (ECCJ) network.[115]

A number of concessions had to be made to secure the political compromise necessary to end the EU CSDDD roller-coaster ride. The most significant concession was the change in scope of the Directive, which decreased the number of companies that fall within the CSDDD's scope by nearly two-thirds. The threshold for the scope of application has been increased from companies with 500 employees to those with 1000 employees and from those with a turnover of €150 million to those with €450 million. In addition, it is now anticipated that a three-year phase-in strategy will be implemented from the date of the CSDDD's adoption, starting with the Directive applying to companies with 5000 employees and €1500 million turnover in 3 years, those with 3000 employees and €900 million turnover in 4 years, and finally those with 1000 employees and €450 million turnover in 5 years. The notion of high-risk sectors has also been removed from the final draft due to pressure from industrial sectors such as mining, agriculture, and manufacture. Unfortunately however, the CSDDD is still not out of the woods. In a rather shocking turn of events, even post its official adoption the CSDDD is still under threat of further dilution within the context of the so-called Omnibus simplification package adopted on 26th February 2025. The EU Commission has framed the Omnibus Initiative as necessary in order to create a more favorable business environment and enhance the competitiveness of EU businesses. In juxtaposition, opponents such as civil society allege that the Omnibus is actually deregulation masquerading as simplification and is a further attempt to water down an already diluted CSDDD.

The ECCJ has been a particularly vocal actor throughout this process. Made up of more than 480 CSOs and NGOs, it is the largest civil society network devoted to BHR and corporate accountability, and its membership includes national coalitions such as the German *CorA-Netzwerk* as well as the Luxembourgish *Initiative Pour un Devoir de Vigilance*.[116] Relying on funding from membership contributions as well as financing from external bodies, the Coalition has been a formidable campaigner for the EU CSDDD. Some of the strategies it has employed in this regard include the following: orchestrating the actions of over 480 CSOs and developing a

112 Fair Trade International, 'A Diluted EU Due Diligence Law is Still Better than None' (15 March 2024), https://www.fairtrade.net/news/a-diluted-eu-due-diligence-law-is-still-better-than-none (last accessed 20 June 2024).

113 Ibid.

114 Belgian Presidency of the Council of the EU, https://belgian-presidency.consilium.europa.eu/en/ (accessed 7 April 2024).

115 European Coalition for Corporate Justice, https://corporatejustice.org (accessed 7 April 2028).

116 ECCJ, "Members", https://corporatejustice.org/members/ (accessed 7 April 2024).

common vision as well as a united voice for corporate accountability issues in Europe; the generation of publicity around the need for an EU Directive as well as other European and national laws and policies; applying (very public) pressure on EU legislators to vote in favour of the CSDDD; sharing information about the legislative process, including by providing easy to access summaries of the various drafts of the Directive.

With the adoption of the CSDDD, European countries, such as Luxembourg, that have not yet enacted an mHRDD law will now be compelled to do so. CSOs such as the *Initiative Pour un Devoir de Vigilance* should seize the day and let these developments at the EU level reinvigorate their advocacy for robust national mHRDD laws. In fact, even when these national mHRDD laws are adopted and finally enter into force, CSOs must continue the struggle for corporate accountability by deploying legal strategies to ensure their effective implementation. This will include bringing legal actions against errant corporations in the home states in question, whether through national administrators such as BAFA in Germany or in courts of law. Ultimately, in order to finally reduce (and eventually close) the corporate accountability gap, CSOs like the *Initiative Pour un Devoir de Vigilance* must not only contribute to mHRDD law-making from below, but they must also actively and ceaselessly participate in the subsequent monitoring and implementation of these laws. Transnational and intersectoral collaborations are key elements for achieving these purposes.

References

Action Solidarité Tiers Monde asbl (ASTM) (2022) Luxembourg's financial centre and its human rights policies. https://www.initiative-devoirdevigilance.org/post/les-droits-humains-et-le-secteur-des-finances-au-luxembourg. Accessed 10 March 2024

Backer LC et al (2015) Democratizing the global business and human rights project by catalyzing strategic litigation from the bottom up. In: Martin J, Bravo KE (eds) The business and human rights landscape: moving forward, looking back. Cambridge University Press, pp 254–287

Birchall D (2020) The role of civil society and human rights defenders in corporate accountability. In: Deva S, Birchall D (eds) Research handbook on human rights and business. Edward Elgar, pp 422–445

Birchall D (2021) Corporate power over human rights: an analytical framework. Bus Hum Rights J 6(1):42–66. https://doi.org/10.1017/bhj.2020.23

Blenkinsop P (2024) EU stalls supply chain law after German, Italian concerns. https://www.reuters.com/markets/europe/eu-postpones-decision-proposed-supply-chain-due-diligince-law-2024-02-09/. Accessed 20 February 2024

Bose D (2023) Decentring narratives around business and human rights instruments: an example of the French Devoir de Vigilance Law. Bus Hum Rights J 8(1):18–42. https://doi.org/10.1017/bhj.2023.6

Bueno N, Bright C (2020) Implementing human rights due diligence through corporate civil liability. Int Comp Law Q 69(4):789–818. https://doi.org/10.1017/S0020589320000305

CDU, CSU, SPD (2018) Ein neuer Aufbruch für Europa. Eine neue Dynamik für Deutschland. Ein neuer Zusammenhalt fürunser Land: Koalitionsvertrag zwischen CDU, CSU und SPD. https://

archiv.cdu.de/system/tdf/media/dokumente/koalitionsvertrag_2018.pdf?file=1. Accessed 20 March 2024

Cossart S, Chaplier J, Beau De Lomenie T (2017) The French law on duty of care: a historic step towards making globalization work for all. Bus Hum Rights J 2(2):317–323. https://doi.org/10.1017/bhj.2017.14

Costa, M. (2024). EU's corporate due diligence rule hits political roadblock. https://greencentralbanking.com/2024/02/19/eu-corporate-due-diligence-directive-delay/. Accessed 10 March 2024

Dehbi F, Martin-Ortega O (2023) An integrated approach to corporate due diligence from a human rights, environment and TWAIL perspective. Regul Gov 17(4):927–943. https://doi.org/10.1111/rego.12538

Deva S (2023) Mandatory human rights due diligence Laws in Europe: a mirage for rightsholders? Leiden J Int Law 36(2):389–414. https://doi.org/10.1017/S0922156522000802

Evans A (2019) Overcoming the global despondency trap: strengthening corporate accountability in supply chains. Rev Int Polit Econ 27(3):658–685. https://doi.org/10.1080/09692290.2019.1679220

Gustafsson MT, Schilling-Vacaflor A, Lenschow A (2023a) The politics of supply chain regulations: towards foreign corporate accountability in the area of human rights and the environment? Regul Gov 17(4):853–869. https://doi.org/10.1111/rego.12526

Gustafsson MT, Schilling-Vacaflor A, Lenschow A (2023b) Foreign corporate accountability: the contested institutionalization of mandatory due diligence in Germany and France. Regul Gov 17(4):891–908. https://doi.org/10.1111/rego.12498

Heindrichs T (2022) Finance sector should be under due diligence law, says NGO. Delano https://delano.lu/article/finance-sector-should-be-under. Accessed 19 January 2024

Hering M (2020) Corporate (Ir)responsibility made in Germany - part II: the unfinished Saga of the Lieferkettengesetz. Doing Business Right Blog. https://www.asser.nl/DoingBusinessRight/Blog/post/corporate-ir-responsibility-made-in-germany-part-ii-the-unfinished-saga-of-the-lieferkettengesetz-by-mercedes-hering. Accessed 10 January 2024

Houerbi S, Muchunguzi JJ (2021) Dialogue on National Action Plans on Business and Human Rights in East and Horn of Africa Region: Tanzania National Dialogue Report. https://www.humanrights.dk/files/media/document/NAP%20Dialogue_Tanzania_Report_ENG_accessible.pdf. Accessed 17 June 2024

Ito K (2024) Challenges to Japan's regulatory approaches for business and human rights. BHRJ Blog. https://bhrj.blog/2024/06/25/challenges-for-japans-regulatory-approaches-for-business-and-human-rights/. Accessed 20 June 2024

Jochnick C (2017) Shifting power on business and human rights: states, corporations and civil society in global governance. In: Rodriguez-Garavito C (ed) Business and human rights: beyond the end of the beginning. Cambridge University Press, pp 128–137

Keck ME, Sikkink K (2018) Transnational advocacy networks in international and regional politics. Int Soc Sci J 68(227–228):65–76. https://doi.org/10.1111/issj.12187

Krajewski M, Dey S (2023) Effective human rights due diligence ten years after Rana plaza? Assessing the complaint against IKEA and Amazon under the German supply chain due diligence act. Verfassungsblog. https://verfassungsblog.de/effective-human-rights-due-diligence-ten-years-after-rana-plaza/. Accessed 10 January 2024

Krajewski M et al (2021) Mandatory human rights due diligence in Germany and Norway: stepping, or striding, in the same direction? Bus Hum Rights J 6(3):550–558. https://doi.org/10.1017/bhj.2021.43

Landau I (2019) Human rights due diligence and the risk of cosmetic compliance. Melb J Int Law 20(1):1–27

Lichuma C (2021) (Laws) made in the first world: a TWAIL critique of the use of domestic legislation to extraterritorially regulate global value chains. Zeitschrift für ausländisches öffentliches Recht und Völkerrecht 81(2):497–532. https://doi.org/10.17104/0044-2348-2021-2-497

Lichuma C (2023) Risky business: critical reflections on the sources of information for risk analysis under the German supply chain law and some ramifications for global south stakeholders. World Comp Law J 56:762–782. https://doi.org/10.5771/0506-7286-2023-4-762

Lichuma C (2024) Mandatory human rights due diligence (mHRDD) Laws caught between rituals and ritualism: the forms and limits of business authority in the global governance of business and human rights. Bus Hum Rights J 2024:1–20. https://doi.org/10.1017/bhj.2023.47

Ling B (2024) Taiwan: business and human rights on the margin of the UN system. BHRJ Blog. https://bhrj.blog/2024/06/10/taiwan-business-and-human-rights-on-the-margins-of-the-un-system/. Accessed 20 June 2024

Macchi C, Bright C (2020) Hardening soft law: the implementation of human rights due diligence requirements in domestic legislation. In: Buscemi M, Lazzerini N, Magi L, Russo D (eds) Legal sources in business and human rights: evolving dynamics in international and European law. Brill, pp 218–247

O'Brien CM et al (2016) National Action Plans: current status and future prospects for a new business and human rights governance tool. Bus Hum Rights J 1(1):117–126. https://doi.org/10.1017/bhj.2015.14

O'Brien CM et al (2021) National Action Plans on business and human rights: an experimentalist governance analysis. Hum Rights Rev 23:71–99. https://doi.org/10.1007/s12142-021-00637-x

Polletta F (2006) It was like a fever: storytelling in protest and politics. University of Chicago Press, Chicago, IL

Ruggie JG (2014) Global governance and "new governance theory": lessons from business and human rights. Glob Gov 20:5–17

Saage-Maaß M (2021) Legal interventions and transnational alliances in the Ali Enterprise case: struggles for workers' rights in global supply chains. In: Saage-Maaß M, Zumbansen P, Bader M, Shahab P (eds) Transnational legal activism in global value chains: the Ali Enterprise fire and the struggle for justice. Springer, pp 25–58. https://doi.org/10.1007/978-3-030-73835-8_3

Savourey E, Brabant S (2021) The French law on the duty of vigilance: theoretical and practical challenges since its adoption. Bus Hum Rights J 6(1):141–152. https://doi.org/10.1017/bhj.2020.30

Sénit CA, Biermann F (2021) In whose name are you speaking? The marginalization of the poor in the global civil society. Global Policy 12:581–591. https://doi.org/10.1111/1758-5899.12997

Shift, Mazars LLP (2015) UN guiding principles reporting framework. https://www.ungpreporting.org/glossary/civil-society-organizations-csos/. Accessed 10 January 2024

Sobieraj S (2011) Soundbitten: the perils of media-centred activism. NYU Press, New York

Vanpeperstraete B (2021) The Rana plaza collapse and the case for enforceable agreements with apparel brands. In: Saage-Maaß M, Zumbansen P, Bader M, Shahab P (eds) Transnational legal activism in global value chains: the Ali Enterprise fire and the struggle for justice. Springer, pp 137–169. https://doi.org/10.1007/978-3-030-73835-8_9

Weihrauch D, Carodenuto S, Leipold S (2023) From voluntary to mandatory corporate accountability: the politics of the German supply chain due diligence act. Regul Gov 17(4):909–926. https://doi.org/10.1111/rego.12501

Caroline Omari Lichuma is a Postdoctoral Researcher at the Centre for Human Rights in Erlangen Nuremberg (CHREN). She received her LLB from the University of Nairobi, her LLM from New York University and her PhD from the Georg-August University of Göttingen (summa cum laude). Her current research is in the broad area of Business and Human Rights (BHR) with a focus on national, regional and international efforts to increase corporate accountability for human rights and environmental abuses. She is particularly interested in the intersection between Third World Approaches to International Law (TWAIL) and BHR.

Strategic Litigation for Corporate Accountability Through (International) Criminal Law: Dutch Legal Dynamics and Litigating Civil Society Organisations

Thomas R. Becker

Abstract This chapter examines the role of civil society organisations (CSOs) engaged in strategic litigation with the aim of closing the corporate criminal enforcement gap for complicity in atrocity crimes. Focusing on the political and legal strategies of CSOs in the Netherlands seeking to influence prosecutorial decision-making through the complaint mechanism that allows CSOs to request a judicial order to prosecute, I examine a case from the Netherlands and two cases of transnational litigation unfolding in other North-Western European countries to assess the practices of and opportunities for CSOs in the field of corporate accountability through criminal law. Drawing on the typologies of the relationship between CSOs and prosecutorial authorities developed by Jeßberger and Steinl, I argue that CSOs fulfil several roles at different stages in the strategic litigation process, each contributing to the institutionalisation of societal questioning of prosecutorial policy in their own way. Through the application of relational typologies to the case studies and Dutch legal dynamics, I argue that strategies solely focused on the litigation process have limited impact in the Dutch criminal justice system due to the doctrinal complexity of determining corporate involvement in atrocity crimes and the courts' position to review prosecutorial prioritisation policies.

I am grateful to Prof. Dr. Brianne McGonigle Leyh and Mr. Tia Yang, as well as the editors, for insightful comments on earlier drafts of this chapter. This manuscript was completed during my Master's degree. Any views expressed in this chapter are my own.

T. R. Becker (✉)
De Brauw Blackstone Westbroek, Amsterdam, The Netherlands
Utrecht University, Utrecht, The Netherlands

R. Grosescu, J. G. Dale (eds.), *Corporate Accountability for Human Rights Violations*, Interdisciplinary Studies in Human Rights 16,
https://doi.org/10.1007/978-3-032-05569-9_11

1 Introduction

International criminal justice is increasingly administered in domestic jurisdictions.[1] The Netherlands is one of these jurisdictions. In part due to the operationalisation of specialised international prosecution units and greater transnational cooperation, domestic trials for international crimes have increased over the last decade.[2] Civil society organisations (CSOs) have an important role in ensuring and advancing international criminal accountability. Not only do they contribute to setting the prosecutorial agenda, but they also collect evidence, file (criminal) complaints, and keep pressure on public authorities to use accountability mechanisms effectively. Such CSOs often direct their efforts to areas they consider overlooked by public authorities. One of these areas is corporate accountability for atrocity crimes, including the role of corporate entities and executives in facilitating, contributing to and profiting from the commission of such crimes.[3] This chapter examines the efforts of CSOs to close what I refer to as an enforcement gap. This is a notion that is closely related to the concept of the accountability gap.[4] The latter usually indicates the absence of legal mechanisms or structures to impose liability. Enforcement gaps, however, concern the situation in which such legal mechanisms are in place but where prosecutorial authorities do not use them when potentially appropriate.

Several CSOs perceive such limited attention to accountability mechanisms in international criminal law as a structural injustice.[5] Hence, they engage in various forms of (litigating) action to address enforcement gaps. Often where criminal proceedings are initiated against corporate entities or their executives, these were instigated in one way or another by CSOs.[6] The criminal complaints brought by NGOs in France against Lafarge for complicity in crimes against humanity and financing terrorism in Syria, and in Sweden against Lundin Petroleum executives for complicity in war crimes in southern Sudan may be indicative of a new frontier of corporate accountability through international criminal norms.[7] This increased activity of CSOs litigating in national courts seeking to apply international criminal law for corporate wrongdoings begs the question which legal avenues such CSOs have

---

[1] Grosescu (2024), Sikkink and Kim (2013, p. 272), Kristjansdottir et al. (2012).

[2] Langer and Eason (2019, p. 781).

[3] See for example Cruvellier and Metenier (2022).

[4] Kaleck and Saage-Maaß (2010, pp. 718–722), Bordeleau-Cass (2019, p. 65).

[5] Cruvellier and Metenier (2022).

[6] Young (2021), ECOS & PAX (2010).

[7] AFP, French Court Upholds Syria "complicity in Crimes against Humanity" Charge against Lafarge. Business and Human Rights Resource Centre, 18 May 2022, https://www.business-humanrights.org/en/latest-news/french-court-upholds-syria-complicity-in-crimes-against-humanity-charge-against-lafarge/ (last accessed 6 March 2024); Truc O, Lundin: serious intimate, Sweden's longest trial sets up for the long haul. Justiceinfo, 21 September 2023, https://www.justiceinfo.net/en/122058-lundin-serious-intimate-sweden-longest-trial-sets-up-for-the-long-haul.html (last accessed 6 March 2024).

available. Furthermore, in this chapter, I pose questions regarding the characterisation of these CSOs and their strategies vis-à-vis prosecutorial authorities.

I begin by discussing the development of CSO activities with a focus on corporate accountability for atrocity crimes (Sect. 2). In Sect. 3, I outline the relevant legal considerations to both opportunities and limitations of criminal trials concerning corporate involvement in such atrocities. Against this background, I propose a typology of litigating CSOs in Sect. 4. Making use of three case studies unfolding in North-Western Europe,[‡] I then explain how various CSOs function in their respective (legal) contexts. I discuss how their strategies relate to their goals and how their interaction with public authorities may determine their mode of operations. This analysis allows me to provide some observations on the space in the Netherlands for using strategic litigation as a means of placing this enforcement gap on the prosecutorial agenda (Sect. 5).

2 International Criminal Justice, Civil Society Organisations and Strategic Litigation

In the past three decades, international criminal law has become a key instrument of CSOs in fighting impunity and challenging accountability and enforcement gaps.[8] CSOs fulfil a bottom-up role in the various stages of investigations and prosecutions through a variety of methods: criminal complaints; media campaigns; the publication of legal research reports; the participation in trials as civil parties; and by acting as private prosecutors.[9]

In this contribution, I consider the use of various legal instruments to influence criminal politics, determining the enforcement of international criminal norms under the notion of strategic litigation. Criminal politics is a concept that refers to the collection of factors that influence prosecutorial policy and decision-making.[10] The notion of strategic litigation is contested in both its meaning and scope.[11] Jeßberger and Steinl refer to those who use this practice in the context of international criminal justice as "[those CSOs] who employ international criminal law not only as an advocacy tool but use litigation to target perpetrators of international crimes as part of a larger juridical-political strategy transcending the individual case."[12]

[‡] Developments in the case studies are up to date as of 4 June 2024.

[8] Buyse et al. (2021, pp. 1–3), McGonigle Leyh (2022, p. 365), Mehta (2024, p. 254).

[9] Buyse et al. (2021, p. 3), Becker and Van Lent (2023, pp. 294–295); for more on private prosecutors, see Mujuzi (2016). Criminal proceedings may, in certain circumstances, be brought by private parties (i.e., private prosecutors) in lieu of the public authorities.

[10] De Lange (2009).

[11] Mehta (2024, pp. 46–47).

[12] Jeßberger and Steinl (2022, p. 379).

Mehta argues that there is a distinction between "tactical" legal interventions and "strategic" legal interventions.[13] Drawing on Knox's military jargon, she contends that strategic litigation should be seen as "the plan to win a *long-term war*" while tactics should be seen as "methods employed to win an individual *immediate battle*."[14] Although these terms are strongly related, the use of tactical approaches to litigation does not inherently correspond to long-term strategic aims. In contrast, strategic litigation transcends a specific legal intervention and generates (or seeks to generate) a structural impact against impunity. This ties into the second aspect of Jeßberger and Steinl's definition referred to above.[15]

This chapter examines the influence of CSOs on prosecutorial decision-making in relation to the concept of strategic litigation. To assess this, it is important to draw a distinction between two general objectives: firstly, (i) litigation aimed at seeking the closure of an enforcement gap; and secondly, (ii) the closure of an accountability gap. Closing an enforcement gap is primarily concerned with diverting prosecutorial resources to criminal conduct that requires attention. The law prohibiting certain behaviour is already in place; it is merely a question of prioritising the enforcement of that particular norm. The objective, in that sense, has extra-legal elements and can be characterised as part of criminal politics.[16] Legal intervention aimed at an accountability gap is more concerned with juridical change. The legal intervention does not concern a question of capacity or priority but rather a question of the law. Generally, litigation of this nature thus seeks to either change the law or alter its interpretation.[17]

Both types of objectives are considered strategic litigation in the literature, although different authors value different aspects. Mégret, on the one hand, appears somewhat dismissive of considering legal interventions to close enforcement gaps as amounting to strategic litigation. He draws a sharp distinction between "litigation whose primary aim is to change the law" and litigation whose primary aim is to "merely obtain its application".[18] On the other hand, Mehta underlines that strategic litigation is primarily concerned with creating political action rather than legal reform.[19] Both approaches, however, seem to emphasise the counter-hegemonic character of strategic litigation. In relation to enforcement gaps, Jeßberger and Steinl describe this concept as the attempt "to counter the asymmetrical enforcement of international criminal law and the innocenting [*sic*] of actors from the Global North through their work."[20] In Mégret's work, this appears rather in his

[13] Mehta (2024, pp. 49–50).

[14] Ibid., p. 48; Knox (2010).

[15] OSJI (2018, p. 19).

[16] Mehta (2024, p. 54 *et seq*).

[17] Mégret (2023, p. 68); see also the distinction between under-regulation and under-enforcement in Kyriakakis (2021, p. 2).

[18] Mégret (2023, p. 68).

[19] Mehta (2024, p. 56).

[20] Jeßberger and Steinl (2022, p. 395).

description of how structural “success” can also be achieved without more singular “victories”.[21] In this narrative, a negative individual legal outcome can, for example, still highlight or render visible systemic injustices in the legal system.[22]

The second constituent element of strategic litigation is naturally the legal intervention itself. Some definitions of strategic litigation restrict its scope to legal action in the court of law.[23] However, some include activities outside of court that still stimulate the strategic aims as determined in this section.[24] Arguably, such a multipolar approach—which covers the road *to* court as well—does more justice to the various ways in which CSOs may obtain strategic juridical-political impact.[25] This is the case even more so in the field of criminal justice. After all, CSOs must generally yield control over the criminal trial to the public authorities. This makes getting to trial just as crucial as steering the proceedings and outcome in their desired direction.

3 The Legal Dynamics

To better understand the different strategies, practices and roles CSOs may fulfil in the strategic litigation process, it is imperative at this point to highlight some of the legal dynamics with which they engage and to which they are subject.[26] Litigating CSOs shape these legal dynamics and are shaped by these legal dynamics. In the first section, I discuss several types of corporate involvement in the commission of atrocity crimes as well as some relevant legal concepts that regulate such behaviour (Sect. 3.1). After discussing some aspects of criminal politics in this field, I discuss the Dutch playing field for strategic litigation through (international) criminal law (Sect. 3.2).

[21] Mégret (2023, p. 68).

[22] Ibid., p. 69.

[23] E.g. Fischer-Lescano (2021, pp. 299–300).

[24] Jeßberger and Steinl (2022, pp. 386–387).

[25] OSJI (2018, pp. 74–76).

[26] I purposefully use the term legal dynamics due to the focus in this contribution on the interaction between the applicable legal frameworks and the strategic legal interventions.

3.1 International Criminal Law and Corporate Accountability for Atrocity Crimes

3.1.1 Corporate Involvement and Complicity in Atrocity Crimes

Corporate actors may get involved in the commission of atrocity crimes in various ways. Often, the corporate actor does not perform the commission of such crimes directly.[27] The direct perpetrators are usually "local police, intelligence agencies or the armed forces".[28] As Kaleck and Saage-Maaß argue, corporate involvement in the commission of atrocity crimes usually arises in two general scenarios: "(1) the cooperation of corporations with military regimes and dictatorships and (2) the involvement of corporations in (civil) war and other conflicts."[29] These categories can be subdivided into several types representing varying degrees in which corporations participate in the commission of crimes.

Perhaps the least direct form of participation designated by Kaleck and Saage-Maaß is that of corporations benefiting from state-sponsored abuses. Examples may include the violent quelling of peaceful protestors which prevent the continued operation of business activities, or the imposition of forced labour from which the corporate actor may profit.[30] Corporate actors may also facilitate or directly support human rights abuses. A well-known example from the Netherlands concerns the logistical support provided by Frans van Anraat to the Iraqi government in the 1980s.[31] More direct corporate action may, for example, take the shape of actively "fuelling conflict through the provision of goods and illicit funds", rather than simply making the commission of particular crimes possible.[32] In another illustrative Dutch case, Guus Kouwenhoven had hired militias through his timber companies and supplied them with the arms used in the massacres of civilians in Liberia under the rule of Charles Taylor.[33] Beyond these types of involvement many more can be considered, such as the silent approval of crimes while not immediately benefiting from them,[34] the investment in projects or governments or State authorities with

[27] Ryngaert (2018, p. 2); although naturally exceptions occur, see Huisman and Van Sliedregt (2010, p. 816).

[28] Huisman and Van Sliedregt (2010, p. 816).

[29] Kaleck and Saage-Maaß (2010, p. 703).

[30] Ibid., pp. 704–705.

[31] Van Anraat was convicted of having assisted chemical attacks by Saddam Hussein against villages in Iraq and Iran in 1987 and 1988. He arranged "the deliveries of large quantities of thiodiglycol (TDG), an important chemical component of mustard gas." For an elaborate discussion of the case, see Sluiter and Shun Ming Yau (2020, pp. 317–320 *et seq*).

[32] Kaleck and Saage-Maaß (2010, p. 707), Young (2021, p. 9).

[33] Court of Appeals The Hague 21 April 2017, ECLI:NL:GHSHE:2017:1760 access via https://uitspraken.rechtspraak.nl/details?id=ECLI:NL:GHSHE:2017:1760

[34] Huisman and van Sliedregt (2010, p. 817).

poor human rights records,[35] or the facilitation of financial transactions by banks or financial institutions.[36]

Most often, corporate actors contribute to or profit from atrocity crimes indirectly. Indirect involvement may be captured in the concept of criminal complicity. Two elements form the main doctrinal thresholds for determining complicity in atrocity crimes: *mens rea* and *actus reus*. *Mens rea* concerns the element of knowledge within the corporation of the perpetrated crimes. Proving the "state of mind" of corporate actors can be challenging due to their nature but sometimes also due to the way in which a corporate entity is structured. Corporations may consist of "impenetrable structures and complex supply-chains" which are made up of subsidiaries, suppliers, and other actors that confuse the determination of criminal intent of an organisation as well as of individual business leaders that operate in this context.[37] This phenomenon is referred to as the "corporate veil".[38]

Additionally, there is debate on the appropriate standard to test which "state of mind" incurs criminal complicity. The subjective element of the intent to enable, exacerbate or facilitate must be present. The corporate actor must either know, should know or be wilfully blind to the risk of such consequences of their agency.[39] The Dutch doctrine presumes, for instance, a *dolus eventualis* standard—accepting the risk that the corporate actor's actions may contribute to the commission of atrocity crimes.[40] This is determined, amongst others, based on the presence of active policies within the legal entity, the daily factual affairs, and the attribution of the actions of individuals to the legal entity as such.[41] Dutch criminal doctrine thus allows the establishment of *mens rea* based on patterns of behaviour in the corporation. The combination of opaque corporate structures and the context of atrocity crimes, which are often complex in nature, makes it difficult to establish those patterns in practice.[42]

The second main element in determining criminal liability for complicity is the *actus reus*, which concerns the criminal act itself. In *Blagojević & Jokić* the Appeals Chamber of the International Criminal Tribunal for Yugoslavia concluded that

---

[35] Marx et al. (2019, p. 5); Mann JK, Money as Complicity: Can Banking and Finance Services Facilitate International Crimes? Rethinking SLIC, 8 June 2020 https://rethinkingslic.org/blog/criminal-law/70-money-as-complicity-can-banking-and-finance-services-facilitate-international-crime (last accessed 6 March 2024).

[36] Vest (2010, p. 852).

[37] Kaleck and Saage-Maaß (2010, p. 722).

[38] The term 'corporate veil' traditionally refers to the separation between the corporate entity and the shareholders in relation to liabilities. See Vandekerckhove (2007), Macey (2019, pp. 1198–1199), Bergkamp and Pak (2001). In the context of this chapter, the 'corporate veil' and its 'piercing' refer to situations in which corporate structures function to frustrate the attribution of criminal accountability. See Stahn (2018, p. 94), Tixeire et al. (2020), and Ottolenghi (1990).

[39] Kaleck and Saage-Maaß (2010, p. 720).

[40] Sluiter and Shun Ming Yau (2020, p. 324).

[41] Kesteloo (2013, pp. 86–89).

[42] See also Stahn (2018, p. 107).

complicity may be established after participation that "substantially affected the commission of that offence".[43] To determine whether the contribution was substantial, one can look at either the result or the way in which the crime was perpetrated. The contribution may be composed of "practical assistance [and] encouragement or moral support".[44] However, the objective threshold for the assessment of substantial contribution remains an issue of contention.[45] This contention manifests itself, amongst others, in the discussion on the neutral assistance defence. This defence concerns the question of when business conduct that in normal circumstances would not be considered criminal, such as the provision of goods or financial means and services, turns into an act of complicity.[46] This question can be answered by investigating whether the occurrence, scale, frequency, efficiency, or type of abuse were affected by the relevant business conduct.[47] Finally, the business conduct must be of sufficient proximity to the commission of the crime on "the causation continuum".[48] In the Netherlands, the Court explicitly mentions that the contribution does not have to be significant or substantial.[49]

3.1.2 The Limitations of Corporate Criminal Accountability Mechanisms

The business and human rights movement is illustrative of increased attention to the responsibility of corporate actors for human rights abuses related to their economic activity. Attempts to capture corporate conduct in the framework of international criminal law, although increasing in number, are, however, not particularly commonplace.[50] This begs the question of to what extent international criminal law is an appropriate instrument to address corporate involvement in the commission of atrocity crimes.[51]

---

[43] *Judgement, Blagojević & Jokić (IT-02-60-A)* (ICTY Appeals Chamber), para. 189; Vest (2010, p. 858).

[44] International Commission of Jurists Expert Legal Panel on Corporate Complicity in International Crimes (2008, p. 11).

[45] Young (2021, p. 10). In the case of Lafarge, a contribution of 13 million dollars to ISIS's funds amounting to 0.65% of its total assets has so far not proven to be insubstantial according to French courts; it is also notable that such contention is fuelled by the fact that differing international and national standards of liability may affect applicable criteria of complicity, see Dale (2007, p. 303).

[46] Stahn (2018, p. 111 *et seq*).

[47] International Commission of Jurists Expert Legal Panel on Corporate Complicity in International Crimes (2008, pp. 8–12).

[48] Ibid., p.13.

[49] Supreme Court 30 June 2009, ECLI:NL:HR:2009:BG4822 (Van Anraat conviction), para. 6.17 access via https://uitspraken.rechtspraak.nl/details?id=ECLI:NL:HR:2009:BG4822; Kelk (2019, p. 496).

[50] Vest (2010, p. 858) and Biggs (2019) note the absence of such attempts at the level of international tribunals.

[51] For some seminal work on this matter, see Kyriakakis (2021), Mavronicola (2024) argues against the centrality of human rights penality from within the human rights framework.

There is still quite some variation across jurisdictions as to how human rights transgressions by corporate actors are addressed.[52] This stems largely from scattered doctrinal and normative perspectives on the accountability of corporate actors under criminal law.[53] Policy considerations are prevalent as well.[54] For example, deliberations to include corporate criminal liability in the 1998 Rome Statute of the International Criminal Court were aborted in part due to the underdeveloped concept of criminal liability for corporate actors, sparking worries about the effectiveness of the complementarity regime.[55] Additionally, participants to the negotiations felt that corporate liability did not fit the main purpose of the Court, namely, to hold those most responsible accountable for humanity's most heinous crimes. Similarly, Bush argues that the non-application of corporate liability at the Nuremberg Tribunal followed more so from political reasons than legal unsoundness.[56] The Special Tribunal for Lebanon, in contrast, did observe in 2015 that "[c]orporate criminal liability is on the verge of attaining, at the very least, the status of a general principle of law applicable under international law".[57] Despite this normative progression since the Nuremberg trials, CSOs criticise the current international regime that maintains the previously discussed enforcement and accountability gaps.[58]

Accordingly, several CSOs have made the conduct of corporations the subject of their attention. This development finds its roots in the increasing potential of companies to influence armed conflicts and human rights abuses.[59] There are several further issues that lead CSOs to plead for increased attention to corporate accountability by means of international criminal law. Firstly, some academics assert that the legal 'fiction' of what is a legal entity serves to shield individuals from accountability and can be further used to obscure the attribution of responsibility in general. This corporate veil plays a role beyond complicating the question of attribution. Kremnitzer, for example, argues that the veil "reduces the personal culpability of the individual perpetrators who are committing a crime in the framework of the corporation for its sake".[60] This warrants, in his view, the imposition of liability for

[52] *Al Jadeed SAL & Ms Khayat Contempt Appeal* (2015) Special Tribunal for Lebanon (Contempt judge) STL-14-05/T/CJ 58, para. 67.

[53] Kyriakakis (2021, pp. 242–249).

[54] Enforcement authorities or legislators might, for example, prefer to focus on non-criminal enforcement due to the benefits of lower reliance on public resources and lower evidentiary thresholds.

[55] Scheffer (2016), Kyriakakis (2021, pp. 106–122).

[56] Bush (2009, pp. 1239–1240), Bush particularly emphasises the preference given to rebuilding the West-German economy over the prosecution of corporations.

[57] *Al Jadeed S.A.L. & Ms Khayat Contempt Appeal* (2015), para, 67. Note that this does not mean that the threshold for obtaining the status of a general principle of international law is reached, see Stahn (2018, p. 124); for more on the position that 'companies cannot commit an offence' see Clapham (2008, p. 900).

[58] Crawford (2019).

[59] Kyriakakis (2021, p. 4).

[60] Kremnitzer (2010, p. 912).

corporate entities, in combination with the original focal point of the international criminal justice project—individual accountability.[61]

Beyond this expressive justification for the promulgation of corporate criminal liability, arguments related to retribution and deterrence support this position as well.[62] The retribution argument draws on the reasoning that corporate actors are bearers of both rights and duties in society.[63] Therefore, if culpable behaviour is attributed to the corporate entity, the entity should also be paying for the damage it has done. This ties in with the deterrence aspect. Although international criminal law is often associated with low enforcement rates, Cryer et al. argue that prosecutions still have a long-term deterrent effect.[64] Scholars perceive more short-term rational actor-based theories in international criminal justice as difficult to substantiate.[65] However, Kyriakakis posits that cost-benefit considerations are more prominent in decision-making by legal entities.[66] This would justify the pursuit of deterrent measures such as financial penalties, but also "penalties such as dissolution of the corporation, prohibition on operating business and permanent closure."[67] Finally, in some jurisdictions, the culpability or attributability of the corporate entity can play a role in determining the *de facto* directorship of individual business leaders over criminal conduct. This is the case in the Netherlands as well.[68]

All in all, these considerations that draw attention to the corporate enforcement and accountability gaps must be weighed against the whole set of factors that determines prosecutorial decision- and policymaking. In the next section, I illustrate the dynamics of such criminal politics in the Netherlands to provide an understanding of the context in which litigating CSOs determine their legal and political strategies. I do this by discussing the space that litigating CSOs have to integrate their strategic objectives into prosecutorial decision-making and policy. This discussion allows me to make observations on the opportunities for the developments set out in Sect. 2 to take root in the Netherlands.

---

[61] Cruvellier and Metenier (2022), Marx et al. (2019, p. 5).

[62] Kyriakakis (2021, p. 256).

[63] Kremnitzer (2010, p. 913).

[64] Cryer et al. (2019, pp. 32–35); although this notion is contested in the literature as well, see Mavronicola (2024, p. 27).

[65] Kyriakakis (2021, p. 262).

[66] Ibid.

[67] Young (2021, p. 13).

[68] Supreme Court 26 April 2016, ECLI:NL:HR:2016:733 access via https://uitspraken.rechtspraak.nl/details?id=ECLI:NL:HR:2016:733

3.2 *The Dynamics of Criminal Politics: The Dutch Criminal Complaints Procedure*[69]

The Dutch Public Prosecutor's Office (DPPO) weighs a combination of legal, political and social factors when it makes the decision to prosecute, dismiss or settle a case.[70] These factors can be roughly divided into two general elements: (i) the feasibility and (ii) the expediency of a prosecution. The first element—rather obviously—refers to the question of whether a prosecution is likely to be successful, which is informed by the evidence obtained, the applicable doctrinal thresholds for criminal liability and the prosecutorial capacity to adequately present the case in court.[71] The second element of prosecutorial decision-making—expediency—is where political and social factors are more prominent. Part of the expediency assessment involves the public interest associated with the crime—i.e., the value of the prosecution for society as a whole.[72] Once again, prosecutorial capacity plays a role. For the benefit of an effective and efficient criminal justice system, the resources spent on the prosecution must not disproportionally outweigh the justifications of the trial, such as deterrence, retribution, and the satisfaction of victims.[73] This signals that there is no complete separation between the expediency and feasibility elements. In essence, criminal politics comes down to determining the allocation of resources to certain criminal cases.[74]

The prosecutorial authorities in the Netherlands have broad discretionary powers to decide which cases to prosecute and which cases to dismiss (or to leave uninvestigated).[75] Additionally, only the DPPO has the right to initiate criminal proceedings.[76] The only legal instrument available to CSOs (and others) to interfere in criminal politics is the complaint mechanism in Article 12 of the Dutch Code of Criminal Procedure (DCCP).[77] This procedure allows those with a legally recognised interest—primarily victims and specialised CSOs—to request an order from the Court of Appeals. After a full review of the prosecutor's decision-making, the

---

[69] This section builds on research published by Dr. Leonie van Lent (Utrecht University) and I, in Becker and Van Lent (2023). The ideas presented here serve mainly to illustrate the socio-legal dynamics of prosecutorial decision-making and policy and how this responds to strategic legal interventions. In that sense, this section and its use in the rest of this contribution provide a refocused perspective on the more doctrinal assessment of strategic litigation opportunities previously published.

[70] Kronenberg and De Wilde (2018, p. 213).

[71] Beckers (2017, p. 39).

[72] De Lange (2009, p. 479).

[73] This is primarily a matter of prosecutorial policy rather than a legal requirement that must be satisfied.

[74] Becker and Van Lent (2023, p. 302).

[75] Article 167 DCCP.

[76] Koning (2022, p. 1).

[77] Ibid.

Court may order the DPPO to initiate a prosecution.[78] This legal instrument was adopted by the legislature as a check on the DPPOs prosecutorial monopoly.[79] It is useful to examine the workings of this procedure since it provides insight into the legal dynamics of prosecutorial prioritisation policy and the ability of CSOs to leave their fingerprints on such policy and enforcement gaps.

Several cases illustrate the procedure's potential as an instrument for strategic litigation. The case of SOBI—an association involved in activism regarding integrity in corporations—complaining about a settlement between the DPPO and the Dutch bank ING concerning the alleged violation of the *Law for the Prevention of Money Laundering and Financing of Terrorism* is one of the most notable. SOBI demanded the prosecution of the legal entity itself and the bank's CEO. The matter concerning the CEO was particularly significant for the purposes of this contribution. In this case, the court ordered that the DPPO should initiate criminal proceedings. In its decision, the Court stated the following:

> The Court considers it of importance that the norm is confirmed in a public criminal trial that directors of a bank cannot go free if they have de facto supervised prohibited conduct. Citizens must be able to see that such actions are not accepted by the government. The Court is aware the prosecution of the accused will be time-consuming and will impose a significant burden on the judiciary. Nevertheless, this should not be decisive. Adjudication also has the objective of norm confirmation. This is related to living together, to social solidarity, to showing what is important in our society, and to what we do not want as a society.[80]

Such considerations are rather uncharacteristic for Dutch Courts. Even though the present doctrine allows the Court to conduct a full review of the prosecutor's decision-making, sensitive cases are usually approached with restraint.[81] The Court in this case, however, fundamentally criticised the DPPO's settlement policy regarding *de facto* directors. By engaging with the public interest aspect of the expediency assessment in such an explicit manner, the Court reflected its willingness to act as a forum for the contestation of enforcement gaps.[82]

Where the pursued change sought by a CSO is of a more juridical nature, the Court, however, does not facilitate the strategic aims of CSOs in the same way. In 2018, a CSO sought an order from the Court to initiate prosecutions against a range of the biggest cigarette producers in the world. Amongst other allegations, the CSO accused the corporations of amongst others attempted murder and the deliberate impairment of health. In the absence of any legislation or case law on the matter, the Court did not consider it appropriate to resolve the matter via the criminal justice

---

[78] Article 12i DCCP.

[79] Van Lent et al. (2016, p. 45).

[80] The Hague Court of Appeals 9 December 2020, ECLI:NL:GHDHA:2020:2344, § 8.8 access via https://uitspraken.rechtspraak.nl/details?id=ECLI:NL:GHDHA:2020:2344 (translation my own).

[81] Supreme Court 1 July 1996, ECLI:NL:HR:1996:ZD0505 access via https://uitspraken.rechtspraak.nl/details?id=ECLI:NL:HR:1996:ZD0505; Van Ham (2011, § 4–5); Kronenberg and De Wilde (2018, pp. 238–239).

[82] Becker and Van Lent (2023, pp. 301–304).

system.[83] A similar approach was discernible in several other cases that illustrate the nature of the procedure's strategic potential such as the complaints procedures against Trafigura and the Dutch Tax Authority.[84]

The Court uses the procedure as a corrective mechanism on the DPPO but does not permit the public interest assessment to be used as a corrective mechanism on the legislator. Koning characterises the potential of the procedure as "a pressure release valve for societal discontent which in the perception of complainants is not sufficiently addressed in the political arena".[85] The procedure allows complainants to make issues—such as enforcement gaps—visible where they were previously invisible or ignored.[86] This function of the procedure quite clearly aligns with Mégret's perception of 'successful' strategic litigation.[87]

In that sense, some elements of counter-hegemonic potential are present in the procedure, but this is also limited.[88] These limitations can be challenged by CSOs by using the procedure as a tool for gathering societal and political attention to the case. Exploring the multi-polar nature of such strategic legal interventions may allow CSOs to further pursue their strategic goals outside of the courtroom. Beckers, for example, describes how media attention and societal uproar may result in the political reality that prosecutions become unavoidable.[89]

4 A Typology of Litigating CSOs

In this section, I provide an understanding of the legal and political strategies of litigating CSOs who seek to challenge corporate enforcement gaps through international criminal law in national jurisdictions. I do this by further elaborating on existing typologies and examining the relationship between CSOs and prosecutorial authorities.

[83] The Hague Court of Appeals 6 December 2018, ECLI:NL:GHDHA:2018:3334 access via https://uitspraken.rechtspraak.nl/details?id=ECLI:NL:GHDHA:2018:3334

[84] The Hague Court of Appeals 12 April 2011 ECLI:NL:GHSGR:2011:BQ1012 (Trafigura) access via https://uitspraken.rechtspraak.nl/details?id=ECLI:NL:GHSGR:2011:BQ1012&showbutton=true&keyword=ECLI%253aNL%253aGHSGR%253a2011%253aBQ1012.&idx=1; The Hague Court of Appeals 13 July 2022, ECLI:NL:GHDHA:2022:1301, § 6.6 access via https://uitspraken.rechtspraak.nl/details?id=ECLI:NL:GHDHA:2022:1301 (Tax Authority).

[85] Koning (2022, p. 2) (translation my own).

[86] Ibid., p. 21.

[87] Mégret (2023, p. 69).

[88] Becker and Van Lent (2023, pp. 303–304).

[89] Beckers (2017, p. 48).

4.1 A Relational Typology of Strategic Litigation Approaches

In their characterisation of different approaches taken by CSOs to strategic litigation, Jeßberger and Steinl focus in significant part on the relationship between the prosecutorial authorities and CSOs.[90] Arguably, this focus can be explained by the counter-hegemonic nature of strategic litigation. Particularly when CSOs attempt to engage with enforcement gaps, the interrelation with the actor holding the ability to shape and control prosecutorial case selection and prioritisation is important. In the case of the Netherlands, this position is predominantly held by the prosecutor itself.[91]

Jeßberger and Steinl distinguish between two main types of strategy: CSOs that function as assistant-prosecutors and those that use more antagonistic methods.[92] The assistant-prosecutor role pertains to the situation in which the CSO collaborates with the prosecutorial authorities. A CSO may do this by providing information, conducting legal analyses, or gathering political support for the case.[93] In some cases, legal intervention is not even required to fulfil this role. For example, Koenig describes how CSOs help investigators and prosecutors collect evidence by gathering open-source intelligence.[94] Criminal complaints by CSOs may also be combined with facilitating access to crucial witnesses of international crimes, as evidenced by several cases in Germany.[95]

For the more antagonistic type of approach, Jeßberger and Steinl describe three *modi operandi*: kickstarters, pacemakers and watchdogs. The kickstarter approach, for example, applies where litigating CSOs file criminal complaints with the prosecutor.[96] CSOs may use their access to information on particular subjects that are not highlighted in the prosecutor's strategy or policy to trigger action when prosecutorial authorities are unwilling to engage in collaborative action. The pacemaker role involves the application of pressure on particular procedures or actors. This can be done by filing complaints but also by joining the prosecution as a civil party, the initiation of certain complaints procedures and the use of media campaigns.[97] Finally, the watchdog type primarily concerns legal interventions in relation to the

---

[90] Jeßberger and Steinl (2022, pp. 389–393).

[91] Other European countries offer more instruments to address a decision not to prosecute, see Verrest and Mevis (2018).

[92] Jeßberger and Steinl (2022, p. 387).

[93] Ibid., p. 390.

[94] Koenig (2022, pp. 829–842), D'Alessandra and Sutherland (2021).

[95] See the cases of Anwar Raslan & Eyad Al-Gharib and Taha al-Jumailly in Becker et al. (2023, pp. 48–49).

[96] Jeßberger and Steinl (2022, p. 391).

[97] See also the threat to initiate civil summary proceedings by SOBI in the Netherlands after securing an order to prosecute from the Court of Appeals in the case of the ING CEO, Van der Boon V and Betlem R, Advocaat Lakeman verwacht dat OM ex-ING-topman Hamers gaat dagvaarden. Financieel Dagblad, 18 March 2024, https://fd.nl/bedrijfsleven/1511243/om-zal-ex-ing-topman-hamers-dagvaarden (last accessed 14 May 2024).

prioritisation question in prosecutorial policy.[98] CSOs seek the prosecution of particular crimes that they deem required by the public interest, especially where the political cost of a prosecution functions as a barrier for the prosecutor to initiate a case.[99] While this distinction is valuable to illustrate the importance of the relationship between the CSO and the prosecutorial authorities, it in no way means that CSOs are limited to one type of strategy, as will be illustrated in the case studies.

4.2 *The Typology and the Case Studies*

In this section, I apply the typology developed by Jeßberger and Steinl to two case studies from France and Sweden. This allows me to make some observations on the determining factors for the chosen strategy and to further expound on the typology as it stands. In Sect. 5, I will then examine a case study from the Netherlands and discuss the extent to which my observations apply in the Dutch context.

The case studies in this section illustrate the development of strategic litigation through international criminal norms in relation to the previously mentioned corporate enforcement gap. Furthermore, they allow for a better understanding of the practices and strategies of litigating CSOs, which facilitates the consideration of a typology. Naturally, these two case studies cannot provide a full picture of the entire field of civil society actors involved in corporate accountability through international criminal law, nor is the selection without bias. It concerns CSOs based in North-Western European countries who act before courts in North-Western European jurisdictions and who have been able to secure (relative) successes. I maintain this selection since it contains—to my awareness—a unique set of factors valuable to the subject of this chapter: charges of atrocity crimes; in a domestic prosecution; against either a legal entity or a corporate executive; after involvement by a CSO; with a strategic component. I discuss the nature of the CSOs, their aims vis-à-vis the enforcement gap, the legal context in which they operate, their relationship with prosecutorial authorities and a specific legal intervention.

4.2.1 PAX, the European Coalition on Oil in Sudan and the Lundin Case

PAX is a peace organisation based in the Netherlands. It is a merger of the Dutch Pax Christi chapter and the Interchurch Peace Council which have been active since the Second World War and the 1960s respectively.[100] The European Coalition on Oil in Sudan (ECOS) was an organisation which, between 2001 and 2012, represented

[98] Jeßberger and Steinl (2022, p. 391).

[99] Ibid.

[100] Who We Are, PAX https://paxforpeace.nl/who-we-are/ (last accessed 6 March 2024).

over fifty CSOs in the peace campaign in relation to the oil conflict in Sudan.[101] Pax held the secretariat of ECOS at the time.[102] Specifically, in the field of business, human rights and conflict, PAX explains its strategic objective as follows:

> [W]e want to contribute to the prevention and remediation of human rights violations by companies in conflict zones. We do this by strengthening the voice and influence of victims in their struggle for truth and remedy, and through the development of and compliance with human rights standards by companies and governments.[103]

PAX's activities in pursuit of this strategic objective vary in nature and include advocacy, campaign initiatives as well as litigation.[104] This broad toolbox allows the CSO to pursue various methods at the same time. The pursuit of strategic litigation through the application of international criminal law in national courts is, in this sense, just one of many tactics available, which allows for a certain level of flexibility. Their involvement in the Lundin Petroleum case is illustrative of this.

In 2008, PAX finished their preliminary report on Lundin's activities in Sudan. This report outlined the company's alleged involvement between 1997 and 2003 in the Sudanese government's seizure by force of a potential oilfield, killing thousands and displacing approximately 200,000 people. The report was originally intended to be used in a political campaign. The aim was to raise awareness and outrage, to motivate shareholders to alter Lundin's behaviour and to provide remedial action.[105] A shift in orientation occurred when the company proved non-cooperative.[106] In 2010, PAX published an updated report which also included an analysis of the possibility of prosecuting Lundin executives in Sweden, where the corporation was based.[107] PAX published the report with an explicit call to the prosecutorial office to investigate the company's involvement. ECOS subsequently submitted a criminal complaint to the Swedish public prosecutor's office, which opened a preliminary investigation in June 2010.[108] Drawing on PAX's report, the research of other CSOs and its own investigation, the prosecutor started proceedings in September 2023,

[101] About Us, Unpaid Debt https://unpaiddebt.org/about/ (last accessed 29 March 2024).

[102] European Coalition on Oil in Sudan (ECOS), https://www.ecosonline.org/ (last accessed 29 March 2024).

[103] Empowering People Building Peace. Strategic Framework 2021–2025, PAX, 11 July 2019 https://paxforpeace.nl/wp-content/uploads/sites/2/import/import/empowering-people-building-peace-pax-strategic-framework-2021-2025.pdf (last accessed 6 March 2024), p. 24.

[104] Ibid., p. 25; Spijkers (2024).

[105] See interview with Egbert Wesselink, one of the authors of the report, Justice Update: Sweden and Sudan, asymmetricalhaircuts, 23 November 2021 https://www.asymmetricalhaircuts.com/episodes/justice-update-sweden-and-sudan/ (last accessed 6 March 2024).

[106] Justice Update: Sweden and Sudan, asymmetricalhaircuts, 23 November 2021 https://www.asymmetricalhaircuts.com/episodes/justice-update-sweden-and-sudan/ (last accessed 6 March 2024).

[107] ECOS & PAX (2010).

[108] Truc O, The Swedish prosecutor who challenged Lundin Oil, Justiceinfo, 10 October 2023 https://www.justiceinfo.net/en/122958-swedish-prosecutor-who-challenged-lundin-oil.html (last accessed 6 March 2024).

charging two Lundin executives with complicity in war crimes.[109] The trial is expected to take several years. Several CSOs, including PAX, remain involved by assisting victims in remedial action and participation in the trial.

Considering the results of this campaign so far, PAX and ECOS seem to have achieved 'victories' in relation to the perceived enforcement gap by ensuring prosecutorial action against the two executives in the home country of the corporation. The legal intervention, which is partially based on the principle of universal jurisdiction, has led to developments in the criminal liability of corporate executives as well.[110] Strategic results in relation to the corporate entity are yet to be determined, considering, amongst others, the role of the criminal case in future litigation on reparations.

4.2.2 The European Center for Constitutional and Human Rights, Sherpa and the Lafarge Case

The European Center for Constitutional and Human Rights (ECCHR) and Sherpa are CSOs that differ somewhat in orientation. The ECCHR is a German CSO and was founded in 2007 by several international human rights lawyers with the aim to protect and enforce civil and human rights "through legal means".[111] Their litigation features a clear counter-hegemonic dimension as featured in Grosescu's description of the CSO:

> Through these proceedings, ECCHER [*sic*] seeks not only to ensure justice for victims, but also to emphasize the inequalities and abuses generated by neoliberal economics and the power of corporations.[112]

Sherpa, founded in 2001 in France, on the other hand, has a more cross-disciplinary approach and "work[s] across four key areas—advocacy, legal action, legal laboratory, capacity sharing—to put an end to the impunity linked to the globalisation of economic and financial exchanges and its consequences for human rights and the environment".[113] The ECCHR thus has a more specific focus on litigation compared to Sherpa. Both CSOs, however, show a strong orientation towards legal intervention regarding the corporate enforcement gap. This is, amongst others, exemplified

[109] Truc O, Lundin, the trial that 'should never have taken place' Justiceinfo, 8 December 2023 https://www.justiceinfo.net/en/125751-lundin-trial-should-never-have-taken-place.html (last accessed 6 March 2024; Truc O, Lundin: serious intimate, Sweden's longest trial sets up for the long haul. Justiceinfo, 21 September 2023, https://www.justiceinfo.net/en/122058-lundin-serious-intimate-sweden-longest-trial-sets-up-for-the-long-haul.html (last accessed 6 March 2024).

[110] Klamberg (2022, pp. 896–901).

[111] Home-page, Ecchr https://www.ecchr.eu/ (last accessed 6 March 2024).

[112] Grosescu (2019, p. 406); see also the ECCHR's view of the function of law Institute for Legal Intervention, ECCHR https://www.ecchr.eu/en/institute-legal-intervention/ (last accessed 13 May 2024).

[113] About Us, Sherpa https://www.asso-sherpa.org/mandate (last accessed 6 March 2024).

by criminal complaints against French arms companies and advocacy efforts regarding human rights due diligence legislation.[114]

In November 2016, ECCHR and Sherpa filed a criminal complaint in France against Lafarge on behalf of eleven former Syrian employees. Their lives had allegedly been endangered by Lafarge by failing to take sufficient precautions against kidnappings and provide evacuation measures when the factory was attacked by ISIS while, at the same time, pressuring them to keep coming to work during the Syrian civil war.[115] Additionally, the CSOs argued that Lafarge had "entered [...] into negotiations with ISIS to purchase ISIS-controlled raw materials".[116] Furthermore, Lafarge, allegedly, had provided the terrorist organisation with around $13 million in funds, in return for the continued exploitation of its cement factory in North-East Syria (then occupied by ISIS forces).[117] In the view of Sherpa and ECCHR, this contributed to the ongoing conflict and hence constituted complicity in crimes against humanity.

The French investigative judges focussed initially on charges of financing terrorist organisations as well as endangerment of people's lives.[118] In 2018, ECCHR and Sherpa were able to convince the investigative judges to include charges for the complicity of the legal entity in crimes against humanity as well. However, in 2019, the investigative judge reduced the scope of the proceedings again.[119] The charges of crimes against humanity would be scrapped.[120] Nevertheless, the CSOs appealed this decision with success. The Court of Appeals confirmed the charges of crimes against humanity against Lafarge as a legal entity and against eight of its executives in 2022.[121] This decision was upheld on the 16th of January 2024 by the Court of

---

[114] Aiding and abetting war crimes in Yemen: Criminal Complaint Submitted against French Arms Companies, Sherpa, 2 June 2022 https://www.asso-sherpa.org/aiding-and-abetting-war-crimes-in-yemen-criminal-complaint-submitted-against-french-arms-companies (last accessed 6 March 2024); Made in Europe, Bombed in Yemen, Ecchr https://www.ecchr.eu/en/case/made-in-europe-bombed-in-yemen/ (last accessed 6 March 2024); Strengthening Corporate Accountability Advocacy Archives, Sherpa https://www.asso-sherpa.org/category/strengthening-corporate-accountability-advocacy (last accessed 6 March 2024).

[115] Tixeire C, Can the Lafarge Case Be a Game Changer? French Multinational Company Indicted for International Crimes in Syria Business and Human Rights Resource Centre, 31 August 2018 https://www.business-humanrights.org/en/blog/can-the-lafarge-case-be-a-game-changer-french-multinational-company-indicted-for-international-crimes-in-syria/ (last accessed 6 March 2024).

[116] Case Report. Lafarge in Syria: accusations of complicity in war crimes and crimes against humanity, Ecchr https://www.ecchr.eu/fileadmin/Fallbeschreibungen/Case_Report_Lafarge_Syria_ECCHR.pdf (last accessed 4 June 2024).

[117] This amounted to 0.65% of ISIS assets at the time, according to Young (2021, p. 10).

[118] Ibid., pp. 5–6.

[119] For more on the powers of the investigative judge in France, see, amongst others, Stevens et al. (2016, pp. 56–60).

[120] Young (2021, pp. 6–8).

[121] Tixeire (2018); AFP, French Court Upholds Syria "complicity in Crimes against Humanity" Charge against Lafarge. Business and Human Rights Resource Centre, 18 May 2022, https://www.business-humanrights.org/en/latest-news/french-court-upholds-syria-complicity-in-crimes-against-humanity-charge-against-lafarge/ (last accessed 6 March 2024).

Cassation following an appeal by Lafarge, confirming for the first time that a legal entity would face such charges.[122] It remains unclear at the time of writing when the proceedings move on to the merit stage.[123] The allocation of prosecutorial resources to the case as well as the confirmation that the crimes against humanity-paradigm is appropriate are indicative of strategic successes related to the enforcement and accountability gap respectively.

4.3 Observations on the Typology Applied

As far as PAX and ECOS are concerned, the CSOs did not immediately pursue the route of criminal justice in the Lundin case. As neither CSOs operate(d) on the basis of one specific method, they pursued several non-criminal approaches as well. By submitting the report on Lundin's activities in Sudan to the Swedish prosecutor, the collaborating CSOs fulfilled a clear kickstarting role in initiating the prosecution. The choice of jurisdiction was based on the company's domiciled status in Sweden and the presence of crimes against humanity and war crimes statutes. However, these statutes are limited to individuals, hence the indictment of two executives and not the corporation itself.[124] At the same time, the legal analysis provided in PAX and ECOS' report fulfils a more supplemental function through the provision of extensive legal analysis and evidence. This fits the activities associated with the assistant-prosecutor role. This illustrates that often, it is difficult to clearly distinguish between assistant-prosecutor and kickstarting roles. The two other types of strategy do not manifestly apply to PAX or ECOS in this particular situation in relation to the enforcement and accountability gap. Although addressing the role of corporate entities in the civil war in Sudan seems to be part of a larger focal point of the CSOs, the watchdog or pacemaker roles were less significant in bringing the alleged criminal behaviour to the attention of the prosecutor.[125]

---

[122] The charge of endangering the lives of others was however thrown out, leaving the charges of 'complicity in crimes against humanity, financing a terrorist organisation and violating an embargo with Syria,' see the press release at ECCHR, 16 January 2024 https://www.ecchr.eu/en/press-release/lafarge-in-syria/ (last accessed 6 March 2024).

[123] Hummel T, Lafarge Can Be Charged with "Complicity in Crimes against Humanity", French Court Says, Reuters, 16 January 2024 https://www.reuters.com/business/lafarge-can-be-charged-with-complicity-crimes-against-humanity-over-syria-plant-2024-01-16/ (last accessed 23 January 2024). The most recent development concerns the terrorist financing charge, see AFP, French prosecutors seek Lafarge trial for terror financing, Justiceinfo, 9 February 2024 https://www.justiceinfo.net/en/128327-french-prosecutors-seek-lafarge-trial-for-terror-financing.html (last accessed 7 March 2024).

[124] Klamberg (2022, p. 930).

[125] Truc O, The Swedish prosecutor who challenged Lundin Oil, Justiceinfo, 10 October 2023 https://www.justiceinfo.net/en/122958-swedish-prosecutor-who-challenged-lundin-oil.html (last accessed 6 March 2024).

The discussion about the role of the ECCHR and Sherpa requires a separation of their respective positions in the trial. While they both kickstarted the proceedings by filing a criminal complaint in 2016, Sherpa was removed from the proceedings as a civil party in 2021, as the French court found the CSO's aims—as formulated in its organisational statutes—insufficiently related to the facts subject to the proceedings.[126] The same happened to the ECCHR regarding the charges of financing a terrorist organisation.

Notwithstanding this limitation, the most dominant role fulfilled by the ECCHR in the Lafarge case is that of the watchdog. This characterisation follows primarily from the legal intervention to ensure that crimes against humanity were reinstated as part of the inquiry. As Mehta describes, one of the main issues standing in the way of this decision was the legal threshold regarding *mens rea.*[127] ECCHR's intervention ensured that the proceedings remained in the human rights paradigm rather than only the counter-terrorism paradigm.[128] The legal context in which the ECCHR operates facilitated this role. In France, a civil party to criminal proceedings has the right to appeal every judicial decision that affects their interests.[129] In that sense, the French jurisdiction is particularly suitable to CSOs with a specific focus on strategic litigation. It should be mentioned that, just as with PAX and ECOS, Sherpa and the ECCHR fulfilled an assisting role here as well by providing information and legal analysis in the judicial inquiry. Although, strictly speaking, the collaborative relationship between the CSOs and the prosecutorial authorities is missing in this case.

Several observations regarding the typology can be made based on these case studies. Firstly, it seems clear that a combination of different types of strategy is pervasive for litigating CSOs and that the difference between them is not always clear-cut. Multiple roles overlap in the activities of litigating CSOs, stressing the multi-polar nature of strategic litigation. The kickstarting role naturally fits the road *to* court best, which in the case studies was triggered by the filing of criminal complaints. The pacemaker role appears more during the procedure itself. The watchdog role seems to have been mostly exercised in the case of Lafarge, facilitated by the legal instruments in place in France. Although it appeared to be less necessary to fulfil the watchdog role in the Lundin case, PAX and other CSOs did exercise this function, particularly by attempting to draw the damage claims of affected civilians within the scope of the criminal proceedings.[130] On the other hand, the assistant-prosecutor role is fulfilled both before and after the trigger of prosecutorial action

---

[126] Historic Victory before French Supreme Court on the Indictment of Multinational Lafarge for Complicity in Crimes against Humanity in Syria. Ecchr, 7 September 2021 https://www.ecchr.eu/en/press-release/historic-victory-before-french-supreme-court-on-the-indictment-of-multinational-lafarge-for-complicity-in-crimes-against-humanity-in-syria/ (last accessed 7 March 2024).

[127] Mehta (2024, pp. 235–239).

[128] Ibid., pp. 229–230.

[129] Becker and Van Lent (2023, pp. 294–295).

[130] The Court throws out the damage claims of war crimes survivors. PAX, 27 November 2023, https://unpaiddebt.org/stockholm-district-court-throws-out-claims-for-damage-of-war-crimes-survivors/ (last accessed 7 March 2024).

through the submission of information and analyses. The assistance may go hand in hand with more antagonistic elements, such as litigation to enforce prosecutorial action.

While the two case studies are not sufficient to make general statements, they suggest that the nature of the actor can play a role in the chosen strategy. PAX—a CSO which is primarily concerned with non-litigious advocacy—seems to firstly question the prosecutor's and court's decision-making through extra-legal avenues, such as political campaigning. In contrast, Sherpa and the ECCHR explicitly committed to pursuing legal action as a primary instrument. These tendencies appear interlinked with the legal context in which the CSOs operate, the available legal instruments and the extent to which the aims pursued by the CSOs remain aligned with those of prosecutorial and judicial authorities. In the case of Lundin, PAX had been able to insert its view on the enforcement gap into prosecutorial decision-making through a combination of advocacy and a kickstarting complaint. The ECCHR (and Sherpa) required more iterations of legal intervention to affect the criminal politics regarding the observed corporate enforcement gap.

Whether eventually successful or not, the previously analysed legal interventions fit the counter-hegemonic narrative of strategic litigation. In both cases, revision of the criminal politics vis-à-vis corporate criminal accountability was sought and required some form of antagonistic approach in defiance of the prosecutorial authorities' allocation of investigative and prosecutorial resources. The case studies show that the criminal politics of prosecutors concerning cases of alleged corporate complicity in atrocity crimes are not always oriented towards the closure of the enforcement gaps perceived by CSOs. Although the limited scope of this contribution does not allow for generalisations, there are sufficient indications that the (extra-)legal issues described in Sect. 3 feed into this (developing) state of criminal politics.[131] The multi-polar strategic litigation efforts of CSOs are directed against this set of criminal political factors that determine the position of the corporate enforcement and accountability gap on the prosecutorial agenda.

5 Strategic Litigation for Corporate Criminal Accountability in the Netherlands: The La Strada International Complaint

The case studies show that the strategies of litigating CSOs require adjustment to the legal and political context in which they operate. Fragmentation in strategies and tactics is, hence, in part, explained by the difference in legal avenues that are present in various jurisdictions. For CSOs interested in opening avenues of justice in the Netherlands, the reference point thus remains the Dutch legal and political system

[131] For the influence of the corporate veil and *mens rea* in the Lafarge case, see: Mehta (2024, pp. 232–239).

with its own opportunities and constraints. Therefore, I discuss the way several CSOs used a recent Article 12 DCCP procedure as a strategic legal intervention concerning the alleged profiting of Dutch shipbuilding companies from forced labour. While the case does not concern the application of international criminal norms, the nature of the complaint is sufficiently analogous to provide concluding observations on the space for strategic litigation in the Netherlands.

La Strada International (LSI) is a platform consisting of around 30 NGOs from Europe oriented at anti-human trafficking initiatives and the cooperation of NGOs in this field.[132] It was officially established in 2004, with a secretariat based in the Netherlands. Starting in 2019, the main purpose of the organisation has been "to strengthen cooperation between civil society organisations, to raise awareness of human trafficking in Europe, to promote anti-trafficking initiatives and the work of NGOs and to engage in joint advocacy and policy work."[133] LSI is active in monitoring and advocacy work, while the member organisations work directly with and for victims of trafficking. The main activities of LSI and its members are not litigation *per se*:

> Our member organisations strengthen trafficked persons' rights through hotlines, education, information provision and campaigns to prevent people from being exploited and having their rights violated. Members provide direct access to assistance and justice to trafficked persons via (legal) support programmes and shelters, and monitor the implementation of international legislation on the ground, while also advocating for changes.[134]

However, in its strategic plan for 2021–2025, LSI has formulated its intention to use strategic litigation.[135] The first steps of such legal intervention were taken in 2020. Based on, amongst others, two academic research reports and a documentary, LSI filed a criminal complaint against two Dutch shipbuilding companies. LSI accused the companies of having profited from human trafficking and forced labour, amongst allegations of money laundering and fencing. The companies had allegedly "acquired ships from Polish shipyards while being aware that these ships were constructed at wharfs employing North-Korean workers under inhumane, exploitative conditions."[136] Following LSI's complaint, the DPPO requested a further substantiation of the benefits which the companies would have enjoyed from the alleged violations, which LSI shared with the DPPO in June 2021.

Due to doubts about proving that the companies had profited from the situation, the DPPO dismissed the case in 2021.[137] LSI, with support from a law firm and the

---

[132] History, LSI, https://www.lastradainternational.org/history-la-strada/ (last accessed 13 May 2024).

[133] Ibid.

[134] Strategic Plan 2021–2025, LSI, September 2021, https://documentation.lastradainternational.org/lsidocs/3432-Strategic%20Plan%202021%20-%202025%20%20100122.pdf (last accessed 13 May 2024), p. 10.

[135] Ibid., p. 17.

[136] North-Korean Forced Labour, LSI, April 2024, https://www.lastradainternational.org/nkforced-labour/ (last accessed 31 May 2024).

[137] Ibid.

Global Legal Action Network, consequently initiated an Article 12-procedure.[138] The strategic aspects of the case were made explicit in press releases and a previous criminal complaint regarding another victim of the same alleged violations. The case includes features related to enforcement and accountability gaps. LSI stated that "[t]he case highlights significant gaps in labour protections within the European Union and the lack of remedies available to affected workers of forced labour".[139] This corresponds with the aim mentioned by Mégret to highlight systematic injustices in the legal system. In relation to the earlier case, the legal intervention is also explicitly connected to an attempt to lift a "veil of impunity surrounding corporate accountability for human rights harms in their supply chains", corresponding both to the notion of the enforcement and the accountability gap.[140] The Article 12-complaint sought to actively engage with the objective of societal norm-setting and matters of criminal politics by including arguments about prosecutorial decision-making regarding investigative capacity in the case.[141]

The Article 12-complaint was dismissed by the Court of Appeals on 15 April 2024.[142] The Court argued that the link between the alleged violations and the conduct of the shipbuilding companies in the Netherlands was insufficient, as the Dutch companies had no active connection to the activities in the Polish shipyards. Moreover, it determined that further investigative action would likely not lead to a successful prosecution due to the date and location of the facts, as well as the current place of residence of the victims.

The reasoning of the Court corresponds to the issues of proximity of the corporation to the facts, as discussed in Sects. 3.1.1 and 3.1.2, while also featuring grounds for dismissal that fall in the feasibility category.[143] Given the rapidly changing political climate on corporate responsibility for human rights violations in supply chains, LSI's effort to integrate such developments into prosecutorial decision-making seems to have been unsuccessful. In its press release following the dismissal, the LSI connected the case to the recently approved EU anti-trafficking Directive, the Forced Labour Regulation and the new Directive on Corporate Sustainability Due Diligence, stating that the judgement 'came around the same time, when the EU

[138] Ibid.

[139] Why is this case so important? LSI, https://www.lastradainternational.org/why-is-this-case-so-important/ (last accessed 13 May 2024).

[140] North Korean labourer files criminal complaint against Dutch shipbuilding firm for alleged profiting from modern slavery, Prakken d'Oliveira, 8 November 2018, https://www.prakkendoliveira.nl/en/news/2018/north-korean-labourer-files-criminal-complaint-against-dutch-shipbuilding-firm-for-alleged-profiting-from-modern-slavery (last accessed 13 May 2024).

[141] The Hague Court of Appeals 15 April 2024, ECLI:NL:GHDHA:2024:844, § 6, access via https://uitspraken.rechtspraak.nl/details?id=ECLI:NL:GHDHA:2024:844

[142] Ibid., § 7.

[143] Similar reasoning was employed by the DPPO in the dismissal of a criminal complaint against Lima Holding lodged by Al-Haq for Riwal's involvement in the construction of the Israeli wall on the West Bank, see No further investigation into crane rental company, DPPO, 14 May 2013, https://www.prakkendoliveira.nl/images/nieuws/2013/130514_om_no_further_investigation_into_crane_rental_company.pdf (last accessed 14 May 2024).

Parliament acknowledged that more is to be done to hold companies liable for severe forms of labour exploitation'.[144] The case, therefore, appears to have the potential of an example of the "success without victory" type of legal intervention, if the "lost battle" were to be used for a further extra-legal campaign to illustrate current presumed inadequacies in present legal dynamics.[145]

As in the previously discussed strategic litigation campaigns, LSI was not the only CSO contributing to the strategic aims in relation to the shipbuilding case: other civil society actors did as well by conducting research into the alleged violations and seeking public attention. Like in the PAX & ECOS campaign, several activities were explored in the non-criminal sphere, both before and after the criminal complaints were lodged. LSI's criminal complaints, supported by the research of other CSOs, feature elements of both the assistant-prosecutor role as well as the kickstarting role. Particularly, the second attempt to assist the prosecutor by providing investigative materials and the DPPO's engagement with LSI after the criminal complaint indicate that a shift towards an antagonistic approach only initiated at the point of the Article 12-complaint procedure. This shift implies both kickstarting and watchdog characteristics, the latter following from the expressed focus on the responsibility of corporations for human rights violations in their supply chains. In Fig. 1, I have provided an overview and typology of the instruments available to

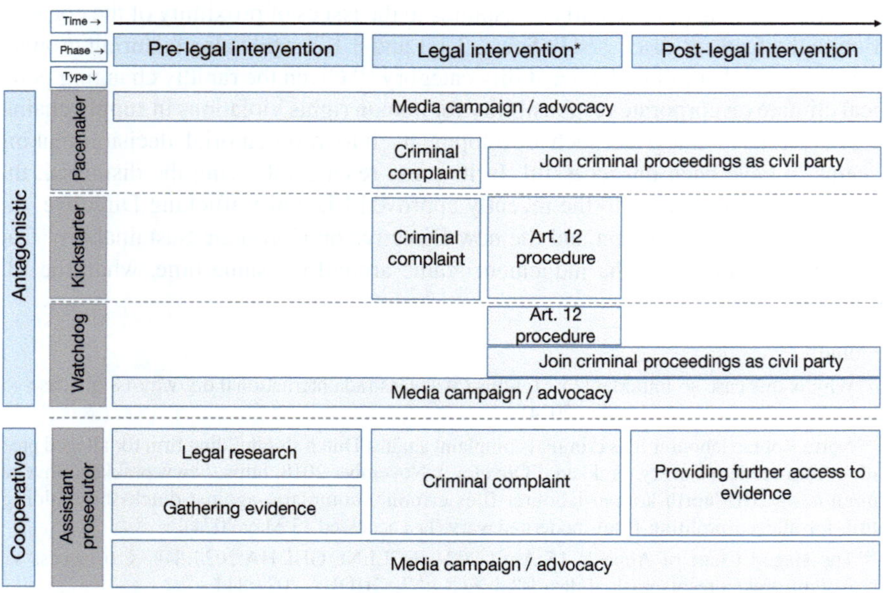

Fig. 1 Typology of litigating CSOs in the Dutch legal context

[144] Why is this case so important? LSI, https://www.lastradainternational.org/why-is-this-case-so-important/ (last accessed 31 May 2024).

[145] See also Lobel (2003).

litigating CSOs in both the legal and extra-legal spheres, particularly focussed on CSOs pursuing strategic litigation through the Article 12-procedure in the Netherlands.

6 Conclusions

The Dutch case study suggests that the potential for instrumental impact of strategic litigation in the Dutch criminal justice system is limited due to two main issues: the doctrinal complexity of showing corporate involvement in atrocities and the judge's willingness to defer to the prosecutor's prioritisation policies. These legal dynamics have implications for strategic litigation in the Netherlands regarding corporate atrocity crimes through the Article 12-procedure.

The legal complexity, the political situation in the place in which the violations have taken place and cross-border elements of such prosecutions can make a prosecution costly in terms of resources. These capacity considerations can weigh heavily in the assessment of prosecutorial policy—although in the ING Bank decision, the Court explicitly distanced itself from such capacity-based reasoning. Since the allocation of resources is primarily the prerogative of the prosecutorial authorities, Courts are inclined to defer questions of prioritisation to the public prosecutor. Becker and Van Lent have previously observed that one of the few ways in which this dynamic can be 'broken' is when the Court is convinced of the fact that the prosecutorial policy or decision-making is inconsistent with already solidifying norms in broader public and political debate.[146] LSI explicitly used such reasoning in their Article 12-procedure, as also mentioned in their press releases. These legal dynamics require CSOs to engage with criminal politics by showing that there is a public interest in diverting resources to the discussed enforcement gap based on societal, practical, and legal considerations. This implies that legal action is just one of several necessary instruments for CSOs to make an instrumental impact. The prevalent question during such strategic legal interventions is thus whether the business and human rights movement has been able to sufficiently show the significance of the norms on corporate accountability for atrocity crimes. In the case of the shipbuilding companies, LSI was unsuccessful in convincing the Court of Appeal that their views on the perceived enforcement and accountability gap should be inserted into criminal politics.

These legal dynamics leave CSOs with two main approaches in their pursuit to influence prosecutorial decision-making and prioritisation in prosecutorial policy in the Netherlands: (i) removing practical obstacles to the initiation of cases springing from limited prosecutorial capacity; (ii) and/or pursuing a more antagonistic approach and demonstrating the inadequacy of prosecutorial prioritisation policy by

[146] Becker and Van Lent (2023, p. 302).

showing the societal need for the closure of a perceived enforcement gap.[147] Present activity of CSOs in the Netherlands highlights a tendency towards using the first approach initially while shifting to the second approach when it becomes clear that their views do not align with those of the prosecutor.[148] However, if an antagonistic intervention through the Article 12-procedure results in an order to prosecute, the relationship with the prosecutorial authorities may shift back to the assistant-prosecutor role to ensure a successful progression of the actual prosecution.

The actor-focused perspective employed in this contribution reveals how shifting relations between CSOs and prosecutorial authorities can be a key determinant in the efforts to close enforcement gaps. CSOs must fulfil several roles, including kick-starters, pacemakers, watchdogs, and assistant-prosecutors, to be successful. Where CSOs' aims regarding the corporate enforcement gap remain aligned with those of prosecutorial and judicial authorities, taking on the assistant-prosecutor role may suffice. Once those aims do not run parallel, however, deploying strategic litigation through antagonistic *modi operandi,* as a counter-hegemonic instrument, is more suitable. In such cases, the Article 12-procedure can be a key instrument to contribute to closing the corporate enforcement gap as part of a multi-polar strategy. However, criminal political features of the complaints procedure can severely limit the potential of such strategic legal interventions.

References

Becker TR, Van Lent L (2023) Strategische procesvoering in de beklagprocedure van artikel 12 Sv. Tijdschrift voor Bijzonder Strafrecht en Handhaving 6:291–304. https://doi.org/10.5553/TBSenH/229567002023009006005

Becker TR et al (2023) Will victims' rights be lost in translation? Bridging the information gap in universal jurisdiction cases. Utrecht J Int Eur Law 38(1):39–61. https://doi.org/10.5334/ujiel.585

Beckers J (2017) Tussen ideaal en werkelijkheid. Een Empirische Studie naar de Strafrechtelijke Aanpak van Organisatiecriminaliteit in Nederland. Erasmus University Rotterdam

Bergkamp L, Pak WQ (2001) Piercing the corporate veil: shareholder liability for corporate torts. Maastricht J Eur Comp Law 8(2):167–188. https://doi.org/10.1177/1023263X0100800204

Biggs M International criminal law and corporate actors—part 2: the Rome statute and its aftermath. Doing Business Right Blog, 21 May 2019. https://www.asser.nl/DoingBusinessRight/Blog/post/international-criminal-law-and-corporate-actors-part-2-the-rome-statute-and-its-aftermath-by-maisie-biggs#_ftn14. Accessed 7 Mar 2024

---

[147] Assuming, of course, that it can be sufficiently substantiated that the suspected actor committed the alleged offences.

[148] See also, for example: Aangifte Ficq tegen Chemours-top om pfas namens ruim 2000 mensen. Financieel Dagblad, 14 augustus 2023 https://fd.nl/bedrijfsleven/1485783/aangifte-ficq-tegen-chemours-top-om-pfas-namens-ruim-2000-mensen (last accessed 7 March 2024); Mol J and Polman J, Topadvocaat Ficq: 'De ceo van Tata Steel moet de gevangenis in'. Financieel Dagblad, 9 juni 2023 https://fd.nl/samenleving/1478339/topadvocaat-ficq-de-ceo-van-tata-steel-moet-de-gevangenis-in#:~:text=In%20het%20kort,gevaar%20alleen%20is%20al%20genoeg (last accessed 7 March 2024).

Bordeleau-Cass JÉ (2019) The 'accountability gap': holding corporations liable for international crimes. PKI Global Justice J 3:65

Bush J (2009) The prehistory of corporations and conspiracy in international criminal law: what Nuremberg really said. Columbia Law Rev 109(5):1094–1262

Buyse A et al (2021) The rule of law from below—a concept under development. Utrecht Law Rev 17(2):1–7. https://doi.org/10.36633/ulr.771

Clapham A (2008) Extending international criminal law beyond the individual to corporations and armed opposition groups. J Int Crim Justice 6(5):899–926. https://doi.org/10.1093/jicj/mqn076

Crawford J Corporate responsibility in war crimes, a new legal battlefield. JusticeInfo, 15 November 2019. https://www.justiceinfo.net/en/42906-corporate-responsibility-war-crimes-new-legal-battlefield.html. Accessed 6 Mar 2024

Cruvellier T, Metenier C (2022) No one really wants corporations to be liable. Justiceinfo. https://www.justiceinfo.net/en/102430-no-one-really-wants-corporations-to-be-liable.html#utm_source=facebook&utm_medium=reseaux-sociaux. Accessed 6 Mar 2024

Cryer R et al (2019) An introduction to international criminal law and procedure. CUP, Cambridge. https://doi.org/10.1017/9781108680455

D'Alessandra F, Sutherland K (2021) The promise and challenges of new actors and new technologies in international justice. J Int Crim Justice 19(1):9–34. https://doi.org/10.1093/jicj/mqab034

Dale JG (2007) Transnational legal conflict between peasants and corporations in Burma: human rights and discursive ambivalence under the US Alien Tort Claims Act. In: Goodale M, Engle Merry S (eds) The practice of human rights. Tracking law between the global and the local. CUP, Cambridge, pp 285–319. https://doi.org/10.1017/CBO9780511819193.012

De Lange T (2009) De beklagprocedure en criminele politiek. Strafblad, pp 477–492

ECOS & PAX (2010) Unpaid Debt: The Legacy of Lundin, Petronas and OMV in Block 5A, Sudan 1997-2003. https://paxforpeace.nl/what-we-do/programmes/unpaid-debt/. Accessed 6 Mar 2024

Fischer-Lescano A (2021) From strategic litigation to juridical action. In: Saage-Maaß M et al (eds) Transnational legal activism in global value chains. Springer, Cham, pp 299–312. https://doi.org/10.1007/978-3-030-73835-8_15

Grosescu R (2019) Transnational advocacy networks and corporate accountability for gross human rights violations in Argentina and Colombia. Glob Soc 33(3):400–418. https://doi.org/10.1080/13600826.2019.1598947

Grosescu R (2024) Justice and memory after dictatorship. Latin America, Central Eastern Europe, and the fragmentation of international criminal law. OUP, Oxford. https://doi.org/10.1093/oso/9780192870346.001.0001

Huisman W, Van Sliedregt E (2010) Rogue traders: Dutch businessmen, international crimes and corporate complicity. J Int Crim Justice 8(3):803–828. https://doi.org/10.1093/jicj/mqq040

International Commission of Jurists Expert Legal Panel on Corporate Complicity in International Crimes (2008) Corporate complicity & legal accountability. Facing the facts and charting a legal path. https://www.icj.org/wp-content/uploads/2012/06/Vol.1-Corporate-legal-accountability-thematic-report-2008.pdf. Accessed 6 Mar 2024

Jeßberger F, Steinl L (2022) Strategic litigation in international criminal justice. J Int Crim Justice 20(2):379–401. https://doi.org/10.1093/jicj/mqac008

Kaleck W, Saage-Maaß M (2010) Corporate accountability for human rights violations amounting to international crimes. The status quo and its challenges. J Int Crim Justice 8(3):699–724. https://doi.org/10.1093/jicj/mqq043

Kelk C (2019) Studieboek materieel strafrecht. Wolters Kluwer

Kesteloo A (2013) De rechtspersoon in het strafrecht. Kluwer

Klamberg M (2022) Prosecuting corporate executives for war crimes in Sudan. NYU J Int Law Polit 54:887–939

Knox R (2010) Strategy and tactics. Finnish Yearbook of International Law 21:193–229. https://doi.org/10.2139/ssrn.1921759

Koenig A (2022) From ‘capture to courtroom’. Collaboration and the digital documentation of international crimes in Ukraine. J Int Crim Justice 20(4):829–842. https://doi.org/10.1093/jicj/mqac046

Koning S (2022) De Ventielfunctie van de Artikel 12 Sv-Procedure: Van Georganiseerd Wantrouwen Naar Gezamenlijk Politiek Project? Netherlands J Legal Philos 51:1–22. https://doi.org/10.5553/NJLP/.000107

Kremnitzer M (2010) A possible case for imposing criminal liability on corporations in international criminal law. J Int Crim Justice 8(3):909–918. https://doi.org/10.1093/jicj/mqq036

Kristjansdottir E, Nollkaemper A, Ryngaert C (2012) International law in domestic courts: rule of law reform in post-conflict states. Intersentia

Kronenberg MJ, De Wilde B (2018) Grondtrekken van het Nederlandse Strafrecht. Wolters Kluwer

Kyriakakis J (2021) Corporations, accountability and international criminal law: industry and atrocity. Edward Elgar, Cheltenham

Langer M, Eason M (2019) The quiet expansion of universal jurisdiction. Eur J Int Law 30(3):779–817. https://doi.org/10.1093/ejil/chz050

Lobel J (2003) Success without victory: lost legal battles and the long road to justice in America. New York University Press, New York

Macey JC (2019) What corporate veil. Mich Law Rev 117(6):1195–1214. https://doi.org/10.36644/mlr.117.6.what

Marx A et al (2019) Corporate accountability mechanisms in EU member states for human rights abuses in third countries - working paper. European Yearbook of Human Rights, pp 1–26

Mavronicola N (2024) The case against human rights Penality. Oxf J Leg Stud 44(3):1–28. https://doi.org/10.1093/ojls/gqae013

McGonigle Leyh B (2022) Using strategic litigation and universal jurisdiction to advance accountability for serious international crimes. Int J Transit Justice 16(3):363–379. https://doi.org/10.1093/ijtj/ijac020

Mégret F (2023) Immunities of foreign officials for international crimes: the dilemmas of strategic litigation. J Hum Rights Pract 15(1):66–83. https://doi.org/10.1093/jhuman/huac067

Mehta K (2024) Strategic litigation and corporate complicity in crimes under international law: a TWAIL analysis. Routledge, New York. https://doi.org/10.4324/9781003405047

Mujuzi JD (2016) Victim participation in the criminal justice system in the European Union through private prosecutions: issues emerging from the jurisprudence of the European court of human rights. Eur J Crime Crim Law Crim Justice 24(2–3):107–134. https://doi.org/10.1163/15718174-24032088

OSJI (2018) Strategic litigation impacts: insights from global experience. https://www.justiceinitiative.org/publications/strategic-litigation-impacts-insights-global-experience. Accessed 6 Mar 2024

Ottolenghi S (1990) From peeping behind the corporate veil, to ignoring it completely. The Modern Law Review 53(3):338–353

Ryngaert C (2018) Accountability for corporate human rights abuses: lessons from the possible exercise of Dutch National Criminal Jurisdiction over multinational corporations. Crim Law Forum 29:1–24. https://doi.org/10.1007/s10609-017-9330-y

Scheffer D (2016) Corporate liability under the Rome statute. Harvard International Law Journal Online Symposium 57(1):35–38

Sikkink K, Kim HJ (2013) The Justice Cascade: the origins and effectiveness of prosecutions of human rights violations. Annu Rev Law Soc Sci 9(1):269–285. https://doi.org/10.1146/annurev-lawsocsci-102612-133956

Sluiter G, Shun Ming Yau S (2020) Aiding and abetting and causation in the Commission of International Crimes. The cases of Dutch businessmen van Anraat and Kouwenhoven. In: Jørgensen NHB (ed) The international criminal responsibility of war’s funders and profiteers. CUP, Cambridge, pp 304–328. https://doi.org/10.1017/9781108692991.013

Spijkers O (2024) Summary proceedings about the delivery from the Netherlands of Parts for F-35 fighter planes to Israel (Part I), Opinio Juris, 5 January 2024. https://opiniojuris.org/2024/01/05/

summary-proceedings-about-the-delivery-from-the-netherlands-of-parts-for-f-35-fighter-planes-to-israel-part-i/. Accessed 6 Mar 2024
Stahn C (2018) Liberals vs romantics: challenges of an emerging corporate international criminal law. Case Western Reserve J Int Law 50(1):91–124
Stevens L et al (2016) De tenlastelegging als grondslag voor de rechterlijke beslissing. Een rechtsvergelijkend onderzoek naar de inrichting van de tenlastelegging en de gebondenheid eraan bij het bewijs, de kwalificatie en de straftoemeting in Nederland, België, Frankrijk, Italië en Duitsland, WODC
Tixeire C et al Holding transnational corporations accountable for international crimes in Syria: update on the developments in the Lafarge case (part II) Opinio Juris, 27 July 2020. http://opiniojuris.org/2020/07/27/holding-transnational-corporations-accountable-for-international-crimes-in-syria-update-on-the-developments-in-the-lafarge-case-part-ii/. Accessed 6 Mar 2024
Van Ham HJA (2011) Beschikking naar aanleiding van het klaagschrift op grond van art. 12 van het Wetboek van Strafvordering betreffend Trafigura. Milieu & Recht 158
Van Lent L et al (2016) Klachten Tegen Niet-Vervolging (Artikel 12 Sv-Procedure). Doorlooptijden, instroom, verwachtingen van klagers en het belang van procedurele rechtvaardigheid. BoomJuridisch
Vandekerckhove K (2007) Piercing the corporate veil. Kluwer Law International, Alphen aan den Rijn
Verrest PAM, Mevis PAM (2018) Rechtsvergelijkende inzichten voor de modernisering van het Wetboek van Strafvordering. Boom juridisch, Den Haag
Vest H (2010) Business leaders and the modes of individual criminal responsibility under international law. J Int Crim Justice 8:851–872. https://doi.org/10.1093/jicj/mqq032
Young M (2021) Lafarge's case cemented: holding corporations liable for crimes against humanity. Emory Int Law Rev Recent Dev 36:1–13

Thomas Becker graduated from University College Utrecht with a double degree in Dutch Law and Liberal Arts and Sciences, specialising in international criminal law and political science. He completed a Legal Research Master's at Utrecht University in 2024 and has, among others, worked on projects related to corporate criminal law, human rights due diligence enforcement mechanisms, and international criminal law and procedure. He has previously published on victims' rights in universal jurisdiction prosecutions, strategic litigation in criminal law and fair trial rights. Presently, he is a lawyer at the Dutch law firm De Brauw Blackstone Westbroek.

Promises and Limitations of Grassroot Activism

Polenta and Cyanide? Investment Arbitration as Prospective Environmental Injustice in Roșia Montană

Stephanie Triefus and Irina Velicu

Abstract Around the world, local communities supported by national and transnational advocacy networks are fighting to defend or preserve their homes and livelihoods from extractivist projects that threaten their environments. In this chapter, we look at Investor-State Dispute Settlement (ISDS) as a form of prospective environmental (in)justice (PEJ). ISDS provides for multinational corporations to sue states when they have a grievance over the state's treatment of their investment. We argue that ISDS continues the structural violence of extractive projects and the pre-project harms resulting from foreign investor-welcoming climates. The chapter draws on empirical research on the Roşia Montană case in Romania to extend the theory of PEJ to scenarios where communities have succeeded in stopping a mining project, but the investor brings arbitration against the state, thus prolonging the "soft" extractive violence. We analyse how grassroots movements formed coalitions with national and foreign NGOs, succeeded in stopping a Canadian mining project based on cyanide extraction, and inscribed Roşia Montană as a UNESCO World Heritage site. In response, the Canadian mining company instigated investment arbitration proceedings against Romania. The case illustrates that, despite the legal victory of the Romanian state, international investment arbitration potentially allows "green crime", rendering it awfully lawful.

Special thanks to the locals of Roşia Montană for opening their hearts to discuss these issues with us. Irina Velicu acknowledges support from the following funding schemes: FCT-PTDC/GET-AMB/29355/2017, PNNR-ULBS, 760077/23.05.2023

S. Triefus (✉)
T.M.C. Asser Institute, The Hague, Netherlands
e-mail: s.triefus@asser.nl

I. Velicu
CES-UC, ULBS, Coimbra, Portugal
e-mail: irinavelicu@ces.uc.pt

R. Grosescu, J. G. Dale (eds.), *Corporate Accountability for Human Rights Violations*, Interdisciplinary Studies in Human Rights 16,
https://doi.org/10.1007/978-3-032-05569-9_12

1 Introduction

Most environmental victories look like nothing happened; the land wasn't annexed by the army, the mine didn't open, the road didn't cut through, the factory didn't spew effluents that didn't give children asthma.[1] All around the world, local communities supported by national and transnational advocacy networks are fighting tooth and nail to defend or preserve their homes and livelihoods from extractivist projects that threaten their environments.[2] When these activists succeed in stopping a harmful project, this is considered to be a 'win' for the community. This was the case in Roşia Montană, Romania, where a local-turned-national and international movement succeeded in stopping a Canadian-owned open-cut gold and silver mine project after a struggle of more than 20 years. The project would have displaced over 1000 people, destroyed thousands of years of cultural heritage, eviscerated four mountains, and threatened the environment with cyanide. Responding to widespread protests around Romania, the Romanian government voted down a law that would have cleared an administrative path for the mine to proceed. Because the mine in Roşia did not go ahead, the potential environmental crimes seemed like they also did not occur. Such non-events obscure the fact that much prospective environmental (in)justice (PEJ) is being done before the ground is ever mined.[3] The concept of PEJ highlights the structural violence that enables such extractive projects to be explored in the first place—that is, extractivism in the unending search for growth perceives (peasant/rural) communities as disposable or displaceable. More so, since 2015, the mining company has been suing Romania in international investment arbitration, alleging that Romania breached the bilateral investment treaties between Romania and Canada and the UK, and seeking over US$5 billion in compensation.[4]

In this chapter, we argue that the *Gabriel Resources v Romania* arbitration is a further dimension of prospective socio-environmental injustice inflicted on the community of Roşia Montană, perpetuating the systemic violence experienced even in the absence of an ongoing extractive project. In this chapter, we expand the concept of PEJ by looking at international investment arbitration as a form of 'green crime', facilitated by a prevailing bias in favour of multinational corporations' interests to the detriment of environmental and human rights.[5] Investment arbitration frequently concerns extractive projects, which inevitably involves lives and livelihoods. Characterised as a private dispute between a company and a state, investment arbitration severely limits the participation of individuals and communities affected

[1] Solnit (2004), p. 74.

[2] Martinez-Alier et al., Nixon (2011), Bullard (1993).

[3] Velicu (2020).

[4] In its initial claim, Gabriel Resources sought $US3.3 billion compensation with compound interest of 4% (Claimant's Memorial 2018, para 931), which would have amounted to over US$5 billion by the time the Award was rendered.

[5] Broad (2015), Shao (2021).

by investment projects. Empirical research reveals that investment arbitration does, in fact, impact these communities.[6] Although some scholars are beginning to examine the impacts of international investment law on local communities affected by investment projects by investigating investment arbitration empirically "from below,"[7] there is much further work to be done in this area. Therefore, we aim to contribute to this emerging literature by focusing on the case study of Roşia Montană and conceptualising these impacts through the framework of PEJ, which gives language to the 'soft' extractive violence inflicted on these communities through investment arbitration. Our argument is further strengthened by the observation that international investment arbitration has come under intense scrutiny as an international economic system with colonial roots[8] that prioritises private corporate interests over public interests and human rights[9] and renders local communities invisible.[10]

The chapter draws on empirical insights gathered from interviews conducted in Roşia Montană and builds on Velicu's active participatory fieldwork in Romania between 2007 and 2013 (30 interviews and virtual/face-to-face discussions with participants in the Salvaţi Roşia Montană movement[11] and eight interviews carried out in Roşia Montană in July 2024 following the arbitral decision in favour of Romania). This research is complemented by interviews conducted in Roşia Montană by Triefus in 2022 after 7 years of arbitration (13 semi-structured interviews with members of the Roşia Montană community who resisted the mine and national and transnational NGOs that supported the movement).[12] In this chapter, we seek to further illustrate the concept of PEJ focusing on the new dimensions of injustice occurring as part of the international investment law processes. Section 2 starts by setting out the theoretical framework of PEJ, extractive violence, green crime and ISDS. Section 3 gives a brief background of the struggle against the gold mine, the local, national and transnational actors involved in stopping the project, and the subsequent investment arbitration case brought in response to this successful struggle. Section 4 draws on interview data to explore the impact of the struggle and arbitration on the community. Section 5 discusses how these impacts can be understood through the lens of PEJ and how doing so contributes both to the debates on environmental injustice as green crime and the backlash against international investment law. Section 6 concludes that ISDS serves to prolong the prospective injustice of extractive projects, keeping communities in limbo as the potential reversal of their successful environmental struggle is debated in a distant forum that excludes their voices and reproduces extractivist violence. The significant struggle

---

[6] Triefus (2024).

[7] Cotula (2020), Perrone (2020), Sierra and Schwartz (2020), Triefus (2024).

[8] Anghie (2005), Sornarajah (2015), Miles (2013).

[9] Arcuri (2019).

[10] Perrone (2019).

[11] Velicu (2014, 2015).

[12] Triefus (2024).

of the people of Roşia Montană and Romanian society to challenge the perceived normalcy of mining highlights the need for continued societal efforts to reshape the discourse surrounding extractive economic activities. These activities pose substantial potential risks to socio-environmental health, necessitating a re-evaluation of how such negotiations are approached and understood.

2 Awfully Lawful? International Arbitration and Prospective Environmental Injustice

If you wanted to convince the public that international trade agreements are a way to let multinational companies get rich at the expense of ordinary people, this is what you would do: give foreign firms a special right to apply to a secretive tribunal of highly paid corporate lawyers for compensation whenever a government passes a law to, say, discourage smoking, protect the environment or prevent a nuclear catastrophe. Yet that is precisely what thousands of trade and investment treaties over the past half century have done, through a process known as "investor-state dispute settlement.[13]

The problem of legal but illegitimate harm to the environment and the definition of the environment itself needs to be examined in the context of the limits and gaps between legality, legitimacy, and justice. Powerful states can and do opt out of attempts to create internationally legally binding environmental controls and agreements. Big businesses often make successful calls for exemption or exceptional leniency regarding environmental regulation labelling as authoritarian even the imposition of penalties on offenders. Green crime is essentially transnational and multifaceted, with nuances of violence and numerous entities at the borders of complex complicity and wrongdoing[14]—which complicates accountability. Therefore, criminal activities have been described as "lawful but awful", recognising that many environmental disruptions are "actually legal and take place with the consent of society".[15]

While such a critical perspective has been a recent development in academia, in parallel, we could observe also an emergent literature that has addressed the problems of the international legal mechanisms that companies may use to complain about harm. International investment law[16] refers to a system of international law that allows foreign investors to sue states directly via arbitration, known as ISDS,

[13] The Economist (2014), p. 78.

[14] South (2014), Iordăchescu and Vasile (2023).

[15] Skinnider (2013), p. 2, see also Passas (2005).

[16] In this article, "international investment law" is used to refer to investor-state arbitration conducted pursuant to bilateral and multilateral investment treaties and contracts between foreign investors and states.

where they consider that their rights under an investment treaty have been breached.[17] These rights typically include, among other rights, the right to property, fair and equitable treatment, non-discrimination, and the same treatment as domestic investors. ISDS has been a relatively new phenomenon in the evolution of international investment law in the 1960s as the World Bank sought to carve out a role for itself in foreign investment promotion, resulting in the establishment of the Convention on the Settlement Investment Disputes between States and Nationals of Other States (ICSID) in 1965. In this new fashion, arbitrators were appointed by the disputing parties while interpreting and applying both national and international laws, with strictly confidential proceedings, and with awards that were not subject to appeal aside from in very limited circumstances.

Arbitration rules developed by the United Nations Commission on International Trade Law (UNCITRAL) in 1976 embraced this model. By 2019, 983 claims were brought to arbitration by foreign investors against over 100 governments, 36% of them having been decided in favour of the state.[18] Usually, foreign investors demonstrate harm by providing evidence that the state expropriated property used for the operation of its business, that policies or actions of the state were discriminatory (based on the nationality of the foreign investor), or by demonstrating that it was treated in a manner that falls below the "international minimum standard of treatment" of foreign investors (violation of customary international law).

Both liberals and conservatives, Global South (Argentina, Ecuador) as well as North (USA, Germany)—in relation to a variety of industries, including tobacco, pharmaceutics, oil, etc.—have been increasingly framing ISDS as an illegitimate legal mechanism. The criticised asymmetry of power is usually related to the fact that cases have overwhelmingly been brought by companies from the Global North against Global South countries. For instance, the US and Canada have initiated over 600 cases, but they have been the target of only 109 claims.[19] The great four European former imperial countries—France, Germany, the Netherlands, and the UK—have initiated together nearly 300 cases; yet, they have been the subject of only five. This system is unusual in international law, which more commonly governs the relationship between states rather than individuals and states and has been found to create "justice bubbles for the privileged."[20] Investment arbitration is asymmetrical in the sense that foreign investors have strong and enforceable rights but few obligations.[21] This is usually discussed as profiling and the double hat dilemma (conflicts of interests and institutional bias)[22]:

> Highly paid corporate lawyers would go back and forth between representing corporations one day and sitting in judgement the next...arbitration is dominated by a few ageing

[17] Sachs and Johnson (2020).

[18] Weghmann and Hall (2021).

[19] Jacobs (2015)

[20] Yilmaz Vastardis (2018).

[21] Arcuri (2019).

[22] Matveev (2015)

> men, …the usual suspects are 'pale, male, and stale'… an invisible college, a mafia, a cartel…just twelve arbitrators have sat on a majority of ICSID tribunals.[23]

Moreover, another major critique refers to the mechanism as weakening the state's capacity to protect the public interest while the investment activities were directly affecting or violating human rights, creating a parallel and preferential legal system which protects new property rights at a cost to the broader public interest. This is usually discussed as the problem of "regulatory chills": the ISDS mechanism, its mere existence which makes states fear being sued, leads to states refraining from even adopting "risky" regulations, such as socio-environmental or public health regulation. While studies of such "cause-effect" possibility are scarce, there is a sense that in terms of environmental policies, states vary in their response to the potential of being sued, depending on their bureaucratic capacity.[24] However, the irony of this international mechanism is, for Kim (2017), that

> democracies are at greater risk of becoming involved in an investment arbitration case than are autocracies. More responsive to popular demands for public policies, democratic governments are often under greater pressure to enact regulatory and policy measures designed to safeguard public health, enhance public safety, promote social welfare, and protect the environment despite their anticipated adverse effects on the interests of foreign investors.[25]

This tension between state responsiveness to democratic input and obligations to foreign investors has formed part of the motivation for European states to withdraw from the Energy Charter Treaty.[26] Cecilia Malmstrom, former European Commissioner for Trade, expressed concern that "the traditional ISDS system … is not fit for purpose in the 21st century…. I want to ensure fair treatment for EU investors abroad, but not at the expense of governments' right to regulate."[27]

Last but not least, individuals and communities affected by investment projects are essentially invisible to international investment law,[28] and concerns about human rights, the environment and other public policy issues tend to be considered irrelevant to the determination of the dispute raised by the investor.[29] This is despite the fact that many investment disputes involve public policy issues and can cause states to alter their approach to making decisions in the public interest due to the threat of arbitration.[30] Investment arbitration awards are often calculated with reference to the imagined lost future profits of the investor, and awards have been handed down in the billions of dollars.[31] Critics such as Jacobs have raised concerns that

---

[23] Jacobs (2015), p. 18, 33.

[24] Berge and Berger (2021).

[25] Kim (2017), p. 301

[26] See generally Verbeek (2023).

[27] Apud. Weghmann and Hall (2021), p. 490.

[28] Perrone (2019)

[29] Triefus (2023).

[30] Tienhaara et al. (2022), Kim (2017).

[31] Bonnitcha and Brewin (2020), Marzal (2021).

> non-democratically-elected individuals decide matters that implicate a sovereign's right to pursue legitimate public policy objectives, such as the restructuring of a society's socio-economy, the provision of essential public services, or the maintenance of the very fabric of public order.[32]

As we will illustrate below, our argument is that this form of arbitration (ISDS) is a form of prospective environmental injustice. As Velicu argued elsewhere,[33] even if actual harm (say, of a mine) has not materialised, numerous places around the world have been placed in a climate of potential (future) harm as well as slow, ongoing injustice. Forever haunted by other possible "development" projects, these places often become uninhabitable or insecure, while from the perspective of markets, the process of "almost doing" a mine established a proper climate for other future investments and profits. This is often described as a socially engineered form of extraction or pacification that precedes the actual mineral extraction: the many faces of environmental injustice beyond pollution may be seen as insidious forms of toxicity, a repertoire of coercive tactics typically employed by state/corporate officials which consists of threats, blackmail, harassment, intimidation, deceit, humiliation, or even physical/verbal violence or restriction of basic rights.[34]

These tactics lead to losses such as a sense of belonging, wellbeing, dignity and self-esteem, or agency which are experienced by individuals as shocks, chronic stress, anger, depression or even suicidal ideation.[35] ISDS is, therefore, a continuation of the same extractive violence with other means, a form of harm that may be "legal" and morally just from the investors´ point of view but certainly toxic and damaging for societies and local communities. As our case will illustrate, what RMGC has created in relation to the Roşia Montană community falls outside typical conceptions of human rights abuse or criminal action—with psychological warfare, lawfare, war of attrition, forcing "consent" through outlasting the opposition being seen as "soft" techniques of violence. Such actions are too insidious to be caught by legalistic notions of abuse but nevertheless incredibly damaging in the long term.

3 The Roşia Montană Movement: Forms of TransNational Engagement and Coalitions

The story of the Roşia Montană project starts in the late 1990s, soon after Romania's transition from communism, when the Toronto-based company Gabriel Resources formed a joint venture with Romanian state-owned enterprise Minvest for the purpose of conducting mining activities in the area of Roşia Montană. The joint venture, named Roşia Montană Gold Corporation (RMGC), is owned 80.69% by

---

[32] Jacobs (2015), p. 25

[33] Velicu (2020).

[34] Arce and Nieto-Matiz (2024), Verweijen and Dunlap (2021), Velicu (2020).

[35] Scheidel et al. (2020).

Gabriel Resources and 19.31% by Minvest. In 1999, RMGC was granted an exploitation licence for the Roşia Montană Project. RMGC planned to use cyanide to process the gold, with the waste produced to be stored in a large tailings facility that would have flooded the Corna Valley with toxic sludge.[36] Several further steps were required under Romanian law to develop the mine, including an urban plan, urban certificate, environmental permit via an environmental impact assessment procedure, archaeological discharge certificates, and the surface rights to the project area.[37]

Most activism in Roşia has been focused on how to counteract the corporate abuse of power, from showing the illegality of the urban permits, revealing the company's capture of nationwide media to counteracting the everyday intimidation that functioned as psychological harassment. The movement succeeded in gathering a critical mass of people and entities transnationally to nurture one of the largest civic movements of post-1989 Romania. The project and the company's approach to executing it divided the local community of Roşia Montană as well as the general population of Romania. People were concerned about the environmental impact of the project, including the use of cyanide, the displacement of the local community, and the destruction of cultural heritage. While many people living in the project area sold their land to the company, many refused to do so and actively resisted the project through public protest and legal action challenging the validity of the plans, permits, and certificates obtained by RMGC. In the following sections, we will briefly introduce the various dimensions of the movements, from the local grassroots to the transnational and from the protests to the juridical forms of activism.

3.1 A Grassroots Movement with Global Partners

On 8 September 2000, a group of local residents and landowners established the association Alburnus Maior, an NGO representing the interests of over 350 families who wanted to stay in Roşia Montană and resisted the mining project.[38] RMGC had started holding meetings in Roşia Montană to promote the project and convince landowners to sell their land to make way for it. Roşia Montană had been a mining region for thousands of years, and many local community members had a great deal of experience with mining passed down through generations. They could, therefore, listen to the plans for the project with a critical ear and decided that they did not trust the company's discourse and offers (for example, what seemed like an obviously

[36] Roşia Montană Gold Corporation (n.d.) 'Report on Environmental Impact Assessment Study: Waste Management Plan', https://web.archive.org/web/20230205071534/https://en.rmgc.ro/Content/uploads/waste-plan.pdf, p. 22.

[37] Gabriel Resources Ltd. and Gabriel Resources (Jersey) v. Romania, ICSID Case No. ARB/15/31; Respondent's Counter-Memorial (2015).

[38] Mining Watch (2006).

exaggerated number of promised jobs).[39] The association was, therefore, set up to coordinate an organised opposition to the mine project. The leaders of Alburnus Maior had little experience organising such an association and so began seeking advice and assistance from other Romanian NGOs such as Terra Mileniul III (which develops awareness programs on sustainable development) and the Mihai Eminescu Trust (dedicated to preserving local cultural heritage).[40] In 2002, French journalist and environmental activist Stephanie Roth heard about the local resistance to the mine through this network of NGOs and began assisting Alburnus Maior to coordinate and escalate the anti-mining campaign, receiving the Goldman Prize in 2005 for her efforts.[41] Together with Alburnus Maior, Roth "mobilised local residents and created a coalition of national non-governmental organisations, archaeological specialists, academics, and clergy to fight the mining proposal."[42]

Alburnus Maior partnered with other Romanian and international NGOs, coming together in a campaign under the slogan of *Salvați Roșia Montană* (Save Roşia Montană). This campaign undertook a variety of activities aimed at stopping the mine project, including legal action, commissioning and disseminating independent research on the harms of the project,[43] protests, petitions, an annual Hay Fest in Roşia, engagement in the media, social media campaigns, documentaries/films, flash mobs, art shows and other types of activism. Alburnus Maior notes on its website that "numerous organisations, institutions, artists, journalists, as well as members of civil society of all ages and from all social strata in Romania and abroad have joined in solidarity."[44] NGOs that were particularly active in their support of *Salvați Roșia Montană* included TERRA Mileniul III, Greenpeace Romania, Mining Watch Romania, Declic, Eco Ruralis, CEE Bankwatch Network, Legal Resources Centre, Roşia Montană Cultural Foundation, and the Independent Center for the Development of Environmental Resources (ICDER). The fight of Alburnus Maior against the gold mine captured the hearts and minds of Romanian society across sectors and regions, and they note that:

> More than ten years of activism have transformed the initiative of the locals from the Apuseni mountains into the largest mobilisation of civil society in Romania. The Save Roşia Montană campaign brings together non-governmental organisations, international

---

[39] Interview by Stephanie Triefus with anonymous resident of Roşia Montană, 13 May 2022, Roşia Montană.

[40] Interview by Stephanie Triefus with anonymous resident of Roşia Montană, 13 May 2022, Roşia Montană.

[41] 2005 Goldman Prize Winner Stephanie Roth: https://www.goldmanprize.org/recipient/stephanie-roth/ (accessed 11 April 2024).

[42] Ibid.

[43] See: Alburnus Maior (2006), Independent Expert Evaluation of the Environmental Impact Assessment Report for the Roşia Montană Mine Proposal: https://issuu.com/stephaniedanielleroth/docs/an_independent_expert_evaluation_of (last accessed 10 February 2024).

[44] See: Salvati Roşia Montană (2024) 'History of the Save Roşia Montană campaign: https://web.archive.org/web/20140111180747/http://Roşiamontana.org/ro/istoricul-campaniei-salvati-Roşia-montana (last accessed 8 April 2024).

heritage protection bodies, academic and scientific institutions, representatives of religious organisations but also ordinary citizens who support the cause of Alburnus Maior.[45]

Alburnus Maior and its NGO partners had already been fighting the mine project for 20 years before support for their efforts suddenly skyrocketed. In June 2013, the Romanian government sought to support the project by submitting the 'Roşia Montană Law' to parliament. This law was specific to the Roşia Montană Project and would have enabled the expropriation of the remaining landowners who did not wish to sell, as well as other legal measures enabling the project to go ahead. However, following the lead of the *Salvați Roşia Montană* campaign, thousands of Romanians took to the streets to protest the law over several months, in what became known as the "Romanian Autumn."[46] Over a period of 4 months, the protests attracted up to 200,000 people across 50 cities in Romania and 30 cities in other countries, particularly Canada.[47] These demonstrations were the largest since the fall of communism in 1989 and "opened the gateway to an overhaul of the relationship between the government and the population: people reclaimed their power and understood that they held influence over political decisions and could call for accountability and transparency about decisions taken against the country's best interests."[48] In June 2014, following a public debate and a Joint Committee Report, the Parliament rejected the law.[49] Following this, RMGC could have continued trying to secure the necessary permits, but it instead commenced arbitration against Romania claiming over US$5 billion in compensation.[50]

3.2 Transnational Activism

The campaign against the Roşia Montană gold project took on a transnational character through engagement with the EU, the international partners of local NGOs, widespread dissemination on social media and active participation of the Romanian diaspora. Romania joined the EU in 2007, and in the years leading up to accession, there was significant pressure on the government to implement EU standards nationally. Alburnus Maior engaged with EU bodies from early on in its resistance to the

[45] See: Salvati Roşia Montană (2024) Salvati Roşia Montană, 'About Alburnus Maior' (machine translated): (machine translated) https://web.archive.org/web/20160526004855/http://www.Roşiamontana.org/node/1899 (Accessed 11 April 2024).

[46] Margarit (2016).

[47] Besliu (2021).

[48] Ibid.

[49] Gabriel Resources Ltd. and Gabriel Resources (Jersey) v. Romania, ICSID Case No. ARB/15/31, Respondent's Counter-Memorial (2018), paras 334, 357–363.

[50] Ibid, para 369.

mine project, and a coalition of NGOs petitioned the EU Parliament contesting the project's Environmental Impact Assessment.[51]

When the *Salvați Roșia Montană* campaign escalated in response to the 2013 law, Romanian communities in most major cities in Romania and abroad began protesting as well as undertaking other forms of protest, including flash-mobs, street painting, exhibits, and informational campaigns.[52] This activism was particularly prevalent in Toronto, Canada, where there is a large concentration of Romanian-Canadians and where Gabriel Resources is listed on the Toronto Stock Exchange.[53] Social media formed an important gathering place for transnational discussion and dissemination of information, and various Facebook groups and pages amassed more than 100,000 followers.[54] The development of social media in the early 2000s was particularly helpful to the campaign in light of RMGC's strategic capture of Romanian media outlets via large advertising contracts that precluded reporting on the opposition to the mine.[55]

Due to the immensely valuable Roman cultural heritage found in Roșia Montană that dates back to 104 AD, a significant part of the *Salvați Roșia Montană* campaign called for Roșia Montană's inscription as a UNESCO World Heritage site.[56] Although the 'Roșia Montană Law' had been voted down, the threat that this decision would be reversed or reappear in a new form remained, particularly in light of the arbitration outlined below. After a number of years of political back and forth, with successive governments supporting then ignoring petitions to submit Roșia Montană to UNESCO, the application was finally submitted in 2017.[57] However, the application was withdrawn by a subsequent government in 2018.[58] The application was then reanimated in 2020 and finally listed as UNESCO world heritage site in 2021.[59]

---

[51] European Parliament (2007).

[52] Bejan et al. (2015), p. 200.

[53] Ibid, p. 201.

[54] See for instance "Roșia Montană in UNESCO World Heritage" [Facebook] Available at: https://www.facebook.com/Roșia.montana.in.unesco and 'Save Roșia Montană' [Facebook] https://www.facebook.com/groups/saveRoșiamontana (accessed 11 April 2024).

[55] Goțiu (2013).

[56] "Roșia Montană in UNESCO".

[57] Predoiu and WNV (2017).

[58] Ciobanu and Stoica (2019).

[59] See: UNESCO, Roșia Montană Mining Landscape: https://whc.unesco.org/en/list/1552/ (accessed 11 April 2024).

3.3 Juridical Activism

A major part of Alburnus Maior and its NGO partners' advocacy strategy was to mount legal challenges at every stage of the project.[60] The scale of this judicial activism was massive, with at least 83 court and administrative petitions brought against the project between 2004 and 2016.[61] These efforts succeeded in substantially delaying the project, as the Environmental Impact Assessment (EIA) process was suspended while there was pending litigation brought by Alburnus Maior concerning the required urban plans and certificates. Alburnus Maior initiated legal proceedings against the Ministry of Culture's decision to grant an archaeological discharge certificate (ADC) to RMGC, which would remove national heritage protection from the Cârnic mountain, an area with the highest gold reserves in the planned exploitation.[62] The Braşov Court of Appeal found irregularities in how the ADC was issued and consequently annulled it,[63] as did the Ploieşti Court of Appeal for the ADC that RMGC had sought to resubmit.[64] Alburnus Maior also challenged the approval of the General Urban Plan (PUG) and the Zonal Urban Plan (PUZ) that declared Roşia Montană a mono-industrial zone and precluded the development of non-mining activities and businesses. The Alba County Court (where Roşia Montană is situated) voided the approval of the plans on the basis that voting local councillors had a conflict of interest.[65] Various Urban Certificates, a necessary basis to apply for construction permits and carry out the environmental permitting procedure, were annulled due to challenges by ICDER.[66] Thefore, the Ministry of Environment decided that it could not continue the environmental impact evaluation procedure while there was no valid Urban Certificate and the project lacked other necessary documentation, such as the endorsement of the Ministry of Culture, approved amended PUZ and while litigation was pending in relation to the ADC and urban plans.[67]

RMGC also tried, unsuccessfully, to use legal proceedings to harass and intimidate opponents of the mine, including filing a complaint against the architects who publicly denounced the company's distorted use of their report, suing a journalist

[60] Mining Watch (2006).

[61] For a list of these proceedings (with many entries censored), see Gabriel Resources Ltd. and Gabriel Resources (Jersey) v. Romania, ICSID Case No. ARB/15/31, Respondent's Memorial, Annex IV.

[62] Gabriel Resources Ltd. and Gabriel Resources (Jersey) v. Romania, ICSID Case No. ARB/15/31, Amicus Curiae Submission (2 November 2018), p. 12.

[63] Braşov Court of Appeal, Sentence No. 157/F/CA (26 November 2007).

[64] Ploieşti Court of Appeal, Decision No. 187 (16 February 2022).

[65] Alba County Court, File No. 1411/107/2007, Judgment 842/CA/2007; Alba Court of Appeal, Judgment 4537/117/2009; *Gabriel Resources v Romania*, Amicus Curiae Submission (2 November 2018), p. 11.

[66] Timişoara Court of Appeal (12 March 2009).

[67] Gabriel Resources Ltd. and Gabriel Resources (Jersey) v. Romania, ICSID Case No. ARB/15/31, Respondent's Counter-Memorial (2018), para 605.

who actively supported the opposition to the project, and challenging the use of the RoşiaMontană.org domain name.[68]

3.4 *The International Arbitration Phase*

In July 2015, Gabriel Resources commenced arbitration, claiming over US$5 billion compensation from Romania for breach of the bilateral investment treaties (BITs) between Romania and the UK and Canada. This case threatened to turn the success of the *Salvaţi Roşia Montană* campaign into a pyrrhic victory by putting enormous pressure on the government to reinstate the mine project. The arbitration, therefore, became another important site of engagement for Alburnus Maior and its NGO partners in their mission to stop the Roşia Montană project. In the arbitration, Gabriel Resources claimed that Romania effectively expropriated its investment and "blocked and prevented implementation of the Project without due process and without compensation, effectively depriving Gabriel entirely of the value of its investments."[69] They contended that the government's actions were politically motivated, and "influenced by anti-project NGOs or others who for political reasons sought to prevent or delay the project."[70] Romania argued, on the other hand, that the project never met the necessary environmental and cultural heritage requirements under Romanian law. They emphasised that the company failed to obtain the social licence to operate, i.e. the community's acceptance and support of the project, as evidenced by the ongoing legal challenges, public protests, and refusal of residents to sell their properties.[71]

The threat of having to pay such enormous amounts of compensation can significantly influence government decision making. As we discussed in the previous section, this is "regulatory chill", where the prospect of being sued or losing an investment arbitration case causes a state to delay or change its orientation on an issue of public interest, such as environmental regulation or the permitting of a project.[72] Proceedings often turn on a technical and technocratic account of the dispute where there is little space or emphasis on the voices of those affected by such projects.[73] Investment arbitration, unlike domestic court proceedings, takes place outside of the respondent state and under relatively secretive circumstances that

[68] Gabriel Resources Ltd. and Gabriel Resources (Jersey) v. Romania, ICSID Case No. ARB/15/31, Amicus Curiae Submission (2 November 2018), p. 6.

[69] Gabriel Resources Ltd. and Gabriel Resources (Jersey) v. Romania, ICSID Case No. ARB/15/31, Request for Arbitration (2015), para 7.

[70] Gabriel Resources Ltd. and Gabriel Resources (Jersey) v. Romania, ICSID Case No. ARB/15/31, Claimant's Memorial (2017), para 167.

[71] Gabriel Resources Ltd. and Gabriel Resources (Jersey) v. Romania, ICSID Case No. ARB/15/31, Respondent's Counter-Memorial (2018).

[72] Tienhaara (2018).

[73] Perrone (2019).

limit public engagement. The *Gabriel Resources v. Romania* tribunal proceedings were publicly broadcast, but only in an overflow room in Washington with a one-hour delay; much of the hearings were held to be confidential and, therefore, censored from the broadcast. Transcripts from the hearing and other documents are available online but also heavily censored.

Alburnus Maior considered engagement with the arbitration to be a continuation of its fight against the gold mine and intervened in the proceedings as an amicus curia.[74] Together with ICDER and Greenpeace Romania and supported by the European Center for Constitutional and Human Rights (ECCHR),[75] Alburnus Maior made an amicus curiae submission, drawing on testimonies of Roşia Montană residents. The testimonies shed light on the impact of the project on the local community, how they were precluded from developing businesses, the campaign of intimidation and harassment perpetrated by RMGC, false promises made by the company to employ those who sold their land, and various pressure and manipulation tactics used by the company to convince people to sell.[76] However, these testimonies were rejected by the tribunal on the basis that they were hearsay, and the witnesses could not be cross-examined, meaning that these voices were excluded from proceedings.[77] As we will discuss in the next section, one member of Alburnus Maior, Mr. Sorin Jurca, was invited by Romania to give evidence at the hearing in Washington. While Mr. Jurca was initially reluctant to "help" the Romanian state's defence, over time he realised that he was not there to "defend" the state but to "tell the truth."[78]

Although the arbitration proceedings continued for 8 years, the NGO network remained engaged throughout the process. In September 2022, ICDER and Greenpeace Romania made a second Amicus Curiae submission communicating to the Tribunal the decision of the Ploieşti Court of Appeal, which had cancelled the last ADC for the mining project in the Cârnic Massif in February 2022.[79] This decision, made after an appeal, confirmed that the mining certificate was issued illegally and, thus, construction work could not have been done in the area. However, neither the Romanian state nor Gabriel Resources informed the Tribunal of this decision. Such information would not have been brought to the Tribunal's attention were it not for the continued advocacy of this coalition of interested NGOs acting in the interest of the local community. Therefore, the organisations were making those

[74] Amicus curiae, or 'friend of the court', refers to a procedure where people or organisations can intervene in an arbitration case where they are not a party to the dispute. The parties to the dispute and the tribunal must approve this intervention.

[75] For ECCHR's engagement with corporate accountability, see also Thomas Becker's chapter in this book.

[76] Gabriel Resources Ltd. and Gabriel Resources (Jersey) v. Romania, ICSID Case No. ARB/15/31, Amicus Curiae Submission (2 November 2018).

[77] Gabriel Resources Ltd. and Gabriel Resources (Jersey) v. Romania, ICSID Case No. ARB/15/31, Procedural Order 19 (2018).

[78] Interview by Stephanie Triefus with Sorin Jurca, Roşia Montană, 12 May 2022.

[79] Mining Watch (2006).

efforts to demand not only the international actors but also the Romanian state to take responsibility with regard to an important decision at the national level, which could be instrumental to the outcome of the arbitration. Such a dimension of procedural injustice fits what we discussed here as PEJ, which we illustrate in the next section.

In March 2024, the Tribunal handed down its decision, finding that Romania had not breached the BITs and that Gabriel Resources should pay half of Romania's legal costs and all of the costs of the Tribunal.[80] This decision was surprising given that the Romanian media had been reporting on statements from Romanian Prime Minister Marcel Ciolacu that Romania had lost the case and would have to pay over US$2 billion to Gabriel Resources.[81] During this time of speculation before the release of the decision, Gabriel Resources' share price doubled, leading to a complaint of corruption being brought against the Prime Minister to the Romanian National Anticorruption Directorate.[82] The rumour that Romania would have to pay US$2 billion raised concerns in political and public fora and led to discussions of restarting the Roşia Montană project.[83] Prime Minister Ciolacu stated that he wanted to organise a referendum to ask Romanians whether they agree with gold mining in Roşia Montană.[84] Marcel Bolos, the Minister of Finance, stated that "there is also the option not to pay anything, but to carry out the exploitation".[85] While this was not legally accurate, it demonstrates the immense pressure that the investment arbitration process put on the Romanian state. The threat of compensation not only presents a genuine concern for governments regarding how they will afford to pay the potential award but also places a tool in the hands of those who would wish to undermine the success of the civil society movement against the mine for their own personal and political gain. The fact that Romania won the case does not mean the arbitration was not harmful. For the 9 years of the arbitration and beyond, as issues of land ownership and land use regulation are sorted out, the community remains in limbo as to the future of Roşia Montană and possibilities for generating livelihood outside of mining. Regarding the impact on the state, respondent states typically spend more in legal costs than they can recover, and Gabriel Resources has reported that it may not be able to pay Romania over US$10 million in legal and arbitration

[80] See: Ministry of Finance (8 March 2024) Romania wins the Roşia Montană case' (machine translated): https://perma.cc/Z58L-JDZ5 (accessed 29 March 2024).

[81] Duţulescu (2024).

[82] See: Digi24.ro (14 March 2024a): https://www.digi24.ro/stiri/actualitate/politica/aur-a-facut-plangere-penala-la-dna-impotriva-lui-ciolacu-bolos-si-ciuca-in-cazul-Roşia-montana-2723103 (accessed 29 March 2024) and Economica.net (11 March 2024): https://www.economica.net/drula-a-depus-plangere-penala-la-dna-impotriva-lui-ciolacu-pentru-manipularea-pietei-abuz-in-serviciu-deturnare-de-fonduri-si-inselaciune-in-cazul-Roşia-montana_731054.html (accessed 11 April 2024)

[83] Digi24.ro (7 March 2024b): https://www.digi24.ro/stiri/actualitate/politica/ciolacu-vrea-referendum-pe-Roşia-montana-sa-vedem-daca-romanii-sunt-de-acord-sa-incepem-exploatarea-aurului-2715051 (accessed 29 March 2024).

[84] Ibid.

[85] Ibid.

costs as the Tribunal ordered.[86] Once it was announced that Gabriel Resources had lost the case, the company lost over US$900 million in share value in a single day.[87] Gabriel Resources is seeking annulment of the decision,[88] prolonging the dispute further.

4 Discussing Investment Arbitration as Prospective Environmental Injustice in Roşia

The prospects of open-cast gold-mining shed light on deep-seated socio-environmental conflicts in Roşia and overall in Romania: more than a decade of waiting for the "actual harm" to happen, rural communities have faced multiple forms of prospective injustices: land-grabbing, slow community disappearance and marginalisation, daily psychological/emotional damage, precarity and disposable futures, disqualification as political subjects, and disavowal of alternatives.[89]As we will illustrate below, these dimensions originate in the early stages of extractive exploration, even before a mine has been dug, insidiously preparing the social groundwork for entrenching abusive relations of control and manipulation. Prospective environmental injustice thus refers to such situations in which development proposals and the actions of state and market actors create injustices even before the projects become a material reality, in phases of mineral explorations and drillings. In this section, we will show how ISDS itself may be seen as a continuation of such prospective injustice: overall, the arbitration case negatively impacts democratic processes, excludes participation of interested parties, and shifts environmental risks and impacts from the powerful to the powerless.[90]

Firstly, by not discussing such long-term harms, investment arbitration validates land-grabbing and slow community disappearance: it is privileging private corporate interests and narratives over those of affected communities. Numerous testimonies of locals illustrate that the techniques used by RMGC in the last two decades have contributed to the internal conflicts and division within the community to obtain surface rights. Company employees harassed and threatened community members who resisted the mine, and the company made it clear that employees who did not show up to meetings to support the project would be fired. Members of the community remember RMGC employees continually pressuring them to sell their land to make way for the project, including coming around to make land valuations without consent. However, the company's behaviour is barely questioned in the

---

86 Nicut (2024); Digital Journal (4 April 2024) https://www.digitaljournal.com/pr/news/access-wire/gabriel-resources-ltd-corporate-update-1721982821.html (accessed 11 April 2024).

87 Friedman (2024).

88 Access Wire (8 July 2024).

89 Velicu 2020.

90 Sachs et al. (2020), para 31.

arbitration, except with reference to its failure to obtain a social licence to operate. The mere existence of such an international arbitration mechanism, allowing corporations to sue states despite the obvious harm produced by the former onto the citizens of the latter, seems to produce oblivion about what constitutes a crime.

> They divided the people enormously... The company had this practice of buying only one brother's share of the property, even though the other brothers had given up their share legally, by notary. So the company came and gave them money to divide them and they divided the families in Roşia Montană, they destroyed a community of people.[91]

> They were sending negotiators to our houses, and they were measuring our yard, houses, and the land book, and we didn't want them to measure, we didn't want to. We told them that we didn't want to, to leave us alone. They counted the trees without asking permission, and we told them that we are not leaving our lands.[92]

Romania merely claims that the company had an obligation to obtain the social licence to operate in relation to the project and failed to do so, for example, because of "grievance and criticism in connection with its relocation efforts".[93] In some cases, there has been corruption and illegal behaviour, such as harassment, and non-compliance with Romanian law in relation to heritage, exhumation of graves etc. RMGC's advertisements were banned from Romanian media in 2013 since they "stimulate a conduit that might damage the population's health or safety".[94] However, in its memorial to the tribunal, Romania does not make any reference to such illegal or "lawful but awful" conduct of the company. It is unknown whether the witness from Roşia Montană was able to speak of this in his witness testimony since it is confidential.

Moreover, the daily psychological and emotional damage wrought by the company continues to affect the community and relationships within, and the physical environment of the community remains difficult, with (heritage) houses falling down around the village and the company's logo at every corner. Heritage and other buildings were destroyed, often without warning, leaving the remaining residents with the feeling that they lived in a war zone, which made many locals refer to the entire situation as a "psychological war". To those who remained, it seemed that this was a deliberate strategy of the company to make the population feel that there was nothing left for them to live with in Roşia Montană. This may be seen as a form of invisible toxicity that degrades everyday life, makes life unliveable, living every day with fear of (home) loss, anger, uncertainty, and generational conflicts:

> It had a devastating impact on the locals... They removed the dead out of the cemeteries without complying with the law...that was part of their plan, that they are already moving to another phase and the cemeteries have no future here. Meaning that the future is in their

[91] Interview by Stephanie Triefus, with anonymous resident of Roşia Montană, Roşia Montană, 13 May 2022.

[92] Interview by Stephanie Triefus with anonymous resident of Roşia Montană, Roşia Montană, 19 May 2022.

[93] Gabriel Resources Ltd. and Gabriel Resources (Jersey) v. Romania, ICSID Case No. ARB/15/31, Respondent's Counter-Memorial (2015), para 102.

[94] Andronache (2013).

> mining…all this contributed to the depopulation of Roşia Montană, to the lack of perspective, to the lack of alternatives.[95]

While the arbitration was ongoing, few alternatives were available to the community to move forward as the company continued to buy and own more and more land and the zoning laws remained tangled up with changes that were made to suit the company. Part of the intimidation tactics has been the continuous discourse about the backwardness of the current lifestyle and livelihood of rural area residents, which further damaged their self-esteem and dignity as humans and political-economic agents. The residents were constantly shamed and ridiculed as primitive, nostalgic communists, with their subsistence economies being constantly devalued. Intangible losses (of self-esteem, peace, health, predictability) have been ignored despite obviously producing enormous harm and grief among the population and led to tangible losses in terms of property, homes, and land.[96] By rendering their everyday lives disposable and unworthy of persistence, the company has already damaged their potential futures in the present. Instead, being a "miner" has been pushed as the main worthy identity, truly a non-choice, despite the uncertainty of such a job in the context of open-cast mining, or the cheap nature of the job and the disavowal of alternatives, making small-scale farming an impossibility and assuming the future is necessarily industrial, urban, or SMART-entrepreneurial. RMGC owns around 80% of the property in Roşia Montană, and many of these (heritage) buildings are falling down. The question of what will happen to this property hangs over those who live there:

> I don't know if [the company] would be interested in keeping them because… or maybe it could also be a punishment for those who are here, to remain poor, to leave them like that. The company is not really interested in the houses.[97]

The international arbitration further disqualified the residents as political subjects, excluding them from taking part in the arbitration and discounting their stories as irrelevant or biased. In that sense, the legal international mechanism of ISDS is part of the global type of consensual politics, denying the political agency and equality of people who could or should produce the society they want to live in. As we mentioned in the previous section, the testimony of Mr. Jurca has been censored in hearing transcripts and is therefore not public. However, he explained in an interview that he agreed to give evidence as:

> a culmination, so to speak, of the hard work I've done, everything that was, everything that I put my soul into, saving Roşia Montană, and I said to myself it was worth it for my voice to also be heard. […] Slowly I became convinced that I was not defending the position of the Romanian State but the position of the locals in Roşia Montană. Because what the Romanian state did was very difficult to cover up. And I was to appear before the court not to cover up lies but to tell the truth.[98]

---

[95] Interview by Stephanie Triefus with Sorin Jurca, Roşia Montană, 12 May 2022.

[96] Tschakert et al. (2019).

[97] Interview by Stephanie Triefus with Sorin Jurca, Roşia Montană, 12 May 2022.

[98] Ibid.

The arbitration was ongoing for 9 years, leaving the Roşia Montană commune in limbo. Neither RMGC nor any Romanian government representatives have been held accountable for their harmful impacts on the community. The Arbitration case further undermines environmental justice in multiple ways, in a blunt disrespect for any "equity and distribution, individual and cultural recognition, political participation, and community functioning".[99] The area remains zoned for mining, making it difficult for the local community to start businesses and generate an economy that does not rely on mining. This means that precious time has been lost in the quest to demonstrate to the Romanian public that Roşia Montană has a future other than mining, and restarting the project should be kept off the table. Although Roşia Montană is now listed as a UNESCO World Heritage site, such a listing is vulnerable to political whims. The listing can be undone if it becomes politically expedient, as demonstrated by the discourse surrounding the outcome of the arbitration.

While interview participants in Roşia Montană describe a sense of justice since the arbitral decision came out in favour of Romania, they continue to feel sceptical and rather reserved about the possibilities of Roşia Montană being a peaceful place to live in the future. They expect Gabriel Resources and other mining companies to "come and go" for profits while they continue to struggle to find ways to make a living, "as it has always been".[100] Most respondents lament the re-election of the same mayor who is only further blocking the development plans for the region from any initiative to improve the quality of life for the locals, from roads, access to potable water for marginalised Roma community to other services necessary to plan sustainable tourism. While some welcome the idea of tourism in the region, others believe that the mining nature of the locality will haunt the place forever. There is a feeling that "when They will want, They will mine", pointing to foreign forces outside the country that have sway over the "weak" Romanian state.[101] Although the mountains scarred from past mining are now starting to regenerate, the local community remain haunted by extraction: they have seen and heard too much through different power regimes to believe that the treasures lying beneath will be left buried.

5 Conclusion

> I am not exotic I am exhausted.[102]

As most literature on environmental justice indicates, the social disarticulation resulting from resource conflicts is associated with distress which reactivates past

---

[99] Schlosberg (2007), p. 52.

[100] Interview by Irina Velicu with anonymous resident of Roşia Montană, Roşia Montană, 23 July 2024.

[101] Ibid.

[102] Perjovschi (2000).

historical intergenerational traumas of wars, dictatorships, or colonisation.[103] While political participation and collective capabilities have often been proposed as complementary environmental justice mechanisms, the ISDS mechanism, composition and procedure is yet another example of how little meaningful change occurs within the patterns that perpetuate disparities.[104] More research has to address the political and economic patterns of control and access to resources and the many forms of harms which cannot even be codified in law for they pervade everyday lives.[105] This chapter is calling attention to "insidious" toxicity as normalised forms of extractive violence in "sacrificial zones", often discussed as "environmental blackmailing",[106] slow/structural/epistemic, hidden in plain sight violence[107] resulting in social/cultural and community disarticulation/annihilation associated with "environmentalism of the poor".[108] Systematic (and traumatic) disruption of the cultural, socio-ecological, and economic bases of the social order emerges as a dimension of environmental injustice in the lives of vulnerable communities facing mining because extractive violence as a social technique to gain consent for mining is harming communities both materially and emotionally since early stages of prospective mining.[109] Entire populations are becoming exposed to "slow violence", dispossessed, displaced, and invisibilised as the growing "glocal" class of "three-nothings: no land, no job, no social security".[110] In other words, the disproportionate harm is not just in the distribution or in failure of recognition, but in the exact production of some people as disposable and places as dispensable, a "surplus" in the ongoing process of exclusion, marginalisation, abandonment and acclimatisation to anxiety and insecure futures.[111]

As our case showed, even though the Romanian state has won in this particular case, investment arbitration outcomes are generally difficult to predict as they are not bound by precedent and outcomes can vary widely. The mere existence of such an international arbitration mechanism may put in danger the possibility of some states to protect their own citizens. Proponents of ISDS consider that investment arbitration and the awards handed down by tribunals do not impact the communities affected by investment projects. However, compensation awards in investment arbitration cases can be extremely high, and a number of tribunals have awarded compensation in the billions of dollars. For instance, Gabriel Resources was claiming over US$5 billion, which amounts to approximately 1.4% of Romania's GDP.[112]

[103] Brulle and Nordgaard (2019).

[104] Pellow (2016).

[105] Pichler et al. (2016).

[106] Bullard (1993).

[107] Davies (2022), Nixon (2011).

[108] Freudenburg (1997), Martinez-Alier (2014).

[109] Velicu (2020), Dunlap (2019).

[110] Li (2010), Nixon (2011).

[111] Velicu 2020, Brulle and Nordgaard (2019).

[112] World Bank (n.d.).

Such an award would have added enormous pressure in circumstances where Romania already struggles to support rural areas in terms of health, social security, or education. If Romania had lost the case, there was also an overwhelming feeling that the Salvați Roșia Montană campaigners would be to blame, adding to the overall climate of harassment which has damaged the lives of residents in the last decades. These pressures come on top of years of attempts to impose mining as inevitable. Challenges to such a future were not even considered valid concerns during the arbitration: nerve-racking controversies on costs and benefits have torn families and communities apart. These occurrences become normalised traumatic experiences and result in a loss of sense of belonging, dignity, wellbeing, or agency. These losses are often experienced as shock, chronic stress, or depression. Prolonged for decades, they present a future challenge for public mental health, becoming intergenerational traumas which haunt collectives and fuel extremism. Communities have thus been dispossessed of basic things they value and for which there may be no commensurable substitute, i.e., intangible values which function as ontological bases of existence, the loss of which leads to various forms of suffering.

Distressed communities have traditionally used a variety of strategies and tactics to address disproportionate exposure to contamination: lawsuits, protests, or good-neighbourhood agreements.[113] Still, this body of scholarship does not sufficiently address the limitations of formal socio-environmental impact assessments, mostly emphasising economic and demographic social data at the expense of emotional/psychological/embodied interpretations of place.[114] Only recently in 2013, as a result of an appeal of the Environmental Defenders Office in Sydney, *solastalgia* (the depression caused by degradation/destruction of environments) was acknowledged in socio-environmental impact assessments of prospective mining.[115] To continue to criticise or even reject ISDS mechanisms would be a way to address their inherent injustice: therefore, what communities and perhaps states themselves have to keep alive is the political discursive struggle about setting of terms of the debate in the communication processes among stakeholders—the political equality of defining what constitutes 'the political' debate in the first place, or the dissensus. In this chapter, we have tried to show the enormous struggle of the Roșia Montană and Romanian society to sustain dissensus with respect to the 'normality' of mining. More societal efforts are needed to transform the way we think about the terms of the debate in which negotiations are taking place when deciding about land grabbing/mining and all the other associated extractivist economic activities which bring about enormous prospective dangers related to socio-environmental health, as described here.

113 Temper et al. (2015).

114 McManus et al. (2014).

115 Kennedy (2016), Albrecht (2007), Ellis and Albrecht (2017).

References

Access Wire (2024) Gabriel Resources Ltd. Corporate update. https://www.accesswire.com/886063/gabriel-resources-ltd-corporate-update. Accessed 15 Jul 2024

Alba County Court, File No. 1411/107/2007, Judgment 842/CA/2007

Alba Court of Appeal, Judgment 4537/117/2009

Albrecht G et al (2007) Solastalgia: the distress caused by environmental change. Australas Psychiatry 15(Suppl 1):S95–S98

Alburnus Maior (2006) Independent expert evaluation of the environmental impact assessment report for the Roşia Montană Mine Proposal. https://issuu.com/stephaniedanielleroth/docs/an_independent_expert_evaluation_of. Accessed 10 Feb 2024

Andronache CM (2013) CNA stops from broadcasting Roşia Montană's commercials. Pagina de Media. https://www.paginademedia.ro/2013/10/cna-stops-from-broadcasting-Roşia-Montanăs-commercials

Anghie A (2005) Imperialism, sovereignty and the making of international law. Cambridge University Press, Cambridge. https://doi.org/10.1017/CBO9780511614262

Arce M, Nieto-Matiz C (2024) Mining and violence in Latin America: the state's coercive responses to anti-mining resistance. World Dev 173:106404. https://doi.org/10.1016/j.worlddev.2023.106404

Arcuri A (2019) The great asymmetry and the rule of law in international investment arbitration. In: Sachs L, Johnson L, Coleman J (eds) Yearbook on international investment law and policy 2018. Oxford University Press, Oxford, pp 394–413

Bejan R et al (2015) Transnational responses to global capitalism: the case study of the Roşia Montană campaign. Trans Soc Rev 5(2):199–207

Berge TL, Berger A (2021) Do investor-state dispute settlement cases influence domestic environmental regulation? The role of respondent state bureaucratic capacity. J Int Dispute Settlement 12(1):1–41. https://doi.org/10.1093/jnlids/idaa027

Besliu B (2021) The Romanian protest wave: a path to a new political era? Green European Journal. https://www.greeneuropeanjournal.eu/the-romanian-protest-wave-a-path-to-a-new-political-era/. Accessed 11 Apr 2024

Bonnitcha J, Brewin S (2020) Compensation under investment treaties: what are the problems and what can be done? IISD. https://www.iisd.org/system/files/2020-12/compensation-investment-treaties-en.pdf

Brasov Court of Appeal, Sentence No. 157/F/CA (2007)

Brulle RJ, Norgaard KM (2019) Avoiding cultural trauma: climate change and social inertia, vol 28. Environ Polit

Broad R (2015) Corporate bias in the World Bank Group's International Centre for Settlement of investment disputes: a case study of a global mining corporation suing El Salvador. U Pa J Int'l L 36:851

Bullard RD (1993) Anatomy of environmental racism and the environmental justice movement. Confronting environmental racism. Voices from the grassroots 15:15–39

Ciobanu C, Stoica M (2019) Roşia Montană: seeds of utopia in town almost lost to gold mining. Al Jazeera. https://www.aljazeera.com/gallery/2019/4/24/Roşia-Montană-seeds-of-utopia-in-town-almost-lost-to-gold-mining. Accessed 11 Apr 2024

Cotula L (2020) Investment disputes from below: whose rights matter? Mining, Environment and Livelihoods in Colombia. IIED. https://www.iied.org/investment-disputes-below-whose-rights-matter

Digi24.ro (2024a) Ciolacu wants a referendum on Roşia Montană: let's see if the Romanians agree to start gold mining. Digi24ro. https://www.digi24.ro/stiri/actualitate/politica/ciolacu-vrea-referendum-pe-Roşia-Montană-sa-vedem-daca-romanii-sunt-de-acord-sa-incepem-exploatarea-aurului-2715051. Accessed 29 Mar 2024

Digi24.ro (2024b) AUR filed a criminal complaint with the DNA against Ciolacu, Boloş and Ciucă in the Roşia Montană case. Digi24.ro. https://www.digi24.ro/stiri/actualitate/politica/

aur-a-facut-plangere-penala-la-dna-impotriva-lui-ciolacu-bolos-si-ciuca-in-cazul-Roșia-Montană-2723103. Accessed 29 Mar 2024
Digital Journal (2024) Gabriel Resources Ltd. Corporate Update Digital Journal. https://www.digitaljournal.com/pr/news/accesswire/gabriel-resources-ltd-corporate-update-1721982821.html. Accessed 11 Apr 2024
Ellis NR, Albrecht GA (2017) Climate change threats to family farmers' sense of place and mental wellbeing: a case study from the Western Australian Wheatbelt. Soc Sci Med 175:161–168. https://doi.org/10.1016/j.socscimed.2017.01.009
Davies T (2022) Slow violence and toxic geographies: 'out of sight' to whom? Environ Plan C: Politics and Space 40(2):409–427
Dunlap A (2019) 'Agro sí, mina NO!' The Tía Maria copper mine, state terrorism and social war by every means in the Tambo Valley, Peru. Polit Geogr 71:10–25
Duțulescu A (2024) Sources: Romania loses the case with Gabriel resources for Roșia Montană. We should pay at least $2 billion Digi24ro. https://www.digi24.ro/stiri/actualitate/justitie/surse-romania-pierde-procesul-cu-gabriel-resources-pentru-Roșia-Montană-ar-trebui-sa-platim-cel-putin-2-miliarde-de-dolari-2670795. Accessed 29 Mar 2024
Economica.net (2024) Drula filed a criminal complaint with the DNA against Ciolacu for market manipulation, abuse of office, misappropriation of funds and fraud in the Roşia Montană case. Economica.net. https://www.economica.net/drula-a-depus-plangere-penala-la-dna-impotriva-lui-ciolacu-pentru-manipularea-pietei-abuz-in-serviciu-deturnare-de-fonduri-si-inselaciune-in-cazul-Roşia-Montană_731054.html. Accessed 11 Apr 2024
European Parliament (2007) Notice to Members: Petition 0344/2006 by Magda Stoczkiewicz (Czech), on behalf of CEE Bankwatch Network, with 35 signatures, on alleged irregularities in the elaboration of the Environmental Impact Assessment for the Roşia Montană (Romania) gold mine development project. https://www.europarl.europa.eu/meetdocs/2004_2009/documents/cm/656/656927/656927en.pdf. Accessed 11 Apr 2024
Freudenburg WR (1997) 1995 MSSA plenary address: the crude and the refined: sociology, obscurity, language, and oil. Sociol Spectr 17(1):1–28
Friedman G (2024) Gabriel resources investors flee after miner loses $4.4-billion arbitration claim against Romania Financial Post. https://financialpost.com/commodities/mining/gabriel-resources-investors-flee-miner-loses-arbitration. Accessed 15 Jul 2024
Gabriel Resources Ltd. and Gabriel Resources (Jersey) v. Romania, ICSID Case No. ARB/15/31: Request for Arbitration (21 July 2015), Claimant's Memorial (30 June 2017), Respondent's Counter-Memorial (22 February 2018), Amicus Curiae Submission (2 November 2018), Procedural Order 19 (7 December 2018), Amicus Curiae Submission (18 September 2022)
Goldman Prize (n.d.) 2005 Goldman prize winner Stephanie Roth. Available at: https://www.goldmanprize.org/recipient/stephanie-roth/. Accessed 11 Apr 2024
Goţiu M (2013) Afacerea Roşia Montană. Tact
Iordăchescu G, Vasile M (2023) Forests of fear: illegal logging, criminalization, and violence in the carpathian mountains. Ann Am Assoc Geogr 113(9):2108–2125. https://doi.org/10.1080/24694452.2023.2209631
Jacobs BL (2015) A perplexing paradox: "De-Statification" of "investor-state" dispute settlement? Emory Int'l L Rev 30:17–49
Kennedy A (2016) A case of place: Solastalgia comes before the court. PAN Philos Act Nat 12:23–33
Kim YK (2017) States sued: democracy, the rule of law, and investor-state dispute settlement (ISDS). Int Interact 43(2):300–325. https://doi.org/10.1080/03050629.2016.1173546
Li TM (2010) To make live or let die? Rural dispossession and the protection of surplus populations. In: The point is to change it: geographies of hope and survival in an age of crisis, pp 66–93
Margarit D (2016) Civic disenchantment and political distress: the case of the Romanian autumn. East Eur Polit 32(1):46–62. https://doi.org/10.1080/21599165.2015.1129945

Martinez-Alier J, Anguelovski I, Bond P, Del Bene D, Demaria F (2014) Between activism and science: grassroots concepts for sustainability coined by environmental justice organizations

Marzal T (2021) Quantum (in)justice: rethinking the calculation of compensation and damages in ISDS. J World Invest Trade 22(2):249–312. https://doi.org/10.1163/22119000-12340209

Matveev A (2015) Investor-state dispute settlement: the evolving balance between investor protection and state sovereignty. UW Austl L Rev 40:348–386

McManus P, Albrecht G, Graham R (2014) Psychoterratic geographies of the upper hunter region, Australia. Geoforum 51:58–65

Miles K (2013) The origins of international investment law: empire, environment and the safeguarding of capital. Cambridge University Press, Cambridge

Mining Watch (2006) Update from Alburnus Maior. Available at: https://miningwatch.ca/news/2006/1/27/update-alburnus-maior. Accessed 11 Apr 2024

Ministry of Finance (2024) Romania wins the Roşia Montană case. Available at: https://perma.cc/Z58L-JDZ5. Accessed 29 Mar 2024

Nicut M (2024) Romania won the process for the gold in Roşia Montană. The Canadians from Gabriel resources are obliged to pay compensation to the Romanian state—the most important statements. Economica.net. Available at: https://www.economica.net/romania-a-castigat-procesul-pentru-aurul-de-la-Roşia-Montană_730594.html. Accessed 11 Apr 2024

Nixon R (2011) Slow violence and the environmentalism of the poor. Harvard University Press

Passas N (2005) Lawful but awful: "legal corporate crimes". J Socio-Econ 34(6):771–786. https://doi.org/10.1016/j.socec.2005.07.024

Pellow DN (2016) Toward a critical environmental justice studies: black lives matter as an environmental justice challenge. Du Bois Rev 13(2)

Perjovschi D (2000) I am not exotic I am exhausted

Perrone NM (2019) The "invisible" local communities: foreign investor obligations, inclusiveness, and the international investment regime. Am J Int Law Unbound 113:16–21. https://doi.org/10.1017/aju.2018.92

Perrone NM (2020) Foreign investment, knowledge and international arbitration: inside a research trip. IIED https://www.iied.org/foreign-investment-knowledge-international-arbitration-inside-research-trip. Accessed 11 Apr 2024

Pichler M (2016) What's democracy got to do with it? A political ecology perspective on socio-ecological justice. In: Fairness and justice in natural resource politics. Routledge

Ploiesti Court of Appeal, Decision No. 187 (16 February 2022)

Predoiu A, WNV (2017) Roşia Montană: How Romanians united to save a mountain village from mining apocalypse. The Ecologist. https://theecologist.org/2017/jan/11/Roşia-Montană-how-romanians-united-save-mountain-village-mining-apocalypse. Accessed 11 Apr 2024

Roşia Montană Gold Corporation (n.d.) Report on environmental impact assessment study: waste management plan. Available at: https://web.archive.org/web/20230205071534/https://en.rmgc.ro/Content/uploads/waste-plan.pdf

Sachs L, Johnson L, Merrill E (2020) Environmental injustice: how treaties undermine human rights related to the environment. La Revue des Juristes de Science Po 18

Save Roşia Montană [Facebook]. Available at: https://www.facebook.com/groups/saveRoşiaMontană. Accessed 11 April 2024

Schlosberg D (2007) Defining environmental justice: theories, movements, and nature. Oxford University Press, Oxford

Shao X (2021) Environmental and human rights counterclaims in international investment arbitration: at the crossroads of domestic and international law. J Int Econ Law 24(1):157–179

Sierra J, Schwartz B (2020) Mining reforms have left Colombia's artisanal miners behind. IIED. Available at: https://www.iied.org/mining-reforms-have-left-colombias-artisanal-miners-behind

Skinnider E (2013) Effect, issues and challenges for victims of crimes that have a significant impact on the environment. United Nations crime prevention and criminal justice Programme network of institutes workshop on 'emerging forms of crime that have an impact on the environment:

lessons learned' United Nations Commission on crime prevention and criminal justice. https://www.unodc.org/documents/commissions/CCPCJ/CCPCJ_Sessions/CCPCJ_22/PNI_Workshop/Paper_ICCLR_CJP_PNI-Workshop.pdf

Scheidel A, Del Bene D, Liu J, Navas G, Mingorría S, Demaria F, Martínez-Alier J (2020) Environmental conflicts and defenders: a global overview. Glob Environ Change 63:102104

Solnit R (2004) River of shadows: Eadweard Muybridge and the technological wild west. Penguin, Bloomsbury

Sornarajah M (2015) Resistance and change in the international law on foreign investment. Cambridge University Press, Cambridge

South N (2014) Green criminology environmental crime prevention and the gaps between law, legitimacy and justice. Revija za kriminalistiko in kriminologijo 65(4):373–381

Temper L, Del Bene D, Martinez-Alier J (2015) Mapping the frontiers and front lines of global environmental justice: the EJAtlas. J Polit Ecol 22(1):255–278

The Economist (2014) Investor-state dispute settlement: the arbitration game. http://www.economist.com/news/finance-andeconomics/21623756-governments-are-souring-treaties-protect-foreign-investorsarbitration

Tienhaara K (2018) Regulatory chill in a warming world: the threat to climate policy posed by investor–state dispute settlement. Transnatl Environ Law 7(2):229–250. https://doi.org/10.1017/S2047102517000309

Tienhaara T, Thrasher R, Simmons A, Galagher K (2022) Investor-state dispute settlement: obstructing a just energy transition. Clim Policy 1

Triefus S (2023) The UNGPs and ISDS: should businesses assess the human rights impacts of investor-state arbitration? Bus Hum Rights J 8(2):329–351. https://doi.org/10.1017/bhj.2023.45

Triefus S (2024) International investment law from below: taking local community rights seriously. Unpublished PhD thesis. Erasmus University Rotterdam

Tschakert P, Ellis NR, Anderson C, Kelly A, Obeng J (2019) One thousand ways to experience loss: a systematic analysis of climate-related intangible harm from around the world. Glob Environ Change 55:58–72

Verweijen J, Dunlap A (2021) The evolving techniques of the social engineering of extraction: introducing political (re) actions 'from above' in large-scale mining and energy projects. Polit Geogr 88:102342

Velicu I (2014) Moral versus commercial economies: Transylvanian stories. New Polit Sci 36(2):219–237. https://doi.org/10.1080/07393148.2014.883804

Velicu I (2015) From mining to Becomings: Roşia Montană's movement for democratic justice. In: Beltrán MJ et al (eds) Political ecology for civil society. ENTITLE—European Network of Political Ecology

Velicu I (2020) Prospective environmental injustice: insights from anti-mining struggles in Romania and Bulgaria. Environ Polit 29(3):414–434. https://doi.org/10.1080/09644016.2019.1611178

Verbeek B-J (2023) The modernization of the energy charter treaty: fulfilled or broken promises? Bus Hum Rights J 8(1):97–102. https://doi.org/10.1017/bhj.2022.39

Weghmann V, Hall D (2021) The unsustainable political economy of investor–state dispute settlement mechanisms. Int Rev Adm Sci 87(3):480–496. https://doi.org/10.1177/00208523211007 89

World Bank (n.d.) Romania overview. Available at: https://www.worldbank.org/en/country/romania/overview

Yilmaz Vastardis A (2018) Justice bubbles for the privileged: a critique of the investor-state dispute settlement proposals for the EU'S investment agreements. Lond Rev Int Law 6(2):279–297. https://doi.org/10.1093/lril/lry020

Stephanie Triefus is a Researcher at the TMC Asser Institute, researching business and human rights and international investment law. She holds PhD (cum laude) from Erasmus University Rotterdam, a Master of Public International Law specialising in Human Rights (cum laude) from Utrecht University and a Bachelor of Laws/Arts (Honours I) from Macquarie University in

Australia. She is admitted as a lawyer in Australia and has practiced commercial and community law.

Irina Velicu is a Researcher working on socio-environmental conflicts in post-communist Europe at the Center for Social Studies, University of Coimbra, Portugal. She has extensively published on social activism, extractivism, food justice, and social (in)justice in journals such as *Environmental Politics, Theory, Culture and Society, Ecological Economics, Geoforum, New Political Science, Globalizations*.

From the International Boomerang to the "Domestic Boomerang": Advocating for Corporate Accountability for Past Human Rights Abuses in Argentina

Gabriel Pereira and Leigh A. Payne

Abstract The scholarship on human rights accountability developed during periods of authoritarian rule emphasises international pressure from the Global North as a key factor for successful advocacy. This chapter questions what could be viewed as an overreliance on transnational actors for advancing contemporary human rights accountability efforts. It contends that international pressure does not always exist to amplify Global South demands for human rights change, particularly in locations distant from the urban centres. It further argues that an international approach overlooks emerging independent accountability dynamics in the Global South. It proposes a complementary and alternative "domestic boomerang" strategy that recognises Global South human rights accountability even in remote locations in the Global South (the "below the below"). The chapter illustrates this novel theoretical framework with a case of corporate accountability in the aftermath of atrocity in Tucumán, Argentina: the "La Fronterita" case.

1 Introduction

Existing approaches to advancing human rights accountability developed during periods of authoritarian rule emphasise international pressure from the Global North as a key factor for successful advocacy.[1] This chapter questions what could be

[1] Keck and Sikkink (1998).

G. Pereira (✉)
Professor of Human Rights at the National University of Tucuman and researcher at the National Scientific and Technical Research Council, Tucumán, Argentina
e-mail: gabriel.pereira@derecho.unt.edu.ar

L. A. Payne
Professor of Sociology and Latin America at St Antony's College, University of Oxford, Argentina
e-mail: leigh.payne@lac.ox.ac.uk

R. Grosescu, J. G. Dale (eds.), *Corporate Accountability for Human Rights Violations*, Interdisciplinary Studies in Human Rights 16,
https://doi.org/10.1007/978-3-032-05569-9_13

viewed as an overreliance on transnational actors for promoting contemporary accountability efforts. It contends, first, that international pressure does not always exist to amplify Global South demands for human rights change; particularly in locations distant from the urban centres, such demands may not reach transnational advocacy networks (TANs) that can promote them. The chapter argues, second, that transnational models overlook emerging accountability dynamics in the Global South that have advanced independently and without direct assistance from TANs. Considering these conditions, the chapter advances a complementary and alternative "domestic boomerang" strategy. It is a complementary strategy in that it recognises that those mobilisations distant from the Global South urban centres always relied on human rights organisations in national cities to promote their demands within TANS. It is an alternative strategy in that it identifies situations in which the "domestic boomerang" can—on its own and without appealing to TANS—promote human rights accountability.

We define the "domestic boomerang" as appeals by victims of human rights abuses or their advocates to powerful human rights organisations in national urban centres to amplify their demands and seek accountability. Those more powerful human rights organisations strengthen the demands of their weaker counterparts by including their claims in reports, engaging in legal mobilisation, and attracting national media attention. At times, these distant appeals, through the "domestic boomerang", reach transnational advocates. At other times, the effective use and influence of the "domestic boomerang" obviates the need for international pressure. Indeed, we contend that the power of these Global South organisations has the potential to bring changes even at the international level, reversing the typical North-to-South direction of human rights change.

The "domestic boomerang" theoretical framework we advance in this chapter emerges from our analysis of an original (and recently updated) Corporate Accountability and Transitional Justice (CATJ) database.[2] We present the framework and apply it here to accountability for economic actors' human rights violations during the recent dictatorships in Argentina (from the mid-1960s to the early-1980s). We have chosen Argentina as our case selection because it is one of the world leaders in achieving corporate accountability.[3] The analysis of those successful cases reveals that many of them involved processes in the provinces located far from the main political and cultural centres of the country and often without any involvement of TANs. The chapter seeks to explain what would seem to be an

[2] The Corporate Accountability and Transitional Justice (CATJ) database tracks accountability mechanisms addressing economic actors in transitional justice contexts. It is segmented into four discrete data sets of mechanisms. The first set involves the historical data of trials for World War II human rights atrocities committed by economic actors in Nazi Germany and Japan. The second set of accountability mechanisms data is official truth commissions. The third data set includes judicial accountability for corporate complicity in violations occurring during authoritarian regimes and armed conflicts of the 1960s to the present. The data set also includes a fourth accountability mechanism used in Colombia. The Justice and Peace process is a transitional justice mechanism designed in the early 2000s to put paramilitary leaders on trial. In their confessions, they mentioned the role that economic actors had in the violence.

[3] Payne et al. (2020).

unlikely outcome of accountability for victims of corporate abuses in distant regions of the Global South. We illustrate the framework using the case study of the "La Fronterita" company in the remote northern region of Tucumán because of the variation in accountability outcomes at different stages over time.

In line with the approach of this volume, our chapter adopts an actor-focused perspective to examine the interaction between national and transnational forms of activism. It highlights the role of national institutional innovators and civil society groups as critical drivers of corporate accountability efforts and the importance of intra-country and inter-sectoral collaborations.[4] Alliances, only sometimes represented in formal partnerships among public prosecutors, public officers, human rights lawyers, and civil society groups, are key to outweigh the power of corporate impunity forces. These collaborations bring together actors who have a national profile and arena of operation with local activists who work exclusively outside the main cities of the countries. In this vein, beyond different local, national, and regional contexts, a variety of ideological views on human rights and economic development, and different professional understandings of accountability processes, our work finds (like Mendiola's chapter in this volume) that domestic geographical borders present another challenge for pro-accountability forces to overcome. Thus, this chapter argues that the mobilisation of civil society and social movements are critical drivers of corporate accountability, especially when it involves national, transnational, and intersectoral action.

We begin the article by discussing the existing approaches to human rights accountability: TANs and the "international boomerang model".[5] We then present our complementary and alternative "domestic boomerang" approach to human rights accountability "from below". This is followed by applying that framework to the "La Fronterita" case. We conclude with reflections on the contribution of this piece, its limitations, and the potential avenues for further research on this topic.

2 Approaching Human Rights Advocacy: From the International Boomerang to the Domestic Boomerang

Keck and Sikkink's[6] seminal work recognises the importance of two factors in advocating human rights justice: transnational advocacy networks (TANs) and the international boomerang. The argument is that local human rights groups need TANs to promote their demand for human rights improvements at the international

[4] By institutional innovators, we refer to actors who translate civil society demands into legal action (Payne et al. 2020). Sometimes, institutional innovators are human rights lawyers representing victims of human rights violations and their relatives. In other cases, institutional innovations are advanced by law enforcement officials such as public prosecutors and judges.

[5] Keck and Sikkink (1998).

[6] Ibid.

level to bring pressure for changes in domestic state practices. TANs engage in information politics, symbolic politics, leverage politics, and accountability politics[7] to bring about human rights change.[8] Through TANs, the demands by civil society groups in the Global South are amplified; "naming and shaming" by international forces reverberate domestically, bringing about changes in states' behaviour in the Global South. Local human rights advocates are key to initiating the international boomerang model. The model recognises that during periods of authoritarian regime control, these local human rights advocates literally risk their lives by mobilising. It further acknowledges that these actors in such a context and on their own are unlikely to be heard or achieve success in advancing human rights claims in authoritarian regimes. TANs offer a way for civil society groups to influence change locally without direct confrontation with repressive states. The model contends that repressive states easily ignore local demands but prove more responsive to external (TAN) forces' pressure to change human rights behaviour. Thus, international boomerang pressure increases the likelihood of human rights change.

Dramatic transformations have occurred in the world during the 25 years since the publication of Keck and Sikkink's path-breaking book. We contend that the arguments developed in it do not fully reflect contemporary human rights dynamics in the context of changes in Global South states and human rights advocacy. We are not alone in this regard; other scholars and practitioners have highlighted the limitations of the international boomerang approach. For example, Dale[9] points out that this model needs to incorporate corporations and market relations to analyse how transnational social movements or transnational advocacy networks exert pressure to change the human rights conditions that motivate their action. Furthermore, Dale claims that the models obscure the transnational pressure that states might exert on transnational corporations. From a different angle, concerns have been raised about how gaining international attention might jeopardise local activism. For example, Bob[10] argues that getting into international actors' radar requires local activists to invest material and symbolic resources. In that quest, they might undermine their original goals or alienate the domestic constituencies they ostensibly represent.

Our critique moves in a slightly different direction. First, in the decades following the end of dictatorships in many countries in the Global South, particularly in Latin America, domestic advocates were able to develop effective means for bringing about change on their own without relying on TANs or the international boomerang.[11] That is not to say that there is no international influence on domestic human rights change in the Global South, but rather that it is more indirect and subtle than the earlier TANs and international boomerang models suggest. Rather than TANs, we contend that domestic institutional innovators—many of them

---

[7] Ibid., pp. 16–25.

[8] This approach has been used and critiqued in several studies addressing corporate accountability, including: Bob (2002); Dale (2011); Saage-Maaß et al. (2021); and Pellow (2007).

[9] Dale (2011).

[10] Bob (2002).

[11] Payne et al. (2020).

"transnationalised" through training, professional roles, and connections in the international arena—work effectively at the local level—"from below'—without needing top-down pressure for change. These transnationalised institutional innovators tend to be located in political and cultural centres of, or the major cities in, the Global South. They may constitute relatively weak actors compared to their Global North counterparts, but they still may have sufficient skills and power to affect human rights accountability without needing to rely on direct pressure from transnational advocacy networks.[12]

Despite this post-transition dynamic of human rights advocacy in the Global South, not all victims of abuses have access to transnationalised "institutional innovators". Fragmentation of pro-accountability forces occurs due to geographical conditions, which, in turn, impacts the access and effectiveness of accountability tools; the demands of victims in regions far from the centres of legal, political, social, and cultural power may not be heard by local and national media or by powerful human rights organisations. In contrast, their adversaries in the human rights struggle, such as economic actors, often possess local and national power as well as transnational power. In these distant regions, municipal and provincial authorities more easily ignore weak and isolated local activists and victims. They also respond positively to powerful local forces with national prominence. Isolated and weak local victims' groups and their advocates are unlikely to win their demands against powerful local veto players who have a national presence and are even less likely to receive attention abroad. Their advocacy is not only "from below;" it is "from below the below".[13] We contend that for these "from below the below" victims to advance human rights accountability, they need to use first a "domestic boomerang" to have their demands amplified by transnationalised institutional innovators. We argue that such a connection may be enough on its own to bring about pressure and thus constitutes an alternative to the international boomerang. But it is only through the "domestic boomerang" and national resonance that these victims are able to access TANs (and potentially benefit from an international boomerang) to have an impact on change, both historically and in the contemporary era. In that sense, we observe cases in which only "domestic boomerang" dynamics occur and others in which the "domestic boomerang" is a precondition for the international one, it complements it.[14]

We have evidence that victims from "below" and "from below the below" in the Global South sometimes win their human rights cases against powerful companies. Moreover, they often do so without directly engaging TANs or the international boomerang. Thus, the third argument made in this article is that a new strategy is underway in the Global South, that offers an alternative to previous forms of transnational advocacy for human rights. We further suggest that the successes of from

[12] Uprimny (2022).

[13] By "below," we refer to the efforts by domestic institutions in the Global South to hold economic actors accountable for complicity in human rights violations during dictatorships and armed conflicts.

[14] A third scenario would involve cases in which only the international boomerang occurs. This chapter does not analyse such cases.

"below" and "from below the below" strategies in Global South courts have the potential to transform Global North human rights accountability. Our model thus flips processes of change. Rather than change depending on international pressure on Global South governments, Global South forces catalysing human rights accountability at the local level have the potential to shape international human rights guarantees.

To clarify, we do not see domestic boomerang and international boomerang as mutually exclusive options or choices. Instead, we recognise that, at times, there is no option for "from below the below" victims and their advocates to access TANs and the international boomerang. In this scenario, they would thus opt for the domestic boomerang alternative. At other times, and even over time, the two strategies may be used together: as an alternative during some moments and as a complementary strategy in other moments. This framework constitutes a strategic and practical rather than a normative or morally driven claim. With this set of arguments presented, we set out the alternative framework below.

3 The "Domestic Boomerang": Tools for Change from Below the Below

"From below" forms of human rights advocacy have been advocated and developed over time. Indeed, the international boomerang process itself begins with and relies on local activists' mobilisation from below. The assumption embedded in that model is that local advocacy in certain (authoritarian) contexts is ineffective without the international boomerang. Our argument is that the international boomerang is not always available to Global South human rights advocates, and thus, alternatives and complementary strategies are imperative.

An innovative "from below" approach has been developed in the last several years using the analogy of Archimedes' Lever.[15] These authors refer to Archimedes' claim that even weak actors can lift up the heavy weight of the world with the appropriate tool—the lever- and the correct placement of the fulcrum on which it rests. These authors use the analogy to examine the effective tools used by weak actors in the Global South to lift up the weight of corporate accountability (the world) in favourable contexts (placement of the fulcrum closer to the weight to be lifted). They emphasise that victims will need increased pressure in unfavourable contexts (when the fulcrum is far from weight to be lifted) and where powerful veto players apply counterpressure to keep the weight down. In these cases, international pressure from TANs may prove crucial in lifting up the weight.

In both favourable and unfavourable contexts, local human rights advocates have worked alongside TANs to promote human rights accountability, even in the

[15] Payne et al. (2020); Tapias Torrado (2020); Shenk (2022).

corporate accountability context.[16] Yet, in cases where the victims are distant from urban centres ("from below the below"), a prior process of resonating with transnationalised innovators through a "domestic boomerang" may be the only way to gain attention from TANs to pressure for change. In these distant contexts, victims' groups usually face formidable veto players or economic actors with local, national, and sometimes international power to "block" or veto human rights accountability. Lifting the weight of accountability from under economic actors' pressure requires a great deal of counterpressure. Those "from below the below" are least likely to have such pressure on their own.

Thus, the tool our empirical research presents as a complement or as an alternative to sole reliance on the international boomerang or TANs is the "domestic boomerang". It is when the demands from those distant victims and advocates—the "from below the below"—are heard by and resonate with institutional innovators in the urban centres of power that they are amplified nationally and internationally. This gives greater weight to the distant victims and their advocates. Those actors distant from urban centres—not only the victims, but also their advocates, lawyers, and judges and public prosecutors—can leverage the necessary pressure—particularly in favourable contexts—to lift the weight of corporate accountability from under economic actors' veto power.

The "domestic boomerang" strategy presented in this article innovates on both the international boomerang and Archimedes' Lever models. It contends that the "domestic boomerang" is an effective tool for those victims and their advocates distant from centres of power. Our research shows that against seemingly impossible odds, the weakest of victims—"from below the below" -, in unfavourable contexts, sometimes makes human rights gains against powerful economic actors. They can do so even without TANs and the international boomerang to leverage their power. Indeed, the same "from below the below" process of engaging the "domestic boomerang" to amplify demands within the country is necessary to amplify demands outside the country, at least for those victims far from urban centres. Without recognition by the institutional innovators in urban centres, TANs will not hear the demands "from the below the below" groups. The international boomerang thus relies on institutional innovators to voice demands in the urban centres in the national context and may succeed in influencing human rights accountability without TANs in favourable conditions. In unfavourable contexts, the "domestic boomerang" enables a process by which transnationalised innovators amplify demands from the most distant victims of human rights violations in the country, gaining resonance and pressure from TANs.

In the next section, we explore how the "domestic boomerang" complements both Archimedes' Lever model and the international boomerang model to advance human rights accountability from below, particularly "from below the below". We analyse the dynamics of the "below the below" for each component: weak actors, the "domestic boomerang" lever, veto players, and the fulcrum or context.

---

[16] Grosescu (2019).

3.1 Weak Actors: Victims of the Global South

Archimedes' Lever model and Keck and Sikkink's[17] TAN model begin with victims' human rights demands. The two frameworks identify these civil society forces in the Global South as "weak actors," tending to lack domestic and international power. Where the two approaches diverge is how to empower these weak actors. In the repressive contexts in which Keck and Sikkink are working, mobilisation by victims is risky, literally life-threatening. Powerful and skilful human rights NGOs, like CELS — the Centre for Legal and Social Studies/Centro de Estudios Legales y Sociales — in Argentina, faced extreme threats from a repressive state, reducing their capacity to defend victims within the country. Thus, strong non-governmental organisations such as CELS joined TANs to amplify human rights demands abroad to bring about changes at home.

While human rights advocacy remains a high-risk profession in much of the Global South, the post-transition context has experienced mobilisation by and for victims that sometimes meets success in advancing human rights accountability. Indeed, in the post-transition context, organisations like CELS in Argentina have become powerful institutional innovators within countries able to bring change often without needing to join TANs. Indeed, these in-country institutional innovators, through their previous engagement of the international boomerang, are themselves transnationalised. They have received substantial funding from abroad for their advocacy work. Their organisations are staffed by individuals who have been trained abroad or have experience working in or with international and regional governmental and non-governmental human rights advocacy groups. They constitute a kind of "transnationalised local advocacy network" (TLAN).

In the current era, some Global South networks, including victims of human rights violations, "name and shame" states directly without appealing to pressure from outside borders to amplify demands. By uniting victims and advocacy groups, they engage in leverage politics locally. They use social and other forms of media for information politics. In Argentina, these groups incorporate the well-known *pañuelos* (headscarves) into public demands for accountability,[18] and they engage in symbolic politics. They use *escraches* (public outings of human rights perpetrators) to employ accountability politics by focusing on rights to justice. Creative strategies

---

[17] Keck and Sikkink (1998).

[18] The white headscarf is an international symbol of the struggle for human rights and the mobilisation of family members, especially women, in public spaces. Before the end of the last dictatorships, a group of women gathered in the Argentine main square, the Plaza de Mayo, to denounce the disappearance of their children and their grandchildren. To identify each other, the women began wearing a white headscarf, representing the diaper of their missing children. The headscarf symbol has been adopted in other parts of the Global South and for a range of other human rights struggles.

to bring forward cases of injustice—using the *tutela, amparo,* and *querella*[19]—are other ways in which local advocacy networks engage in accountability politics, directly accessing the justice system.

While both Archimedes' Lever and the international boomerang models begin with civil society demand, they do not end there. Both models recognise the limitations of victim-demand alone to transform human rights. To enhance the power of civil society groups in Keck and Sikkink's model, TANs play a critical role in promoting an international boomerang effect. In Archimedes' Lever model, civil society groups work with TLANs, or institutional innovators in their own country, to bring about change. They may continue to seek international pressure to bolster local human rights accountability, but they may not find such support and, instead, may rely on a "domestic boomerang" model.

The argument made in this chapter is that the weakest human rights victims in the Global South do not have access to TANs or the international boomerang. Indeed, they are so distant from the locus of global human rights advocacy that their demands are not even heard by TLANs within their country. Thus, in addition to the strategies developed locally, they need to add a new set of strategies with a national scope to attract TLANs capable of amplifying their voices within the country and even internationally. A missing process in the TANs/international boomerang model is how the weakest sets of victims—the "from below the below"—must engage TLANs to advance accountability. Archimedes' Lever may also tend to focus on victims' groups in the urban centres, overlooking the difficulties faced by those located in the provinces and rural periphery of the country. The distant location of the weakest human rights victims requires them to make links to TLANs through the "domestic boomerang" to lift the weight of human rights accountability. Once TLANs amplify their demands, they may even win support internationally that is crucial in unfavourable contexts.

3.2 The Domestic Boomerang as Lever

With the transition from authoritarian rule, opportunities opened up for civil society forces to mobilise. The emergence of "institutional innovators" put new tools for advancing accountability in the hands of civil society forces. We define "institutional innovators" as actors in positions that allow them to use creative methods, interpret and apply legal and political instruments, overcome counterpressure from powerful groups and individuals (veto power), and advance accountability on behalf

[19] The *tutela* or *amparo* allows individual citizens to take cases of violation of constitutional rights to high courts in certain Latin American countries. Under Argentine criminal procedure law, victims, relatives, and civil society organisations have the right to participate actively in criminal prosecutions and trials as *querellantes*. For example, they can bring new evidence, request the judge to collect new evidence, and make their accusations, which could be distinct from those of the public prosecutor.

of victims. Innovators emerge from different sectors: human rights and legal advocacy groups, NGOs, lawyers for plaintiffs, public prosecutors, and judges. Our research shows that these innovators bring creative processes to the work of civil society groups, combining international human rights law with domestic criminal and civil law. These groups also have a different level of access to institutions through elite alliances as well as through historical experiences.

Civil society groups linked to these institutional innovators with specialised human rights expertise are more likely to bring about change. Indeed, we suggest that without these inter-sectoral alliances between civil society groups and institutional innovators from different sectors, those groups distant from urban centres will likely fail at advancing accountability. Successful accountability efforts "from below the below" rely on a "domestic boomerang" in which their demands resonate with institutional innovators in the urban centres who are then able to promote them and pressure for changes in governmental policies and practices. These institutional innovators operating in urban centres and with connections with TANs resulting from their own national struggles are able on their own, in favourable contexts, to advance human rights accountability even from those in distant locations. They are also able, in unfavourable contexts, to employ the international boomerang model: they amplify victims' demands at the global level, bringing pressure from abroad on the side of the lever of the weak actors, thus lifting up human rights accountability. This additional pressure on the side of the "below the below" victims and their advocates is aiding in lifting up the weight of human rights accountability from under the power of domestic veto players.

3.3 Veto Players

Veto players are comprised of those civil society forces that are opposed to human rights accountability. In the case of corporate accountability for human rights abuses, these are likely to include members of the business community. They could be individual owners or managers, or business associations, or other economic actors. They engage in direct processes of blocking advances through threats to, or actual physical violence against human rights advocates and delegitimising advocates through media and other forms of campaigns against them. They are also engaged in less direct processes of blocking accountability by funding or otherwise promoting institutional actors who protect their interests. Examples include lobbying for certain high court judges who are likely to decide against human rights accountability cases or prosecutors who have previously defended businesses against human rights claims.

These veto players often have extraordinary power levels in remote regions away from the urban centres. In sub-national contexts, economic actors tend to form part of conservative elite groups with strong influence in social, political, and cultural spheres. They are in a position to veto accountability efforts through political and social linkages. Ideological viewpoints, shared economic interests, and social connections with key politicians and judges provide them with social class, culture, and financial proximity to politically powerful individuals and groups that can shape viewpoints and outcomes, increasing their power. Not all businesses have veto power, but those with connections to political or judicial authorities enhance their influence over judicial processes. They thus present heavy pressure to counter efforts to lift up human rights accountability.[20]

It is in this context, that the "domestic boomerang" is essential to "below the below" struggles for change. They need the national weight of institutional innovators to assist in lifting up the weight of human rights accountability. In favourable contexts, the added support of institutional efforts may be enough to lift up that weight. In unfavourable contexts, institutional innovators will unlikely be enough. One of those unfavourable contexts is the provincial one in which economic actors have not only economic power but also influence over local political and judicial decisions. It is in this context, therefore, that TANs can play a critical role. They have the potential to apply additional pressure to demands already amplified by institutional innovators, thereby promoting the demands of the weakest actors ("below the below") and lifting up human rights accountability.

By recognising the role of local veto players, Archimedes' Lever model suggests that in some contexts, TANs may not be necessary to lift up the weight of human rights accountability. In other —unfavourable— contexts, TANs may provide the additional pressure necessary for lifting up that weight. But TANs are only likely to be able to play that role if the demands of the weak actors resonate. For weak victims in distant locations, they may need to have transnationalised institutional innovators in urban centres of the country to amplify their demands. This is the "domestic boomerang": TLANs that represent the demands "from below the below" with their allies within TANs to pressure from abroad and bring human rights accountability. The context is thus critical to the need for TANs to advance change. It reflects the complementary uses of the domestic and the international boomerangs.

3.4 Fulcrum or the Context of Human Rights Accountability

One of the main issues about the applicability of the TANs framework and the international boomerang is the question of a change of context. The argument we make is that TANs, so critical to advocacy during the period of dictatorships, may have become less necessary in the post-transition era and particularly with the rise of human rights expertise within the Global South. To put this in Archimedes' Lever framework, the more favourable context following the democratic transitions and the development of powerful transnationalised domestic institutional innovators (TLANS) may not require TANs to amplify the voices for change.

[20] Such power of economic actors exists in national urban centres, but we contend that it is often even greater in the provinces because of tighter connections between economic, social, and political elites.

Yet, those who are distant from these urban and transnationalised domestic institutional innovators are unlikely to find a favourable context. They face powerful businesses that have historical, cultural, social, political, and economic links within and beyond their region. Without the transnationalised institutional innovators' amplification of their demands at the national level, they would be unlikely to advance even in more favourable contexts in the post-dictatorship. With institutional innovators on their side, however, they may acquire the power necessary to lift up the weight of human rights accountability in these favourable contexts. In unfavourable contexts, those transnationalised institutional innovators can add pressure on the side of victims by resonating with TANs.

This suggests that the global context may be more neutral or less favourable for lifting up human rights accountability. Similarly, the political shifts domestically mean that, at times, the fulcrum may be closer to, and at other times further away from, human rights accountability. In favourable moments, "domestic boomerang" processes may work very well on their own; in less favourable contexts, the alliance of civil society and institutional innovator TLAN forces may be necessary to bolster their demands with TANs.[21]

4 From Below the Below and the "Domestic Boomerang": The "La Fronterita" Case[22]

Argentina has been seen as a "human rights protagonist"[23] because of the successful mobilisation by victims and their advocates for accountability for the abuses of the 1976–1983 dictatorship. Regarding corporate accountability, a more mixed view of the context is evident. Veto players in the form of economic actors are part of a powerful conservative elite with strong influence in social, political, and cultural spheres. Not all businesses have veto power, but those with connections to political or judicial authorities possess enhanced influence over accountability processes.

Yet, the power of economic actors in remote provinces makes such groups even stronger veto players. Argentina is a federal but highly centralised country. Provincial authorities in this context are susceptible to institutional, media and social actors with a national scope, and less responsive to local provincial pressure. Accountability forces, both human rights groups and institutional innovators, need to seek out national actors and agencies for support, solidarity, resonance, and pressure to influence the litigation process of corporate complicity cases.

---

[21] Grosescu (2019).

[22] The analysis in this section is based, among other sources, on direct observation of the accountability process. Pereira is one of the lawyers representing Ortíz's family. Also, Payne and Pereira have developed action-research projects around this case in Argentina. If the trial starts and reaches that point, Payne will serve as an expert witness in the trial hearings.

[23] Sikkink (2008).

Our case study is the litigation process of the “La Fronterita” case, which involves a sugar mill’s alleged involvement in crimes against humanity committed against at least 68 victims in the province of Tucumán, Argentina, from 1975 to 1978. Although the last Argentine dictatorship overthrew the constitutional government in March 1976, the Argentine Truth Commission (CONADEP) and several judicial cases showed in the 1980s—after the fall of the last dictatorship—that systematic state violence or “state terrorism”, as it is called in Argentine public debate, started prior to the coup, in February 1975, if not earlier (see Basualdo’s chapter in this volume). At that time, the pre-coup democratic national government had signed a decree implementing the so-called Operativo Independencia (Operation Independence), which was the first massive intervention by the country’s armed and security forces in the context of a systematic plan of human rights violations.

The evidence collected by the accusers suggested that the “La Fronterita” company made substantial contributions to the perpetration of crimes against humanity, such as kidnapping people from their homes or places of work, illegal detention in a clandestine centre, torture, and sexual abuse. The company’s collaboration consisted mainly of providing material resources and information to the armed forces that led to the disappearance and torture of victims. Also, the company allowed the authoritarian government to mount a clandestine detention centre on its premises. After the end of the dictatorship, the company remained silent about the crimes. It did not provide any information to the provincial and national truth commission nor was any evidence presented to the judiciary. This silence contributed to impunity.

Tucumán, the province where the crimes were committed and the judicial case was litigated, is distant from the country’s principal political centres, posing great barriers to human rights accountability efforts.[24] Victims and their advocates needed to draw national and international attention to the case to generate solidarity and support for human rights claims. Their work, moreover, unfolded in a provincial context in which the economic actors accused of corporate complicity enjoyed social, economic, and political privileges that enabled them to block accountability efforts. The strength of these veto players increased over time, particularly within a political context unfavourable to corporate accountability, as we describe below. The case remains open at the time of the preparation of this chapter in 2024. Through the stop-and-go process of litigating the alleged human rights violations of the company, the case shows both the potential and the limitations of the “domestic boomerang”.

[24] Tucumán is considered one of the most affected provinces by state terrorism in Argentina. It is the province where the country’s first clandestine centre was mounted, the place with the largest documented mass grave, and where state terrorism formally started in Argentina with the Independence Operation. This operation included territorial occupation of the villages and towns in the southwest of Tucumán province until 1979. The military occupied certain urban and rural public and private realms, such as sugar mills and schools. As the military intervened and regulated all social activities, these areas became large open-air concentration camps in which all citizens were captives. For a reference to these aspects, see Nassif (2016, 2018).

The ongoing "La Fronterita" case particularly reveals the dynamics of the "domestic boomerang" strategy, including its different implementation methods, limitations, and short- and medium-term impact on the litigation process. It also shows how institutional innovators' accountability strategies change to respond to political changes, different levels of veto power, and the absence of strong civil society mobilisation. It shows how the transnational component is also relevant and complements the efforts of domestic actors. The accountability forces bridged the domestic and international borders and sectoral divisions to fight against corporate accountability.

In analysing the use of the "domestic boomerang" in this case, we nuance the notion of "success". For practical and analytical purposes, we do not judge "success" as a final conviction or adverse civil judgment. Transitional judicial processes, and most human rights judicial processes in the Global South, are lengthy and non-linear, marked by advances, reversals, and paralysis. In such contexts, particularly when cases are still pending final decisions, success might be translated into the progress toward a subsequent phase of the litigation process, mainly when impunity forces are strong and the political context is negative for accountability. When the odds against judicial action are so high, these advances mark momentum toward justice. Also, sometimes, claimants' main goal is not a final conviction but strengthening political actions, drawing public attention to current abuses, or providing victims a platform to make their voices heard—particularly in strategic litigation settings.[25] In measuring success, we consider the litigation process's particularities and the litigants' ultimate goal.

In this case, the "domestic boomerang" succeeded in a critical moment of the litigation process, but its effects were limited at a later phase of the litigation process. When the prosecutorial investigation reached an impasse, accountability forces from different sectors resorted to the "domestic boomerang" strategy, and the case was unblocked and moved toward trial hearings. In addition to institutional innovators' efforts, national media played a crucial role in the strategy of information politics. Despite this momentum, the case reached another impasse just before the initiation of trial hearings. At this stage, international actors were integrated into the "domestic boomerang" strategies. The litigation process advanced again. Even so, the "domestic boomerang" strategy in the long term has not yet ended in convictions. The Minnetti family, owners of the sugar mill and the multinational economic group, the veto players in this case, have increased efforts to counterbalance accountability forces. The case remains pending.

[25] As Siri Glopen argues, "Even if the case is not decided in favor of the claimant, litigation might have a transformative impact. and when courts provide a platform for social rights concerns, this might generate or intensify popular debate and create political momentum." Authorities threatened with court action may settle out of court. Courts providing a platform for social rights concerns might generate or intensify popular debate and create political momentum.

4.1 *The Litigation Process*[26]

Accountability forces from three different sectors joined together to advance the litigation process. The federal public prosecutor in the province of Tucumán, Pablo Camuña, initiated a preliminary investigation against six board members and high-ranking company officers accused of these crimes in 2015, 40 years after the crimes were committed. The Tucumán-based human rights organisation Andhes (Abogados y Abogadas del Noroeste Argentino en Derechos Humanos y Estudios Sociales/ Lawyers of Northwest Argentina for Human Rights and Social Studies) filed a *querella* on behalf of Mr. Fidel Jacobo Ortiz's family.[27] Ortíz was a union leader working for "La Fronterita" who disappeared in 1976.[28] In 2020, the Human Rights Secretariat of the Ministry of Justice of the National Government (Secretaría de Derechos Humanos de la Nación) also presented its *querella* file on behalf of other victims.

Both the prosecutor and Andhes pressed charges and requested the judge to indict four of the accused in 2018.[29] The pretrial prosecutorial investigation and trial preparation proceedings finished in early 2022. However, the trial date has been postponed for more than a year due to the Tribunal's packed agenda and lack of administrative and clerical staff to support the trial development. As of March 2024, the "La Fronterita" case has been delayed nearly 8 years in reaching the final trial stage.

The litigation process unfolded in three phases, as illustrated in Fig. 1. The initial phase started at the beginning of the investigation and lasted until the public

[26] The judicial proceedings in the case advanced slowly after the conclusion of this chapter's investigation in December 2023. Following dilatory motions filed by the defense and unjustified delays attributable to the court, a date was set in July 2024 for the preliminary hearing to begin in February 2025. However, the defense subsequently filed additional motions that prevented the hearing from taking place. Once these motions were resolved, no further appeals remained pending, and at the time of this review (August 2025), the case was awaiting the scheduling of the trial's start date.

[27] ANDHES is an Argentinean NGO working in Jujuy, Salta, and Tucuman, three impoverished Provinces in North Argentina. The organisation was created in 2000 by law students from the University of Tucuman. Andhes focuses on anti-impunity for state terrorism crimes but also current state violence and promotes the rights of impoverished communities and indigenous populations through civil litigations and educational campaigns.

[28] A company worker and a recognised union leader, Ortíz defended victims of state terrorism at the time. He made formal presentations to authorities in defence of the kidnapped workers who, during their captivity, were fired by the company. Ortíz sought to avoid wrongful dismissals as well as the release of his colleagues from detention. In April 1976, Ortíz was kidnapped for the first time from his home in the colonias. He was transported in a company vehicle to the clandestine detention centre that operated in the mill. He was released but kidnapped again in June of that year. During his first kidnapping, the company notified the corresponding state agency that Ortíz had voluntarily resigned from his position. This claim is highly unlikely, given that the resignation would have occurred, according to the company's own dates, during his detention.

[29] Initially, the investigation was against six high officers and shareholders of the company. However, by the time of the indictment, one of them passed away and another one became non-fit to be subject to a prosecutorial investigation.

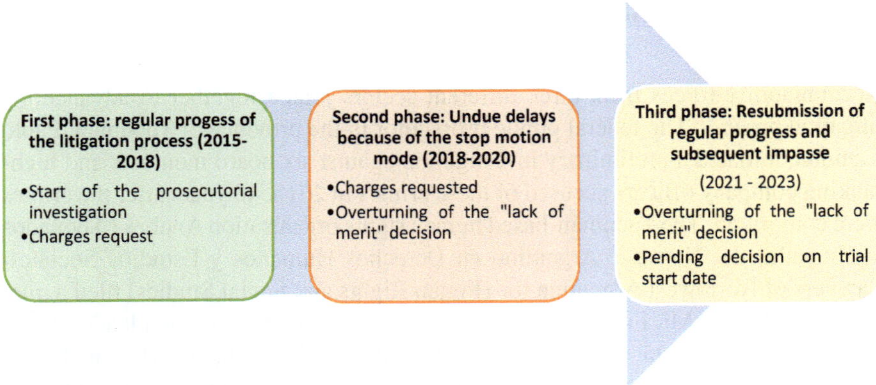

Fig. 1 The three phases of the La Fronterita case

prosecutor and Andhes pressed charges in May 2018.[30] It evolved smoothly, and no undue delays occurred. Thus, the accountability process advanced in this stage.

The second phase lasted from the moment the accusers pressed charges in May 2018 to December 2020. During this phase, the accountability process reached an impasse due to the veto players' strategies, but accountability forces managed to counterbalance such power, and the case moved to a further stage. The litigation process switched to a *stop-motion* effect in which veto players deployed their tactics to delay the decision on the charges for more than 24 months.[31] The stop-motion mode turned on from the very moment the prosecutors requested the indictment. Although the procedural codes gave him only 10 days, it was not until May 2019—nearly a year after—that the intervening judge ruled that there was insufficient evidence to prosecute the accused and ordered the investigation to be redirected toward crimes committed by the state rather than economic actors. The decision triggered an appeals spiral. The accusers appealed to an upper tribunal, which denied the appeal in June 2020—2 years after the request for an indictment. This tribunal

[30] Two of the accused were removed from the judicial process due to death and physical inability to be subject to a judicial process.

[31] As Jasinsky (2020) discusses, the stop-motion effect results from a series of judicial decisions made in the investigative phase by first-instance investigative judges and appeals tribunals. When charges are pressed, judges can either acquit, accept charges, or establish that there is insufficient evidence to either press charges or dismiss the case. The last option is technically called a "lack-of-merit" decision which initiates a long spiral of appeals as these decisions can be appealed to Appeals Chambers. If that second instance confirms a lack of merit, the Criminal Cassation Chamber must review the appeal of that decision and ultimately by the Supreme Court of Justice. This path is not linear but instead zigzags from one instance to another. A higher instance confirming a lack-of-merit decision returns the case to a lower court, so more evidence must be collected. Even when public prosecutors collect further evidence, nothing prevents the same lower judge from reissuing a lack-of-merit decision. Meanwhile, when the higher instance overturns such a decision, it does not replace it with a new one. Instead, it overturns the ruling and returns the case to the lower court so that its judge must rule again on the indictment. A new ruling might be issued after several months. Additionally, although procedural rules establish deadlines, appeals Chambers and Criminal Cassation Chambers do not usually follow them. Lack-of-merit decisions and the spiral of appeals produce a stop-motion effect.

confirmed the "lack of merit" decision on all grounds, including the recommendation to investigate only state actors. Then, the Cassation Chamber overturned the "lack of merit" decision in December 2020 and requested the lower tribunal, not the first judge, to issue a new ruling.[32] Notably, the Cassation Chamber asserted that the first judge and the Appeal Tribunal's decisions constituted a deviation from the standard evidentiary interpretation and regular judicial practices in general and in crimes against humanity cases in particular.[33]

The third stage run from December 2020 to December 2023, during the writing of this chapter. Accountability advanced, but it reached a new impasse. The litigation process moved on with no undue delays during the first part of this stage. In compliance with the Cassation Tribunal's decision, the Appeal Tribunal indicted the accused in September 2021. Then, the first instance judge referred the case to a Trial Tribunal. The proceedings before the start of the trials began in May 2022, almost 8 years after the public prosecutor initiated the investigation. Since then, the litigation process had slowed down and reached an impasse again in 2023. The Tribunal did not set the start date alleging that it had a packed trial agenda and lacked the staff to undertake the trial hearing until the completion of hearings for other ongoing trials.

As we will demonstrate further, the ongoing litigation process of the "La Fronterita" company reveals how the components of Archimedes' Lever interacted with the "domestic boomerang" strategy. It shows that the case advanced towards accountability without any international pressure. It further underlines, however, that the unfavourable context and the particular power of local economic actors rendered appeal to TANs a critical strategy for overcoming an accountability impasse.

4.2 A Changing Political Context

The three phases of the litigation process occurred during three different political moments, corresponding to three different administrations, as illustrated in Fig. 2. In the first phase, the case was initiated in a favourable political context for corporate accountability when the Kirchner administration (YEAR) undertook wide public policies of reckoning with the dictatorial pasts. During this period, the Argentine government and Supreme Court repealed the amnesty law for state perpetrators, and their prosecution began with few political constraints,[34] and institutional reforms related to corporate accountability were also implemented. For example, the Central Bank of Argentina created a human rights unit to collect information about financial

[32] Cassation Federal Chamber, "Recurso Queja N° 6–IMPUTADO: FIGUEROA MINETTI, JORGE Y OTROS s/AVERIGUACION DE DELITO QUERELLANTE: ORTIZ, HORTENCIA."

[33] Cassation Federal Chamber.

[34] Argentina's transitional justice process has followed an 'ebb and flow' pattern. The initial opening to judicial accountability of human rights violations in the early 1980s was gradually restricted by two amnesty laws and eventually foreclosed during the 1990's by presidential decrees. It was not until the 2000s that both the Congress and the Supreme Courts repelled those laws and decrees subsequently: Engstrom and Pereira (2012).

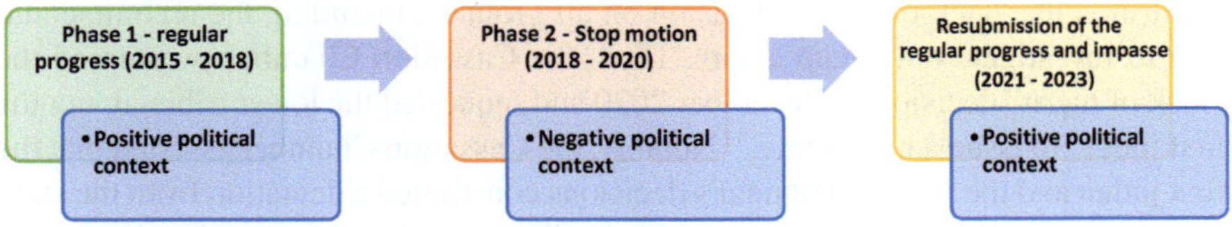

Fig. 2 The political context of the La Fronterita Case

activities that might have facilitated state terrorism, and the Financial Information Unit incorporated into its remit the investigation of the links between money laundering activities and crimes against humanity. Also, in 2015, new legislation established that any civil actions connected to crimes against humanity against natural and legal persons were not subject to statutes of limitations.[35] The same year, less than a month before the right-wing politician and businessman Mauricio Macri was elected President, a truth commission on corporate responsibility for past human rights abuses was created by law. The context was propitious for human rights groups and their advocates to attempt to advance corporate accountability in the courts with at least some expectation of success.[36]

The second—stop-motion—phase marked a negative context for corporate accountability. This was the beginning of President Macri's administration in December 2015. During this administration, human rights policies experienced severe restrictions regarding scope, financing, and personnel.[37] The Supreme Court also took a restrictive stance regarding the scope and sanctions in trials for crimes against humanity.[38] In addition, public rhetoric was sustained by frontline government officials seeking to delegitimise transitional justice trials.[39] Although these restrictions did not entirely stop the pursuit of judicial accountability, they posed critical constraints.[40] The political context was more adverse to corporate accountability. The Macri government's links with business elites and their shared interests

---

[35] Payne et al. (2017).

[36] Indeed, more than twenty cases of corporate complicity were initiated in this period. Significant prosecutorial activity pushed this case along into the litigation process, and the public prosecutor presented charges in several criminal cases. Pereira and Doz (2020).

[37] Centro de Estudios Legales y Sociales (2017); Lessa (2018).

[38] Pereira and Doz (2020).

[39] Centro de Estudios Legales y Sociales, "Derechos Humanos En La Argentina: Informe 2017," 2017, https://www.cels.org.ar/web/publicaciones/derechos-humanos-en-la-argentina-informe-2017/. (accessed October 22, 2024)

[40] Procuraduría de Crímenes contra la Humanidad, "Informe Estadístico Sobre El Estado de Las Causas Por Delitos de Lesa Humanidad En Argentina Diagnóstico 2018," 2018, https://www.fiscales.gob.ar/wp-content/uploads/2018/12/LESA_informe-estadistico-anual-2018.pdf. (accessed October 22, 2024)

are well documented.[41] The number of critical public office posts in Macri's government held by high-profile business community members is unparalleled in recent Argentine history.[42] Policies enabling corporate accountability were, not surprisingly, put on hold during this period. For instance, the truth commission on economic actors approved by Congress in 2015 was not implemented; the human rights unit of the Central Bank of Argentina was dismantled; and the Financial Information Unit that investigated corporate complicity was decommissioned.[43]

The stop-motion effect was deactivated when the political context became positive for corporate accountably again. President Alberto Fernández took power in December 2019 and reinstated some transitional justice policies that had been discontinued during his predecessor's administration. Also, in 2020 the Human Rights Secretary created a specialised unit dedicated to fostering corporate accountability in the transitional justice context. The Unit was comprised of prominent academics and activists dedicated to promoting corporate accountability. The Secretariat began performing the role of *querellante* in criminal cases, including the "La Fronterita" trial. Furthermore, the Unit signed an innovative agreement with the National Research Council to foster research in the field. Additionally, the National Government signed a friendly settlement with representatives of victims of crimes against humanity before the Inter-American Commission on Human Rights, in which Argentina acknowledged its legal responsibility for not providing access to justice to those who sued companies in labour courts.[44] It committed to implementing a truth commission on corporate complicity repelling the judicial application of statutes of limitations to civil and labour damages claims, providing symbolic and restorative reparations for the victims of the case, and implementing a mechanism to determine financial reparations, among other measures. It was in December 2020, almost 1 year after Fernández took power, that the Cassation Chamber overturned

[41] Graciela Mochkofsky, "What's Next for Mauricio Macri, Argentina's New President? | The New Yorker," *The New Yorker*, December 15, 2015, https://www.newyorker.com/news/news-desk/whats-next-mauricio-macri-argentinas-new-president; Nathaniel Parish Flannery, "What Can Investors Expect From Argentina's Economy In 2018?," *Forbes*, June 28, 2018, https://www.forbes.com/sites/nathanielparishflannery/2018/06/29/what-can-investors-expect-from-argentinas-economy-in-2018/#6e049c9b1755; Kenneth Rapoza, "President Macri's Theme Song: Definitely Cry For Me, Argentina," *Forbes*, September 6, 2018, https://www.forbes.com/sites/kenrapoza/2018/09/06/argentinas-president-macri-setting-the-table-for-future-peronista-government/#47d503573d02. (accessed October 22, 2040)

[42] Castellani (2018).

[43] Centro de Estudios Legales y Sociales, "Derechos Humanos En La Argentina: Informe 2017.", 2017. Not surprisingly, during these years, the overall corporate accountability process languished. At least 17 cases remained in the same procedural stage they had reached in the previous period under a favourable political context. In addition, excessive delays were observed in further 17 cases. The number of adverse decisions increased: three acquittals, two of them still pending review, and at least three decisions were issued establishing the lack of evidence to continue with the processes. Pereira et al. (2022), "Justice from Below: Corporate Accountability in Argentina."

[44] Further information on the report and the friendly settlement please can be found here: https://www.argentina.gob.ar/noticias/el-estado-argentino-firmara-un-acuerdo-ante-la-comision-interamericana-por-el-caso-de-un (accessed October 22, 2040)

the precedent decisions on "La Fronterita" case blocking the path to accountability.[45]

4.3 The Domestic and International Boomerang Strategies against Veto Players[46]

Accountability efforts increased over the course of the litigation process in the "La Fronterita" case, as illustrated in Fig. 3. During the first phase of the litigation process, neither national nor international actors were directly involved in the mobilising strategy inside and outside the courtroom. Traditional "naming and shaming" strategies in the province of Tucumán were enough to move the case forward. While the case received support and solidarity from local activists, the case did not attract the solidarity necessary to mobilise a robust and national civil society demand for justice.

However, the mobilisation strategy changed in 2020 when the case was switched to stop-motion in phase two. Andhes collaborated with national and international partners to give visibility to the case and exert pressure on judges, pursuing a domestic and international boomerang strategy. In 2020, CELS, the prominent "transnationalised" Latin American human rights organisation, and the European Center for Constitutional and Human Rights, known for its involvement in business and human rights cases worldwide, submitted an amicus curiae brief before the Criminal Cassation Chamber. Submitting amicus briefs meant expanding the range of mobilisation strategies to include legal mobilisation tools based on direct participation in judicial processes.

In conjunction with the public prosecutor, Andhes also resorted to other innovative litigation strategies to amplify the boomerang effect. They proposed that

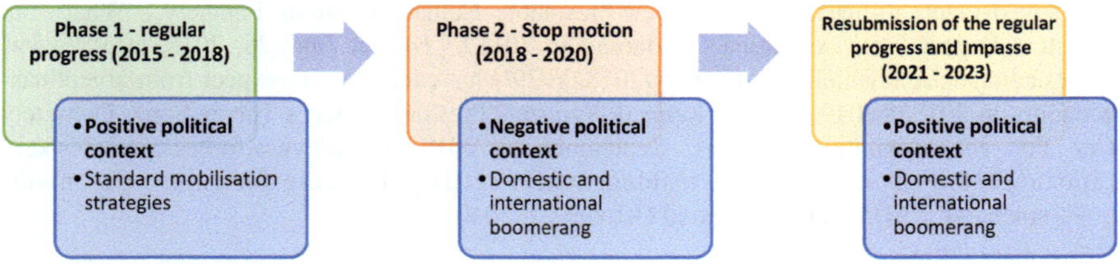

Fig. 3 Mobilisation strategies

[45] In December 2023, Javier Milei assumed the presidency of Argentina. His administration has adopted an adverse stance toward accountability for crimes against humanity. This recent political shift is not examined here, as our data collection concluded at the end of 2023.

[46] The analysis of this subsection is based on direct observation of the accountability process. As stated in a previous footnote, Pereira and Payne have direct participation in the litigation process.

well-known experts make testimony before the Tribunal during the trial hearings if the trial happens to start. Experts and contextual witnesses have been incorporated into trials for crimes against humanity since 2005 in Argentina. This is an innovative legal mobilisation strategy in which widely recognised legal and social science experts discuss technical issues relevant to the case brought to court. Such testimonies are considered as evidence by tribunals. The public prosecutor and Andhes requested the Tribunal to allow the participation of national and international scholars in the field of social science, including Argentine historian Victoria Basualdo and UK sociologist Leigh Payne, along with well-known national and international practitioners from CELS, the International Commission of Jurists, and the European Center for Constitutional and Human Rights.

The case also captured media attention from national newspapers and other media outlets during the second and third phases. The participation of national and international figures and organisations in the case attracted national media attention. In addition, Andhes developed a more aggressive media campaign, publishing regular op-eds and audiovisual material and reaching out to journalists from the national media. In parallel, the Human Rights Secretariat developed audiovisual outlets to call attention to the case and the litigation process.

Finally, Andhes brought another national actor on board. It requested the national government to implement a process of "signposting" in front of the company's headquarters, as illustrated in Image 1. As part of its memory policy, the National Human Rights Secretariat has placed signs at sites where crimes against humanity were committed. Those signs are aimed at making the public aware of atrocities committed during the period of state terror. This signposting policy has gained

Image 1 Signposting of La Fronterita Sugar Mill

national attention through extensive media campaigns. The signpost at "La Fronterita" was placed in September 2023.

The public prosecutor's innovative investigative approach to the case also included "domestic boomerang" strategies, particularly since the case got stuck in stop-motion mode. He used the institutional support structure provided by the National Attorney General's Office of Crimes against Humanity and the Office of Economic Investigation and Financial Analysis. These agencies provided crucial technical advice to the prosecutors' team, made official visits to the province, and participated in specific proceedings of the litigation process.

During the third phase, the public prosecutor made a controversial, innovative move to bring another national agency on board of the case. In 2022, the accuser knew that the defendants were selling off portions of their assets connected to the crimes. The public prosecutor requested the freezing of those assets, mainly land and buildings in which human rights violations had occurred. The prosecutor called on the General Directorate for Asset Recovery and Forfeiture of Assets of the Attorney General's Office to design such a strategy. This national agency also made formal interventions in the litigation process.

The judge overseeing the investigation granted the request. This measure, the first of its kind in corporate complicity cases in Argentina, was grounded on the need to secure assets that would serve as evidence during the trial and to protect victims' rights to reparation. In practice, this step also aimed to place an economic burden on the company's owners, as it prevented them from selling their assets. It further sought to pressure the trial Tribunal to resume the litigation process. These developments brought media attention to the case.

Meanwhile, the accused increased their efforts at veto power as the case moved forward in the litigation process, and the political context turned more positive for corporate accountability, as shown in Fig. 4. Initially, they did not need to exert strong power to block judicial prosecution, at least until the stop-motion effect was switched off and the case moved to the third litigation phase. They invested their effort in their judicial strategies to block accountability by attempting to freeze the judicial process rather than obtaining judicial exoneration.

The accused's legal team was reluctant to provide key evidence to the public prosecutor. For example, in 2009, in response to the investigation into the forced disappearance of workers in a previous judicial investigation which targeted state

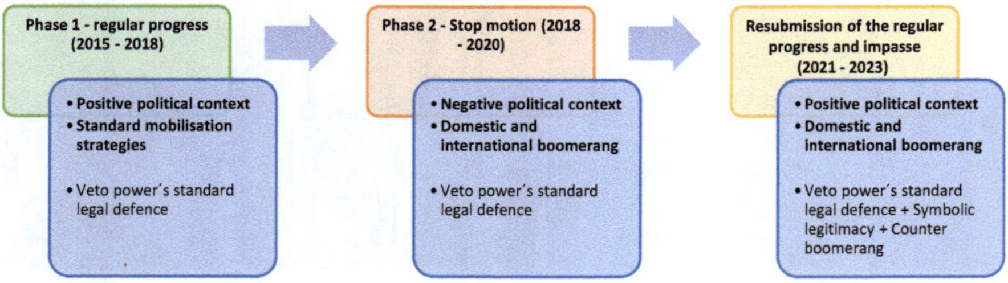

Fig. 4 Veto players' strategies

officials, the company provided false information regarding the management of the mill in 1975. Similarly, in 2015, it falsely denied that it had employed one group of workers. Moreover, in 2016, the company ignored the prosecutor's request for documents, prompting a search ordered by the judge in 2016. This behaviour led the public prosecutor to require the judge to indict the company for "procedural fraud." The strategy put forward by the company significantly delayed the investigation.

The accused have also relied on their economic power and privilege to access highly efficient professional legal services. Initially, they hired one of the most prominent, well-connected, and experienced lawyers in the province. In addition to his professional abilities, the lawyer was an influential figure in the federal and provincial judiciary: he advised leading politicians and possessed an extensive network of contacts with officials, prosecutors, and judges. Eventually, the accused relied on a new legal team with vast experience in defending crimes against humanity in trial hearings. This team had greater technical expertise appropriate to the new phase of the litigation process.

As the case moved to the pretrial proceedings, the accused also resorted to new strategies to increase their symbolic and political power and, possibly, exert public pressure on the trial tribunal. One of the main accused, Figueroa Minetti, received an award for model citizen from the mayor of Famaillá City. Famaillá is the city where the "La Fronterita" is located and where most of the crimes were committed according to the accusation. Somewhat paradoxically, the mayor of Famaillá was a prominent member of the provincial branch of the Peronist Party, the main party of the Frente de Todos coalition in power between 2019 and 2023 which favoured transitional justice policies. The award is assumed to be the result of the power exerted by the accused over the mayor.

The accused's legal team also resorted to an innovative legal defence. They developed a counterstrategy in response to the prosecutor's request to freeze assets. Because such a request touched not only the assets of the individual accused but also the company's, they formally requested the company to be part of the judicial process and future trial hearings, should they ever begin. The company itself was not a party to the criminal prosecution because, under Argentine criminal law, only individual company officers can be prosecuted, and the company is a legal entity. However, for the purpose of the trial discussion on the use of the assets to perpetrate crimes, the defendants brought the company's legal team to the trials. This means that two legal teams will be involved in the future trial: the accused individuals' and the company's representatives. Coca-Cola Bottling Company of Latin America acquired "La Fronterita" in 2016. Counting on two legal teams might contribute, at least hypothetically, to a stronger and more effective defence of the defendants´ interests.

"La Fronterita" case shows that for initiating and maintaining corporate accountability, judicial cases require renewed mobilisation capable of attracting nationwide social support and exerting public pressure on judges and prosecutors. Both innovators from civil society and state innovators have developed domestic and international boomerang strategies to unblock the litigation process and move the case to the trial stage. Although the outcome of their efforts is still pending, the case reveals how this strategy has been used. National media is a crucial component of the strategy as part of information politics. Meanwhile, veto players increased the power of their strategies to counterbalance the initiatives put forward by institutional innovators and limit the effect of a positive political context.

5 Analysis

This chapter reflected on how corporate accountability models have been developed in the Global South, especially in Argentina, using a combination of local civil society demand bolstered by institutional innovators applying creative tools that blend domestic law with international human rights norms. It contended that international forces and transnational advocacy do not always exist to amplify Global South demands for human rights change, particularly in locations distant from the urban centres. Also, it argued that transnational models overlook emerging accountability dynamics in the Global South that have advanced without transnational advocacy networks.

Considering these conditions, the chapter advanced a complementary and alternative "domestic boomerang" strategy. The weakest victims—those located far from urban centres of power within countries—use visibility strategies to gain attention from powerful allies. Together, these forces from below develop information, symbolic, leverage, and accountability politics to overcome veto players' obstacles to accountability. We have argued that these processes underway in some parts of the Global South have advanced corporate accountability even beyond what has been achieved in the Global North.[47]

We used the "La Fronterita" case here to test our theoretical proposal. In this case, the "domestic boomerang" succeeded on its own and without pressure from the international boomerang and TANs at an early critical moment of the litigation process. At that stage, it was sufficient to use TLANs national promotion of the case to advance the cause. When, at a later phase of the litigation process, the case stalled, the "domestic boomerang" strategy was successful deployed again. TLANs continued to bring pressure, attracting attention crucial to information politics. However, the case reached another impasse just before trial hearings would have begun. At this point, TANs formed part of the international boomerang process to advance the litigation process. A third impasse seems to have been reached in which the positive outcome of convictions remains stalled. Veto players have doubled down on efforts to counterbalance the domestic and international boomerang forces and avoid an accountability outcome.

This analysis highlighted the role of national institutional innovators and civil society groups as critical drivers of corporate accountability efforts and the importance of intra-country and inter-sectoral collaborations. Thus, the chapter argued that the mobilisation of civil society and social movements are critical drivers of corporate accountability, especially when it becomes national, transnational, and intersectoral.

[47] Payne et al. (2020).

6 Conclusion

While still preliminary, our theoretical contribution aimed to shed light on transformations in efforts at human rights accountability. We suggest that complementary and alternative strategies to the sole reliance on an international boomerang and TANs overlook the power of human rights organisations and their advocacy in national urban centres and "from below the below" contexts. Transnationalised local advocacy networks have proved capable of applying enough pressure on their own "from below" in favourable human rights contexts to advance accountability efforts. In this case, they become alternative strategies to the sole reliance on international boomerang and TANs. In unfavorable contexts, human rights groups operating "from below the below" are the cornerstone of accountability efforts. However, their geographical and political distance from national urban centers limits their capacity to generate broader pressure for change. In such contexts, TLANs play a critical supporting role. Without them, those "from below the below" human rights groups would not be able to bring to bear added pressure for change from TANs and the international boomerang. In both favourable and unfavourable scenarios, TLANs promote demands "from below the below" to bring effective national attention to advance accountability on their own or enhance pressure for change through transnational advocacy strategies. Future research will involve more systematic empirical analysis. This would include the area of corporate accountability for past human rights abuses, business and human rights, and other subfields of human rights accountability with powerful veto players resisting change. Such research will reveal the importance of varying human rights contexts over time, even in a single country. It will explore factors contributing to the success or failure of domestic boomerangs and transnational advocacy in the region. It will also examine how and when human rights advocates enable or not the "domestic boomerang" and the most effective strategies for its success.

References

Bob C (2002) Merchants of morality. Foreign Policy 32(4):36–45

Castellani A (2018) Cambiemos SA Exposición a Los Conflictos de Interés En El Gobierno Nacional. Los Funcionarios Con Participación En Empresas Privadas a Junio de 2018. Buenos Aires. http://noticias.unsam.edu.ar/wp-content/uploads/2018/08/Informe-N5-Observatorio.pdf

Centro de Estudios Legales y Sociales (2017) Derechos Humanos En La Argentina: Informe 2017. https://www.cels.org.ar/web/publicaciones/derechos-humanos-en-la-argentina-informe-2017/

Dale JG (2011) Free Burma: transnational legal action and corporate accountability. University of Minnesota Press

Engstrom P, Pereira G (2012) From amnesty to accountability: the ebbs and flows in the search for justice in Argentina. In: Lessa F, Payne LA (eds) Amnesty in the age of human rights accountability: comparative and international perspectives. Cambridge University Press, Cambridge

Grosescu R (2019) Transnational advocacy networks and corporate accountability for gross human rights violations in Argentina and Colombia. Glob Soc 33(3):400–418. https://doi.org/10.1080/13600826.2019.1598947

Keck M, Sikkink K (1998) Activists beyond Borders: advocacy networks in international politics. Cornell University Press, Ithaca
Lessa F (2018) Investigating crimes against humanity in South America: present and future challenges. Latin American Center, University of Oxford, Oxford. https://www.lac.ox.ac.uk/files/lacpolicybriefenglish0pdf
Nassif S (2016) Tucumán En Llamas. In: El Cierre de Los Ingenios y La Lucha Obrera Contra La Dictadura (1966–1973). Universidad Nacional de Tucumán, Tucumán
Nassif S (2018) Terrorismo de Estado En La Argentina: Tucumán y La Ofensiva Contra Los Obreros de La Agro-Industria Azucarera. Rev Interdiscip Estud Agrar 48
Payne LA, Pereira G, Bernal-Bermúdez L, Costa J (2017) Can a treaty on business and human rights help achieve transitional justice goals? Homa Pública–Rev Int Derechos Hum Emp 1(2)
Payne LA, Pereira G, Bernal-Bermúdez L (2020) Transitional justice and corporate accountability from below: deploying Archimedes' lever. Cambridge University Press, Cambridge. https://doi.org/10.1017/9781108564564
Pellow DN (2007) Resisting global toxics: transnational movements for environmental justice. MIT Press
Pereira G, Payne LA, Bermúdez LB (2022) Justice from below: corporate accountability in Argentina. Int J Human Rights 26(8):1418–1454. https://doi.org/10.1080/13642987.2022.2027764
Pereira G, Doz CJ (2020) Hacia una política de verdad y justicia sobre la complicidad de actores económicos en delitos de lesa humanidad en el marco del terrorismo de estado en la Argentina: Aportes desde la sociedad civil. ANDHES, Tucumán
Saage-Maaß M, Zumbansen P, Bader M, Shahab P (eds) (2021) Transnational legal activism in global value chains: the Ali Enterprises factory fire and the struggle for justice. Springer Nature. https://doi.org/10.1007/978-3-030-73835-8
Shenk JL (2022) Democratization from below: citizen-activated participatory democracy in Colombia's extractive industries. Sociology. Dissertation,. Jesus College
Sikkink K (2008) From pariah state to global protagonist: Argentina and the struggle for international human rights. Latin Am Pol Soc 50(1):1–29. https://doi.org/10.1111/j.1548-2456.2008.00002.x
Tapias Torrado NR (2020) Indigenous women leading the defence of human rights from the abuses by mega-projects in Latin America, in the face of extreme violence. Sociology. Dissertation, University of Oxford, St Antony's College
Uprimny R (2022) Conclusion: the past, the present and the future of accountability of corporate complicity in gross human rights violations. In: Payne LA, Bernal-Bermúdez L, Pereira JR (eds) Economic actors and the limits of transitional justice: truth and justice for business complicity in human rights violations. British Academy Scholarship Online, London, pp 265–279

Gabriel Pereira is a permanent researcher at the Consejo Nacional de Investigaciones Científicas y Tecnológicas of Argentina (CONICET) and a Human Rights Professor at the National University of Tucumán (Argentina). He is also an affiliated researcher to the Latin American Centre of the University of Oxford. He completed his PhD in Politics at the same University in 2014, and holds a Master's Degree in Social Science (Democracy and Democratization) from the University College London, and a Law Degree from the National University of Tucuman. He has written in journals and in books on fields including transitional justice, business and human rights, human rights, and judicial politics, and recently co-authored two books on corporate complicity in transitional justice contexts. He is also a founder and president of the human rights organisation Andhes. He has recently co-authored two books in the field of corporate accountability: *Economic Actors and the Limits of Transitional Justice: Truth and Justice for Business Complicity in Human Rights Violations.* (Oxford University Press, 2024); Transitional Justice and Corporate Accountability from Below: Deploying Archimedes' Lever. (Cambridge University Press, 2021).

Leigh A. Payne is Professor of Sociology and Latin America at St Antony's College, University of Oxford. She has published numerours books, articles and books chapters on transitional justice and corporate accountability. She has recently co-authored the following volumes *Economic Actors and the Limits of Transitional Justice: Truth and Justice for Business Complicity in Human Rights Violations.* (Oxford University Press, 2024); Transitional Justice and Corporate Accountability from Below: Deploying Archimedes' Lever. (Cambridge University Press, 2021) and The Right against Rights in Latin America. (Oxford University Press, 2023). Based on her research findings, Payne has been involved in numerous academic-practitioner impact projects around the world. For her academic research and policy impact work, she has received grants from foundations including Open Society, Ford, Oak, Newton, and Zennström. She has also received funding from research councils, including the Economic and Social Research Council (UK), Arts and Humanities Research Council (UK), British Academy, and National Science Foundation (US).

Forced Labour in Spain Under Franco's Rule: Public Debates Over Corporate Accountability in the Twenty-First Century

Fernando Mendiola and Juan Carlos García-Funes

Abstract This chapter examines the treatment of corporate responsibility for forced labour within public memory policies in Spain during the twenty-first century, with a particular focus on legislation pertaining to the accountability of private companies. First, we provide a comprehensive overview of the legislation on this issue since the end of the dictatorship, with a special emphasis on the measures implemented by both the central government and the autonomous communities. Second, we consider the role of social movements, particularly memory associations and trade unions, and their corporate accountability initiatives, particularly in autonomous communities, but also in the case of the public railway company, RENFE. We argue that corporate accountability efforts are at a very incipient stage in Spain due to the general impunity concerning Francoist crimes, the veto power of corporate actors, and the alliances they forge with political elites, especially right-wing ones. However, intersectoral and cross-regional civil society mobilizations have succeeded in moving forward the debate, an aspect facilitated by the decentralised Spanish political and administrative system.

1 Introduction

Memory policies concerning the legacy of the Franco dictatorship in Spain have been the subject of significant public debate. While progress has been made, it is evident that much work remains to be done, and that corporate accountability initiatives, especially regarding forced labour, have been limited. Nonetheless, recent developments—such as the enactment of a new law on democratic memory in 2022—underscore the ongoing importance of this issue. This chapter aims to elucidate how Spain has addressed corporate responsibility concerning forced labour

F. Mendiola (✉) · J. C. García-Funes
Universidad Pública de Navarra - Nafarroako Unibertsitate Publikoa,
Iruñea - Pamplona, Spain
e-mail: fernando.mendiola@unavarra.es; juancarlos.garcia@unavarra.es

R. Grosescu, J. G. Dale (eds.), *Corporate Accountability for Human Rights Violations*, Interdisciplinary Studies in Human Rights 16,
https://doi.org/10.1007/978-3-032-05569-9_14

under the Franco regime. To achieve this goal, we draw upon the theoretical framework of “Archimedes’ lever”,[1] which posits the importance of local actors in shaping post-dictatorial justice and memory. We examine not only the evolution of the legal framework, but also various social initiatives that have emerged at the level of the autonomous provinces.

For this purpose, the text has been divided into two parts. The first part analyses the evolution of memory policies in relation to forced labour from the end of Franco’s dictatorship to the adoption of the 2022 Democratic Memory Law, taking into account both national legislation and the different kinds of policies carried out by the governments of the autonomous communities.[2] Indeed, the tension between the national government and the autonomous communities has been one of the key elements that explains the evolution of the legislation surrounding memory policies. The second part examines both the factors that explain why impunity regarding forced labour remains widespread, and aspects—mainly related to grassroots mobilisations—that have allowed for accountability to progress. Crucially, we understand accountability here to mean not only the right to justice, which should result in reparations or criminal convictions, but also the right to truth, which can be achieved through truth commissions, public reports or social initiatives interested in condemnation and visibility.

2 The Public Memory of Forced Labour Under Franco: Debates Around Legislation

The establishment and perpetuation of the Francoist dictatorship (1936–1975) relied heavily on repression and violence against dissenting populations,[3] including forced labour as a means of subjugation and control.[4] Initiated in 1937 through a decree[5] concerning the work of prisoners and prisoners of war (POWs), forced labour manifested in two main forms: concentrationary and penitentiary. The former, managed by the Inspección de Campos de Concentración de Prisioneros[6]

[1] Payne et al. (2021); See also the chapter by Payne and Pereira in this volume.

[2] The Spanish constitution recognises the legislative powers of different regions (autonomous communities), as long as their exercise does not clash with national legislation.

[3] To conceptualise Franco’s repression, terms such as Spanish Holocaust (Preston 2011), political cleansing (Mikelarena 2016), extermination policy (Espinosa 2002) or genocidal practices (Miguez 2015) have been used. For an update of the quantitative death toll, see Espinosa (2021).

[4] Mendiola (2013a) and García-Funes (2022).

[5] Decreto núm. 281.- Concediendo el derecho al trabajo a los prisioneros de guerra y presos por delitos no comunes, bajo las condiciones que se establecen. *Boletín Oficial del Estado*: núm. 224, de 01/06/1937, https://www.boe.es/datos/pdfs/BOE//1937/224/A01698-01699.pdf (last accessed 4 April 2024).

[6] Orden.- Dispone la constitución de una Comisión que procesa a la creación de Campos de concentración de prisioneros, designando para Presidente al Coronel D. Luis Martín Pinillos y Blanco de Bustamante, designando para auxiliarle al personal que indica. *Boletín Oficial del Estado*: núm.

(Inspectorate of Prisoners of War Concentration Camps), organised prisoners of war into various labour units, such as the Batallones de Trabajadores (Workers' Battalions), the Batallones Disciplinarios de Soldados Trabajadores (Disciplinary Battalions of Worker Soldiers) or other smaller units.[7] The latter, based on the Sistema de Redención de Penas por el Trabajo (System of Redemption of Sentences through Work), involved labour both outside (Militarised Penal Colonies, until 1960, and Penal Detachments, until 1970) and within penitentiary facilities.[8]

This system of captive labour reached its peak in 1940, with approximately 109,000 workers, the majority of whom were part of the concentrationary system, after which the number began to decline. By 1943, there were 32,684 captive workers, most of whom were prisoners integrated into the penitentiary system, with the last concentration camp closing in 1948.[9] Forced labour primarily benefited the public sector, with the military overseeing much of the labour, but also the private sector. Although companies employing POWs or prisoners theoretically had to pay a salary to the state for the concession of these workers, the actual benefits were diverse, depending on the sector, geographical location, legal modality, year in question or and variations in productivity. The relative scarcity of labour at certain times, the need for a disciplined workforce, the ease of relocating workers to sparsely populated regions, and the demand for skilled personnel for specific tasks were among the reasons for companies to opt for captive labour.[10]

Despite the importance of this form of repression, forced labour has played a relatively minor role in the framework of the memory policies implemented in Spain after the end of the dictatorship.[11] These policies can be differentiated between those that took place in the twentieth century as part of the framework of transitional justice, and evolutions during the twenty-first century, considered to be part of post-transitional justice processes.[12]

Within transitional justice, the 1977 Amnesty Law[13]—which granted pardons to individuals involved in Francoist repression—represents both an example of the lack of willingness to provide accountability for rights violations during the

258, de 05/07/1937, página 2219, https://www.boe.es/datos/pdfs/BOE//1937/258/A02219-02219.pdf (last accessed 4 April 2024).

[7] García-Funes (2022).

[8] García-Funes (2022), Acosta Bono et al. (2004) and Gomez Bravo (2008).

[9] For a description and quantification of the various forms of penitentiary labour, see Mendiola (2013a). For a quantification of forced labour in concentrationary system, refer to García-Funes (2022).

[10] For a detailed explanation of the variations in business strategies regarding forced labour across different sectors, regions, and circumstances, see Mendiola (2013b, 2017) and García-Funes (2022).

[11] For different approaches to memory policies in Spain after the end of the dictatorship, see Alonso Olea and Belaustegi (2021), Aguilar (2008a, b), Espinosa (2006, 2015), Fernández et al. (2020), Jimeno Aranguren and Aguilar (2022), Juliá (2006) and Sánchez León and Izquierdo (2017). For the specific case of forced labour, see Mendiola (2021).

[12] Aguilar (2008b).

[13] Ley 46/1977, de 15 de octubre, de Amnistía, *Boletín Oficial del Estado*, 248, https://www.boe.es/eli/es/l/1977/10/15/46/con (last accessed 4 April 2024).

dictatorship, and as a framework that has hindered, and continues to hinder, the fulfilment of the rights of the victims of the dictatorship as a whole and, in particular, of those subjected to various forms of forced labour.[14] In fact, the impunity resulting from the law was amplified by the difficulty of engaging in historiographical analysis due to the delayed opening of the archives related to the repression, which remains incomplete in 2024,[15] late and limited reparation measures, and a lack of institutional will to identify places of memory of Franco's repression. In this respect, organisations such as Amnesty International,[16] the UN Special Rapporteur Pablo de Greiff[17] and the UN Human Rights Council[18] have pointed out, on various occasions, that the victims of Franco's regime have not seen their rights to truth, justice and reparation recognised, even after the 2007 memory law, on which we elaborate below.

Consequently, during the twentieth century, there was no explicit recognition of the specificity of forced labour in any type of legislation, ignoring the criteria of the Nuremberg trials, which had incorporated forced labour as a category of crimes against humanity, leading to trials and sentences,[19] going beyond the 1930 International Labour Organization's Convention on Forced Labour. Regarding reparation measures, the 1990 Budget Law[20] included some compensation for people who had spent years in prison for political reasons during the dictatorship, but did not mention forced labour at all: hence, POWs from labour battalions dependent on the concentration camp system were left without compensation.[21] This lack of recognition of work in captivity must also be linked to the persistence in Spanish penal

[14] For an analysis of the Amnesty Law and its implications for the politics of memory, see Aguilar (2008a) and Jimeno (2018). In her analysis of the impact of amnesty laws on transitional justice processes, Olsen (2022) points out that these laws have not always been an obstacle to developing specific corporate accountability policies. In addition, she also argues that transition processes that stem from military dictatorships are more likely to implement this type of policies.

[15] Espinosa (2019).

[16] Amnistía Internacional (2012) Casos cerrados, heridas abiertas. El desamparo de las víctimas de la Guerra Civil y el franquismo en España. Amnistía Internacional, Madrid. https://doc.es.amnesty.org/ms-opac/doc?q=mssearch_fld41%3A%22justicia+universal%22&start=15&rows=1&sort=msstored_title%20asc&fq=norm&fv=siai&fo=and (last accessed 1 July 2024).

[17] de Greiff P (2014) Informe del Relator Especial sobre la promoción de la verdad, la justicia, la reparación y las garantías de no repetición, Pablo de Greiff - Misión a España. Naciones Unidas, Oficina del Alto Comisariado para los Derechos Humanos. www.congreso.es/docu/docum/ddocum/dosieres/sleg/legislatura_12/spl_24/pdfs/7.pdf (last accessed 1 July 2024).

[18] UN Human Rights Council (2017) Report of the Working Group on Enforced or Involuntary Disappearances, Addendum: Follow-up report to the recommendations made by the Working Group: Missions to Chile and Spain, A/HRC/36/39/Add.3 www.refworld.org/docid/59bfb4b84.html (last accessed 1 July 2024).

[19] Wiessen (2001) and Payne et al. (2022).

[20] Ley 4/1990, de Presupuestos Generales del Estado para 1990. *Boletín Oficial del Estado*, 156, www.boe.es/boe/dias/1990/06/30/pdfs/A18669-18710.pdf(last accessed 1 July 2024).

[21] Mendiola (2021). In the Basque Autonomous Community, the decision not to include concentrationary labour in the cases of compensation was explicitly endorsed by the autonomous government, which led to a strong controversy, analysed in depth by Urquijo (2006). In any case, this political action differs greatly from that carried out in Germany regarding forced labour. See Authers (2006) and Payne et al. (2022).

and penitentiary law of the System of Redemption of Sentences through Labour, which was created in 1938 and maintained, with some modifications, until the adoption of a new criminal code in 1995.[22] In other words, it was difficult to implement corporate accountability measures when the system by which companies accessed forced labour remained in place for two decades after the dictator's death.

This general situation of impunity and silence surrounding Franco's repression was largely shattered at the grassroots level with the emergence of a broad social mobilisation in the early years of the twenty-first century, and the establishment of strong organisations, including the Asociación por la Recuperación de la Memoria Histórica (Association for the Recovery of Historical Memory)[23] and the Foro por la Memoria (Forum for Memory), which later became the Federación Estatal de Foros por la Memoria (Federation of Forums for Memory).[24] These organisations have combined the condemnation of the impunity resulting from the Amnesty Law with activities designed to raise awareness about the effects of Francoist repression. They have also promoted the search for disappeared persons through the exhumations of mass graves, using archaeology and forensic anthropology—activities that sparked sustained media attention that placed them at the centre of the political debate.[25] In the case of forced labour, the Andalusian initiative around the so-called Canal de los Presos (Prisoners' Canal), which we explore in more detail below, also brought to light the reality of forced labour, a reality that gained further visibility in the debates over the Francoist mausoleum of Cuelgamuros, the so-called Valle de los Caídos (Valley of the Fallen), built in part through the labour of prisoners.[26]

At the beginning of the century, at a juncture in which both Spanish and global issues related to the traumatic memory of dictatorships were gaining increasing prominence, the socialist government of Rodríguez Zapatero enacted, in 2007, the so-called Ley de Memoria Histórica (Historical Memory Law)[27]—a law that placed the rights to truth, justice and reparation on the national agenda, but which was criticised for its limited progress[28] and shortcomings, observable in the case of forced labour, among others.[29] Not only that, but the Amnesty Law remained in place and

---

[22] Ley Orgánica 10/1995 del Código Penal. *Boletín Oficial del Estado*, 281, www.boe.es/buscar/pdf/1995/BOE-A-1995-25444-consolidado.pdf (last accessed 4 April 2024). See also Mendiola (2013a).

[23] For further information, https://memoriahistorica.org.es/ (last accessed 4 April 2024).

[24] www.foroporlamemoria.info/ (last accessed 4 April 2024).

[25] Ferrándiz (2023).

[26] Sueiro (1976), Olmeda (2009), Sanchez Albornoz (2012), Hepworth (2014) and Stockey (2013).

[27] Ley 52/2007, de 26 de diciembre, por la que se reconocen y amplían derechos y se establecen medidas en favor de quienes padecieron persecución o violencia durante la guerra civil y la dictadura, Boletín Oficial del Estado, 310, www.boe.es/eli/es/l/2007/12/26/52/con (last accessed 4 April 2024).

[28] For an analysis of this law, see Martín Pallín and Escudero Alday (2009). From the point of view of the satisfaction of rights, see the reports by Amnesty International (2012) and Pablo de Greiff (2014).

[29] The analysis of the draft bill is also useful for understanding the law after its approval in 2007, as no meaningful changes were made to it during the parliamentary process. See Mendiola (2006).

blocked any kind of justiciability, and advances in the field of the right to truth and reparation were also very weak. The law only mentioned that "public administrations may provide subsidies for the creation of censuses of buildings and public works carried out" by captive labour, without any state commitment to facilitate or promote such initiatives, and without public signposting or musealisation. At most, the state could facilitate subsidies to entities and groups involved in such activities. Furthermore, with respect to the compensation of victims, the law did not introduce any changes compared to what had been outlined in 1990, and did not involve the companies that benefited from forced labour in any way: there was no obligation to open their archives, nor to contribute funds for compensation, reparation measures or research projects.[30]

In the years following the enactment of the law, memorial initiatives developed in which two parallel dynamics converged, ushering in legislative innovation at the level of the autonomous communities. On the one hand, various social initiatives related to forced labour emerged. On the other hand, various autonomous communities governed by the Socialist Party (Partido Socialista Obrero Español—PSOE) adopted regional legislation to address the unresolved gaps in the 2007 Law. For example, Law 2/2017 on the Historical and Democratic Memory of Andalusia[31] expressly mentioned the beneficiaries of forced labour for the first time, stating in Article 19 that "the Administration of the Junta de Andalucía will promote actions to involve the organisations that used forced labour to their benefit in the measures of recognition and reparation." Similar formulations would subsequently be used in the legislation of other autonomous communities, including the País Valencià,[32] Aragón,[33] and Extremadura.[34] Moreover, various movements concerned with justice and memory for Francoist crimes, united under the Coordinadora Estatal de Apoyo a la Querella Argentina (CEAQUA, State Coordinating Committee in Support of the Argentinean Complaint), to file a collective lawsuit in Argentina in 2010, taking advantage of the principle of universal jurisdiction for crimes against humanity.[35] In this case, too, there were attempts to address forced labour, including one initiative promoted by a trade union, Confederación General del Trabajo (General

[30] Mendiola (2006).

[31] Ley 2/2017, de 28 de marzo, de Memoria Histórica y Democrática de Andalucía, *Boletín Oficial del Estado*, 95, www.boe.es/eli/es-an/l/2017/03/28/2 (last accessed 4 April 2024).

[32] Ley 14/2017, de 10 de noviembre, de Memoria Democrática y para la Convivencia de la Comunitat Valenciana, *Boletín Oficial del Estado*, 23/12/2017, www.boe.es/eli/es-vc/l/2017/11/10/14/con, article 35.5 (last accessed 4 April 2024).

[33] Ley 14/2018, de 8 de noviembre, de memoria democrática de Aragón, *Boletín Oficial del Estado*, 14 (www.boe.es/eli/es-ar/l/2018/11/08/14), Article 10. It must be noted that this law was derogated in February 2024 by right-wing regional government of Aragon: www.boe.es/eli/es-ar/l/2018/11/08/14/con (last accessed 4 April 2024).

[34] Ley 1/2019, de 21 de enero, de memoria histórica y democrática de Extremadura, article 23, *Boletín Oficial del Estado*, 38, www.boe.es/eli/es-ex/l/2019/01/21/1 (last accessed 4 April 2024).

[35] Messuti (2013).

Confederation of Work), and by former prisoners subjected to forced labour.[36] The lawsuit has not resulted in any guilty verdicts yet, but Argentinean judges issued several international arrest warrants against former Francoist officials.[37] None, however, concerned the forced labour issue.

On the other hand, in the face of institutional inaction, different associations and researchers began to draw up censuses of forced labour sites. As a result, in some autonomous communities, we have access to exhaustive lists of forced labour sites, as is the case for Andalusia,[38] Navarre,[39] Castilla – León[40] or the Basque Autonomous Community.[41] Except for the latter, in which the regional government commissioned a collective publication linked to places of memory,[42] the censuses were carried out without any state institutional support or impetus.

Consequently, not only in terms of forced labour, but the politics of remembrance as a whole, the 2007 Law was heavily contested, both by memory activists and various political parties and by the right-wing media, which described it as a revanchist or "civil war" law. The law thus became an insufficient instrument for one segment of society, and an unnecessary one for another. Moreover, the right-wing government, led by the Partido Popular (Popular Party), halted the implementation of the law from 2011 to 2018. As a result, after the arrival of socialist Pedro Sánchez as head of government in 2018, the new left-wing governmental coalition formed by the PSOE and Unidas Podemos (Together we can), began to promote the adoption of a new law, leading to the publication of a preliminary draft of the Law on Democratic Memory (LDM)[43] in 2020, and its subsequent approval in November 2022.

The publication of the draft in 2020 gave new impetus to a wider societal debate on memory policies, including surrounding forced labour, in relation to which the LDM introduced a number of innovations compared to the 2007 Law. While the preamble explicitly referred to forced labour, the reference was to the International Labour Organization's 1930 Convention, without any consideration of the practice as a crime against humanity as envisaged by the Nuremberg Charter, or as a crime against humanity or war crime as defined by the 1998 Rome Statute of the International Criminal Court.[44] The absence of any reference to the System for the Redemption of Sentences, the Penal Detachments or prison labour left ambiguous

---

[36] This is the case of Félix Padín and Luis Ortiz Alfau, whose experiences are the subject of two memoirs: Padín (2017) and Izagirre (2016).

[37] Grosescu (2024), pp. 159–180.

[38] Gutiérrez and Martínez (2007).

[39] Mendiola (2012).

[40] García-Funes (2016).

[41] Mendiola (2015).

[42] Agirreazkuenaga and Urquijo (2015).

[43] Ley 20/2022, de 19 de octubre, de Memoria Democrática, *Boletín Oficial del Estado*, 252, www.boe.es/eli/es/l/2022/10/19/20/con (last accessed 4 April 2024).

[44] For further information: https://www.un.org/spanish/law/icc/statute/spanish/rome_statute(s).pdf (last accessed 4 April 2024).

whether prison labour during Franco's regime was even considered forced labour under the law. Consequently, there was no change in terms of remedying the absence of justiciability or creating systems of compensation (a matter that now increasingly affects fewer and fewer people).

An innovation introduced by the LDM was Article 32.2, which dealt with forced labour, which stipulated that,

> the General State Administration, in collaboration with the other public administrations, shall draw up an inventory of the buildings and works carried out by members of the Disciplinary Battalions of Labour Soldiers, as well as by prisoners in concentration camps, Workers' Battalions and prisoners in Militarised Penal Colonies.

Moreover, it introduced a provision previously stipulated in the Andalusian law with regard to corporate responsibility, that,

> the General State Administration will promote actions for the recognition and reparation of the victims who carried out forced labour, such as the signposting of places directly related to forced labour, in such a way as to enable their identification and the remembrance of what happened, as well as promotion of initiatives by organisations or companies for which it is established, through a census, that they used forced labour to their advantage, so that they adopt measures to this end.

These provisions, already included in the 2020 draft law, gave rise to a series of protests and positions on the matter. The platform Encuentro Estatal de Colectivos de Memoria Histórica y de Víctimas del franquismo[45] (State Meeting of Historical Memory Collectives and Victims of the Franco Regime), made up of a hundred associations, denounced the draft law for not recognising "the patrimonial responsibility of the State, nor of institutions, organisations, entities and individuals, which benefited from Franco's plundering and forced labour"[46] or guaranteeing "the opening and free access to all public and private archives on Franco's repression".[47] The lack of access to information hindered the victims' right to truth, justice, and reparation. In addition, several activists criticised the lack of regulation in relation to corporate responsibility. For instance, Cecilio Gordillo, one of the promoters of the initiative Canal de los Presos, in Andalusia, replied to a journalist in 2020: "What is 'encouraging' companies to take measures. 'Encouraging'? What is this 'encouraging' in a law?"[48] Similarly, several scholars[49] have highlighted a 2000 German law as a counterexample, which established the Erinnerung, Verantwortung und Zukunft Foundation[50] with the purpose of promoting reparations through the contribution of some 5000 private companies, the opening of business archives to researchers, and

[45] For further information: www.encuentroporlamemoria.org/ (last accessed 4 April 2024).

[46] See www.encuentroporlamemoria.org/2021/02/02/la-ley-de-memoria-que-necesitamos/ (last accessed 4 April 2024).

[47] Ibid.

[48] See www.infolibre.es/politica/gobierno-abre-melon-represion-economica-franquismo-protege-pago-indemnizaciones_1_1187461.html (last accessed 4 April 2024).

[49] Maestre (2019) and García-Funes and Mendiola (2020).

[50] See www.stiftung-evz.de/en/ (last accessed 4 April 2024).

the creation of a fund for educational initiatives about forced labour under Nazi rule. Likewise, trade unions have also lobbied to include corporate accountability for forced labour in the law, or denounced, as in Navarre, that "companies that benefited from slave labour are exempt [in the draft law] from any type of financial responsibility, reparation or compensation".[51]

The new law has thus not met the expectations of memory activist groups, and has fallen far short in comparison to the engagement of other countries on the subject of corporate accountability (including Germany, but also Argentina, as examined by Basualdo in this volume). However, the LDM is still a small milestone in the right direction, given that national legislation has for the first time acknowledged the involvement of corporations and state institutions in the use of forced labour and referred to their potential duty to engage in reparations and the uncovering of historical truth. Nevertheless, this was a mere declaration of intent, expressed in desiderative terms, with no de facto normative character as required of a law. What is undeniable is that the introduction of these innovations in the law were the result of a series of social mobilisations in favour of accountability, while its limitations occurred due to the persistence of a corporate veto over this issue.

The narrative is currently open, in a historic moment in which the rise of far-right parties has become another factor of resistance against corporate accountability. Indeed, unlike in Andalusia, where the ascent of the Popular Party to government did not mean the repeal of the LDM, in Aragón, the new regional government, which includes the far-right Vox party, repealed the regional law on Historical Memory in 2024.[52] Aragón thus stands as an example of what a more right-wing government could mean for Spain as a whole. Moreover, after this shift in Aragón, Partido Popular and Vox announced their intention to replace the existing laws on historical or democratic memory with so-called "Laws of Concord" in several autonomous communities where they governed in 2024, such as the Balearic Islands and País Valencià. Paradoxically, it is now on the regional level that setbacks are occurring in relation to memory policies, with the Spanish government even denouncing regional non-compliance with national legislation on these issues at the EU and the UN. As a result, three UN Special Rapporteurs have urged the Spanish government to act against these regional proposals, as they pose a threat to the rights of the victims of Francoism.[53] The evolution of these memory policies, and thus the question of accountability, remains an open and ongoing matter, subject to continu-

[51] The full text of the campaign: https://steilas.eus/wp-content/uploads/2021/04/Memoria-Demokratikoa-_-Eskuorria-gaz-2_compressed.pdf (last accessed 4 April 2024).

[52] LEY 1/2024, de 15 de febrero, de derogación de la Ley 14/2018, de 8 de noviembre, de memoria democrática de Aragón. *Boletín Oficial del Estado*, 61, https://www.boe.es/eli/es-ar/l/2024/02/15/1 (last accessed 4 April 2024).

[53] Salvioli F, Baldé A, Tidball-Binz M (2024) Mandatos del Relator Especial sobre la promoción de la verdad, la justicia, la reparación y las garantías de no repetición; del Grupo de Trabajo sobre las Desapariciones Forzadas o Involuntarias y del Relator Especial sobre ejecuciones extrajudiciales, sumarias o arbitrarias (Ref.: OL ESP 4/2024; https://spcommreports.ohchr.org/TMResultsBase/DownLoadPublicCommunicationFile?gId=29036) (last accessed 1 July 2024).

ous negotiation and contestation between forces defending impunity (such as right-wing political parties and many business actors) and the persistent social mobilization in favour of the rights to truth, justice, and reparation. This is a complex conflict, which we explain in greater depth in the next section.

3 The Keys to Impunity and Social Mobilisation

Beyond the legal framework surrounding accountability, it is crucial to understand the complex dynamics influencing both the persistent impunity observed among major companies that utilized forced labour and the advances achieved through social pressure. In the following sections, we delve into the factors contributing to these contrasting outcomes, shedding light on key determinants shaping accountability within this context.

3.1 Veto Power and Incremental Impunity of Corporate Actors

Impunity and the lack of corporate accountability for forced labour must be understood within a broader historical context, notably the absence in Spain's public memory policies of debates surrounding corporate involvement in the preparation and financing of the 1936 coup d'état. This stands in contrast to countries with similar transitional processes, such as Argentina and Brazil, where such discussions have taken place.[54] Furthermore, the historical ties between certain businessmen and the Franco regime, including businessmen holding political positions, did not hinder their receipt of honorary distinctions after the fall of the dictatorship—as exemplified by Félix Huarte, vice-president of the Provincial Council of Navarra and a deputy member of Spanish parliament from 1964 to 1971, who was awarded the Navarre regional government's medal for his role in industrializing the region in 2014.[55]

The focus on sectors where forced labour had significant weight, such as Bizkaia (in the Basque Country),[56] reveals a concerning lack of visibility and acknowledge-

[54] CELS (2015), Pereira (2022) and Colla de Amorim et al. (2022).

[55] Huarte was a successful businessman closely associated with the Franco regime, serving as Vice President of the Provincial Council of Navarra from 1964 to 1971, as well as a deputy member of Spanish parliament during the same period (Paredes 1997). He was awarded Navarre regional government's medal in 2014 for his contribution to the industrialization of Navarre. The award caused widespread controversy, with strong opposition coming from social movements related to historical memory, including organization such as Autobús de la Memoria (2014). The Spanish government eventually announced its intention to withdraw the medal in November 2022.

[56] In Bizkaia, forced labour in iron mines and the steel industry was one of the tools that enabled the reorganization of the economy following the Francoist occupation in 1937, redirecting it towards military production for the war efforts (Mendiola 2012).

ment of this historical reality. Despite opportunities within the context of deindustrialization, initiatives to manage Bizkaia's industrial heritage remain sparse compared to other European regions.[57] Furthermore, there is a noticeable lack of interest in addressing the issue of forced labour within local and regional initiatives, particularly concerning areas linked to the Basque industrial bourgeoisie. A striking example is the mining region near Bilbao, which has been repurposed into a recreational area featuring a mining museum and nature interpretation centres known as Ekoetxeak. Despite attracting thousands of visitors annually for picnics and trekking, these spaces lack any reference to their concentrationary past. This omission extends even to the Museo de la Minería del País Vasco[58] (Mining Museum of Basque Country), which, despite financing a research project on forced labour in the mines in 2009,[59] failed to incorporate this aspect into its permanent exhibition or educational materials.

In a climate of limited social pressure, the Basque Government's enactment of a new Law on historical and democratic memory in 2023 represented a concerning regression compared to the progress observed in other autonomous communities, particularly Andalusia and its 2022 Law on Democratic Memory.[60] In terms of the Basque law, despite an acknowledgement of those who carried out forced labour, notably in Article 4, a conspicuous absence persists regarding entities that profited from this repressive practice. Remarkably, the same political parties, PSOE and the Basque Nationalist Party (PNV), that had previously championed the 2022 national law also promoted this legislation at the autonomous level. The absence of corporate accountability in the new law can be attributed to the formidable influence of the business sector, particularly in a region where private enterprises were deeply involved in forced labour, coupled with the relative weakness of the associative fabric. Unlike in other autonomous communities, the issue of forced labour has not been effectively placed at the forefront of memory policies in the Basque region, highlighting a missed opportunity for a comprehensive historical reckoning.

Another sector deeply implicated in the exploitation of captive labour, yet notably absent from accountability efforts or attempts to engage in investigative and reparation measures, is the construction industry. This sector's involvement extended to not only to urban and monumental projects, but also hydraulic or transport infrastructures. However, its complicity has been largely obscured, sometimes through mergers and acquisitions, continuous growth, and the corporate concentration experienced in the latter decades of the twentieth century. An illustrative example of the social invisibility surrounding a company's involvement in forced labour is the Banús family, owners of one of the largest construction business empires during the

---

[57] Ruzafa (2022).

[58] For further information, www.meatzaldea.eus/ (last accessed 4 April 2024).

[59] Pastor (2010).

[60] Ley 9/2023, de 28 de septiembre, de Memoria Histórica y Democrática de Euskadi, Boletín Oficial del Estado, 274, de 16 de noviembre de 2023, https://www.boe.es/diario_boe/txt.php?id=BOE-A-2023-23216 (last accessed 4 April 2024).

dictatorship, with a more than twenty year history of using prison labour.[61] Despite facing an economic crisis in the 1970s, the public image of José Banús remains associated with business success and luxury tourism, marked by tributes such as a statue in his honour in Puerto Banús (Marbella, Málaga) and a foundation for the promotion of culture that carries his name.[62] In contrast, there is a conspicuous absence of public acknowledgement linking this prosperity to captive labour under the dictatorship.

Within the construction industry, Dragados y Construcciones was another major company that profited from prison labour. Similar to the Banús family, the growth of Dragados y Construcciones coincided with its close ties to the Franco regime, exemplified by its directors Luis Sánchez-Guerra Sainz and Antonio Durán Tovar.[63] Durán Tovar was awarded the title of Marqués de la Ribera del Sella in 2003, "for his purported contributions to the advancement and internationalization of Spain's construction sector, as well as the personal and professional development of workers".[64] Unlike Banús, however, Dragados y Construcciones weathered the crises of the 1970s and expanded into an internationally recognized business group, ultimately acquired by the ACS Group in 2002. Furthermore, the historical responsibility of Dragados y Construcciones intersects with its use of forced labour and the financing of the 1936 coup d'état by the Spanish Banca March, whose heirs still hold a significant stake (18.2%) in the bank.[65] Banca March's involvement in funding the coup d'état underscores the broader issue of corporate impunity during the Franco era,[66] a topic that remains insufficiently highlighted in the public discourse, despite the cultural prestige of the foundation associated with the bank.[67]

Furthermore, it is crucial to note that certain construction companies used captive labour for the expansion and construction of railway infrastructure. Among these companies was MZOV, which participated in constructing the railway to Galicia.[68] In 1997, MZOV was integrated into the Acciona group, which also included Entrecanales y Távora. Notably, Entrecanales y Távora oversaw the construction of the Seville Collector during the war, using captive labour.[69] Public outcry over their involvement, along with subsequent publications highlighting their

---

[61] The participation of Banús in the construction of the Valley of the Fallen is documented in the Memoirs of the Directorate General of Prisons, and analysed by authors such as Sueiro (1976), Olmeda (2009) and Sanchez Albornoz (2012). For an analysis of the business career of Juan Banús, see Gutiérrez Molina (2017).

[62] For more information: www.fundacionbanus.com/ (last accessed 4 April 2024).

[63] Sáenz Ridruejo and Maestre (2019).

[64] Real Decreto 818/2003, de 23 de junio, por el que se concede el título de Marqués de la Ribera del Sella a don Antonio Durán Tovar. *Boletín Oficial del Estado*, 150, www.boe.es/diario_boe/txt.php?id=BOE-A-2003-12597 (last accessed 4 April 2024).

[65] Maestre (2019), p. 109.

[66] Sanchez Asiáin (2014).

[67] For more information: www.march.es/es/fundacion (last accessed 4 April 2024).

[68] Mendiola (2013c).

[69] Gordillo (2014).

role,[70] prompted Acciona, which acquired Entrecanales y Távora in 1997, to remove any reference to their business activities between 1931 and 1948 from its website's history section.[71] This exemplifies a business strategy of denying the use of forced labour, in contrast to the approach of German companies that profited from forced labour. After decades of trying to obscure their complicity, German companies have acknowledged this responsibility, although justifying it as the result of the historical circumstances under National Socialism. Starting in 1958, and definitively from 2000, with the mentioned Erinnerung, Verantwortung und Zukunft Foundation, various German companies have participated in compensating former forced labourers and facilitating historical research on the subject.[72]

In Spain, legal and social impunity in relation to the use of forced labour still benefits most companies regardless of their sector and historical trajectory. In Bizkaia, industrial decline, bankruptcies and the disappearance of many companies stand as an obstacle to the demand for accountability. In the case of construction companies, on the contrary, corporate growth and concentration are key processes reinforcing Archimedes' lever and thus the corporate veto over memory policies.[73]

3.2 *Grassroot Mobilization: Catalyst for Advancements in Corporate Accountability*

As shown in Sect. 2, some advancements toward the social recognition of forced labour and corporate involvement did occur in certain Spanish regions and economic sectors. However, none has yet resulted in judicial or economic accountability for the implicated companies. Nevertheless, these developments represent notable progress within the Spanish context and serve as valuable reference points for future endeavours. One case, in particular, was highly influential for the adoption of the 2022 Law of Democratic Memory, and also highlights some of the elements in the Archimedes' lever approach. Launched in 2002 by the trade union Confederación General del Trabajo (CGT), a social initiative centred around the Canal del Guadalquivir in Seville, Andalusia—famously known as the Canal de los Presos (Prisoners' Canal)—became the pioneering social campaign in Spain to address forced labour. This initiative has not only contributed to scholarly

---

[70] Maestre (2019).

[71] Domínguez (2020). ACCIONA website: https://www.acciona.com/es/nuestro-proposito/historia/?_adin=0183579827 (last accessed 4 April 2024).

[72] For the evolution of the strategy engaged in by German companies regarding their Nazi past and forced labour, see Wiessen (2001). For negotiations over accountability and compensation, see Authers (2006) and Payne et al. (2022). An example of this business strategy in Germany is analysed by Gregor (2001) with regard to the entrepreneur Karl Dielh. An example of this exculpatory strategy can be found on the website of this business group: www.diehl.com/group/en/company/history/ (last accessed 4 April 2024).

[73] Payne et al. (2021).

understanding through its rigorous research, but also significantly influenced public awareness on the issue, marking a crucial milestone in the advancement of corporate accountability in Spain.[74] Although directed by a public institution, the Servicio de Colonias Penitenciarias Militarizadas (Military Penitentiary Colonies Service), the construction of the canal between 1940 and 1962 gave way to private interests by converting thousands of hectares of rain-fed land owned by large Sevillian landowners into irrigated land. This emphasis on private gains has become a central point of the campaign, voiced prominently by the CGT and Andalusian memory associations. In this vein, Gutiérrez Molina, director of the Todos los nombres project, denounced such private interests more than a decade ago: "Slave labour is still not recognised and… the companies that took advantage of the slave labour [that was] provided by the Patronato de Redención de Penas por el Trabajo have not been asked [to take] financial responsibility, but rather [to acknowledge] what happened".[75]

In addition, activists have emphasised other instances of forced labour involving private companies, including the Campo del Colector in the Heliópolis neighbourhood of Seville. Established in July 1937 by the Seville City Council and managed by Entrecanales y Távora, this project aimed to construct sewage infrastructure to divert discharge into the Guadalquivir.[76] Since 2001, the CGT working group has advocated for the recognition of such sites, with efforts culminating in 2016 with the installation of a monument, funded by the group and public contributions, on land donated by the town council.

The active social initiative surrounding the Canal del Guadalquivir had a profound impact, especially in the legislative sphere. It is noteworthy that the Law on Historical and Democratic Memory of Andalusia, adopted in 2017, spurred by such grassroots mobilisations, became the first in Spain to explicitly mention the beneficiaries of forced labour. This legislative milestone underscored the direct influence of the social initiative on shaping policy responses to historical injustices. Moreover, the law mandated the inclusion of forced labour sites in censuses and inventories of places of memory. Notably, this provision was enacted in specific cases such as the Canal de los Presos in Seville[77] and the island of Saltés in Huelva.[78] While these sites did not involve private companies, only state-owned companies, their inclusion in memory initiatives signifies a crucial step towards acknowledging and preserving the memory of forced labour experiences in Andalusia.

Despite the institutional interventions that have paralyzed initiatives in Andalusia since the election of the right-wing Partido Popular to the regional government in 2019, the resilience and strength of grassroots movements have continued to exert influence beyond the region's borders. These initiatives have not only shaped

[74] Acosta Bono et al. (2004) and Acosta Bono (2010).

[75] Gutiérrez Molina (2010), p. 9.

[76] Gordillo (2014).

[77] See www.juntadeandalucia.es/organismos/turismoculturaydeporte/areas/cultura/memoria-democratica/lugares-memoria-democratica/paginas/canal-presos.html(last accessed 4 April 2024).

[78] See www.juntadeandalucia.es/organismos/turismoculturaydeporte/areas/cultura/memoria-democratica/lugares-memoria-democratica/paginas/isla-saltes.html(last accessed 4 April 2024).

legislative developments, but also served as a beacon of inspiration for social mobilisations in other parts of Spain. For instance, in Navarre, the Memoriaren Bideak[79] (Paths of Memory) association has collaborated with Andalusian organisations since its inception in 2004. This collaboration underscores the cross-regional solidarity and enduring impact of grassroots efforts in advancing the cause of historical memory and accountability.

The mobilisations in Navarre were rooted in a specific historical context. The region's position at the Pyrenean border with France made it a strategic site for military fortification, leading to the construction of numerous bunkers and mountain roads.[80] Between 1939 and 1942, approximately 14,000 POWs were integrated into Workers' Battalions and Disciplinary Battalions of Working Soldiers. While all forced labour in Navarre was directed and executed by concentrationary units under military control, with no involvement of private enterprises, the collaborative efforts at memorial work between various social groups and the administration set a benchmark at the state level. This progress resulted from a combination of institutional support and robust social mobilization—in addition to Memoriaren Bideak, an association of historians, the Gerónimo de Uztariz Institute, and the video-activist collective Eguzki Bideoak have also participated. Their efforts resulted in a website, a travelling exhibition with a catalogue that became an edited volume on forced labour in Spain,[81] several documentaries[82] and the placement of a sculpture in the Artesiaga Pass.

With the formation of a new centre-left government in Navarre in 2015, and especially since the creation of the Navarre Institute of Memory in 2017,[83] various campaigns were carried out around the mountain fortifications, including archaeological activities with the participation of young volunteers, collaboration with educational institutions, the development of a new international exhibition on forced labour in the Pyrenean fortification[84] and the reconstruction of a POW barracks[85] in Igal. These results were further reinforced in April 2019 by the declaration of the Igal-Vidángoz road as an official Site of Memory in Navarre.[86]

Moreover, in October 2022, the Navarre Institute of Memory signed an agreement with the Secretary of State for Democratic Memory to promote the project

---

[79] For more information: https://memoriarenbideak.eus/ (last accessed 4 April 2024).

[80] Mendiola and Beaumont (2006) and Mendiola (2012). There are also two documentaries on the use of forced labour on these roads (Eguzki Bideoak 2007 and Eguzki Bideoak 2011a).

[81] Mendiola and Gastón (2007).

[82] Eguzki Bideoak (2007, 2011a, b).

[83] For more information: https://pazyconvivencia.navarra.es/es/instituto-navarro-de-la-memoria (last accessed 4 April 2024).

[84] For further information: www.fronterasdehormigon.com/ (last accessed 4 April 2024).

[85] For further information: www.navarra.es/home_es/Actualidad/Sala+de+prensa/Noticias/2018/09/29/igal+barracon+prisioneros+franquismo.htm (last accessed 4 April 2024).

[86] For further information: https://bon.navarra.es/es/anuncio/-/texto/2019/97/13/ (last accessed 4 April 2024).

Fronteras de Hormigón (Frontiers of Concrete),[87] with the development of several mountain cycling and road routes to visit these infrastructure sites. During the inauguration of the barracks in Igal, regional Minister Ana Ollo underscored the significance of the collaboration between Memoriaren Bideak, the Gerónimo de Uztariz Institute and Eguzki Bideoak, as a key factor in these memory achievements.[88] These results thus symbolized the cooperative efforts of different grassroot organisations in addressing the historical legacy of forced labour in Navarre. They serve as a tangible reminder of past injustices and highlight the importance of collective action in confronting such atrocities. Furthermore, they demonstrate the potential of collaboration between civil society organisations and governmental entities in fostering meaningful change and promoting the social recognition of forced labour issues.

In addition, other associations have promoted memorial projects on forced labour on the Pyrenean border itself. Starting in 2007, in Gipuzkoa province, in the Basque Country, the Kattin Txiki and Lezo Memoria associations reconstructed one barrack in 2024, advocated for the conservation of the ruins of others as spaces of memory, and produced two documentaries (in 2015 and 2017)[89]—despite the lack of any public institutional support. This collaboration between agents at the regional level has also been complemented by a joint initiative between Memoriaren Bideak and the CEAQUA to enhance cooperation between associations from different autonomous communities and international networks. In this case, CEAQUA –strengthened by a lawsuit filed in Argentina in 2010 against various Francoist officials accused of crimes against humanity—lodged, together with Memoriaren Bideak, the first lawsuit over forced labour in Spain, "against persons who may be responsible for conduct that may be characterized as war crimes and crimes against humanity" during in the construction of a mountain road in the Pyrenees between 1939 and 1941.[90] The complaint was presented in Navarre on 20 October 2022 by the relatives of twelve prisoners of war who were part of Work Battalions organized by the

[87] For further information: www.navarra.es/es/-/nota-prensa/relaciones-ciudadanas-y-la-secretaria-de-estado-de-memoria-democratica-firman-un-convenio-para-el-desarrollo-en-navarra-del-proyecto-fronteras-de-hormigon- (last accessed 4 April 2024).

[88] "The inauguration of these barracks today required various efforts. Historians played a crucial role in recovering the history of the road's construction and revealing the harsh living conditions experienced by hundreds of captives here. The association Memoriaren Bideak, in collaboration with the Gerónimo de Uztariz Institute and Eguzki Bideoak, actively participated in its dissemination. Local residents from the Salazar and Roncal valleys provided their testimonies and experiences, and the owners of this piece of land also contributed significantly to preserving this memory. Additionally, witnesses of the atrocities were essential in providing their testimonies to ensure this history is remembered." In www.noticiasdenavarra.com/opinion/2019/03/22/vicente-luis-memoria-2418696.html (last accessed 4 April 2024).

[89] Kattin Txiki (2015) and Mendizabal (2017).

[90] For more information see: https://elpais.com/espana/2023-10-20/doce-familiares-de-esclavos-del-franquismo-se-querellan-contra-el-gobierno.html, https://www.eldiario.es/navarra/familias-presos-republicanos-presentan-primera-querella-trabajos-forzados-franquismo_1_10613006.html, or https://todaytimeslive.com/politics/421842.html (last accessed 4 April 2024).

Inspectorate of Prisoner Concentration Camps. The complaint was accompanied by an expert report with precise information on the construction of the road.[91] However, the court of first instance in Aoiz (Navarra) and the Court of Justice of Navarre rejected the complaint, invoking the 1977 Amnesty Law. The judicial path nonetheless remains open after a subsequent appeal to the Constitutional Court, whose decision is still pending as of summer 2024. This case might in the future become a reference for lawsuits in other regions, including cases involving private companies. In addition, the initiative has received the support of the councils of the Salazar Valley and some villages in Roncal Valley, where the road is located. The Parliament of Navarre,[92] the prisoners' localities of origin and the vast majority of trade unions in Navarre also support the lawsuit.[93] The complaint is, therefore, a specific case of a grassroots initiative supported by national memory and justice networks, such as CEAQUA, and local and state institutions.

Finally, it should be stressed that the public railway company RENFE[94] is the only company thus far to promote the public visibility of forced labour. Although Spanish railways have not yet been held accountable, nor have they participated in reparations, there have been attempts to bring to light the reality of both forced labour and the general repression suffered by the company's workers under Franco's regime. A pivotal tool in this endeavour was the Memoria Histórica Ferroviaria website[95] (Historical Memory of the Railways), launched in 2020, which provides information on the different types of repression under the dictatorship suffered in the railway sector. In relation to forced labour, the website devotes a section to one of the railway penal detachments, Bustarviejo,[96] in the northern mountains of Madrid. Additionally, it offers a comprehensive historical overview[97] of forced labour's significance in shaping railway infrastructure under Franco's regime, based on a previous report by Mendiola and García Funes.[98]

[91] Mendiola et al. (2023).

[92] See: https://parlamentodenavarra.es/es/noticias/el-parlamento-de-navarra-muestra-su-apoyo-la-querella-interpuesta-para-que-el-r%C3%A9gimen-del-0 (last accessed 4 April 2024).

[93] See: www.noticiasdenavarra.com/sociedad/2023/12/26/juzgado-aoiz-inadmite-querella-trabajo-7681314.html (last accessed 4 April 2024).

[94] The public business entity RENFE OPERADORA is itself made up of four public limited companies www.renfe.com/es/es/informacion-legal/renfe-operadora (last accessed 4 April 2024).

[95] For further information: https://memoriahistoricaferroviaria.org (last accessed 4 April 2024).

[96] See https://memoriahistoricaferroviaria.org/trabajo-forzado/destacamento-penal-de-bustarviejo/ (last accessed 4 April 2024).

[97] See https://memoriahistoricaferroviaria.org/otras-represiones/trabajo-forzado/ (last accessed 4 April 2024).

[98] Mendiola (2013c, 2017) and García-Funes (2022).

3.3 One Special Case: The Public Railway Company (RENFE)

Despite the inherent limitations of existing initiatives, it is imperative to dissect the key factors that have contributed to addressing historical injustices, particularly concerning forced labour under Franco's regime. Within this framework, a nuanced understanding of various factors, many of which align with the conceptual framework of Archimedes' lever, becomes essential. Notably, the role of former victims, memorial associations, trade unions, university researchers, and institutional innovators emerges as pivotal. These actors have played distinct yet interconnected roles, with former victims sharing their experiences, memorial associations advocating for recognition and remembrance, trade unions mobilizing grassroots support, university researchers providing scholarly insights, and institutional innovators driving policy changes and initiatives. Intersectoral collaboration has thus been a key element in moving forward the debates concerning forced labour in Spain. Furthermore, it is crucial to acknowledge the influence of both the political and business contexts in shaping the trajectory of these efforts. Political dynamics, including shifts in governance and policy frameworks, have undoubtedly impacted the landscape of addressing corporate accountability.

In the realm of railway labour exploitation, grassroots efforts have played a crucial role in shedding light on historical injustices. Testimonies and condemnations of labour exploitation within the railway sector first surfaced in the accounts of former forced labourers, documented in memoirs.[99] In a poignant tribute to these narratives, the Altsasu town council (Navarre), in collaboration with the internationalist Whipala association, envisioned placing a sculpture at the railway station in Altsasu—a site mentioned in former forced labourer Isaac Arenal's memoirs. However, their plans were met with bureaucratic hurdles, as permission from the public company ADIF was refused. Undeterred, the sculpture found its place in a town square in 2008, with Arenal himself present at the inauguration ceremony.[100]

Beyond these individual efforts, the most important collective initiative around forced labour on the railway concerned the penal detachment of Bustarviejo, on the railway line from Madrid to Burgos, where several thousand prisoners worked between 1943 and 1952.[101] An archaeological intervention in 2006, that brought to light the huts in which the prisoners' families stayed,[102] was followed by a tribute to forced labourers in 2013, the production of a documentary,[103] and the publication of a book on the history of the detachment and the subsequent memory initiatives in 2022.[104]

---

[99] Larch (1975) and Arenal (1999).

[100] See http://ahaztuak1936-1977.blogspot.com/2008/05/alsasua-recuerda-los-batallones-de.html (last accessed 3 July 2024).

[101] Mendiola (2013c).

[102] Falquina et al. (2008).

[103] Cabello (2013).

[104] Riesco (2022).

These grassroots efforts have also found support within certain sectors of RENFE, though only after the arrival of a more favourable political constellation. In 2004, at the behest of the trade unions Comisiones Obreras and Unión General de Trabajadores, the RENFE Board of Directors decided to promote initiatives aimed at recovering the memory of oppressed families. Although primarily symbolic, this initial step laid the groundwork for further action. In 2018, again under the PSOE government, a new agreement was signed, involving ADIF and RENFE Operadora,[105] with the backing of the Ministry of Public Works and Transport. This agreement signalled a renewed commitment to the cause, culminating in plans to erect a statue at Madrid's main railway station, Atocha-Almudena Grandes. The statue was inaugurated in 2008, together with a dedicated website.[106]

In the case of RENFE and railway infrastructure, in addition to trade union pressure and the company's disposition, certain figures within railway historical heritage management were particularly concerned with acknowledging and rectifying the historical debt owed by the railway companies to those repressed by the dictatorship. This concern has been further facilitated by the existence of the Railway Historical Archive, which encompasses documentation from private railway companies predating the creation of RENFE in 1941. This archival resource has greatly supported historical research efforts, especially since the establishment of the Fundación de los Ferrocarriles Españoles (Foundation of Spanish Railways) in 1985. In addition, two foundation directors, who can be described as "institutional innovators" within the theoretical framework of the Archimedean lever,[107] conducted historical research on repression within the railway system.[108] Undoubtedly, both Polo Muriel's work as director of the Museo del Ferrocarril and Miguel Muñoz's activities at the Fundación de los Ferrocarriles Españoles have been fundamental to the launch and development of above-mentioned initiatives on historical memory, which are unique in the Spanish business world.[109]

RENFE's engagement with historical memory can also be attributed to changes in the political landscape. The public nature of RENFE makes it particularly sensitive to political shifts. For instance, RENFE's promotion of initiatives for the recovery of historical memory was met with support during PSOE governments, but was largely sidelined during the Popular Party's administration between 2011 and 2018. It was only with the resurgence of a PSOE-led government in 2018 that the initiative gained renewed impetus. This highlights how changes in political leadership can significantly impact the prioritization and progress of initiatives within public companies like RENFE.

---

[105] RENFE was divided in 2005, giving way to two new public companies, one managing railway infrastructure (ADIF) and the other one in charge of passenger and freight transport (RENFE Operadora).

[106] See https://memoriahistoricaferroviaria.org/ (last accessed 3 July 2024).

[107] Payne et al. (2021).

[108] Polo Muriel (2019) and Muñoz Rubio (2020a).

[109] Muñoz Rubio (2020b).

While RENFE is a case of particular importance at the national level, another initiative at the Basque level illustrates how the strength of the associative networks, and the existence of railway heritage professionals sensitive to the recovery of historical memory made the history of forced labour visible. The collaboration between the associative network of Gernika (Bizkaia), the Association of Professionals and Students of Criminology of the Basque Country, the Basque Museum on Railways, and public institutions such as the town council of Gernika and the Basque Government, led to a tribute, exhibition and book on the role of prisoners and POWs in the reconstruction of Gernika and the opening of the Sukarrieta-Bermeo railway in 2022.[110] However, this initiative is not yet strong enough to introduce issues related to corporate accountability into Basque regional legislation.

4 Conclusions

The assessment of corporate responsibility and accountability for forced labour in Spain has to be contextualized in the broader framework of memory policies surrounding Franco's dictatorship. The pervasive impunity granted to individuals and institutions associated with the regime's repression inevitably extends to corporations. Moreover, this impunity not only pertains to potential criminal liability, but also to social (un)awareness of business complicity in labour exploitation practices and to the restricted access to company archives. In this regard, the issue of forced labour has been largely overlooked or even rendered invisible in the sparse legal measures aimed at recognising repression against individuals. Even with the modest advancements in legislation witnessed in the twenty-first century, achieving corporate accountability has remained elusive. In only a handful of instances, and always with limited outcomes, have corporations been held to account for their complicity in forced labour.

In addition to overarching factors shaping the characteristics of memory policies in post-dictatorial Spain, specific contextual elements further elucidate this invisibility. First, there is a societal perception that legal deficiencies in addressing forced labour were comparatively less significant than those pertaining to other forms of repression, such as extrajudicial killings or forced disappearances. Second, within the realm of economic accountability, impunity has extended into various spheres, including the financing of the coup, the close ties of certain companies with Franco's regime, and the private profiteering resulting from the expropriation of property from repressed individuals. Consequently, the lack of accountability for forced labour must be contextualized within a broader context of economic actors' impunity.

In this sense, the business veto that the literature has identified as an obstacle to corporate accountability has operated in the Spanish case above all through large

[110] Leonet (2022).

construction companies that have maintained influential relations with political institutions not only during the dictatorship, but also after its fall. It is within these large construction companies that some of the enterprises that benefited from captive labour were integrated, following takeovers and mergers. Paradoxically, however, this veto is not exclusively connected to the strength of the companies after the fall of the dictatorship, insofar as the economic crisis of the 1980s and the process of deindustrialisation also led to the dissolution of various companies and, consequently, to a lack of accountability. Moreover, the legal system that allowed prison labour to occur during the dictatorship, namely the System of Redemption of Sentences through Work, was maintained in Spain, albeit with certain modifications, until the adoption of the new criminal code in 1995. It is reasonable to surmise that companies benefiting from a system that endured for two decades after the demise of the dictatorship would not face legal prosecution or be held accountable.

Hence, it was not until the enactment of the Law on Democratic Memory at the end of 2022 that national legislation articulated the need for companies that profited from captive labour to engage in public acknowledgement of this historical reality. Nonetheless, this provision remains more aspirational than prescriptive, lacking normative force, as it does not compel companies to assume any specific form of corporate responsibility. Moreover, at the moment of writing, the rise of the extreme right in some parts of Spain threatens the gains made in the past decade, with the danger of repealing the current legislation on historical and democratic memory.

The modest legislative changes regarding the accountability of companies that used forced labourers during the dictatorship cannot be understood without considering the activism of civil society. These initiatives are closely linked to the influence of certain trade unions and social memorialist movements, prominent in particular regions, such as Andalusia or Navarre. Additionally, the responsiveness of regional institutions and public entities, such as RENFE, to these demands has played a significant role in pushing legislative changes forward.

The accomplishments in addressing forced labour have primarily been the identification of workplaces and culpable companies, alongside the commemoration of these specific locations. Furthermore, significant efforts have been directed at fostering research, particularly on the railway sector. Notably, progress has predominantly occurred in the legislative sphere at the regional level, capitalizing on opportunities offered by the decentralized Spanish political system. These initiatives mark formative strides towards compelling companies to assume their share of the costs and responsibilities stemming from societal awareness of this repressive past.

In conclusion, the limited progress observed in Spain concerning corporate responsibility for forced labour under Franco's regime is closely intertwined with the overarching characteristics of memory policies regarding the dictatorship and the pervasive impunity enjoyed by perpetrators of human rights violations. Private companies have largely evaded legal obligations in this regard. Nevertheless, modest progress has been driven by three key factors: the political opportunities offered by decentralization; heightened receptiveness within public companies; and crucially, social pressure exerted by associations and trade unions advocating for truth, justice, and reparation. This social pressure, bolstered by collaboration among associations from different autonomous communities and influenced by international legal actions such as the lawsuit in Argentina, has served as a catalyst for initiating accountability. Most clearly, this social activism reflects the significance of ongoing efforts to enhance scientific and social acknowledgement of forced labour in Spain.

References

Acosta Bono G (2010) Los Merinales, un lugar para la memoria. Un largo proceso reivindicativo. In: AMHYJA (ed) VI Jornadas Campos de Concentración y Trabajo Esclavo en Andalucía. Asociación Memoria Histórica y Justicia de Andalucía, Sevilla

Acosta Bono G, Gutiérrez Molina JL, Martínez Macías L, Del Río SÁ (2004) El Canal de los Presos (1940-1962), Trabajos forzados: de la represión política a la explotación económica. Crítica, Barcelona

Agirreazkuenaga J, Urquijo M (eds) (2015) Senderos de la memoria. Relación de espacios vinculados a la memoria de la guerra civil. Eusko Jaurlaritza—Gobierno Vasco, Vitoria—Gasteiz

Aguilar P (2008a) Políticas de la memoria y memorias de la política. El caso español en perspectiva comparada. Alianza Editorial, Madrid

Aguilar P (2008b) Transitional or post-transitional justice? Recent developments in the Spanish case. South Eur Soc Politics 13(4):417–433

Alonso Olea E, Belaustegi U (eds) (2021) La memoria pública a debate: la memoria pública de la Guerra Civil, el franquismo y la Transición (1936-2019). Silex, Madrid

Arenal I (1999) 95 Batallón de Trabajadores, Madrid. http://memoriarenbideak.eus/isaac-arenal-cardiel

Authers J (2006) Making good again: German compensation for forced and slave laborers. In: de Greiff P (ed) The handbook of reparations. Oxford University Press, Oxford

Autobús de la Memoria (2014) Medalla de Oro de Navarra: apología del franquismo. In: Autobús De La Memoria, Simbología golpista en Navarra. Memoria y presencia del franquismo. Pamiela—Autobús de la Memoria/Oroimenaren Autobusa, Iruñea—Pamplona

Cabello P (2013) Los sonidos y los silencios de Bustarviejo. Documental. Arqueología de la Guerra Civil Española. (documentary film). http://guerraenlauniversidad.blogspot.com.es/2013/12/los-sonidos-y-silencios-de-bustarviejo.html

CELS (2015) Responsabilidad empresarial en delitos de lesa humanidad: represión a trabajadores durante el terrorismo de Estado. Infojus / Facultad Latinoamericana de Ciencias Sociales (FLACSO-Argentina) / Programa Verdad y Justicia y la Secretaría de Derechos Humanos, (Ministerio de Justicia y Derechos Humanos), Buenos Aires

Colla de Amorim F, Sion V, Machado R (2022) Accountability for Volkswagen's role in the Brazilian dictatorship. In: Payne L, Pereira G, Bernal-Bermúdez L (eds) Economic actors and the limits of transitional justice. Truth and justice for business complicity in human rights violations. Oxford University Press, Oxford

Domínguez D (2020) Acciona trata de borrar el pasado de la compañía durante la posguerra en su página web, La Marea. www.yoibextigo.lamarea.com/informe/acciona/que-es/acciona-borrar-pasado-posguerra-web/

Eguzki Bideoak (2007) Desafectos, esclavos de Franco en el Pirineo. (documentary film). www.channels.com/episodes/show/3600017/Desafectos#/episodes/show/3600017/Desafectos

Eguzki Bideoak (2011a) 827 kilómetros sin retorno. Iruñea—Pamplona. (documentary film)

Eguzki Bideoak (2011b) Disciplina y resistencia: trabajos forzados en la España de Franco - Discipline and resistance: Forced labour in Franco's Spain (Compilation of documentary films)

Espinosa F (2002) Julio de 1936. Golpe militar y plan de exterminio. In: Casanova J, Espinosa F, Mir C, Moreno F (eds) Morir, matar, sobrevivir: la violencia en la dictadura de Franco. Crítica, Barcelona

Espinosa F (ed) (2006) Contra el olvido. Historia y memoria de la guerra civil. Crítica, Barcelona
Espinosa F (2015) Lucha de historias, lucha de memorias: España 2002-2015. Aconcagua, Sevilla
Espinosa F (2019) La lucha por el acceso a los archivos del franquismo. De los «Fondos Especiales» del Tribunal de Cuentas a los «10.000 documentos» del Ministerio de Defensa. In: González Quintana A, Galvez S, Castro, L (eds) El acceso a los archivos en España, Fundación Francisco Largo Caballero, Fundación 1° de Mayo, Madrid
Espinosa F (2021) "La investigación de la represión franquista 40 años después (1979-2020)", Memoriapaper(ak): Documentos de trabajo del Fondo Documental de la Memoria Histórica en Navarra. Nafarroako Oroimen Historikoari Buruzko Fondo Dokumentalaren langaiak, 9
Falquina Á, Fermín P, González A, Marín C, Quintero A, Rolland J (2008) Arqueología de los destacamentos penales franquistas en el ferrocarril Madrid-Burgos: El caso de Bustarviejo. Complutum 19:175–195
Ferrándiz F (2023) Unmaking forgotten mass graves and honorable burial: engaging with the Spanish civil war legacy. In: Parra RC, Ubelaker DU (eds) Anthropology of violent death: theoretical foundations for forensic humanitarian action. John Wiley & Sons, London
García-Funes JC (2016) A recoger bombas. Batallones de trabajo forzado en Castilla y León (1937–1942). Atrapasueños, Sevilla
García-Funes JC (2022) Desafectos. Batallones de trabajo forzado en el franquismo. Comares, Granada
García-Funes, JC, Mendiola F (2020) Historia y memoria del trabajo forzado del sistema concentracionario franquista. Cahiers de civilisation espagnole contemporaine, 24
Gomez Bravo G (2008) La redención de penas: la formación del sistema penitenciario franquista. Los libros de la Catarata, Madrid
Gordillo C (2014) Campo de concentración «El Colector». Heliópolis (Sevilla). In: López Fernández R (ed) Lugares de la memoria. Golpe militar, represión y resistencia en Sevilla. Itinerarios. Aconcagua, Sevilla
Gregor N (2001) Vergangenheitspolitik, CSU-style: the memory of forced labour in Nuremberg. J Holocaust Educ 10(3):83–104
Grosescu R (2024) Justice and memory after dictatorship. Central Eastern Europe, Latin America and the fragmentation of international criminal law. Oxford University Press, Oxford
Gutiérrez JL, Martínez L (2007) El trabajo esclavo de los presos políticos del franquismo en Andalucía. In: Historia y Memoria. Todos los Nombres, Mapa de Fosas y Actuaciones de los Tribunales de Responsabilidades Políticas en Andalucía. Universidad de Almería, Almería
Gutiérrez Molina JL (2010) El trabajo esclavo en Andalucía: análisis de una realidad existente. In: AMHYJA (ed) VI Jornadas. Campos de concentración y trabajo esclavo en Andalucía. AMHYJA, Sevilla
Gutiérrez Molina JL (2017) José Banús Masdeu (1906-1984). In: Torres E (ed) Cien empresarios españoles. LID Editorial Empresarial, Madrid
Hepworth A (2014) Site of memory and dismemory: the valley of the fallen in Spain. J Genocide Res 16:4
Izagirre A (2016) El siglo de Luis Ortiz Alfau. Eusko Jaurlaritzaren Argitalpen Zerbitzu Nagusia / Servicio Central de Publicaciones del Gobierno Vasco, Bilbao
Jimeno R (2018) Amnesties, pardons and transitional justice Spain's pact of forgetting. Routledge, New York
Jimeno Aranguren R, Aguilar P (2022) De la «memoria histórica» a la «memoria democrática». La evolución de las políticas públicas de memoria y justicia transicional en España. In: Penadés A, Garmendia A (eds) Informe sobre la democracia en España 2022. El largo plazo. Fundación Alternativas, Madrid
Juliá S (2006) Memoria, historia y política de un pasado de guerra y dictadura. In: Juliá S (ed) Memoria de la guerra y del franquismo. Taurus, Madrid
Kattin Txiki (2015) Trabajadoriak, esclavos del franquismo en Oarsoaldea. Oiartzun, Kattin Txiki (documentary film)
Leonet D (ed) (2022) Gernika—Bermeo trenbidea—ferrocarril. Gobierno Vasco, Departamento de Planficación Territorial, Vivienda y Transportes—APECPV/EHPIKE, Vitoria-Gasteiz
Maestre A (2019) Franquismo S.A. Akal, Madrid

Martín Pallín JA, Escudero Alday R (2009) De malas leyes, peores reglamentos: el desarrollo de la Ley de la memoria histórica. Jueces para la Democracia 66:9–25
Mendiola F (2006) Se mantiene el manto de silencio: proyecto de ley y trabajos forzados bajo el franquismo. Cuadernos para el Diálogo 14:6–15
Mendiola F (2012) El impacto de los trabajos forzados en la economía vasconavarra (1937—1945). Investigaciones de Historia Económica - Economic History Research 8(2):104–116
Mendiola F (2013a) «La consideración de ser explotado»: trabajo forzado y trabajo en cautividad en la España del siglo XX. In: Oliver Olmo P (ed) El siglo de los castigos. Prisión y formas carcelarias en la España del siglo XX. Anthropos, Barcelona
Mendiola F (2013b) Forced labor, public policies, and business strategies during Franco's dictatorship: an interim report. Enterprise Soc 14(1):182–213
Mendiola F (2013c) El trabajo forzado en infraestructuras ferroviarias bajo el franquismo (1938-1957): una estimación cuantitativa. Transportes, Servicios y telecomunicaciones 25:40–62
Mendiola F (2015) Lugares públicos y privados donde se utilizó el trabajo forzado. In: Agirreazkuenaga J, Urquijo M (eds) Senderos de la memoria. Relación de espacios vinculados a la memoria de la guerra civil. Eusko Jaurlaritza—Gobierno Vasco, Vitoria—Gasteiz
Mendiola F (2017) Of firms and captives: railway infrastructures and the economics of forced labour (Spain, 1937-1957). Revista de Historia Industrial 68:165–192
Mendiola F (2021) Políticas de memoria en torno al trabajo forzado: El franquismo en perspectiva comparada. In: Alonso Olea E, Belaustegi U (eds) La memoria pública a debate: la memoria pública de la Guerra Civil, el franquismo y la Transición. Sílex, Madrid, pp 1936–2019
Mendiola F, Beaumont E (2006) Esclavos del franquismo en el Pirineo. Txalaparta, Tafalla
Mendiola F, Gaston JM (eds) (2007) Los trabajos forzados en la dictadura franquista. Iruñea-Pamplona, Memoriaren Bideak
Mendiola F, Beaumont E, García-Funes JC, Rodríguez I (2023) La carretera Igal-Vidángoz-Roncal (Navarra, 1939—1941): trabajo forzado concentracionario y legislación internacional. memoriapaper(ak) 15
Mendizabal M (2017) Frankismoaren esklaboei omenaldia Lezon. Lezo, Etxetxo Lezoko Memoria Historikoaren Elkartea, (documentary film)
Messuti A (2013) La querella Argentina: la aplicación del principio de justicia universal al caso de las desapariciones forzadas. In: Escudero R, Pérez González C (eds) Desapariciones forzadas, represión política y crímenes del franquismo. Trotta, Madrid
Miguez A (2015) Genocidal genealogy of Francoism: violence, memory and impunity. London School of Economics, London
Mikelarena F (2016) Sin piedad. Limpieza política en Navarra, 1936. Pamiela, Iruñea-Pamplona
Muñoz Rubio M (2020a) "Ochocientos brazos". El movimiento obrero en el ferrocarril durante el franquismo. Editorial Anexo, Madrid
Muñoz Rubio M (2020b) Memoria histórica en el ferrocarril. Revista del Ministerio de Fomento 701:62–65
Olmeda F (2009) El Valle de los Caídos: una memoria de España. Península, Barcelona
Olsen TD (2022) Business as usual? The legacy of transitions to democracy on corporate accountability. In: Payne L, Pereira G, Bernal-Bermudez L (eds) Economic actors and the limits of transitional justice. Truth and justice for business complicity in human rights violations. Oxford University Press, Oxford
Padín F (2017) República, guerra y campos de concentración. Memorias de un anarquista bilbaíno. Fundación Anselmo Lorenzo, Madrid
Paredes J (1997) Félix Huarte, 1896—1971. Ariel, Barcelona
Pastor F (2010) El Batallón Minero n° 1 en las minas de Vizcaya. Beta III Milenio, Bilbao
Payne L, Pereira G, Bernal-Bermudez L (2021) Justicia transicional y la rendición de cuentas de actores económicos, desde abajo: desplegando la palanca de Arquímedes. Bogotá, Dejusticia
Payne L, Beall M, Hutchinson A (2022) The roots of corporate accountability: from the holocaust and beyond. In: Payne L, Pereira G, Bernal-Bermudez L (eds) Economic actors and the limits of transitional justice. Truth and justice for business complicity in human rights violations. Oxford University Press, Oxford

Pereira G (2022) Corporate accountability in Argentina: fighting corporate impunity in provincial transitional justice contexts. In: Payne L, Pereira G, Bernal-Bermudez L (eds) Economic actors and the limits of transitional justice. Truth and justice for business complicity in human rights violations. Oxford University Press, Oxford
Polo Muriel F (2019) La depuración del personal ferroviario durante la Guerra Civil y el Franquismo (1936–1975). Fundación de los Ferrocarriles Españoles, Madrid
Preston P (2011) Spanish holocaust: inquisition and extermination in twentieth-century Spain. Harper Collins, London
Riesco S (2022) El destacamento penal de Bustarviejo. Lugar de memoria. Asociación de Memoria Histórica «Los Barracones», Bustarviejo
Ruzafa R (2022) El tratamiento museográfico de la desindustrialización en el País Vasco. In: Vega R, Diaz I (eds) Desindustrialización: memoria, patrimonio y representaciones. Trea - Universidad de Oviedo - Fundació Cipriano García - Arxiu Històric de CCOO de Catalunya, Oviedo
Sanchez Albornoz N (2012) Cárceles y Exilios. Anagrama, Barcelona
Sanchez Asiáin JÁ (2014) La financiación de la guerra civil. Crítica, Barcelona
Sánchez León P, Izquierdo J (2017) La guerra que nos han contado y la que no: memoria e historia de 1936 para el siglo XXI. Postmetropolis Editorial, Madrid
Stockey G (2013) Valley of the fallen, the (n)ever changing face of general Franco's monument. Cultural and Communications Press, Nottingham, Critical
Sueiro D (1976) La verdadera historia del Valle de los Caídos. Editorial Sedmay, Madrid
Urquijo M (2006) La memoria negada. La encrucijada de la vía institucional en el caso del Gobierno Vasco y las víctimas del franquismo. Hispania Nova: Revista de historia contemporánea 6:196–225
Wiessen J (2001) West German industry and the challenge of the Nazi past, 1945-1955. University of North Carolina Press, Chapel Hill

Fernando Mendiola is a Researcher at the Public University of Navarra, Spain. His research work can be divided into two main fields: the first focused on family economies during industrialization, attending to migratory movements, co-residence strategies and labour markets. The second, initiated in 2002, is aimed at revealing the political and economic logic of forced labour under Francoism. He is member of the *Study Group on the History of Prison and Punitive Institutions*, the *Spanish Network of Labour History*, the research team of the *Documentary Fund of Historical Memory in Navarra* and the *Working Group Labour and Coercion within the European Labour History Network*. He is author, amongst other publications, of "Forced labour, public policies, and business strategies during Franco's dictatorship: An interim report," *Enterprise and Society* (2013), and "Of Firms and Captives: Railway Infrastructures and the Economics of Forced Labour (Spain, 1937–1957)," *Revista de Historia Industrial* (2017).

Juan Carlos García-Funes is a Lecturer in History at the Public University of Navarra, Spain. He received his PhD in 2017 from the same university with the thesis "Espacios de castigo y trabajo forzado del sistema concentracionario franquista," for which he was awarded the Extraordinary Doctorate Prize in Humanities and Social Sciences in 2022. He was a lecturer in history at the UFR d'Études ibériques et latinoaméricaines of the Faculty of Arts of Sorbonne Université (2019–2020) and is currently a team member in the *Study Group on the History of Prison and Punitive Institutions* and the *Documentary Fund of Historical Memory in Navarra*. Among other publications, he is the author of *"A recoger bombas": batallones de trabajo forzado en Castilla y León (1937–1942)* (Atrapasueños, 2016) and *Desafectos. Batallones de trabajo forzado en el franquismo* (Comares, 2022).

MIX
Papier aus verantwortungsvollen Quellen
Paper from responsible sources
FSC® C105338

If you have any concerns about our products,
you can contact us on
ProductSafety@springernature.com

In case Publisher is established outside the EU,
the EU authorized representative is:
Springer Nature Customer Service Center GmbH
Europaplatz 3, 69115 Heidelberg, Germany

Printed by Libri Plureos GmbH
in Hamburg, Germany